Text Linguistics of Qur’ani Discourse

Text Linguistics of Qur’anic Discourse is an in-depth investigation of the fabric of Qur’anic discourse. It unravels the texture of the macro Qur’anic text; its cohesion and coherence systems; the notions of intertextuality, semantic relatedness, and thematic sequentiality; the macro textual features of ellipsis, repetition, and argumentation structure; and the contextual, co-textual, grammatical, and semantic factors involved in the macro Qur’anic text. This book is a valuable and methodologically consistent learning and teaching academic resource for universities worldwide in this intriguing new discipline. Through its methodologically coherent discussion and in-depth analysis that is hinged upon modern European text linguistics, *Text Linguistics of Qur’anic Discourse* provides an insight into the newly established discipline of text linguistics and explores the different layers of the macro Qur’anic text as an academic requirement.

Hussein Abdul-Raof (formerly Leeds University) is a Professor of Linguistics and Translation Studies, Department of Languages and Translation, Taibah University, Saudi Arabia.

Culture and Civilization in the Middle East

General Editor: Ian Richard Netton

Professor of Islamic Studies, University of Exeter

This series studies the Middle East through the twin foci of its diverse cultures and civilisations. Comprising original monographs as well as scholarly surveys, it covers topics in the fields of Middle Eastern literature, archaeology, law, history, philosophy, science, folklore, art, architecture and language. While there is a plurality of views, the series presents serious scholarship in a lucid and stimulating fashion.

Muslims and Christians in Norman Sicily
Arabic-Speakers and the End of Islam
Alexander Metcalfe

Modern Arab Historiography
Historical Discourse and the Nation-State
Youssef Choueiri

The Philosophical Poetics of Alfarabi, Avicenna and Averroes
The Aristotelian Reception
Salim Kemal

Published by Routledge

57. Arabs and Iranians in the Islamic Conquest Narrative
Memory and Identity Construction in Islamic Historiography, 750–1050
Scott Savran

58. The Chaldean Catholic Church
Modern History, Ecclesiology and Church-State Relations
Kristian Girling

59. Text Linguistics of Qur'anic Discourse
An Analysis
Hussein Abdul-Raof

For a full list of books in the series, please go to: www.routledge.com/middleeast studies/series/SE0363

Text Linguistics of Qur'anic Discourse

An Analysis

Hussein Abdul-Raof

Routledge
Taylor & Francis Group
LONDON AND NEW YORK

First published 2019
by Routledge
2 Park Square, Milton Park, Abingdon, Oxon OX14 4RN

and by Routledge
605 Third Avenue, New York, NY 10017

First issued in paperback 2020

Routledge is an imprint of the Taylor & Francis Group, an informa business

British Library Cataloguing-in-Publication Data
A catalogue record for this book is available from the British Library

Library of Congress Cataloging-in-Publication Data
Names: Abdul-Raof, Hussein, author.
Title: Text linguistics of Qur'anic discourse : an analysis / Hussein Abdul-Raof.
Description: London ; New York, NY : Routledge, 2018. | Series: Culture and civilization in the Middle East ; 59 | Includes bibliographical references and index.
Identifiers: LCCN 2018029467 | ISBN 9781138946224 (hardback)
Subjects: LCSH: Qur'an—Language, style. | Arabic language—Rhetoric. | Arabic language—Discourse analysis.
Classification: LCC PJ6696.Z5 R45185 2018 | DDC 492.7/5—dc23
LC record available at https://lccn.loc.gov/2018029467

ISBN 13: 978-0-367-73323-0 (pbk)
ISBN 13: 978-1-138-94622-4 (hbk)

Typeset in Times New Roman
by Apex CoVantage, LLC

For Emily and Elaine

Contents

Preface

Text Linguistics of Qur'anic Discourse provides an insight into the fabric of the Qur'anic text. It explains why specific lexical, grammatical, and stylistic forms are employed and for what pragmatic function they are used. The present book provides a thorough examination of Qur'anic Arabic, a systematic account of the constituent standards that form Qur'anic textuality, a fresh exploration of the Qur'anic macro text in the light of text linguistics, and an awareness of the multifarious layers of the macro Qur'anic text.

Text Linguistics of Qur'anic Discourse provides a methodical account of the major components of the Qur'anic text, such as the texture of the macro Qur'anic text, the cohesion and coherence systems of the Qur'anic text, the macro Qur'anic textual constituents like intertextuality, semantic relatedness, and thematic sequentiality, ellipsis, repetition, and argumentation structure. The book also discusses the contextual, co-textual, grammatical, and semantic factors involved in the macro Qur'anic text.

Text Linguistics of Qur'anic Discourse is the first publication in English and Arabic on the prototypical feature of argumentation structure in Qur'anic discourse. The book provides a comprehensive account of the network of argumentation in Qur'anic genre and explores the thematic level within a few consecutive sentences where a tenet of faith is presented, either argued for to validate it or argued against to rebut it, and the narrative discourse level within a Qur'anic parable where a tenet of faith is debated between discourse participants.

In a methodical manner, the present book explores the notions of premise and conclusion of an argument. A premise is a statement (a proposition) of an argument which the arguer puts forward to the audience as true. Thus, it is a statement which aims to induce or justify a conclusion. The premise, therefore, is an assumption that something is true. However, a conclusion is a statement which the arguer wants his/her audience to accept and believe in as true. However, the proof of a true conclusion depends on both the truth of the premises and the validity of the argument.

Text Linguistics of Qur'anic Discourse also deals with Aristotle's modes of persuasion (ethos, pathos, and logos) and whether we can encounter these modes in the macro Qur'anic text. The current book has put the modes of persuasion into practice through an in-depth analysis of examples taken from Qur'anic discourse.

These examples are like the debate between God and Satan, Abraham and his people, Moses and Pharaoh, as well as several other Prophets and their relevant nations. The syntactic structures employed by discourse participants will also be analyzed in order to pin-point some stylistic facts about what type of lexical items God is using compared to Satan's words or the stylistic patterns employed by Moses compared to those used by Pharaoh. Are passive voice structures, adjectives, active participles used by the opponent or by the arguer? And why do they do that?

Text Linguistics of Qur'anic Discourse is the first publication in English and Arabic on this newly established academic research discipline, which I launched in 2001. The present book plugs a research gap in an innovative and methodologically coherent approach and will meet market academic needs in Qur'anic text linguistics for undergraduate and postgraduate students, researchers, and scholars.

Acknowledgements

I would like to express my sincere gratitude to all authors whose published research has been the primary source for the discussion of the present book. To all the names that have appeared in the Bibliography at the end of this book, a big *Thank You* for your valuable contributions to text linguistics, theoretical linguistics, and Qur'anic and Islamic studies which have made this work available to readers. For their generous time and valuable details, my special thanks are also due to those who I met with for debate and consultation during my research trips. I am also grateful to those who let me borrow their books from their personal libraries.

Arabic transliteration system

In terms of transliteration of examples, we have transferred the Qur'anic expression in full but, at times, we separate some conjunctive particles like (wa, fa) in the interest of clarity. Throughout the present work, the Library of Congress transliteration system has been consistently employed whenever an Arabic expression is quoted. The following table explains the Arabic transliteration system for Arabic consonants and vowels:

Transliteration	*Arabic*	*Transliteration*	*Arabic*
t	ط	a	أ
z	ظ	'	ء
ʿ	ع	b	ب
gh	غ	t	ت
f	ف	th	ث
q	ق	j	ج
k	ك	h	ح
l	ل	kh	خ
m	م	d	د
n	ن	dh	ذ
h	هـ	r	ر
w	و	z	ز
y	ي	s	س
sh	ش		
s	ص		
d	ض		

Arabic short – long vowels and case endings:

Transliteration	*Arabic*	*Transliteration*	*Arabic*
-an	ـً	a	ا
-un	ـٌ	u	ـو
-in	ـٍ	i	ـي
		a	ـَ
u	ـُ		
i	ـِ		

Introduction

Text Linguistics of Qur'anic Discourse is an investigation of the fabric of the Qur'anic text. According to Halliday and Hasan (1976:142), language does not function in isolation; it functions as TEXT, in actual situations of use. Thus, it is imperative to account for the constituent standards that form textuality.

Rationale

Qur'anic text linguistics is a new academic discipline. There have been no publications either in Arabic or in English on this discipline in a book form. Lack of such a book constitutes a research gap in this intriguing new discipline which will be of value to Qur'anic and Islamic studies, Qur'anic exegesis, Arabic studies, European theoretical linguistics, contrastive linguistics, corpus and computational linguistics, discourse analysis, and translation studies. Our claim is based on facts on the ground (the classroom) and my own personal teaching and research experience. Most importantly, the value of European theoretical linguistics to the investigation of the Qur'anic text at a macro level has been overlooked. Qur'anic discourse can greatly benefit from European text linguistics. Thus, for learning, teaching, and research needs, a fresh analysis of the Qur'anic macro text in the light of text linguistics is required. The different layers of the macro Qur'anic text need to be explored as an academic requirement.

To deprive Qur'anic discourse of a text linguistics approach constitutes a research gap. A book on Qur'anic text linguistics will provide an academic resource for American and European universities, as well as for several other universities worldwide where Islamic studies courses are taught at undergraduate level and where PhD students are studying. A book on Qur'anic text linguistics needs to have breadth, in-depth analysis, and the insight into putting European text linguistics into practice through a detailed analysis of a large number of micro and macro Qur'anic text examples.

There has been an academic and market need for a book on Qur'anic text linguistics, which accounts for the following major components of the text:

i the texture of the macro Qur'anic text,
ii the cohesion and coherence systems of the Qur'anic text,

iii the major notions of the macro Qur'anic text such as intertextuality, semantic relatedness, and thematic sequentiality,
iv the macro Qur'anic textual features of ellipsis, repetition, and argumentation structure, and
v the contextual, co-textual, grammatical, and semantic factors involved in the macro Qur'anic text.

About this book

Text Linguistics of Qur'anic Discourse: An Analysis provides a valuable academic resource and a valuable pool of text linguistics information for the following research and academic categories:

i Arabic and English contrastive text linguistics,
ii Arabic and Qur'anic/Islamic studies,
iii translation studies, and
iv corpus and computational linguistics.

The present book enjoys an academic international appeal since it constitutes:

i a major research gap in the macro textual features and the constituents of texture and intertextuality of the macro Qur'anic text, and
ii a market need for undergraduate/postgraduate students of linguistics and of Arabic and Islamic studies, researchers, and scholars of Islamic and Qur'anic studies.

My premise is based on the following academic and market facts:

1. Undergraduate and postgraduate students' interest in Arabic and Qur'anic text linguistics. This is based on my past teaching experience in Leeds University (1993–2012).
2. The present book addresses the learning and academic needs of undergraduate and postgraduate students, researchers, and scholars.
3. This book will be in high demand by a large number of PhD students, researchers, and scholars who are either studying or researching in Arabic/Islamic/Qur'anic studies, European theoretical linguistics, contrastive linguistics, corpus and computational linguistics, discourse analysis, Qur'anic exegesis, and translation studies.
4. The present book is of interest to students and researchers working on Qur'anic software programs.
5. Concerns have been expressed by undergraduate and postgraduate students about the lack of learning resources related to Qur'anic text linguistics. While there are a few books on European text linguistics, there is no book available on Qur'anic text linguistics.
6. There is a growing academic and research international interest in the linguistic constituents and the texture of Qur'anic discourse.

7 There have been no consistent academic teaching materials on the language of Qur'anic discourse at the macro level for undergraduate and postgraduate students studying Islamic and Arabic studies and for scholars who are the module leaders of such courses.
8 There are highly important linguistic topics which have been overlooked in the syllabus of Islamic and Arabic studies courses taught in European, American, and Australian universities as well as in most overseas universities where Islamic and Arabic studies courses are taught such as Malaysia, Indonesia, India, Pakistan, Turkey, Iran, South Africa, and the American University of Sharjah (UAE). Based on the above, *Text Linguistics of Qur'anic Discourse* is a valuable and methodologically consistent learning and teaching resource.

Through its methodologically coherent discussion and in-depth analysis that is hinged upon modern European text linguistics, this book provides an insight into the newly established academic discipline of text linguistics.

Overview of the work

This is an in-depth account of the constituent components of the Qur'anic text. This book includes an introduction and eight well-researched chapters whose analysis is based on European text linguistics.

Introduction

This provides an informative bird's eye view of the eight chapters that constitute the book. It will introduce the reader to the analysis of Qur'anic discourse in terms of European text linguistics.

Chapter 1: Text linguistics

This is an account of what text linguistics focuses on and the major theoretical topics related to it. It gives a detailed definition of text linguistics as well as the major notions of text linguistics such as the text, its texture, its typology, its qualities, its macro functions, its illocutionary force, its audience, its phases of production, its context, the difference between the subtext and the paratext, the cohesive ties of the text, the notion of textuality and its standards, how a text should be analyzed, textual progression, and what Qur'anic text linguistics is concerned with.

Chapter 2: Qur'anic macro text

This chapter accounts for a macro text–level analysis of Qur'anic discourse prototypical features. The present chapter will account for context and co-text functions within the macro text and their impact on the macro level due to the occurrence of specific lexical items. The major text linguistic feature of intertextuality will be discussed thoroughly, and examples of Qur'anic leitmotifs will be provided to explain this notion. Also, the coherent presentation of the Qur'anic tenets of faith, the coherent stylistic presentation between consecutive āyahs, and the coherent stylistic presentation between consecutive sūrahs will be discussed.

Also, the textual feature of recurrent Qur'anic syntactic structures will be accounted for. This includes the following forms of repetition in the macro Qur'anic text:

- i the repetition of lexical items (content words and function words),
- ii the repetition of different types of conjunctive particles,
- iii the repetition of frozen syntactic structures (formulas),
- iv the repetition of leitmotifs (tenets of faith), and
- v the repetition of Qur'anic parables.

Chapter 3: Argumentation structure in Qur'anic discourse

Argumentation is a prototypical feature of Qur'anic discourse. It occurs at two levels:

1 the thematic level within a few consecutive sentences where a tenet of faith is presented, either argued for to validate it or argued against to rebut it, and
2 the narrative discourse level within a Qur'anic parable where a tenet of faith is debated between discourse participants.

The present chapter will account for the notions of premise and conclusion of an argument. A premise is a statement (a proposition) of an argument which the arguer puts forward to the audience as true. Thus, it is a statement which aims to induce or justify a conclusion. The premise, therefore, is an assumption that something is true. However, a conclusion is a statement which the arguer wants his/her audience to accept and believe in as true. However, the proof of a true conclusion depends on both the truth of the premises and the validity of the argument.

This chapter will also deal with Aristotle's modes of persuasion and whether we can encounter these modes in the macro Qur'anic text. Aristotle's modes of persuasion are:

- i ethos (the ethical appeal, i.e., convincing the opponent through the good charismatic character of the speaker),
- ii pathos (persuading the opponent by appealing to his/her emotions and self-interest), and
- iii logos (the logical appeal, i.e., persuading the opponent by the use of logical reasoning and supportive evidence).

In order to argue effectively and convince the opponent, the speaker/writer needs to introduce a commonplace statement which the opponent (listener/reader) accepts with no hesitation. The chapter will also account for Qur'anic commonplaces. Some examples of commonplaces include (everyone dies – kullu nafsin dhā'iqatu al-mawti). These commonplaces are statements which no one can refute – not even the opponent of an idea.

The present chapter will put the modes of persuasion into practice through an in-depth analysis of examples taken from Qur'anic discourse. These examples are like the debate between God and Satan, Abraham and his people, Moses and Pharaoh, as well as several other prophets and their relevant nations. The syntactic structures employed by discourse participants will also be analyzed in order to pinpoint some stylistic facts about what type of lexical items God is using compared to Satan's words or the stylistic patterns employed by Moses compared to those used by Pharaoh. Are passive voice structures, adjectives, active participles used by the opponent or by the arguer? And why do they do that?

We will explain why specific lexical, grammatical, and stylistic forms are used and for what pragmatic function they are employed.

Chapter 4: Ellipsis in Qur'anic discourse

The present chapter provides an in-depth account of ellipsis as a linguistic and rhetorical feature of Qur'anic discourse. It also provides a thorough and explicated account of the different types of ellipsis. The discussion will also deal with the distinction between ellipsis (al-ḥadhf) and succinctness (al-ījāz) and their different pragmatic roles in Qur'anic discourse. The grammatical and contextual factors of ellipsis will also be accounted for.

Among the major types of ellipsis that will be syntactically and semantically analyzed are:

1 ellipsis at the conjunctive particle level,
2 ellipsis at the word level,
3 ellipsis at the grammatical case level,
4 ellipsis at the grammatical function level,
5 ellipsis at the clause level,
6 ellipsis at the sentence level, and
7 ellipsis at the narrative text level.

Chapter 5: Coherence in Qur'anic discourse

This chapter will investigate the ways in which Qur'anic themes and relations are linked and used to achieve effective communication with the reader. Different types of relations in Qur'anic discourse will be discussed, such as causality, enablement, reason, purpose, and time. Each type of relation will be thoroughly accounted for with many different examples. This chapter also accounts for the Qur'anic text at the micro level (consecutive sentences) and at the macro level (consecutive sūrahs). This analysis achieves two aims:

i to unravel the textual cohesion of Qur'anic discourse, and
ii to demonstrate the sequential connectivity and thematic progression that bond the Qur'anic āyahs and sūrahs.

The notion of texture will be accounted for in this chapter. Both the unity of the Qur'anic text and the semantic interdependence within the Qur'anic text are hinged upon the notion of texture. The notion of semantic interdependence will be dealt with in terms of thematic sequentiality, semantic connectivity, and progression of Qur'anic text.

Examples will illustrate that without texture, the macro Qur'anic text is no more than jumbled up and semantically unrelated sentences which seriously lack thematic relatedness to each other either within a given sūrah or between consecutive sūrahs. Thus, Qur'anic intertextuality is highly significant for the discussion of texture and coherence of Qur'anic discourse.

The present chapter refers to the text linguistic notion of intertextuality through which the Qur'anic text achieves conceptual chaining and semantic relatedness. The present discussion argues that Qur'anic discourse features a textually coherent presentation technique that is hinged upon leitmotifs and thematic allusions.

The present account also investigates two textual features:

1 macro textual progression: This includes the conceptual and intertextual links among a number of consecutive sūrahs, and
2 presentation technique: This includes the presentation of tenets of faith in Qur'anic discourse.

Chapter 6: Cohesion in Qur'anic discourse

This chapter accounts for the text linguistic notion of cohesion in Qur'anic discourse. The analysis of the cohesion system will benefit from the work of both Halliday and Hasan on cohesion in English (1976, 1979, 1985). The present chapter will provide an in-depth account of the cohesion constituents in Qur'anic discourse. These include the grammatical notions, such as reference, ellipsis, substitution, conjunction, and lexical cohesion. These grammatical notions are semantic ties and constitute a set of linguistic resources which link one part of a text to another. We will investigate whether this is the same in Qur'anic Arabic. The grammatical notions are like the glue which holds different parts of a text together. They are the only factor in making a text coherent. Thus, they are concerned with the cross-referencing of pronouns, particles, and some types of adverb, as in: (The man went to town. However, he did not stay long) (Crystal 2003:81). The present chapter will demonstrate how the grammatical and lexical elements can form semantic connections between Qur'anic text components. These grammatical notions also refer to grammatical or semantic relations except the lexical cohesion device which refers to lexical relations.

The discussion of Qur'anic cohesion aims to account for the surface continuity of the Qur'anic text composition. Thus, the current chapter will also account for the Qur'anic cohesive devices and their grammatical and semantic role in a given sentence. We will argue that Qur'anic cohesion is also concerned with the texture of the Qur'anic text and whether it is a cohesive text.

Chapter 7: Linguistic inimitability of Qur'anic discourse

This is a detailed account of the historical development of the theological notion of inimitability of Qur'anic discourse and how this notion can be integrated into Qur'anic text linguistics. Thus, the analysis is of value to comparative-contrastive text linguistics with other languages. However, the theological orientation to inimitability falls outside the scope of the present chapter. In terms of text linguistics, we will argue that the notion of inimitability of Qur'anic discourse is multi-faceted:

- i It is concerned with macro Qur'anic text analysis.
- ii It is linguistically and stylistically oriented in terms of the cohesion system.
- iii It is intertextuality oriented in terms of Qur'anic exegesis.
- iv It is hinged upon linguistic and paralinguistic levels of analysis.
- v It is an approach that attempts to capture the macro Qur'anic text features.

The present chapter will also deal with the cohesion system problems on the grammatical, semantic, rhetorical, and phonetic levels and their impact on the meaning of a given sentence. The linguistic analysis of different examples will also demonstrate how Arab grammarians appoint different grammatical functions to the same Qur'anic grammatical constituent. Thus, we can argue that Arabic grammar has not regulated grammar-based Qur'anic interpretation. As a result, there is always room for grammatical manoeuvrability through which one can prove a given theological point of view which may be contrary to the canons of Qur'anic exegesis. The discussion will also account for the semantically and stylistically based analysis of grammatically and semantically ambiguous sentences and Qur'anic expressions. This chapter will also investigate the different Qur'anic syntactic structures. This discussion has a direct bearing on applied semantics. We will also account for several morpho-syntactic problems, semantically oriented assonance especially at sentence-final position, the semantically based active participle and passive participle, the stylistic selection of specific lexical items to deliver a specific pragmatic function, and the notion of intertextuality and connectivity of Qur'anic leitmotifs within a given sūrah or between consecutive sūrahs. All these notions are major constituents of linguistic and stylistic Qur'anic discourse that need to be raised during the investigation of the notion of inimitability.

Chapter 8: General observations on Qur'anic text linguistics

This chapter provides a bird's-eye view of the discussion raised in the previous chapters and furnishes highly useful recommendations and various conclusions.

Bibliography

The discussion of each of the chapters of the present book will be hinged upon the following resources that can be effectively employed for comparative and contrastive Arabic and English text linguistic analysis. Most importantly, the resources that follow will be of great value to undergraduate and postgraduate students, PhD students, researchers, and scholars of Arabic, Islamic, and Qur'anic studies, corpus and computational linguistics, discourse analysis, contrastive linguistics, and translation studies.

1 Text linguistics

1.1 Introduction

This is an account of what text linguistics is concerned with. The discussion provides the major notions of text linguistics such as the text, the qualities of the text, its macro functions, the different types of text, the text's pragmatic function, the relationship between the text producer (writer/speaker) and the text receiver (reader/listener), the relationship between the text and its context, the role of coherence and cohesion in the creation of a text, the cohesive ties involved in the text such as reference, substitution, ellipsis, conjunction, and lexical cohesion. This chapter also deals with the standards of textuality, how the text progresses, and what Qur'anic text linguistics is about.

1.2 What is text linguistics?

Text linguistics emerged during the 1970s as a new discipline but has remained a branch of mainstream linguistics. It is concerned with the description and analysis of macro spoken and written texts. In other words, the text is the major and largest linguistic sign/unit which is worthy of analysis rather than its constituent single words, phrases, or sentences. Text linguistics studies the communicative relationship through texts between the text producer (writer/speaker) and the text receiver (reader/hearer). It studies the communicative employment of cohesive devices in the construction of a given text. Text linguistics is concerned with the flow of information intra-sententially (within the same sentence) and inter-sententially (among different sentences) by looking at text linguistic features of the text like coherence, cohesion, the organization of old/given/known (unmarked) information and new/unknown (marked) information which are constituents of the text structure. In text linguistics, we focus on the linguistic processes of text cohesion and text coherence.

In text linguistics, the text is a communication system and has a communication function. In the view of Dirven and Vespoor (2004:180), text linguistics is concerned with the study of how a writer/speaker and a reader/hearer manage to communicate through texts. In other words, how the text producer and the text receiver can go beyond the text, i.e., how they effectively employ cohesive devices (adawāt al-rabṭ), such as (wa – and), (bisabab – because), (thumma – then), and (walākin – but), in order to construct sentential and paragraph relations within a given text.

Text linguistics is different from traditional structural linguistics. The latter focuses on sentence grammar, i.e., sentence structure, and is concerned primarily with the sentence as the largest linguistic unit in linguistic analysis. However, text linguistics views the sentence as a micro unit of language and is concerned with the text structure and textuality. Linguistic analysis should be carried out at the macro level, the text, and the sentence is only a part of the macro text.

For more details, see Dressler (1978:21); Trask (1997:219); Beaugrande and Dressler (1981:ii, 3); Crystal (2003:234–235, 462); and Hatim and Munday (2004:350).

1.3 Major notions in text linguistics

The major notions in text linguistics include: text, subtext, context of situation, texture, cohesive ties, standards of textuality, and macro functions of text (field, tenor, and mode), and text types. These are discussed in what follows.

1.3.1 Text

The word 'text' is derived from the Latin verb (texere) meaning to weave, to compose, or to contrive. In other words, the words are woven together in a text. A text enjoys inherent lexicogrammatical and stylistic hallmarks which reflect the social and cultural context in which a specific text occurs. A text should constitute a congruent discourse (kalām mutalā'im). A text should be well formed (faṣīḥ) and be free from rhetorical deficiency (ᶜuyūb balāghiyyah) and sluggish sentences (jumal mutanāfirah). A text should also enjoy continuity and progression. On the lexical, grammatical, and stylistic levels, the text is influenced by its social event. Thus, the context of situation is the womb of the text. On the stylistic level, the text should avoid distasteful style and unnaturalness (ᶜadam al-istirsāl, al-takalluf). A text should enjoy grammatical, semantic, and stylistic congruity. On the rhetorical level, a text should avoid verbosity (al-iṭnāb) to elevate its illocutionary force and not to undermine informativity.

A text is the linguistic outcome of a specific interaction, such as a particular speech (or part of a speech), a book (or a chapter or a paragraph from a book) (McCabe 2011:390). According to Halliday and Hasan (1976:1–2), a text has the following prototypical features:

1 It is any passage, spoken or written, of whatever length, that forms a unified whole.
2 It is a unit of language in use.

3 It is any form of a communicative or meaningful event.
4 It is not a grammatical unit like a sentence or a clause.
5 It is a semantic unit (a unit of meaning).
6 It does not consist of sentences but is realized by (encoded in) sentences.
7 It is not defined by its size.
8 It has texture which distinguishes it from something that is not a text.
9 It is coherent and cohesive.
10 A text has cohesive properties through which it can be analyzed, and that some items within the text function cohesively (Halliday and Hasan 1976:3–4).
11 A text is a communicative occurrence which should meet seven standards of textuality: cohesion, coherence, intentionality, acceptability, informativity, situationality, and intertextuality (Beaugrande and Dressler 1981:3).
12 Texts are seen as vehicles for the expression of a range of socio-cultural meanings (Hatim and Munday 2004:86).
13 A text must be relevant to other texts in the same discourse and not just to participants' intentions and to the situational setting (Beaugrande and Dressler 1981:188).

The notion of 'text' has been discussed further by linguists. For Halliday and Hasan (1976:23), a text is a passage of discourse which is coherent with respect to the context of a situation, and it is coherent with respect to itself and therefore cohesive. In general, any unit which is structured hangs together so as to form text. All grammatical units – sentences, clauses, groups, words – are internally 'cohesive' simply because they are structured. A text is realized in the form of related sentences as a semantic unit, i.e., a unit of meaning, and its semantic unity lies in the cohesion among its constituent sentences (ibid:1, 2, 293). In other words, a text is not a unit of form and, therefore, it is not a grammatical unit. However, for van Dijk (1977:3), a text is a grammatical unit. It is a larger unit of reconstructed utterances which can be assigned textual structure and are acceptable discourses of the language, i.e., are well formed and interpretable (ibid).

For McCabe (2011:82), a text is the linguistic outcome of a specific interaction. According to Brown and Yule (1996:190), a text is the verbal record of a communicative event. For Trask (1997:219), the text is a continuous stretch of spoken or written language, but particularly one which forms a discrete unit by itself and has some recognizable internal structure.

Thus, we can argue that the major components of a communicative text are coherence and cohesion. The text should be cohesive in terms of grammatical patterns. The text should also be logically presented, i.e., its sentences are linked coherently. The notion of 'text' is also related to the notion of 'text processing', i.e., the use of a text in communication with the minimum expenditure of effort by the addressee (text receiver, hearer/reader). For an efficient textual communication, the text producer needs to make his/her text processed (thoroughly understood) by the text receiver (the reader/listener).

In terms of sentence structure, some texts favour short and simple sentences with coordination conjunctive particles. Such sentences are paratactic. However, other texts favour long and complex sentences with subordination conjunctive particles. Such sentences are hypotactic. For more details, see Section 1.3.10. For Barthes (1973:31), the text can, if it wants, attack the canonical structures of the language itself: lexicon, syntax. Then it becomes language. This applies to Qur'anic discourse in terms of foregrounding for saliency reasons. For more details, see Chapter 5, Section 5.7. However, in terms of text types and cross-cultural communication, Hatim and Munday (2004:303) argue that texts, genres, and discourses are macro-signs within which we do things with words. Words, thus, become instruments of power and ideology. For Barthes (1973:13, 14, 31), the text transcends prattle, comes from culture and does not break with it, and the text can, if it wants, attack the canonical structures of the language itself: lexicon, syntax. Then it becomes language.

Based on Qur'anic discourse, a text dovetails with another text in the same discourse to attain sequentiality (connectivity) of themes (leitmotifs). Thus, coherence is achieved. This is evident in Qur'anic discourse where the tenets of faith dovetail with each other in a sequential manner. For more details, see Chapter 5, Section 5.10.1.2.

1.3.1.1 Text illocutionary force

Each text is produced for a perlocutionary force on the reader/hearer. Perlocution is concerned with the impact of the text upon its receivers. The impact of the text is achieved through its words. Thus, the text involves an illocutionary force. In other words, we can say the following:

> Text Producer → Text → Illocutionary Force → Perlocutionary Effect → Audience.

Although the text receiver is expected to possess acute discernment (nafādh baṣīrah), a pragmatically (communicatively) effective text should enjoy specific rhetorical characteristics so that the text's illocutionary act (the impact of words) is employed to the maximum. We believe that the text's illocutionary force is fortified by the following rhetorical characteristics, which can elevate the illocutionary force of the text, i.e., raise the text's influence upon the text receivers and achieve the text producer's desired perlocutionary force:

1 the minimum use of allusion (hidden meaning),
2 the minimum use of structural and semantic ambiguity,
3 the minimum use of amphigouri (periphrasis) and bombast (pointless, redundant discourse – kalām ajwaf malī' bil-ḥashu),
4 the minimum use of catachresis (excessive allegory – al-ta^{c}assuf al-majāzi),
5 the minimum use of complete non-relatedness (lack of coherence – kamāl al-inqiṭā^{c}) whose antonym is complete relatedness (consonance – kamāl al-ittiṣāl),

6 the minimum use of coding (al-ilghāz), i.e., blinding when using metonymy,
7 the minimum use of complex assonance (al-saj[c] al-mu[c]aqqad),
8 the minimum use of implicatures,
9 the words employed should have explicatures (ma[c]ānī wāḍiḥah),
10 the minimum use of inkhorn expressions (al-fāẓ gharībah),
11 the minimum use of lexical oddity (gharābat al-alfāẓ),
12 the use of elegance of discourse (ḥusn al-kalām),
13 the use of elegance of introduction (ḥusn al-istihlāl),
14 compatibility between the register of discourse and the psychological state of the audience,
15 the use of grammatical, morphological, semantic, and stylistic congruity,
16 a pragmatically effective and appropriate text should enjoy stylistic purity (al-jazālah), should employ a sublime style (islūb rafi[c]), and should avoid verbosity (iṭnāb),
17 a pragmatically effective and appropriate text should be decorated by embellishments ([c]ilm al-badī[c]) and figures of speech ([c]ilm al-bayān) to promote the text's figure of thought (al-ṣūrah al-bayāniyyah lil-naṣṣ), and
18 the illocutionary force of the text can be enhanced through the employment of foregrounding a sentence constituent and bringing it into a prominent perspective.

1.3.1.2 Text receiver

This is referred to in Arabic as (al-mutalaqqī). Texts are not produced haphazardly. Each text is purpose centred and has a targeted audience. However, each text addresses a given category of readers/listeners. Based on the type of audience, the text producer (al-mubdi[c]) designs the genre, which involves specific linguistic and stylistic mechanisms through which the text's intended message is relayed to the targeted category of text audience.

Although the text receiver is expected to possess acute discernment (nafādh baṣīrah), an informative text, we believe, should enjoy the following characteristics:

i the use of minimum allusion (hidden meaning),
ii the use of minimum structural and semantic ambiguity,
iii the use of minimum amphigouri (pointless discourse).

In Qur'anic discourse, we encounter different categories of text receivers, such as:

1 disbelievers (kāfirūn): This is a major category of Qur'anic text receivers. They can be sub-classified into:

   i the polytheists (al-mushrikūn): This category of Qur'anic text receivers are deniers (munkirūn) of the Qur'anic intended message, namely, monotheism and Muḥammad's prophethood. The polytheists represent idol worshippers, i.e., believers in different gods. However, they believe in the hereafter. Example: (wajadnā ābā'anā laha ᶜābidīn . . . – We found our fathers worshippers of them (idols), Q21:53).

ii the heretics (al-mulḥidūn): This category of Qur'anic text receivers are deniers (munkirūn) of the Qur'anic intended message, namely, monotheism, Muḥammad's prophethood, eschatology, and reward and punishment. The heretics are not idol worshippers, i.e., they are disbelievers in any god. Example: (mā hiya illā ḥayatunā al-dunyā namūtu wanaḥyā wamā yuhlikunā illā aldahr – This is not but our worldly life. We die and live and nothing destroys us except time, Q45:24).

iii the Jews (al-yahūd, banū isrā'īl): This category of Qur'anic text receivers are deniers (munkir) of the Qur'anic intended message of monotheism and Muḥammad's prophethood. However, they are believers in eschatology and reward and punishment.

iv the Christians (al-naṣārā): This category of Qur'anic text receivers are deniers (munkir) of the Qur'anic intended message of monotheism and Muḥammad's prophethood. However, they are believers in eschatology and reward and punishment.

v the hypocrites (al-munāfiqūn): This category of Qur'anic text receivers are sceptical (mutaraddid) of the Qur'anic intended message of monotheism and Muḥammad's prophethood, eschatology, and reward and punishment. However, they are not heretical. The hypocrites have a shaky belief in Islam, i.e., they are undecided. In other words, they pretend the belief in the Qur'anic intended message (as a lip service) but are not firm believers. They are described as:

> yukhādiᶜūna allāh walladhīna āmanū, fī qulūbihim maraḍun, hum al-mufsidūn, ṣummun bukmun ᶜumyun – They think to deceive God and those who believe but they do not except themselves and perceive it not, Q2:9, 10, 12, 18)

Also in:

> idhā laqaw alladhīna āmanū qālū āmannā wa'idhā khalaw ilā shayāṭīnihim qālū innā maᶜakum innamā naḥnu mustahzi'ūn – When they meet those who believe, they say: 'We believe', but when they are alone with their evil ones, they say: 'Indeed, we are with you. We were only mockers', Q2:14

The hypocrites are fake believers. Thus, they are considered Muslims but not believers because (innahum kafarū billāhi warasūlih – They disbelieved in God and His messenger, Q9:84) and they are (ashaddu kufran wanifāqan – They are stronger in disbelief and hypocrisy, Q9:97). Thus, the hypocrites are described as (rijsun – evil, Q9:95).

2 the believers (al-mu'minūn): This category of Qur'anic text receivers are open-minded (khāli al-dhihn) towards the Qur'anic intended message of monotheism, Muḥammad's prophethood, eschatology, and reward and punishment.

For more details on the text receiver and argumentation within discourse participants, see Chapter 3, Section 3.9. For more details on the genre of different discourse participants, see Chapter 3, Section 3.9.2.

1.3.1.3 Text qualities

A text should enjoy three qualities: efficiency, effectiveness, and appropriateness (Beaugrande and Dressler 1981:11):

- i The efficiency of a text depends on its use in communicating with a minimum expenditure of effort by the participants, i.e., to ease the processing of the text.
- ii The effectiveness of a text depends on its leaving a strong impression and creating favourable conditions for attaining a goal, i.e., the intense use of resources to deliver the goal successfully.
- iii The appropriateness of a text is the agreement between its setting and the ways in which the standards of textuality are upheld, i.e., the relationship between the context of situation and the standards of textuality.

1.3.1.4 Phases of text production

Prior to its production, the text goes through different phases (Beaugrande and Dressler 1981:39–40):

- i Planning: This phase involves the text producer's intention to pursue a given goal through the text, such as admonition and monotheism, for the Qur'anic text.
- ii Ideation: This phase involves the presentation of an idea to the text receivers.
- iii Development: This involves the expansion, specifying, elaborating, and interconnecting of the ideas (messages) relayed to the text audience.
- iv Expression: This is the stage of releasing the content of the text.
- v Parsing: This phase involves the arrangement of the lexical elements into grammatical dependencies and arranging the latter in a linear format for the surface text, i.e., the lexical elements are linearized in a grammatical manner and arranged next to each other grammatically.

1.3.2 Subtext

A subtext is characterized by the following prototypical features:

1. It is any passage which is a transition that takes place within the main text,
2. It is outside the context of the main text,
3. It functions as an independent text in its own right,
4. It displays no cohesion with what has preceded it, and
5. It is characterized by loose texture.

An example of a subtext is *The Queen of Hearts* in the final chapter of *Alice in Wonderland* (Halliday and Hasan 1976:296). It is worthwhile to note that the Qur'an does not have any subtext. In the view of Halliday and Hasan (1976:296), the subtext is characterized by loose texture where fewer cohesive ties are employed.

1.3.3 Paratext

A paratext represents the additional elements such as titles, captions, headings, and footnotes. These are considered additional elements to the main body of the text (Hatim and Munday 2004:345). It is worthwhile to note that the Qur'an does not have any paratext.

1.3.4 Context of situation

This is referred to in Arabic as (al-maqām, muqtaḍā al-ḥāl). A major prerequisite of a successful text is the compatibility of discourse with context. The context of situation is the womb of the text. For Halliday and Hasan (1985:3–46), the context of situation is the immediate socio-cultural environment in which a text functions and unfolds.

Thus, the reader/hearer misunderstands the intentionality, i.e., the intended meaning, of the text if he/she is unaware of the text's context of situation. In other words, the text unfolds and its meaning becomes clear when analyzed in terms of its context of situation. In a similar vein, van Dijk (1977:3) stresses the systematic relation between text and context. The notion of context of situation is regarded as a semantic notion by Lyons (1977, 2:572), but for Carnap (1956, cf. Lyons 1977, 1:116 and 2:572) it is a pragmatic notion. Although Katz and Fodor (1963, cf. Lyons 1977, 2:573) acknowledge the importance of context of situation in the interpretation of what one writes or says, they believe that semantics should be concerned with the meaning of sentences without reference to their context of situation. The reason why Katz and Fodor do not recognize the role of context of situation in the determination of the text's meaning is attributed to the fact that they are both sentence-based linguists, i.e., they are not text linguists.

For Hatim and Munday (2004:336), context is the multi-layered extra-textual environment which exerts determining influence on the language used. The subject matter of a given text, for example, is part of a context of situation. The ideology of the speaker, on the other hand, would form part of the context of culture.

Context is concerned with the decisions as to the appropriateness of certain ways of speaking or choosing a word that is more appropriate in a given context and situation. It is to do with the best language or the 'correct' way of speaking (McCabe 2011:4).

For more details on the influential role of the context of situation (communication) and the emergence of different genres or text types, see Section 1.3.9.

1.3.5 Texture

Texture is the semantic interdependence within text. A text which lacks texture is a non-text because its sentences have no relationship to each other. Each sentence in any text should be linked coherently to the previous sentence. Thus, we have sequentiality, i.e., linear sequence, among the constituent sentences of a text. This leads to the progression of the text, i.e., coherence, while the internal ties within the text are semantic in nature and lead to cohesion. The texture of the text can be produced if coherence and cohesion are maintained; thus, it is coherence and cohesion that give a text texture (Halliday and Hasan 1976:23). For Halliday and Hasan (ibid:7), sentences, clauses, and words are structured because they are internally 'cohesive'; thus, structure is one means of expressing texture. Texture, in the view of Halliday and Hasan (ibid:2) is also created through coreferentiality, which is a cohesive agency, as in: (I saw John and told him about the exam), where coreferentiality holds between (John) and the anaphoric item (him); thus, texture is achieved by cohesion as a linguistic means. The speaker/writer employs cohesion to signal texture, and the listener/reader reacts to it in his/her interpretation of texture (ibid:293, 295). A word coheres with another word either through collocation, reiteration, or synonymy, and so such a word contributes to the texture of the text (ibid:319).

For Halliday and Hasan (1976:9), the cohesive devices (adwāt al-rabṭ) between sentences in the text stand out more clearly because they are the only source of texture. A text should be unified whose units – words and sentences – are connected together in a cohesive manner through the cohesive devices, like (thumma – then; wa – and; li'anna – because; qabla – before) that make the text hang together and create its unique texture and total unity. Other linguistic processes which also have a role in the realization of a text's texture or textuality are: reference, substitution, and ellipsis. According to Martin (2015:61), texture is one aspect of the study of coherence, which takes the social context of texture into consideration.

Halliday and Hasan (1976:295–297) make a distinction between two types of texture: 'tight and loose texture'. A fair indication of something that is a general feature of texts of all kinds, we encounter variation in texture. In 'tight texture', we find dense clusters of cohesive ties which serve to signal that the meanings of the parts are strongly interdependent and that the whole forms a single unity. However, in other texts, we find 'loose texture', where fewer cohesive ties are used, perhaps just one or two. This is a feature of subtexts which occur within a text. For Halliday and Hasan (ibid:296), the portions that are less closely knit, i.e., with loose texture, with the remainder of the main text constitute the subtext; thus, loose texture is a feature of subtexts.

1.3.6 Cohesive ties

A text needs to be internally cohesive through ties which represent cohesive relations. The cohesive ties are cohesive devices, i.e., they are intra- and inter-sentential links. A tie has a cohesive function between a pair of cohesively related items, as

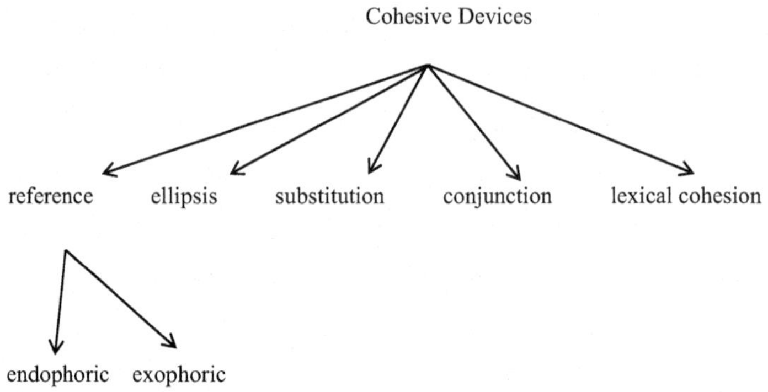

Figure 1.1 Intra- and inter-sentential cohesive links

in: (I met my friends in the library and showed them my essay), where the relation between (them) and (my friends) constitutes a tie. Therefore, for a thorough cohesion-based text analysis, we look for the cohesive ties which enable the text to be cohesive. For Halliday and Hasan (1976:4), there are different kinds of cohesive ties in a text: reference, substitution, ellipsis, conjunction, and lexical cohesion. These are illustrated in Figure 1.1.

The cohesive ties are outlined as follows:

1 Reference: Through reference, we can identify interrelated items within a text. Reference includes nouns, determiners, pronouns (personal and demonstrative), and adverbs. Reference is classified into endophoric and exophoric. Endophoric reference includes:

 i Cataphoric reference: This is the use of a linguistic item to refer forward to subsequent elements in the text (e.g., In *her* speech, *Theresa May* reassured the Europeans that . . .).
 ii Anaphoric reference: This takes place when a noun occurs first then is followed by its reference pronoun.
 iiii Personal reference: This refers to personal pronouns (he, she, it, they, you).
 iv General reference: This refers to items like (other one, another one, other ones, the first, the latter, one of them), as in:

 > I bought two books, one on linguistics and the other on semantics. The first was written in English and the latter was written in French. Last week, John asked me to borrow one of them.

 v Demonstrative reference: This refers to demonstrative pronouns (this, that, these, those).
 vi Comparative reference: This refers to items like (more/most, fewer/less, better/worse).

2 Ellipsis: This refers to anything that is left unsaid in the second sentence. For Beaugrande and Dressler (1981:66), ellipsis is a cohesive device that contributes to the text's compactness and efficiency. There are three types of ellipsis:

i Nominal ellipsis, as in (John and Peter are students. Both came to the party) where we have nominal ellipsis because the nouns (John and Peter) are ellipted in the second sentence and instead (both) is employed.
ii Verbal ellipsis, as in (John came to the party. Peter did not) where verbal ellipsis is represented by the missing verb (come) in the second sentence.
iii Clausal ellipsis, as in (Have you finished your essay? Yes) where clausal ellipsis is represented by the missing clause (have finished the essay) in the second sentence.

3 Substitution: This is the replacement of a word or phrase to avoid the repetition of the same word or phrase. There are three types of substitution:

i Nominal substitution: This is represented by (one) or (ones), as in (I gave you red, green, and yellow colouring pencils. Give back the green ones only) where substitution is represented by the word (ones) that stands for the noun (colouring pencils). The word (same) also functions as a nominal substitute, as in:

(A): I will buy a new red car.
(B): I will buy the same.

ii Verbal substitution: This is realized by (do), as in:

(A): I hope you understood my point.
(B): I did.

where (did), which is used by the second speaker (B), substitutes the verb (understood).

iii Clausal substitution: This refers to the substitution of an entire clause through the word (so), as in:

(A): Did John pass his driving test?
(B): I was told so.

4 Conjunction: This is realized through different types of conjunctive elements, such as additive conjunction (and), adversative conjunction (although), causal conjunction (so), and temporal conjunction (then). Beaugrande and Dressler (1981:71) refer to conjunctions as junctive expressions.
5 Lexical cohesion: This is achieved through the selection of vocabulary, such as the use of general nouns as cohesive elements (man, woman, boy, girl, person, people). There are three types of lexical cohesion:

i Reiteration: The employment of the same word repeatedly achieves a link between the various parts of a text. The word has the same referent as the item which it represents, as in (Peter bought a BMW. It is the most expensive car in the street). Beaugrande and Dressler (1981:54) refer to reiteration as lexical recurrence.

ii Collocation: Some lexical items co-occur regularly, as in (pound . . . penny), (poor . . . rich), (hospital . . . doctor).

iii Synonymy: This refers to words which are either equivalent or partially equivalent in their meaning, such as (holiday/vacation), (kid/child), and (courageous/brave).

iv Antonymy: This refers to the oppositeness of meaning, as in (hot/cold).

1.3.7 Standards of textuality

As language functions as TEXT, in actual situations (Halliday and Hasan 1976:142), it is important to account for the constituent standards that form textuality. There are seven standards of textuality whose presence in a text helps the realization of a communicative text. The seven standards of textuality were introduced by Beaugrande and Dressler (1981:3). These are:

1 Cohesion: For Halliday and Hasan (1976:4–5), cohesion is a semantic relation and is defined as the relations of meaning that exist within the text and that define it as a text. It is the grammatical or lexical relationship that binds different parts of a text together. Cohesion is expressed partly through the grammar and partly through the vocabulary. Thus, there is grammatical cohesion and lexical cohesion (ibid:5–6). For Beaugrande and Dressler (1981:3), cohesion depends on grammatical dependencies. This means that the surface components (words) of the text depend upon each other according to grammatical forms and conventions, i.e., the words are mutually connected within a sequence. Although cohesion plays a pivotal role in textuality, there must be interaction between cohesion and other standards of textuality to make communication efficient (ibid:4). In the view of Beaugrande and Dressler (1981:55–56), lexical recurrence (repetition) contributes to cohesion. As for Hatim and Munday (2004:336), cohesion is the requirement that a sequence of sentences display grammatical and/or lexical relationships which ensure the surface continuity of text structure. Yule (1985:140) defines cohesion as the ties and connections which exist within texts. It refers to the different cohesive devices that are necessary for any text units to be strongly connected together. Cohesive devices are defined by Salkie (2005:9) as those certain words and expressions which any cohesive text should include. They are necessary in linking the sentences together. They are like the glue which holds different parts of a text together and the only factor in making a text coherent.

2 Coherence: Coherence is the spirit of the text, is what makes the text semantically meaningful, and is considered the most significant element in text linguistics. van Dijk (1977:93) points out that the notion of coherence can be defined as a semantic property of discourse. For Hatim and Munday (2004:335), coherence is a standard which all well-formed texts must meet

and which stipulates that grammatical and/or lexical relationships 'hang together' and make overall sense as text. According to Beaugrande and Dressler (1981:84), coherence represents a continuity of senses among the knowledge activated by the expressions of the text. For them (ibid), the continuity of senses constitutes the foundation of coherence. Manser (2006:141) argues that coherence is a feature of good style. Tanskanen (2006:7) argues that coherence is the outcome of a dialogue between the text and its listener/reader.

In terms of Qur'anic discourse, coherence is hinged upon thematic sequentiality and textual relatedness. For more details, see Chapter 5.

3 Intentionality: This is concerned with the intentions (attitude) of text producers. In the view of Beaugrande and Dressler (1981:116), intentionality designates all the ways in which text producers utilize texts to pursue and fulfil their intentions.

4 Acceptability: This refers to the text receivers' attitude in communication. In other words, text receivers must accept a language configuration as a cohesive and coherent text capable of utilization (Beaugrande and Dressler 1981:129).

5 Informativity: This is concerned with the extent to which a presentation is new or unexpected for the receivers (Beaugrande and Dressler 1981:139). Thus, informativity is to do with the content of the text. In terms of textuality, informativity is more interrelated to coherence than cohesion, which is viewed as subsidiary (not given prominence) to coherence. In other words, our attention is focused on the coherence of concepts and relations (ibid). However, we can claim that informativity goes beyond coherence. We believe informativity should correlate with the quantity and value of the information provided to the satisfaction and best interest of the text receiver. A text is not informative: (i) if it does not provide enough details about the unknown and (ii) if the details provided are of no value, false, or misleading. Informativity is also concerned with the unknown (new) information versus the known (old) information.

6 Situationality: This is concerned with the factors which render a text relevant to a current or recoverable situation of occurrence. The Arabic proverb can be of value to situationality: (likulli maqālin maqām) meaning 'for every discourse, there is a context'. In other words, the text producer needs to take into account what is said, why, when, where, and how. According to Beaugrande and Dressler (1981:179), whether a text is acceptable may depend not on the 'correctness' of its 'reference' to the 'real world' but rather on its believability and relevance to the participants' outlook regarding the situation.

7 Intertextuality: It is the property which texts have of referring, implicitly or explicitly, to other texts. It is the dependence of one text on another. For Beaugrande and Dressler (1981:10), a text is dependent upon the knowledge of one or more previously encountered texts. It subsumes the ways in which the production and reception of a given text depends upon the participant's

> knowledge of other texts (ibid:182). According to Hatim and Munday (2004:343), intertextuality is a precondition for the intelligibility of texts, involving the dependence of one text upon another. Therefore, texts are intertextually related. It is a processing mechanism through which textual elements convey meaning by virtue of their dependence on other relevant texts (Bakhtin 1981; Beaugrande 1980).

A text alludes to other texts, i.e., a text harks back to another text. Thus, text allusion is related to intertextuality. In the view of Beaugrande and Dressler (1981:10), allusion is related to the ways people use or refer to well-known texts. In principle, a text producer can draw upon any available prior text. However, in practice, well-known texts are more suitable as being more readily accessible to the receiver audience (ibid:186). In Qur'anic discourse, intertextuality is primarily concerned with 'thematic reference'. Thematic (conceptual) reference is a Qur'an-specific feature. It is allusion to a given Qur'anic theme (concept, leitmotif, notion). Through Qur'anic intertextuality, thematic chaining within Qur'anic discourse is achieved.

1.3.8 Macro functions of text

The text as a communicative occurrence occurs in a written or spoken language form. It aims to establish bridges of interpersonal relations. However, these bridges vary from one group of people to another. In other words, a writer/speaker engaged with a reader/listener may use different forms of language according to their age, sex, status, relationship, formality, or informality. Thus, language performs three major functions:

1. Field: It refers to a classification of registers in terms of subject matter, e.g., the fields of biology, religion, mathematics (Crystal 2003:145; Hatim and Munday 2004:339).
2. Tenor: It is the relationship between interlocutors (McCabe 2011:390). Tenor is an aspect of register that refers to formality or informality as an aspect of the register to which a text belongs (Hatim and Munday 2004:350). In other words, tenor is concerned with the relations in a text among the participants in a language activity, especially the level of formality they adopt, i.e., whether it is colloquial or formal (Crystal 2003:352).
3. Mode: It is the channel of communication, e.g., written, spoken, etc. Mode is an aspect of register which builds on the basic distinction spoken versus written (Hatim and Munday 2004:344). In other words, mode refers to the medium of the text, i.e., the language activity, which determines the role played by the language in a situation (Crystal 2003:227).

1.3.9 Text typology

There are different types of text such as religious, narrative, journalistic, scientific, instructional, expository, argumentative, descriptive, advertisement, letter, and poetic.

Although these different text types share some but not all features, they fulfil the same standards of textuality. They have different producers and different consumers. They also have different settings of occurrence and different functions. The lexical components of any text type are mutually connected within a sequence. When the words of any text type are disturbed, the text gets disturbed, too. Beaugrande and Dressler (1981:183) assert that a typology of texts must be correlated with typologies of discourse actions and situations.

For Trosborg (1997), the notion of 'text type' refers to a 'mode of discourse' or a 'mode of presentation' which aims to fulfil a rhetorical and communicative purpose. Texts are classified either in terms of their field (domain, subject matter) of discourse (Crystal and Davy 1969; Beaugrande and Dressler 1981:183–186) or in terms of their rhetorical purposes Hatim and Mason (1990:138). Following is an outline of each text type:

1 Qur'anic text type: We can argue that the Qur'an is a text type (genre) in its own right whose subject matter is admonition (wa^c^ẓ). However, the Qur'an also includes Islamic legal rulings (aḥkām), which are legal, narrative passages such as the stories of Prophets (qaṣaṣ al-anbiyā') whose communicative function is admonition, and instructional passages.
2 Religious (liturgy) text type: This is like a Friday prayer sermon (khuṭbat al-jum^c^ah).
3 Scientific text type: A scientific/technical text is marked by factual details but void of emotive, connotative, and figurative expressions and can involve foreign scientific loan words.
4 Journalistic text type: This refers to media reports.
5 Advertisement text type: Advertisements are marked by persuasive discourse, the use of emotive and eye-catching expressions.
6 Narrative text type: This refers to the novel, the short story, and drama and is characterized by dialogue, emotive expression, and figures of speech.
7 Letter text type: This can be divided into (i) formal letters which do not employ figurative, connotative, or emotive expressions, and (ii) informal (personal) letters in which we encounter emotive expressions and figurative language and is sent to friends and relatives.
8 Poetic text type: This can be classified into two: (i) rhymed (fixed rhyme) poetry and (ii) free verse.
9 Instructional text type: Instructional texts are marked by the imperative form of sentences which show the reader/hearer how to do things.
10 Descriptive text type: A descriptive text expresses the writer/speaker's personal view points; thus, it is subjective. In a descriptive text, we encounter emotive, connotative, and figurative expressions.
11 Expository text type: An expository text type includes academic reports, summit reports, police reports, personal reports, and critical reports.
12 Argumentative text type: This includes editorial comments, texts which express the writer's points of view, and letters sent by readers to the editor of a newspaper.

1.3.10 Text analysis

For McCabe (2011:128–129), a text analysis is based on the understanding of clauses and how they relate to each other. There are two types of clause relations: parataxis and hypotaxis (Halliday and Hasan 1976:222–224). These are syntactic means through which clause relations can be established.

1 A paratactic sentence has one clause (a clause simplex). Clauses that can be combined as equals, express different kinds of meaning, and are related to each other in this way are in a paratactic relationship. The paratactic relation is that of coordination, i.e., we have coordinating conjunctions (and, or, but, so).
2 A hypotactic sentence has more than one clause (a clause complex). Clauses which are in an unequal relationship to each other, have a subordination relationship (main clause/subordinate clause), and the clause order can be reversed are in a hypotactic relationship. The hypotactic relation is that of subordination, i.e., we have subordinating conjunctions (if, when, while, until, before, after, if, unless, since, because, where, whereas, so that, in order to, although).

1.3.11 Textual progression

Textual progression is a textual property of the micro and macro Qur'anic text. Textual progression is concerned with coherence and textual cohesion. The investigation of textual progression provides:

i an in-depth account of the conceptual and intertextual links among āyahs (at the micro level) and among sūrahs (at the macro level) and
ii an interpretation of the presentation technique of Qur'anic tenets of faith (monotheism, prophethood, eschatology, and reward and punishment).

The major aim of textual progression is to verify that a text does not lack linear thematic connection, i.e., it is logically connected, and is free of disjointedness. A theme represents a proposition, i.e., a topic of conversation. For a text to progress conceptually, themes (leitmotifs) need to be intertextually related (connected) within it and in relation to the surrounding texts. Thus, the macro text (a sūrah plus a set of consecutive sūrahs) attain intertextuality, which is a major standard of textuality.

Micro level textual progression is well represented through a tenet of faith, such as monotheism (Q2:21), which is backed up by contextual leitmotifs like God's omnipotence (Q2:22), which provides substantiating details for monotheism. At the micro level textual progression, we need to take the macro context into account to see whether or not there is sequentiality (thematic connectivity) between an āyah with a set of preceding or following āyahs, as in Q17:97–99 and Q17:100. Let us consider the following micro level textual progression:

innamā anā basharun mithlukum yūḥa ilaiya annama ilāhukum ilāhun wāḥidun faman kāna yarjū liqā'a rabbihi falyaᶜmal ᶜamalan ṣāliḥan walā

> yushriku bi^cibādati rabbihi aḥadan – I am only a man like you, to whom has been revealed that your god is one God. So whoever would hope for the meeting with his Lord – let him/her not associate in the worship of his/her Lord anyone, Q18:110

where we have the following tenets of faith as constituent units:

- i prophethood (innamā anā basharun mithlukum yūḥā ilaiya – I am only a man like you, to whom has been revealed),
- ii monotheism (annama ilahukum ilahun wahidun – That your god is one God),
- iii eschatology (faman kāna yarjū liqā'a rabbihi – So whoever would hope for the meeting with his/her Lord), and
- iv monotheism (walā yushriku bi^cibādati rabbihi aḥadan – Let him not associate in the worship of his/her Lord anyone).

Another example is:

> ghāfir al-dhanb waqabil al-tawb shadīd al-^ciqāb dhī al-ṭawl lā ilāha illā hū ilaihi al-maṣīr – The forgiver of sin, acceptor of repentance, severe in punishment, owner of abundance. There is no deity except Him; to Him is the destination, Q40:3.

where the major constituents of this āyah are:

- i reward and punishment (ghāfir al-dhanb waqābil al-tawb shadīd al-^ciqāb dhī al-ṭawl – The forgiver of sin, acceptor of repentance, severe in punishment, owner of abundance),
- ii monotheism (lā ilāha illā hū – There is no deity except Him), and
- iii eschatology (ilaihi al-maṣīr – To Him is the destination).

It is worthwhile to note that in Qur'anic discourse, presentation technique is directly related to textual progression. In other words, some tenets of faith co-occur with a given leitmotif. The tenet of faith of monotheism, for instance, is accompanied by other leitmotifs such as God's omnipotence. However, the tenet of faith of reward and punishment is occasionally accompanied by antithesis, as in:

> inna al-abrāra lafī na^cīm wa'inna al-fujjāra lafi jaḥīm – Verily, the pious believers will be in paradise, and verily, the wicked will be in hell, Q82:13–14.

In macro level textual progression, the tenet of faith of monotheism, for instance, is the only constituent of a sūrah like Q112, but we also encounter two major tenets of faith (eschatology and reward and punishment) in Q101:1–5 and Q101:6–11 respectively. Similarly, in long sūrahs, the tenets of faith occur recurrently and at different places to attain macro level textual progression and intertextuality.

1.4 Qur'anic text linguistics

Since the Qur'an is a genre in its own right, i.e., it is a text type of its own, we can claim that its textual analysis requires additional linguistic notions in order to achieve a thorough Qur'anic text linguistic analysis. This means that the notions discussed earlier and provided by the European theory of text linguistics cannot capture the ad hoc textual features of the Qur'anic text. I can claim that the Qur'anic text can be illuminated by a further text linguistic notion, namely textual progression.

In Qur'anic text linguistics, we can put forward the following observations:

i The Qur'anic text progresses thematically through the leitmotifs (themes) which recur within it and which are in relation to the surrounding texts. Thus, the macro text, i.e., the sūrah and a set of consecutive texts (sūrahs) attain intertextuality.
ii Intertextuality is demonstrated through the leitmotifs which hark back to each other and establish thematic connectivity within the sūrah.
iii The intra and inter-thematic relations are shared by neighbouring texts which are intertextually interconnected.
iv The textuality of the Qur'an is entrenched in the thematic and textual chaining (dovetailing) of propositions. Thus, through textual progression and thematic sequentiality, the Qur'anic text has attained continuity of meaning and intertextual relations at intra-sentential and inter-sentential levels (the micro level) and at the inter-sūrah level (the macro level of consecutive sūrahs).
v The thematic bonds at the micro and macro levels are semantic in nature. Through these bonds, intertextual relatedness and textual allusions in the Qur'anic text are achieved.
vi The Qur'anic text has two inherent features: (a) coherence, which represents the meaning relations that reflect thematic sequentiality and intertextuality, and (b) texture, which represents the grammatical and lexical cohesion of Qur'anic discourse.
vii The notions of thematic sequentiality and intertextuality in Qur'anic discourse should be investigated through the linguistic tools of context and co-text.
viii Co-text is the linguistic context and the textual environment in which a word or a sentence occurs. It is concerned with the internal structuring of the text constituents.

1.5 Summary

Text linguistics deals with the communicative relationship through texts between the text producer (the interlocutor, the speaker, the writer) and the text receiver (the listener, the reader) – in other words, how a speaker/writer and a hearer/reader manage to communicate successfully through a text. A text can be written or spoken; it is a unit of language, consists of sentences, and is both cohesive and coherent, i.e., the text has cohesive ties within its sentences, and the sentences are logically linked to each other. If it is a book, the chapters should also be logically related. The text carries the intended meaning of its producer, and this is the pragmatic function of the text.

Therefore, the text can influence its receiver. A successful text should enjoy the seven standards of textuality: cohesion (which deals with the cohesive devices that link the sentences together and which represent cohesive relations among sentences), coherence (which represents the continuity of senses in a text and the logical relationship among the text segments), intentionality (which is the intended meaning of the text producer), informativity (which is the quantity of information provided by the text), acceptability (which refers to the text receiver's attitude towards accepting or rejecting a text), situationality (which deals with how a text is relevant to a situation), and intertextuality (which deals with the relationship between different texts and how a text explains a previously encountered text).

There are many text types, but each text type has a field of a particular subject matter, a tenor (formal/informal), and a mode through which the text is channelled (spoken text/written text). A text should enjoy textual progression which demonstrates its conceptual continuity and relatedness. The macro Qur'anic text is characterized by conceptual (thematic) relatedness (sequentiality, chaining, dovetailing). Thematic relatedness is shared by the neighbouring text segments which share an intertextual relationship of a particular notion (theme, concept). This intertextual relationship has established textual progression and chaining (dovetailing) of Qur'anic themes (concepts, leitmotifs, notions).

2 Qur’anic macro text

2.1 Introduction

The present chapter provides an overview of the most recurrent Qur’anic macro text features which have contributed to the textuality of the Qur’an. In terms of text linguistics, we encounter frequent recurrence of macro text features like: (1) occurrence (of sentences, set formulas, grammatical patterns, and specific lexical items in terms of their number and sentence position), (2) synonymy, (3) repetition (of content words and function words), (4) formulas, (5) epithets, (6) leitmotifs, (7) Qur’anic parables, (8) premise and rebuttal, (9) deductive argument, (10) shift (word order, sentence-final verb, contextual shift, number, particle), (11) noun-initial sentences, (12) mutashābihāt, (13) thematic coherence, (14) relevance-based lexical items, (15) intertextuality, (16) God’s omnipotence argumentation technique, and (17) tenets of faith. The examples discussed here are of value to Qur’anic corpus linguistics.

2.2 Macro text features

This is an account of the macro text features of Qur’anic discourse. The analysis is concerned with the macro text level. This investigation involves lexical, grammatical, and stylistic features.

2.2.1 Macro text occurrence

The present discussion accounts for the occurrence of either lexical items or sentences on the macro level. The lexical items are either content words or function words. It also accounts for the lexical item’s position in the sentence, i.e., whether it occupies initial, middle, or final sentence position.

1 Occurrence of sentences once: There are sentences that have occurred only once in the Qur’an, as in sentence 89 of Q20, which is the only sentence in the Qur’an that starts with the interrogative phrase (afalā yarawna – did they not see?). Sentence 95 of Q21 is the only sentence in the Qur’an which starts with the verb (wa ḥarāmun – and there is prohibition). Sentence 64

of Q39 is the only sentence in the Qur'an which begins with (qul afaghair – is it other than). Q24:20 is the only sentence in the Qur'an in which the nominal sentence (allāhu ra'ūfun raḥim – God is kind and merciful) occurs. Q60:11 is the only sentence in the Qur'an in which the verb (dhahabat – went, feminine, singular) occurs. Sentence 15 of Q18 is the only sentence in the Qur'an which starts with the demonstrative pronoun (hā'ulā'i – these). Q42:5 (inna allāha huwa al-ghafūr al-raḥīm – Unquestionably, it is God who is the forgiving, the merciful) is the only syntactic structure with (inna + subject + pronoun + two adjectives) in the Qur'an in this stylistic pattern.

2 Occurrence of sentences twice: There are sentences that have occurred only twice in the Qur'an, as in sentences Q2:274–275 in which the relative pronoun (alladhīna – those who) occurs in sentence-initial position in sentences immediately after each other only twice in the Qur'an. The pronoun (huwa – He (God)) occurs in sentence-initial position in sentences immediately after each other only twice in the Qur'an, as in Q3:6–7. The additive conjunctive particle (wa) + the preposition (ᶜalā – on) → (wa ᶜalā – and on) occurs in sentence-initial position only twice in the Qur'an, as in Q6:146 and Q16:118. The compound conjunctive particle (ammā . . . fa): ammā + relative pronoun + verb + complement → (ammā alladhīna kafarū . . . fa – but as for those who disbelieved) occurs in sentence-initial position only twice in the Qur'an, as in Q30:16 and Q45:31.

3 Occurrence of formulas twice: The phrase formula (inna lil-muttaqīna – indeed, for the righteous) occurs sentence-initially only twice in the Qur'an, as in Q68:34, Q78:31. The phrase formula (lillāhi mulku al-samāwāti wal-arḍi – to God belongs the dominion of the heavens and the earth) occurs sentence-initially only twice in the Qur'an, as in Q5:120 and Q42:49. The phrase formula (al-ḥaqqu min rabbika – the truth is from your Lord) occurs in sentence initial position only twice in the Qur'an, as in Q2:147 and Q3:60.

4 Occurrence of syntactic patterns twice: The syntactic structure: inna + subject noun → (inna rabbakum allāhu – Indeed, your Lord is God) occurs in sentence-initial position only twice in the Qur'an, as in Q7:54 and Q10:3. The syntactic structure: in + nominal sentence → (in kānat illā saiḥatan wāḥidatan – it was not but one shout) occurs in sentence-initial position only twice in the Qur'an, as in Q36:29 and Q36:53. The syntactic structure: in + verbal sentence → (in tadᶜūhum – if you invite them) occurs in sentence-initial position only twice in the Qur'an, as in Q7:193 and Q7:198. The syntactic structure: in + verbal sentence → (in yurīdū – if they intend) occurs in sentence-initial position only twice in the Qur'an, as in Q8:62 and Q8:71. The syntactic structure: in + verbal sentence → (in yamsaska allāhu biḍurrin falā kāshifa lahu illā hū – if God should touch you with adversity, there is no remover of it except Him) occurs in sentence-initial position only twice in the Qur'an, as in Q6:17 and Q10:107. The syntactic structure: verb → (fa'awjasa – and he felt) occurs in sentence-initial position only twice in the Qur'an, as in Q20:67 and Q51:28. The syntactic structure: verb + subject + object → (jaᶜalnā al-laila – We (God) have made the night) occurs in

sentence-initial position only twice in the Qur'an, as in Q17:12 and Q78:10. The syntactic structure: passive voice verb + prepositional phrase → (yuṭāfu ᶜalaihim – there will be circulated among them) occurs sentence-initially only twice in the Qur'an, as in Q37:45 and Q43:71. The syntactic structure: imperative verb → (falyanẓur – look at) occurs sentence-initially only twice in the Qur'an, as in Q80:24 and Q86:5. The syntactic structure: verb (qāla) + object + subject → (qāla lahum mūsā – Moses said to them) occurs in sentence-initial position only twice in the Qur'an, as in Q20:61 and Q26:43. The syntactic structure: conjunctive particle (qad) + verb → (qad khasira – have lost) occurs in sentence-initial position only twice in the Qur'an, as in Q6:31 and Q6:140. The syntactic structure with a negation particle (lā) + imperative verb → (lā taqūlū – do not say) occurs sentence-initially only twice in the Qur'an, as in Q2:154 and Q16:116. The syntactic structure with a negation particle (mā) + verb → (mā ahlaknā – We (God0 did not destroy) occurs sentence-initially only twice in the Qur'an, as in Q15:4 and Q26:208. The syntactic structure with a negation particle (laisa) + nominal sentence → (laisa ᶜalaikum junāḥ – there is no blame upon you) occurs sentence-initially only twice in the Qur'an, as in Q2:198 and Q24:29. The syntactic structure with the vocative → (yā nisā'a al-nabiy – O wives of the Prophet) occurs in sentence-initial position only twice in the Qur'an, as in Q33:30 and Q33:32. The syntactic structure: vocative → (yā qawmi lā – O my people do not) occurs sentence-initially only twice in the Qur'an, as in Q11:29 and Q11:89. The syntactic structure: relative pronoun + verb → (alladhīna hājarū – those who immigrated) occurs in sentence-initial position only twice in the Qur'an, as in Q16:41 and Q22:58. The syntactic structure: relative pronoun + passive voice verb → (alladhīna yutawaffawna – those who are taken in death) occurs in sentence-initial position only twice in the Qur'an, as in Q2:234 and Q2:240. The syntactic structure: prepositional phrase + prepositional phrase → (lakum fīhā – for you therein) occurs sentence-initially only twice in the Qur'an, as in Q22:33 and Q43:73.

5 Occurrence of lexical items or sentences three times: The masculine plural active participle noun (sā'ilīn – the needy petitioners) occurs only three times in the Qur'an, as in Q2:177, Q12:7, and Q41:10. There are only three sentences in the Qur'an which occur consecutively with the initial vocative word (rabbanā – our Lord): Q3:192, 193, and 194.

There are only three sentences in the Qur'an which occur consecutively with the initial word (dhālika – that): Q22:60, 61, and 62. There are only three sentences in the Qur'an which occur with the initial passive voice verb (qutila – are destroyed), as in Q51:10, Q80:17, and Q85:4. There are only three sentences in the Qur'an which occur with the initial noun (salāmun – peace), as in Q13:24, Q36:58, and Q97:5.

6 Occurrence of lexical items or sentences four times: The masculine singular active participle noun (sā'il – the needy petitioner) occurs only four times in the Qur'an, as in Q51:19, Q70:1, Q70:25, and Q93:10. There are only four sentences in the Qur'an which occur with an initial third person masculine plural pronoun (hum – they): Q3:163, Q36:56, Q48:25, and Q63:7.

7 Occurrence of a word once in sentence-final position in a sūrah: Q78:40 is the only sentence which concludes with the word (turābā – dust). Q3:5, Q14:24, and Q14:38 are the only sentences which conclude with the word (al-samā' – the sky).

2.2.2 Macro text synonyms

Synonymy is a semantic macro text feature of Qur'anic discourse. For instance, the noun phrase (yawm al-qiyāmah – the day of resurrection), which refers to eschatology (resurrection) as a tenet of faith has the following synonyms in the Qur'an:

(yawm al-dīn – the day of recompense) Q1:4
(al-yawm al-ākhir – the last day) Q2:177
(yawm al-ḥasrah – the day of regret) Q19:39
(yawm al-baᶜth – the day of resurrection) Q30:56
(yawm al-ḥisāb – the day of account) Q38:53
(yawm al-talāq – the day of meeting) Q40:15
(yawm al-azifah – the approaching day) Q40:18
(yawm al-tanād – the day of calling) Q40:32
(yawm taqūm al-sāᶜah – the day the hour appears) Q40:46
(yawm al-jamᶜ – the day of assembly) Q42:7
(yawm al-waᶜīd – the day of the threat) Q50:20
(yawm al-khulūd – the day of eternity) Q50:34
(yawm al-khurūj – the day of emergence) Q50:42
(al-wāqi ᶜah – the (day of) occurrence) Q56:1
(yawm al-taghabun – the day of deprivation) Q64:9
(al-ḥāqqah – the (day of) inevitable reality) Q69:3
(al-qāri ᶜah – the (day of) striking calamity) Q69:4
(yawm al-faṣl – the day of judgement) Q77:38
(al-ṭāmmah – the (day of) overwhelming calamity) Q79:34
(al-ṣākhkhah – the (day of) deafening blast) Q80:33
(al-ghāshiyah – the (day of) overwhelming event) Q88:1

2.2.3 Macro text repetition

Repetition is a prototypical stylistic feature of Qur'anic genre. The major rhetorical functions of repetition in Qur'anic discourse are diaphora (al-tawkīd al-lafẓī) and epizeuxis (al-tikrār al-tawkīdī). Linguistically, repetition is context sensitive and is employed to achieve lexical cohesion. In Qur'anic genre, repetition includes content words and function words.

2.2.3.1 Repetition of content words

The stylistic technique of repeating certain words is a stylistic macro textual feature of Qur'anic discourse. Linguistically, the lexical items are content words like nouns, verbs, adjectives, or adverbs. This kind of stylistic technique is explained in the following examples:

> qāla mā mana^c^aka allā tasjuda . . ., qāla anā khairun minhu . . ., qāla fahbiṭ minhā . . ., qāla anẓirnī ilā yawmi al-dīn . . ., qāla innaka min al-munẓarīn . . ., qāla fabimā aghwaitanī la'aq^c^udanna lahum . . . – (God) said: 'What prevented you from prostrating . . . ', (Satan) said: 'I am better than him (Adam) . . . ', (God) said: 'Descend from it (paradise) . . . ', (Satan) said: 'Reprieve me until the day they are resurrected'. (God) said: 'Indeed, you are of those reprieved'. (Satan) said: 'Because You (God) have put me in error, I will surely sit in wait for them . . . ', Q7:12–16.

where the verb (qāla – said) is repeated six times.

> lā a^c^budu mā ta^c^budūn . lā antum ^c^ābidūna mā a^c^bud. lā ana ^c^ābidun mā ^c^abadtum. lā antum ^c^ābidūna mā a^c^bud . . . – I do not worship what you worship, nor are you worshipping of what I worship, nor will I be a worshipper of what you worship, nor will you be worshippers of what I worship, Q109:2–5.

where the content lexical items are the verb (a^c^bud – to worship) and the noun (^c^ābid – worshipper) have been repeated.

> qul a^c^ūdhu birabbi al-nāss. maliki al-nāss. ilāhi al-nāss. min sharri al-waswās khannāss. alladhī yuwaswisu fī ṣudūri al-nāss. min al-jinnati wa al-nāss – Say: 'I seek refuge in the Lord of mankind, the Sovereign of mankind, the God of mankind, from the evil of the retreating whisperer who whispers evil into the breasts of mankind, from among the jinn and mankind', Q114:1–6.

Throughout this Qur'anic chapter, the content word (al-nāss – mankind), which is a noun, is repeated five times.

2.2.3.2 Repetition of function words

These linguistic items are function words like conjunctive particles, prepositions, pronouns, and relative pronouns. This kind of stylistic technique is explained in the following examples:

i conjunctive particles like (idhā – when), (idh – when), (inna – indeed, verily), (lā – no), (laqad – certainly), as in the following examples:

> idhā qīla lahum lā tufsidū . . . idhā qīla lahum āminū . . . idhā laqū alladhīna āmanū . . . – When it is said to them: 'Do not make mischief . . .' When it is said to them 'Believe . . .' When they meet those who believe, . . ., Q2:11–14

The particle (idhā) also occurs in Q81:1–13.

idh ibtalā ibrāhīmu rabbuhu . . ., idh ja^{c}alnā al-baita . . ., idh qāla ibrāhīmu . . ., idh yarfa^{c}u ibrāhīmu al-qawā^{c}ida . . . – When Abraham was tried by his Lord . . ., When We (God) made the House (the Ka^{c}bah) . . ., When Abraham said . . ., When Abraham was raising the foundations . . ., Q2:124–127

where the temporal conjunctive particles (idhā – when) and (idh – when) are repeated.

inna alladhīna yaktumūna . . ., inna alladhīna kafarū . . ., inna fi khalqi alsamāwāti wal-arḍi . . . – Indeed, those who conceal . . ., Indeed, those who disbelieve . . ., Indeed, in the creation of the heavens and the earth . . ., Q2:159–164

where the affirmation particle (inna – indeed) is repeated.

lā a^{c}budu mā ta^{c}budūn . lā antum ^{c}ābidūna mā a^{c}bud. lā anā ^{c}ābidun mā ^{c}abad-tum. lā antum ^{c}ābidūna mā a^{c}bud . . . – I do not worship what you worship, nor are you worshipping of what I worship, nor will I be a worshipper of what you worship, nor will you be worshippers of what I worship, Q109:2–5

where the negation particle (lā – no) is repeated four times.

laqad makkannākum fī al-arḍi . . ., laqad khalaqnākum . . . – Certainly, We (God) have established you upon the earth . . . Certainly, We (God) have created you . . ., Q7:10–11

where the affirmation particle (laqad – certainly) is repeated.

Other repeated particles are those like (am – or) as in Q52:30–43, (ammā – as for) as in Q93:9–11, and (fa – and) as in Q101:2–5.

ii prepositions like (min – from), as in the following examples:

min sharri mā khalaq, min sharri ghāsiqin . . . min sharri al-naffāthāti . . . min sharri ḥāsidin idhā ḥasad – From the evil of that which He (God) created, from the evil of darkness . . ., from the evil of the blowers . . ., from the evil of an envier when he envies, Q113:2–5

iii pronouns such as (huwa – he), as in the following examples:

huwa alladhī yuṣawwirukum fī al-arḥāmi . . ., huwa alladhī anzala ^{c}alaika al-kitāba . . . – It is He (God) who forms you in the wombs . . ., It is He (God) who has sent down to you (Muḥammad) the Book . . ., Q3:6–7

huwa alladhī khalaqakum min ṭīnin . . ., huwa allāhu fī al-samāwāti wafī al-arḍi . . . huwa alladhī ja^{c}ala lakum al-nujūma . . ., huwa alladhī ansha'akum min nafsin wāḥidatin . . ., huwa alladhī arsala min al-samā'i mā'an . . . – It is He who created you from clay . . ., He is God the only deity in the heavens and the earth . . ., It is He (God) who placed for you the stars . . ., It is He (God) who produced you from one soul . . ., It is He (God) who sends down rain from the sky . . ., Q6:2–3 and Q6:97–99 iv relative pronouns, as in the following examples:

alladhīna yunfiqūna fī al-sarrā'i wal-ḍarrā'i . . ., alladhīna idhā fa^calu fāḥishatan . . . – Who spend in the cause of God during ease and hardship . . ., Who, when they commit an immorality . . ., Q3:134–135

alladhīna yabītūna lirabbihim . . ., alladhīna yaqūlūna . . ., alladhīna idhā anfaqū . . ., alladhīna lā yad^cūna ma^ca allāhi ilāhan ākhara . . . – Who spend part of the night to their Lord . . ., Who say . . ., Who, when they spend . . ., Who do not invoke with God another deity . . ., Q25:64–68

Other repeated relative pronouns are those like (amman – who), as in:

amman khalaqa al-samāwāti wal-arḍa . . . amman ja^cala al-arḍa qarāran . . . amman yujību al-muḍṭarra idhā da^cāhu . . . amman yahdīkum fī ẓulumāti al-barri wal-baḥri . . . amman yabda'u al-khalqa thumma yu^cīduhu . . . – Is it He (God) not best who created the heavens and the earth . . . Is it He not best who made the earth a stable ground . . . Is it He not best who responds to the desperate one when he calls upon Him (God) . . . Is it He not best who guides you through the darkness of the land and sea . . . Is it He not best who begins creation and then repeats it . . ., Q27:60–64.

2.2.4 Macro text formulas

Linguistically, a formula is a fixed (frozen) expression which features in Qur'anic discourse and can be repeated in consecutive sentences, as in:

ilāhukum ilāhun wāḥidun – Your God is one God.

The above Qur'anic set formula has occurred in Q2:163, Q16:22, Q18:110, Q21:108, Q22:34.

ilā allāhi (rabbikum) marji^cukum jamī^can – Your return all together is to God.

The above formula has occurred in Q5:48, Q6:60, 164, Q11:4, and Q39:7.

ilā allāhi turja^cu al-umūr – All matters are returned to God.

The above set formula has occurred in Q2:210, Q3:109, Q8:44, Q22:76, Q35:4, and Q57:5.

yā qawmi u^cbudū allāha mā lakum min ilāhin ghairuhu – O my people, worship God; you have no deity other than Him.

The above set formula has occurred four times in Q7:59, 65, 73, 85. This formula has also occurred three times in Q11:50, 61, 84.

inna fī dhālika la'āyatan/wamā kāna aktharuhum mu'minīn/wa inna rabbaka lahuwa al-^cazīzu al-raḥīm – Indeed, in that is a sign/but most of them were not to be believers./Indeed, your Lord, He is the exalted in might, the merciful, Q26.

In the above example, the repetition of the fixed formulas occurs eight times in Q26:8–9, 67–68, 103–104, 121–122, 139–140, 158–159, 174–175, and 190–191.

a'ilāhun ma^{c}a allāh – Is there a deity with God?

The above formula has occurred five times in Q27:60–64.

fabi'aiyi ālā'i rabbikumā tukadhdhibān – So which of the favours of your Lord would you deny? Q55.

The above Qur'anic formula has occurred 31 times in Q55, such as Q55:13, 16, 18, 21, 23.

ittakhadhū min dūni allāhi ālihatan – They have taken besides Him (God) deities.

The above formula has occurred in Q18:15, Q19:81, Q21:24, Q25:3, Q36:23, and Q36:74.

inna rabbaka lahuwa al-^{c}azīzu al-raḥīmu – Indeed, your lord – He is the exalted in might, the merciful.

The above Qur'anic set formula has occurred eight times in Q26:9, 68, 104, 122, 140, 159, 175, 191.

2.2.5 Macro text epithets

The macro Qur'anic text is marked by recurrent reference of epithet couplets, as in the following examples:

al-raḥmānu al-raḥīm – the entirely merciful, the especially merciful.

The above has occurred several times, as in Q1:1, 3, QQ2:163, Q27:30, Q59:22, and Q27:30, 41:2.

al-ghafūr al-raḥīm – the forgiving, the merciful.

The above has occurred several times, as in Q2:173, 182, 192, 199, 218, 225, 226, Q3:31, 89, 129, Q4:25, Q5:3, 34, 39, 74, 98, 101, Q9:27, 91, 99, 102, Q16:18, 110, 115, 119, Q24:5, 22, 33, 62, and Q35:28, 30, 34, 53.

al-^{c}alīm al-ḥakīm – the knowing, the wise.

The above has occurred several times, as in Q2:32, Q4:26, Q8:71, 75, Q9:15, 28, 97, 106, 110, Q12:6, 83, 100, Q15:25, Q22:52, and Q24:18, 59.

al-^{c}azīz al-raḥīm – the exalted in might, the merciful.

The above has occurred several times, as in Q30:5, Q32:6, Q36:5, and Q44:42.

al-^{c}aziz al-ḥakīm – the exalted in might, the wise.

The above has occurred several times, as in Q2:129, 209, 220, 228, 240, 260, Q3:6, 18, 62, 126, Q5:38, 118, Q8:10, 49, 63, 67, Q9:40, 71, Q29:26, 42, Q31:9, 27, and Q45:2, 37.

2.2.6 Macro text leitmotifs

On the macro text level, Qur'anic discourse is marked by sentences that are structurally and stylistically different but are thematically and conceptually similar on the one hand and are intertextually related on the other. Through such sentences, Qur'anic discourse achieves two major text linguistic features: intertextuality and textual cohesion. The following sentences demonstrate how they are intertextually and thematically (conceptually) related:

> walā taqtulū awlādakum min imlāqin naḥnu narzuqukum wa'iyyāhum – Do not kill your children out of poverty. We (God) will provide for you and them, Q6:151

The leitmotif (killing own children) of the above sentence is repeated in a different style. Thus, Q6:151 is intertextually related to the following sentence, which has the same theme:

> walā taqtulū awlādakum khashyata imlāqin naḥnu narzuquhum wa'iyyākum – Do not kill your children for fear of poverty. We (God) will provide for them and for you, Q17:31.

Similarly, the leitmotif (Satan's refusal to prostrate to God) is expressed in different styles establishing intertextuality among the stylistically different but conceptually similar sentences as demonstrated in the following examples:

> fasajadū illā iblīsa abā wastakbara wakāna min al-kāfirīn – They prostrated except for Satan. He refused and was arrogant and became among the disbelievers, Q2:34.
> illā iblīṣa abā – Except for Satan. He refused, Q20:116
> illā iblīsa istakbara wakāna min al-kāfirīn – Except for Satan. He was arrogant and became among the disbelievers, Q38:74.
> illā iblīsa lam yakun min al-sājidīn – Except for Satan. He was not of those who prostrated, Q7:11.
> illā iblīsa abā an yakūna min al-sājidīn – Except for Satan. He refused to be with those who prostrated, Q15:31.
> illā iblīsa qāla a'asjudu liman khalaqta ṭīnā – Except for Satan. He said: 'Should I prostrate to one You (God) created from clay?', Q17:61.

2.2.7 Macro text parables

Qur'anic discourse is marked by parables. Their major features are:

i On the macro level, parables occur at different places throughout the Qur'anic text,
ii Qur'anic parables are of different lengths,
iii They are of different styles although they talk about the same theme, and
iv They serve the text linguistic functions of intertextuality and textual cohesion.

In terms of stylistic shift, only Q12 (sūrat yūsuf) occurs once, i.e., it is not repeated elsewhere in the Qur'an.

The repetition of parables involves either:

i The occurrence of a parable very briefly in a couple of lines only, or
ii The occurrence of the same parable in detail but in a different style.

For instance, the parable of Noah has occurred in the Qur'an 23 times: Q4:163, Q6:84, Q7:59–64, Q9:70, Q10:71–73, Q11:25–49, Q14:9, Q17:17, Q21:76–77, Q23:23–30, Q26:105–122, Q29:14–15, Q33:7, Q37:75–82, Q40:5, Q42:13, Q50:12–14, Q51:46, Q53:52, Q54:9–16, Q57:26, Q66:10, and Q71:1–28. It is interesting to note that although the parable of Noah has occurred 23 times at different places and in varying lengths, in all these 23 instances, different stylistic patterns and linguistic structures have been employed. The parable of Moses has occurred 10 times in the Qur'an: Q7:103–157, Q10:75–93, Q11:96–101, Q20:9–99, Q23:45–68, Q27:7–14, Q3–44, Q40:23–56.

2.2.8 Macro text premise and rebuttal

Argumentation is a major Qur'anic macro text feature. Throughout the Qur'an, we encounter both God's (protagonist's) thesis and the opponent's (antagonist's) (denier, rejecter – munkir) thesis (premise). In Qur'anic argumentation, the response to opponents' premises is through rebuttal techniques which are usually represented by God's omnipotence details, as will be explained in the following examples. Let us first consider God's premises and how they are substantiated (defended/rebutted):

Example 1

God's premise on monotheism: ilāhukum ilāhun wāḥidun lā ilāha illā huwa al-raḥmānu al-raḥīimu – Your god is one God. There is no deity worthy of worship except Him, the entirely merciful, the exceptionally merciful, Q2:163.

Substantiation to premise: inna fī khalqi al-samāwāti wal-arḍi wakhtilāfi al-laili wal-nahāri wal-fulki allatī tajrī fī al-baḥri bimā yanfaᶜu al-nāsa wamā anzala allāhu min al-samā'i min mā'in fa'aḥyā bihi al-arḍa baᶜda mawtihā wabaththa fīhā min kulli dābbatin wataṣrīf al-riyāḥi wal-saḥābi al-musakh-khari baina al-samā'i wal-arḍi la'āyātin liqawmin yaᶜqilūn – Indeed, in the creation of the heavens and the earth, and the alternation of the night and the day, and the ships which sail through the sea with that which benefits people, and what God has sent down from the heavens of rain, giving life thereby to the earth after its lifelessness and dispersing therein every kind of moving creature, and his directing of the winds and the clouds controlled between the heaven and earth are signs for a people who use reason, Q2:164

Example 2

God's premise on monotheism: inna rabbakumu allāhu – Indeed, your Lord is God, Q7:54.

Substantiation to premise: khalaqa al-samāwāti wal-arḍa fī sittati aiyāmin thumma istawā ᶜalā al-ᶜarshi yughshī al-laila al-nahāra yaṭlubuhu ḥathīthā wal-shamsa wal-qamara wal-nūjuma musakhkharātin bi'amrihi alā lahu al-khalqu wal-amru tabāraka allāhu rabbu al-ᶜālamīn – He created the heavens and earth in six days and then established Himself above the throne. He covers the night with the day another night chasing it rapidly, and He created the sun, the moon, and the stars, subjected by His command. Unquestionably, His is the creation and the command, blessed is God, Lord of the worlds, Q7:54.

Example 3

God's premise on resurrection and reward and punishment: qad aflaḥa al-mu'minūn . . . ulā'ika hum al-wārithūn alladhīna yarithūna al-firdawsa – Certainly will the believers have succeeded . . . Those are the inheritors who will inherit paradise, Q23:1–11.

Substantiation to premise: laqad khalaqnā al-insāna min sulālatin min ṭīn thumma jaᶜalnāhu nuṭfatan . . . thumma khalaqnā al-nuṭfata ᶜalaqatan . . . fakasawnā al-ᶜiẓama laḥman . . . thumma innakum baᶜda dhālika lamaiyitūn thumma innakum yawa al-qiyāmati tubᶜathūn – Certainly the believers will have succeeded . . . Those are the inheritors who will inherit the highest part of paradise . . . Certainly We (God) created man from an extract of clay. Then We (God) placed him as a sperm-drop in a womb. Then We (God) made the sperm-drop into a clinging clot . . . We (God) covered the bones with flesh . . . Then indeed, after that you are to die. Then indeed, on the day of resurrection, you will be resurrected, Q23:12–16.

Example 4

God's premise on monotheism: mattakhadha allāhu min waladin wamā kāna maᶜahu min ilāh – God has not taken any son, nor has there ever been with Him any deity, Q23:91.

Substantiation to premise: idhan ladhahaba kullu ilāhin bimā khalaqa walaᶜalā baᶜḍuhum ᶜalā baᶜḍ – If there had been, then each deity would have taken what it created, and some of them would have sought to overcome others, Q23:91.

Example 5

God's premise on monotheism: aqim wajhaka lildīni ḥanīfan – Direct yourself towards the religion, inclining to truth, Q30:30.

Substantiation to premise: fiṭrata allāhi allatī faṭara al-nāsa ᶜalaihā/lā tabdīla likhalqi allāhi/dhālika al-dīnu al-qaiyimu/walākinna akthara al-nāsi ḷā yaᶜlamūn – Adhere to the inherent nature of mankind (fiṭrah) given by God and upon which He has created all people. No change should there be in the creation of God. That is the correct religion, but most of the people do not know, Q30:30.

However, we also encounter opponents' premises and how they are rebutted. The following are examples of this macro text feature:

Example 1

The opponent's premise is about his denial of resurrection: annā yuḥyi hādhihi allāhu ba^{c}da mawtihā – How will God bring this to life after its death?, Q2:259

Rebuttal to opponent's thesis: unẓur ilā al-^{c}iẓāmi kaifa nunshizuhā thumma naksūhā laḥmā – Look at the bones how We (God) raise them and then We cover with flesh, Q2:259.

Example 2

The opponent's premise is about his denial of resurrection: a'idhā mitnā wakunnā turāban dhālika raj^{c}un ba^{c}īd – When we have died and have become dust, will we return to life? That is unlikely to happen, Q50:3.

Rebuttal to opponent's thesis: afalam yanẓurū ilā al-samā'i fawqahum kaifa banaināhā . . . wal-arḍa madadnāhā . . . wa'anbatnā fīhā min kulli zawjin bahīj . . . wanazzalnā min al-samā'i mā'an mubārakan fa'anbatnā bihi jannātin waḥabba al-ḥaṣīd . . . wa'aḥyainā bihi baldatan maitan kadhālika al-khurūj – When we have died and have become dust will we return to life? That is unlikely to happen . . . Have they not looked at the heaven above them – how We (God) structure it . . . and the earth – We (God) spread it out . . . and made grow therein something of everything beautiful kind . . . and We (God) have sent down blessed rain from the sky and made grow thereby gardens and grain from the harvest . . . and We (God) have given life thereby to a dead land. Thus is the resurrection, Q50:6–11.

For more details on premise and rebuttal in argumentation, see Chapter 4.

2.2.9 Macro text deductive argument

The deductive argument (reasoning scheme) is a major Qur'anic macro text feature. Throughout the Qur'an, we encounter God's omnipotence details functioning as a deductive argument through which the reader/listener is persuaded and enabled to reach a conclusion that supports God's premise, as in the following example:

> It is He (God) who created heavens and earth . . . He created man from a sperm-drop . . . He has created the livestock for you . . . and created the horses, mules, and donkeys for you . . . It is He who sends down rain from the sky . . . He causes to grow for you thereby the crops, olives, palm trees . . . Indeed in that is a sign for a people who give thought. He has subjected for you the night and day and the sun and moon, and the stars are subjected by His command. Indeed in that are signs for a people who reason. He has subjected whatever

> He multiplied for you on the earth of varying colours. Indeed in that is a sign for a people who remember. It is He who subjected the sea for you to eat from it tender meat and to extract from it ornaments which you wear . . . He has cast into the earth firmly set mountains . . . And landmarks. And by the stars they are also guided. Then is He (God) who creates like one who does not create?, Q16:3–17

In the above text segments, we are introduced to the sign topic (āyah (singular) or āyāt (plural)) as a Qur'anic macro text feature. The deductive argument above has listed twelve signs which are the foundation of the logical reasoning that leads to the conclusion prescribed in Q16:17 (afaman yakhluqu kaman lā yakhluq – Then is He (God) who creates like one who does not create?) and the hearer/reader will also be persuaded to believe in the initial premise (annahu lā ilāha illā anā fattaqūn – There is no deity except Me (God), so fear Me, Q16:2) and the subsequent premise (ilāhukum ilāhun wāḥidun – Your god is one God, Q16:22). Thus, the 12 signs and their characteristics are employed for persuasion and the verification (substantiation) of the text producer's thesis (argument, premise). The 12 signs are: (the creation of the heavens and earth, the creation of mankind, the creation of livestock, the creation of horses, mules, and donkeys, the sending down of water for drink and for growing trees, making the night, the day, the sun, the moon and the stars of benefit to mankind, making the many-coloured things on earth of benefit to mankind, making the sea of benefit to mankind, making the mountains stand firm on the earth, making rivers on the earth, making paths on the earth for people to find their way, and the creation of stars to guide people through the desert or the sea at night).

Another example of a deductive argument is:

> inna fī khalqi al-samāwāti wal-arḍi wakhtilāfi al-laili wal-nahāri wal-fulki allatī tajrī fī al-baḥri bimā yanfaᶜu al-nāsa wamā anzala allāhu min al-samā'i min mā'in fa'aḥyā bihi al-arḍa baᶜda mawtihā wabaththa fihā min kulli dābbatin wataṣrīf al-riyāḥi wal-saḥābi al-musakhkhari baina al-samā'i wal-arḍi la'āyātin liqawmin yaᶜqilūn – Indeed, in the creation of the heavens and the earth, and the alternation of the night and the day, and the ships which sail through the sea with that which benefits people, and what God has sent down from the heavens of rain, giving life thereby to the earth after its lifelessness and dispersing therein every kind of moving creature, and His directing of the winds and the clouds controlled between the heaven and earth are signs for a people who use reason, Q2:164

where many God's omnipotence details are listed and are employed to substantiate God's premise on monotheism: (ilāhukum ilāhun wāḥidun lā ilāha illā huwa al-raḥmānu al-raḥīmu – Your god is one God. There is no deity worthy of worship except Him, the entirely merciful, the exceptionally merciful, Q2:163). These examples are: (khalqi al-samāwāti wal-arḍi – the creation of the heavens and the earth), (ikhtilāf al-lail wal-nahār – the alternation of the night and the day), (al-fulk allatī tajrī fī al-baḥri bimā yanfaᶜu al-nāsa – the ships which sail through the sea with that which benefits people), (mā anzala allāhu min al-samā'i min mā'in fa'aḥyā bihi al-arḍa baᶜda mawtihā – what God has sent down from the heavens of rain, giving life thereby to the earth after its lifelessness), (baththa fīhā min kulli dābbatin – dispersing therein every kind of moving creature), (taṣrīf al-riyāḥ – His directing of the winds), and (al-saḥābi al-musakhkhari baina al-samā'i wal-arḍ – the clouds controlled between the heavens and earth). Thus, these signs (āyāt) are the foundation of the logical reasoning that leads to the deduction (conclusion, inference) that supports God's premise on monotheism.

2.2.10 Macro text shift

The grammatical process of shift occurs throughout the Qur'anic discourse whether at micro (sentence) level or at macro (text) level. The macro text level shift is concerned with shift that occurs in different places of the Qur'anic discourse and it has different types. The macro text types of shift are discussed in what follows.

2.2.10.1 Word order shift

The word order (Verb + Subject + Complement) in a number of consecutive sentences may change to other word orders, as in:

> atā amru allāhi falā tastaᶜjilūh . . . yunazzilu al-malā'ikata bilrūḥi min amrihi . . . khalaqa al-samāwāti wal-arḍa bil-ḥaqqi . . . khalaqa al-insāna min nuṭfatin . . . al-anᶜāma khalaqahā. lakum fīhā dif'un . . . lakum fīhā jamālun . . . taḥmilu athqālakum . . . al-khaila wal-bighāla wal-ḥamīra litarkabūhā . . . ᶜalā allāhi qaṣda al-sabīl . . . huwa alladhī anzala min al-samā'i mā'an . . . yunbitu lakum bihi al-zarᶜa . . . sakhkharā lakum al-laila wal-nahāra . . . – The command of God is coming, so do not be impatient for it . . . He sends down the angels, with His revelation . . . He created the heavens and earth in truth . . . He created man from a sperm-drop . . . He created the grazing livestock for you, in them there is warmth . . . For you in them, there is the enjoyment of beauty . . . They carry your loads . . . The horses, mules, and donkeys are for you to ride . . . Upon God is the direction of the right way . . . It is He who sends down rain from the sky . . . He causes to grow for you thereby the crops . . . He has subjected for you the night and day . . ., Q16:1–12.

where we have: (Verb + Subject + Complement) syntactic structures represented by verb-initial sentences (atā – is coming), (yunazzilu – send down), (khalaqa – created), (khalaqa – created). Then we have a word order shift to thematic structures: (Object + Verb + Subject + Coreferential Pronoun + Complement), as in:

> al-anᶜāma khalaqahā – He created the grazing livestock, Q16:5.

where (al-anᶜāma – the grazing livestock) is the object noun; then a word order shift to a no-main-verb nominal sentence:

> lakum fihā dif'un – In them there is warmth, Q16:5.
>
> lakum fihā jamālun – For you in them, there is the enjoyment of beauty, Q16:6.

Then we have another word order shift to: (Verb + Subject + Complement), as in: taḥmilu athqālakum – They carry your loads, Q16:7

Then we have a word order shift to thematic structures: (Object + Verb + Subject + Coreferential Pronoun + Complement), as in:

> al-khaila wal-bighāla wal-ḥamīra litarkabūhā – The horses, mules, and donkeys are for you to ride, Q16:8.

where we have three object nouns: (al-khaila/al-bighāla/al-ḥamīra).

Then we have a word order shift to a no-main-verb nominal sentence with a foregrounded prepositional phrase (ᶜalā allāhi – upon God), as in:

> ᶜala allāhi qaṣda al-sabīl – Upon God is the direction of the right way, Q16:9.

Then another word order shift to: (huwa (He – God) + Relative Pronoun + Verb + Complement), as in:

> huwa alladhī anzala min al-samā'i mā'an – It is He who sends down rain from the sky, Q16:10.

Then we have a word order shift to: (Verb + Subject + Complement), as in:

> yunbitu lakum bihi al-zarᶜa – He causes to grow for you thereby the crops, Q16:11.
>
> sakhkhara lakum al-laila wal-nahāra – He has subjected for you the night and day, Q16:12.

2.2.10.2 Sentence-final verb shift

This is a macro level stylistic shift that usually occurs within a given sūrah. Let us consider the following examples:

> dhālikum waṣṣakum bihi laᶜallakum taᶜqilūn – This He (God) has instructed you that you may use reason, Q6:151
> dhālikum waṣṣakum bihi laᶜallakum tadhakkarūn – This He (God) has instructed you that you may use reason, Q6:152
> dhālikum waṣṣakum bihi laᶜallakum tattaqūn – This He (God) has instructed you that you may use reason, Q6:153

where we have identical syntactic structures but are stylistically different because of the occurrence of different verbs at the end of each sentence.

The same problem is encountered in Q30:

> inna fī dhālika la'āyātin liqawmin yatafakkarūn – Indeed in that are signs for a people who give thought, Q30:21.
> inna fī dhālika la'āyātin liqawmin yasmaᶜūn – Indeed in that are signs for a people who listen, Q30:21.
> inna fī dhālika la'āyātin liqawmin yaᶜqilūn – Indeed in that are signs for a people who use reason, Q30:21.

The above three sentences have identical syntactic structures but are stylistically different because of the occurrence of different verbs at the end of each sentence.

2.2.10.3 Context-sensitive style shift

At the macro text level of Qur'anic discourse, we encounter syntactic structures whose meaning may be similar but whose stylistic patterns are different, as in:

> lā ilāha illā hū khāliqu kulli shai' – There is no deity except Him (God), the creator of all things, Q6:102

> khāliqu kulli shai' lā ilāha illā hū – The creator of all things, there is no deity except Him (God), Q40:62

Structurally, each of the above examples consists of two linguistic units. The order of example one is:

> (lā ilāha illā hū) + (khāliqu kulli shai') Q6:102

The order of example two is:

> (khāliqu kulli shai') + (lā ilāha illā hū) Q40:62.

The shift in the above order of units is attributed to the context in which each sentence is embedded. In Q6:102, we have the leitmotif of monotheism (al-tawḥīd) placed sentence-initially. This is due to the impact of Q6:101 in which there is reference to the leitmotif of polytheism (al-shirk). Thus, Q6:102 has the pragmatic function of substantiation of monotheism through sentence-initial position (lā ilāha illā hū – There is no deity except Him (God)). However, the stylistic shift in Q40:62 is also due to the influence of context. We have reference to the notion of creation in Q40:57 and to the notion of God's omnipotence in Q40:60–61. This context has led to the syntactic structure in Q40:62 where the leitmotif of creation (khāliqu kulli shai' – the creator of all things) is placed first before the notion of monotheism.

2.2.10.4 Number shift

This is a macro level stylistic shift that usually occurs either within the same sūrah or between different sūrahs. In other words, we encounter identical syntactic structures at different places of the Qur'anic text which are stylistically distinct due to the occurrence of the noun in the singular form in one sentence but in the plural form in the other sentence. The number shift occurs in Qur'anic discourse for contextual and co-textual reasons. Let us consider the following examples:

> uballighukum risālāt rabbī – I convey to you the messages of my Lord, Q7:62, 68, 93, 144.
>
> ablaghtukum risālat rabbī – I convey to you the message of my Lord, Q7:79.

In the above examples, the noun (risālāt – messages) is in the plural in Q7:62, 68, 93, and 144, but the noun changes to the singular form (risālat – message) in Q7:79. This is due to the context of situation which impacted the noun form. In Q7, we have reference to some Prophets' parables like Noah (Q7:59–64), Hud (Q7:65–72), Shuᶜaib (Q7:85–93), Moses (Q7:103–145), and Salih (Q7:73–79). We have observed that the plural noun (risālāt – messages) occurs in the parables of Noah, Hud, Shuᶜaib, and Moses. This is due to the contextual fact that each parable refers to a number of moral lessons and admonition details. Stylistically, the plural noun is the most compatible form in this context of situation. However, in the context of the parable of the Prophet Salih (Q7:73–79), there is reference to only one moral lesson, which is that of the she-camel. Therefore, the employment of the singular form noun (risālat – a message) in Q7:79 is stylistically more compatible for this context of situation.

Having discussed the impact of context on the number shift, we now turn to the impact co-text on the number shift:

> fa'aṣbaḥū fī dārihim jāthimīn – They became within their home corpses fallen prone, Q7:78, 91 and Q29:37.
>
> fa'aṣbaḥū fī diyārihim jāthimīn – They became within their homes corpses fallen prone, Q11:67, 94.

The noun (dār – home) in Q7:78, 91 and Q29:37 occurs in the singular form because reference has been made to a singular noun (al-rajfah – earthquake). Also, this noun collocates with the singular noun (al-arḍ – the earth). Therefore, sentences Q7:78, 91 and Q29:37 employ the singular noun (dār – home). However, the noun (diyār – homes) occurs in the plural form in sentences Q11:67 and 94. This is because the noun (al-ṣaiḥah – the blast) designates a phenomenon that takes place in (al-samā' – the skies, heavens). Since the Arabic noun (al-samā') can be made plural (al-samāwāt), the plural noun (diyār – homes) occurs.

2.2.10.5 Particle shift

This is a macro level stylistic shift that usually occurs within different sūrahs. In other words, we encounter identical syntactic structures at different places of the

Qur'anic text which are stylistically distinct due to the ellipsis of a particle from one of them. Let us consider the following examples:

> yaṭūfu ᶜalaihim wildānun mukhalladūn – There will circulate among them young boys made eternal, Q56:17.

> wa yaṭūfu ᶜalaihim wildānun mukhalladūn – And there will circulate among them young boys made eternal, Q76:19.

In the first example, the verb (yaṭūfu – circulate) has no additive conjunction particle (wa – and) before it while the same verb (yaṭūfu) in the second example is preceded by (wa). The reason of the ellipsis or addition of the additive conjunction particle (wa) is attributed to the grammatical process of coordination (al-ᶜaṭf) between the adjacent sentences. For instance, Q56:17 is not coordinated to the previous sentences. However, Q76:19 is coordinated to (maᶜṭūfah ᶜala), the previous sentence Q76:15, which is thematically related to sentence Q76:19. The same case applies to Q52:24, which has the conjunctive particle (wa – and) (wa yaṭūfu ᶜalaihim – and there will circulate among them). The occurrence of the (wa) is due to the fact that Q52:24 is coordinated to the previous sentence Q52:22 on the one hand and because Q52:22 and Q52:24 are thematically related.

Let us consider the following two examples:

> wa yaqtulūna al-nabiyyīna bighairi al-ḥaqqi – And they kill the Prophets without right, Q2:61.

> wa yaqtulūna al-nabiyyīna bighairi ḥaqqin – And they kill the Prophets without right, Q3:21.

Although structurally similar, the above two sentences are stylistically distinct. This is because Q2:61 employs the noun (al-ḥaqqi – literally 'the right') with a definite article (al – the) while in Q3:21 the same noun occurs as indefinite (ḥaqqi – right). The definite/indefinite particle shift is attributed to co-text. In Q2:61, the co-text abounds with definite nouns such as Q2:42, 71, 91, 109, 119, 121, 144, 146, 147, 149, 151, 176, 213, 252, and 282, where we have the definite noun (al-ḥaqqi). To achieve grammatical and stylistic symmetry throughout the macro text of Q2, the noun (al-ḥaqqi) should occur in the definite case. The impact of the macro grammatical co-text also applies to Q3:21 where the indefinite noun (ḥaqqin) occurs in Q3:86 and 102.

2.2.10.6 Passive/active voice shift

> annā lā nadrī asharrun urīda biman fī al-arḍi am arāda bihim rabbuhum rashadā – We do not know whether evil is intended for those on earth, or whether their Lord intends a right course for them, Q72:10.

where in the first part of the sentence, we have a passive voice verb (urīda – is intended, is wanted) while in the second part we have an active voice verb (arāda – to intend, to want). This shift from the passive voice (urīda) to the active voice (arāda) is conditioned by the performative intent (the intended meaning) of the text producer. Because the word (sharrun – evil, misfortune) occurs in the first part of the sentence, it is not tactful of the speaker to use the word (allāh – God) or (rabb – the Lord) adjacent to the connotatively negative word (sharrun). Thus, to avoid this unpleasant stylistic outcome, the passive voice is adopted where we understand that the implicit (deleted) subject is (rabbuhum – their Lord). However, in the second part of the sentence, a connotatively positive word (rashadā – right, guidance) is employed, and the active voice verb (arāda) can be used with the word (rabbuhum).

2.2.11 Macro text noun-initial sentences

As a macro text syntactic feature, we encounter two recurrent syntactic structures:

i (Subject + Verb + Complement), and
ii (allāhu + Relative Pronoun (alladhī) + Verb + Complement)

The above two grammatical patterns are stylistic techniques which have two pragmatic functions:

a to substantiate God's omnipotence (qudrat allāh), and
b to highlight God's blessings (niᶜam allāh) bestowed upon mankind.

This is explained in what follows:

First structure: Subject + Verb + Complement

allāhu anzala min al-samā'i mā'an fa'aḥyā bihi al-arḍa baᶜda mawtihā . . . allāhu khalaqakum thumma yatawaffākum . . . allāhu faḍḍala baᶜḍakum ᶜalā baᶜḍ fī al-rizq . . . allāhu jaᶜala lakum min anfusikum azwājan . . . allāhu akhrajakum min buṭūni ummahātikum . . . allāhu jaᶜala lakum min buyūtikum sakanan wajaᶜala lakum min julūdi al-anᶜāmi buyūtan . . . allāhu jaᶜala lakum mimmā khalaqa ẓilālan wajaᶜala lakum min al-jibāli aknānan . . . – God has sent down rain from the sky and given life thereby to the earth after its lifelessness. God created you; then He will take you in death . . . God has favoured some of you over others in provision . . . God has made for you from yourselves mates . . . God has extracted you from the wombs of your mothers . . . God has made for you from your homes a place of rest . . . God has made for you, from that which He has created, . . . shades and has made for you from the mountains, shelters . . ., Q16:65–81

allāhu khalaqa kulla dābbatin min mā' – God has created every living creature from water, Q24:45

Second structure: allāhu + Relative Pronoun (alladhī) + Verb + Complement

allāhu alladhī rafaᶜa al-samāwāti bighairi ᶜamadin tarawnahā – God is the one who erected the heavens without pillars that you can see, Q13:2

allāhu alladhī yursilu al-riyāḥa fatuthīru saḥāban fī al-samā'i . . . allāhu alladhī khalaqakum min ḍaᶜfin thumma jaᶜala . . . – God is the one who sends the winds, and they stir the clouds in the sky . . . God is the one who created you from weakness, then He made . . ., Q30:48, 54

2.2.12 *Macro text mutashabihat*

This is concerned with the stylistically different but thematically and grammatically similar structures referred to as (al-mutashābihāt) in Arabic. At the macro text level of Qur'anic discourse, we encounter two syntactic structures which occur at different places but are intertextually related through the common leitmotif (theme) shared by the two sentences, as in:

> dhālika bi'anna allāha huwa al-ḥaqqu wa'anna mā yadᶜūna min dūnihi huwa al-bāṭilu wa'anna allāha huwa al-ᶜaliyyu al-kabīr – That is because God is indeed the truth, and that which they call upon other than Him is indeed falsehood, and because God is the most high, the grand, Q22:62.
>
> dhālika bi'anna allāha huwa al-ḥaqqu wa'anna mā yadᶜūna min dūnihi huwa al-bāṭilu wa'anna allāha huwa al-ᶜaliyyu al-kabīr – That is because God is indeed the truth, and that which they call upon other than Him is falsehood, and because God is the most high, the grand, Q31:30.

The above two sentences are intertextually related since both express the same leitmotif of monotheism. However, they are stylistically different because Q22:62 employs the pronoun (huwa) twice, once before the noun (al-ḥaqq – the truth) and the other before the noun (al-bāṭilu – falsehood). The pronoun (huwa) occurs once in Q31:30 before the noun (al-ḥaqq – the truth) but is ellipted before the noun (al-bāṭil – falsehood). The pronoun (huwa) literally means 'he', which can refer to human, non-human, animate, and inanimate nouns. However, in the context of Q22:62, the pronoun (huwa) means 'indeed it is, surely'. In other words, it is employed for the pragmatic purpose of affirmation, i.e., affirming the notion that 'what they call upon other than God is indeed falsehood'. Having investigated the grammatical co-text of Q22:62, one can conclude that the recurrent employment of other forms of affirmation particles creates a stylistic environment which requires the employment of an affirmation pronoun (huwa) in the second part of sentence 62. The use of (huwa) before the noun (al-bāṭilu – falsehood) has achieved stylistic harmony with the surrounding sentences of Q22:62. The other forms of affirmation particles used are:

i the affirmation letters (lām – the initial affirmation letter /l/) and (nūn – the consonant nasal sound /n/) used in the verb (layarzuqannahum – will indeed provide for them) in Q22:58,

ii the affirmation letter (lām) and the affirmation pronoun (huwa) used in (lahuwa) in Q22:58,

iii the affirmation letters (lām) and (nūn) used in the verb (layudkhilannahum – will surely cause them to enter) in Q22:59, and

iv the affirmation particles (lām), (inna), and (nūn) used in Q22:60, 64, 66.

However, Q31:30 lacks the grammatical co-text requirement. Thus, there is no stylistic need for the affirmation pronoun (huwa) to be used before the noun (al-bāṭilu – falsehood) in Q31:30.

> tukhriju al-ḥaiyah min al-maiyiti wa tukhriju al-maiyita min al-ḥai – You bring the living out of the dead, and You bring the dead out of the living, Q3:27, Q10:31 and Q30:19.
>
> yukhriju al-ḥaiyah min al-maiyiti wa mukhriju al-maiyiti min al-ḥai – You bring the living out of the dead, and You bring the dead out of the living, Q6:95.

The first syntactic structure involves a sentence-initial verb (tukhriju – (you) bring out) in the second person masculine (you) referring to God, while the second example involves a sentence-initial verb in the third person masculine (he) referring also to God. This is a minor shift between the two stylistic patterns.

However, a major shift takes place at the morphological level: The first example employs another verb (tukhriju – to bring out), which is the same as the first verb. The second example involves a morphological shift where Q6:95 employs an active participle (mukhriju – the one who brings out). This word form is used to match the two active participles (fāliq – the cleaver) that occur in the same sentence Q6:95 and also in the following sentence Q6:96. In other words, the lexical co-text in Q6:95–96 has impacted on the employment of an active participle (mukhrij) although preceded by a verb (yukhrij). Thus, stylistic and grammatical symmetry is achieved between sentences 95 and 96 of Q6.

One may wonder, however, whether Arabic grammar allows the combination between a verb (yukhrij) and an active participle (mukhrij) in Q6:95. Grammatically, the active participle (ism al-faᶜil) has the function of either a verb or a noun. Therefore, grammatically, the active participle (mukhrij) can coordinate with a verb (yukhrij) through the conjunctive particle (wa – and) within the same sentence Q6:95.

In Q3:27, Q10:31, and Q30:19, only verbs have been used, and the stylistic purpose of this is to achieve lexical and grammatical symmetry among the lexical items of the relevant sentences within the same lexical environment. A lexically based textual analysis of the macro text of Q3, Q10, and Q30 will reveal that there is heavy occurrence of verbs in Q3:26–28, Q10:30–31, and Q30:19–21. This is the lexical co-text that justifies the occurrence of:

> (tukhriju – bring out . . . + tukhriju – bring out . . .) → (verb . . . + verb . . .) in Q3:27, Q10:31 and Q30:19.

2.2.13 Macro text thematic coherence

At the Qur'anic macro text, the tenets of faith (mabādi' al-īmān) occur in a coherent manner. There are four major tenets of faith: monotheism (al-tawhid), prophethood (al-nubuwwah), eschatology (al-baᶜth, al-maᶜād), and reward and punishment (al-thawāb wal-ᶜiqāb). In between these tenets of faith, we may encounter other themes like God's omnipotence (qudrat allāh), admonition for morality (mawᶜiẓah wa akhlaq), or Islamic legal rulings (aḥkam). Let us consider Q23 for textual analysis. This sūrah consists of the following tenets of faith:

i prophethood (Q32:2–3) represented by the word (al-kitāb – the Book, the Qur'an) and the implicit reference to Muḥammad (iftarāhu – he (Muḥammad) invented it).

ii monotheism (Q32:3) represented by the word (allāh – God).

iii God's omnipotence (Q32:3–9) where reference has been made to: the creation of the heavens and the earth, the arrangements God makes of matters from the heavens to the earth, God's being the knower of the unseen and the seen, the perfection of His creation, the creation of man from clay, the making of man's posterity out of the extract of a liquid, the proportioning of man, the breathing of God into man, the making of man's hearing, vision, and heart.

iv eschatology (Q32:10–12) represented by the theme of resurrection after death and meeting God.

v reward and punishment (Q32:13–14) represented by reference to hell and punishment.

vi prophethood (Q32:15) represented by the word (yu'min – to believe [in the prophethood of Muḥammad]).

vii monotheism (Q32:15–16) represented by the word (rabbahum – their (one) Lord).

viii admonition (Q32:16) represented by the expression (mimmā razaqnāhum yunfiqūn – they spend to help the needy from what God has provided them).

ix reward and punishment (Q32:17) represented by the expression (qurrata aᶜyun – what has been hidden for the believers of comfort in paradise).

x prophethood (Q32:18) through the word (mu'min – believer (in Muḥammad's prophethood)).

xi prophethood + reward and punishment (Q32:22) through reference to (alladhīna āmanū – those who believed in Muḥammad's prophethood), (jannāt – paradise), (fasaqū – those who defiantly disobeyed Muḥammad's prophethood), (al-nār – the fire), (al-mujrimūn – the criminals, i.e., those who disbelieved Muḥammad's prophethood), and (muntaqimūn – retribution).

xii admonition (Q32:23–24) through reference to Moses, the Children of Israel, and the theme of patience.

xiii eschatology (Q32:25) represented by the expression (yawm al-qiyāmah – the day of resurrection).

xiv admonition (Q32:26) through reference to the many generations which God destroyed in the past.

xv God's omnipotence (Q32:27) represented by reference to the water in the clouds, how the barren land gives crops for living.

xvi eschatology (Q32:28–29) represented by the word (al-fatḥ – day of judgement).

xvii prophethood (Q32:30) through the imperative verb (aᶜriḍ – (you Muḥammad) turn away (from the disbelievers)) directed to Muḥammad.

However, a whole short sūrah may present one tenet of faith only such as Q112 where monotheism occurs.

Coherence between two or more sūrahs runs throughout the Qur'anic discourse in terms of the initial or final theme of the consecutive sūrahs.

Types of coherence between Qur'anic sūrahs are:

1 coherence between beginning and end of a Qur'anic sūrah, as in Q11 where the beginning and the end of this sūrah is about monotheism:

> A.L.R. This is a Book whose āyahs are decisive, and have been set forth in detail in the presence of someone who is wise, informed so that you will serve only God alone: 'I am a warner, a herald from Him to you', Q11:1–2.
>
> God holds the unseen in heaven and earth, and unto Him does every matter return; so serve Him, and rely on Him. Your Lord is not unmindful of what you all are doing, Q11:123

2 logical sequence between the end of a sūrah and the beginning of the following sūrah, as in Q56 whose end is attuned to the beginning of Q57 as illustrated below:

> Therefore, O Muḥammad, praise the name of your Lord, Q56:96.
>
> All that is in the heavens and the earth glorify God; and He is the mighty, the wise, Q57:1.
>
> where both the end of Q56 and the beginning of Q57 are about praising and glorifying God.

3 logical sequence between two consecutive sūrahs, as in Q51 and Q52 where both are characterised by similar linguistic structures and both refer to the state which the righteous are promised to enjoy:

> The righteous will be in gardens and springs, Q51:15.
>
> The righteous will be in gardens and bliss, Q52:17.

4 logical sequence between two consecutive sūrahs where the latter provides elaboration for matters raised in the former, as in Q2 and Q3. Q3 elaborates on what has been mentioned briefly in Q2 like the Book, i.e., the Qur'an, other divine Books, i.e., the Torah and the Bible, the battle of Uhud, those who are killed in battles for the sake of God, interest, pilgrimage, and the process of creation of man.

2.2.14 Macro text relevance-based lexical items

This is a semantic macro text feature that recurrently occurs in the Qur'an. This is concerned with the occurrence of a specific word due to its relevance and through which coherence and continuity of thought are achieved. Let us consider the following examples:

> allāhu anzala min al-samā'i mā'an fa'aḥyā bihi al-arḍa baᶜda mawtihā inna fī dhālika la'āyātin liqawmin yasmaᶜūn – God sends down rain from the sky

> and gives therewith life to the earth after its death; verily in this is a sign for those who listen, Q16:65.

Stylistically, one wonders why the verb (yasmaᶜūn – listen) is used in a sentence which talks about the rain. Therefore, the reader expects verbs like (yanẓurūn – to see (the rain)) or (yubṣirūn – to look at (the rain)). Stylistically, the verb (yasmaᶜūn – listen) is the most appropriate (relevant) word in this context through which the message can be delivered. The macro text of Q16:65 unravels the semantic significance of this style. The pagan Arabs have been described in the Qur'an as arrogant people who associate other deities with God, do not listen to the message of the Qur'an, and do not believe in eschatology (al-baᶜth). The pagans are admonished by Q16:65 to ponder upon the rain as conclusive evidence, manifestation of God's omnipotence, and God's existence. If they 'listen' to this premise put forward by Q16:65, the pagans can logically conclude that God exists and resurrection will surely take place. The logical conclusion is also established by the example given in the same sentence: The earth (al-arḍa), which has been dry for a long time, is now 'revived and brought back to life again by the rain sent down by God'. Thus, the dead for a long time can also be resurrected and brought back to life by God. If the pagans 'listen' to this argument, they will believe in eschatology. Therefore, stylistically, there is a good semantic reason for using the verb (yasmaᶜūn – listen). The presentation is, thus, coherent.

> yawma taqūmu al-sāᶜatu yuqsimu al-mujrimūna mā labithū ghaira sāᶜah – On the day that the hour of reckoning will be established, the transgressors will swear that they had remained but an hour, Q30:55.

This sentence employs pun through the word (sāᶜatu – hour), which is semantically a polyseme meaning either (i) the hour of reckoning, i.e., the day of resurrection (eschatology), or (ii) an hour (60 minutes). The coherent presentation of words is achieved through the following:

i the employment of polysemy (sāᶜatu),
ii the employment of pun (sāᶜatu),
iii the employment of (yuqsimu – to swear, take oath), and
iv the employment of intertextuality.

The semantic componential features of (yuqsimu) are: [+ Human], [+ Animate], and most importantly [+ Truthful]. It is the third semantic feature [+ Truthful] that we are concerned with in terms of verifying whether Q30:55 exhibits a coherent stylistic presentation and is successful at rebutting the transgressors. If someone takes oath, he/she must be truthful. However, the transgressors swear, but they are not truthful because they provide false information that they have only been dead for an hour, which is not true. On the intertextual level, the word (yuqsimu – to take oath, swear) is intertextually related to the word (kadhdhaba – to disbelieve) and its morphological derivatives, which have occurred 281 times in the Qur'an as in Q3:137, Q56:51, Q77:15, and Q85:19. The transgressors used to disbelieve their relevant Prophets and describe them as (liars – kādhib). In Q30:55, the truth unfolds as the transgressors are proven to be untruthful, i.e., liars.

Also, we encounter two opposite words where the word with a positive meaning is explained by the neighbouring word with a negative meaning, as in:

> man khashiya al-raḥmāna bil-ghaibi wa jā'a biqabin salīm. idkhūluhā bisalāmin . . . – Who feared the most merciful unseen and came with a heart returning in repentance. Enter it in peace, Q50:33–34.

The word (al-raḥmāna – the mercy-giving) may seem stylistically unsuitable in this sentence and should not be placed next to the verb (khashiya – to live in awe of). However, the word (khashiya) has occurred in the co-text of (al-raḥmāna) in order to signify the considerable rewards endowed by God upon the person whose heart is full of respect-based fear of Him since the adjective (al-raḥmāna) signifies the ample mercy of God. Then the expression (bisalāmin – peacefully) is employed to consolidate the connotatively positive meanings of the word (al-raḥmāna) and to highlight the sharp semantic contrast between the two words (peace) and (to live in awe of).

2.2.15 Macro text foregrounding

Foregrounding is a major textual feature of Qur'anic genre. It is a stylistic technique through which a word or a phrase is placed sentence-initially in order to make it more prominent and salient than other sentence constituents. Halliday (1973) has characterized foregrounding as motivated prominence in order to make a text segment stand out in some way. It is the phenomenon of linguistic highlighting. For Simpson (2004), the foregrounded element draws attention to itself. In the view of Childs and Fowler (2006), foregrounding is readily identified with linguistic deviation, i.e., the violation of rules and conventions. Therefore, we can argue that since foregrounding is a linguistic deviation, foregrounding leads to a marked (unusual) word order which is a linguistic deviation from the unmarked (usual) word order. The foregrounded text segment aids memorability and invites interpretation.

Examples

iyyāka na[c]budu – You (God) we worship, Q1:5.
ilaihi turja[c]ūn – To Him you will be returned, Q2:245.
ilā allāh al-maṣir – To God is the destination, Q3:28.
lillāhi yasjudu mā fī al-samāwāti wal-arḍi – To God prostrates whatever is in the heavens and whatever is on the earth, Q16:49.
allāhu khalaqakum – God created you, Q16:70.
ilaiyah al-maṣir – To Me is the destination, Q22:48.

The above underlined sentence constituents are foregrounded elements and have acquired saliency and prominence.

2.2.16 Macro text intertextuality

Qur'anic intertextuality is primarily concerned with thematic reference. Thematic (conceptual) reference is a Qur'an-specific feature. It is primarily concerned with allusion to a given Qur'anic theme (concept, leitmotif, notion). Qur'anic intertextuality deals with invoking a thematic (conceptual) relatedness (chaining, dovetailing) between two Qur'anic notions where one of them harks back to the other, thus reminding the reader of the text producer's performative intent. Intertextuality creates a thematic interrelationship between different text segments of the Qur'an and generates related understanding in separate parts of the Qur'anic text. Through Qur'anic intertextuality, thematic chaining within Qur'anic discourse is achieved. Thus, intertextuality in Qur'anic discourse makes the reader understand a given theme in different parts of the Qur'an. Without this pre-understanding or success to grasp the thematic link between two text segments, our understanding of the text segments is hampered. Separate Qur'anic text segments are expected to express mutual relevance to each other in terms of thematic relatedness and sequentiality. The utilization of one text segment depends on prior knowledge of one or more previously encountered text segments.

Qur'anic intertextuality is a macro text feature. It is encountered within the same Qur'anic chapter and between two or more separate chapters. Intertextuality has been taken as a separate approach in Qur'anic exegesis. Based on this macro text feature, Qur'anic intertextual exegesis has emerged (tafsir al-qur'an bil-qur'an). Qur'anic intertextuality can be explained through the following examples:

Example 1

in kuntum fī raibin mimmā nazzalnā ᶜalā ᶜabdinā – If you are in doubt about what We have sent down upon Our servant, Q2:23.

where the word (ᶜabdinā – Our servant) is intertextually related (explained by):

amanū bimā nuzzila ᶜalā Muḥammad – They believed in what has been sent down upon Muḥammad, Q47:2.
ᶜabdinā → Muḥammad.

Example 2

ᶜindahu mafātiḥ al-ghaib – With Him are the keys of the unseen, Q6:59.

where the expression (mafātiḥ al-ghaib – the keys of the unseen) is intertextually related (explained by):

inna allāha ᶜindahu ᶜilmu al-sāᶜati wayunazzilu al-ghaitha wayaᶜlamu mā fī al-arḥām – Indeed, God has knowledge of the hour and sends down the rain and knows what is in the womb Q31:34.

mafātiḥ al-ghaib → ^{c}ilmu al-sā^{c}ati/yunazzilu al-ghaitha/ya^{c}lamu mā fī al-arḥām.

It is worthwhile to note that the presupposed meaning of the ellipted element(s) can also be retrieved through intertextuality, as in the elliptical sentence Q2:173 and Q2:57 and 172; Q6:42 and Q35:4.

For more details on ellipsis and intertextuality, see Chapter 4, Section 4.7.

2.2.17 Macro text God's omnipotence

God's omnipotence details which are a Qur'anic argumentation technique which deliver the following types of illocutionary force:

- i signs to ponder upon,
- ii example for deductive reasoning,
- iii substantiation of God's might,
- iv substantiation of monotheism,
- v proof of divinity,
- vi substantiation of God's mercy to mankind since the details refer to causes of sustenance and benefits to all human and non-human creatures, and
- vii rebuttal to deniers who disbelieve in the tenets of faith (monotheism, prophethood, eschatology, and reward and punishment).

Having said the above, let us consider the following examples:

Example 1

wamin āyātihi an yursila al-riyāḥa mubashshirātin waliyudhīqakum min raḥmatihi walitajriya al-fulku bi'amrih walitabtaghū min faḍlih wala^{c}allakum tashkurūn – Another of His (God's) signs is that He sends out the winds bearing good news, giving you a taste of His grace, making the ships sail at His command, enabling you to journey in search of His bounty so that you may be grateful, Q30:46.

Example 2

allāhu alladhī yursilu al-riyāḥa fatuthīru saḥāban fayabsuṭuhu fī al-samā' kaifa yashā' wayaj^{c}aluhu kisafan fatarā al-wadqa yakhruju min khilālih . . . – It is God who sends the winds, and they stir the clouds and spread them in the sky however He wills, and he makes them fragments so you see the rain emerge from within them . . ., Q30:48.

where God's omnipotence details refer to the wind and the ships in Q30:47 and to the winds, the clouds, and the rain in Q30:48. However, in the following statement:

walaqad arsalnā min qablika rusulan ilā qawmihim fajā'ūhum bil-baiyināti fantaqamnā min alladhīna ajramū . . . – Before you (Muḥammad), We sent

> messengers, each to their own people; they brought them clear proofs and then We punished the evildoers . . ., Q30:47.

reference is made to sending Prophets to past unbelieving nations, but they denied their message and continued to be evildoers. Thus, the textual structure of Q30:46, 47, and 48 is like the following:

> God's omnipotence details → past unbelieving nations → God's omnipotence details

Thus, Q30:46 and 48 refer to God's omnipotence details as a Qur'anic argumentation technique to admonish the reader about God's might, monotheism, divinity, His mercy to mankind, since God's omnipotence details refer to the causes of sustenance and benefits to all human and non-human creatures and rebuttal to deniers who disbelieve in monotheism, prophethood, eschatology, and reward and punishment.

Through God's omnipotence details, people are informed that they should be grateful for God's blessings bestowed upon them through the many causes of bounty, sustenance, and welfare, such as the wind, the rain, the sea, the sun, the night, and the daylight. If not, God will take retribution from those who commit evil deeds and incumbent upon God, as they are informed by Q30:47 (fantaqamnā min alladhīna ajramū – We punished the evildoers).

Example 3

> inna rabbakumu allāhu alladhī khalaqa al-samāwāti wal-arḍa fī sittati aiyāmin thumma istawā ᶜalā al-ᶜarshi yughshī al-laila al-nahāra yaṭlubuhu ḥathīthā wal-shamsa wal-qamara wal-nujūma musakhkharātin bi'amrihi alā lahu al-khalqu wal-amru tabāraka allāhu rabbu al-ᶜālamīn – Indeed, your Lord is God who created the heavens and earth in six days and then established Himself above the throne. He covers the night with the day, chasing it rapidly, and He created the sun, the moon, and the stars, subjected by His command. Unquestionably, His is the creation and the command, blessed is God, Lord of the worlds, Q7:54.

Example 4

> It is He (God) who created heavens and earth . . . He created man from a sperm-drop . . . He has created the livestock for you . . . and created the horses, mules and donkeys for you . . . It is He who sends down rain from the sky . . . He causes to grow for you thereby the crops, olives, palm trees . . . Indeed in that is a sign for a people who give thought. He has subjected for you the night and day and the sun and moon, and the stars are subjected by His command. Indeed in that are signs for a people who reason. He has subjected whatever He multiplied for you on the earth of varying colours. Indeed in that is a sign for a people who remember. It is He who subjected the sea for you to eat from it tender meat and to extract from it ornaments which you wear . . . He has

> cast into the earth firmly set mountains . . . and landmarks. And by the stars they are also guided. Then is He (God) who creates like one who does not create?, Q16:3–17.

where the focus of the above example is on monotheism and divinity through the 12 signs: the creation of the heavens and earth, the creation of mankind, the creation of livestock, the creation of horses, mules, and donkeys, the sending down of water for drink and for growing trees, making the night, the day, the sun, the moon, and the stars of benefit to mankind, making the many-coloured things on earth of benefit to mankind, making the sea of benefit to mankind, making the mountains stand firm on the earth, making rivers on the earth, making paths on the earth for people to find their way, and the creation of stars to guide people through the desert or the sea at night.

For more details on the function of God's omnipotence details in argumentation, see Chapter 3.

2.2.18 Macro text tenets of faith

There are four tenets of faith (mabādi' al-īmān): monotheism (al-tawḥīd), prophethood (al-nubuwwah), reward and punishment (al-thawāb wal-ᶜiqāb), and eschatology (resurrection) (al-maᶜād, al-baᶜth). The four tenets of faith have occurred several times throughout the Qur'anic text in all the Qur'anic chapters.

For more details on the macro occurrence of the four tenets of faith, see Chapter 5, Section 5.10.1.2.1.

2.3 Summary

Qur'anic macro text means the Qur'anic text as a whole, i.e., the larger text rather than the Qur'anic word or sentence. Also, Qur'anic macro text means the most common features which we encounter in Qur'anic discourse such as specific words, synonyms, formulas, epithets, leitmotifs, and parables that have occurred in different numbers and in different places of the Qur'anic text. We also encounter the macro text feature of shift, no-main-verb nominal sentences, mutashābihāt (grammatically similar but stylistically dissimilar sentences), and text segments that are coherently and intertextually linked.

There are content words (like verbs, nouns, adjectives) and function words (like prepositions, pronouns) that have occurred in varying numbers and places throughout the Qur'an. Formulas (fixed expressions) are also repeatedly employed in Qur'anic discourse. The Qur'anic macro text also includes numerous examples of argumentative texts which involve premises, their rebuttal, substantiation, and conclusion. Most of the argumentative texts are based on deductive reasoning where rebuttal or substantiating details (God's omnipotence details) are provided to enable the listener/reader to reach a sound conclusion and, eventually, persuade him/her to accept the text producer's premise or response as true and valid. A specific word is selected and made salient in the sentence because it represents high-value information, contributes effectively in the achievement of coherence, and makes the sentence progress in terms of continuity of thought. Such words have occurred in different places of the Qur'anic text. Similarly, these words and sentences in different places of the Qur'anic text hark back to (allude to) each other. Thus, they have established Qur'anic intertextuality.

3 Argumentation structure in Qur'anic discourse

3.1 Introduction

This is a textual analysis of the argumentation techniques encountered in Qur'anic discourse. In an argumentative text, we encounter two major characters: the protagonist (the active supporter of a cause or idea) and the antagonist (an opponent to the protagonist's cause or idea). A successful interlocutor (protagonist) should be able to provide a satisfactorily defended standpoint based on a high level of truth value to persuade the opponent (antagonist) to accept the standpoint as true. A valid argument is free from fallacy, i.e., free from mistakes in reasoning which make the protagonist's argument invalid (false). In the present discussion of argumentation structure of Qur'anic discourse, the protagonist and the antagonist are God and the disbelievers. The present discussion is concerned with the argumentative text which represents an event of a difference of opinion where one discussant puts forward an opinion and the other discussant calls that idea into question, i.e., the fallacy of begging the question (Eemeren and Grootendorst 2004:176).

The examples provided in this chapter are argumentative text segments which represent advancing a standpoint and calling a standpoint into question. This chapter provides informative details on the components of an argument, the premise and conclusion, the nature of the deductive argument, the no-main-verb nominal statement in different Qur'anic argumentative texts, the mood and topos in an argumentative text, the persuasive techniques in Qur'anic argumentation, the types of audience and their cognitive status in Qur'anic argumentative discourse, and the types of Qur'anic argumentative texts.

3.2 What is argumentation?

Argumentation is the study of how conclusions can be reached through logical reasoning. It includes debate, negotiation, dialogue, court trial by lawyers, presentation, and persuasion. Thus, an argument has audience or readership. In other words, there is a text producer (speaker/writer) and a text receiver (listener/reader), each contending differing points of view and trying to persuade each other. Based on the cognitive status of the text receiver, there are three categories of audience:

i open-minded (impartial),
ii sceptical (undecided, a floater), and
iii denier (opponent).

Argumentation is concerned with reaching a conclusion that is acceptable to the opponent or any category of audience. In Qur'anic discourse, we encounter two major types of addressee:

i the polytheists who worship deities other than God, and
ii the Scripturists who are the followers of Judaism or Christianity.

It is worthwhile to note that the opponent in argumentation is at times referred to as (al-insān – man), which is a generic noun meaning (the disbeliever), as in Q19:67 (awalā yadhkuru al-insānu innā khalaqnāhu min qablu walam yaku shai'ā – Does man not remember that We (God) created him/her when he/she was nothing before?). Argumentation is also concerned with the testing of the validity of some evidence. A true or false claim is based on a premise. It is important to note that an argument must have a method of reasoning or deduction. An inference must hold between the premise and the conclusion. This is a common practice in Qur'anic argumentation represented by God's omnipotence details employed as an argumentation technique for either substantiation or rebuttal. God's omnipotence details are employed for deductive reasoning. Deductive reasoning also requires a strong relationship between the premise(s) and the conclusion. The purpose of God's omnipotence details is to help the reader/listener make an inference to reach the conclusion, which is usually monotheism. However, the conclusion can also be other tenets of faith such as prophethood or eschatology (resurrection).

We often encounter deductive inferences in Qur'anic argumentation. A deductive inference represents an argument that the truth of its premises guarantees the truth of its conclusion. In deductive inferences, the premise provides support to its conclusion. In English argumentation, linguistic indicators are employed. A linguistic indicator is the keyword that flags the conclusion (a conclusion indicator) and is employed to connect the premise to the conclusion, i.e., the linguistic indicator is a discourse flag in English which indicates the logical relationship of claim. English linguistic indicators are like (therefore, thus, wherefore, accordingly, we may conclude). However, in Qur'anic argumentation, such linguistic indicators are not used. The Qur'anic argument employs indicator words like (idhan – therefore, then, for this reason, as in Q23:91), (kadhālika – likewise, thus, therefore, as in Q50:11), (subḥana – God is exalted, as in Q17:93, Q21:22, Q23:91), and (alaisa – therefore, as in Q36:81 and Q75:40), which flag the conclusion. Let us consider the following examples of Qur'anic argumentation:

Example 1

aw kalladhī marra ᶜalā qaryatin wahiya khāwiyatun ᶜalā ᶜurūshihā qāla annā yuḥyi hādhihi allāhu baᶜda mawtihā fa'amātahu allāhu mi'ata ᶜāmin thumma baᶜathahu qāla kam labithta qāla labithtu yawman aw baᶜḍa yawmin qāla bal labithta mi'ata ᶜāmin fanẓur ilā ṭaᶜāmika washarābika lam yatasannah wanẓur ilā ḥimārika walinajᶜalaka āyatan lil-nāsi wanẓur ilā al-ᶜiẓāmi kaifa nunshizuhā thumma naksūhā laḥmā falammā tabaiyana lahu qāla aᶜlamu anna allāha ᶜalā kulli shai'in qadīr – Or consider such an example as the one who passed by a township which had fallen into ruin. He said: 'How will God bring this to life after its death?' So God caused him to die for a hundred years; then He revived him. He said: 'How long have you remained?' He (the man) said: 'I have remained a day or part of a day'. God said: 'Rather, you have remained one hundred years. Look at your food and your drink; it has not changed with time. And look at your donkey; and We will make you a sign for the people. And look at the bones (of this donkey) – how We raise them and then We cover them with flesh'. And when it became clear to him, he said: 'I know that God is over all things competent', Q2:259.

where the opponent's premises are about his denial of resurrection and the conclusion is (anna allāha ᶜalā kulli shai'in qadīr – God is competent over all things). The conclusion is flagged by the expression (falammā tabaiyana lahu – when it has become clear to him).

Example 2

a'idhā mitnā wakunnā turāban dhālika rajᶜun baᶜīd . . . afalam yanẓurū ilā al-samā'i fawqahum kaifa banaināhā . . . wal-arḍa madadnāhā . . . wa'anbatnā fīhā min kulli zawjin bahīj . . . wanazzalnā min al-samā'i mā'an mubārakan fa'anbatnā bihi jannātin waḥabba al-ḥaṣīd . . . wa'aḥyainā bihi baldatan maitan kadhālika al-khurūj – When we have died and have become dust, will we return to life? That is unlikely to happen . . . Have they not looked at the heaven above them – how We (God) structure it . . . and the earth – We (God) spread it out . . . and made grow therein something of everything beautiful kind . . . and We (God) have sent down blessed rain from the sky and made grow thereby gardens and grain from the harvest . . . and We (God) have given life thereby to a dead land. Thus is the resurrection, Q50:3–11.

where the antagonist's (opponents') premises are about their denial of resurrection (a'idhā mitnā wakunnā turāban dhālika rajᶜun baᶜīd – When we have died and have become dust, will we return to life? That is unlikely to happen).

The rebuttal to their argument is represented by God's omnipotence details: (afalam yanẓurū ilā al-samā'i fawqahum kaifa banaināhā . . . wal-arḍa madadnāhā . . . wa'anbatnā fīhā min kulli zawjin bahīj . . . wanazzalnā min al-samā'i mā'an mubārakan fa'anbatnā bihi jannatin wahabba al-ḥaṣid . . . wa'aḥyainā bihi baldatan maitan – Have they not looked at the heaven above them – how We (God) structure it . . . and the earth – We (God) spread it out . . . and made grow therein something of everything beautiful kind . . . and We (God) have sent down blessed rain from the sky and made grow thereby gardens and grain from the harvest . . . and We (God) have given life thereby to a dead land).

The conclusion is: (kadhālika al-khurūj – Thus is the resurrection). The conclusion is flagged by the linguistic indicator (kadhālika – thus, likewise).

The same applies to Q36:78–83 where the premise is a denial of resurrection (man yuḥyī al-ᶜizāma wahiya ramīm – Who will give life to bones while they are disintegrated?, Q36:78). A rebuttal to the opponent's premise is through God's omnipotence details (Q36:79–82). The conclusion of the argument is: (fasubhana alladhī biyadihi kulli shai'in wa'ilaihi turjaᶜūn – So exalted is He (God) in whose hand is the realm of all things, and to Him you will return after resurrection, Q36:83). The conclusion is flagged by the linguistic indicator: (subḥāna – God is exalted).

Example 3

qad aflaha al-mu'minūn . . . ulā'ika hum al-wārithūn alladhīna yarithūna al-firdawsa . . . laqad khalaqnā al-insāna min sulālatin min ṭīn thumma jaᶜalnāhu nuṭfatan . . . thumma khalaqnā al-nuṭfata ᶜalaqatan . . . fakasawnā al-ᶜiẓāma laḥman . . . thumma innakum baᶜda dhālika lamaiyitūn thumma innakum yawa al-qiyāmāti tubᶜathūn – Certainly the believers will have succeeded . . . Those are the inheritors who will inherit the highest part of paradise . . . Certainly We (God) created man from an extract of clay. Then We (God) placed him as a sperm-drop in a womb. Then We (God) made the sperm-drop into a clinging clot . . . We (God) covered the bones with flesh . . . Then indeed, after that you are to die. Then indeed, on the day of resurrection, you will be resurrected, Q23:1–16.

where the premises of the speaker (God) focus on resurrection. First, we are told about who the believers (al-mu'minūn) are and then we are told that they will inherit paradise (ulā'ika hum al-wārithūn alladhīna yarithūna al-firdawsa). This is an implicit reference to their death and resurrection. Thus, the major premise is resurrection. Then we are given substantiation for this premise through details on God's omnipotence in terms of the stages of the creation of man. Then we are told that man will die. The conclusion that is linked to the previous premises is (innakum yawa al-qiyāmāti tubᶜathūn – Indeed, you will be resurrected on the day of resurrection). In other words: (innakum maiyitūn – You will definitely die) → (innakum tubᶜathūn – You will definitely be resurrected).

Argumentation, for Hatim and Munday (2004:334), is a text type in which concepts and/or beliefs are evaluated. The two basic forms of argumentation are:

1 Counter-argumentation: This is where a thesis is presented and then challenged and
2 Through-argumentation: This is where a thesis (a premise) is presented and defended.

For more details on counter-argumentation and through-argumentation, see Section 3.10.

3.2.1 Components of an argument

An argument has the following major components:

i Premise: An argument has either one premise or many premises consolidating each other. The premise must provide consistent claims so that we have a consistent conclusion.
ii Rebuttal: These are statements which may occur on their own or be part of the premise(s). Rebuttal is an argumentation technique that aims to invalidate the opponent's claim or argument.
iii Substantiation/rebuttal: These are statements that belong to the premise and primarily aim to give validity to the text producer's thesis (premise) and lead the audience or the opponent to accept the premise without qualms.
iv Quantifiers: They express the text producer's degree of force or certainty concerning the claim or the argument. The major quantifiers in Qur'anic discourse are the sentence-initial affirmation particles: (inna/qad – indeed, certainly, undoubtedly) and the letter /l/ (lām al-tawkīd). These are referred to by Searle and Vanderveken (1985) as 'illocutionary force indicating devices' (IFIDs).
v Conclusion: An argument usually has one conclusion. The conclusion is derived from the premise. In other words, the conclusion follows logically from the premise(s). The consistency of the conclusion depends on the consistency of the premise(s). An illogical (inconsistent) conclusion is the result of illogical (inconsistent) premise(s).

3.3 The premise and the conclusion

Effective premises make the text producer reach his/her intended conclusion. The premise highlights the text producer's thesis (performative intent, main argument). It is through the premise that the text producer's conclusion is accepted as true or rejected as false by the text receivers (audience). When the premise is directed towards the right audience, i.e., the speaker/writer is aware of the cognitive status of the audience, the premise will not be questioned by the audience. For instance, 'Interest on loans is causing financial hardship to borrowers. Therefore, there should be no interest on loans'. If the audience are people with mortgages or loans, the premise (Interest on loans is causing financial hardship to borrowers) will be taken as true and the conclusion (Therefore, there should be no interest on loans) will be accepted without qualms. However, if the same premise is directed to bankers and money lenders, the premise constitutes a weak argument, i.e., false, and its conclusion will be rejected by bankers and money lenders. Thus, an inference must hold between the premise and the conclusion.

Based on Qur'anic discourse, we can make the following observations about the premise(s) and the conclusion:

1 The premise is an assertion that reflects the text producer's performative intent. In other words, the thesis statement (the premise) represents the main argument of the text producer.
2 A premise is a proposition upon which an argument is based or from which a conclusion is drawn. In other words, the premise leads the reader to the conclusion.
3 There is a subtle difference between the premise and the conclusion: The premise is the claim that functions as the reason to accept the main point. The conclusion is the claim that expresses the main point.
4 The text producer has to make sure that the text receivers (audience) will accept the premise as true. Thus, the premise is the pivotal part in argumentation. In other words, when a premise is rejected by the audience, the conclusion will be rejected, too, and the whole argument will fall apart.
5 When constructing the premise, the text producer needs to be aware of the cognitive status of the text receiver, i.e., the state of mind of the audience. In other words, whether the argument is made for an open-minded, a sceptical, or a denier audience. Thus, it is imperative to consider the rationales and beliefs of the opponents.
6 Having known the cognitive status of the audience, the text producer can fortify the argument with affirmation devices. This is because in Qur'anic presentation of argumentation, the number and type of affirmation devices depend on the type of the audience. This is a Qur'an-specific argumentation feature. The major cohesive devices in Qur'anic argumentation are the affirmation /l/ letter (lām al-tawkīd) and the particles (inna) and (qad). The major argumentative cohesive devices in English are (therefore, for this reason, thus, however). Examples are like:

    inna rabbaka lasarīᶜ al-ᶜiqābi/annahu laghafūrun raḥīm – Your Lord is swift in penalty/Indeed, he is forgiving and merciful, Q7:167

  where the argumentation is about the antagonists (opponents) who are described as (those who forgot that by which they had been reminded . . . are insolent about that which they had been forbidden, Q7:165–166). Thus, the cognitive status of the audience is a denier (munkir). Therefore, a high level of assertiveness should be employed (more than one affirmation tool should be employed). Thus, we have the linguistic assertive particle (inna) + the affirmation /l/ letter + the active participles (sarīᶜu/ghafūr/raḥīm) + the no-main-verb nominal grammatical status of the statement.

    inna rabbaka lashadīd al-ᶜiqāb – Indeed, your Lord is severe in penalty, Q13:6

  where the argumentation is about the antagonists (opponents) who deny eschatology (resurrection): → (when we are dust, will we indeed be brought into a new creation?, Q13:5). Thus, the cognitive status of the audience is a denier. For this reason, the level of assertiveness should be high, and affirmation tools are required: particle (inna) + the affirmation /l/ letter + the active participles (shadid) + the no-main-verb nominal grammatical status of the statement.

7 The proof of a conclusion depends on both the truth of the premise(s) and the validity of the argument.

8 In Qur'anic argumentation, both the premise and the conclusion statements rely heavily on the employment of the nominal sentence, which enjoy a powerful illocutionary force for both substantiation and rebuttal. This is a Qur'an-specific argumentation feature. For further details, see Section 4.4.

9 In Qur'anic argumentation, both the premise and the conclusion statements employ the nominal sentence fortified with the active participle. This is a Qur'an-specific argumentation feature. For further details, see Section 4.4.

10 In Qur'anic argumentation, substantiation of a premise can be made through antithesis, as in the following example:

> Premise: yaᶜbudū allāha mukhliṣīna lahu al-dīn – To worship God, being sincere to Him in religion, Q98:5
>
> Substantiation: inna alladhīna kafarū min ahli al-kitābi wal-mushrikīna fī nāri jahannama khālidīna fīhā ūlā'ika hum sharru al-bariyyah. inna alladhīna āmanū wacamilū al-ṣāliḥāti ulā'ika hum khairu al-bariyyah. jaža'an cinda rabbihim jannātu cadnin . . . khālidīna fihā . . . – Indeed, they who disbelieved among the People of the Scripture and the polytheists will be in the fire of hell abiding eternally therein. Those are the worst of creatures. Indeed, they who believed and done righteous deeds – those are the best of creatures. Their reward with God will be gardens of perpetual residence . . . wherein they will abide forever, Q98:6–8
>
> Conclusion: dhālika liman khashiya rabbahu – That is for whoever has feared his/her Lord, Q98:8

11 A premise must have an illocutionary force. This is concerned with the communicative (pragmatic) impact of a statement (an argument) on the addressee (text receiver/hearer/reader), as in:

> allāhu shadīdu al-ᶜiqāb – God is severe in penalty, Q3:11

which may be taken either as a warning for punishment or a reassurance for security. Searle and Vanderveken (1985) have introduced illocutionary force indicating devices (IFID) such as word order, stress, intonation contour, punctuation, and the mood of the verb. At times, In Qur'anic discourse, the past tense is employed as an illocutionary force indicating device, as in:

> atā amru allāhi falā tastaᶜjilūh – The command of God is coming, so do not be impatient for it, Q16:1
>
> iqtarabat al-sāᶜatu wanshaqqa al-qamar – The hour has come near, and the moon has split in two, Q54:1

kāna allāhu ᶜafuwwan ghafūrā – God is ever forgiving and merciful, Q4:99

where the mood is expressed through the past tense in (atā – came) and (iqtarabat – came near) whose illocutionary force includes:

i affirmation and certainty of something that will take place, and
ii warning for what will take place in the future.

Similarly, the past tense auxiliary verb (kāna) delivers the illocutionary force of eternity and continuity.

In Qur'anic argumentation, word order is employed by the text producer as an illocutionary force indicating device. This includes foregrounded lexical items such as noun-initial statements and sentence-initial prepositional phrases, as in the following examples:

allāhu yarzuqu man yashā'u bighairi ḥisāb – God gives provision to whom He wills without account, Q2:212

allāhu yaᶜṣimuka min al-nāss – God will protect you from the people, Q5:67

biyadika al-khair – In Your hand is all good, Q3:26

ilā allāhi al-maṣīr – To God is the final destination, Q3:28

We can safely claim that Qur'anic argumentation employs more illocutionary force indicating devices which are Qur'an specific. The Qur'an-specific illocutionary force indicating devices are:

1 the active participle, as in:

anna allāha mūhin kaid al-kāfirīn – God will weaken the plot of the disbelievers, Q8:18

where the active participle (mūhin – will weaken) enjoys the illocutionary force of [+ Permanency] and [+ Continuity]. However, a verb cannot replace the active participle since the verb has a different illocutionary force, and this will undermine the performative intent of the premise. The verb's illocutionary force includes [– Permanency] and [– Continuity].

2 antithesis: This is an illocutionary force indicating device whose performative intent (communicative force) is persuasion and admonition, as in:

al-shaiṭānu yaᶜidukum al-faqra waya'murukum bil-fahshā'i wa allāhu yaᶜidukum maghfiratan minhu wafaḍla – Satan threatens you with poverty and orders you to immorality, while God promises you forgiveness from Him and bounty, Q2:268

inna rabbaka ladhū maghfiratin wadhū ᶜiqābin alīm – Your Lord is a possessor of forgiveness and a possessor of painful penalty, Q41:43

3 the nominal status of the statement: It is also interesting to note that Q2:268 has employed the nominal status of the premise as an IFID where noun-initial (al-shaiṭānu – Satan) and (allāhu – God) are used.

Similarly, Q41:43 has employed two types of IFID: antithesis and the affirmation tools, which are (inna), the affirmation letter /l/ in (ladhū), as well as the nominal status of the premise.

12 Qur'anic discourse uses reasoning with universal quantifiers. In other words, the Qur'an constructs valid arguments through the employment of the universal quantifier. It is worthwhile to note that the meaning of the quantifier remains intuitive. For instance, when we say: (All men are mortal. Jeremy is a man). Therefore, by intuition, the meaning of (Jeremy is a man) leads us to infer (conclude) that (Jeremy is mortal). Thus, the premise, i.e., thesis, argument (All men are mortal) has employed the universal quantifier, which has led to a valid conclusion. It is through reasoning that we have intuitively reached the valid conclusion. Let us consider the following examples of arguments with universal quantifiers:

> inna al-insāna layaṭghā. an ra'āhu istaghnā – Indeed, man transgresses because he sees himself self-sufficient, Q96:6.

The premise is: (inna al-insāna layaṭghā).

The inference is: Because X is a Man, X will have (ṭughyān – transgression).

The conclusion is: Every X will have (ṭughyān) when X has (istighnā' – self-sufficiency).

> inna allāha lā yaghfiru an yushraka bihi wayaghfiru mā dūna dhālika liman yashā' waman yushrik billāhi faqad ḍalla ḍalalan baᶜīdā – God does not forgive association with Him, but He forgives what is less than that for whom He wills. And he who associates others with God has certainly gone far astray, Q4:116

The premise is: (inna allāha lā yaghfiru an yushraka bihi wayaghfiru mā dūna dhālika liman yashā' – God does not forgive association with Him, but He forgives what is less than that for whom He wills).

The conclusion is: (waman yushrik billāhi faqad ḍalla ḍalālan baᶜīdā – And he who associates others with God has certainly gone far astray).

Similarly, in:

The premise is: (man yaᶜmal min al-ṣāliḥāti min dhakarin aw unthā wahuwa mu'minun – Whoever does righteous deeds, whether male or female, while being a believer, Q4:124) → when male/female X does good deeds + is a believer.

The conclusion is: (ulā'ika yadkhulūna al-jannata walā yuẓlamūna naqīrā – Those will enter paradise and will not be wronged even as much as the spike on a date seed, Q4:124) → male/female X enters paradise.

13 The Qur'an, during the occurrence of universal quantifiers, employs phrases like (inna fī dhālika la'āyātin liqawmin yaᶜqilūn – Indeed in that are signs for a people who use reason, Q30:24), (inna fī dhālika laᶜibratan li'ulī al-abṣār – Indeed in that is a lesson for those of vision, 3:13, Q24:44), (ᶜibratun li'ulī al-albāb – a lesson for those of understanding, Q12:111), (liqawmin yatafakkarūn – for a people who give thought, Q10:24), (li'uli al-albāb – for those of understanding, Q3:190). These universal quantifier phrases affirm the importance of intuition, inference (deduction), and logical reasoning to arrive at the valid conclusion of the unity of God (the oneness of God), that God is the creator of humans, the heavens, and the earth. In other words, if a particular object has a property, then someone/something has that property. This rule is called 'existential generalization'. It takes an instance and then generalizes to a general claim. We are informed through God's omnipotence details that God has the unique property of reviving the dead; therefore, He must have the property of resurrection, i.e., eschatology is verified, as in Q23:12–14 where God's omnipotence details are introduced first followed by reference to eschatology (resurrection) in Q23:15–16, and in Q36:78 where reference is made to the opponent's premise about their denial of eschatology and is followed by a rebuttal where God's omnipotence is presented in Q36:79–81. We are informed through God's omnipotence details that God has the unique property of creation, then He must have the property of being the creator, as in:

> awalaisa alladhī khalaqa al-samāwāti wal-arḍa biqādirin ᶜalā an yakhluqa mithlahum – Is it not (i.e., therefore) He who created the heavens and the earth able to create the likes of them?, Q36:81
>
> alaisa dhālika biqādirin ᶜalā an yuḥyiya al-mawtā? – Is not (i.e., therefore) that creator able to give life to the dead, Q75:40

where the interrogative word (alaisa) is equivalent to the English conclusion indicators: (therefore, wherefore, accordingly, we may conclude, entails that, hence, thus, consequently, we may infer that, it must be that, whence, so, it follows that, implies that).

14 We can claim that the premise → (shows, indicates, proves, entails, implies, or establishes) that the conclusion is X Y Z. We can also claim that a conclusion → (is shown, is indicated, is proven, is entailed, is established) by the premise. The conclusion is what the argument is trying to prove.

15 English employs linguistic indicators (words or phrases) that indicate premises. Also, a linguistic indicator is the keyword that flags the conclusion and is employed to connect the premise to the conclusion, i.e., the linguistic indicator is a discourse flag which indicates the logical relationship of claim. These are: (since, if, because, as indicated by, for, in that, may be inferred from, as, seeing that, for the reason that, for these reasons, inasmuch as, given that, may be concluded from, the reason that, due to the fact that, from which it follows). English also employs indicator words and phrases

that indicate a conclusion. These are: (therefore, wherefore, accordingly, we may conclude, entails that, hence, thus, consequently, we may infer that, it must be that, whence, so, it follows that, implies that).

16 Unlike English, Qur'anic argumentation does not employ similar linguistic indicators through which the premises are flagged. The Qur'anic argument employs conclusion indicator words and conjunctives such as: (idhan – therefore, then, for this reason, as in Q23:91), (the interrogative word alaisa – therefore, wherefore, accordingly, Q75:40, Q95:8), the conjunctive particle (fa – then, therefore), and (kadhālika – likewise, thus, therefore, as in Q50:11), which flag the conclusion. Similarly, the Qur'anic argument employs indicator phrases used sentence-initially through which the premise is flagged, such as (wamin āyātihi – of His signs, Q30:20–23, 46) and the grammatical structure (huwa alladhī – it is He who, Q30:27), (allāhu alladhī – it is God who, Q30:48, 54), and (inna rabbakumu allāhu alladhī – Indeed, your lord is God, Q7:54). We also encounter the indicator word: (lākinna – however, Q30:30).

17 Unlike English, Qur'anic argumentation does not employ similar indicator words through which the conclusion is flagged. The Qur'anic argument employs indicator phrases sentence-initially through which the conclusion is indicated, such as: (tabāraka – blessed, Q7:54), (subḥānahu – He (God) is far above this (polytheistic claim), He is exalted, Q2:116), and (subḥānahu wataᶜālā – He is exalted and high above, Q6:100).

18 The Qur'anic indicator word (subḥānahu) is an argumentative theological signal for deanthropomorphism (al-tanzīh), which has occurred 14 times in Qur'anic discourse. It is employed for rebutting the polytheistic claims such as (ittakhādhā allāhu waladā – God has taken a son, Q10:68) and (yajᶜalūna lillāhi al-banāt – They attribute daughters to God, Q16:57). Thus, a rebuttal is signalled by (subḥānahu), as in (waqālu ittakhādhā allāhu waladan subḥānahu – They say: 'God has taken a son'. He is exalted!, Q2:116), (lā ilāha illā hū subḥānahu ᶜammā yushrikūn – There is no deity except Him. He is exalted and He is above whatever they associate with Him, Q9:31), (yajᶜalūna lillāhi al-banāt subḥānahu – They attribute to God daughters, Q16:57).

19 Statements of an argument have different moods which are expressed through the verbs. The moods are indicative, imperative, and subjunctive. For more details on mood, see Section 3.5.

20 The purposeful configuration of sentence constituents as a major grammatical mechanism of coherence plays a vital role in the substantiation of a thesis and in introducing the conclusion of a deductive argument, as in:

> qul allāhumma mālika al-mulki tu'tī al-mulka man tashā'u watanziᶜu al-mulka mimman tashā'u watuᶜizzu man tashā'u watudhillu man tashā'u biyadika al-khairu innaka ᶜalā kulli shai'in qadīr – Say: 'O God, owner of sovereignty, You give sovereignty to whom You will and You take sovereignty away from whom You will. You honour whom You will and You humble whom You will. All that is good lies in Your hand. Indeed, You are over all things competent', Q3:26

where we have an argument whose premises have specific characteristics of God. The premises are backed up by subsequent text segments that have employed the configuration of specific segments to sustain the premises:

> (allāhu mālika al-mulki/allāhu yu'tī al-mulka man yashā'u/allāhu yanziᶜu al-mulka mimman yashā'u/allāhu yuᶜizzu man yashā'u/allāhu yudhillu man yashā'u – God is the owner of sovereignty/God gives sovereignty to whom He wills/God takes sovereignty away from whom He wills/ God honours whom He wills/God humbles whom He wills).

In the above example, we have foregrounded expressions in the ayah-final no-main-verb nominal sentences: (biyadika al-khairu – All that is good lies in Your hand) and (innaka ᶜalā kulli shai'in qadīr – Indeed, You are over all things competent). The foregrounded expressions are: (biyadika – in Your hand) and (ᶜalā kulli shai'in – over all things), which have contributed to the continuity of the premises and have substantiated them, too. To consolidate the premises, the foregrounding of the text segments (biyadika) and (ᶜalā kulli shai'in) has become a prerequisite for the conclusion and has consolidated the truth value of the premises.

21 Qur'anic discourse includes narrative argumentation where in the Prophets' parables, we encounter the opponent's (denier – munkir) premises. Examples of narrative argumentation is found in Q7 where there are five narrative argumentative texts: Q7:59–64 (Noah's parable), Q7:65–72 (Hud's parable), Q7:73–79 (Ṣāliḥ's parable), Q7:80–84 (Lot's parable), and Q7:85–95 (Shuᶜaib's parable).

Similarly, Q26 involves eight Prophets' stories, Q26:2–9 (Muḥammad's parable), Q26:10–68 (Moses's parable), Q26:69–104 (Abraham's parable), Q26:105–122 (Noah's parable), Q26:123–140 (Hud's parable), Q26:141–159 (Ṣāliḥ's parable), Q26:160–175 (Lot's parable), and Q26:176–191 (Shuᶜaib's parable).

22 Qur'anic discourse involves two major types of argumentation:

i through-argumentation, and
ii counter-argumentation.

For more details, see Section 4.8.

23 Qur'anic discourse involves three major types of audience in argumentation:

i open-minded (khāli al-dhihn),
ii sceptical (mutraddid), and
iii denier (munkir).

Each category of audience reflects the cognitive status of the listener/reader. For more details, see Section 4.7.1.

24 Qur'anic discourse employs specific argumentation techniques, sentence structures, and affirmation tools for each type of audience.

25 Qur'anic discourse employs different para-linguistic rebuttal and substantiation techniques. These include different modes of persuasion, such as:

i admonition (Q39:7–8, 53–61),
ii admonition through reference to Prophets' parables and stories of past unbelieving nations (Q10:71–74, Q10:75–93, Q26:10–191, Q39:25–26),
iii God's omnipotence (Q39:5–6, 21),
iv reward and punishment (Q39: end of 8–10, 15–20, 71–74), and
v eschatology (Q39:24, 60, 68).

For more details on modes of persuasion, see Section 4.6.1

26 Qur'anic discourse employs different linguistic rebuttal and substantiation techniques. These include the nominalized noun (subḥānahu – He (God) is exalted, Q39:4) and the no-main-verb nominal sentence, as in (huwa allāhu al-wāḥidu al-qahhār – He is God, the one, the prevailing, Q39:4), (dhālikum allāhu rabbukum lahu al-mulk – That is God, your Lord, to Him belongs dominion, Q39:6), and (lā ilāha illā hū – There is no deity except Him, Q39:6).

27 In Qur'anic argumentation, there are two major types of addressee: (i) the polytheists worshipping gods other than God and (ii) the People of the Book (the Jews and the Christians).

28 In Qur'anic argumentation, we encounter different types of opponents' premises:

i the oneness (unity) of God, i.e., partners are ascribed to God,
ii disbelief in eschatology, i.e., rejecting the notions of resurrection (al-baᶜth) and reward and punishment (al-thawāb wal-ᶜiqāb), and
iii rejecting the prophethood (al-nubuwwah) of a given Prophet and disbelieving both his message and the Scripture he claims to be a revelation from God.

29 In Qur'anic argumentation, the counter-argument to an opponent's premise is heavily based on details about God's omnipotence as a mode of persuasion, i.e., using the deductive reasoning technique, as in Q39:5–6.

30 In Qur'anic argumentation, the counter-argument to an antagonist's (opponent's) premise is based on details about reward and punishment as a mode of persuasion, as in Q44:35–36 (antagonist's premises), which are counter-argued by reward and punishment details in Q44:37–57.

31 An argument must be presented logically to the addressee; otherwise, it will be rejected because it becomes a fallacy. A fallacy is an often plausible argument using either false, illogical reasoning or a stick. Abraham presents to his polytheist father a logical argument based on deductive reasoning: (lima taᶜbudu mā lā yasmaᶜu walā yubṣiru walā yughnī ᶜanka shai'an – Why do you worship that which does not hear, does not see, and will not benefit you at all?, Q19:42. However, his father responds with a fallacy that is an argument backed by a stick: (la'in lam tantahi la'arjumannaka wahjurnī

maliyyā – If you do not desist, I will surely stone you. So, keep out of my way, Q19:46), i.e., his father has employed force and resorted to threat without evidence in order to have his standpoint accepted by his son.

3.3.1 Analysis of Qur'anic argumentation

The present analysis provides examples of different types of argumentation which reflect different premises, different rebuttal details, different conclusions, and different types of audience.

Example 1

inna rabbakumu allāhu alladhī khalaqa al-samāwāti wal-arḍa fī sittāti aiyāmin thumma istawā ᶜalā al-ᶜarshi yughshī al-laila al-nahāra yaṭlubuhu ḥathīthā wal-shamsa wal-qamara wal-nujūma musakhkhāratin bi'amrihi alā lahu al-khalqu wal-amru tabāraka allāhu rabbu al-ᶜālamīn – Indeed, your Lord is God who created the heavens and earth in six days and then established Himself above the throne. He covers the night with the day chasing it rapidly, and He created the sun, the moon, and the stars, subjected by His command. Unquestionably, His is the creation and the command; blessed is God, Lord of the worlds, Q7:54.

where the premises are: (inna rabbakumu allāhu alladhī khalaqa al-samāwāti wal-arḍa fī sittāti aiyāmin – Indeed, your Lord is God who created the heavens and earth in six days), (istawā ᶜalā al-ᶜarshi – He established Himself above the throne), (yughshī al-laila al-nahāra yaṭlubuhu ḥathīthā – He covers the night with the day chasing it rapidly), (wal-shamsa wal-qamara wal-nujūma musakhkhāratin bi'amrihi – the sun, the moon, and the stars, subjected by His command), and (alā lahu al-khalqu wal-amru – Unquestionably, His is the creation and the command) followed by the conclusion: (tabāraka allāhu rabbu al-ᶜālamīn – Blessed is God, Lord of the worlds).

Example 2

innahu man yattaqi wayasbir fa'inna allāha lā yuḍīᶜu ajra al-muḥsinīn – Indeed, he who fears God and is patient, then indeed God does not allow the reward of those who do good to be lost, Q12:90.

where the premise is: (innahu man yattaqi wayaṣbir – Indeed, he who fears God and is patient) and the conclusion is: (fa'inna allāha lā yuḍīᶜu ajra al-muḥsinīn – then indeed God does not allow the reward of those who do good to be lost). The conclusion is flagged by the linguistic indicators (fa + inna – then indeed).

Example 3

mattakhādhā allāhu min waladin wamā kāna maᶜahu min ilāh idhan ladhahaba kullu ilāhin bimā khalaqa walaᶜalā baᶜḍuhum ᶜalā baᶜḍ – God has not taken

> any son, nor has there ever been with Him any deity. If there had been, then each deity would have taken what it created, and some of them would have sought to overcome others. God is exalted and he is above what they describe concerning Him, Q23:91.

where the premises are (mattakhādhā allāhu min waladin –/wamā kāna ma^cahu min ilāh – God has not taken any son/nor has there ever been with Him any deity) and their conclusion is (idhan ladhahaba kullu ilāhin bimā khalaqa wala^calā ba^cḍuhum ^calā ba^cḍ – If there had been, then each deity would have taken what it created, and some of them would have sought to overcome others). The conclusion is flagged by the linguistic indicator (idhan – then, therefore).

Example 4

> wakam ahlaknā min qaryatin baṭirat ma^cīshatahā fatilka masākinuhum lam tuskan min ba^cdihim illā qalīlā wakunnā naḥnu al-wārithin. wamā kāna rabbuka muhlika al-qurā ḥattā yab^catha fī ummihā rasūlan yatlū ^calaihim āyātinā wamā kunnā muhlikī al-qurā illā wa'ahluhā ẓālimūn – We have destroyed many a community that once revelled in its wanton wealth and easy living. Since then their dwelling places have barely been inhabited. We are the only heir. Your Lord would never destroy towns without first raising a messenger in their midst to recite Our messages to them, nor would We destroy towns unless their inhabitants were evildoers, Q28:59.

where the premises are: (wakam ahlaknā min qaryatin baṭirat ma^cīshatahā fatilka masākinuhum lam tuskan min ba^cdihim illā qalīlā wakunnā naḥnu al-wārithin. wamā kāna rabbuka muhlika al-qurā ḥattā yab^catha fī ummihā rasūlan yatlū ^calaihim āyātinā – We have destroyed many a community that once revelled in its wanton wealth and easy living. Since then, their dwelling places have barely been inhabited. We are the only heir. Your Lord would never destroy towns without first raising a messenger in their midst to recite Our messages to them) and the conclusion is: (wamā kunnā muhlikī al-qurā illā wa'ahluhā ẓālimūn – We would never destroy towns unless their inhabitants were evildoers).

Example 5

> aqim wajhaka lildīni ḥanīfan fiṭrata allāhi allatī faṭara al-nāsa ^calaihā lā tabdīla likhalqi allāhi dhālika al-dīnu al-qaiyimu walākinna akthara al-nāsi ḷā ya^clamūn – So direct yourself toward the religion, inclining to truth. Adhere to the fitrah of God upon which He has created all people. No change should there be in the creation of God. That is the correct religion. However, most of the people do not know, Q30:30.

where we have an argument with an imperative mood through the imperative verb (aqim – direct) followed by the premises: (aqim wajhaka lildīni ḥanīfan – direct yourself towards the religion, inclining to truth), (fiṭrata allāhi allatī faṭara al-nāsa ᶜalaihā – Adhere to the fitrah of God upon which He has created all people), (lā tabdīla likhalqi allāhi – No change should there be in the creation of God), and (dhālika al-dīnu al-qaiyimu – That is the correct religion). The conclusion is introduced by the indicator word (lākinna – however, but): (lākinna akthara al-nāsi ḷā yaᶜlamūn – However, most of the people do not know).

Example 6

āti dhā al-qurbā ḥaqqahu wal-miskīna wabna al-sabīl dhālika khairun lilladhīna yurīdūna wajha allāhi wa'ulā'ika hum al-mufliḥūn – Give the relative his right, as well as the needy and the traveller. That is best for those who desire the countenance of God; it is they who will be the successful, Q30:38.

where the argument is initiated by the imperative mood represented by the imperative verb (āti – give). The premises are: (āti dhā al-qurbā ḥaqqahu wal-miskīna wabna al-sabīl – Give the relative his right, as well as the needy and the traveller) and (dhālika khairun lilladhīna yurīdūna wajha allāhi – That is best for those who desire the countenance of God) followed by the conclusion: (ulā'ika hum al-mufliḥūn – It is they who will be the successful).

Example 7

an askhur lillāh waman yashkur fa'innamā yashkuru linafsihi waman kafara fa'inna allāha ghaniyyun ḥamīd – Be thankful to God. Whoever is grateful is grateful for the benefit of himself. Whoever denies God's favour – then indeed God is free of need and praiseworthy, Q31:12.

where the premises are: (an askhur lillāh – Be thankful to God) and (man yashkur fa'innamā yashkuru linafsihi – Whoever is grateful is grateful for the benefit of himself) followed by the conclusion: (fa'inna allāha ghaniyyun ḥamīd – God is free of need and praiseworthy). The conclusion is flagged by the linguistic indicator (fa + inna – then, indeed).

Example 8

law arāda allāhu an yattakhidha waladan laṣṭafā mimmā yakhluqu mā yashā' subḥānahu huwa allāhu al-wāḥidu al-qahhār – If God had intended to take a son, He could have chosen from what he creates whatever He willed. He is exalted. He is God, the one, the prevailing, Q39:4.

where the premises are: (law arāda allāhu an yattakhidha waladan laṣṭafā mimmā yakhluqu mā yashā' – If God had intended to take a son, He could have chosen from what he creates whatever He willed) followed by the conclusion: (subḥānahu – He is exalted), (huwa allāhu al-wāḥidu al-qahhār – He is God, the one, the prevailing) where the conclusion is flagged by the linguistic indicator: (subḥānahu).

Example 9

waqtaraba al-wa^{c}du al-ḥaqqu fa'idhā hiya shākhiṣatun abṣāru alladhīna kafarū yāwailatanā qad kunnā fī ghaflatin min hādhā bal kunnā ẓalimin. innakum wamā ta^{c}budūna min dūn allāh ḥaṣabu jahannama antum lahā wāridūn. law kāna hā'ulā'i ālihatan mā waradūhā wakullun fihā khālidūn – When the true promise draws near, the disbelievers' eyes will stare in terror, and they will say: 'Woe to us! We were not aware of this at all. We were wrong'. You (disbelievers) and what you worship instead of God will be fuel for hell; that is where you will go. If those idols had been real gods, they would not have come to it, but all are eternal therein, Q21:97–99.

Since the idols which the polytheists have been worshipping are not real gods, therefore, both you and them will be the fuel for hell. Thus, the conclusion is: (law kāna hā'ulā'i ālihatan mā waradūhā wakullun fihā khālidūn – If those idols had been real gods, they would not have come to it, but all are eternal therein).

Q21:99 is similar to Q21:22 (law kāna fihimā ālihatun illā allāhu lafasadatā – Had there been within the heavens and earth gods besides God, they both would have been ruined). Since there are no deities, the heavens and the earth have not been ruined and are still intact. Therefore, God is exalted and He is the Lord of the throne and He is above what they describe, i.e., God is above the opponents' (polytheists') scepticism and allegations: (fasubhana allāhi rabbi al-^{c}arshi ^{c}ammā yaṣifūn).

Q21:99 is also similar to Q7:40 (inna aladhīna kadhdhabū bi'āyātinā wastakbarū ^{c}anhā lā tufattaḥu lahum abwābu al-samā'i walā yadkhulūna al-jannata ḥattā yalija al-jamalu fī sammi al-khiyāṭ – Indeed, those who deny Our revelations and are arrogant towards them, the gates of heaven will not be opened for them, nor will they enter paradise until a camel enters into the eye of a needle). The premise which we can make for this argument is: Those who deny God's revelations and are arrogant towards them will enter the gates of heaven when the camel enters through the eye of a needle. In other words: Since the camel cannot enter through the eye of a needle, therefore, the conclusion is: Those who deny God's revelations and are arrogant towards them will never enter paradise. This is argument from analogy or argument from example. For more details on this, see Section 3.3.2, points (iii) and (iv).

Example 10

shahida shāhidun min ahlihā in kāna qamīṣuhu qudda min qubulin faṣadaqat wahuwa min al-kāfirīn. wa'in kāna qamīṣuhu qudda min duburin fakadhabat wahuwa min al-ṣādiqīn. falammā ra'ā qamīṣuhu qudda min duburin qāla innahu min kaidikunna – A witness from her family testified: 'If Joseph's shirt is torn from the front, then she has told the truth, and he is of the liars. However, if his shirt is torn from the back, then she has lied, and he is of the truthful'. So, when her husband saw Joseph's shirt torn from the back, he said: 'Indeed, it is women's plan. Indeed, your plan is vehement', Q12:26–28.

We have two premises: shāhida shāhidun min ahlihā – A witness from her family testified and (qamīṣuhu qudda min duburin – His shirt is torn from the back). Therefore, the conclusion is: (falammā ra'ā qamīṣuhu qudda min duburin qāla innahu min kaidikunna – When her husband saw Joseph's shirt torn from the back, he said: 'Indeed, it is women's plan. Indeed, your plan is vehement'), i.e., (hiya kādhibah wahuwa ṣādiq – She is a liar and he is truthful). The conclusion is based on deductive reasoning. In other words, Joseph ran away from her but she held him from the back of his shirt and tore it. Because the shirt is torn from the back, it must be her who was chasing him. The conclusion is flagged by the linguistic indicator (fa – then, indeed).

Example 11

in hiya illā mawtatunā al-ūlā wamā naḥnu bimunsharīn. fa'tū bi'ābā'inā in kuntum ṣādiqīn – There is nothing beyond our one death. We will not be resurrected. If what you say is true, bring back our forefathers, Q44:35–36.

The polytheists' premises are: (in hiya illā mawtatunā al-ūlā / mā naḥnu bimunsharīn – There is nothing beyond our one death. We will not be resurrected, Q44:35). Their conclusion is based on deductive reasoning: (Because you cannot bring back our forefathers, therefore, there is no resurrection, i.e., what you say about resurrection is not true) → (fa'atū bi'ābā'ina in kuntum ṣadiqīn – If what you say is true, bring back our forefathers, Q44:36)

Example 12

wakadhālika nuriya ibrāhīma malakūta al-samāwāti wal-arḍi waliyakūna min al-mūqinīn. falammā janna ᶜalaihi al-lailu ra'ā kawkaban qāla hādhā rabbī falammā afala qāla lā uḥibbu al-āfilīn. falammā ra'ā al-qamara bāzighan qāla hādhā rabbī falammā afalā qāla la'in lam yahdiyani rabbī la'akūnanna min al-qawmi al-ḍallīn. falammā ra'ā al-shamsa bāzighatan qāla hādhā rabbī hādhā akbar falammā afalat qāla yā qawmi innī barī'un mimmā tushrikūn. innī wajjahtu wajhiya lilladhi faṭara al-samāwāti wal-arḍa ḥanīfan wamā anā min al-mushrikīn – Thus, did We show Abraham the realm of the heavens and the earth that he would be among the certain in faith. So, when the night covered him with darkness, he saw a star. He said: 'This is my lord'. But when it disappeared, he said: 'I do not like those that disappear'. When he saw the moon rising, he said: 'This is my lord'. But when it disappeared, he said: 'Unless my Lord guides me, I will surely be among the people gone astray'. When he saw the sun raising, he said: 'This is my lord. This is greater'. But when it disappeared, he said: 'O my people, indeed I am free from what you associate with God. Indeed, I have turned myself toward He who created the heavens and the earth, inclining toward truth, and I am not of those who associate others with God', Q6:75–79.

Through deductive reasoning, Abraham reaches the conclusion: (innī wajjahtu wajhiya lilladhī faṭara al-samāwāti wal-arḍa ḥanīfan wamā anā min al-mushrikīn – Indeed, I have turned myself towards he who created the heavens and the earth, inclining towards truth, and I am not of those who associate others with God). This is because he has witnessed the fact that the star, the moon, and the sun disappear after a short period of time and he is left with nothing to worship or to ask for help. By deductive reasoning, God should be permanent and available all the time. Thus, the previous premises have led him to abandon the false gods and declare: (innī barī'un mimmā tushrikūn – Indeed I am free from what you associate with God). Abraham wanted to inform his people that these false gods (the star, the moon, and the sun) are not worthy of worship and that whoever created the heavens and the earth is worthy of worship. By deductive reasoning, God has created the heavens and the earth. Thus, God alone is worthy of worship. For more details on deductive reasoning, see Section 3.3.2.

3.3.2 Qur'anic deductive argument

Deductive reasoning (logical deduction) is a cognitive activity, i.e., a type of reasoning, which goes from general to specific. If the premises are true, then the reasoning should be valid. For instance: (Because all humans are mortal, and Jeremy is a human, therefore Jeremy is mortal). Another example: (It is dangerous to drive on icy streets. The streets are icy now. So it is dangerous to drive now). Thus, deductive reasoning is the process of reasoning taken from one or more statements (premises) in order to reach a logical (true) conclusion (Sternberg 2009:578). In other words, the premises are linked with the conclusion through the process of deductive reasoning.

Deductive reasoning adopts the classic reasoning pattern of (A = B and B = C, therefore A = C). However, deductive reasoning follows other reasoning patterns such as: (Be careful around bees, they might sting you). Based on deductive reasoning, we understand the statement, i.e., we infer from the statement, that: (All bees might sting). Another example: (I need an hour to get to work. I leave home at 7 a.m.). Based on deductive reasoning, I can safely conclude that: (I will reach my office by 8 a.m.). Through deductive reasoning, we can draw conclusions from specific statements (premises). In other words, it is hinged upon the premise(s).

Thus, we use deductive reasoning to have a better understanding of the world around us.

The Qur'anic deductive argument has the following features:

i The deductive argument is based on a sound definition: We encounter in Qur'anic discourse a deductive argument with an explicit definition of God, as in:

Example 1

allāhu lā ilāha illā huwa al-ḥāiyu al-qaiyūmu lā ta'khudhuhu sinatun walā nawm lahu mā fī al-samāwāti wamā fī al-arḍi man dhā alladhī yashfaᶜu ᶜindahu illā bi'idhnih yaᶜlamu ma baina aidīhim wamā khalfahum walā yuḥīṭuna bishai'in min ᶜilmihi illā bimā shā' wasiᶜa kursiyyuhu al-samāwāti wal-arḍa walā ya'ūduhu ḥifẓuhumā wahuwa al-^{c}aliyyu al-^{c}aẓīm – God, there is no deity except Him, the ever living, the sustainer of all existence. Neither drowsiness overtakes Him nor sleep. To Him belongs whatever is on the earth. Who is it that can intercede with Him except by His permission? He knows what is presently before them and what will be after them, and they do not encompass a thing of His knowledge except for what He wills. His chair extends over the heavens and the earth, and their preservation does not tire Him. He is the most high, the most great, Q2:255

Example 2

tanzīlu al-kitābi min allāh → al-^{c}azīz/al-^{c}alīm/ghāfir al-dhanb/qābil al-tawb/shadīd al-^{c}iqāb/dhi al-ṭawl/lā ilāha illā hū/ilaihi al-maṣīr – The revelation of the Qur'an is from God → the exalted in might/the knowing/the forgiver of sin/the acceptor of repentance/the severe in punishment/the owner of abundance/there is no deity except Him/to Him is the destination, Q40:2–3

Example 3

huwa allāhu alladhī lā ilāha illā hu ^{c}ālimu al-ghaibi wal-shahādati huwa al-raḥmānu al-raḥīmu huwa allāhu alladhī lā ilāha illā huwa al-maliku al-quddūsu al-salāmu al-mu'minu al-muhaiminu al-^{c}azīzu al-jabbāru al-mutakabbiru . . . huwa allāhu al-khāḷiqu al-bāri'u al-muṣawwiru lahu al-asmā'u al-ḥusnā yusabbiḥu lahu mā fī al-samāwāti wal-arḍi wahuwa al-^{c}zīzu al-ḥakīmu – He is God, other than whom there is no deity, knower of the unseen and the witnessed. He is the entirely merciful, the especially merciful. He is God, other than whom there is no deity, the Sovereign, the pure, the perfection, the bestower of faith, the overseer, the exalted in might, the compeller, the superior, . . . He is God, the creator, the inventor, the fashioner; to Him belong the best names. Whatever is in the heavens and earth is exalting Him. And He is the exalted in might, the wise, Q59:22–24

ii The deductive argument refers to the nature of things and their specific characteristics: Let us consider the following example that represents a deductive argument with specific characteristics of God and those who are besides God (the partners worshipped by polytheists).

Q3:26 provides an example of premises with specific characteristics of God and are linked with the conclusion through the process of deductive reasoning. The premises are fortified by subsequent text segments that have opted for the configuration of specific segments to prop up the main thought:

> qul allāhumma mālika al-mulki tu'tī al-mulka man tashā'u watanzi^{c}u al-mulka mimman tashā'u watu^{c}izzu man tashā'u watudhillu man tashā'u biyadika al-khairu innaka ^{c}alā kulli shai'in qadīr – Say: 'O God, owner of sovereignty, You give sovereignty to whom You will and You take sovereignty away from whom You will'.

> You honour whom You will and You humble whom You will. All that is good lies in Your hand. Indeed, You are over all things competent.

In the above example, we have foregrounded expressions in the āyah-final no-main-verb nominal sentences: (biyadika al-khairu – All that is good lies in Your hand) and (innaka ᶜalā kulli shai'in qadīr – Indeed, You are over all things competent). In these nominal sentences, the foregrounded expressions are: (biyadika – in Your hand) and (ᶜalā kulli shai'in – over all things), which have contributed to the continuity of the pivotal thought at the beginning of the statement and have substantiated it, too. The premises are:

> (allāhu mālika al-mulki/allāhu yu'tī al-mulka man yashā'u/allāhu yanziᶜu al-mulka mimman yashā'u/allāhu yuᶜizzu man yashā'u/allāhu yudhillu man yashā'u – God is the owner of sovereignty/God gives sovereignty to whom He wills/God takes sovereignty away from whom He wills/ God honours whom He wills/God humbles whom He wills).

To consolidate the premises, the foregrounding of the text segments (biyadika) and (ᶜalā kulli shai'in) has become a prerequisite for the conclusion and has elevated the truth value of the premises.

Similarly, in:

> huwa alladhī khalaqakum min nafsin wāḥidatin wajaᶜalā minhā zawjahā liyaskuna ilaihā falammā taghashshāhā ḥamalat ḥamlan khafīfan famarrat bihi falammā athqalat daᶜū allāha rabbahumā la'in ātaitanā ṣāliḥan lanakūnanna min al-shākirīn. falammā ātāhumā ṣāliḥan jaᶜalā lahu shurakā'a fīmā ātāhumā fataᶜālā allāhu ᶜammā yushrikūn. ayushrikūna mā lā yakhluqu shai'an wahum yukhlaqūn? walā yastaṭīᶜūna lahum naṣran walā anfusahum yanṣurūn? in tadᶜūhum ilā al-hudā lā yattabiᶜūkum sawā'an ᶜalaikum adaᶜawtumūhum am antum ṣāmitūn. inna alladhīna tadᶜūna min dūni allāhi cibādun amthālukum fadᶜūhum falyastajībū lakum in kuntum ṣadiqīn. alahum arjulun yamshūna bihā am laham aidin yabṭishūna bihā am laham aᶜyunun yubṣirūna bihā am lahum ādhānun yasmaᶜūna bihā qul idᶜū shurakā'akum thumma kīdūni falā tunẓirūn. inna waliyiya allāhu alladhī nazzala al-kitāba wahuwa yatawallā al-ṣāliḥīn. walladhīna tadᶜūna min dūnihi lā yastaṭīᶜūna naṣrakum walā anfusahum yanṣurūn – It is He who created you from one soul and created from it its mate that he (man) might dwell in security with her. When he covers her, she becomes pregnant and continues therein. When it becomes heavy, they both invoke God, their Lord: 'If you should give us a good child, we will surely be among the grateful'. But when He (God) gives them a good child, they ascribe partners to Him concerning that which He has given them. God is exalted and above what they associate with Him. Do they associate with Him those who create nothing and they are themselves created? They (the false deities) are unable to give them help, nor can they help themselves. If you (believers) invite them to guidance, they will not follow you. It is all the same for you whether you invite them or you are silent. Indeed, those you (polytheists) call upon besides God are creations

> like you. So call upon them and let them respond to you, if you should be truthful. Do they have feet by which they walk? Or do they have hands by which they strike? Or do they have eyes by which they see? Or do they have ears by which they hear? Say (O Muḥammad): 'Call your partners and then conspire against me and give me respite. Indeed, my protector is God who has sent down the Book. He is an ally to the righteous'. Those you call upon besides Him are unable to help you, nor can they help themselves, Q7:189–197

In the above example, specific characteristics of God are outlined in addition to those of the false gods which the disbelievers have taken for worship other than the Lord. We are informed that God is the creator of all humans from one soul, He is able to give people children, that people can call upon Him and he can answer their call, that He can see, strike, and hear, that He can protect the righteous, and He can help them. However, the partners worshipped by the polytheists are depicted as being unable to create, they are like us as humans (who, of course, are created by God as we are informed), who are unable to provide help to the polytheists, who are unable to help themselves, who cannot be called upon, and who can neither see, strike, or hear. Thus, the logical reasoning is based on the conclusion that God is far above the partners which the polytheists set up alongside Him. In other words, the conclusion is that God alone is worthy of worship.

Q9:67 is an interesting example of a deductive argument which refers to the specific characteristics of the hypocrites:

> al-munāfiqūna wal-munāfiqātu ba^{c}ḍuhum min ba^{c}ḍin ya'murūna bil-munkari wayanhawna ^{c}an al-ma^{c}rūfi wayaqbiḍūna aidiyahum nasū allāha fanasiyahum inna al-munāfiqīna hum al-fāsiqūn – The hypocrites, both men and women, are all the same: they order what is wrong and forbid what is right; they are tight-fisted. They have ignored God, so He has ignored them. The hypocrites are the disobedient ones.

where the premises are: (al-munāfiqūna wal-munāfiqātu ba^{c}ḍuhum min ba^{c}ḍin/ya'murūna bil-munkari/wayanhawna ^{c}an al-ma^{c}rūfi/wayaqbiḍūna aidiyahum/nasū allāha fanasiyahum/ – The hypocrites, both men and women, are all the same: they order what is wrong and forbid what is right; they are tight-fisted. They have ignored God, so He has ignored them) and their conclusion is: (inna al-munāfiqīna hum al-fāsiqūn – The hypocrites are the disobedient ones).

A common argumentation or reasoning scheme in Qur'anic discourse is also encountered in the argumentation text segments which introduce the sign topic (āyah (singular) or āyāt (plural)), as in the following example:

> It is He (God) who created heavens and earth . . . He created man from a sperm-drop . . . He has created the livestock for you . . . and created the horses, mules and donkeys for you . . . It is He who sends down rain from the sky . . . He causes to grow for you thereby the crops,

> olives, palm trees . . . Indeed in that is a sign for a people who give thought. He has subjected for you the night and day and the sun and moon, and the stars are subjected by His command. Indeed in that are signs for a people who reason. He has subjected whatever He multiplied for you on the earth of varying colours. Indeed in that is a sign for a people who remember. It is He who subjected the sea for you to eat from it tender meat and to extract from it ornaments which you wear . . . He has cast into the earth firmly set mountains . . . And landmarks. And by the stars they are also guided. Then is He (God) who creates like one who does not create?, Q16:3–17.

The deductive argument above has listed 12 signs which are the foundation of the logical reasoning that leads to the conclusion prescribed in Q16:17 (afaman yakhluqu kaman lā yakhluq – Then is He (God) who creates like one who does not create?) and the hearer/reader will also be persuaded to believe in the initial premise (annahu lā ilāha illā anā fattaqūni – There is no deity except Me (God), so fear Me, Q16:2) and the subsequent premise (ilāhukum ilāhun wāḥidun – Your god is one God, Q16:22). Thus, the 12 signs and their characteristics are employed for persuasion and the verification (substantiation) of the text producer's thesis (argument, premise). The 12 signs are:

> the creation of the heavens and earth,
> the creation of mankind,
> the creation of livestock,
> the creation of horses, mules, and donkeys,
> the sending down of water for drink and for growing trees,
> making the night, the day, the sun, the moon and the stars of benefit to mankind,
> making the many coloured things on earth of benefit to mankind,
> making the sea of benefit to mankind,
> making the mountains stand firm on the earth,
> making rivers on the earth,
> making paths on the earth for people to find their way, and
> the creation of stars to guide people through the desert or the sea at night.

We can summarise the above example as:

> (premise) → (signs) → (conclusion).

Similarly, in:

> It is God who made for you the grazing animals upon which you ride, and some of them you eat. And for you therein are other benefits . . . and upon them and upon ships you are carried. He (God) shows you His signs. So which of the signs of God do you deny?, Q40:79–81.

iii The deductive argument includes analogies and comparisons: Let us consider the following examples:

Example 1

huwa alladhī yursilu al-riyāḥa bushran baina yadai raḥmatihi ḥattā idhā aqallat saḥāban thiqālan suqnāhu libaladin maiyitin fa'anzalnā bihi al-mā'a fa'akhrajnā bihi min kulli al-thamarāti kadhālika nukhriju al-mawtā la^{c}allakum tadhakkarūn – It is He (God) who sends the winds as good tidings before His mercy (rainfall) until they have created heavy rainclouds. We drive them to a dead land and We send down rain therein and bring forth thereby some of all the fruits. Thus will We bring forth the dead, perhaps you may be reminded, Q7:57.

where an analogy is made between the rain as the cause of bringing life back to a dead land and the dead person and how he will be brought back to life. Based on this comparison, the text receiver will have the logical inference that resurrection is certain to take place.

Example 2

allāhu alladhī khalaqakum thumma razaqakum thumma yumītukum thumma yuḥyīkum hal min shurakā'ikum man yaf^{c}al dhālikum min shai' subḥānahu wata^{c}ālā ^{c}ammā yushrikūn – God is the one who created you, then provided for you, then will cause you to die, and then will give you life. Are there any of your partners who does anything of that? He is exalted and above what they associate with Him, Q30:40.

The comparison is between God and the partners: God is able to create, provide for people, cause death to them, and resurrect them. However, the partners are depicted through the rhetorical question as unable to do so. Thus, by logical reasoning, one can conclude that God is superior to the partners (deities, idols) and polytheism is wrong.

Example 3

inna alladhīna yulḥidūna fī āyātinā lā yukhfawna ^{c}alainā . . . afaman yulqā fī al-nāri khairun am man ya'tīya āminan yawma al-qiyāmah . . . – Indeed, those who inject deviation into Our āyāt are not concealed from Us . . . So, is he who is cast into fire better or he who comes secure on the day of resurrection? . . ., Q41:40.

where a comparison is made between two choices: Is it better to go to heaven or to be thrown in the hell fire? By deductive reasoning, the answer is to go to heaven. The conclusion is: Those who inject deviation into God's āyāt (revelations or signs) are wrong.

Example 4

khalaqa al-samāwāti bighairi ^{c}amadin tarawnahā wa'alqā fī al-arḍi rawāsiya an tamīda bikum wabaththa fīhā min kulli dābbatin wa'anzalnā min al-samā'i mā'an fa'anbatnā fīhā min kulli zawjin karīm. hādhā khalqu allāhi fa'arūnī mādhā khalaqa alladhīna min dūnihi bal al-ẓālimūna fī ḍalālin mubīn – He created the heavens without pillars that you see and has cast into the earth firmly set mountains, lest it should shift with you, and dispersed therein from every creature. We sent down rain from the sky and made grow therein plants of every noble kind. This is the creation of God. So show Me what those other than Him have created. Rather, the wrongdoers are in clear error, Q31:10–11

where God's omnipotence is introduced first to set the scene for the reader/listener about God's ability. This is followed by the comparison between God who is depicted as the able and the creator and (alladhīna min dūnihi – those other than Him, which literally means 'those below Him') who are implicitly introduced as 'have not been able to create anything'. Thus, by deductive reasoning, one concludes that God is the creator.

Example 5

wanazzalnā min al-samā'i mā'an mubārakan fa'anbatnā bihi jannātin waḥabba al-ḥaṣīd. wal-nakhla bāsiqātin lahā ṭalᶜum naḍīd. rizqan lil-ᶜibād wa'aḥyainā bihi baldatan maitan kadhālika al-khurūj – We (God) have sent down blessed rain from the sky and made grow thereby gardens and grain from the harvest. And lofty palm trees having fruit arranged in layers – as provision for the servants, and We have given life thereby to a dead land. Thus, is the resurrection, Q50:9–11.

where the lexeme (kadhālika) means (likewise, thus, in a similar fashion), which is a linguistic indicator employed to introduce the conclusion and the text segment upon which the logical conclusion is hinged.

iv The deductive argument cites parallel examples: This is illustrated through the following examples:

Example 1

inna fī khalqi al-samāwāti wal-arḍi wakhtilāfi al-laili wal-nahāri wal-fulki allatī tajrī fī al-baḥri bimā yanfaḍu al-nāsa wamā anzalā allāhu min al-samā'i min mā'in fa'aḥyā bihi al-arḍa baᶜda mawtihā wabaththa fīhā min kulli dābbatin wataṣrīf al-riyāḥi wal-saḥābi al-musakhkhari baina al-samā'i wal-arḍi la'āyātin liqawmin yaᶜqilūn – Indeed, in the creation of the heavens and the earth, and the alteration of the night and the day, and the great ships which sail through the sea with that which benefits people, and what God has sent down the heavens of rain, giving life thereby to the earth after its lifelessness and dispersing therein every kind of moving creatures, and His directing of the winds and the clouds controlled between the heavens and earth are signs for a people who use reason, Q2:164

where many God's omnipotence examples are listed which are employed to substantiate the previous statements: (ilāhukum ilāhun wāḥidun lā ilāha illā huwa al-raḥmānu al-raḥīmu – Your god is one God. There is no deity worthy of worship except Him, the entirely merciful, the especially merciful,

Q2:163). These examples are: (khalqi al-samāwāti wal-arḍi – the creation of the heavens and the earth), (wakhtilāfi al-laili wal-nahāri – the alteration of the night and the day), (wal-fulki allatī tajrī fī al-baḥri bimā yanfa^{c}u al-nāsa – the great ships which sail through the sea with that which benefits people), (wamā anzalā allāhu min al-samā'i min mā'in fa'aḥyā bihi al-arḍa ba^{c}da mawtihā wabaththa fīhā min kulli dābbatin – what God has sent down the heavens of rain, giving life thereby to the earth after its lifelessness and dispersing therein every kind of moving creatures), (wataṣrīf al-riyāḥi – the directing of the winds), and (wal-saḥābi al-musakhkhari baina al-samā'i wal-arḍi – the clouds controlled between the heavens and earth).

Example 2

fa'ajā'aha al-makhaḍu ilā jidh^{c} al-nakhlati . . . wahuzzī ilaiki bijidh^{c}i al-nakhlati tusāqiṭ ^{c}alaiki ruṭaban janiyyā – When the pains of childbirth drove her to cling to the trunk of a date palm . . . If you shake the trunk of the palm tree towards you, it will deliver fresh ripe dates for you, Q19:23, 25.

where we have Mary's story and its parallel example of the trunk of a date palm tree. In other words, Mary is having a baby and the dry, lifeless trunk of a date palm tree is giving fresh ripe dates. We can make the following observations to set the scene for our deductive reasoning:

1 We need to consider the relevance of the word (jidh^{c} – trunk) to the story of the fresh ripe dates.
2 The two statements could have ignored (jidh^{c}) and employed only the word (al-nakhlati – a date palm).
3 The word (jidh^{c}) semantically entails it had no leaves (sa^{c}fu al-nakhlati) and no head (ra'su al-nakhlati); it was just a lifeless trunk of a palm tree with no fresh dates on.
4 The place was barren, and there were no surrounding date palm trees.
5 Because there were no trees near the dead palm tree, we can conclude that there was no male date palm tree.
6 Because there was no male palm tree nearby, the trunk could not have been fertilized. Therefore, it could not have been able to produce fresh dates.

Therefore, through deductive reasoning, we can make three inferences:

i Mary had no physical contact with a male partner (a man). Yet she got pregnant and gave birth to a baby boy, Jesus.
ii The dry date palm trunk was the only tree in that place and there was no male date palm tree nearby to get the female dead palm tree fertilized and be able to produce fresh dates.
iii The trunk's situation is identical to Mary's. Both have had no contact with a male partner, but both have managed to produce.
iv It was God who caused Mary to give birth to a baby boy, and it was God who caused the date palm trunk to produce fresh dates.

v By deductive reasoning, the two stories entail God's omnipotence.

vi The two stories point to Q19:35 (mā kāna lillāhi an yattakhidha min waladin subḥānahu idhā qaḍā amran fa'innamā yaqūlu lahu kun fayakūn – It would not befit God to have a child. He is far above that: when He decrees something, He says only: 'Be' and it is). In other words, we can infer the notion of monotheism from the two stories.

Example 3

fanẓur ilā athāri raḥmat allāh kaifa yuḥyī al-arḍa baᶜda mawtihā inna dhālika lamuḥyī al-mawtā wahuwa ᶜalā kulli shai'in qadīr – So observe the effects of the mercy of God – how He gives life to the earth after its lifelessness. Indeed, that same one will give life to the dead, and He is competent over all things, Q30:50.

where (yuḥyī al-arḍa baᶜda mawtihā – He gives life to the earth after its lifelessness) is an analogy used to substantiate (lamuḥyī al-mawtā – that same one will give life to the dead), i.e., eschatology (resurrection). In similar vein, the following are examples of a deductive argument which cites parallel examples:

> huwa alladhī yursilu al-riyāḥa bushran baina yadai raḥmatih ḥattā idhā aqallat saḥāban thiqālan suqnāhu libaladin maiyitin fa'anzalnā bihi al-mā'a fa'akhrajnā bihi min kulli al-thamarāti kadhālika nukhriju al-mawtā laᶜallakum tadhakkarūn – It is He who sends the winds as good tidings before rainfall until when they have carried heavy rainclouds, We drive them to a dead land and We send down rain therein and bring forth thereby some of all the fruits. Thus, We will bring forth the dead, perhapse you may be reminded, Q7:57.

> allāhu alladhī arsalā al-riyāḥa fatuthīru saḥāban fasuqnāhu ilā baladin maiyitin fa'aḥyainā bihi al-arḍa baᶜda mawtihā kadhālika al-nushūr – It is God who sends the winds, and they stir the clouds, and We drive them to a dead land and give life thereby to the earth after its lifelessness. Thus is the resurrection, Q35:9.

> wamin āyātihi annaka tarā al-arḍa khāshiᶜatan fa'idhā anzalnā ᶜalaihā al-mā'a ihtazzat warabat. inna alladhī aḥyāhā lamuḥyī al-mawtā innahu ᶜalā kulli shai'in qadīr – Of His signs is that you see the earth stilled, but when We send down upon it rain, it quivers and grows. Indeed, He who has given it life is the giver of life to the dead. Indeed, He is competent over all things, Q41:39.

v The deductive argument provides cause and consequence: This is explained in the following examples:

Example 1

inna alladhīna lā yarjūna liqā'anā waraḍū bilḥayāti al-dunyā waṭma'annū bihā walladhīna hum ᶜan āyātinā ghāfilūn ulā'ika ma'wāhum al-nāru bimā kānū yaksibūn – Indeed, those who do not expect the meeting with Us and are satisfied with the life of this world and feel secure therein and those who are heedless of Our signs – For those their refuge will be the fire because of what they used to earn, Q10:7–8

Cause: inna alladhīna lā yarjūna liqā'anā waraḍū bilḥayāti al-dunyā waṭma'annū bihā walladhīna hum ᶜan āyātinā ghāfilūn – Indeed, those who do not expect the meeting with Us and are satisfied with the life of this world and feel secure therein and those who are heedless of Our signs.

Effect: ma'wāhum al-nāru bimā kānū yaksibūn – their refuge will be the fire because of what they used to earn.

Example 2

watarā al-arḍa hāmidatan fa'idhā anzalnā ᶜalaihā al-mā'a ihtazzat warabat wa'anbatat min kulli zawjin bahīj – You see the earth barren, but when We send down upon it rain, it quivers and swells and grows something of every beautiful kind, Q22:5.

Cause: al-mā' – rain.

Effect: ihtazzat warabat wa'anbatat min kulli zawjin bahīj – It (the barren earth) quivers and swells and grows something of every beautiful kind.

Example 3

Through cause and effect premises, the subsequent premises in Q22:6–7 are substantiated through deductive reasoning:

> dhālika bi'anna allāha huwa al-ḥaqqu wa'annahu yuḥyi al-mawtā wa'annahu ᶜalā kulli shai'in qadīṛ. wa'anna al-sāᶜata ātiyatun lā raiba fīhā wa'anna allāha yabᶜathu man fī al-qubūr – That is because God is the truth and because He gives life to the dead and because He is competent over all things. And that they may know that the hour is coming – no doubt about it – and that God will resurrect those in the grave, Q22:6–7 where eschatology is substantiated.

Example 4

wakam ahlaknā min qaryatin baṭirat maᶜīshatahā fatilka masākinuhum lam tuskan min baᶜdihim illā qalīlā wakunnā naḥnu al-wārithīn. wamā kāna rabbuka muhlika al-qurā ḥattā yabᶜatha fī ummihā rasūlan yatlū ᶜalaihim āyātinā wamā kunnā muhlikī al-qurā illā wa'ahluhā ẓālimūn – We have destroyed many a community that once reveled in its wanton wealth and easy living. Since then their dwelling places have barely been inhabited. We are the only heir. Your Lord would never destroy towns without first raising a messenger in their midst to recite Our messages to them, nor would We destroy towns unless their inhabitants were evildoers, Q28:59.

where the premises are: (wakam ahlaknā min qaryatin baṭirat maᶜīshatahā fatilka masākinuhum lam tuskan min baᶜdihim illā qalīlā wakunnā naḥnu al-wārithīn. wamā kāna rabbuka muhlika al-qurā ḥattā yabᶜatha fī ummihā rasūlan yatlū ᶜalaihim āyātinā – We have destroyed many a community that once reveled in its wanton wealth and easy living. Since then, their dwelling places have barely been inhabited. We are the only heir. Your Lord would never destroy towns without first raising a messenger in their midst to recite Our messages to them). The conclusion to these premises is: (wamā kunnā muhlikī al-qurā illā wa'ahluhā ẓālimūn – We would never destroy towns unless their inhabitants were evildoers). Thus, based on the premises, we can establish the following cause and consequence of the above deductive argument:

Cause: (1) baṭirat maᶜīshatahā – to revel or be insolent in one's way of living, and (2) al-ẓulm – wrongdoing.

Effect: al-halāk – destruction.

vi The deductive argument provides testimony, authority, and expert opinions: This is explained by the following examples:

Example 1

qālū yā mūsā . . . – The magicians said: 'O Moses, either you throw your staff first or we will'. He said: 'You throw', and they did, casting a spell on people's eyes, striking fear into them, and bringing about sorcery. Then, We inspired Moses: 'Throw your staff', and it devoured their fakery. The truth was confirmed and what they had produced came to nothing; they were defeated and utterly humiliated. The sorcerers fell to their knees and said: 'We believe in the Lord of the worlds, the Lord of Moses and Aaron'. However, Pharaoh said: 'How dare you believe in Him (God) before I have given you permission? This is a plot you have hatched to drive the people out of the city! Soon you will see, I will cut off your alternate hands and feet and then crucify you all'. The magicians said: 'So, we shall return to our Lord. Your only grievance against us is that we believed in the signs of our Lord when they came to us. Our Lord, pour steadfastness upon us and let us die in devotion to You', Q7:115–126.

where the magicians' statements (Q7:121–122) represent testimony, authority, and expert opinion. Similarly, statements 123–124 represent Pharaoh's standpoint towards the magicians. This is followed by the magicians' testimony (Q7:125–126). The same applies to Q26:47–48 (The sorcerers declared: 'We believe in the Lord of the worlds, the Lord of Moses and Aaron'). More statements are provided by the sorcerers and Pharaoh in Q20:70–76 (. . . Pharaoh said: 'This must be your master, the man who taught you witchcraft . . . You will know for certain which of us has the fiercer and more lasting punishment'. The sorcerers said: 'We shall never prefer you to the clear signs that has come to us, nor to Him who created us. So decide whatever you will. You can only decide matters of this present life. We believe in our Lord, hoping He may forgive us our sins and the sorcery that you forced us to practice. God is better and more lasting').

Example 2

fa'alqā al-saḥaratu sājidīn. qālū āmannā birabbi al-ᶜālamīn. rabbi mūsā wahārūn – The sorcerers fell to their knees and said: 'We believe in the Lord of the worlds, the Lord of Moses and Aaron', Q26:46–48

where (al-saḥaratu – the magicians) represent testimony, authority and expert opinion because of their high social status as we are told by Q7:113–114 (wajā'a al-saḥaratu firᶜawna qālū a'inna lanā la'ajran in kunnā naḥnu al-ghālibīn. qāla naᶜam wa'innakum lamina al-muqarrabīn – The magicians came to Pharaoh. They said: 'Indeed for us is a reward if we are the predominant?' He (Pharaoh) said: 'Yes, and moreover you will be among those made near to me'). Thus, the magicians are depicted with the social status of the elite (innakum lamina al-muqarrabīn – You (magicians) will be among those made near to me (Pharaoh), i.e., you will join my inner court). For this reason, they appeal to their credible personality (ethos), and their statements acquire authority because of their expertise in magic and due to their charismatic character as dignitaries. Their premises are Q20:70–73: (āmannā birabbi hārūna wamūsā – We have believed in the Lord of Aaron and Moses), (lan nu'thiraka ᶜalā mā jā'anā min al-baiyināti walladhī faṭaranā – Never will we prefer you over what has come to us of clear proofs and over He who created us), (faqḍi mā anta qāḍin innamā taqḍi hādhihi al-ḥayāta al-dunyā – So decree whatever you are to decree. You can only decree for this worldly life), (innā āmannā birabbinā liyaghfira lanā khaṭāyāna wamā akrahtanā ᶜalaihi min al-siḥri – Indeed, we have believed in our Lord that He may forgive us our sins and what you compelled us to do of magic), and their conclusion is Q20:73: (allāhu khairun wa'abqā – God is better and more enduring).

Example 3

qāla mūsā liqawmihi istaᶜīnū billāhi waṣbirū inna al-arḍa lillāhi yūrithuhā man yashā'u min ᶜibādihi wal-ᶜāqibatu lil-muttaqīn – Moses said to his people: 'Turn to God for help and be steadfast; the earth belongs to God. He gives it as their own to whichever of His servants He chooses and the happy future belongs to those who are mindful of Him', Q7:128.

Moses enjoys a charismatic and upright character. Thus, his premises (statements) are based on ethos. Ethos refers to the ethical appeal of the speaker/writer, who is expected by the listener/reader to be a credible charming character with expertise and sound knowledge and, most importantly, worthwhile to listen to. The conclusion of Moses' argument is: (al-ᶜāqibatu lil-muttaqīn – the happy future belongs to those who are mindful of Him (God)).

3.4 The pivotal statement in argumentation

In Qur'anic discourse, the premise, as the text producer's assertion and performative intent, and the conclusion, which the text receiver will not readily accept, are more often than not presented through the nominal sentence. It is also interesting to note that the nominal sentence for an argumentation purpose are embedded with active participle lexemes (ism al-fāᶜil) as further linguistic defences for consolidating the premise and for making the audience accept the conclusion without qualms, i.e., accepting the conclusion as true. 'The active participle is the centerpiece which features heavily in the no-main-verb nominal sentences' (Abdul-Raof 2018:167). The nominal-sentence–based premise leads the reader/listener to the conclusion. Thus, the premise should enjoy a solid illocutionary force to make the audience accept willingly the conclusion. The major features of the illocutionary force of the nominal sentence are [+ Continuity] and [+ Permanency]. As mentioned, the nominal sentence is fortified with active participle lexemes as added value linguistic defences to make either the premise or the conclusion acceptable.

It is worthwhile to note that the illocutionary force of the nominal sentence and the active participle are employed for two reasons:

i the substantiation of the text producer's (own) thesis, and
ii the rebuttal of opponent's thesis.

We need to distinguish between two important matters:

1 The nominal sentence is of two types: (a) no-main-verb nominal sentence and (b) noun-initial with a main verb sentence, and
2 The active participle as the pivotal sentence constituent employed as a defence added value.

One may wonder, however, why the verb-initial sentence structure is avoided. This is due to the pragmatic fact that the nominal sentence has a powerful illocutionary force which the verb-initial sentence lacks. Thus, the latter sentence structure is avoided, as in the following examples:

> allāhu laṭīfun biᶜibādih – God is gentle with His servants, Q42:19.

To change the above nominal sentence to a main-verb sentence (allāhu yalṭufu biᶜibādih), the illocutionary force will disappear, and the performative intent of the text producer will not be delivered. In other words, the verbal sentence entails the meaning: (God's gentleness to people is not permanent, not continuous, and is renewed every now and then).

Let us consider the following example:

> anā al-tawwābu al-raḥīmu – I am the accepting of repentance, the merciful, Q2:160.

where we have a combination of a no-main-verb nominal sentence plus the active participles (al-tawwābu – the accepting of repentance) and (al-raḥīmu – the merciful) substantiation linguistic techniques which endorse the truth value of what has been said in Q2:160, which is initiated by the exception particle (illā – except, unless).

However, Q2:159 sets the scene for Q2:160: (As for those who hide the proofs and guidance We send down, after We have made them clear to people in the Scripture, God rejects them, and so do others, unless they repent, make amends, and declare the truth. I will certainly accept their repentance: I am the accepting of repentance, the most merciful).

Similarly, in:

> ilāhukum ilāhun wāḥid lā ilāha illā huwa al-raḥmān al-raḥīm – Your god is one God. There is no deity except Him, the entirely merciful, the especially merciful, Q2:163.

where we have two no-main-verb nominal sentences: (ilāhukum ilāhun wāḥid – Your god is one God) and (lā ilāha illā huwa al-raḥman al-raḥīm – There is no deity except Him, the entirely merciful, the especially merciful) with the second having two active participles. The two no-main-verb nominal sentences reflect the text producer's performative intent of monotheism and are employed as substantiation linguistic techniques to validate monotheism and rebut polytheism.

Having made reference to polytheism: (the polytheists have attributed to God partners – the jinn – while He has created them. They have fabricated for God sons and daughters, Q6:100), the text producer introduces a rebuttal through the substantiation linguistic techniques of the no-main-verb nominal sentences:

> badīᶜu al-samāwāti wal-arḍ/annā yakūnu lahu waladun walam takun lahu ṣāḥibatun/huwa bikulli shai'in ᶜalīm – God is the originator of the heavens and the earth/How could He have a son when He does not have a wife/He is knowing of all things, Q6:101.

In Q33:72, we are informed that God has offered the heavens, the earth, and the mountains to accept the obligations and obedience to Him. However, they have declined to bear this responsibility. Yet man has undertaken to bear it. To demonstrate how unjust and ignorant man is, the text producer needs to present the conclusion to the earlier premise through a no-main-verb nominal sentence:

> innahu kāna ẓalūman jahūlā – Indeed, man was unjust and ignorant, Q33:72.

Thus, substantiation has been made to the premise through the substantiation linguistic techniques of the no-main-verb nominal sentence in addition to the active participles (ẓalūman – unjust) and (jahūlā – ignorant).

An interesting text linguistic observation about argumentation and the substantiation linguistic techniques through the no-main-verb nominal sentence is encountered in Q26:8–9, 67–68, 103–104, 121–122, 139–140, 158–159, 174–175, and 190–191:

> inna fī dhālika la'āyatan/mā kāna aktharuhum mu'minīn/inna rabbaka lahuwa al-ᶜazīzu al-raḥīmu – Indeed, in that is a sign/But most of them were not to be believers / Indeed, your Lord is the exalted in might, the merciful.

The substantiation linguistic technique of the no-main-verb nominal sentence is also encountered to substantiate the notion of prophethood, as in:

> mā kāna muḥammadun abā aḥadin min rijālikum walākin rasūl allāh wakhātam al-nabiyyīn wakāna allāhu bikulli shai'in ᶜalīmā – Muḥammad is not the father of anyone of your men, but he is the messenger of God and the last of the Prophets. God knows everything, Q33:40.

similarly, in:

> inna hādhā lahuwa al-qaṣaṣu al-ḥaqq/mā min ilāhin illā allāh/inna allāha lahuwa al-cazīzu al-ḥakīmu – Indeed, this is the true narration. And there is no deity except God. And indeed, God is the exalted in might, the wise, Q3:62.

where the notions of prophethood and monotheism are highlighted through the no-main-verb-nominal sentence.

As a prerequisite for a successful conclusion that will not be questioned by the audience, there should be more than one premise, as in the following example:

> inna rabbukum allāhu alladhī khalaqa al-samāwāti wal-arḍa fī sittāti aiyāmin thumma istawā ᶜalā al-ᶜarsh yughshī al-laila al-nahāra yaṭlubuhu ḥathīthan wal-shamsa wal-qamara wal-nujūma musakhkharātun bi'amrih alā lahu al-khalqu wal-amru tabāraka allāhu rabbu al-ᶜālamīn – Indeed, your Lord is God who created the heavens and earth in six days and then established Himself above the throne. He covers the night with the day, chasing it rapidly; and He created the sun, the moon, and the stars, subjected by His command. Unquestionably, His is the creation and the command. Blessed is God, Lord of the worlds, Q7:54.

where we have more than one premise (inna rabbukum allāhu – Indeed, your Lord is God), (alladhī khalaqa al-samāwāti wal-arḍa fī sittāti aiyāmin thumma istawā ᶜalā al-carsh – who created the heavens and earth in six days and then established Himself above the throne), (yughshī al-laila al-nahāra yaṭlubuhu ḥathīthan – He covers the night with the day, chasing it rapidly), (wal-shamsa wal-qamara wal-nujūma musakhkharātun bi'amrih – He created the sun, the moon, and the stars, subjected by His command). These premises are vital for the audience whose cognitive status is a denier. It is also worthwhile to note that the initial premise is a no-main-verb nominal sentence (inna rabbukum allāhu – Indeed, your Lord is God) plus the fact that it has employed the affirmation device (inna) to consolidate the effectiveness of the premise and its performative intent that God is indeed your Lord and that He is the creator of the heavens and earth. The conclusion is represented by two statements. The first is a no-main-verb nominal sentence: (alā lahu al-khalqu wal-amru – Unquestionably, His is the creation and the command) and the second is a verbal sentence (tabāraka allāhu rabbu al-ᶜālamīn – Blessed is God, Lord of the worlds) whose verb has the illocutionary force of [+ Abundance of God's Blessings] (kathrat khairāt allāh), [+ God's Glorification] (al-taqdīs) and [+ Deanthropomorphism] (al-tanzīh). Thus, although the second conclusion statement is verbal, it has used a verbal lexeme that in fact theologically supports the premise.

Let us consider Q9:67 which is a deductive argument that refers to the characteristics of the hypocrites:

> al-munāfiqūna wal-munāfiqātu baᶜḍuhum min baᶜḍin ya'murūna bil-munkari wayanhawna ᶜan al-maᶜrūfi wayaqbiḍūna aidiyahum nasū allāha fanasiyahum inna al-munāfiqīna hum al-fāsiqūn – The hypocrites, both men and women, are all the same: they order what is wrong and forbid what is right; they are tight-fisted. They have ignored God, so He has ignored them. The hypocrites are the disobedient ones.

where the initial premise is presented through the nominal sentence: (al-munāfiqūna wal-munāfiqātu baᶜḍuhum min baᶜḍin – The hypocrites, both men and women, are all the same) and the conclusion is also presented through the nominal sentence with the employment of the active participle: (inna al-munāfiqīna hum al-fāsiqūn – The hypocrites are the disobedient ones) with the employment of the affirmation tool (inna – indeed) and the active participle (al-fāsiqūn – the disobedient ones).

In Q28:58–59, we are given the premises on the communities that have been destroyed because they have been insolent in their way of life and because of their evildoing. The conclusion to these premises is: (wamā kunnā muhlikī al-qurā illā wa'ahluhā ẓālimūn – We would never destroy towns unless their inhabitants were evildoers). What we can observe is the fact that the conclusion is decorated by: (i) the nominal sentence structure, and (ii) the employment of the active participles (muhlik – destroyer) and (ẓalim – evildoer, unjust) to validate the conclusion and rebut the opponent's argument.

The substantiation linguistic technique of the no-main-verb nominal sentence is also encountered to describe the notion of reward and punishment, as in:

> inna jahannama kānat mirṣādā. lilṭāghīna ma'ābā. lābithīna fīhā aḥqābā . . . inna lil-muttaqīna mafāzā. ḥadā'iqa wa'aᶜnābā. wakawāᶜiba atrābā. waka'san dihāqā – Indeed, hell has been lying in wait. For the transgressors, a place of return, in which they will remain for ages unending . . . Indeed, for the righteous is attainment, gardens and grapevines, and full-breasted companions of equal age and a full cup, Q78:21–23, 31–34.

3.5 Mood in Qur'anic argument

An argument is made of statements (premises), and each statement may employ a verb; thus, we get a verbal sentence. However, some statements do not employ a verb; thus, we get a no-main-verb sentence (a nominal sentence without a main verb).

Moods are important constituents in an argument because the mood expresses the text producer's (speaker/writer) performative intent and how the thought of the statement is expressed. We encounter three different moods in Qur'anic discourse: indicative, imperative, and subjunctive.

1 Indicative mood: In Qur'anic argument, the indicative mood has the illocutionary force of either stating a fact or denying a fact. The indicative mood in Qur'anic discourse is not always expressed by a verb. The indicative mood can be expressed by a present tense main verb: (yamḥaqu allāhu al-ribā wa yurbī al-ṣadaqāt – God destroys interest and gives increase for charities, Q2:276), a past tense auxiliary verb (kāna – was): (kāna allāhu samīᶜan ᶜalīmā – God is ever hearing and knowing, Q4:148), by a no-main-verb nominal sentence: (allāhu lā ilāha illā huwa al-ḥaiyu al-qaiyūm – God – there is no deity except Him, the ever-living, the sustainer of all existence, Q2:255), or by a statement with an active participle (ghāfir al-dhanb wa qābil al-tawb – (God is) the forgiver of sin, the acceptor of repentance, Q40:3). In terms of Arabic rhetoric, this represents reporting statements.

2 Imperative mood: This is a command mood which gives a command or advises the audience (listener/reader) to do something. In terms of Arabic rhetoric, this represents informing statements, as in:

> khudh al-ᶜafwa wa'mur bil-ᶜurfi waᶜriḍ ᶜan al-jāhilīn – Take what is given freely, enjoin what is good, and turn away from the ignorant, Q7:199.

where the imperative mood is represented by the verbs (khudh – take), (a'mur – enjoin), and (aᶜriḍ – turn away).

> aqim wajhaka lildīni ḥanīfan fiṭrata allāhi allatī faṭara al-nāsa ᶜalaihā la tabdīla likhalqi allāhi dhālika al-dīnu al-qaiyimu walākinna akthara al-nāsi ḷā yaᶜlamūn – So direct yourself toward the religion, inclining to truth. Adhere to the fiṭrah of God upon which He has created all people. No change should there be in the creation of God, Q30:30.

where we have an argument with an imperative mood through the imperative verb (aqim – direct).

> āti dhā al-qurbā ḥaqqahu wal-miskīna wabna al-sabīl dhālika khairun lilladhīna yurīdūna wajha allāhi wa'ulā'ika hum al-mufliḥūn – So give the relative his right, as well as the needy and the traveller. That is best for those who desire the countenance of God, and it is they who will be the successful, Q30:38

where the imperative mood is represented by the imperative verb (āti – give).

An interesting example of a series of the imperative mood is encountered in Q31:13–19.

3 Subjunctive mood: The subjunctive mood is represented by the word (yālaita – I wish). This mood represents hypothetical or contrary to fact things which might be a wish, a desire, a doubt, or an imaginary situation. In terms of Arabic rhetoric, this represents informing satements, as in:

> yā laitanī mittu qabla hādhā wakuntu nasyan mansiyyā – Oh, I wish I had died before this and was in oblivion, forgotten, Q19:23
>
> yā laita lanā mithla mā ūtiya qārūn innahu ladhū ḥaẓẓin ʿaẓīm – Oh, would that we had like what was given to Qārūn. Indeed, he is one of great fortune, Q28:79
>
> yā laita qawmī yaʿlamūn – I wish my people could know, Q36:26
>
> yālaitani kuntu turābā – I wish that I were dust, Q78:40
>
> yālaitahā kānat al-qadiyah – I wish my death had been the decisive one, Q69:27

3.6 Topos in Qur'anic argument

In order to argue effectively and convince the opponent, the speaker needs to introduce a commonplace statement the opponent accepts with no hesitation. Topos (plural (topoi)) is a Greek term which literally translates into English as 'places' but is more commonly known as 'topics'. This inaccurate translation developed because, in ancient times, rhetorical students would read these topics off of papyrus rolls. The students would have to search on these rolls for specific topoi, which would be in specific places (Aristotle 1924:1356b). The location of the topoi became the definition of the term. Over time, however, the more appropriate translation of 'topics' has emerged in its place (Crowley and Hawhee 2008:117). A topos is required in defending or arguing against a thesis. It is used to clarify or substantiate an argument. The topos provides related ideas and supportive data for the argument. If an argument has a missing or a weak topos to support it, it can be rebutted and invalidated easily by the opponent's effective argument which enjoys a logical topos and credibility. The topos is a general argumentative form or pattern, and the concrete arguments are instantiations of the general topos.

Generally speaking, an Aristotelian topos ('place', 'location') is an argumentative (reasoning) scheme that enables a dialectician or rhetorician to construe an argument for a given conclusion. But while in earlier rhetoric a topos was understood as a complete pattern or formula that can be mentioned at a certain stage of the speech to produce a certain effect, most of the Aristotelian topoi are general instructions saying that a conclusion of a certain form can be derived from premises of a certain form (Allen 2007).

A common topos is a topos which is universally applicable to any rhetorical situation. They are also known as commonplaces, such as (kulli nafsin dhā'iqatu al-mawti – Every soul will taste death, Q3:185), (inna allāha lā yuṣliḥu ʿamal al-mufsidīn – Indeed, God does not amend the work of corruptors, Q10:81), (kulli ḥizbin bimā ladaihim fariḥūn – Every faction rejoices in what it has, Q30:32), (wamā tadrī nafsun mādhā taksibu ghadan – No soul perceives what it will earn tomorrow, Q31:34), (wamā tadrī nafsun bi'aiyi arḍin tamūt – No soul perceives in what land it will die, Q31:34), and (in taᶜuddū niᶜmat allāhi lā tuḥṣūhā – If you should count the favours of God, you could not enumerate them, Q16:18).

These commonplaces are statements which no one can refute – not even the antagonist, someone on the opposing side of an issue. A commonplace, or a common ground in this context, refers to any related ideas shared by the opponents on an issue. Another ancient account of argumentation (reasoning) schemes is that given in the Rhetoric to Alexander (about 340 BC), believed to be authored by Anaximenes of Lampsacus (Braet 1996). This contains a list of proofs (pisteis) and other types of argumentation which may be seen as the oldest surviving typology of argumentation schemes (avant la lettre). We can claim that the oldest typology is identical to recent classifications. Modern scholars, like Walton et al. (2008), have also classified argumentation schemes but have provided a shorter list than that provided by Aristotle.

Aristotle has listed 28 commonplaces, some of which are applicable to Qur'anic argumentation, such as:

i Opposites: This is concerned with antonyms (opposite meaning of words), as in:

> wamā yastawī al-aᶜmā wal-baṣīr. walā al-ẓulumātu walā al-nūr. walā al-ẓillu walā al-ḥarūr. wamā yastawī al-aḥyā'u walā al-amwātu – Not equal are the blind and the seeing, Nor are the darknesses and the light, Nor are the shade and the heat, and not equal are the living and the dead. Indeed, God causes to hear whom He wills, but you cannot make hear those in the graves, Q35;19–22
>
> tu'tī al-mulka man tashā' watanziᶜu al-mulka mimman tashā' watuᶜizzu man tashā' watudhillu man tashā' – You give sovereignty to whom You will and You take sovereignty away from whom You will. You honour whom You will and You humble whom You will, Q3:26

ii Incentives and deterrents: This is represented by the antithesis statements that refer to the notion of reward and punishment, as in:

> wasīqa alladhīna kafarū ilā jahannama zumarā . . . wasīqa alladhīna ittaqaw rabbahum ilā al-jannāti zumarā – Those who disbelieved will be driven to hell in groups . . . Those who feared their Lord will be driven to paradise in groups, Q39:71–73
>
> fawailun yama'idhin lil-mukadhdhibīn . . . yawma yudaᶜᶜūna ilā nāri jahannama daᶜᶜā. hādhihi al-nāru allatī kuntum bihā tukadhdhibūn . . . inna al-muttaqīna fī jannātin wanaᶜīm . . . – Then woe, that day, to the deniers, who are amusing themselves in empty discourse. The day they are thrust toward the fire of hell with a violent thrust, its angels will say: 'This is the

fire which you used to deny . . . Indeed, the righteous will be in gardens and pleasure, enjoying what their Lord has given them, and their Lord protected them from the punishment of hellfire', Q52:11–18

iii Definition: This is concerned with highlighting the characteristics or features of someone, as in:

huwa allāhu alladhī lā ilāha illāhū ᶜālimu al-ghaibi wal-shahādati huwa al-raḥmānu al-raḥīmu huwa allāhu alladhī lā ilāha illā huwa al-maliku al-quddūsu al-salāmu al-mu'minu al-muhaiminu al-ᶜazīzu al-jabbāru al-mutakabbiru . . . huwa allāhu al-khāḷiqu al-bāri'u al-muṣawwiru lahu al-asmā'u al-ḥusnā yusabbiḥu lahu mā fī al-samāwāti wal-arḍi wahuwa al-ᶜzizu al-ḥakīmu – He is God, other than whom there is no deity, knower of the unseen and the witnessed. He is the entirely merciful, the especially merciful. He is God, other than whom there is no deity, the Sovereign, the pure, the perfection, the bestower of faith, the overseer, the exalted in might, the compeller, the superior, . . . He is God, the creator, the inventor, the fashioner; to Him belong the best names. Whatever is in the heavens and earth is exalting Him. He is the exalted in might, the wise, Q59:22–24

iv Meeting slander: This is represented by slander statements, as in:

qālat rabbi annā yakūnu lī waladun walam yamsasnī basharun – She said: 'My Lord, how will I have a child when no man has touched me?', Q3:47

badī ᶜu al-samāwati wal-arḍi annā yakūnu lahu waladun walam takun lahu ṣāḥibatun wakhalaqa kulla shai'in wahuwa bikulli shai'in ᶜalīm – He (God) is the originator of the heavens and the earth. How could He have a son when He does not have a wife and He created all things? He is knowing of all things, Q6:101

qāla inna rasūlakum alladhī ursila ilaikum lamajnūn – (Pharaoh) said: 'Indeed, your messenger (Moses) who has been sent to you is mad', Q26:27

yaqūlūna a'innā latārikū ālihatinā lishāᶜirin majnūn – They say: 'Are we to leave our gods for a mad poet (Muḥammad)?', Q37:36

v Ambiguous terms: This is concerned with words whose meaning is unclear, as in: (fāṭir – creator, Q6:14) and (abban – grass, Q80:31).

kharaqū lahu banīna wabanātin bighairi ᶜilmin – They have fabricated for Him (God) sons and daughters without knowledge, Q6:100

where the verb (kharaqa – to create) is a rarely used word (gharīb) whose alternative word that is recurrently employed is (khalaqa – to create).

vi Cause to effect (result): This is concerned with statements that have the cause and the effect, as in:

tarā al-arḍa hāmidatan fa'idhā anzalnā ᶜalaihā al-mā'a ihtazzat warabat wa'anbatat min kulli zawjin bahīj – You see the earth barren, but when We

> send down upon it rain, it quivers and swells and grows of every beautiful kind, Q22:5

Cause: (al-mā'a – rain).

Effect: (ihtazzat warabat – quivers and swells) and (wa'anbatat min kulli zawjin bahīj – grows of every beautiful kind).

> wanazzalnā min al-samā'i mā'an mubārakan fa'anbatnā bihi jannātin waḥabba al-ḥaṣīd . . . wa'aḥyainā bihi baldatan maitan – We have sent down blessed rain from the sky and made grow thereby gardens and grain from the harvest, and We have given life thereby to a dead land, Q50:9–10

Cause: (mā'an – rain).

Effect: (jannātin waḥabba al-ḥaṣīd – gardens and grain from the harvest) and (aḥyainā bihi baldatan maitan – We have given life thereby to a dead land).

vii Sign: This is represented by the Qur'anic expression (āyah (singular) or āyāt (plural)). Let us consider the Qur'anic signs below:

> It is He who sends down rain from the sky . . . He causes to grow for you thereby the crops, olives, palm trees . . . Indeed in that is a sign for a people who give thought. He has subjected for you the night and day and the sun and moon, and the stars are subjected by His command. Indeed in that are signs for a people who reason. He has subjected whatever He multiplied for you on the earth of varying colours. Indeed in that is a sign for a people who remember, Q16:10–13

> wamin āyātihi annaka tarā al-arḍa khāshiᶜatan fa'idhā anzalnā ᶜalaihā al-mā'a ihtazzat warabat inna alladhī aḥyāhā lamuḥyī al-mawtā innahu ᶜalā kulli shai'in qadīr – Of His signs is that you see the earth stilled, but when We send down upon it rain, it quivers and grows. Indeed, He who has given it life is the giver of Life to the dead. Indeed, He is competent over all things, Q41:39

3.7 The skilful initiation of locution

This is concerned with the skilful techniques of initiating (opening, launching) any type of discourse. We can claim that the skilful initiation of locution is concerned with argumentation. First, we need to distinguish between locution, illocution, and perlocution (Ogiermann 2009:7):

i Locution refers to 'what is said, i.e., our speech (our argument, our premise)',
ii Illocution refers to 'what is meant by our locution, i.e., the intention (the intended (implicit) meaning) of our speech', and
iii Perlocution is concerned with 'what happens to the addressee as a result of our locution, i.e., the impact and power of our speech on the addressee'.

Locution is a speech act, i.e., an act of communication between an interlocutor (text producer, writer/speaker) and an addressee (text receiver, reader/listener). However, illocution is a skilful act of speaking or writing which bears, as speakers/writers, our intended action, such as ordering, promising, threatening, warning, or advising (admonishing).

In terms of the argumentation notion of the skilful initiation of locution, we can claim that Qur'anic discourse observes this notion in the initiatory (opening) statement or section of sūrahs. For instance, the initiation of a sūrah, like Q2, Q15, and Q28, with cryptic letters is to achieve the illocutionary force of suspense for the addressee (reader/hearer) since neither stylistic usage nor the meaning of cryptic letters is known to the addressee.

A case in point is Q1 and the relationship between Q1:2–3 and Q1:5. The opening sūrah of the Qur'an, Q1, presents an interesting example of gentle argumentation where the interlocutor is the human and the addressee is the Lord. As a Qur'anic presentation technique with an illocutionary force, Q1 initiates the discourse with introducing God's epithets (al-raḥmān al-raḥīm – the entirely merciful, the especially merciful, Q1:1) as a depiction of God's compassion and mercy to creation in general (human and non-human, believers and unbelievers) and to His worshippers in particular. It is worthwhile to note that God's epithets are employed in the active participle to designate the illocutionary force of [+ Continuity], i.e., God's mercy to His creation will never cease, and the illocutionary force [+ Permanency], i.e., mercy is a perpetual status of God. Grammatically, the two epithets (al-raḥmān al-raḥīm) are adjectives to the noun (allāh – God) in Q1:1. Later on, an interlocutor (the human worshipper) pleads to his/her creator (the Lord, God). In terms of argumentation, Q1 can be taken as an example of Qur'anic skilful initiation of locution where Q1 is the gate to the whole Qur'an. However, we are concerned here only with Q1 argumentation presentation technique. Let us consider the skilful argumentation techniques and the means to achieve impressive locution:

1 The human speaker (interlocutor) has initiated his/her discourse by skilfully addressing his/her creator (God) through gentle epithets that describe God's perpetual mercy that covers all His creation regardless of their colour or race (rabb al-ᶜālamīn – the Lord of the worlds).
2 The second skilful technique of locution which the human speaker has employed is the no-main-verb sentences: (al-ḥamdu lillāhi rabb al-ᶜālamīn/al-raḥmān al-raḥīm/maliki yaw al-dīn – All praise is due to God, Lord of the world/the entirely merciful, the especially merciful/sovereign of the day of resurrection, Q1:2–4).
3 The employment of the word (al-ḥamdu – all praise is due) as a nominalized noun (al-maṣdar) to achieve the illocutionary force of [+ Continuity] to the theological notion of deanthropomorphism (al-tanzīh). The nominalized noun (al-ḥamdu) also achieves the illocutionary force of [+ Monotheism]. Had the speaker used the verb form in the singular or plural form: (aḥmidu – I praise/naḥmidu – we praise), the illocutionary force [+ Continuity] to the

theological notion of deanthropomorphism will not be achieved. The verb entails [– Continuity].

4 Coherence and continuity of thought are achieved through (iyyāka naᶜbudu/iyyāka nastaᶜīn – It is you we worship/it is you we ask for help, Q1:5).

5 Q1:5 sets the scene for a bargaining argumentation technique where the vendor is the interlocutor (the human speaker appealing to his/her Lord) and the purchaser (the addressee, the listener) is God. The vendor (the human worshipper) has realized that his/her worship is imperfect. Thus, he/she pleads to the purchaser to accept his/her bargain as a wholesale, i.e., sold as seen. This wholesale bargain includes both perfect and imperfect items. As a purchaser, the bargain can either be accepted as it is or be rejected. However, according to Islamic law, the purchaser cannot pick up the perfect items and reject the defective ones. To sell the items as a whole, the vendor (the human worshipper) has employed the verbs in the plural form: (naᶜbudu – we worship) and (nastaᶜīn – we ask for help) instead of the singular form: (aᶜbudu – I worship) and (astaᶜīn – I ask for help). This is a skilful initiation of locution on the part of the speaker to include the vendor's worship plus the other humans' worship so that the purchaser will accept the bargain as it is. In other words, not all worshippers are perfect. Yet they all ask for God's help. The question is: Will the Lord fulfil their wish?, i.e., will God accept the bargain?

6 The acceptance of the bargain as a whole befits God's mercy and compassion towards His creation.

7 The skilful initiation of speech in Q1 has demonstrated that God's epithets are introduced first to designate compassion and sympathy as a prelude to the bargain (the request) in: (iyyāka naᶜbudu/iyyā nastaᶜīn – It is you we worship/it is you we ask for help, Q1:5), which the vendor aims to be accepted by the purchaser.

3.8 Persuasion in argumentation

A forceful and persuasive speaker/writer needs to have three means of persuasion as rhetorical styles:

i His/Her character should be charismatic, upright, and ethically based,

ii The audience's emotions and needs should be measured and addressed accurately, and

iii Ability to reason logically with his/her audience.

It is also imperative to note that in order to persuade the audience, it is important that the argument put forward should have a balance of ethos, pathos, and logos (Leighton 1982, 2009).

The strategies of discourse (the rhetorical triangle) used by a persuasive speaker/writer were dealt with by Aristotle (2007) years ago who developed a comprehensive theory of persuasion (Fahnestock and Secor 1983). In the view of Aristotle, persuasive interlocutors employ three strategies to persuade their audience:

1 by the appeal of their reason,
2 by the appeal of their emotion, and
3 by the appeal of their personality.

However, it is worthwhile to note that each discourse strategy is appropriate for a particular circumstance. In other words, the cognitive status of the addressee influences the discourse strategy adopted by the speaker/writer.

3.8.1 Modes of persuasion

This is a discussion of the art of rhetoric and how to employ effectively the three major rhetorical and stylistic strategies in a persuasive act. The strategies taken by a persuasive speaker are based on logical reasoning (logos), character (ethos), and emotions (pathos). Persuasion is a communication skill which the text producer (speaker/writer) needs to possess to enable him/her to influence the audience to change their belief or attitude. Thus, it is the function of the art of rhetoric which has the power of observing the means of persuasion. For more details on the practical analysis of Arabic rhetoric and modes of persuasion, see Section 4.6.1.2.

In the view of Corbett (1990:37), Aristotle has stated that three essential pillars are utilized to persuade others:

i to appeal to people's reason (logos),
ii to appeal to our credible personality (ethos), and
iii to appeal to people's emotions (pathos).

Linguistically, 'persuasion requires linguistic wit and linguistic powers' (Abdul-Raof 2006: xiii). 'If language is the weapon, words are the bullets' (ibid:1). The modes of persuasion have been discussed by Aristotle which are also called 'appeals' (Aristotle 1924:1356a). A statement is persuasive and credible either because it is directly self-evident or because it appears to be proved from other statements that are so. In either case it is persuasive because there is somebody whom it persuades (ibid). The terms (logos, ethos, and pathos) have been coined by Aristotle, who refers to them as 'the three artistic proofs' (Aristotle 1924:1356a). These modes are meant to help the text producer (speaker/writer) to create an effective argument which leads to convince his/her audience. In other words, in any persuasive act (rhetorical act, communication act), three modes of persuasion (three appeals) are required by the speaker/writer.

These three rhetorical styles are discussed in what follows (Cockcroft and Cockcroft 2005; Walton 2006, 2007; Walton et al. 2008; Ice 2012; Burton 2013):

i Logos: This is Aristotle's favourite appeal. Logos (Greek for 'word') refers to the internal consistency of the message, the clarity of the thesis (statement, premise), the logic of its reasons, and the effectiveness of its supporting evidence. The impact of logos on the audience is called 'the argument's logical appeal' or 'persuading by the use of reasoning'. Logos refers to the logical appeal and deals with the matter of the case in a persuasive act (rhetorical circumstance). It uses the arguments of the case itself to appeal to the audience's reason. Logos also depends on 'the proof, or apparent proof, provided by the words of the speech itself' (Aristotle 1924:1356a). A forceful speaker/writer should be able to provide a proof or an apparent proof to substantiate his/her argument. This means convincing the audience by the use of logic or reason. In other words, the speaker/writer adopts logical reasoning to persuade through proof, facts, and reason. In this situation, the speaker/writer attempts to prove a truth or an apparent truth by means of a persuasive argument which represents a series of premises which are appropriate to the case in question. A forceful argument needs to cite facts, statistics, and historical and literal analogies and to cite certain authorities on a subject. According to Corbett (1990), humans are forced to follow reasons because it is obviously foolish not to do so and it is said if you can't hear you will feel.

ii Ethos: It is related to the character of the speaker/writer in a persuasive act. In other words, to achieve persuasion through the speaker's/writer's trustworthy character traits. He/She should be a morally correct, trustworthy, ethical, and credible speaker/writer. Ethos is the Greek word for 'character'. The word 'ethic' is derived from ethos. When an argument is based on the speaker's own character, the mode of ethos is created through which the speaker employs his/her personal 'trustworthiness or credibility' to persuade the listeners to believe the argument put forward to them on a particular topic (Ramage and Bean 1998:81–82). Thus, it refers to the ethical appeal of the speaker/writer, who is expected by the listener/reader to be a credible charming character with expertise, sound knowledge, and most importantly, worthwhile to listen to. It is a human nature that people are readily persuaded by a person who is ethically right, honest, and known to be unbiased and truthful. The charismatic character of the speaker is particularly crucial for persuasion when people are sceptical and their opinions are divided. Thus, (ethical appeal) → (credibility, integrity, likeable character, worthy of respect, worthy to read/listen to). It is human nature that we believe people whom we respect. For this reason, the impact of ethos is called the argument's 'ethical appeal' or the 'appeal from credibility' (Cockcroft and Cockcroft 2005).

Because ethos is also related to choosing the appropriate level of language (vocabulary, style, and sentence structure), it can be claimed that ethos is directly related to the sound employment of language in any act of communication that aims for persuasion. 'If language is the weapon, words are the bullets' (Abdul-Raof 2006:1).

iii Pathos: (Greek for 'suffering' or 'experience'), pathos deals with the emotions of the audience in a persuasive act. It is the power of emotion to sway the mind of the audience. In other words, pathos is associated with emotional appeal (motivational appeals, vivid language, emotional language, and numerous sensory details) when persuading an audience by appealing to their emotions. A successful speaker/writer should be able to invoke sympathy from his/her audience in order to drive his/her message home, influence their belief, and convince them to change their opinion and attitude. Pathos is a persuasion technique which invokes sympathy from an audience, i.e., to make the audience feel what the speaker/writer wants them to feel. The speaker/writer adopts emotions to persuade by putting the audience into a certain emotional frame of mind. This appeal can be achieved by the use of metaphors, storytelling, or general passion. In order to appeal to an audience's emotions during the delivery of a speech, the speaker must first take the audience's emotion into account during the early invention phase (Ice 2012). In Qur'anic discourse, the most common way of conveying a pathetic appeal is through a narrative or a story (Prophets' parables).

3.8.1.1 Analysis of modes of persuasion

The following is a practical analysis of the three modes of persuasion: logos, ethos, and pathos.

Example 1: the text segment is taken from Q3:26–28.

Ethos: qul allāhumma mālika al-mulki tu'tī al-mulka man tashā' watanzi^{c}u al-mulka mimman tashā' watu^{c}izzu man tashā' watudhillu man tashā' biyadika al-khair innaka ^{c}alā kulli shai'in qadīr – Say: 'O God, owner of sovereignty, You give sovereignty to whom You will and You take sovereignty away from whom You will. You honour whom You will and You humble whom You will. In Your hand is all good. Indeed, You are over all things competent', Q3:26

Logos: tūliju al-laila fī al-nahāri watūliju al-nahāra fī al-laili watukhriju al-ḥaiya min al-maiyiti watukhriju al-maiyita min al-ḥaiyi watarzuqu man tashā'u bighairi ḥisāb – You cause the night to enter the day, and You cause the day to enter the night, and You bring the living out of the dead, and You bring the dead out of the living, and You give provision to whom You will without limit, Q3:27

Pathos: lā yattakhidh al-mu'minūna al-kāfirīna awliyā'a min dūni al-mu'minīna waman yaf^{c}al dhālika falaisa min allāhi fī shai'in illā an tattaqū minhum tuqāt wayuḥadhdhirukum allāhu nafsahu wa'ilā allāhi al-maṣīr – Let not believers take disbelievers as allies rather than believers. Whoever does that has nothing with God, except when taking precaution against them in prudence. God warns you of Himself, and to God is the final destination, Q3:28

Example 2: The text segment is taken from Q22:54–65.

Ethos: waliya^{c}lama alladhīna ūtū al-^{c}ilma annahu al-ḥaqqu min rabbika fayu'minū bihi fatubkhita lahu qulūbuhum wa'inna allāha lahādi alladhīna āmanū ilā ṣirāṭin mustaqīm – So, those who were given knowledge may know that it is the truth from your Lord and therefore believe in it and their hearts humbly submit to it. Indeed, God is the guide of those who have believed to a straight path, Q22:54

Pathos: walā yazālu alladhīna . . . – But those who disbelieved will not cease to . . ., Q22:55

Pathos: al-mulku yawma'idhin lillāh . . . – All sovereignty that day is for God . . ., Q22:56

Pathos: walladhīna kafarū wakadhdhabū . . . ᶜadhābun muhīn – and they who disbelieved and denied . . . a humiliating punishment, Q22:57

Pathos: walladhīna hājarū fī sabīl allāh thumma . . . wa'inna allāha lahuwa khairu al-rāziqīn – And those who emigrated for the cause of God and then . . . Indeed, it is God who is the best of providers, Q22:58

Pathos: liyudkhilannahum mudkhalan yarḍawnah wa'inna allāha laᶜalīmun ḥalīm – He will surely cause them to enter an entrance with which they will be pleased, and indeed, God is knowing and forbearing, Q22:59

Pathos: dhālika waman ᶜāqaba . . . inna allāha laᶜafuwwun ghafūr – That is so, and whoever responds to injustice with the equivalent of that with which he was harmed, . . . God is pardoning and forgiving, Q22:60

Logos: dhālika bi'anna allāha yūliju . . . wa'anna allāha samīᶜun baṣīr – That is because God causes the . . . and because God is hearing and seeing, Q22:61

Ethos: dhālika bi'anna allāha huwa al-ḥaqqu . . . wa'anna allāha huwa al-ᶜaliyyu al-kabīr – That is because God is the truth . . . and because God is the most high and great, Q22:62

Logos: alam tara anna allāha anzalā min . . . inna allāha laṭīfun khabīr – Do you not see that God has sent down from . . . Indeed, God is subtle and acquainted, Q22:63

Pathos: lahu mā fī al-samāwāti wamā fī al-arḍ wa'inna allāha lahuwa al-ghaniyyu al-ḥamīd – To Him belongs what is in the heavens and what is on the earth. Indeed, God is free of need, the praiseworthy, Q22:64

Logos: alam tara anna allāha sakhkhara lakum mā fī al-arḍi wal-fulka tajrī . . . inna allāha bil-nāsi lara'ūfun raḥīm – Do you not see that God has subjected to you whatever is on the earth and the ships which run . . . Indeed, God is kind and merciful to people, Q22:65

Example 3: The text segment is taken from Q23:1–22.

Pathos: qad aflaḥa al-mu'minūn. . . . alladhīna yarithūna al-firdawsa hum fīhā khālidūn – Certainly the believers will have succeeded . . . who will inherit the highest part of paradise and will abide therein eternally, Q23:1–11

Logos: walaqad khalaqnā al-insāna min sulālatin min ṭīn thumma ja^{c}alnāhu . . . fatabāraka allāhu aḥsanu al-khāliqīn – We certainly did create man from an extract of clay, then We placed him . . . So, God is blessed, the best of creators, Q23:12–14

Pathos: thumma innakum ba^{c}da dhālika lamaiyitūn thumma innakum yawma al-qiyāmati tub^{c}athūn – Then, indeed after that you are to die, then indeed, on the day of resurrection, you will be resurrected, Q23:15–16

Logos: walaqad khalaqnā fawqakum sab^{c}a ṭarā'iqa wamā . . . wa^{c}alaihā wa^{c}alā al-fulki tuḥmalūn – We have created above you seven layered heavens, and never . . . And you are carried upon them and on ships, Q23:17–22

Example 4: The text segment is taken from Q35:3–17.

Ethos: People, remember God's grace towards you. Is there any creator other than God to give you sustenance from the heavens and earth? There is no god but Him. How can you be deluded? If they call you a liar (Prophet), many messengers before you were also called liars: it is to God that all things will be returned. People! God's promise is true, so do not let the present life deceive you. Do not let the deceiver deceive you about God: Satan is your enemy – so treat him as an enemy – and invites his followers only to enter the blazing fire, Q35:3–6

Pathos: Those who disbelieve will be punished severely; those who believe and do good deeds will be forgiven, and richly rewarded. What about those whose evil deeds are made alluring to them so that they think they are good? God leaves whoever He will to stray and guides whoever He will. (Prophet), do not waste your soul away with regret for them: God knows exactly what they do, Q35:7–8

Logos: It is God who sends forth the wind. They raise up the clouds. We (God) drive them to a dead land and with them revive the earth after its death: such will be the resurrection . . . It is God who created you from dust and later from a drop of fluid, then He made you into two sexes; no female conceives or gives birth without His knowledge; no person grows old or has his life cut short, except in accordance with a record: all this is easy for God. The bodies of water are not alike – one is palatable, sweet, and pleasant to drink, the other salty and bitter – yet from each you eat fresh fish and extract ornaments to wear, and in each you see the ships ploughing their course so that you may seek God's bounty and be grateful. He makes the night merge into the day and the day into the night. He has subjected the sun and the moon – each runs for an appointed term, Q35:9–13

Ethos: Such is God your Lord: all control belongs to Him. Those you invoke beside him do not even control the skin of a date stone. If you call them, they cannot hear you. If they could hear, they could not answer you. On the day of resurrection they will disown your idolatry. None can inform you (Prophet) like the one God who is all aware. People! It is you who stand in need of God – God needs nothing and is worthy of all praise. If He wills, he can do away with you and bring in a new creation. That is not difficult for God, Q35:13–17

Example 5: The text segment is taken from Q11:109–123.

Ethos: lā taku fī miryatin mimmā yaᶜbudu hā'ulā' mā yaᶜbudūna illā kamā yaᶜbudu ābā'uhum min qablu wa'innā lamuwaffūhum naṣībahum ghaira manqūṣ – So do not be in doubt, (O Muḥammad), as to what these polytheists are worshipping. They worship not except as their fathers worshipped before. Indeed, We will give them their share undiminished, Q11:109

Pathos: walaqad ātainā mūsā al-kitāba fakhtulifa fīhi . . . innahum lafī shakkin minhu murīb wa'innā kullan lammā layuwaffiyannahum rabbuka aᶜmālahum . . . – We had certainly given Moses the Scripture, but it came under disagreement . . . Indeed they are, concerning the Qur'ān, in disquieting doubt. Indeed, each of the believers and disbelievers – your Lord will fully compensate them for their deeds. Indeed, He is acquainted with what they do . . ., Q11:110–111

Ethos: istaqim kamā umirta waman tāba maᶜaka walā taṭghaw . . . lā tarkanū ilā alladhīna ẓalamū . . . aqim al-ṣalāta ṭarafai al-nahāri . . . aṣbir . . . – So remain on a right course as you have been commanded, you and those who have turned back with you to God, and do not transgress . . . Do not incline toward those who do wrong . . . Establish prayer at the two ends of the day . . . and be patient . . ., Q11:112–115

Pathos: lawlā kāna min al-qurūni min qablikum ulū baqiyyatin yanhawna ᶜan al-fasādi fī al-arḍi illā qalīlan mimman anjainā minhum wattabaᶜa alladhīna ẓalamū mā utrifū fīhi wakānū mujrimaīn wamā kāna rabbuka liyuhlika al-qurā biẓulmin wa'ahluhā muṣliḥūn walaw shā'a rabbuka lajaᶜala al-nāsa ummatan wāḥidatan . . . watammat kalimatu rabbika la'amla'anna jahannama min al-jinnati wal-nāsi ajmaᶜīn wakullan naquṣṣu ᶜalaika min anbā'i al-rusuli mā nuthabbitu bihi fu'ādaka wajā'aka fī hādhihi al-ḥaqqu wamawᶜiẓatan wadhikrā lil-mu'minīn waqul lil-ladhīna la yu'minūna iᶜmalū ᶜalā makānatikum innā ᶜāmilūn wantaẓirū innā muntaẓirūn – So why were there not among the generations before you those of enduring discrimination forbidding corruption on earth – except a few of those We saved from among them? But those who wronged pursued what luxury they were given therein, and they were criminals. Your Lord would not have destroyed the cities unjustly while their people were reformers. If your Lord had willed, He could have made mankind one community . . . But the word of your Lord is to be fulfilled that: 'I will surely fill Hell with jinn and men all together'. Each story We relate to you from the news of the messengers is that by which We make your heart firm. There has come to you, in this, the truth

> and an instruction and a reminder for the believers. Say to those who do not believe: 'Work according to your position; indeed, we are working. Wait, indeed, we are waiting', Q11:116–122
>
> Logos: lillāhi ghaibu al-samāwāti wal-arḍi wa'ilaihi yurjaᶜu al-amru kulluhu faᶜbudhu watawakkal ᶜalaihi wamā rabbuka bighāfilin ᶜammā taᶜmalūn – To God belong the unseen aspects of the heavens and the earth and to Him will be returned the matter, all of it, so worship Him and rely upon Him. Your Lord is not unaware of that which you do, Q11:123

3.8.1.2 Persuasion and Arabic rhetoric

Arabic rhetoric is of value to the appreciation of the stylistic strategies in a persuasive act. In Arabic rhetoric, we have two types of statement (premise):

1 An informing statement (al-inshā'): This represents mood in a premise of an argument. An informing premise is that which does not qualify to be true or false.
2 A reporting statement (al-khabar): This represents mood of an argument. The reporting premise can be either true or false and is related to something that already exists.

There are two types of an informing speech act. These are request informing and non-request informing:

1 Request informing (al-inshā' al-ṭalabī): This category of informing entails something requested that has not taken place at the time of request. This type of discourse includes five categories of request informing, which are interrogative (al-istifham), imperative (al-amr), prohibition (al-nahi), vocative (al-nidā'), and wish (al-tamannī).
2 Non-request informing (inshā' ghair ṭalabī): This category of informing does not entail something requested. This form of discourse involves (i) praise and dispraise statements, (ii) astonishment statements, (iii) hope constructions (al-rajā'), (iv) oath statements, and (v) legal statements. For more details on informing and request statements, see Abdul-Raof (2006) Chapter 4, Sections 4.5 and 4.6.

Let us consider the following example:

> qul allāhumma mālika al-mulki tu'tī al-mulka man tashā' watanziᶜu al-mulka mimman tashā' watuᶜizzu man tashā' watudhillu man tashā' biyadika al-khair innaka ᶜalā kulli shai'in qadīr – Say: 'O God, owner of sovereignty, You give sovereignty to whom You will and You take sovereignty away from whom You will. You honour whom You will and You humble whom You will. In Your hand is all good. Indeed, You are competent over all things', Q3:26.

We can make the following observations:

- a This is a request informing (inshā' ṭalabī) whose category is imperative (al-amr) through the verb (qul – Say!).
- b Because it is an informing speech act, it does not qualify to be true or false. Thus, it is a skilful technique to force the opponent to accept the premise and believe it as true.
- c The stylistic mechanism of foregrounding provides the illocutionary force of specificity to God.
- d The stylistic mechanism represents the ethos of the argument.

One may wonder how the above four observations contribute to the truth value of Q3:26 in terms of persuasion and rebuttal to opponents whose cognitive status is classified as deniers. Because it is in the imperative form, Q3:36 makes it obligatory for the text receiver to accept it as a fact. The truth value of the imperative premise Q3:36 is backed up by the following text linguistic mechanisms:

- i Intertextuality: Q3:36 is intertextually supported by Q6:73, Q35:13, and Q39:6 (lahu al-mulk – To Him belongs the dominion).
- ii The stylistic mechanism of foregrounding in the subsequent text segments which are thematically related to Q3:26 are employed to rebut the scepticism of the deniers (munkir): (biyadika al-khair – In Your hand is all good, Q3:26) and (innaka ᶜalā kulli shai'in qadīr – Indeed, You are competent over all things, Q3:26).
- iii Substantiation through God's omnipotence details in the subsequent statement Q3:27 (tūliju al-laila fī al-nahāri watūliju al-nahāra fī al-laili watukhriju al-ḥaiya min al-maiyiti watukhriju al-maiyita min al-ḥaiyi watarzuqu man tashā'u bighairi ḥisāb – You cause the night to enter the day, and You cause the day to enter the night. You bring the living out of the dead, and You bring the dead out of the living; and You give provision to whom You will without account).

We are informed by the request informing premise in Q3:26 about the illocutionary force of specificity, i.e., the qualities of 'giving sovereignty', 'taking away sovereignty' and 'all good' are made God-specific.

3.8.2 Persuasion and implicit audience

This is related to the pragmatic notion of conversational implicature, which is an indirect or implicit speech act where what is meant by a speaker's statement is not part of what is explicitly said in the statement. Thus, it is related to context and inference, i.e., to pragmatics and semantics, and, of course, to relevance theory, or the principle of relevance (Sperber and Wislon 1986; Clark 2013). In the view of Eemeren and Grootendorst (2004:183), the requirement of clarity neither means that the text producer must necessarily formulate his/her intentions explicitly and directly nor that it is enough for the text receiver to attribute a literal meaning to the words of the protagonist (speaker/writer). It is normal for all kinds of things to remain implicit in ordinary language or for intentions to be conveyed indirectly. Implicit and indirect speech acts do not entail any problems. By making use of background knowledge, it will be easy to ascertain what is intended from the context.

The present discussion demonstrates that implicit (intended) audience is a gentle persuasion technique employed in Qur'anic argumentation as a strategy for persuasion, i.e., how to convince an antagonist (opponent) without addressing him/her directly. Let us consider the following examples which demonstrate two types of audience: the explicit and the implicit audience.

Example 1

> wamāliya lā a^{c}budu alladhī faṭaranī wa'ilaihi turja^{c}ūn. a'attakhidhu min dūnihi ālihatan in yuridni al-raḥmānu bidurrin lā tughni ^{c}annī shafā^{c}atuhum walā yunqidhūni. innī idhan lafī dhalālin mubīn – Why should I not worship He (God) who created me and to whom you will be returned? Should I take other than Him false deities while if the most merciful intends for me some adversity, their intercessors will not avail me at all, nor can they save me. Indeed, I would then be in manifest error, Q36:22–24.

The explicit audience is the speaker himself. To persuade his opponents about the notion of monotheism, the speaker employs the implicit audience technique of persuasion. He does not criticize them or blame them about their polytheistic practices. Instead, he speaks about himself as an explicit audience: (wamāliya lā a^{c}budu alladhī faṭaranī – Why should I not worship He (God) who created me), which, in fact, is directed to his disbelieving opponents. This is what is meant by 'the implicit audience'. In other words, his statement should read: {wamalākum lā ta^{c}budū alladhī faṭarakum wa'ilaihi turja^{c}ūn – Why should you not worship He (God) who created you and to whom you will be returned?}. The speaker has successfully put forward his argument to his opponent with regards to monotheism but in an indirect way. He is informing his opponents indirectly that the one who has created me is worthy of worship rather than the false gods who cannot create but rather they are created by their own worshippers. His persuasion goes on: (in yuridni al-raḥmānu biḍurrin lā tughni ^{c}annī shafā^{c}atuhum walā yunqidhūni – If the most merciful intends for me some adversity, their intercessors will not avail me at all, nor can they save me) + (inni idhan lafi dhalalin mubin – Indeed, I would then be in manifest error). He refers in both statements to himself while the intended audience are his disbelieving opponents. Therefore, the explicit meaning of the two statements is: {in yuridkum al-raḥmānu biḍurrin lā tughni ^{c}ankum shafā^{c}atuhum walā yunqidhūnakum – If the most merciful intends for you some adversity, their intercessors will not avail you at all, nor can they save you} + {innakum idhan lafī dhalālin mubīn – Indeed, you would then be in manifest error}.

Example 2

walaqad ūḥiya ilaiyaka wa'ilā alladhīna min qablika la'in ashrakta layaḥbaṭanna ᶜamaluka walatakūnanna min al-khāsirīn – It was already revealed to you and to those before you that if you should associate anything with God, your work would surely become worthless, and you would surely be among the losers, Q39:65.

The explicit addressee is Muḥammad and the past Prophets. However, Muḥammad and the past Prophets are messengers sent delivering the pivotal notion of monotheism. So how can Q39:65 address Muḥammad and the past Prophets? In fact, the implicit audience are the believers who are warned about polytheism. Q39:65 should read: {walaqad ūḥiya ilaiyaka wa'ilā alladhīna min qablika la'in ashraktum layaḥbaṭanna ᶜamalukum walatakūnū min al-khāsirīn – It was already revealed to you and to those before you that if you (i.e., the believers) should associate anything with God, your (i.e., the believers') work would surely become worthless, and you (i.e., the believers) would surely be among the losers}. Thus, the implicit audience are warned about polytheism rather than Muḥammad and the past Prophets.

Similarly, we encounter expressions whose implicit audience are the disbelievers, as in:

wamā yadhdhakkaru illā ulū al-albāb – None will remember except those of understanding, Q2:269.
wadhikrā li'ulī al-albāb – It is a reminder for those of understanding, Q38:43.
kadhālika nufaṣṣilu al-āyāti liqawmin yatafakkarūn – Thus do We explain in detail the signs for a people who give thought, Q10:24.
inna fī dhālika la'āyātin liqawmin yatafakkarūn – Indeed in that are signs for a people who give thought, Q13:3.
qad faṣṣalnā al-āyāti liqawmin yafqahūn – We have detailed the signs for a people who understand, Q6:98.

The intended meanings of the above expressions are: (al-kāfirūna lā yatadhakkarūn/ lā yatafakkarūn/lā yafqahūn – The disbelievers do not remember/do not give thought/do not understand), (al-kāfirūna lā albāba lahum – The disbelievers are not people of understanding), (al-kāfirūna lā yantafiᶜūn min āyāt allāh – The disbelievers do not benefit from God's signs).

Example 3

fariḥa al-mukhallafūna bimaqᶜadihim khilāfa rasūl allāh wakarihū an yujāhidū bi'amwālihim wa'anfusihim fī sabīl allāh waqālū lā tanfirū fī al-ḥarri qul nāru jahannama ashaddu ḥarran law kānū yafqahūn – Those who remained behind rejoiced in the staying at home after the departure of the messenger of God and disliked to strive with their wealth and their lives in the cause of God and said: 'Do not go forth in the heat'. Say: 'The fire of hell is more intense in heat' – if they would but understand, Q9:81.

This statement refers to the Battle of Tabūk (9/630), when the hypocrites made excuses not to go with the Muslim army and preferred to stay with their families. It is common knowledge that the heat of hell is more intense than the heat of the sun. However, the intended meaning is that 'the hypocrites will be punished in the hell fire'. Thus, Q9:81 has the illocutionary force of threat. In other words, Q9:81 is not meant to inform about the difference in temperature but is a threat to the hypocrites.

Example 4

rabbī innī limā anzalta ilaiyya min khairin faqīr – My Lord, indeed I am in need for whatever good You would send down to me, Q28:24.

This is about Moses after he left Egypt because he was wanted for murder. Moses unintentionally struck a man and killed him. As a result, he left Egypt. In Q28:24, Moses prays to God to grant him a secure place of living, a secure source of income, and the chance to get married. Moses' supplication was made immediately after he helped the two young girls with giving water to their flocks. After the girls left home, Moses went back to the shade and said the above statement. Because Q28:24 was said immediately after this incident, we can claim that the intended meaning is 'my Lord, I am in need for a secure place of living, a secure source of income, and getting married'. This intended meaning is supported by the following statement: (fajā'athu iḥdāhumā tamshī ᶜalā istiḥyā' qālat inna abī yadᶜūka liyajziyaka ajra mā saqaita lanā – Then one of the two women came to him walking with shyness. She said: 'Indeed, my father invites you that he may reward you for having watered for us', Q28:25). The employment of the conjunctive particle (fa) prefixed to the verb (-jā'athu – she came to him) provides further support to the intended meaning of Moses' statement. In other words, the conjunctive particle (fa) signifies 'immediately after', i.e., immediately after Moses has made his request to his Lord. Thus, his wish has come true. Moses gets married to one of the two girls, gets a secure job, and a place to live in.

3.9 The text and its audience

This is an account of successful communication and the relationship between the communicator and his/her audience. Thus, it is of value to translation studies. For more details, see Section 7.4.1. The linguistic approach in Qur'anic exegesis accounts for the pragmatic functions of semantic syntax in Arabic discourse. Thus, syntax and pragmatics become inextricable. The theory of word order put forward by al-Jurjānī is based on the notion of linguistic deviation from the norm due to contextual and pragmatic factors, which is referred to as *al-khurūj ᶜalā muqtaḍā al-ẓāhir*. Thus, al-Jurjānī has, thus, established the intimate pragmatic relationship between the communicator (the text producer) and his/her audience (the text receiver). The text producer needs to be aware of the psychological and ideological state of the text receiver in terms of his/her preparedness to accept or reject the proposition put forward. For a successful communication, the text producer needs to make some assumptions about the text receiver's cognitive abilities and contextual resources. Word order change is directly linked to context, which is a psychological construct, a subset of the hearer's assumptions about the world. Different word orders have distinct pragmatic interpretations. Thus, we need to integrate the properties of the context with the semantic properties of the speech act. A proposition does not only relay thoughts but also uncovers the communicator's attitudes to the thought expressed. Various orders of sentence constituents can be employed for different communicative functions. Although the verb-initial pattern is stylistically the unmarked (common) word order in Arabic, this linguistic mechanism is abandoned for pragmatic reasons in order to achieve a given communicative function. In other words, Arabic employs noun-initial stylistic patterns when there is a good pragmatic function which the communicator aims to achieve. In Arabic rhetoric, when the communicator wants to relay an important message to the addressee, he/she adopts the stylistic technique of foregrounding, i.e., fronting (al-taqdīm), the noun. Thus, the noun (noun phrase) occupies the initial position of the sentence. The foregrounded noun is referred to as al-musnad ilaihi. It should be pointed out that the foregrounded noun does not pose a translation problem. The only loss that occurs in the target language (TL) is attributed to the fact that the rhetorically important pragmatic functions of foregrounding the noun cannot be conveyed by the target text. Foregrounding of the musnad ilaihi occurs as a feature of God's omnipotence. It is a Qur'an-specific stylistic mechanism that aims to achieve praise to Allah, i.e., the fronted noun, and to highlight a feature in order to eliminate doubt in the addressee's mind. Thus, through foregrounding the noun Allāh, the Qur'an achieves two interrelated pragmatic functions:

i rebuttal of opponent's thesis, and
ii substantiation of God's omnipotence are achieved.

However, the alternative verb-initial structures will not be able to deliver these communicative functions. This is due to the fact that in Arabic rhetoric, the initial verb signifies non-continuity. Noun-initial structures beginning with (Allāh) are context sensitive. In other words, they occur in the context of denial statements such as the denial of Allāh's favours, accepting polytheism, denial of the prophethood of Muḥammad, or disbelief in eschatology. This is illustrated by the following sentences in Q16:65, 70, 71, 72, 78, 80, and 81:

> allāhu anzala min al-samā'i mā'an . . . – It is God who sends water down from the sky . . .
> allāhu khalaqakum . . . – It is God who has created you . . .
> allāhu faḍḍalā ba^cḍakum ^calā ba^cḍ fī al-rizq . . . – It is God who has given some of you more provision than others.

> allāhu ja^cala lakum min anfusikum azwājan . . . – It is God who has given you spouses from among yourselves.
> allāhu akhrajakum min buṭūni ummahātikum . . . – It is God who brought you out from the wombs of your mothers . . .
> allāhu ja^cala lakum min buyūtikum sakanan . . . – It is God who has given you a place of rest in your homes . . .
> allāhu ja^cala lakum mimmā khalaqa ẓilālan . . . – It is God who has given you shade from what He has created . . .

This also applies to Q40:60, 64, and 79. Similarly, the pragmatic functions of substantiation of monotheism and God's omnipotence as well as the rebuttal of antagonist's (opponent's) views are also achieved by the initial musnad ilaihi explicit pronoun (huwa – He, i.e., Allāh – God), as in Q40:67 and 68.

The translator, as a text analyst, should be aware of the fact that there is an underlying level of semantics within the rhetorical level of Arabic discourse. The surface structure meaning of a given syntactic construction provides the outward rhetorical façade of the proposition. However, the same proposition has an underlying signification that matches the intended message of the text producer. Through the rhetorical means of semantic syntax (word order), Arabic can stylistically achieve this communicative goal (cf. Abdul-Raof 2006). Consider Q7:29:

> amara rabbī bil-qisṭi wa'aqīmū wujūhakum ᶜinda kulli masjidin – My Lord has ordered justice and that you maintain yourselves at every place of prostration, Q7:29.

Linguistically, there are two grammatical units in this speech act: the first unit starts with the verb (amara – to order) and ends with the prepositional phrase (bil-qisṭi – with justice), which includes the preposition (bi – with) and the nominalization form (al-qisṭi). Unit two is (aqīmū . . . – to maintain . . .), which is conjoined to (maᶜṭūfah ᶜalā) unit one. However, the first lexical item of unit two (aqīmū – to maintain) occurs in the verb form and not in the nominalization form as we have expected to match the grammatical pattern of unit one. Therefore, stylistically, unit two should have been (iqāmah), so that we get:

> (amara rabbī {bil-qisṭi wa'iqāmat} wujūhakum ᶜinda kulli masjidin).

The word order, i.e., the stylistic pattern, in Q7:29 is not without a good communicative reason. Rhetorically, this speech act is divided into two modes of discourse:

i a request-reporting mode (al-khabar al-ṭalabī) where the past tense verb form is employed (amara rabbī bil-qisṭ), and
ii a request-informing mode (al-inshā' al-ṭalabī) where the imperative verb form (aqīmū) is employed.

The rhetorical reason for this particular word order is that the employment of a request reporting in unit one has the possibility of being true or false. In other words, the communicator is reporting to the addressee what he/she is required to do. The addressee may believe or disbelieve the communicator. However, to highlight the value of 'praying' to the addressee, the text producer intentionally selects the mode of request informing that does not allow the possibility of being true or false. In other words, the shift in mode of discourse from the reporting (al-khabar) in unit one to informing (al-inshā') in unit two is primarily to eliminate the addressee's verdict of true or false on the communicator's statement. Although statements like Q7:29 do not pose a translation problem, the pragmatic functions conveyed by the Arabic sentence are not present in the English translation.

Denial reporting (al-khabar al-inkāri) is a mode of discourse which is employed in the Qur'an for a stubborn addressee who rejects outright the proposition and denies it as false. Thus, there is a huge yawning gap and ideological clash between the text producer and the text receiver. For this reason, we encounter excessive use of linguistic affirmation tools which aim to substantiate the claim put forward by the text producer. Thus, the statement acquires a high level of evaluativeness (affirmation). On the macro textual level, repetition of expressions, which is a form of lexical cohesion, is also regarded as an affirmation technique in Qur'anic rhetoric, as in surat al-raḥmān (Q55) where the formulaic expression (fabi'aiyi ālā'i rabbikumā tukadhdhdibān – so which of the favours of your Lord would you deny?) is repeated 31 times, and the formulaic instructional sentence (u^{c}budū allāha mā lakum min ilāhin ghairuhu – worship God; you have no deity other than Him) in Q7, which is repeated four times.

3.9.1 Affirmation in communication

Rhetorically, affirmation (evaluativeness) can be realized through other linguistic techniques such as:

1. The nominal sentence, as in (rabbanā ya^{c}lamu – our Lord knows) and (innā ilaikum lamursalūn – we are messengers to you) in Q36:16 where affirmation (al-ta'kīd) is employed to refute the opponents' premise that 'prophets cannot be humans'.
2. The use of negation plus exception is another technique of affirmation which occurs in denial reporting, as in (mā antum illā basharun mithlunā – You are nothing more than humans like us, Q16:15) where the negation particle (mā) and the exception particle (illā) are used to reject the proposition put forward by the first speaker who claims (antum basharun mithlunā – You are humans like us (thus, you cannot be prophets)).
3. Affirmation plays a significant role in Qur'anic genre. Affirmation particles are language specific and may not be possible to convey in translation. The particle (qad), for instance, is employed for affirmation especially when the context refers to the hypocrites. However, this affirmation feature is lost in some Qur'an translations of the following statements:

qad ya^{c}lamu allāhu alladhīna yatasallalūna minkum liwādhan – God is indeed aware of those of you who steal away surreptitiously, Q24:63.

qad ya^{c}lamu allāhu al-mu^{c}awwiqīna minkum – God is indeed aware of those of you who hinder others, Q33:18

where the particle (qad) is rendered as (indeed). Apart from the translations of Ali and Asad, other Qur'an translators have overlooked this significant rhetorical aspect in the source language.

4 The occurrence of assertive linguistic tools (affirmation particles) is not random in Qur'anic genre. They are context-sensitive and geared towards the addressee's state of mind and his/her ideological point of view. In Qur'anic rhetoric, the employment of affirmation tools is not required for an open-mind addressee (khālī al-dhihn) who is neither sceptical nor a denier of the text producer's, i.e., speaker/writer, statement. Therefore, the sentence should be minimally evaluative. This is called initial reporting (al-khabar al-ibtidā'ī). However, it is preferable to employ one affirmation particle to a sceptical audience (mutradid) who are 'floaters' unable to make up their mind about the thesis put forward to them. This is called request reporting (al-khabar al-ṭalabī). Most importantly, it is stylistically compulsory to employ several affirmation tools when addressing a denier (al-munkir) who disbelieves the proposition given by the text producer. This is referred to as denial reporting (al-khabar al-inkārī). These affirmation tools are employed by the text producer in the reporting mode of discourse due to the fact that reporting (al-khabar) can be either true or false. In other words, the text producer in his/her reporting statement conveys either correct or incorrect information to the addressee. The text receiver, however, is at liberty to accept or reject the message. In Qur'anic discourse, we encounter denial reporting statements with many affirmation particles, as in:

inna rabbaka lahuwa al-^{c}azīzu al-raḥīmu – Your Lord alone is the almighty, the merciful, Q26:9

The stylistic pattern of denial reporting is linked to the overall context that precedes it. The preceding statements (Q26:2–7) refer to disbelief in and ridicule of the Prophet Muḥammad. There is, therefore, a sharp ideological gap between the communicator and the addressee. Therefore, the Qur'an employs affirmation tools such as (inna), (anna), (qad), the initial (la), (the affirmation letter /l/), the detached pronoun like (huwa), the absolute object (kallama allāhu mūsā taklīmā – God spoke to Moses with direct speech, Q4:164) in order to substantiate the premise of prophethood and rebut the addressee's scepticism. It is also interesting to note that the Qur'anic word order system (al-naẓm) has employed the two musnads (al-^{c}azīzu al-raḥīmu) in the definite form for the pragmatic function of restriction (al-ḥaṣr) in order to strictly specify the exclusive features of (^{c}azīz) and (raḥīm) to Allāh only and that these features co-occur recurrently with Him at all times. The ordinary non-Qur'anic stylistic pattern {rabbuka ʿazīzun raḥīmun} cannot deliver these pragmatic and semantic functions. Unfortunately, this is what has happened in the translation of Q26:9 earlier.

5 In terms of the rhetorical discipline of word order (ʿilm al-maʿāni), affirmation in Qur'anic Arabic is also achieved through the order system (al-naẓm) of the sentence. Thus, through the foregrounding of a word, a given notion is highlighted, i.e., given focus or saliency, as in (alladhīna hum birabbihim lā yushrikūna, Q23:59). This is a marked (stylistically uncommon) word order which aims, through the foregrounding of (birabbihim), to achieve the pragmatic function of affirmation, i.e., it affirms 'the negation of polytheism – nafī al-shirk' on the part of this particular group of people. However, the unmarked (stylistically common) word order {alladhīna lā yushrikūna birabbihim} does not achieve the same communicative function of affirmation. All Qur'an translators have opted for the latter unmarked word order to accommodate for the structural norms of the target language. Thus, we get: (Those who do not ascribe partners to their Lord) where the source language foregrounded expression (birabbihim – their Lord) has become backgrounded in the translation.

3.9.2 Categories of audience

This is concerned with the compatibility of the stylistic structure with the cognitive status of the addressee. In other words, we can claim that the cognitive status of the audience dictates the structural pattern of the locution of the text producer (the speech, the statements made by the speaker/writer). To discuss the categories of audience, we need to focus on two matters:

1 The stylistic structure of the sentence:

i The intended meaning and stylistic structure: The stylistic pattern of the sentence depends on its intended meaning, the illocutionary force behind it, the context, and most importantly the cognitive status of the addressee. For instance, the sentence: (iʿmalū mā shi'tum innahu bimā taʿmalūna baṣīr – Do whatever you will. Indeed, He (God) is seeing of what you do, Q41:40) can be understood as an imperative statement commanding people to do whatever they wish. However, one needs to investigate its context, the speaker's intended meaning, and the type of addressee spoken/written to. The context of situation of Q41:40 refers to a category of disbelievers who are rejecters of the Prophethood of Muḥammad, who used to fabricate some Qur'anic āyahs, and used to provide wrong interpretations to some āyahs to mislead the public. Therefore, the text segment mentioned above should be re-analysed and put into context:

> inna alladhīna yulḥidūna fī āyātinā lā yakhfawna ʿalainā afaman yulqā fī al-nāri khairun am man ya'tī āminan yawma al-qiyāmati

iᶜmalū mā shi'tum innahu bimā taᶜmalūna baṣīr – Those who distort the meaning of Our message are not hidden from Us. Is he who is hurled into the fire better, or he who comes through safely on the day of resurrection? Do whatever you want. God certainly sees everything you do, Q41:40

Having read the context in which the small text segment occurs and having known the type of the cognitive status of the addressee, we are now in a position to discern the performative intent of the text producer (the speaker). We can claim that the small text segment (iᶜmalū mā shi'tum innahu bimā taᶜmalūna baṣīr – Do whatever you will. Indeed, He (God) is seeing of what you do, Q41:40) has the illocutionary force of [+ Threat] to the category of people mentioned in the larger context. Thus, the intended meaning is not positive, i.e., it is not giving liberty to people to enjoy what they want to do. Rather, it bears a threat with the punishment in the fire for their evil deeds which have been witnessed by God.

ii The exception sentence structure (lā . . . illā . . . – no . . . except . . .): This is employed to achieve the illocutionary force of affirmation of the text producer's performative intent, as in: (an lā taᶜbudū illā allāh – That you should not worship except God, Q11:26). Alternative stylistic structures are ruled out because they lack assertiveness: {an aᶜbudū allāh – That you worship God} or {uᶜbudū allāh – Worship God}.

iii The no-main-verb nominal stylistic structure: This stylistic pattern enhances the text producer's performative intent in terms of delivering the illocutionary force of affirmation, as in (innahum mughraqūn – Indeed, they are to be drowned, Q11:37) where the nominal grammatical status affirms the fate of those who disbelieved Noah. Also, in (allāhu ᶜalā kulli shai'in qadīr – God is competent over all things, Q3:29) where the illocutionary force is focused on God's power. A main verb alternative stylistic pattern would fail to deliver the text producer's performative intent (allāhu yaqdiru ᶜalā kulli shai'in/yaqdiru allāh ᶜalā kulli shai'in – God is competent over all things).

2 Affirmation tools: Texts display varying degrees of evaluativeness (affirmation). Depending on the cognitive status of the addressee, the degree of evaluativeness (affirmation tools) can be decided for each sentence. For instance, if I am only informing you about the current situation of (Sālim), I should say: (Sālimun mujtahidun – Sālim is hard-working), where I have employed zero affirmation tools because there is no need to affirm anything to the addressee who is an open-minded person (khālī al-dhihn). Thus, we have a low degree of evaluativeness (low evaluative discourse). If I am responding to a question about (Sālim), I should say: (inna sāliman mujtahidun – Indeed, Sālim is hard-working) where I have employed one affirmation tool (inna – indeed) because the addressee is a sceptical person. Therefore, my statement needs to be slightly affirmed. Thus, we have a mid degree of evaluativeness (mid evaluative discourse). However, if I am

rebutting a false claim that denies Salim the hard work he has been doing and classifies him as a lazy person, I should say: (inna sāliman lamujtahidun – Indeed, Sālim is definitely hard-working), where I have employed two affirmation tools: (inna – indeed) and the affirmation /l/ (lām al-tawkīd) to rebut the allegation made by the denier (munkir) against Sālim. Thus, we have a high degree of evaluativeness (highly evaluative discourse).

Thus, I have produced three responses which are informing statements, each suitable for a specific addressee based on his/her cognitive status:

i Plain informing (khabar ibtidā'ī): As in (Sālimun mujtahidun – Salim is hard-working). Plain informing does not employ any affirmation tools because the audience are open-minded and impartial and, most importantly, they believe the information told to them and accept it as true. However, the speaker may employ one affirmation tool if he/she believes the addressee is slightly sceptical, as in:

> walā tukhaṭibnī fī alladhīna ẓalamū innahum mughraqūn – Do not plead with Me (God) for those who have done evil – indeed, they will be drowned, Q11:37

where the addressee is Noah and the speaker is God. Having realized that Noah has a slight hesitation and suspense, God puts forward the statement with one affirmation tool (inna – indeed) prefixed to (-hum – they). Also, because Noah is impatient with regards to finding out about the fate of those who have been doing evil, the speaker employs one affirmation tool to confirm the outcome of the evildoers.

It is interesting to note that, at times, Qur'anic discourse employs no affirmation tools while the addressee is a denier. One may wonder why the Qur'an uses plain informing (a statement without affirmation tools) while the audience are deniers. The illocutionary force of such statements is sarcasm and belittling the audience. For instance, in: (dhālika al-kitābu lā raiba fīhi – This is the Scripture in which there is no doubt, Q2:2), the audience are the unbelievers who are deniers of the prophethood of Muḥammad and the Qur'an. However, Q2:2 does not employ any affirmation tool. The text producer's performative intent is that the revelation of the Qur'an to Muḥammad is a fact and bears a truth value. Thus, it is too foolish to deny such a fact. Because it is a fact, according to the text producer, the statement put forward to the denier audience does not need to be affirmed. Thus, the speaker ignores the cognitive status of the audience and treats them as open-minded.

It is also worthwhile to note that, at times, plain informing is employed with a sceptical addressee who is treated as open-minded and no affirmation tools are employed, as in:

> qāla kadhālika allāhu yafʿalu mā yashā' – He (the angel) said: 'Such is God. He does what He wills', Q3:40

which is a response to the sceptical statement made by Zachariah:

> qāla rabbi annā yakūnu lī ghulāmun waqad balaghaniya al-kibaru wamra'atī ᶜāqir – He (Zacharia) said: 'My Lord how will I have a boy when I have reached old age and my wife is barren', Q3:40

Exactly the same thing takes place with the sceptical statement of Mary: (qālat rabbi annā yakūnu lī waladun walam yamsasnī bashar – She (Mary) said: 'My Lord, how will I have a child when no man has touched me?!', Q3:47) where a plain informing statement is used which has no affirmation tools because Mary is treated as an open-minded addressee (qāla kadhālika allāhu yakhluqu mā yashā'u – He (the angel) said: 'Such is God. He creates what He wills').

ii Request reporting (khabar ṭalabī): As in (inna sāliman mujtahidun – Indeed, Sālim is hard-working). Request informing employs one affirmation tool because the audience are sceptical and the information given to them needs to be slightly affirmed to persuade them and accept the statement as true. In Q20:12–15, we encounter a unique example of a sceptical addressee who is Moses. To make the sceptical Moses believe in what and who the speaker is, the speaker (God) employs one affirmation tool (inna) plus a nominal sentence: (innī anā rabbuka – Indeed, I am your Lord, Q20:12), (innaka bilwādi al-muqaddasi ṭuwā – You are in the sacred valley of Ṭuwā, Q20:12), (innanī anā allāhu/lā ilāha illā anā – Indeed, I am God/there is no deity except Me, Q20;14). Although Moses is not a denier (munkir), the speaker has raised the level of evaluativeness and employed more than one affirmation tool.

iii Denial reporting (khabar inkārī): As in (inna sāliman lamujtahidun – Indeed, Sālim is definitely hard-working) or (wallāhi inna sāliman lamujtahidun – By God, indeed, Sālim is definitely hard-working). Denial informing employs two or more affirmation tools because the audience are deniers. Thus, the statement put forward to them needs to be highly evaluative (heavily affirmed) to win the hearts and minds of the deniers and persuade them about the truth value of the information relayed to them.

Among the linguistic devices of affirmation (evaluativeness) are: oath expressions such as (wal-ᶜaṣri – by time, Q103:1); antithesis statements; the auxiliary verb (inna – indeed); the /l/ letter (lām al-tawkīd); the attached pronoun (ḍamīr al-faṣl) like (huwa – he); the particle (qad – indeed, certainly) and (laqad – indeed, certainly); the /sīn/ that designates future tense; the no-main-verb nominal sentence as in Q59:22–24 to affirm monotheism, and (innamā anā basharun mithlukum – I am indeed only a man like you, Q18:110) and (innā ilaikum lamursalūn – We are messengers to you, Q36:16) to affirm prophethood; the noun-initial with a main verb nominal sentence; the repetition of the same word as in (al-qāriᶜatu. ma al-qāriᶜatu. wamā adrāka mā al-qāriᶜatu – The striking calamity. What is the striking calamity? What can make you know what the striking calamity is?, Q101:1–3) where the word (al-qāriᶜatu – the striking calamity) is repeated three times. In the view of

Beaugrande and Dressler (1981:55), recurrence (repetition) is prominently used to assert and re-affirm one's viewpoint.

An example of a statement with a high degree of evaluativeness is: (inna hādhā lahuwa al-qaṣaṣu al-ḥaqq – Indeed, this is the true narration, Q3:63) where we have four linguistic devices of evaluativeness: (inna – indeed), (lām al-tawkīd – the /l/ prefixed to the attached pronoun (-huwa – it)), the attached pronoun (ḍamīr al-faṣl) (huwa – it, i.e., the Qur'an), and the no-main-verb nominal sentence itself.

Other examples of the employment of more than one affirmation tool are:

> innā lanaḥnu al-ṣāffūn / innā lanaḥnu al-musabbiḥūn – Indeed, we are those who line up for prayer / indeed, we are those who exalt God, Q37:165–166.
> inna naḥnu nuḥyi al-mawtā – Indeed, it is We who bring the dead to life, Q36.
> inna al-sā^cata la'ātiyatun walākinna akthara al-nāsi lā ya^clamūn – Indeed, the hour is coming – no doubt about it – but most of the people do not believe, Q40:59.
> innaka lamin al-mursalīn – indeed you (Muḥammad) are from among the messengers, Q36:3.
> hum ^can al-ākhirati hum ghāfilūn – They, of the hereafter, are unaware, Q30:7.
> innā lananṣuru rusulanā . . . – Indeed, We will support Our messengers . . ., Q40:51.
> inna al-abrāra lafī na^cīm/inna al-fujjāra lafī jaḥīm – Indeed, the righteous will be in pleasure/Indeed, the wisked will be in hellfire, Q82:13–14.

It is interesting to note that, at times, Qur'anic discourse employs affirmation tools while the addressee is not a denier. One may wonder why the Qur'an uses denial informing (a statement with many affirmation tools) while the audience are not deniers. The illocutionary force of such statements is reassurance and confirmation of close ties and friendship with the addressee. For instance, in: (innā ma^cakum innamā naḥnu mustahzi'ūn – Indeed, we are with you, we were only mockers, Q2:14), which is the speech of the hypocrites to their audience who are the evil ones (shayāṭīn). The hypocrites are speaking to their allies. Therefore, their statement should not have employed any affirmation tools because the addressee is open-minded, i.e., believing whatever the speaker says. However, the hypocrites have employed the affirmation tools (inna) to reassure their evil allies. The hypocrites have treated their audience (the evildoers) as deniers of their friendship, and, thus, have employed affirmation tools. Similarly, in Q22:58, we have reference to those who emigrated for the cause of God and were killed or died. This category of people is reassured and told: 'God will surely provide for them a good provision'. To reassure them more, a highly evaluative (heavily affirmed) message is provided: (inna allāha lahuwa khairu al-rāziqīn – Indeed, it is God who is the best of provision, Q22:58) whose stylistic pattern is:

> inna + noun + affirmation letter /l/ + noun phrase with an active participle.

The high level of evaluativeness lies in the following facts:

i the grammatical status of the sentence: a no-main-verb nominal sentence, and
ii the affirmation tools.

Based on the cognitive status of the addressee (listener/reader), there are three types of audience:

1 Open-minded (khālī al-dhihn): This category of audience does not pass on any judgement on the claim or statement put forward to them. They are impartial and easily persuaded. Thus, there is no need for the speaker to employ any linguistic assertive particles (affirmation tools), as in:

   dhālika al-kitābu lā raiba fīhi hudan lil-muttaqīn alladhīna yu'minūna bil-ghaibi wayuqīmūna al-ṣalāta wamimmā razaqnāhum yunfiqūn – This is the Scripture in which there is no doubt, containing guidance for those who are mindful of God, who believe in the unseen, keep up the prayer, and give out of what We (God) have provided for them, Q2:2–3

   tilka āyātu al-kitābi al-mubīn – There are the statements of the Scripture that makes things clear, Q26:2

   nazalā bihi al-ruḥū al-amīn. ᶜalā qabika litakūna min al-mundhirīn, bilisānin ᶜarabiyyin mubīn – The trustworthy Spirit (Gabriel) brought it down to your (Muḥammad's) heart, so that you could bring warning in clear Arabic language, Q26:193–195

   where affirmation tools are not employed because the statements address an open-minded audience.

2 Sceptical (mutaraddid): This category of audience is sceptical and undecided about their position whether to accept the speaker's claim (statement) or not. However, their hearts and minds can be won through making the statement slightly affirmed. In other words, because they have not made up their minds, the speaker needs to employ a mid degree of assertiveness, i.e., using one affirmation tool like (inna/anna – indeed), as in:

   anna allāha huwa al-ḥaqqu/annahu yuḥyī al-mawtā/annahu ᶜalā kulli shai'in qadīr/anna al-sāᶜata ātiyatun/anna allāha yabᶜathu manfī al-qubūr – God is the truth/He brings the dead back to life/He has power over everything/Indeed, the last hour is bound to come/Indeed, God will raise the dead from the graves, Q22:6–7

   which is a response to the sceptical audience mentioned in Q22:5 (yā aiyuhā al-nāsu in kuntum fī raibin min al-baᶜthi . . . – O people, if you are in doubt about resurrection . . .) where in sentences 6–7 we have a series of statements using one affirmation particle (anna).

   inna allāha yudāfiᶜu ᶜan alladhīna āmanū – Indeed, God defends those who have believed, Q22:38

where we have the affirmation particle (inna – indeed) because the speaker wants to eliminate any trace of scepticism which may have afflicted the audience.

In Q26:154, the people of Prophet Ṣāliḥ are sceptical of his prophethood. Therefore, their response to him involves the employment of one affirmation tool, which is the exception sentence structure (mā . . . illā – no . . . but): (mā anta illā basharun mithlunā – You are nothing but a man like us).

It is worthwhile to note that, at times, the denier addressee is explicitly specified, as in (yā aiyuhā al-nāsu in kuntum fī raib min al-baᶜth . . . – O people, if you are sceptical about the resurrection . . ., Q22:5) where the expression (raib – in doubt, scepticism) is employed. Thus, we have one affirmation particle (inna – indeed) which occurs in the substantiation part (Q22:5) this is (inna + the plural pronoun merged with it) (innā – Indeed, We (God)).

3 Denier (munkir): This category of audience rejects the speaker's statement and does not accept it as true. The stylistic strategy which the speaker should employ is to use more than one affirmation tool like (inna – indeed), the affirmation /l/ (lām al-tawkīd, meaning 'definitely'), and the detached pronoun (ḍamīr al-faṣl) to rebut the charge made by the deniers and substantiate the speaker's argument, as in:

> inna ᶜadhāba rabbika lawāqiᶜ – Indeed, the punishment of your Lord will definitely occur, Q52:7

where the statement is addressing antagonists who deny resurrection and reward and punishment. Thus, we have a high degree of assertiveness: (inna – indeed) and the affirmation /l/ (i.e., definitely) prefixed to the word (wāqiᶜ) → (lawāqiᶜ – will definitely occur). The high level of assertiveness employed with the denier audience is also encountered in Q36:13–16.

Similarly, the statement: (anna mā yadᶜūna min dūnihi huwa al-bāṭil – Whatever else they invoke is sheer falsehood, Q22:62) refers to a denier audience. Therefore, more affirmation tools are required in the subsequent substantiating statements: (anna allāha huwa al-ᶜaliyyu al-kabīr . . . inna allāha lahuwa al-ghaniyyu al-ḥamīd – It is God who is the most high, the most great . . . Indeed, God is the free of need, the praiseworthy, Q22:62, 64).

3.9.3 Categories of people

This is a faith-based classification of people in the Qur'an. In terms of faith, we encounter the following text receivers:

1 Disbelievers (kāfirūn): This is a major category of Qur'anic text receivers. They can be sub-subclassified into:

i the polytheists (al-mushrikūn): This category of Qur'anic text receivers are deniers (munkirūn) of the Qur'anic intended message, namely, monotheism and Muḥammad's prophethood. The polytheists represent idol worshippers, i.e., believers in different gods. However, they believe in the hereafter. Example: (na^cbudu mā ya^cbudu ābā'unā . . . – We worship what our fathers worshipped, Q11:62). In terms of their cognitive status, the polytheists are deniers.

ii the heretics (al-mulḥidūn): This category of Qur'anic text receivers are deniers (munkirūn) of the Qur'anic intended message, namely, monotheism, Muḥammad's prophethood, eschatology, and reward and punishment. The heretics are not idol worshippers, i.e., they are disbelievers in any god. Example: (qālū mā hiya illā ḥayātunā al-dunyā namutu wanaḥyā wa mā yuhlikunā illā al-dahr – They said: 'There is not but our worldly life; we die and live (i.e., replaced by other people) and nothing destroy us except time', Q45:24). In terms of their cognitive status, the heretics are deniers.

iii the Jews (the Children of Israel – banū isrā'īl, al-yahūd): This category of Qur'anic text receivers are deniers (munkir) of the Qur'anic intended message of monotheism and Muḥammad's prophethood. However, they are believers in eschatology and reward and punishment. In terms of their cognitive status, the Jews are deniers.

iv the Christians (al-naṣārā): This category of Qur'anic text receivers are deniers (munkir) of the Qur'anic intended message of monotheism and Muḥammad's prophethood. However, they are believers in eschatology and reward and punishment. In terms of their cognitive status, the Christians are deniers. Both the Jews and the Christians are Scripturists and are referred to as (ahl al-kitāb – the People of the Book).

v the hypocrites (al-munāfiqūn): This category of Qur'anic text receivers are sceptics (mutaraddid) of the Qur'anic intended message of monotheism and Muḥammad's prophethood, eschatology, and reward and punishment. However, they are not heretical. The hypocrites have a shaky belief in Islam, i.e., they are undecided. In other words, they pretend the belief in the Qur'anic intended message (as a lip service) but are not firm believers. They are described as: (yukhādi^cūna allāh walladhīna āmanū/ fī qulūbihim maraḍun/hum al-mufsidūn/ṣummon bukmun ^cumyun – They deceive God and those who believe/in their hearts is disease/they are the corrupters/deaf, dumb, and blind, Q2:9, 10, 12, 18) and (idhā laqaw alladhīna āmanū qālū āmannā wa'idhā khalaw ilā shayāṭīnihim qālū innā ma^cakum innamā naḥnu mustahzi'ūn – When they meet those who believe, they say: 'We believe', but when they are alone with their evil ones, they say: 'Indeed, we are with you; we are only mockers', Q2:14). The hypocrites are fake believers. Thus, they are considered as Muslims but not believers because (innahum kafarū billāhi warasūlih – They disbelieved in God and His messenger, Q9:84) and they are (ashaddu kufran wanifāqan – They are stronger in disbelief and hypocrisy, Q9:97).

Thus, the hypocrites are described as (rijsun – evil, Q9:95). In terms of their cognitive status, the hypocrites are sceptics.

2 The believers (al-mu'minūn): This category of Qur'anic text receivers are open-minded toward the Qur'anic intended message of monotheism, Muḥammad's prophethood, eschatology, and reward and punishment. In terms of their cognitive status, the believers are open-minded.

3.10 Types of argumentation in Qur'anic discourse

We can identify two types of argumentation (Hatim 1997:39–40). These are discussed in what follows:

1 Through-argumentation: This type of argumentation is initiated by stating own viewpoint (text producer's premise) to be argued through, and there is no explicit reference to an opponent. The format of through-argumentation is:

Thesis to be supported → Substantiation → Conclusion

Example 1

Own thesis cited: yā aiyuhā al-nāsu in kuntum fī raibain min al-baᶜth – O people, if you should be in doubt about the resurrection, Q22:5

Substantiation: innā khalaqnakum min turābin thumma min nutfatin thumma min calaqatin thumma min mudghatin . . . nuqirru fī al-arḥāmi mā nashā' ilā ajalin musammā thumma nukhrijukum ṭiflan thumma litablughū ashuddakum . . . watarā al-arḍa hāmidatan fa'idhā anzalnā ᶜalaihā al-mā'a ihtazzat warabat wa'anbatat min kulli zawjin bahīj – Indeed, We created you from dust, then from a sperm-drop, then from a clinging clot, and then from a lump of flesh, formed and unformed – that We may show you. We settle in the wombs whom We will for a specified term, then We bring you out as a child, and then We develop you that you may reach your time of maturity. Among you is he who is taken in early death, and among you is he who is returned to the most decrepit old age so that he knows nothing, after once having knowledge. You see the earth barren, but when We send down upon it rain, it quivers and swells and grows something of every beautiful kind, Q22:5–6

Conclusion: dhālika bi'anna allāha huwa al-ḥaqqu wa'annahu yuḥyī al-mawtā wa'annahu ᶜalā kulli shai'in qadīr. anna al-sāᶜata ātiyatun lā raiba fīhā wa'anna allāha yabᶜathu man fī al-qubūr – That is because God is the truth and because He gives life to the dead and because He is competent over all things, and that the hour is coming – no doubt about it – and that God will resurrect those in the graves, Q22:6–7

Example 2

law arāda allāhu an yattakhidha waladan laṣṭafā mimmā yakhluqu mā yashā'. subḥānahu. huwa allāhu al-wāḥidu al-qahhār. khalaqa al-samāwāti wal-arḍa bil-ḥaqqi yukawwiru al-laila ᶜalā al-nahār wayukawwiru al-nahāra ᶜalā al-lail wasakhkhara al-shamsa wal-qamar kullun yajrī li'ajalin musammā alā huwa al-ᶜazīz al-ghaffār. khalaqakum min nafsin wāḥidatin thumma jaᶜalā minhā zawjahā wa'anzalā min al-ānᶜami thamāniyata azwāj yakhluqukum fī buṭūni ummahātikum khalqan min baᶜdi khalq fī ẓulumātin thalāth dhālikum allāhu rabbukum lahu al-mulk lā ilāha illā hū fa'annā tuṣrafūn – If God had intended to take a son, He could have chosen from what he creates whatever He willed. He is exalted, the one, the prevailing. He created the heavens and earth in truth. He wraps the night over the day and wraps the day over the night and has subjected the sun and the moon, each running its course for a specified term. Unquestionably, he is the exalted in might, the perpetual forgiver. He created you from one soul. Then, He made from it its mate, and he produced for you from the grazing livestock eight mates. He creates you in the wombs of your mothers, creation after creation, within three darknesses. That is God, your Lord, to Him belongs dominion. There is no deity except Him, so how are you averted?, Q39:4–6

The text producer's thesis in the above example is 'God has no son', i.e., monotheism (Q39:4). In other words, the text producer's thesis is (allāhu al-wāḥidu – God is the one). This is substantiated through the following techniques:

i deductive reasoning: (law arāda allāhu an yattakhidha waladan laṣṭafā mimmā yakhluqu mā yashā' – If God had intended to take a son, He could have chosen from what he creates whatever He willed). God has not chosen from what he has created. Therefore, God has no son.

ii substantiation through the theological expression (subḥānahu – God is exalted). This means God is far above the opponent's false claim that God has a son. This is a rebuttal expression and theologically stands for deanthropomorphism.

iii substantiation through the linguistic mechanism via the employment of the active participle that designates God's epithets: (al-wāḥidu – the one), (al-qahhār – the prevailing), (al-ᶜazīz – the exalted in might), and (al-ghaffār – the perpetual forgiver).

iv substantiation through God's omnipotence details. These include: the creation of the heavens and earth, wrapping of the night around the day, the wrapping of the day around the night, the subjection of the sun and the moon to run their courses for an appointed time, the creation of people from a single being, the creation of the livestock in pairs, the creation of mankind in the womb, and reference to the three-fold depths of darkness.

v substantiation through the linguistic mechanism which is hinged upon the no-main-verb nominal sentence: (dhālikum allāhu rabbukum – That is God, your Lord), (lahu al-mulk – to Him belongs dominion), and (lā ilāha illā hū – There is no deity except Him).

vi substantiation through the interrogative statement: (fa'annā tuṣrafūn – So, how are you averted?), which is a form of sarcasm. The antagonist is ridiculed due to his/her false premise that God has a son.

Conclusion: lā ilāha illā hū – There is no deity except Him.

Example 3

Own thesis cited: tabāraka alladhī nazzala al-furqāna ᶜalā ᶜabdihi liyakūna lil-ᶜālamīna nadhīrā – Blessed is He who sent down the criterion upon His servant that he may be a warner to the worlds, Q25:1

Substantiation: lahu mulku al-samāwāti wal-arḍi/lam yattakhidh waladan/lam yakun lahu sharīkun fī al-mulk/khalaqa kulla shai'in faqaddarahu taqdīrā – He to whom belongs the dominion of the heavens and the earth and who has not taken a son and has not had a partner in dominion and has created each thing and determined it with precise determination, Q25:2

Conclusion: anzalahu alladhī yaᶜlamu al-sirra fī al-samāwāti wal-arḍi – Say, (O Muḥammad): 'It has been revealed by He who knows every secret within the heavens and the earth. Indeed, He is ever forgiving and merciful', Q25:6

Example 4

allāhu khāliqu kulli shai'in wahuwa ᶜalā kulli shai'in wakīl. lahu maqālīdu al-samāwāti wal-arḍ walladhīna kafarū bi'āyāti allāhi ulā'ika hum al-khāsirūn. qul afaghair allāh ta'murūnnī aᶜbudu aiyuhā al-jāhilūn. walaqad ūḥ§iya ilaika wa'ilā alladhīna min qablika la'in ashrakta layaḥbaṭanna ᶜamaluka walatakūnanna min al-khāsirīn. bal allāha faᶜbud wakun min al-shākirīn – God is the creator of all things, and He is, over all things, disposer of affairs. To Him belong the keys of the heavens and the earth. They who disbelieve in the verses of God – it is those who are the losers. Say, (O Muḥammad): 'Is it other than God that you order me to worship, O ignorant ones?' It was already revealed to you and to those before you that if you should associate anything with God, your work would surely become worthless, and you would surely be among the losers. Rather, worship only God and be among the grateful, Q39:62–66

Own thesis cited: allāhu khāliqu kulli shai'in wahuwa ᶜalā kulli shai'in wakīl – God is the creator of all things, and He is, over all things, disposer of affairs, Q39:62

Substantiation: lahu maqālīdu al-samāwāti wal-arḍ walladhīna kafarū bi'āyāti allāhi ulā'ika hum al-khāsirūn. qul afaghair allāh ta'murūnnī aᶜbudu aiyuhā al-jāhilūn. walaqad ūḥiya ilaika wa'ilā alladhīna min qablika la'in ashrakta layaḥbaṭanna camaluka walatakunanna min al-khāsirīn – To Him belong the keys of the heavens and the earth. They who disbelieve in the verses of God – it is those who are the losers. Say, (O Muḥammad): 'Is it other than God that you order me to worship, O ignorant ones?' It was already revealed to you and to those before you that if you should associate anything with God, your work would surely become worthless, and you would surely be among the losers, Q39:63–65

Conclusion: bal allāha faᶜbud wakun min al-shākirīn – Rather, worship only God and be among the grateful, Q39:66

Example 5

Own thesis cited: afattakhadhtum min dūnihi awliyā' – Have you then taken besides Him allies?, Q13:16

Substantiation: lā yamlikūna li'anfusihim nafᶜan walā ḍarran/hal yastawī al-aᶜmā wal-baṣīr?/am hal tastawī al-ẓulumātu wal-nūr?/am jaᶜalū lillāhi shurakā'a khalaqū kakhalqihi fatashābaha al-khalqu ᶜalaihim – Not possessing even for themselves any benefit or any harm/Is the blind equivalent to the seeing?/Or is darkness equivalent to light?/Or have they attributed to God partners who created like His creation so that the creation of each seemed similar to them?, Q13:16

Conclusion: allāhu khāliqu kulli shai'in wahuwa al-wāḥidu al-qahhār – God is the creator of all things, and He is the one, the prevailing, Q13:16

Example 6

Own thesis cited: yaᶜbudū allāha mukhliṣīna lahu al-dīn – They worship God, being sincere to Him in religion, inclining to truth, Q98:5

Substantiation: inna alladhīna kafarū min ahli al-kitābi wal-mushrikīna fī nāri jahannama khālidīna fīhā ūlā'ika hum sharru al-bariyyah. inna alladhīna āmanū waᶜamilū al-ṣāliḥāti ulā'ika hum khairu al-bariyyah. jazā'an ᶜinda rabbihim jannātu ᶜadnin . . . khālidīna fīhā . . . – Indeed, they who disbelieved among the People of the Scripture and the polytheists will be in the fire of hell, abiding eternally therein. Those are the worst of creatures. Indeed, they who have believed and done righteous deeds – those are the best of creatures. Their reward with God will be gardens of perpetual residence . . . wherein they will abide forever, Q98:6–8

Conclusion: dhālika liman khashiya rabbahu – That (i.e., the gardens of perpetual residence) is for whoever has feared his Lord, Q98:8

2 Counter-argumentation: This type of argumentation is initiated by stating an antagonist's viewpoint (thesis, premise), followed by a counter-claim, a rebuttal to substantiate own claim, and finally a conclusion. The format of counter-argumentation is:

Thesis cited to be rebutted → Rebuttal → Substantiation of counter-claim → Conclusion

Example 1

Antagonist's premises: (al-jinnu shurakā' lillāhi – The jinn are partners with God, Q6:100) and (kharaqū banina wabanatin lillāhi – They attributed sons and daughters to God).

Thus, the cognitive status of the antagonist is a denier who rejects monotheism.

Rebuttal to antagonist's premises: Rebuttal to the opponent's premises is cited in the following text segments:

i In Q6:95–99 where God's omnipotence is listed in terms of God's ability in bringing out the living from the dead and the dead from the living, making the dawn break, the creation of the stars, the creation of people, and the sending down of water from the sky.
ii Rebuttal is also cited in Q6:100 (khalaqahum – It was God who created the jinn).
iii In Q6:100 (bighair ᶜilm – without any true knowledge, i.e., the polytheists made the jinn partners with God without any true knowledge, i.e., without any evidence, lack of proof to their premise).
iv In Q6:100 through the theological expression (subḥānahu – Glory be to God) that affirms the oneness of God (monotheism): (subḥānahu wataᶜālā ᶜammā yushrikūn – Glory be to Him! He is far higher than what they ascribe to Him).
v Rebuttal through the no-main-verb nominal sentences (Q6:101–102), which affirm the notion of monotheism: (badīᶜu al-samāwāti wal-arḍ – The creator of the heavens and earth), (huwa bikulli shai'in ᶜalīm – He has full knowledge of all things), (dhālikum allāhu rabbukum – This is God, your Lord), (lā ilāha illā hū – There is no deity except Him), (khāliqu kulli shai'in – The creator of all things), (huwa ᶜalā kulli shai'in wakīl – He is in charge of everything).
vi Rebuttal through the denial interrogative question: (annā yakūnu lahu waladun walam takun lahu ṣāḥibatun – How could God have children when He has no spouse, when He created all things, and He has full knowledge of all things, Q6:101). Conclusion: (khāliqu kulli shai'in faᶜbudūhu huwa ᶜalā kulli shai'in wakīl – The creator of all things. So, worship Him. He is in charge of everything). Thus, the jinn are not in charge of anything.

Example 2

Antagonist's premise: ittakhadha allāhu waladā – God has taken a son, Q10:68

Rebuttal to antagonist's premises: subḥānahu/huwa al-ghaniy/lahu mā fī al-samāwāti wamā fī al-arḍ/in ᶜindakum min sulṭānin bihādhā / ataqūlūna ᶜalā allāhi mā lā taᶜlamūn – He is exalted/He is free of need/To Him belongs whatever is in the heavens and whatever is in the earth/You have no authority for this claim/Do you say about God that which you do not know?, Q10:68

Conclusion: inna alladhīna yaftarūna ᶜalā allāhi al-kadhiba lā yufliḥūn – Indeed, those who invent falsehood about God will not succeed, Q10:69

Example 3

Antagonist's premises: lan nu'mina laka ḥattā tafjura . . . ḥattā tunazzila ᶜalainā kitāban naqra'uhu – We will not believe you until you break open for us . . . until you bring down to us a book we may read, Q17:90–93

Rebuttal to antagonist's premises: subḥāna rabbī hal kuntu illā basharan rasūlā/wamā manaᶜa al-nāsa an yu'minū idh jā'ahum al-hudā illā an qālū abaᶜatha allāhu basharan rasūlā/qul law kāna fī al-arḍi malā'ikatun yamshūna muṭma'innīna lanazzalnā ᶜalaihim min al-samā'i malakan rasūlā – 'Exalted is my Lord! Was I ever but a human messenger?' What prevented the people from believing when guidance came to them except that they said: 'Has God sent a human messenger?' Say: 'If there were upon the earth angels walking securely, We would have sent down to them from the heaven an angel as a messenger', Q17:93–95

The above rebuttal (Q17:93–95) is intertextually backed up by Q34:9:

in nasha' nakhsif bihim al-arḍa aw nusqiṭ ᶜalaihim kisafan min al-samā' – If We should will, We could cause the earth to swallow them or could let fall upon them fragments from the sky, Q34:9

Conclusion: kafā billāhi shahīdan bainī wabainakum/innahu kāna biᶜibādihi khabīran baṣīrā – Sufficient is God as witness between me and you/Indeed He is ever, concerning His servants, acquainted and seeing, Q17:96

Example 4

Antagonist's premise: a'idhā kunnā ᶜiẓāman warufātan a'innā lamabᶜūthūna khalqan jadīdan – When we are bones and crumbled particles, will we truly be resurrected in a new creation?, Q17:98

Rebuttal to opponent's premise: awalam yaraw anna allāha alladhī khalaqa al-samāwāti wal-arḍa qādirun ᶜalā an yakhluqa mithlahum/jaᶜala lahum ajalan lā raiba fīhi – Do they not see that God who created the heavens and earth is able to create the likes of them/He has appointed for them a term about which there is no doubt, Q17:99

Conclusion: abā al-ẓālimūna illā kufūrā – The wrongdoers refuse anything except disbelief, Q17:99

Example 5

Antagonist's premise: ittakhadha al-raḥmānu waladā – The most merciful has taken a son, Q21:26

Rebuttal to antagonist's premises: subḥānahu/bal ᶜibādun mukramūn/lā yasbiqūnahu bil-qawl/hum bi'amrihi yaᶜmalūn/yaᶜlamu mā baina aidīhim wamā khalfahum/lā yashfaᶜūna illā liman irtaḍā/hum min khasyatihi mushfiqūn – He is exalted/They are but honoured servants/They cannot precede Him in word/ They act by His command/He knows what is presently before them and what will be after them/They cannot intercede except on behalf of one whom He approves/They are apprehensive from fear of Him, Q21:26–28

Conclusion: man yaqul minhum innī ilāhun min dūnihi fadhālika najzīhi jahannam – Whoever of them should say: 'Indeed, I am a god besides Him' – that one We would recompense with hell, Q21:29

Example 6

Antagonist's thesis: qāla alladhīna kafarū hal nadullukum ᶜalā rajulin yunabbi'ukum idhā muzziqtum kulla mumazzaqin innakum lafī khalqin jadīd. iftarā ᶜalā allāhi kadhiban am bihi jinnatun – But those who disbelieve say: 'Shall we direct you to a man who will inform you that when you have disintegrated in complete disintegration, you will then be recreated in a new creation? Has he invented about God a lie or is there in him madness?', Q34:7–8

Rebuttal to opponent's thesis: alladhīna lā yu'minūna bil-ākhirāti fī al-ᶜadhābi wal-ḍalāli al-baᶜīd. afalam yaraw ilā mā baina aidīhim wamā khalfahum min al-samā'i wal-arḍi in nasha' nakhsif bihim al-arḍa aw nusqiṭ ᶜalaihim kisfan min al-samā' – Rather, they who do not believe in the hereafter will be in the punishment and are in extreme error. Then, do they not look at what is before them and what is behind them of the heaven and earth? If We should will, We could cause the earth to swallow them or could let fall upon them fragments from the sky, Q34:8–9

Conclusion: inna fī dhālika la'āyatan likulli ᶜabdin munīb – Indeed, in that is a sign for every servant turning back to God, Q34:9

Example 7

We also encounter the opponent's thesis presented, but the rebuttal comprises the consequence to their rejection, i.e., cause and effect argumentation where the opponent's premises cause their fate, as in:

Antagonist's thesis (Cause): qālū innamā anta min al-musaḥḥarīn. wamā anta illā basharan mithlunā wa'in naẓunnuka lamina al-kādhibīn. fasqiṭ ᶜalainā kisfan min al-samā' in kunta min al-ṣādiqīn . . . fakadhdhabūhu – They said: 'You are only of those affected by magic. You are but a man like ourselves, and indeed, we think you are among the liars. So cause to fall upon us fragments of the sky, if you should be of the truthful . . . They denied him', Q26:185–189

Rebuttal to antagonist's thesis (Effect): fa'akhadhahum ᶜadhābu yawmi al-ẓullati innahu kāna ᶜadhaba yawmin ᶜaẓīm. inna fī dhālika la'āyatan wamā kāna aktharuhum mu'minīn. wa'inna rabbaka lahuwa al-ᶜzīz al-raḥīm – So the punishment of the day of the black cloud seized them. Indeed, it was the punishment of a terrible day. Indeed in that is a sign, but most of them were not to be believers. Indeed, your Lord – He is the exalted in might, the merciful, Q26:189–191

Conclusion: fa'akhadhahum ᶜadhābu yawmi al-ẓullāti – the punishment of the day of the black cloud seized them, Q26:189

Example 8

Antagonist's premise: in hiya illā mawtatunā al-ūlā wamā naḥnu bimunsharīn. fa'tū bi'ābā'inā in kuntum ṣādiqīn – There is not but our first death, and we will not be resurrected. Then, bring back our forefathers, if you should be truthful, Q44:35–36

Rebuttal to antagonist's premises: This is achieved through details on reward and punishment in Q44:37–49.

Conclusion: inna hādhā mā kuntum bihi tamtarūn – Indeed, this is what you used to dispute, Q44:50

Example 9

Antagonist's premise: aiyyāna yawmu al-qiyāmah – When will the day of resurrection be?! (i.e., a denial question), Q75:6

Rebuttal to antagonist's premise: This is achieved through God's omnipotence details and antithesis Q75:7–39

Conclusion: alaisa dhālika biqādirin ᶜalā an yuḥyiya al-mawtā – Is not that creator able to give life to the dead, Q75:40

3.11 Summary

An argumentative text involves a protagonist who puts forward a standpoint (opinion) and an antagonist who calls into question the proposed standpoint. In a persuasive argument, the protagonist's main goal is to convince the antagonist of the validity of the opinion put forward to him/her. For an argument to be successful and accepted as valid, the speaker should provide sound evidence, facts, logical reasons, and examples when appropriate. The speaker needs to know what type of audience he/she is addressing and what solutions (such as reward and punishment) he/she can provide. The speaker should be able to appeal to the listener's ethos (the sense of ethics), the pathos (emotions), and the logos (sense of reason, logic).

A premise is a proposition upon which an argument is based or from which a conclusion is drawn. The proof of a conclusion depends on both the truth of the premise(s) and the validity of the argument. The premise is the claim that functions as the reason to accept the main point. The conclusion is the claim that expresses the main point. Unlike English, in Qur'anic argumentation, there are limited indicator words through which the premises and conclusions are flagged. The argument includes:

i a premise (thesis, standpoint, opinion),
ii a rebuttal (to attack and invalidate the antagonist's (opponent's) thesis (opinion) or to substantiate own opinion),
iii affirmation tools, and
iv a conclusion.

The premises are linked with the conclusion through deductive reasoning. Through deductive reasoning, the listener can draw a conclusion. The speaker provides a topos (a topic) to defend or refute (rebut) a premise. In terms of audience (listeners/ readers), we encounter open-minded, sceptic, and denier audiences. Qur'anic discourse provides:

a through-argumentation where the protagonist puts forward his/her premise followed by substantiating details and a conclusion, and
b counter-argumentation where the antagonist's (opponent's) standpoint is cited first in order to be rebutted (attacked) by the protagonist.

4 Ellipsis in Qur'anic discourse

4.1 Introduction

This chapter provides a comprehensive account of the text linguistic mechanism of ellipsis in Qur'anic discourse. A detailed list of examples will be given to illustrate the three types of ellipsis and their pragmatic functions. Among the major ellipsis notions investigated are cataphoric and anaphoric ellipsis, the four pragmatic functions of ellipsis, the major types of ellipsis (nominal ellipsis and verbal ellipsis), clausal ellipsis, the relationship between ellipsis and micro/macro intertextuality, ellipsis and presupposition, and contextual ellipsis. The sentences between brackets () represent non-elliptical (ellipsis-free) sentences and are non-Qur'anic. The presupposed ellipted elements are placed between curly brackets {}.

4.2 What is ellipsis?

Ellipsis is a Greek word meaning 'to leave out'. Thus, ellipsis is related to any word or phrase omitted from the sentence in order to avoid redundancy and produce an effective text structure. Ellipsis is a cohesive device which has a lexico-grammatical relation in which a word or a phrase is specified through the use of a grammatical signal, indicating that this word or phrase is to be recovered from what has gone before, i.e., to be retrieved from the preceding text (Halliday and Hasan 1976:308; Salkie 1995:57). In other words, ellipsis is the leaving out of a word or a phrase instead of repeating the same word or phrase. Thus, there is a gap, but as readers, we can make sense of the ellipted (left out) items through the background information which we derive from the same, i.e., the previous, text or from the subsequent text we are reading. Therefore, ellipsis is a form of anaphoric and cataphoric cohesion where we presuppose something by means of what is implied or unsaid.

Ellipsis is a form of presupposition. In other words, it is a tool to specify someone/something through referring it to someone/something:

i that has already been mentioned in the previous text (statement). Thus, ellipsis is anaphoric,
ii that is known to the reader/hearer. Thus, ellipsis is based on presupposition,

iii that the reader/hearer can recover it (someone/something) from the following text. Thus, ellipsis is cataphoric, and
iv that the reader is able to recover someone/something through intertextuality. Thus, ellipsis is either anaphoric or cataphoric, i.e., depending on the position of the ellipsis-based sentence within the Qur'anic text.

Based on these reasons, we will understand why ellipsis contributes to the semantic structure of the text (discourse). It is worthwhile to note that ellipsis is somewhat similar to substitution because both involve referring to someone/something that has been mentioned earlier in the previous text. Whereas in substitution a particular word refers, in ellipsis there is a 'gap' in the text. It is this 'gap' that refers to someone/something in the previous text (Salkie 1995:57). For Beaugrande and Dressler (1981:66), ellipsis is a cohesive device that contributes to the text's compactness and efficiency.

In Chapter 6, Section 6.5.5.2, we have claimed that reiterating (repeating) a word or a phrase (lexical repetition) is a cohesive mechanism in discourse. We can also claim that leaving out a word or a phrase (ellipsis) is another cohesive mechanism in discourse. Throughout the present discussion, the position of the ellipted element(s) will be indicated by curly brackets {}.

4.2.1 *Anaphoric ellipsis*

Anaphoric ellipsis takes place when the context sentence from which our presupposed meaning of the ellipted element is retrieved occurs first followed by the elliptical sentence (a sentence which involves ellipsis), as in:

> a'idhā mitnā wakunnā turāban waᶜiẓāman a'innā lā mabᶜūthūn? awa'ābā'unā al-awwalūn? qul naᶜam {} wa'antum dākhirūn – When we have died and become dust and bones, are we indeed to be resurrected? And our forefathers as well? Say: 'Yes, {} and you will be rendered contemptible', Q37:16–18.

The context sentence is (a'idhā mitnā wakunnā turāban waᶜiẓāman a'innā lā mabᶜūthūn? – When we have died and become dust and bones, are we indeed to be resurrected?, Q37:16). This is followed by the elliptical sentence (qul naᶜam {} wa'antum dākhirūn – Say: 'Yes, and you will be rendered contemptible', Q37:18). The ellipted element in Q37:18 is a verb {tubᶜathūn – to be resurrected} which is retrieved from (mabᶜūthūn – resurrected, Q37:16) that has occurred in the previous context sentence. The position of the ellipted verb {tubᶜathūn} comes after the response word (naᶜam – yes).

> a'idhā mitnā wakunnā turāban waᶜiẓāman a'innā lā mabᶜūthūn? → context sentence
>
> qul naᶜam {} wa'antum dākhirūn → elliptical sentence

Thus, to rewrite the elliptical sentence Q37:18, we get an ellipsis-free sentence:

> (a'idhā mitnā wakunnā turāban wᵃciẓāman a'innā lā mabᶜūthūn? awa'ābā'unā al-awwalūn? qul naᶜam {tubᶜathūn} wa'antum dākhirūn – When we have died and become dust and bones, are we indeed to be resurrected? And our forefathers as well? Say: 'Yes, {you will be resurrected} and you will be rendered contemptible', Q37:16–18).

Another example of anaphoric ellipsis is Q75:3, which is the context sentence from which we can retrieve our presupposed elliptical element that has occurred in the elliptical sentence which is Q75:4 as explained here:

> ayaḥsabu al-insānu allan najmaᶜa ᶜiẓāmahu? balā {} qādirīna ᶜalā an nusawiya banānahu – Does man think that We will not assemble his bones? Yes, {} we are able to proportion his fingertips, Q75:3–4.
>
> ayaḥsabu al-insānu allan najmaᶜa ᶜiẓāmahu? → context sentence
>
> balā {} qādirīna ᶜalā an nusawiya banānahu → elliptical sentence

Through the context sentence (Q75:3), we can retrieve the presupposed ellipted element {najmaᶜuhā – to assemble them (i.e., the bones)}. The position of the ellipted element in the elliptical sentence Q75:4 is after the response word (balā – yes), which signals an ellipted verb. The verb (najmaᶜu – to assemble), which has occurred in the context sentence, has made possible for the reader/listener to provide the meaning of the ellipted element.

Thus, to rewrite the elliptical sentence Q75:4, we get an ellipsis-free sentence:

> (balā {najmaᶜuhā} qādirīna ᶜalā an nusawiya banānahu – Yes, {We will assemble them (the bones)} and we are able to proportion his fingertips, Q75:4).

4.2.2 Cataphoric ellipsis

Within the Qur'anic text, cataphoric ellipsis occurs when the elliptical sentence (a sentence which involves ellipsis) occurs first followed by a sentence which is either immediately after the elliptical sentence or in a far-away place in the same macro text. In other words, the following sentence that comes after the elliptical sentence constitutes the context for the retrieval of the presupposed meaning of the ellipted element, as in:

> {} ṣummon bukmun ᶜumyun – Deaf, dumb and blind, Q2:18.
> walā taḥsabanna alladhīna qutilū fī sabīl allāh amwātan bal {} aḥyā' ᶜinda rabbihim yurzaqūn – And never think of those who have been killed in the cause of God as dead. Rather, {} are alive with their Lord, receiving provision, Q3:169.

waqālū ittakhadha al-raḥmānu waladan subḥānahu bal {} ᶜibādun mukramūn – And they say: 'The Most Merciful has taken a son' Exalted is He. Rather honoured servants, Q21:26.
waqālat {} ᶜajūzun ᶜaqīm – And said: 'A barren old woman', Q51:29.
{} nārun ḥāmiyah – A fire, intensely hot, Q101:11.
{} nāru allāhi al-mūqadah – {} The fire of God, fueled, Q104:6.

The ellipted personal pronouns in the above elliptical sentences are:

({hum} ṣummon bukmun ᶜumyun – {They} are deaf, dumb and blind, Q2:18).
(. . . {hum} aḥyā' ᶜinda . . . – . . . Rather {they} are alive with . . ., Q3:169).
(. . . {hum} ᶜibādun mukramūn – . . . {they} are honoured servants, Q21:26).
(. . . {anā} ᶜajūz ᶜaqīm – . . . {I} am a barren old woman, Q51:29).
({hiya} narun . . . – {It} is a fire . . ., Q101:11).
({hiya} narun . . . – {It} is the fire of . . ., Q104:6).
{} fī sidrin makhḍūd – {The companions of the right} are among lote trees with thorns removed, Q56:28.
{aṣḥābu al-yamīn} fī sidrin makhḍūd – {The companions of the right} are among lote trees with thorns removed, Q56:28.
{} fajā'athu iḥdāhumā tamshī ᶜalā istiḥyā' – {} Then one of the two women came to him walking with shyness, Q28:25.

Our presupposition about the ellipted information is based on the context of Q28:25. The context is about Moses when he was in Midian, the two women who wanted to water their flocks but could not because of a crowd of men watering their flocks, and their father. Thus, we presuppose the ellipted details as: {fadhahabatā ilā abīhimā waqaṣṣatā ᶜalaihi mā jarā maᶜa mūsā wamusāᶜadathu lahumā fa'arsalā al-abu ibnatahu ilā mūsā – The two girls went back home to their father and told him of Moses' assistance to them. The father sent his daughter to Moses}. Thus, putting the presupposed ellipted information, we get: ({fadhahabatā ilā abīhimā waqaṣṣatā ᶜalaihi mā jarā maᶜa mūsā wamusāᶜadathu lahumā fa'arsalā al-abu ibnatahu ilā mūsā} fajā'athu iḥdāhumā tamshī ᶜalā istiḥyā' – {The two girls went back home to their father and told him of Moses' assistance to them. The father sent his daughter to Moses}. Then one of the two women came to him walking with shyness).

Cataphoric ellipsis can occur sentence-initially and represents verbal ellipsis where the verb {idhkur – remember (imperative, second person masculine)} is the presupposed meaning. The particle (idh – when) signals this form of ellipsis, as in:

{} idh qāla rabbuka lil-malā'ikāti – {} when your Lord said to the angels, Q2:30.
{} idh yamkuru bika – {} when plotted against you, Q8:30.
{} idh yaḥkumān fī al-ḥarth – {} when they judged concerning the field, Q21:78.

To bring back the ellipted verbal element, we get:

> ({idhkur} idh qāla rabbuka lil-malā'ikāti – {Remember} when your Lord said to the angels, Q2:30).
> ({idhkur} idh yamkuru bika – {Remember} when plotted against you, Q8:30).
> ({idhkhur} idh yaḥkumān fī al-ḥarth – {Remember} when they judged concerning the field, Q21:78).

4.3 Pragmatic functions of ellipsis

In Qur'anic discourse, ellipsis is employed for different perlocutionary effects, such as (i) warning, (ii) specification, (iii) rebuke, and (iv) glorification.

4.3.1 Ellipsis for warning

Ellipsis also takes place when the ellipted element designates the pragmatic function of warning (al-taḥdhīr wal-takhwīf). For instance, the ellipted verb (verbal ellipsis) in the imperative form (ihdhar – Beware!, i.e., I warn you) signals the illocutionary force of a serious warning whose defiance leads to destruction, as in:

> faqāla lahum rasūl allāh {} nāqata allāhi wasuqyāhā – The messenger of God said to them: '{} The she-camel of God or her drink', Q91:13.

Based on macro level intertextuality (Q7:73), the presupposed meaning of the ellipted element is {iḥdharū – be warned!}, which signifies a warning meaning (dharū – leave her alone (i.e., do not kill her)). Thus, we get (faqāla lahum rasūl allāh {iḥdharū} nāqata allāhi wasuqyāhā – The messenger of God said to them: '{Be warned} about the she-camel of God and about her drink', Q91:13).

> qāla hādhihi nāqatun lahā shirbun walakum shirbu yawmin ma^clūm wa {} lā tamassūhā bisū'in faya'khudhakum ^cadhābu yawmin ^caẓīm – He said: 'This is a she-camel. For her is a drink, and for you is a drink on a known day. {} Do not touch her with harm lest you be seized by the punishment of a terrible day', Q26:155–156.

When we put back the ellipted elements in Q26:155–156, we get:

> (qāla hādhihi nāqatun lahā shirbun walakum shirbu yawmin ma^clūm wa {iḥdharū} lā tamassūhā bisū'in faya'khudhakum ^cadhābu yawmin ^caẓīm – He said: 'This is a she-camel. For her is a drink, and for you is a drink on a known day. And {be warned} not to touch her with harm lest you be seized by the punishment of a terrible day', Q26:155–156).

where the presupposed ellipted meaning is {iḥdharū – be warned!} as a warning to the people of Prophet Ṣāliḥ. This meaning of the ellipted verb (verbal ellipsis) is based on macro text intertextuality represented by Q7:78 and Q91:14 as explained here:

> fa'akhadhathum al-rajfatu fa'aṣbaḥū fī dārihim jāthimīn – So the earthquake seized them, and they became within their home corpses fallen prone, Q7:78.
>
> fakadhdhabūhu fa^caqarūhā fadamdama ^calaihim rabbuhum bidhanbihim fasawwāhā – But they denied him and killed her. So their Lord brought down upon them destruction for their sin and made them equal in destruction, Q91:14.

4.3.2 Ellipsis for specification

The ellipted element can also designate the pragmatic function of specification (al-ikhtiṣāṣ or al-takhṣīṣ). For instance, the ellipted verb (verbal ellipsis), which is (aᶜnī – I mean, specifically, or i.e.), signals the illocutionary force of specifying a given meaning, as in:

> qālū ataᶜjabīna min amri allāh raḥmatu allāhi wabarakātuhu ᶜalaikum {} ahla al-baiti – They said: 'Are you amazed at the decree of God? May the mercy of God and His blessings be upon you {}, people of the home', Q11:73.
> wa'ātainā mūsā al-kitāba wajaᶜalnāhu hudan libanī isrā'īla allā tattakhidhū min dūnī wakīlā {} dhurriyyata man ḥamalnā maᶜa nūḥ – We gave Moses the Scripture and made it a guidance for the Children of Israel that you not take other than Me as Disposer of affairs {} O descendants of those We carried with Noah, Q17:2–3.
> innamā yurīdu allāhu liyudhhiba ᶜankum al-rijsa {} ahla al-baiti – God intends only to remove from you the impurity {} O people of the household, Q33:33.
> inna al-abrāra yashrabūna min ka'sin kāna mizājuhā kāfurā {} ᶜainan yashrabu bihā ᶜibādu allāhi – Indeed, the righteous will drink from a cup whose mixture is of kāfūr {}. A spring of which the servants of God will drink, Q76:5–6.

where the presupposed meaning of the ellipted word is {(aᶜnī – I mean, specifically, or i.e.)}. Thus, we get:

> qālū ataᶜjabīna min amri allāh raḥmatu allāhi wabarakātuhu ᶜalaikum {aᶜnī} ahla al-baiti – They said: 'Are you amazed at the decree of God? May the mercy of God and His blessings be upon you {I mean} the people of the home', Q11:73.
> wa'ātainā mūsā al-kitāba wajaᶜalnāhu hudan libanī isrā'īla allā tattakhidhū min dūnī wakīlā {aᶜnī} dhurriyyata man ḥamalnā maᶜa nūḥ – We gave Moses the Scripture and made it a guidance for the Children of Israel that you not take other than Me as Disposer of affairs. {I mean} the descendants of those We carried with Noah, Q17:2–3.
> innamā yurīdu allāhu liyudhhiba ᶜankum al-rijsa {aᶜnī} ahla al-baiti – God intends only to remove from you the impurity. {I mean} the people of the household, Q33:33.

> inna al-abrāra yashrabūna min ka'sin kāna mizājuhā kāfūrā {aᶜnī} ᶜainan yashrabu bihā ᶜibādu allāhi – Indeed, the righteous will drink from a cup whose mixture is of kāfūr {I mean} a spring of which the servants of God will drink, Q76:5–6.

For this reason, the verb {aᶜnī} has made the noun (ahla – the people of) in Q11:73 and Q33:33, the noun (dhurriyyata – the descendants of) in Q17:3, and the noun (ᶜainan – a spring) in Q76:6 in the accusative case objects.

4.3.3 Ellipsis for rebuke

Ellipsis in Qur'anic discourse takes place for the illocutionary force of rebuke, as in:

> {} imra'atu al-ᶜazīzi turāwidu fatāhā ᶜan nafsih – {} The wife of the governor is seeking to seduce her slave, Q12:30.

where the interrogative particle {a} is ellipted and whose position is at the beginning of Q12:30.

> ({a} imra'atu al-ᶜazīzi turāwidu fatāhā ᶜan nafsih? – Is the wife of the governor seeking to seduce her slave?).

The ellipsis of the interrogative particle {a} is to achieve the illocutionary force of rebuke and astonishment through the elliptical statement: (imra'atu al-ᶜazīzi turāwidu fatāhā ᶜan nafsih – The wife of the governor is seeking to seduce her slave, Q12:30). In other words, the pragmatic functions of rebuke and astonishment will not be achieved if the interrogative particle {a} is employed.

4.3.4 Ellipsis for glorification

The illocutionary force of glorifying the Lord is achieved through the ellipsis of the vocative particle (yā – O) called (al-nidā' – exclamation). The vocative sentence structure does not indicate a command or an order by the speaker to the addressee. Thus, a vocative sentence with (yā) does not lack tact or thoughtfulness on the interpersonal communication level between the Lord and the human addressee. The vocative particle (yā) has been used in Qur'anic discourse several times, as in (yā aiyuhā alladhīna āmanū – O you who have believed, Q2:153), (yā banī isrā'īl – O Children of Israel, Q2:122), and (yā aiyuhā al-nāssu – O mankind, Q2:21). However, on the interpersonal textual level, to demonstrate the intimate relationship with the Lord, the human speaker takes out the vocative (yā) to achieve the illocutionary force of glorification of the Lord, as in:

> {yā} rabbanā akhrijnā min hādhihi al-qaryāti al-ẓālimi ahluhā – {O} our Lord take us out of this city of oppressive people, Q4:75.
>
> qālat {yā} rabbī innī ẓalamtu nafsī – She said: '{O} my Lord, indeed I have wronged myself', Q27:44.

where the human speaker appeals to his/her Lord using an elliptical sentence structure that does not include the vocative particle {yā} in order to achieve the pragmatic purpose of glorifying the Lord and depicting the intimate relationship with God.

Similarly, on the interpersonal level of communication, the ellipsis of the vocative particle {yā} is used to demonstrate humbleness on the part of the human speaker towards his/her Lord, as in:

> {} rabbī lā tadharnī fardan – {} My Lord, do not leave me alone, Q21:89.
>
> qāla {} rabbī ighfir lī wahab lī mulkan – He said: '{} My Lord, forgive me and grant me a kingdom', Q38:35.

where the speakers (Zachariah in Q21:89 and Solomon in Q38:35) leave out the vocative particle {yā} to achieve the illocutionary force of humbleness towards their Lord.

4.4 Types of ellipsis

In Qur'anic Arabic, we encounter three types of ellipsis: (i) nominal ellipsis, (ii) verbal ellipsis, and (iii) clausal ellipsis.

4.4.1 Nominal ellipsis

Nominal ellipsis is concerned with the leaving out of either (i) a personal pronoun, (ii) a noun, or (iii) an adjective.

i Ellipsis of a personal pronoun: Examples of nominal ellipsis where the personal pronoun is left out are:

> {} ṣummun bukmun ᶜumyun – Deaf, dumb and blind, Q2:18
>
> walā taḥsabanna alladhīna qutilū fī sabīl allāh amwātan bal {} aḥyā' ᶜinda rabbihim yurzaqūn – Never think of those who have been killed in the cause of God as dead. Rather, {} are alive with their Lord, receiving provision, Q3:169
>
> waqālū ittakhādhā al-raḥmānu waladan subḥānahu bal {} ᶜibādun mukramūn – They say: 'The Most Merciful has taken a son' Exalted is He. Rather honoured servants, Q21:26
>
> waqālat {} ᶜajūzun ᶜaqīm – She said: 'A barren old woman', Q51:29
>
> {} nārun ḥāmiyah – A fire, intensely hot, Q101:11
>
> {} nāru allāhi al-mūqadah – {} The fire of God, fueled, Q104:6

The ellipted personal pronouns in the above elliptical sentences are:

> {hum} ṣummun bukmun ᶜumyun – {They} are deaf, dumb and blind, Q2:18
>
> walā taḥsabanna alladhīna qutilū fī sabīl allāh amwātan bal {hum} aḥyā' ᶜinda rabbihim yurzaqūn – Never think of those who have been killed in

the cause of God as dead. Rather, {they} are alive with their Lord, receiving provision, Q3:169

waqālū ittakhadha al-raḥmānu waladan subḥānahu bal {hum} ᶜibādun mukramūn – They say: 'The Most Merciful has taken a son' Exalted is He. Rather {they} are honoured servants, Q21:26

waqālat {anā} ᶜajūzun ᶜaqīm – She said: '{I} am a barren old woman', Q51:29

{hiya} nārun ḥāmiyah – {It (she, referring to the fire (a feminine noun))} is a fire, intensely hot, Q101:11

{hiya} nāru allāhi al-mūqadah – {It (she, referring to the fire (a feminine noun))} is the fire of God, fueled, Q104:6

ii Ellipsis of a noun: Examples of nominal ellipsis where the noun is left out are:

awakullamā ᶜāhadū {} ᶜahdan nabadhahu farīqun minhum – Is it not that every time they took a covenant {} a party of them threw it away?, Q2:100

was'al {} al-qaryata – And ask {} the city, Q12:82

kallā idhā balaghat {} al-tarāqī – No! When {} has reached the collar bones, Q75:26

ḥāṭṭā tawārat {} bil-ḥijāb – Until {} disappeared into the curtain of darkness, Q38:32

wajaᶜala lakum sarābīla taqīkum al-ḥarra {} – And He has made for you garments which protect you from the heat {}, Q16:81

qāla faman rabbukumā yā mūsā {}? – He said: 'So who is the Lord of you two, O Moses {}?', Q20:49

wal-rāsikhūna fī al-ᶜilmi yaqūlūna {} āmannā bihi – But those firm in knowledge say:

{} 'We believe in it', Q3:7

{} fī sidrin makhḍūd – {} Among lote trees with thorns removed, Q56:28

fa'atāhum {} allāhu min ḥaithu lam yaḥtasibū – {} God came upon them from where they had not expected, Q59:2

man ᶜamila ṣāliḥan fa {} linafsih waman asā'a faᶜalaihā – Whoever does righteousness, {} is for his soul, and whoever does evil does so against it, Q41:46

The ellipted nouns in the above elliptical sentences are:

awakullamā ᶜāhadū {allaha} ᶜahdan nabadhahu farīqun minhum – Is it not that every time they took a covenant with {God} a party of them threw it away?, Q2:100

was'al {ahl} al-qaryata – And ask {the people} of the city, Q12:82

kallā idhā balaghat {al-rūḥu/al-nafsu} al-tarāqī – No! When {the soul} has reached the collar bones, Q75:26

ḥāṭṭā tawārat {al-shamsu} bil-ḥijāb – Until {the sun} disappeared into the curtain of darkness, Q38:32

waja^c^ala lakum sarābīla taqīkum al-ḥarra {wal-bard} – And He has made for you garments which protect you from the heat {and the cold}, Q16:81

qāla faman rabbukumā yā mūsā {wa hārūn}? – He said: 'So who is the Lord of you two, O Moses {and Aaron}?', Q20:49

wal-rāsikhūna fī al-^c^ilmi yaqūlūna {rabbanā} āmannā bihi – But those firm in knowledge say: '{Our Lord} we believe in it', Q3:7

{aṣḥābu al-yamīn} fī sidrin makhḍūd – {The companions of the right} are among lote trees with thorns removed, Q56:28

fa'atāhum {amru} allāhi min ḥaithu lam yaḥtasibū – {The decree} of God came upon them from where they had not expected, Q59:2

man ^c^amila ṣāliḥan fa {^c^amalahu} linafsih waman asā'a fa^c^alaihā – Whoever does righteousness, {his work} is for his soul, and whoever does evil does so against it, Q41:46

Let us compare the ellipsis that has taken place in Q16:24 and Q16:30:

idhā qīla lahum mādhā anzala rabbukum qālū {} asāṭīru al-awwalīn – When it is said to them: 'What has your Lord sent down?' They say: '{} legends of the former people', Q16:24

In Q16:24, we have nominal ellipsis. The ellipted element is the subject pronoun {huwa – it (i.e., the Qur'an)}. Thus we can have the following non-ellipted sentence:

(idhā qīla lahum mādhā anzala rabbukum qālū {huwa} asāṭīru al-awwalīn – When it is said to them: 'What has your Lord sent down?' They say: '{It} is the legends of the former people').

This is because (asāṭīru – legends, fables) is in the nominative case (marfū^c^); thus, we cannot have an ellipted verb (anzala – to send down). This is because if we assume a verb, we should have (asāṭīra) in the accusative case (manṣūb), and this is not allowed since the meaning will dramatically change. Thus, the ellipsis in Q16:24 above is nominal.

However, the ellipsis in Q16:30 is verbal:

qīla lilladhīna ittaqaw mādhā anzala rabbukum qālū {} khairan – It will be said to those who feard God: 'What did your Lord send down?' They will say: 'Good', Q16:30

The ellipsis in Q16:30 is verbal because the ellipted element is a verb {anzala – to send down} whose object noun (khairan – good) is in the accusative case where we have an ellipted verb (verbal ellipsis) → (anzala) after the word (qālū – they said) and the word (khairan – good) is in the accusative case due to the ellipted verb. The non-ellipted sentence is:

(qīla lilladhīna ittaqaw mādhā anzala rabbukum qālū {anzala} khairan – It will be said to those who feard God: 'What did your Lord send down?' They will say: '{He sent down} Good') where (anzala) is a verb.

iii Ellipsis of an adjective: Examples of nominal ellipsis where the adjective is left out are:

(wakam min qaryatin {} ahlaknāhā – And how many {} cities have We destroyed, Q7:4).

(huwa alladhī ja^c^ala lakum al-laila {} litaskunū fīhi wal-nahāra mubṣirā – It is He who made for you the night {} to rest therein and the day giving sight, Q10:67).

(wakāna warā'ahum malikun {} ya'khudhu kulla safīnatin ghaṣbā – There was after them a {} king who seized every ship by force, Q18:79).

The ellipted adjectives in the above elliptical sentences are:

wakam min qaryatin {ẓālimatin} ahlaknāhā – And how many {unjust} cities have We destroyed, Q7:4

huwa alladhī ja^c^ala lakum al-laila {muẓliman} litaskunū fīhi wal-nahāra mubṣiran – It is He who made for you the night {dark} to rest therein and the day giving sight, Q10:67

wakāna warā'ahum malikun {ẓālimun} ya'khudhu kulla safīnatin ghaṣbā – There was after them an {unjust} king who seized every ship by force, Q18:79

4.4.2 Verbal ellipsis

Verbal ellipsis is concerned with the deletion of a main verb. However, it is worthwhile to note that the Arabic verb includes an implicit subject like (qāma – He stood up), and that we may encounter a verbal construction including an object, like (sa'alahum – He asked them). Having said that, we have treated such grammatical examples as instances of verbal ellipsis for the sake of the argument concerning verbal ellipsis, i.e., ignoring the implicit subject and the attached object pronoun. Therefore, verbal ellipsis in Qur'anic Arabic should be distinguished from clausal ellipsis discussed in Section 4.4.3 below. Verbal ellipsis in Qur'anic discourse is illustrated by the following examples:

Example 1

wa'idh istasqā mūsā liqawmihi faqulnā aḍrib bi^c^aṣāka al-ḥajar {} fanfajarat minhu ithnatā ^c^ashrata ^c^ainan – When Moses prayed for water for his people, so We said: 'Strike the stone with your staff. {} And there gushed forth from it twelve springs', Q2:60.

where the presupposed meaning of the ellipted element is {daraba – to strike}. Thus, we get the following ellipsis-free sentence:

(wa'idh istasqā mūsā liqawmihi faqulnā aḍrib biᶜaṣāka al-ḥajar {faḍaraba} fanfajarat minhu ithnatā ᶜashrata ᶜainan – And when Moses prayed for water for his people, so We said: 'Strike the stone with your staff. {And he struck} and there gushed forth from it twelve springs', Q2:60). The same applies to Q26:63.

Example 2

wa'idh yaḍaᶜu ibrāhīmu al-qawāᶜida min al-baiti wa'ismāᶜīlu {} rabbanā taqabbal minnā – And when Abraham was raising the foundations of the house and Ishmael. {} 'Our Lord accept this from us', Q2:127.

where the ellipted element in Q2:127 is the active participle {qā'ilīn – saying}. Thus, to retrieve the ellipted verb and put it back in the above elliptical sentence, we get:

(wa'idh yaḍaᶜu ibrāhīmu al-qawāᶜida min al-baiti wa'ismāᶜīlu {qā'ilīn} rabbanā taqabbal minnā – When Abraham was raising the foundations of the house and Ishmael. {Saying}: 'Our Lord accept this from us', Q2:127).

Example 3

alladhīna yadhkurūna allāha qiyāman waquᶜūdan . . . {} rabbanā mā khalaqta hādhā bāṭilan – Who remember God while standing or sitting . . . {} 'Our Lord, You did not create this aimlessly', Q3:191.

where the presupposed ellipted element is the verb {yaqūlūna – they say}. Thus, we get:

(alladhīna yadhkurūna allāha qiyāman waquᶜūdan . . . {yaqūlūna} rabbanā mā khalaqta hādhā bāṭilan – Who remember God while standing or sitting . . . {They say}: 'Our Lord, You did not create this aimlessly', Q3:191).

Example 4

wal-malā'ikatu yadkhulūna ᶜalaihim min kulli bāb {} salamūn ᶜalaikum – And the angels will enter upon them from every gate {}: 'Peace be upon you', Q13:23–24.

where the presupposed ellipted element is the active participle {qā'ilīn – saying}. Thus, we get the following non-ellipted sentence:

(wal-malā'ikatu yadkhulūna ᶜalaihim min kulli bāb {qā'ilīn} salamūn ᶜalaikum – And the angels will enter upon them from every gate. {Saying}: 'Peace be upon you', Q13:23–24).

Example 5

> qīla lilladhīna ittaqaw mādhā anzalā rabbukum qālū {} khairan – It will be said to those who feard God: 'What did your Lord send down?' They will say: 'Good', Q16:30.

where we have an ellipted verb (verbal ellipsis) {anzala – send down} after the word (qālū) and the word (khairan) is in the accusative case due to the presupposed ellipted verb: (qīla lilladhīna ittaqaw mādhā anzala rabbukum qālū {anzala} khairan – It will be said to those who feard God: 'What did your Lord send down?' They will say: 'Good' {was sent down}, Q16:30).

Example 6

> fa'aqim wajhaka lil-dīni ḥanīfan {} fiṭrata allāhi allatī faṭara al-nāsa ᶜalaihā – So direct your face toward the religion inclining to truth. {} The natural disposition of God which He has instilled in people, Q30:30.

The presupposed meaning of the ellipted word is the imperative verb {alzimū – adhere to} or {ittabiᶜū – follow}. Thus, the ellipsis-free sentence is:

> (fa'aqim wajhaka lil-dīni ḥanīfan {alzimū} fiṭrata allāhi allatī faṭara al-nāsa ᶜalaihā – So direct your face toward the religion inclining to truth. {Adhere} to the natural disposition of God which He has instilled in people, Q30:30).

This is backed up by the grammatical fact that the noun (fiṭrata) is in the accusative case acting as an object of the ellipted verb {alzimū}.

It is worthwhile to note that the ellipsis-free sentence syntactic structure needs to be altered in some cases of verbal ellipsis, as in:

> fa'idhā laqītum alladhīna kafarū fa {} ḍarba al-riqāb – So when you meet those who disbelieve, {} strike necks, Q47:4.

after we have included the ellipted verb {aḍrib – strike (in the imperative form)}, we get the following slightly different grammatical pattern due to the addition of the verb:

> (fa'idhā laqītum alladhīna kafarū fa {aḍrib} ḍarba al-riqāb – So when you meet those who disbelieve, {strike} their necks in a striking way, Q47:4) where (ḍarba – striking) is a nominalized noun (maṣdar) in the accusative case because it is the object of the ellipted verb {ḍaraba – to strike}.

Similarly:

> innā zaiyannā al-samā'a al-dunyā bizīnatin al-kawākib wa {} ḥifẓan min kulli shaiṭānin mārid – Indeed, We have adorned the nearest heaven with an adornment of stars. And {} as protection against every rebellious devil, Q37:6–7.

after we have included the ellipted verb {ḥafaẓa – to protect}, we get the following slightly different grammatical pattern due to the addition of the verb:

> (innā zaiyannā al-samā'a al-dunyā bizīnatin al-kawākib wa {ḥafaẓnāhā} ḥifẓan min kulli shaiṭānin mārid – Indeed, We have adorned the nearest heaven with an adornment of stars. And {protected it} as protection against every rebellious devil, Q37:6–7) where (ḥifẓan – protection) is a nominalized noun (maṣdar) in the accusative case because it is the object of the ellipted verb {ḥafaẓa – protect}.

The same applies to Q30:6 where the presupposed ellipted verb is {waᶜada – to promise} whose direct object in the accusative case is the nominalized noun (waᶜd – a promise). Thus the grammatical structure of Q30:6 will be changed to: (waᶜada allāhu waᶜdan – God promised a promise).

4.4.2.1 Observations on verbal ellipsis

Having discussed verbal ellipsis, we can make the following observations about its most common environment:

1 Verbal ellipsis occurs in WH-questions (Yes/No questions) whose answer is (naᶜam/balā – yes) after which the presupposed ellipted element occurs, as in:

> qāla awalam tu'min? qāla balā {} walākin liyaṭma'inna qalbī – God said: 'Have you not believed?' Abraham said: 'Yes, {} only that my heart may be satisfied', Q2:260

where the presupposed meaning of the ellipted verbal element is (āmantu – believe). Thus, we get the following ellipsis-free sentence:

> (qāla awalam tu'min? qāla balā {āmantu} walākin liyaṭma'inna qalbī – God said: 'Have you not believed?' Abraham said: 'Yes, {I believed} only that my heart may be satisfied', Q2:260).

Another example of verbal ellipsis is encountered in Q7:44:

> wanādā aṣḥābu al-jannaati aṣḥāba al-nāri an qad wajadnā mā waᶜadanā rabbunā ḥaqqan fahal wajadtum mā waᶜada rabbukum ḥaqqan? qālū naᶜam – The companions of paradise will call out to the companions of the fire: 'We have already found what our Lord promised us to be true. Have you found what your Lord promised to be true?' They will say: 'Yes', Q7:44

An elliptical verbal group presupposes one or more words from a previous verbal group (Halliday and Hasan 1976:167). In other words, in the verbal group, there is only the verb itself like (wajada – to find) in the embedded question (hal wajadtum mā waᶜada rabbukum ḥaqqan? qālū naᶜam {wajadnā mā waᶜadanā rabbunā ḥaqqan} – Have you found what your Lord promised to be true? They will say: 'Yes, we have found what our Lord promised us to be true') of the above example.

> a'idhā mitnā wakunnā turāban waᶜiẓāman a'innā lā mabᶜūthūn? awa'ābā'unā al-awwalūn? qul naᶜam {} wa'antum dākhirūn – When we have died and become dust and bones, are we indeed to be resurrected? And our forefathers as well? Say: 'Yes, {} and you will be rendered contemptible', Q37:16–18

where the ellipted element which is a verb {tubᶜathūn – to be resurrected} is retrieved from (mabᶜūthūn – resurrected, Q37:16). The position of the ellipted verb {tubᶜathūn} comes after the response word (naᶜam – yes). Thus, to rewrite Q37:18, we get an ellipsis-free sentence:

> (a'idhā mitnā wakunnā turāban waᶜiẓāman a'innā lā mabᶜūthūn? awa'ābā'unā al-awwalūn? qul naᶜam {tubᶜathūn} wa'antum dākhirūn – When we have died and become dust and bones, are we indeed to be resurrected? And our forefathers as well? Say: 'Yes, {you will be resurrected} and you will be rendered contemptible', Q37:16–18).

Another WH-question is Q75:3, which leads to ellipsis in Q75:4, which is the response sentence:

> ayaḥsabu al-insānu allan najmaᶜa ᶜiẓāmahu? balā {} qādirīna ᶜalā an nusawiya banānahu – Does man think that We will not assemble his bones? Yes, {} we are able to proportion his fingertips, Q75:3–4

where in Q75:4 we encounter the response word (balā – yes), which signals an ellipted verb {najmaᶜuhā – to assemble them (i.e., the bones)}. Our presupposed meaning of the ellipted verb {najmaᶜuhā} is retrieved from the previous sentence Q75:3 where the verb (najmaᶜu – to assemble) occurs. Thus we get:

> (ayaḥsabu al-insānu allan najmaᶜa ᶜiẓāmahu? balā {najmaᶜuhā} qādirīna ᶜalā an nusawiya banānahu – Does man think that We will not assemble his bones? Yes, {We will assemble them (the bones)} and we are able to proportion his fingertips, Q75:3–4).

Similarly, we have a WH-question in Q40:16, and the presupposed meaning of the ellipted element is a verb, as in:

> liman al-mulku al-yawma? {} lillāhi al-wāḥidi al-qahhār – To whom belongs sovereignty this day? {} To God, the one, the prevailing, Q40:16

where the ellipted element is a verb {yaqūlūn – say}; thus, we get a non-elliptical sentence:

> (liman al-mulku al-yawma? {yaqūlūn} lillāhi al-wāḥidi al-qahhār – To whom belongs sovereignty this day? {They say}: 'To God, the one, the prevailing', Q40:16).

2 Verbal ellipsis occurs after the verb (qāla – say) in all its different forms like (qul – say (imperative second person masculine singular), Q2:219, Q6:91, Q17:50, Q34:24), (yaqūlanna – say (third person masculine

plural), Q29:63, Q31:25, Q43:87), and (qālū – say (third person masculine plural), Q16:30, Q51:25).

3 Verbal ellipsis occurs before the temporal conjunctive particle (idh – when). In this linguistic environment of verbal ellipsis, we encounter a sentence-initial ellipted imperative verb (idhkur – remember (imperative, second person singular)), which is the presupposed meaning. Thus, this is verbal ellipsis whose environment is the particle (idh – when), which signals this form of verbal ellipsis, as in the following examples:

{} idh qāla rabbuka lil-malā'ikāti – {} when your Lord said to the angels, Q2:30

{} idh yamkuru bika – {} when plotted against you, Q8:30

{} idh yaḥkumān fī al-ḥarth – {} when they judged concerning the field, Q21:78

To bring back the presupposed ellipted imperative verbal element {idhkur – remember}, we get the following non-elliptical (ellipsis-free) sentences:

({idhkur} idh qāla rabbuka lil-malā'ikāti – {Remember} when your Lord said to the angels, Q2:30).

({idhkur} idh yamkuru bika – {Remember} when plotted against you, Q8:30).

({idhkur} idh yaḥkumān fī al-ḥarth – {Remember} when they judged concerning the field, Q21:78).

4 Verbal ellipsis also occurs in oath sentences beginning with the oath particles (al-wāw) and (al-fā'). In oath sentences, the verb is deleted which should have come after the oath particle, as in the following examples:

wa {} al-samā'i wa {} al-ṭāriq – {} by the sky and {} the night comer, Q86:1

wa {} al-shamsi wa {} ḍuḥāhā – {} By the sun and {} its brightness, Q91:1

wa {} al-laili idhā yaghshā – {} By the night when it covers, Q92:1

fa {} biᶜizzatika . . . – {} By Your might . . ., Q38:82

The presupposed ellipted oath verbs which come after an oath particle are either {aḥlif – to swear by} or {uqsim – to swear by}. To bring back the ellipted verb and place it after the oath particle, we get the following non-elliptical sentences:

(wa {aḥlif} bil-samā'i wa {aḥlif} bil-ṭāriq – {I swear} by the sky and {I swear} by the night comer, Q86:1).

(wa {aḥlif} bil-shamsi wa {aḥlif} biḍuḥāha – {I swear} by the sun and {} its brightness, Q91:1).

(wa {aḥlif} bil-laili idhā yaghshā – {I swear} by the night when it covers, Q92:1).

(fa {uqsim} biᶜizzatika . . . – {I swear} by Your might . . ., Q38:82).

For more details on ellipsis in oath sentences, see Section 4.6.

4.4.3 Clausal ellipsis

We can claim that the major purpose of clausal ellipsis in Qur'anic discourse is to achieve brevity, which is a feature of Arabic rhetoric and stylistic elegance. Let us consider the following examples, which involve a series of elliptical sentences:

1 Clausal ellipsis at parable level: This is context-based macro level ellipsis which occurs in a Qur'anic parable. The presupposed meaning of the ellipted clauses is retrieved from the context of the parable, as in the following examples:

Example 1

qālū idᶜu lanā rabbaka yubaiyin lanā mā hiya inna al-baqara tashābaha ᶜalainā wa'innā in shā' allāh lamuhtadūn – They said: 'Call upon your Lord to make clear to us what it is. Indeed, all cows look alike to us. Indeed, if God wills, we will be guided', Q2:70

This is the parable of Moses and the Children of Israel who ask Moses three questions (Q2:68–70) about what cow specifically the Lord has asked them to slaughter. After asking God, Moses informs them:

musallamatun lā shiyata fīhā qālū al'āna ji'ta bil-ḥaqqi {} fadhabaḥūhā – One free from fault with no spot upon her. They said: 'Now you have come with the truth'. {} So they slaughtered her, Q2:71

There are six sentences that have been ellipted before they slaughtered the cow. These are: (i) They have been told about the features of the cow, (ii) They went to look for one, (iii) They spent a long time and eventually they found one with the same features, (iv) However, the owner refused to sell them the cow, (v) They offered him a good price and he agreed to sell it to them, and (vi) The Children of Israel brought the cow to Moses.

Example 2

faqulnā aḍribūhu bibaᶜḍihā {} kadhālika yuḥyi allāhu al-mawtā wayurīkum āyātihi laᶜallakum taᶜqilūn – So We said: 'Strike him with part of it'. {} Thus, does God bring the dead to life, and He shows you His signs that you might reason, Q2:73

In this Qur'anic parable, there are three ellipted sentences: (i) They struck him, (ii) He came back to life, and (iii) he told them about his murderer.

Example 3

anā unabbi'ukum bita'wīlihi fa'arsilūn {} – I will inform you of its interpretation, so send me forth {}, Q12:45–46

There are three sentences that have been taken out from the parable: (i) They agreed to send him to meet Joseph in the prison, (ii) He goes to the prison to meet Joseph, and (iii) He meets Joseph in the prison.

2 Clausal ellipsis at comparative sentence level: This is comparative context-based ellipsis which occurs within a sentence. The ellipted elements bear comparative information to what has already been said, as in the following examples:

Example 1

afaman kāna ᶜalā baiyinatin min rabbihi {} wayatlūhu shāhidun mihu wamin qablihi kitābu mūsā imāman waraḥmatan – So is one who upon a clear evidence from his Lord {}? And a witness from Him follows it, and before it was the Scripture of Moses to lead and as mercy, Q11:17

where the presupposed meaning of the ellipted clausal elements is {kaman laisa ᶜalā baiyinatin min rabbih – similar to the one who is not upon a clear evidence from his Lord}. Thus, we get the following ellipsis-free sentence:

(afaman kāna ᶜalā baiyinatin min rabbihi {kaman laisa ᶜalā baiyinatin min rabbih} wayatlūhu shāhidun mihu wamin qablihi kitābu mūsā imāman waraḥmatan – So is one who upon a clear evidence from his Lord {similar to the one who is not upon a clear evidence from his Lord}? And a witness from Him follows it, and before it was the Scripture of Moses to lead and as mercy, Q11:17).

Example 2

afaman sharaḥa allāhu ṣadrahu lil-islām fahuwa ᶜalā nūrin min rabbih {} fawailun lil-qāsiyāti qulūbuhum min dhikr allāh – So is one whose breast God has expanded to Islam and he is upon a light from his Lord? {} Then woe to those whose hearts are hardened against the remembrance of God, Q39:22

where the presupposed meaning of the ellipted clausal elements is {kaman qasā qalbuhu – similar to the one whose heart is hardened}. Thus, we get:

(afaman sharaḥa allāhu ṣadrahu lil-islām fahuwa ᶜalā nūrin min rabbih {kaman qasā qalbuhu} fawailun lil-qāsiyāti qulūbuhum min dhikr allāh – So is one whose breast God has expanded to Islam and he is upon a light from his Lord {similar to the one whose heart is hardened}? Then woe to those whose hearts are hardened against the remembrance of God, Q39:22).

3 Clausal ellipsis at sentence level: This is context-based ellipsis which occurs within a sentence, as in the following examples:

Example 1

wajā'a al-saḥaratu firᶜawna qālū inna lanā la'ajran in kunnā naḥnu al-ghālibīn? qāla naᶜam {} wa'innakum lamin al-muqarrabīn – The magicians came to Pharaoh. They said: 'Indeed for us is a reward if we are the predominant?' He said: 'Yes, and you will be among those made near', Q7:113–114 where the presupposed meaning of the ellipted clausal elements is {inna lakum la'ajran – indeed, you will be given a reward}. Thus, we get the following non-ellipted sentence:

(wajā'a al-saḥaratu fir^{c}awna qālū inna lanā la'ajran in kunnā naḥnu al-ghālibīn? qāla na^{c}am {inna lakum la'ajran} wa'innakum lamin al-muqarrabīn – The magicians came to Pharaoh. They said: 'Indeed for us is a reward if we are the predominant?' He said: 'Yes, {indeed, you will be given a reward} and you will be among those made near', Q7:113–114).

Example 2

falammā tarā'ā al-jam^{c}āni qāla aṣḥābu mūsā innā lamudrakūn. qāla kallā {} inna ma^{c}ī rabbī sayahdīn – As soon as the two sides came within sight of one another, the companions of Moses said: 'Indeed, we are to be overtaken'. He said: 'No! {} Indeed, with me is my Lord', Q26:61–62

where the presupposed meaning of the ellipted clausal elements is {lan tudrakū – you will not be overtaken}. Thus, we get:

(falammā tarā'ā al-jam^{c}āni qāla aṣḥābu mūsā innā lamudrakūn. qāla kallā {lan tudrakū} inna ma^{c}ī rabbī sayahdīn – When the two companies saw one another, the companions of Moses said: 'Indeed, we are to be overtaken'. He said: 'No! {You will not be overtaken}. Indeed, with me is my Lord', Q26:61–62).

Example 3

qul yā qawmi i^{c}malū ^{c}alā makānatikum innī ^{c}āmilun {} fasawfa ta^{c}lamūn man ya'tīhi ^{c}adhābun yukhzīhi – Say: 'O my people, work according to your position. Indeed, I am working, and you are going to know to whom will come a torment disgracing him', Q39:39–40

where the presupposed meaning of the ellipted clausal elements is {^{c}alā makānāti – according to my position}. Thus, we get the following ellipsis-free sentence:

(qul yā qawmi i^{c}malū ^{c}alā makānatikum innī ^{c}āmilun {^{c}alā makānatī} fasawfa ta^{c}lamūn man ya'tīhi ^{c}adhābun yukhzīhi – Say: 'O my people, work according to your position. Indeed, I am working {according to my position}, and you are going to know to whom will come a torment disgracing him', Q39:39–40).

Example 4

inna alladhīna kafarū bil-dhikri lammā jā'ahum {} wa'innahu kitābun ^{c}azīz – Indeed, those who disbelieve in the message after it has come to them {}. Indeed, it is a mighty Book, Q41:41

where the presupposed meaning of the ellipted clausal elements is {lā yakhfawna ᶜalainā – they cannot hide from Us}. Thus, we get the following ellipsis-free sentence:

(inna alladhīna kafarū bil-dhikri lammā jā'ahum {lā yakhfawna ᶜalainā} wa'innahu kitābun ᶜazīz – Indeed, those who disbelieve in the message after it has come to them {they cannot hide from Us}. Indeed, it is a mighty Book, Q41:41).

Example 5

mā re we have a marked (unusuaaṣāba min muṣībatin {} illā bi'idhn allāh – No disaster strikes {} except by permission of God, Q64:11

where the presupposed meaning of the ellipted clausal elements is {fī al-arḍi walā fī anfusikum – upon the earth or among yourselves}. Thus, we get the following ellipsis-free sentence:

(mā aṣāba min muṣībatin {fī al-arḍi walā fī anfusikum} illā bi'idhn allāh – No disaster strikes {upon the earth or among yourselves} except by permission of God, Q64:11).

4.5 Ellipsis in conditional sentences

Ellipsis occurs in conditional sentences of Qur'anic discourse. There are two types of elliptical conditional clauses: (i) verbal ellipsis and (ii) clausal ellipsis. These are illustrated in what follows:

i Verbal ellipsis in conditional clauses: This occurs when the verb is ellipted in a conditional clause, as explained in the following examples:

Example 1

ainamā takūnū yudrikukum al-mawtu walaw kuntum fī burūjin mushaiyadatin {} – Wherever you may be, death will overtake you, even if you should be within towers of lofty construction {}, Q4:78

where the presupposed meaning of the ellipted element is {la'adrakakum – overtake}. Thus, we get the following ellipsis-free sentence:

(ainamā takūnū yudrikukum al-mawtu walaw kuntum fī burūjin mushaiyadatin {la'adrakakum} – Wherever you may be, death will overtake you, even if you should be within towers of lofty construction {you will be overtaken (by death)}, Q4:78).

Example 2

lawlā faḍlu allāhi ᶜalaikum waraḥmatuhu {} – If not for the favour of God upon you and His mercy {}, Q24:10

where the presupposed meaning of the ellipted element is {laᶜāqabakum – punish you, or lahalaktum – be destroyed}. Thus, we get the following non-ellipted sentence:

(lawlā faḍlu allāhi ᶜalaikum waraḥmatuhu {laᶜāqabakum} – If not for the favour of God upon you and His mercy, {He would have punished you}, Q24:10). This also applies to Q24:20.

Example 3

ḥattā idhā jā'ūhā wafutiḥat abwābuhā waqāla lahum khazanatuhā salāmun ᶜalaikum {} . . . – When they reach it while its gates have been opened and its keepers say: 'Peace be upon you {} . . .', Q39:73

where the presupposed meaning of the ellipted element is {iṭma'innū – be reassured}. Thus, we get the following ellipsis-free sentence:

(ḥattā idhā jā'ūhā wafutiḥat abwābuhā waqāla lahum khazanatuhā salāmun ᶜalaikum {iṭma'innū} . . . – When they reach it while its gates have been opened and its keepers say: 'Peace be upon you and {be reassured} . . .', Q39:73).

ii Clausal ellipsis in conditional clauses: This takes place when a whole clause is ellipted within a conditional clause, as demonstrated by the following examples:

Example 1

walaw annahum raḍū mā ātāhum allāhu warasūluhu {} waqālū . . . – If only they had been satisfied with what God and His messenger gave them {} and said: . . ., Q9:59

where the presupposed meaning of the ellipted elements is {lakāna khairan lahum – it would have been better for them}. Thus, we get the following ellipsis-free sentence:

(walaw annahum raḍū mā ātāhum allāhu warasūluhu {lakāna khairan lahum} waqālū . . . – If only they had been satisfied with what God and His messenger gave them {it would have been better for them} and said: . . ., Q9:59).

Example 2

walaw tarā idh wuqifū ᶜalā al-nāri {} faqālū . . . – If you could but see when they are made to stand before the fire {} and will say . . ., Q6:27

where the presupposed meaning of the ellipted elements is {lashāhadta amran ᶜaẓīman – you would have seen something horrible, or lara'aita sū'ḥālihim – you would have seen the horrible situation they were in}. Thus, we get the following non-elliptical sentence:

(walaw tarā idh wuqifū ᶜalā al-nāri {lashāhadta amran ᶜaẓīman} faqālū . . . – If you could but see when they are made to stand before the fire {you would have seen something horrible} and will say . . ., Q6:27). This also applies to Q6:30, Q32:12, and Q34:31.

Example 3

law anna lī bikum quwwatan aw āwī ilā ruknin shadīd {} – If only I had against you some power or could take refuge in a strong support, Q11:80

where the presupposed meaning of the ellipted elements is {lamanaᶜtukum wabālaghtu fī dafᶜikum – I would have resisted you and exaggerated in pushing you away}. Thus, we get the following ellipsis-free sentence:

(law anna lī bikum quwwatan aw āwī ilā ruknin shadīd {lamanaᶜtukum wabālaghtu fī dafᶜikum} – If only I had against you some power or could take refuge in a strong support {I would have resisted you and exaggerated in pushing you away}, Q11:80).

Example 4

law anna qur'ānan suyyirat bihi al-jibālu aw quṭṭiᶜat bihi al-arḍu aw kullima bihi al-mawtā {} – If there was any Qur'an by which the mountains would be removed or the earth would be broken apart or the dead would be made to speak {}, Q13:31

where the presupposed meaning of the ellipted elements is {lakāna hādhā al-qur'ān – it would have been this Qur'an}. Thus, we get the following ellipsis-free sentence:

(law anna qur'ānan suyyirat bihi al-jibālu aw quṭṭiᶜat bihi al-arḍu aw kullima bihi al-mawtā {lakāna hādhā al-qur'ān} – If there was any Qur'an by which the mountains would be removed or the earth would be broken apart or the dead would be made to speak, {it would have been this Qur'an}).

Example 5

wa'andhir al-nāsa yawma ya'tīhim al-ᶜadhābu fayaqūl alladhīna ẓalamū rabbanā akhkhirnā ilā ajalin qarīb {} nujib daᶜwataka wanattibiᶜ al-rusul – Warn the people of a day when the punishment will come to them and those who did wrong will say: 'Our Lord, delay us for a short term {}; we will answer Your call and follow the messenger', Q14:44

where the presupposed meaning of the ellipted elements is {fa'in akhkhartanā – if you delay us}. Thus, we get the following non-elliptical sentence:

(wa'andhir al-nāsa yawma ya'tīhim al-ᶜadhābu fayaqūl alladhīna ẓalamū rabbanā akhkhirnā ilā ajalin qarīb {fa'in akhkhartanā} nujib daᶜwataka wanattibiᶜ al-rusul – Warn the people of a day when the punishment will come to them and those who did wrong will say: 'Our Lord, delay us for a short term. {If you delay us}, we will answer Your call and follow the messengers', Q14:44).

4.6 Ellipsis in oath sentences

There are 81 oath sentences in the Qur'an: 63 oath sentences in Makkan sūrahs but only 18 in Madīnan sūrahs. Oath particles are (al-wāw, al-fā', al-bā', al-tā', and al-lām). Most of the oath sentences where the verb is deleted are those which start with (al-wāw) oath particle, but we also encounter other oath particles before the ellipted element, as in:

wa {} al-samā'i wa {} al-ṭāriq – {} by the sky and {} the night comer, Q86:1.
wa {} al-shamsi wa {} ḍuḥāhā – {} By the sun and {} by its brightness, Q91:1.
wa {} al-laili idhā yaghshā – {} By the night when it covers, Q92:1.
fa {} bi^cizzatika . . . – {} By Your might . . ., Q38:82.
{} la'in lam tantahi la'arjumannaka – {} If you do not desist, I will surely stone you, Q19:46.
{} la'u^cadhdhibannahu – {} I will surely punish him, Q27:21.

Ellipted oath represents verbal ellipsis where the oath verb is taken out. The presupposed ellipted oath verbs which come after an oath particle are either {aḥlif – to swear by} or {uqsim – to swear by}. The ellipted oath verb comes after the oath particle (al-wāw) as in Q86:1, Q91:1, and Q92:1, and also after the oath particle (al-fā') as in Q38:82. The ellipted oath verb can also occur before the oath particle (al-lām) as in Q19:46 and Q27:21. It is also worthwhile to note that a minor stylistic change is required after the addition of the oath verb {aḥlif} which comes after the oath particle (al-wāw) where the preposition (al-bā' / bi/) is prefixed to the first and second noun, as we can observe in Q86:1, Q91:1 and Q92:1. Having brought back the ellipted oath verbs, we get the following ellipsis-free sentences:

(wa {aḥlif} bil-samā'i wa {aḥlif} bil-ṭāriq – {I swear} by the sky and {I swear} by the night comer, Q86:1).
(wa {aḥlif} bil-shamsi wa {aḥlif} biḍuḥāhā – {I swear} by the sun and {I swear} by its brightness, Q91:1).
(wa {aḥlif} bil-laili idhā yaghshā – {I swear} by the night when it covers, Q92:1).
(fa {uqsim} bi^cizzatika . . . – {I swear} by Your might . . ., Q38:82).
({uqsim} la'in lam tantahi la'arjumannaka – {I swear} if you do not desist, I will surely stone you, Q19:46).
({uqsim} la'u^cadhdhibannahu – {I swear} I will surely punish him, Q27:21).

However, in:

qāff wal-qur'āni al-majīd {} – Qāff. By the honoured Qur'an {}, Q50:1.

we have details in Q50:3 which will help us retrieve the presupposed meaning of the ellipted element. Based on Q50:3, we manage to bring back the taken-out (ellipted) elements {latubᶜathunna – you will definitely be resurrected}. Thus, we can provide an ellipsis-free sentence:

(qāff wal-qur'āni al-majīd {latubᶜathunna} – Qāff. By the honoured Qur'an {you will definitely be resurrected}, Q50:1).

4.7 Ellipsis and intertextuality

Ellipsis, presupposed exegetical meaning, and intertextuality are interrelated to each other. Ellipsis can be retrieved either from a previous text or from a subsequent text within Qur'anic discourse. For this reason, ellipsis is concerned with either the macro or the micro Qur'anic text. In other words, our presupposition about the meaning of an ellipted element(s) is entirely hinged upon either the same sentence (micro level) or upon the surrounding larger (macro) text rather than confined to a micro level only, i.e., the same sentence where ellipsis has taken place. The following discussion illustrates our claim.

4.7.1 Ellipsis and macro intertextuality

The grammatical process of ellipsis is accounted for at the macro level. In other words, the presupposed meaning of the ellipted element is retrieved through macro level intertextuality. This is explained in the following examples:

Example 1

innamā ḥarrama ᶜalaikum {} al-maitata – He has only forbidden to you {} dead animals, Q2:173.

where the ellipted elements are {an ta'kulū – to eat, the eating of}. Thus, it is 'the eating' of a dead animal that is forbidden. This ellipted presupposed meaning is based on the macro text where we encounter the verb (kulū – eat) in: (yā aiyuhā alladhīna āmanū kulū min ṭaiyibāṭī mā razaqnākum – O you who have believed, eat from the good things which We have provided for you, Q2:57 and 172). The presupposed meaning of the ellipted element is retrieved through macro level intertextuality. thus, the non-elliptical sentence is:

(innamā ḥarrama ᶜalaikum {an ta'kulū} al-maitata – He has only forbidden to you {to eat} dead animals).

Example 2

walaqad arsalnā ilā umamin min qablika {} fa'akhadhnāhum bil-ba'sā'i wal-ḍarrā'i – We have already sent to nations before you. Then, We seized them with poverty and hardship, Q6:42.

where the presupposed meaning of the ellipted element {fakadhdhabūhum – disbelieved them} can be retrieved from macro level intertextuality found in the following sentence:

> wa'in yukadhdhibūka faqad kudhdhibat rusulun min qablika – And if they disbelieve you, already were messengers disbelieved before you, Q35:4.

When we bring back the ellipted element to Q6:42, we get the following ellipsis-free sentence:

> (walaqad arsalnā ilā umamin min qablika {fakadhdhabūhum} fa'akhadhnāhum bil-ba'sā'i wal-ḍarrā'i – We have already sent messengers to nations before you. {They disbelieved them}; then, We seized them with poverty and hardship, Q6:42).

Example 3

> mā aṣāba min muṣībatin {} illā bi'idhni allāh – No disaster strikes {} except by permission of God, Q64:11.

where the presupposed meaning of the ellipted elements can be retrieved through macro level intertextuality found in the following sentence:

> mā aṣāba min muṣībatin fī al-arḍi walā fī anfusikum illā fī kitāb – No disaster strikes upon the earth or among yourselves except that it is in a register, Q57:22.

Thus, to put back the ellipted elements in Q64:11, we get the following non-ellipted sentence:

> (mā aṣāba min muṣībatin {fī al-arḍi walā fī anfusikum} illā bi'idhni allāh – No disaster strikes {upon the earth or among yourselves} except by permission of God, Q64:11).

Example 4

> wala'in sa'altahum man khalaqa al-samāwāti wal-arḍa layaqūlanna {} allāh – And if you asked them: 'Who created the heavens and earth?', they would say: 'God', Q31:25.

where the ellipted element is the verb {khalaqahunna – create}, which is a verbal ellipsis: (wala'in sa'altahum man khalaqa al-samāwāti wal-arḍi layaqūlanna {khalaqahunna} allāh – And if you asked them: 'Who created the heavens and earth?', they would say: 'God' {created them}). This presupposed meaning is based on the macro level intertextuality between Q31:25 and Q43:9 (wala'in sa'altahum man khalaqa al-samāwāti wal-arḍa layaqūlunna khalaqahunna al-ᶜazīz al-^{c}alīm – If you should ask them: 'Who has created the heavens and the earth?' They would surely say: 'They were created by the exalted in might, the knowing', Q43:9) where the verb (khalaqahunna – create) is employed.

Example 5

> ṣād wal-qur'āni dhi al-dhikr {} – Ṣād. By the Qur'an containing reminder {}, Q38:1–2.

where the ellipted elements are the verb + its object noun {lanuhlikanna a^{c}dā'aka – We will destroy your enemies}, which is a verbal clause ellipsis. Thus, we get the following ellipsis-free sentence:

> (ṣād wal-qur'āni dhi al-dhikr {lanuhlikanna a^{c}dā'aka} – Ṣād. By the Qur'an containing reminder {We will destroy your enemies}).

This meaning is based on the macro level intertextuality between Q38:1–2 and Q6:6 (alam yaraw kam ahlaknā min qablihim min qarnin makkannāhum fī al-arḍi mā lam numakkin lakum wa'arsalnā al-samā'a ^{c}alaihim midrāran waja^{c}alnā al-anhāra tajrī min taḥtihim fa'ahlaknāhum bidhunūbihim . . . – Have they not seen how many generations We destroyed before them which We had established upon the earth as We have not established you? And We sent rain from the sky upon them in showers and made rivers flow beneath them; then We destroyed them for their sins . . ., Q6:6) where the verb (ahlaka – destroy) occurs twice.

Example 6

> fa'idhā nazala {} bisāḥatihim – But when {} descends in their territory, Q37:177.

where the ellipted element is the subject noun {al-^{c}adhābu – the punishment}, which is a nominal ellipsis: (fa'idhā nazala {al-^{c}adhābu} bisāḥatihim – But when {the punishment} descends in their territory). This meaning is based on the macro level intertextuality between Q37:177 and Q37:176 (afabi^{c}adhābinā yasta^{c}jilūn – Then for Our punishment they are impatient?, Q37:176) where the noun (^{c}adhāb – punishment) occurs.

Example 7

> lam yalbathū illā sā^{c}atan min nahārin {} balāgh – As though they had not remained in the world except an hour of a day. {} Notification, Q46:35.

where the ellipted item is the demonstrative pronoun {hadhā – this}, which is a nominal ellipsis. Thus, we get the following non-ellipted sentence:

> (lam yalbathū illā sā^{c}atan min nahārin {hadhā} balāgh – As though they had not remained in the world except an hour of a day. {This is} notification).

The above presupposed meaning is based on the macro level intertextuality between Q46:35 and Q14:52 (hādhā balāgh lil-nāss – This is notification for the people) where the demonstrative pronoun (hadhā) occurs.

Example 8

wajāhidū fī allāhi ḥaqqa jihādihi huwa ijtabākum wamā ja^{c}ala ^{c}alaikum fī al-dīni min ḥarajin {} millata abīkum ibrāhīmu – And strive for God with the striving due to Him. He has chosen you and has not placed upon you in the religion any difficulty. {} The religion of your father, Abraham, Q22:78.

where the ellipted word is {alzimū – adhere to} or {ittabi^{c}ū – follow}, whose presupposed meaning is retrieved from the macro level intertextuality. Thus, we get the following ellipsis-free sentence::

(wajāhidū fī allāhi ḥaqqa jihādihi huwa ijtabākum wamā ja^{c}ala ^{c}alaikum fī al-dīni min ḥarajin {alzimū} millata abīkum ibrāhīmu – And strive for God with the striving due to Him. He has chosen you and has not placed upon you in the religion any difficulty. {Follow} the religion of your father, Abraham, Q22:78).

where the presupposed ellipted word {ittabi^{c}ū – follow} is intertextually related to (ittaba^{c}ūhu – followed him) as well as the intertextual relationship between the words (millata – religion). The words {ittabi^{c}ū – follow} and (millata) form a collocation:

inna awlā al-nāsi bi'ibrāhīma lalladhīna ittaba^{c}ūhu – Indeed, the most worthy of Abraham among the people are those who followed him, Q3:68.
. . . wattaba^{c}a millata ibrāhima ḥanīfā – . . . follows the religion of Abraham, inclining toward truth, Q4:125.
wattaba^{c}tu millata ābā'ī ibrāhīma . . . – and I have followed the religion of my fathers, Abraham . . ., Q12:38.

Example 9

Sentence-initial verbal ellipsis (cataphoric ellipsis) where the verb (idhkur – remember) is the presupposed meaning and is also an example of macro intertextuality ellipsis. The particle (idh – when) signals this form of ellipsis, as in:

{} idh qāla rabbuka lil-malā'ikāti – {} when your Lord said to the angels, Q2:30
{} idh yamkuru bika – {} when plotted against you, Q8:30
{} idh yaḥkumān fī al-ḥarth – {} when they judged concerning the field, Q21:78

To bring back the ellipted verbal element, we get the following ellipsis-free sentences:

({idhkur} idh qāla rabbuka lil-malā'ikāti – {Remember} when your Lord said to the angels, Q2:30).

({idhkur} idh yamkuru bika – {Remember} when plotted against you, Q8:30). ({idhkur} idh yaḥkumān fī al-ḥarth – {Remember} when they judged concerning the field, Q21:78).

This is intertextually based on a similar syntactic structure which keeps the verb (idhkur – remember), as in:

idhkurū idh kunkum qalīlan – Remember when you were few, Q7:86.

idhkur akhā ᶜādin idh andhara qawmahu – Remember the brother of ᶜĀd when he warned his people, Q46:21.

4.7.2 Ellipsis and micro intertextuality

Micro level intertextuality is concerned with the retrieval of the presupposed meaning of an ellipted element within the same sentence as illustrated in the following examples:

Example 1

wal-baladu al-ṭaiyibu yakhruju nabātuhu {} bi'idhni rabbih – And the good land, its vegetation emerges {} by permission of its Lord, Q7:58.

The presupposed meaning of the ellipted element is {ṭaiyiban – good}, which is an adverb. Thus, we get the following ellipsis-free sentence:

(wal-baladu al-ṭaiyibu yakhruju nabātuhu {ṭaiyiban} bi'idhni rabbih – And the good land, its vegetation emerges {good} by permission of its Lord).

This is an example of a presupposed ellipted element {ṭaiyiban} based on a micro text intertextuality because the same word (al-ṭaiyibu – good) has occurred in the same sentence.

Example 2

It is worthwhile to note that the meaning of the presupposed ellipted verb can be retrieved from the same sentence, and this will establish micro level intertextuality. This form of verbal ellipsis occurs in WH-questions whose answer is (naᶜam/balā – yes) after which the presupposed ellipted element occurs, as in:

a'idhā mitnā wakunnā turāban waᶜiẓāman a'innā lā mabᶜūthūn? awa'ābā'unā al-awwalūn? qul naᶜam {} wa'antum dākhirūn – When we have died and become dust and bones, are we indeed to be resurrected? And our forefathers as well? Say: 'Yes, {} and you will be rendered contemptible', Q37:16–18 where we retrieve the ellipted element (the verb) {tubᶜathūn – to be resurrected} based on the passive participle (ism mafᶜūl) word (mabᶜūthūn – resurrected). The position of the ellipted verb {tubᶜathūn} comes after the response word (naᶜam – yes). Thus, we get the following ellipsis-free sentence represented by Q37:18:

> (a'idhā mitnā wakunnā turāban waᶜiẓāman a'innā lā mabᶜūthūn? awa'ābā'unā al-awwalūn? qul naᶜam {tubᶜathūn} wa'antum dākhirūn – When we have died and become dust and bones, are we indeed to be resurrected? And our forefathers as well? Say: 'Yes, {you will be resurrected} and you will be rendered contemptible', Q37:16–18).

Example 3

Similarly, in Q75:3, we have a WH-question and in Q75:4, we get the response sentence:

> ayaḥsabu al-insānu allan najmaᶜa ᶜiẓāmahu? balā {} qādirīna ᶜalā an nusawiya banānahu – Does man think that We will not assemble his bones? Yes, {} we are able to proportion his fingertips, Q75:3

where in Q75:4 we encounter the response word (balā – yes), which signals an ellipted verb {najmaᶜuhā – to assemble them (i.e., the bones)} based on the micro level intertextuality where the verb (najmaᶜu – to assemble) occurs. Thus we get the following ellipsis-free sentence:

> (ayaḥsabu al-insānu allan najmaᶜa ᶜiẓāmahu? balā {najmaᶜuhā} qādirīna ᶜalā an nusawiya banānahu – Does man think that We will not assemble his bones? Yes, {We will assemble them (the bones)} and we are able to proportion his fingertips, Q75:3).

4.8 Presupposed context-based ellipsis

There is also context-based presupposition of what is to be said, i.e., of what has been ellipted from the sentence. In other words, we can presuppose the ellipted information without assistance from either the micro or the macro text. Instead, we establish our presupposition of context, as in the following examples:

Example 1

walaqad jā'akum mūsā bil-baiyināṭī thumma ittakhadhtum al-ᶜijla {} min baᶜdihi wa'antum ẓālimūn – And Moses had certainly brought you clear proofs. Then you took the calf {} after he left, while you were wrongdoers, Q2:92.

The verb (ittakhadhtum – take) has two objects: The first direct object is mentioned, which is (al-ᶜijla – the calf), but the second direct object {ilāhan – a god} is ellipted. Based on this grammatical analysis and the context, we can retrieve the presupposed meaning of the ellipted second direct object {ilāhan}. Thus, we get the following ellipsis-free sentence:

> (walaqad jā'akum mūsā bil-baiyinātī thumma ittakhadhtum al-ᶜijla {ilāhan} min baᶜdihi wa'antum ẓālimūn – And Moses had certainly brought you clear proofs. Then you took the calf {a god} after he left, while you were wrongdoers, Q2:92).

Example 2

> was'al {} al-qaryata allatī kunnā fihā – Ask {} the city in which we were, Q12:82.

The presupposed context-based meaning of the ellipted element is {ahl – people}, which is a nominal ellipsis:

> (was'al {ahl} al-qaryāti allatī kunnā fīhā – Ask {the people} of the city in which we were).
>
> faqabaḍtu qabaḍatan min athar {} al-rasūl – I took a handful of dust from the track of {} the messenger, Q20:96.

The presupposition of the meaning of the ellipted elements is retrieved from the context of Q20:96. The ellipted words are {ḥāfir faras – the horse's hoof}. Thus, the ellipsis-free sentence is:

> (faqabaḍtu qabaḍatan min athar {ḥāfir faras} al-rasūl – I took a handful of dust from the track of {the horse's hoof} of the messenger, Q20:96).

Example 3

> {} fajā'athu iḥdāhumā tamshī ᶜalā istiḥyā' – {} Then one of the two women came to him walking with shyness, Q28:25.

This is another example of context-based presupposed meaning of ellipted elements.

Our presupposition about the ellipted information is based on the context of Q28:25. The context is about Moses when he was in Midian, the two women who wanted to water their flocks but could not because of a crowd of men watering their flocks, and their father. Thus, we presuppose the ellipted details as:

> {fadhahabatā ilā abīhimā waqaṣṣatā ᶜalaihi mā jarā maᶜa mūsā wamusāᶜadathu lahumā fa'arsalā al-abu ibnatahu ilā mūsā – The two girls went back home to their father and told him of Moses' assistance to them. The father sent his daughter to Moses}.

Thus, when we include the presupposed ellipted information, we get the following non-ellipted sentence:

> ({fadhahabatā ilā abīhimā waqaṣṣatā ᶜalaihi mā jarā maᶜa mūsā wamusāᶜadathu lahumā fa'arsalā al-abu ibnatahu ilā mūsā} fajā'athu iḥdāhumā tamshī ᶜalā

istiḥyā' – {The two girls went back home to their father and told him of Moses' assistance to them. The father sent his daughter to Moses}. Then one of the two women came to him walking with shyness, Q28:25).

Example 4

{} watilka niᶜmatun tamunnuhā ᶜalaiya an ᶜabbadta banī isrā'īl – This is a favour of which you remind me, that you have enslaved the Children of Israel, Q26:22.

As it stands, Q26:22 is a statement rather than an interrogative structure. Our presupposed meaning is context based, i.e., we should have an interrogative particle {a}, which is (hamzat al-istifhām – the interrogative particle) at the beginning of the sentence:

({a} watilka niᶜmatun tamunnuhā ᶜalaiya an ᶜabbadta banī isrā'īl – Is this a favour of which you remind me, that you have enslaved the Children of Israel?).

Thus, we have got an ellipsis-free interrogative grammatical structure.

Example 5

falammā janna ᶜalaihi al-lailu ra'ā kawkaban qāla {} hādhā rabbī – So when the night covered him, he saw a star. He said: 'This is my Lord', Q6:76.

As it is, Q6:76 involves an ellipted element and is not an interrogative grammatical structure. Our presupposed meaning is both context based and co-text based. To retrieve the presupposed meaning, we need to bring back the ellipted interrogative particle {a}. Thus, we have the following non-ellipted sentence:

(falammā janna ᶜalaihi al-lailu ra'ā kawkaban qāla {a} hādhā rabbī? – So when the night covered him, he saw a star. He said: 'Is this my Lord?'). The co-text (the surrounding linguistic environment in which a sentence occurs) presupposes the occurrence of the ellipted interrogative particle {a}. This is supported by the occurrence of interrogative particles in the surrounding linguistic environment, as in: a tattakhidhu aṣnāman ālihatan? – Do you take idols as gods?, Q6:74,
a tuḥājjūnnī fī allāhi waqad hadāni? – Do you argue with me concerning God while He has guided me?, Q6:80,
a falā tatadhakkarūn? – Will you not remember?, Q6:80, and
kaifa akhāfu mā ashraktum walā takhāfūna annakum . . . ? – How should I fear what you associate while you do not fear that you have . . ., Q6:81.

Thus, we can claim that Q6:76 is originally an interrogative structure rather than a statement.

Example 6

walladhīna tabawwa'ū al-dāra wa {} al-īmāna – And those who were settled in the home (i.e., Madinah) and the faith, Q59:9.

The presupposed context-based meaning of the ellipted element is {iᶜtaqadū – adopt}, which is a verbal ellipsis represented by the following ellipsis-free sentence:

> (walladhīna tabawwa'ū al-dāra wa {iᶜtaqadū} al-īmāna – And those who were settled in the home (i.e., al-Madīnah) and {adopted} the faith, Q59:9).

Based on context, the collocation takes place between the verb (tabawwa'a – to settle down + a place → tabawwa'a + al-dāra = to settle down in a place). However, the noun (al-īmāna – faith) is not a place and cannot collocate with the verb (tabawwa'a). Therefore, we presuppose the ellipted verb for (tabawwa'a) is {iᶜtaqada} → iᶜtaqada + al-īmāna = to adopt, believe a faith.

4.9 Contextual ellipsis

This is an account of what we call 'contextual ellipsis', which is concerned with the influence of context on the ellipsis of specific words or phrases and the non-ellipsis of the same words or phrases in other sentences. In other words, contextual ellipsis deals with how context decides the occurrence or non-occurrence of the same words or phrases in a similar sentence in Qur'anic discourse. Therefore, 'contextual ellipsis' is distinct from presupposed context-based ellipsis discussed in Section 5.8, where we establish our own presupposition of context. Let us consider the following examples of contextual ellipsis:

Example 1

huwa alladhī jaᶜala lakum al-laila litaskunū fīhi wal-nahāra mubṣirā – It is He who made for you the night so that you can rest in it and the daylight giving sight, Q10:67.

Prior to our textual analysis, we are required to make the following observations:

1. The objects are (al-laila – the night) and (al-nahāra – the day), whose verb is (jaᶜala – made).
2. There are two text segments, (al-laila litaskunū fīhi/wal-nahāra mubṣirā), which can be divided into two structural units:

   Unit one: (al-laila litaskunū fīhi – the night so that you can rest in it)
   Unit two: (al-nahāra mubṣirā – the daylight giving sight)

3. There is antithesis between the two units: (al-laila – the night) versus (al-nahāra – the day).
4. Both units are elliptical, i.e., involve ellipsis.
5. We expect what is mentioned with (al-laila) to occur with (al-nahāra) and what is mentioned with (al-nahāra) to occur with (al-laila). However, this has not taken place because of the process of ellipsis.

6 The verbal clause (litaskunū fīhi – so that you can rest in it) occurs with the noun (al-laila), explaining the purpose of (al-laila).
7 The noun (al-nahāra – the day) does not have a verbal clause explaining its purpose. Thus, the verbal clause is ellipted.
8 The status of (al-laila) is ellipted in unit one. We are not informed about the purpose of (al-laila).
9 The status of (al-nahāra) is mentioned, which is (mubṣirā – giving light).
10 Based on the above, ellipsis has taken place in both units for the rhetorical function of succinctness, through which stylistic elegance has been delivered.

Analysis of unit one

In unit one, we have the verbal clause (litaskunū fīhi – so that you can rest in it). This is evident through the employment of the reason particle (li – so that), which is the initial letter /l/ prefixed to the verb (taskunū). Thus, the reason particle /li/ requires a verbal sentence (taskunū fīhi – you can rest in it), which is followed by a [+ Action] result, i.e., to rest. In other words, we have the Cause (al-laila) followed by its Effect (result) → (litaskunū fīhi):

Cause (al-laila) → Effect (litaskunū fīhi)

It is important to note that we do not have the night's status in unit one. The night's status should be mentioned as an adjective (muẓlimā – giving darkness), but this adjective is ellipted. Thus, we should have {al-laila (muẓlimā) litaskunū fīhi – the night (giving darkness) so that you can rest in it}. It is worthwhile to note that we have a reason particle, which is the initial letter /l/, prefixed to the verb (taskunū) to introduce the night's status (purpose).

Analysis of unit two

However, in unit two, the day's status is mentioned, which is the adjective (mubṣirā – giving light). However, there is no reason particle in unit two; this particle is ellipted. Thus, unit two is not a Cause + Effect construction. Compared to unit one, the effect of (al-nahāra) should be stated as (lita^c^malū fīhi – to work in it), but the latter is ellipted. In other words, the verbal clause (lita^c^malū fīhi – to work in it) does not occur with the noun (al-nahāra) explaining the purpose of (al-nahāra). This is illustrated in what follows:

Table 4.1 Cause and effect in contextual ellipsis

	Effect	*Status*
Unit one	mentioned	ellipted
Unit two	ellipted	mentioned

It is worthwhile to note that although ellipsis is involved twice in Q10:67, the illocutionary force of the statement has not been impinged. The text producer's performative intent has been delivered through the pivotal lexical elements (litaskunū – so that you can rest) and (mubṣirā – giving light). The latter two expressions designate the illocutionary force of God's blessings bestowed upon His creation. In other words, the semantic entailment of unit one is the blessing of (al-sukūn – resting) rather than (al-ẓulmah – darkness). However, the semantic entailment of unit two is the blessing of (al-ẓiyā' – light) rather than (al-ḥarakah wal-ᶜamal – moving about and work).

Example 2

sayarā allāhu ᶜamalakum wa rasūluhu thumma turaddūna ilā ᶜālimi al-ghaibi wal-shahādati fayunabbi'ukum bimā kuntum taᶜmalūn – God and His messenger will observe your deeds; then you will be taken back to the knower of the unseen and the witnessed and He will inform you of what you used to do, Q9:94.

qul iᶜmalū fa sayarā allāhu ᶜamalakum warasūluhu wal-mu'minūn wa saturaddūna ilā ᶜālimi al-ghaibi wal-shahādati fayunabbi'ukum bimā kuntum taᶜmalūn – Say: Do as you will, for God, His messenger, and the believers will see your deeds; then you will be taken back to the knower of the unseen and the witnessed and He will inform you of what you used to do, Q9:105.

There are two cases of ellipsis:

1 The ellipsis of the definite plural subject noun (al-mu'minūn – the believers) in Q9:94 and the non-ellipsis of the definite plural subject noun (al-mu'minūn – the believers) in Q9:105: Although the verb (yarā – to observe, see) occurs in both sentences 49 and 105, we observe two subjects for this verb in sentence 94 (allāhu wa rasūluhu – God and His messenger), but there are three subjects in sentence 105 (allāhu wa rasūluhu wal-mu'minūn – God, His messenger, and the believers).

   The main problem is the ellipsis of the definite plural noun (al-mu'minūn – the believers) in Q9:94 and the non-ellipsis of the definite plural noun (al-mu'minūn – the believers) in Q9:105. To account for the non-ellipsis (occurrence) of the definite plural noun (al-mu'minūn) in Q9:94, we need to consider the context in which this statement has occurred. The context of sentence 94 is about the hypocrite Muslims who did not join the Muslim army during the Battle of Tabūk (9/630) and who provided false excuses for their staying back in Madīnah and preferred to stay with their families rather than joining the Muslim army. The main reasons for the ellipsis of the noun (al-mu'minūn – the believers) in Q9:94 are attributed to the following contextual reasons:

   i The believers are not aware of the true intentions of the hypocritical Muslims, i.e., the believers do not possess the knowledge of the unseen. This is God-specific knowledge, ii The believers used to believe the hypocrites' false excuses for not joining the army,

iii God has informed Muḥammad of the intentions of the hypocrites, and he is aware of why they refused to join the Muslim army: (qad nabba'anā allāhu min akhbārikum – God has already informed us of the news concerning you (the hypocrites), Q9:94),

iv It is only God who has the knowledge of the unseen and the witnessed, and

v It is only God who will inform the believers and the hypocrites on the day of judgement of what they used to do.

Based on these contextual reasons, the noun (al-mu'minūn – the believers) is ellipted in sentence 94 because the believers cannot be the subject of the verb (yarā – to observe, to see). In other words, sentence 94 is focused on the hypocrites and their deeds and, therefore, the only subjects who can 'see and observe the hypocrites and their deeds' are (allāhu wa rasūluhu – God and His messenger).

However, the context of sentence 105 is about the true believers who are urged in the previous sentences (Q9:103–104) to do good deeds, and Muḥammad is also instructed to take from their wealth a charity and to invoke God's blessings upon them. The context also refers to virtuous deeds like prayer, repentance, and God's epithets 'accepting of repentance and the merciful'. Because the good deeds which the believers are doing such as prayer and charity can be witnessed and experienced, i.e., seen (yarā), by the believers themselves, sentence 105 mentions the subject noun (al-mu'minūn – the believers) in addition to the other subjects (allāhu wa rasūluhu – God and His messenger). Thus, the three subjects occur in Q9:105 because the believers are involved as a subject in the action of the verb (yarā).

2 The ellipsis of the temporal conjunctive particle (thumma – then) occurs in sentence 94 before the verb (turaddūna – to be taken back) but not in 105. Instead, we observe the additive conjunctive particle (wa – and) employed in 105 before the verb (saturaddūna – will be taken back). Sentence 94 focuses on the hypocrites and has two text segments:

> Text segment 1: sayarā allāhu ᶜamalakum wa rasūluhu – God and His messenger will observe your deeds.
>
> Text segment 2: turaddūna ilā ᶜālimi al-ghaibi wal-shahādati fayunabbi'ukum bimā kuntum taᶜmalūn – You will be taken back to the knower of the unseen and the witnessed and He will inform you of what you used to do.

The two text segments are separated by the temporal conjunctive particle (thumma – then). The illocutionary force of (thumma) is [+ Threat], which designates their punishment in the hereafter for their deeds such as double standards, dishonesty, and lying. However, sentence 105 employs the additive conjunctive particle (wa – and). This sentence focuses on the believers and has two text segments:

Text segment 1: qul i^{c}malū fa sayarā allāhu ^{c}amalakum warasūluhu wal-mu'minūn – Say: Do as you will, for God, His messenger, and the believers will see your deeds.

Text segment 2: saturaddūna ilā ^{c}ālimi al-ghaibi wal-shahādati fayunabbi'ukum bimā kuntum ta^{c}malūn – You will be taken back to the knower of the unseen and the witnessed and He will inform you of what you used to do.

The two text segments are separated by the additive conjunctive particle (wa – and), whose illocutionary force is [+ Promise of Reward] in the hereafter. It is for this reason that the conjunctive particle (fa) is prefixed to the verb (fa sayarā – will see) as a backup to the promised reward to the believers. Thus, the two text segments are conjoined to (ma^{c}ṭūf ^{c}alā) each other as if they were one unit since the three subject nouns share the same verb (yarā – to see).

Example 3

walākinna akthara al-nāsi lā yashkurūn – But most of the people do not show gratitude, Q2:243, Q40:61.

walākinna aktharahum lā yashkurūn – But most of them do not show gratitude, Q10:60, Q27:73.

where in Q2:243 and Q40:61, the subject noun (al-nāsi – people) occurs. However, in Q10:60, Q27:73, the noun (al-nāsi) is ellipted and substituted by its coreferential (anaphoric) pronoun (-hum – they) of the word (aktharu + hum – most of + them). The main reason for the occurrence of the noun (al-nāsi) in Q2:243 is attributed to the fact that there is no mention of the noun (al-nāsi) for the last 18 sentences, i.e., since sentence Q2:225. For this reason, it is stylistically more appropriate to mention the noun (al-nāsi) than its pronoun (-hum). In Q40:57 and 59, the lexical co-text (environment) has influenced the sentence structure of sentence 61. In Q40:57, 59 and 61, we encounter the same stylistic pattern:

walākinna + akthara + al-nāsi + lā + verb (ya^{c}lamūn/yu'minūn/yashkurūn).

Thus, sentences 57, 59, and 61 of Q40 have achieved stylistic symmetry. Similarly, lexical co-text has also influenced the employment of the anaphoric pronoun (-hum – they) instead of the noun (al-nāsi) in Q10:60. The occurrence of the noun (al-nāsi) at the beginning of sentence 60 of Q10 and at the beginning of sentence 73 of Q27 necessitates the replacement of the noun (al-nāsi) by its anaphoric pronoun (-hum):

inna allāha ladhū faḍlin ^{c}alā al-nāsi walākinna aktharahum lā yashkurūn – Indeed, God is full of bounty to the people, but most of them are not grateful, Q10:60.

inna rabbaka ladhū faḍlin ^{c}alā al-nāsi walākinna aktharahum lā yashkurūn – Indeed, your Lord is full of bounty to the people, but most of them are not grateful, Q27:73.

4.10 Summary

Ellipsis (deletion) is a linguistic process that makes the sentence cohesive and hang well together. We presuppose that something like a word, a phrase, or a clause is ellipted (taken out) from the sentence. As readers/listeners, we should be able to retrieve the ellipted (missing) element(s).

An ellipted element means an element that has been taken out from the sentence. An elliptical sentence is a sentence that involves ellipsis. Ellipsis can be either anaphoric or cataphoric. In anaphoric ellipsis, the first part of the sentence, or the first part of a text segment that can be more than one sentence, acts as the context from which we can recover the ellipted (missing, presupposed) elements. In cataphoric ellipsis, the elliptical sentence which has a missing element occurs first, followed by a sentence which acts as the context from which we can recover the ellipted (missing, presupposed) elements. There is also nominal ellipsis and verbal ellipsis. Nominal ellipsis deals with the ellipsis of a noun, a pronoun, or an adjective. Verbal ellipsis is concerned with the deletion of a main verb. Verbal ellipsis occurs in Yes/No questions whose answer is (naᶜam/balā – yes) or (kallā – no), after the verb (qāla – say), in conditional clauses, and in oath sentences. There is a relationship between ellipsis, presupposed meaning, and intertextuality, i.e., ellipsis can be retrieved either from a previous text or from a subsequent text within Qur'anic discourse. We have also 'contextual ellipsis', which refers to context which has influenced the ellipsis of specific words or phrases and the non-ellipsis of the same words or phrases in other sentences. Therefore, we are dealing with how context decides the occurrence or non-occurrence of the same words or phrases in a similar sentence in Qur'anic discourse.

5 Coherence in Qur'anic discourse

5.1 Introduction

The present chapter accounts for the text linguistic feature of coherence in Qur'anic discourse. It provides an in-depth investigation of the ways in which Qur'anic themes and meaning relations are linked and used to achieve effective communication between the text producer and the text receiver (reader/listener). It demonstrates how the continuity (sequentiality or chaining) of the text producer's thought (theme or leitmotif) is achieved through different mechanisms. It accounts for the coherence network, continuity of thought, leitmotif configuration, and how the text segments hang well together. This chapter deals with how coherence is achieved through different grammatical mechanisms that give a text's segment potency. Fifteen mechanisms of linguistics-based coherence are discussed with examples. The chapter also accounts for the interrelationship between coherence and relevance, coherence and saliency, coherence and context, and the two major types of coherence: micro level coherence and macro level coherence. The sentences between brackets () represent statements which lack coherence and are non-Qur'anic.

5.2 What is coherence?

Coherence is a text-centred notion and is a constitutive principle of effective communication. In any textual communication, coherence plays a pivotal role in the fulfilment of the text producer's communicative goals at the interpersonal communication level and at a persuasion process level. The interlocutor's communicative goal is his/her *thought* which he/she wants to deliver to the hearer/reader. The appropriate arrangement of *thoughts* in a given text makes it easy for the *thought* to get across to the text receiver and to be processed. In other words, the configuration of words (word order) through which the text producer's concepts are relayed to the text receiver plays a major role in the delivery of the illocutionary force of the message involved in the text. Thus, we can argue that coherence is concerned with the hierarchical arrangement of textual units into structured entities. Coherence is not merely concerned with 'sticking to the point'. Rather, it is concerned with the semantic relatedness and continuity of senses between the segments of the text, be it a single word, two consecutive sentences, or a larger text. In other words, coherence is concerned with:

i the relationships among the constituent lexemes of a sentence (proposition),
ii the relationships among the consecutive sentences, and
iii the relationships among different macro texts such as the consecutive chapters of a book or the consecutive sūrahs of Qur'anic discourse.

This means that coherence is concerned with how a text hangs well together. The logical order of the text's segments is only one element through which we achieve coherence. Saliency is another element from which coherence stems. Coherence plays a pivotal role in interpersonal communication and in persuasive discourse. Thus, saliency aids coherence to deliver the intended illocutionary force of the text producer. Making a text's segment salient is a clear sign to the text receiver that this particular segment is important and represents the underlying idea of the text. In Qur'anic discourse, saliency is an achieved through specific grammatical processes. For more details, see Section 5.7.

An in-depth account of coherence should be based on three different levels:

1 intra-sententially, i.e., at word level where the appropriateness of a word is investigated and how far a lexeme fits in well in a sentence,
2 inter-sententially, i.e., at sentence level where the logical organization and the development of the sentence's thematic content are taken into consideration, and
3 intertextually, i.e., at macro text level where the logical organization and the development of the consecutive Qur'anic chapter's thematic content are taken into consideration.

A coherent text has conceptual (thematic) unity. The text's unity is hinged upon:

a the text's underlying ideas (notions, leitmotifs),
b the logical organization of these ideas, and
c the development of the text's conceptual (thematic) content.

For Carter and Malmkjær (2002:544), coherence concerns the way in which the things that the text is about are mutually accessible and relevant. In the view of Henri Weil (1844, 1887), the relations of *thoughts* to each other affect the arrangement of words in sentences (cf. Beaugrande and Dressler 1981:20). For Beaugrande and Dressler (ibid:84), a text 'makes sense' because there is a continuity of senses among the knowledge activated by the expressions of the text. A 'senseless' or 'non-sensical' text is one in which text receivers can discover no such continuity, usually because there is a serious mismatch between the configuration of concepts and relations expressed and the receivers' prior knowledge of the world. They (ibid:94) argue that knowledge and meaning are context sensitive. Based on this view, Beaugrande and Dressler suggest that this can be a candidate model for text coherence. Also, they (ibid:95) claim that the concepts expressed in the text are the steps in the construction of the continuity of sense.

Coherence is also concerned with 'relational coherence where smaller textual units combine into larger ones' (Egg and Redeker 2012:1). For Martin (2015:62), coherence is the process whereby a reading position is naturalized by texts for listeners and readers. Thus, without coherence, communication slows down and may break down.

The continuity of senses is a prototypical feature of coherence. This is illustrated by the following example:

> 1. walā tadᶜu maᶜa allāhi ilāhan ākhar – Do not invoke with God another deity → 2. lā ilāha illā hū – There is no deity except Him → 3. kullu shai'in hālikun illā wajhahu – Everything will be destroyed except His face → 4. lahu al-ḥukmu – He is the judgement → 5. ilaihi turjaᶜūn – To Him you shall all be brought back, Q28:88.

where we have a series of different messages (text segments) each with a similar thought and intended meaning, and, most importantly, all point to the same illocutionary force intended by the text producer, namely 'monotheism'. We are instructed by the initial message not to invoke with God another deity. This is the pivotal thought of the interlocutor (text producer). The underlying sense of this command continues in the subsequent messages. However, the text producer needs to undertake four important decisions hinged upon text linguistics:

- i coherence and continuity of senses among the different messages that occur after each other,
- ii organization of the constituent segments of each message,
- iii making salient a specific segment of each message through which the continuity of senses and coherence are realized, and
- iv substantiation of the pivotal thought through syntactic mechanisms that can deliver coherence.

In text (2), the no-main-verb nominal sentence is employed, which gives saliency to monotheism as the major thought of the macro text (Q2:88). Also, the affirmation stylistic technique of negation + exception (lā (no) + illā (except)) to deliver the illocutionary force of affirmation of monotheism. The no-main-verb nominal sentence is employed to demonstrate the semantic componential features [+ Continuity] and [+ Permanency] of the notion (theme) of monotheism. In text (3), we encounter the no-main-verb nominal sentence + foregrounding (placing a text's segment sentence-initially) + the employment of the active participle (ism al-fāᶜil) in order to give saliency to monotheism, the eternity of God, and the destruction of everything. Thus, (kullu shai'in – Everything) is placed sentence-initially. It is worthwhile to note that the active participle (hālik – is destroyed) has an underlying meaning of a passive participle (ism mafᶜūl), since it means (muhlak – will be destroyed (sayatimmu fanā'uh)). In text (4), the illocutionary force of specificity (al-takhṣiṣ) is achieved through the saliency and foregrounding of the prepositional phrase (lahu – to Him (God)). This organization of segments has led to the continuity of senses and the substantiation of the thought of monotheism. The same applies to text (5) where we have saliency and foregrounding of the propositional phrase (ilaihi – to Him (God)) to achieve specificity of this notion, i.e., it is God specific.

5.3 Coherence and cohesion

A cohesive text is not necessarily coherent, but a coherent text is necessarily cohesive. This entails that cohesion is a prerequisite of coherence. For more details on cohesion, see Chapter 6. Let us put our claim to the test. Consider the following examples:

Example 1

> qālat rabbi annā yakūnu lī waladun walam yamsasnī basharun qāla **kadhālik** allāhu yakhluqu mā yashā' – She (Mary) said: 'My Lord, how will I have a child when no man has touched me?' The angel said: '**Such** is God. He creates what He wills. When He decrees a matter, He only says to it: "Be", and it is', Q3:47.

In this text, the word (kadhālik – such) is the cohesive tie that has made the text cohesive and substituted for a whole clause. To remove (kadhālik), the text will not hang together, i.e., it will have neither cohesion nor coherence:

> (qālat rabbi annā yakūnu lī waladun walam yamsasni basharun qāla {**yakūnu laki waladun walam yamsaski basharun**} allāhu yakhluqu mā yashā' – She (Mary) said: 'My Lord, how will I have a child when no man has touched me?' The angel said: {**You will have a child when no man has touched you**}. God creates what He wills. When He decrees a matter, He only says to it: "Be", and it is').

Example 2

> man kāna yurīdu al-ᶜājilata ᶜajjalnā lahu fihā . . . man arāda al-ākhirata wa saᶜā lahā saᶜyahā wahuwa mu'minun . . . kullan numiddu **hā'ulā'** wa **hā'ulā'** min ᶜaṭā'i rabbika – Whoever should desire the immediate, We (God) hasten for him from it . . . But whoever desires the hereafter and exerts the effort due to it while he is a believer . . . To each category, We (God) extend, to **those** and to **those**, from the gift of your Lord, Q17:18–20.

where the first demonstrative pronoun (hā'ulā' – those) substitutes for the clause (man kāna yurīdu al-ᶜājilata – whoever should desire the immediate), while the second (hā'ulā' – those) substitutes for the clause (man arāda al-ākhirata wa saᶜā lahā saᶜyahā wahuwa mu'minun – whoever desires the hereafter and exerts the effort due to it while he is a believer). Due to the substitution process through the demonstrative pronoun (hā'ulā'), the text has attained cohesion. However, to replace what (hā'ulā') has substituted, we get the following text, which lacks both cohesion and coherence:

> (man kāna yurīdu al-ᶜājilata ᶜajjalnā lahu fihā . . . man arāda al-ākhirata wa saᶜā lahā saᶜyahā wahuwa mu'minun . . . kullan numiddu {**liman kana yuridu al-ᶜājilata**} wa {**liman arāda al-ākhirata wa saᶜā lahā saᶜyahā wahuwa mu'minun**} min ᶜaṭā'i rabbika – Whoever should desire the immediate, We (God) hasten for him from it . . . But whoever desires the hereafter and exerts the effort due to it while he is a believer. . . . To each category, We (God) extend, to {**whoever should desire the immediate**} and to {**whoever desires the hereafter and exerts the effort due to it while he is a believer**}, from the gift of your Lord).

Example 2

> wal-qur'ān dhi al-dhikr . . . **huwa** naba'un ᶜaẓīmum . . . in **huwa** illā dhikrun lil- cālamīn – By the Qur'an containing reminder . . . **It** is great news . . . **It** is but a reminder to the world, Q38:1, 67 and 87.

The above text includes nominal substitution where the pronoun (huwa – it) substitutes for the noun phrase (al-qur'ān dhi al-dhikr – the Qur'an containing reminder). If we bring back what the pronoun (huwa) has substituted, the result will be the following text that lacks both cohesion and coherence:

> (al-qur'ān dhi al-dhikr . . . {**al-qur'ān dhi al-dhikr**} naba'un ᶜaẓimum . . . in {**al-qur'ān dhi al-dhikr**} illā dhikrun lil-ᶜālamīn – By the Qur'an containing reminder . . . {**The Qur'an containing reminder**} is great news . . . {**The Qur'an containing reminder**} is but a reminder to the world).

Example 3

> huwa alladhī yabda'u al-khalqa thumma yuᶜīduh wa **huwa** ahwanu ᶜalaih – It is He who begins creation, then He repeats it, and that is easier for Him, Q30:27.

This text involves verbal substitution where the pronoun (huwa – that) substitutes for the verbal clause (yabda'u al-khalqa thumma yuᶜīduh – He (God) begins creation, then He repeats it). To replace what the pronoun (huwa) substitutes will result in the following text that lacks cohesion and coherence:

> (huwa alladhī yabda'u al-khalqa thumma yuᶜīduh wa {**bad'u al-khalqi thumma iᶜādatihi**} ahwanu ᶜalaih – It is He (God) who begins creation, then He repeats it, and {**the beginning of creation and repeating it**} is easier for Him).

Example 4

wamin āyātihi yurīkum al-barqa khawfan waṭamaᶜan wayunazzilu min al-samā'i mā'an fayuḥyi bihi al-arḍa baᶜda mawtihā inna fī **dhālika** la'āyāt liqawmin yaᶜqilūn – And of His (God's) signs is that He shows you the lightning causing fear and aspiration, and He sends down rain from the sky by which he brings to life the earth after its lifelessness. Indeed, in that are signs for a people who use reason, Q30:24

where the demonstrative pronoun (dhālika) substitutes for the verbal clauses (yurīkum al-barqa khawfan waṭamaᶜan – He shows you the lightning causing fear and aspiration) and (wayunazzilu min al-samā'i mā'an fayuḥyī bihi al-arḍa baᶜda mawtihā – He sends down rain from the sky by which he brings to life the earth after its lifelessness). To bring back what the pronoun (dhālika) has substituted will create the following text that lacks cohesion and coherence:

(wamin āyātihi yurīkum al-barqa khawfan waṭamaᶜan wayunazzilu min al-samā'i mā'an fayuḥyi bihi al-arḍa baᶜda mawtihā inna fī {**ira'atakum al-barqa khawfan waṭamaᶜan wa'an yunazzila min al-samā'i mā'an fayuḥyi bihi al-arḍa baᶜda mawtihā**} la'āyāt liqawmin yaᶜqilūn – And of His (God's) signs is that He shows you the lightning causing fear and aspiration, and He sends down rain from the sky by which he brings to life the earth after its lifelessness. Indeed, in {showing you the lightning causing fear and aspiration, and sending down rain from the sky by which he brings to life the earth after its lifelessness} are signs for a people who use reason).

Example 5

The cohesion process of reference (co-referentiality – ᶜawdat al-ḍamir ᶜalā al-ism) plays a pivotal role in the realization of a cohesive and a coherent text, as illustrated by the following example:

allāhu lā ilāha illā huwa . . . lā ta'khudhuhu sinatun walā nawmun lahu mā fī al-samāwāti . . . man dha alladhī yashfaᶜu ᶜindahu illā bi'idhnihi yaᶜlamu mā baina aidīhim wamā khalfahum walā yuḥīṭūn bishai'in min ᶜilmihi illā bimā shā' . . . wasiᶜa kursiyyuhu al-samāwāt wal-arḍ wa lā ya'uduhu ḥifẓihimā wa huwa al-ᶜaliyyu al-ᶜaẓim – God – there is no deity except Him . . . Neither drowsiness overtakes Him nor sleep. To Him belongs whatever is in the heavens . . . Who is it that can intercede with Him except by His permission? He knows what is present before them and what will be after them, and they do not encompass a thing of His knowledge except for what He wills . . . His kursi extends over the heavens and the earth and their preservation does not tire Him, and He is the most high, the most great, Q2:255

The above text enjoys both cohesion and coherence where the pronouns (huwa – He, Him), (-hu – Him) of (ta'khudhuhu – overtake Him), (-hu – Him) of (lahu – to

Him), (-hu – Him) of (ᶜindahu – with Him), (-hi – His) of (bi'idhnihi – by His permission), the implicit pronoun (huwa – He) in the verb (yaᶜlamu – He knows), the pronoun (-hi – His) of (ᶜilmihi – His knowledge), the implicit pronoun (huwa – He) of (shā' – He wills), the pronoun (-hu – His) of (kursiyyuhu – His kursi), and the pronoun (-hu – Him) of (ya'uduhu – tire Him) refer to (allāhu – God). The pronoun (-humā – their (dual)) of (ḥifẓihimā – their preservation) refer to (al-samāwāt wal-arḍ – the heavens and the earth). However, the pronouns (-him – them/their) of (aidīhim – (literally) their hands), (-hum – them) of (khalfahum – after them), and the implicit masculine plural pronoun (-un – they) of (yuḥīṭūn – they encompass) refer to the plural noun represented by the exegetically based clause (all those who have the intellect and are living either in the heavens or on earth). However, if we take out all the elements of reference from the above text, the result will be a text that has neither cohesion nor coherence:

> (allāhu lā ilāha illā {**allah**} . . . lā ta'khudh {**allah**} sinatun walā nawmun li {**allah**} mā fī al-samāwāti . . . man dha alladhī yashfaᶜu ᶜinda {**allah**} illā bi'idhn {**allah**} yaᶜlam {**allah**} mā baina aidihim wamā khalfahum walā yuḥīṭūn bishai'in min ᶜilm {**allah**} illā bimā shā' {**allah**} . . . wasiᶜa kursiyyu {**allah**} al-samāwāt wal-arḍ wa lā ya'udu {**allah**} ḥifẓihimā wa {**allah**} al-ᶜaliyyu al-ᶜaẓim – God – there is no deity except {**God**} . . . Neither drowsiness overtakes {**God**} nor sleep. To {**God**} belongs whatever is in the heavens . . . Who is it that can intercede with {**God**} except by {**God's**} permission? {**God**} knows what is present before them and what will be after them, and they do not encompass a thing of {**God's**} knowledge except for what {**God**} wills . . . {**God's**} kursi extends over the heavens and the earth and their preservation does not tire {**God**}, and {**God**} is the most high, the most great).

Example 6

However, not all cohesion processes affect the coherence of a text. For instance, the absence of the cohesion process of reiteration and lexical cohesion does not affect the coherence of the text, as in the following example:

> bal kadhdhabū bil-sāᶜati wa'aᶜtadnā liman kadhdhaba bil-**sācati** saᶜirā – But they have denied the hour, and We have prepared for those who deny the **hour** a blaze, Q25:11

where the noun (sāᶜati – hour) is repeated for lexical cohesion. Thus, it flouts the cohesion process of reference. In other words, the co-referential pronoun (-hā – it (the hour)). Thus, we should have:

> (bal kadhdhabū bil-sāᶜati wa'aᶜtadnā liman kadhdhaba bi{**hā**} saᶜirā – But they have denied the hour, and We have prepared for those who deny {**it**} a blaze). However, both types of text are coherent.

Example 7

Similarly, the absence of the cohesion process of ellipsis does not affect the coherence of the text, as in:

> laisa ᶜalā al-aᶜmā ḥarajun wa **lā ᶜalā** al-aᶜraji **ḥarajun** wa **lā ᶜalā** al-maridi **ḥarajun** wa **lā ᶜalā** anfusikum an ta'kulū min buyūtikum aw . . . – There is not upon the blind any constraint **nor upon** the lame **constraint**, **nor upon** the ill **constraint**, **nor upon** yourselves when you eat from own homes or . . ., Q24:61

where the negative particle (lā – not) + the preposition (ᶜalā – upon) and the noun (ḥarajun – constraint) are repeated, but their repetition can be avoided, i.e., they can be ellipted. Thus, we have:

> (laisa ᶜalā al-aᶜmā wal-aᶜraji wal-marīḍi wa'anfusikum ḥarajun an ta'kulū min buyūtikum aw . . . – There is not upon the blind, the lame, the ill, and yourselves any constraint when you eat from own homes or . . .).

However, ellipsis is avoided to achieve reiteration.

Example 8

alladhīna lā yu'tūna al-zakāta wa **hum** bil-ākhirati **hum** kāfirūn – Those who do not give zakāt, and in the hereafter they are disbelievers, Q41:7

where we have the pronoun (hum – they) used for reiteration and lexical cohesion. However, to remove (hum), the text will remain both cohesive and coherent:

> (alladhīna lā yu'tūna al-zakāta wa bil-ākhirati kāfirūn – Those who do not give zakāt, and disbelieve in the hereafter).

However, the illocutionary force of affirmation is missing.

5.4 Grammatical mechanisms of coherence

In Qur'anic discourse, coherence is achieved through different grammatical mechanisms that give a text's segment potency. The organization of Qur'anic textual units involves the following mechanisms:

i The purposeful configuration of sentence constituents: This is concerned with the planning of word order. This is concerned with the configuration of the constituent units of the text, such as nouns, verbs, adjectives (God's epithets in particular), prepositional phrases, and noun phrases. The positioning of a sentence constituent is highly significant for the delivery of a given illocutionary force. Thus, foregrounding (al-taqdīm) and backgrounding (al-ta'khīr) are frequently employed in Qur'anic discourse. Similarly, the placement of a subject noun before the verb, i.e., the employment of a noun at sentence-initial position, has an illocutionary force (communicative, pragmatic function).

ii The purposeful selection of grammatical form: The selection of a given grammatical form rather than the other is well planned for a specific pragmatic and communicative function. This involves the selection of the following mechanisms:

1 an active participle rather than a passive participle,
2 the selection of a noun rather than a verb,
3 the selection of a hyperbole adjective rather than an active participle,
4 the selection of a passive voice rather than an active voice or vice versa,
5 the selection of a no-main-verb nominal sentence, and
6 the selection of a nominalized noun (maṣdar) rather than a verb.

iii The purposeful selection of conjunctive particles and confirmation tools: The selection of a specific cohesive device or confirmation tools like the detached pronoun (huwa – He (God)) and the confirmation /l/ (lām al-tawkīd) are not haphazardly done.

iv The purposeful selection of lexical items: There is a close relationship between the word and the coherence of the message. The word is a major constituent unit of the statement, and its selection is purposeful in order for the illocutionary force to be effectively and successfully delivered.

We can argue that the planning of word order, the purposeful selection of grammatical form, of conjunctive particles, of confirmation tools, and of lexical items contribute to the continuity of senses. For more details, see Sections 5.5.1 and 5.8.

5.5 Coherence and linguistics

The different disciplines of linguistics (syntax, semantics, morphology, word order (style), and phonetics) play a pivotal role in the attainment of coherence. This constitutes a research gap. In other words, the impact of the different disciplines of linguistics on the attainment of coherence has not been accounted for in text linguistics. To fill in this research gap, we will provide an investigation of grammar-based, semantics-based, morphology-based, stylistics-based, and phonetics-based contextual coherence, i.e., a link between coherence and grammar, semantics, morphology, style, and phonetics and how these different disciplines of linguistics play a role in saliency and potency of a text's segment. Our approach accounts for saliency, communicative prominence, and how the text producer attains coherence and continuity of senses through linguistics-based mechanisms such as the employment of a noun-initial main verb sentence, a verb-initial sentence, a sentence-initial prepositional phrase, an active participle, a passive participle, a grammatical pattern of sentence-initial emphatic (inna) + a noun modifier of the subject noun + main verb, configuration of text segments, the morphological form of a lexeme, and the phonetic features of a lexeme. Through the linguistic mechanisms, coherence can be achieved, and the illocutionary force of the message is delivered to the text receiver.

5.5.1 Mechanisms of linguistics-based coherence

Let us consider the following mechanisms of linguistics-based coherence:

1 **Coherence through a prepositional phrase sentence-initially rather than the verb**: This is explained in the following examples:

Example 1

bil-ākhirati hum yūqinūn – In the hereafter they firmly believe, Q2:4

where we have a sentence-initial prepositional phrase (bil-ākhirati – in the hereafter) rather than a verb-initial sentence {yūqinūn bil-ākhirati – They firmly believe in the hereafter}. The context is about 'those conscious of God, who believe in the unseen, Q2:2–3'. Thus, to achieve coherence, saliency is given to eschatology as a tenet of faith 'in the hereafter' since it is the focus of the text producer's message rather than the verb (yūqin – believe firmly).

Example 2

ilaihi marjiᶜukum jamīᶜan – To Him (God) is your return all together, Q10:4

where we have a marked (unusual) sentence structure with a foregrounded (sentence-initial) prepositional phrase (ilaihi – to Him) rather than an unmarked (expected, usual) word order {marjiᶜukum jamīᶜan ilaihi – your return all together is to Him}. To achieve continuity of senses and contextual coherence, (ilaihi) is made salient through its position sentence-initially to reinforce the illocutionary force of (resurrection being made specifically to God and no one else). The continuity of senses: (substantiation of God's omnipotence in Q10:3) → (a command urging people to worship their Lord in Q10:3) → (the return will be specifically to Him).

Example 3

lillāhi yasjudu man fī al-samāwāti wal-arḍi – To God prostrates whoever is within the heavens and the earth, Q13:15

where the propositional phrase (lillāhi – to God) is employed sentence-initially rather than a verb-initial sentence {yasjudu lillāhi man fī al-samāwāti wal-arḍi ṭawᶜan wakarhan – Prostrating to God whoever is within the heavens and the earth}. We observe that the sentence-initial prepositional phrase (lillāhi – to God) is given saliency to attain contextual coherence and continuity of senses. The macro context (Q13:1–14) is about the revelation being the truth from the Lord yet people do not believe, statements substantiating God's omnipotence (2–4, 8, 12–13), and reference to the sceptics and deniers (5–7, 14). The foregrounding of the prepositional phrase (lillāhi – to God) gives it saliency, which enhances the illocutionary force of specificity, i.e., (the prostration of whoever is within the heavens and the earth is specifically made to God and no one else).

Example 4

lahu al-mulk/lahu al-ḥamd/huwa ᶜalā kulli shai'in qadīr – To Him belongs dominion / To Him belongs praise / He is over all things competent, Q64:1

In the above marked (unusual) word order, we have three salient text segments: the two prepositional phrases (lahu – to Him (God)) and (ᶜalā kulli shai'in – over all things). Thus, specificity (al-ikhtiṣāṣ) has been achieved through the salient text segments: dominion is God-specific, praise is God-specific, and total control over all things is God-specific. Saliency is a text linguistic feature.

For more details on saliency, see Section 6.7.

Example 5

Let us consider the following interesting examples:

1 bil-ḥaqqi anzalnāhu – With truth We have sent it (the Qur'an) down, Q17:105
2 bil-ḥaqqi nazal – With truth it has descended, Q17:105

where the sentence-initial prepositional phrase (bil-ḥaqqi – with truth) is given saliency to attain contextual coherence and continuity of senses.

Now let us compare Q17:105 with the following examples:

3 anzalnā ilaika al-kitāba bil-ḥaqqi – We have revealed to you the Book in truth, Q5:48
4 khalaqa al-samāwāti wal-arḍa bil-ḥaqqi – He created the heavens and earth in truth, Q16:3

where Q5:48 and Q16:3 above have unmarked (usual) word order with the verb sentence-initially and the prepositional phrase (bil-ḥaqqi – in truth) at sentence-final position. The actions denoted by the verbs (anzala – to reveal, send down) and (khalaqa – to create) are highlighted (made salient) rather than the prepositional phrase. Thus, the latter is placed at its usual position because it is not made salient.

It is worthwhile to note that foregrounding in Qur'anic discourse is semantically and pragmatically oriented. Through foregrounding, we attain the following results:

i We get a marked (unusual) word order,
ii The text producer's performative intent is delivered,
iii We achieve the illocutionary force of specificity,

iv We attain the text linguistic feature of saliency, and
v We establish the stylistic feature of affirmation.

2 **Coherence through the active participle (ism al-fāᶜil)**: The active participle has the pragmatic functions of [+ Permanency], [+ Continuity], [+ Renewability], the verb has the pragmatic functions of [+ Action Taking Place], [+ Renewability], [– Continuity], and [– Permanency], and the comparative adjective designates the pragmatic functions of [+ Better Than]. Let us consider the following examples:

Example 1

dhālika al-kitābu lā raiba fīhi hudan lil-muttaqīn. alladhīna yu'minūna bil-ghaibi wayuqīmūna al-ṣalāta wamimmā razaqnāhum yunfiqūn. walladhīna yu'minuna bima unzila ilaika wamā unzila min qablika wabil-ākhirati hum yūqinūn. ulā'ika ᶜalā hudan min rabbihim wa'ulā'ika hum al-mufliḥūn – This is the Book about which there is no doubt, a guidance for those conscious of God, who believe in the unseen, establish prayer, and spend out of what We have provided for them. And who believe in what has been revealed to you, (O Muḥammad), and what was revealed before you, and of the hereafter they are certain in faith. Those are upon the right guidance from their Lord, and it is those who are the successful, Q2:2–5

where we have the active participle (muttaqūn – the conscious of God) rather than the alternative verb form (yattaqūn) or the alternative grammatical pattern (alladhīna yattaqūn – who are conscious of God), which can form a stylistic symmetry with the following relative clauses (alladhīna yu'minūna . . . – who believe in . . .) and (alladhīna yu'minūna . . . – who believe in . . .). However, syntax-based coherence requires the active participle to fulfil the sequentiality of thoughts, and the illocutionary force of [+ Continuity] and [Permanency], which represent the text producer's intended meaning. The use of the active participle in sentence 2 is also backed up by the active participle (al-mufliḥūn – the successful) in sentence 5. Based on sentence 2, the Qur'an (al-kitābu – the Book) is a guidance for a specific category of people labelled (muttaqūn), and in the concluding sentence 5, they are also referred to in the active participle and defined as (mufliḥūn). This particular section of people (muttaqūn) enjoys specific character traits, which are listed in sentences 3–4:

i yu'minūna bil-ghaibi – believe in the unseen,
ii yuqīmūna al-ṣalāta – establish prayer,
iii mimmā razaqnāhum yunfiqūn – spend out of what We have provided for them,
iv yu'minuna bimā unzila ilaika – believe in what has been revealed to you,
v yu'minūna bimā unzila min qablika – believe in what was revealed before you, and
vi bil-ākhirati hum yūqinūn – of the hereafter they are certain in faith.

Then, in the concluding sentence 5, the (muttaqūn) are described as:

a ulā'ika ᶜalā hudan min rabbihim – Those are upon the right guidance from their Lord, and
b ulā'ika hum al-mufliḥūn – Those who are the successful.

Furthermore, in sentence 2, the Book (al-kitābu) is described as (hudan – a guidance) for the (muttaqūn) and in 5, as part of continuity of thoughts, the (muttaqūn) are described as (ᶜalā hudan min rabbihim – are upon the right guidance, i.e., they are following their Lord's guidance). Thus, such section of the community should possess specific characteristics that enjoy the pragmatic features [+ Continuity] and [+ Permanency] in order to qualify for what has been concluded in sentence 5: (ᶜalā hudan min rabbihim) and (mufliḥūn). Having said this, it is inappropriate to use the verb (yattaqūn) instead of the active participle (muttaqūn). The verb has the features [– Continuity] and [– Permanency]. Thus, the active participle has contributed effectively in the attainment of coherence.

Example 2

allāhu khāliqu kulli shai'in – God is the creator of all things, Q13:16

where the active participle (khāliqu – Creator) occurs rather than a verb (yakhluqu – to create), and the sentence remains stylistically and grammatically sound. This is coherent because it fits in well with the other active participle (al-wāḥid – the one) and hyperbole form (al-qahhār – the prevailing) of the same complex sentence → (wa huwa al-wāḥid al-qahhār – He (God) is the One, the Prevailing, Q13:26). The continuity of senses stems from the rebuttal to (people who have taken allies besides God, these allies do not possess for themselves any benefit or any harm, these allies are likened to the blind and to darkness, and these allies cannot create anything). Thus, the active participle delivers an illocutionary force that substantiates God's ability to be → (khāliqu kulli shai'in – the creator of all things). The active participle stimulates the illocutionary force of a habitual action and a permanent characteristic.

Example 3

When there is a context of challenge and the text is argumentative involving the text producer (protagonist) and an opponent (antagonist), the text producer resorts to the employment of the active participle as a defensive tool of rebuttal and substantiating own thesis, as in:

afara'aitum mā taḥruthūn? a'antum tazraᶜūnahu am naḥnu al-zāriᶜūn? . . . am naḥnu al-munzilūn? . . . am naḥnu al-munshi'ūn? – Have you seen that seed which you sow? Is it you who make it grow, or are We (God) the grower? . . . or is it We (God) who bring it down? . . . or are We (God) the producer?, Q56:63–64, 69, 72 where coherence is context sensitive in the above text segments of argumentation. Thus, the active participles (al-zāri^{c}ūn – the grower, al-munzilūn – the one who brings water down, al-munshi'ūn – the producer) are appropriately selected for the illocutionary force of rebuttal and substantiation of own proposition.

3 **Coherence through the hyperbole adjective (ṣīghat al-mubālaghah)**: It is worthwhile to note that the hyperbole forms are like (fa^{c}ūl), (mif^{c}āl), (fa^{c}īl), (fa^{cc}āl), and (fa^{c}il). Let us consider the appropriate selection of the hyperbole adjective (kafūr) and its illocutionary force:

> innā hadaināhu al-sabīla immā shākiran wa'immā kafūrā – Indeed, We (God) guided him (men and women) to the way, be he/she grateful or be he/she ungrateful, Q76:3

> lā tuṭi^{c} minhum āthiman aw kafūrā – Do not obey from among them a sinner or ungrateful, Q76:24

In terms of text linguistics, the purposeful selection of the hyperbole adjective (ṣīghat al-mubālaghah on the morphological form (fa^{c}ūl) ⟶ (kafūr – ungrateful)) in Qur'anic discourse is for a good reason. This is a hyperbole form that achieves coherence. Pragmatically, the hyperbole adjective designates [+ Preference], [+ Multitude], [+ Repetition], and [+ Permanency]. Semantically, it has two meanings: (i) hyperbole in disbelief as in Q22:66 and (ii) hyperbole in being ungrateful as in Q76:3. Thus, to change the hyperbole adjective (kafūr) to an active participle (kāfir – a disbeliever), the intended meaning of the text producer's message would have been seriously undermined. Grammatically and stylistically, as text receivers, we have expected to encounter (active participle (shākir) + active participle (kāfir)) in Q76:3 and (active participle (āthim) + active participle (kāfir)) in Q76:24. However, it is only through the hyperbole form (kafūr) that the illocutionary force of hyperbole in disbelief or in being ungrateful can be delivered. In terms of coherence, the same applies to Q11:107 where the hyperbole adjective (fa^{cc}āl – the effecter) is employed rather than its counterpart the verb (yaf^{c}al – to affect). However, the verb would have failed to deliver the illocutionary force of the hyperbole adjective through its features of [+ Multitude], [+ Repetition], and [+ Permanency].

It is interesting to note that cohesion is dependent on the morphological pattern of the lexeme that is to be made salient in the text. For instance, (ẓallām – is not ever unjust, Q3:182, Q8:51, Q22:10, Q41:46, Q50:29), clothes the text with cohesion through the pragmatic role and illocutionary force which it plays, which is that of hyperbole. It delivers more hyperbole to the text than its alternative active participle form (ẓālim – unjust), which fails to deliver the same pragmatic goal. Thus, cohesion cannot be achieved by the active participle (ẓālim).

4 **Coherence through the superlative adjective (ism al-tafḍīl), i.e., the superlative af^{c}al form (ṣighat af^{c}al al-tafḍīl)**: To achieve continuity of thought,

contextual coherence can best be achieved by a no-main-verb nominal sentence which is further fortified by the superlative af^{c}al morphological form. Let us consider the appropriate selection of the superlative adjective (a^{c}lam) and its illocutionary force:

> allāhu a^{c}lam bimā waḍa^{c}at – God was most knowing of what she delivered, Q3:36
>
> inna rabbaka huwa a^{c}lam man yaḍillu ^{c}an sabīlih wahuwa a^{c}lam bil-muhtadīn – Indeed, your Lord is most knowing of who strays from His way, and he is most knowing of the rightly guided, Q6:117
>
> allāhu a^{c}lam ḥaithu yaj^{c}alu risālatah – God is most knowing of with whom He places His message, Q6:124
>
> allāhu a^{c}lam bi'īmānihinna – God is most knowing as to their faith, Q60:10

where the superlative adjective (ism al-tafḍīl) → (a^{c}lam – most knowing, knows best) is the salient segment of these texts through which the text receiver decodes it as 'God is most knowledgeable' rather than Mary's mother who is a sceptic because she is concerned about the value of the baby's female gender she has given birth to. In other words, God knows best about the future that the baby girl named Mary will be the mother of a Prophet called Jesus. However, the sceptics are different in Q6:117 and 124. The salient superlative adjective is employed to rebut the polytheists and the People of the Book who have serious doubt about the revelation and the Prophethood of Muḥammad. Thus, the text is given potency and communication momentum through the segment (a^{c}lam), which is a superlative adjective. It is also worthwhile to note that the salient lexeme is further supported by the nominal status of the statement, i.e., Q6:117 and 124 are nominal sentences which designate [+ Continuity], [+ Permanency] of a given feature, namely 'God being the most knowing' → (a^{c}lam), i.e., saliency of God's knowledge and wisdom with regards to where the role of prophethood is assigned. However, saliency, and consequently cohesion, will not be achieved had we changed the hyperbole lexeme (a^{c}lam) to a verb form (ya^{c}lam – to know).

A unique example of continuity of senses and contextual coherence is Q60:10 (allāhu a^{c}lam bi'īmānihinna – God is most knowing as to their faith), which represents continuity (sequentiality, chaining) to the beginning of the same āyah (yā aiyuhā alladhīna āmanū idhā jā'akum al-mu'mināṭu muhājirātin famtaḥinūhunna – O you who have believed, when the believing women come to you as emigrants, test them).

It is worthwhile to note that lexemes like (a^{c}lam) are referred to in Arabic grammar as the superlative af^{c}al form (ṣighat af^{c}al al-tafḍil), which acquire saliency in their relevant text and achieve coherence due to the fact that they perform two types of illocutionary force: (i) hyperbole, and (ii) preference over other things. However, it should be noted that the superlative af^{c}al form (aẓlam) enjoys a lesser degree of hyperbole than its counterpart lexeme (ẓallām), which has a higher degree of hyperbole.

Among the lexemes which have the superlative afᶜal form are (aẓlam – most unjust, Q2:114), which has occurred 16 times in the Qur'an, (aḥraṣu – the most greedy, Q2:96), (aḥabbu – the most beloved, Q12:8), (akhfā – the most hidden, Q20:7), (abqā – the most enduring, Q87:17).

5 **Coherence through the nominal sentence**: A reporting speech act can be made coherent through the stylistic technique of affirmation where the grammatical pattern of the speech act is changed. There are two grammatical techniques of affirmation which deliver coherence. These are:

i coherence through the no-main-verb nominal sentence: The employment of a no-main-verb nominal sentence is a stylistic technique for the achievement of coherence and the illocutionary force of affirmation. The continuity of senses and coherence is achieved through the nominal sentences without a main verb, as in:

> al-ḥamdu lillāh rabb al-ᶜālamīn – All praise is due to God, Lord of the worlds, Q1:2

where this nominal sentence is initiated by a nominalised noun (maṣdar) → (al-ḥamdu) in order to designate the illocutionary force of [+ Continuity] and [+ Permanency] of our praise to God, i.e., the praise is continuous and there is no interruption whatsoever of our praise to the Lord. However, this illocutionary force ceases through the alternative verbal form: {naḥmid allāh rabb al-ᶜālamīn – We give all due praise to God, Lord of the worlds}. This verbal syntactic form designates the illocutionary force of [+ Renewability], which does not befit God. In other words, the verb-initial text means our praise to the Lord is interrupted and not continuous. On the interpersonal level of communication, the nominalised noun stylistic pattern is pragmatically more affirmative than its counterpart verbal pattern.

> dhālikum allāhu rabbukum – That is God, your Lord, Q10:3 where the continuity of senses is achieved through this affirmative sentence that is coherently linked to the previous intra-sentential context of Q10:3 and is a continuation to it where (rabbukum – your Lord) is presented as (alladhī khalaqa al-samāwāti wal-arḍa – who created the heavens and the earth). Thus, the text producer's communicative interest lies in the doer of the creation, i.e., (allāhu – God), rather than in the action of creation represented by the verb (khalaqa – to create). Similarly, the affirmative no-main-verb sentence (dhālikum allāhu rabbukum) is followed by an imperative verbal sentence (faᶜbudūh – Worship Him (God)) rather than {faᶜbudū allāha rabbakum – Worship God, your Lord}.

Other examples of coherence delivered through the no-main-verb nominal sentence are:

> dhālika al-kitābu lā raiba fīhi hudan lil-muttaqīn – This is the Book about which there is no doubt, a guidance for those conscious of God, Q2:2

dhālikum allāḥu rabbukum – That is God, your Lord, lā ilāha illā hū – There is no deity except Him, khāliqu kulli shai' – The Creator of all things, Q6:102

mā naḥnu bitāriki ālihatinā ᶜan qawlika – We will not forsake our gods on the grounds of what you have said, Q11:53

mā naḥnu laka bimu'minīn – We are not believers in you, Q11:53; ilāhukum ilāhun wāḥidun – Your God is the One God, Q16:22

qur'ānan ᶜarabiyyan ghaira dhī ᶜiwajin – It is an Arabic Qur'an, without any deviance, Q39:28

mā khalqukum wamā baᶜthukum illā kanafsin wāḥidatin – Your creation and your resurrection will not be but as that of a single soul, Q31:28

al-ḥamdu lillāhi fāṭir al-samāwāti wal-arḍi jāᶜil al-malā'ikati rusulan ulī ajniḥatin mathnā wathulātha warubāᶜ – All praise is due to God, creator of the heavens and the earth, who made the angels messengers having wings, two or three or four, Q35:1

Through Q35:1, we can observe two interesting text linguistics facts:

1 This is a no-main-verb nominal sentence whose illocutionary force is affirmation of God's omnipotence,
2 Q35:1 is the spearhead of conceptual sequentiality, i.e., there is a chain of senses. These senses hark back to each other under the umbrella of God's omnipotence as the pivotal theme (thought) of the macro text. Q35:1 has set the scene for the continuity of thought.

The thought of God's omnipotence is made salient through the no-main-verb nominal sentence (inna allāha ᶜalā kulli shai'in qadīr – God is over all things competent, Q35:1), which is employed as the first backup to the initial part of the nominal sentence Q35:1, which flags up the major thought of God's omnipotence. The chain of senses continues. In Q35:2, we are informed about God being able to grant or withhold mercy to people; in Q35:3, we are admonished about God as the only provider of provision to humanity; in Q35:9, we are informed about God's omnipotence with regards to the winds, how they stir the clouds, and how the rain gives back life to a dead land; in Q35:11, we are told about how people are created from dust, then from a sperm-drop; in Q35:12, we are informed about God's omnipotence with regards to the two different types of water: the fresh, sweet and palatable versus the salty and bitter water; and finally, in Q35:13, we read about a series of God's omnipotence: how God causes the night to enter the day, how God causes the day to enter the night, and how God has subjected the sun and the moon, each running its course for a specified term. Thus, the continuity of senses (coherence) has been maintained and linked to the initial no-main-verb nominal sentence (Q35:1).

Also, a series of no-main-verb nominal sentences is encountered in Q59:22–24, which has contributed to contextual coherence and continuity of the thought (theme) of prophethood referred to in Q59:21.

ii coherence through the noun-initial nominal sentence with a main verb: This is where the subject (al-fa^c^il) of a given sentence is placed sentence-initially (foregrounded) before its verb in order to achieve the illocutionary force of affirmation. Thus, we attain the affirmation mode of discourse, as in:

> allāhu nazzala aḥsana al-ḥadīthi kitāban mutashābihan mathānī – God has sent down the best statement: a consistent Book wherein is reiteration, Q39:23

where the subject noun (allāhu – God) is placed before its verb (nazzala – sent down) for the illocutionary force of affirmation. Affirmation is achieved through the explicit noun (allāhu) and the implicit co-referential pronoun (huwa – He (God)) that refers to (allāhu). Thus, reference has been made twice to (allāhu). Other examples are:

> allāhu yastahzi'u bihim – God mocks them, Q2:15

> allāhu ya^c^lamu mā tusirrūna wamā tu^c^linūn – God knows what you conceal and what you declare, Q16:19

> allāhu khalaqakum thumma yatawaffākum – God created you; then He will take you in death, Q16:70

> allāhu faḍḍala ba^c^ḍakum ^c^alā ba^c^ḍin fī al-rizq – God has favoured some of you over others in provision, Q16:71

> allāhu ja^c^ala lakum min anfusikum azwājan . . . – God has made for you from yourselves mates, Q16:72

> allāhu akhrajakum min buṭūni ummahātikum lā ta^c^lamūna shai'an – God has extracted you from the wombs of your mothers, Q16:78

> allāhu ja^c^ala lakum min buyūtikum sakanan – God has made for you from your homes a place of rest, Q16:80

> allāhu ja^c^ala lakum mimmā khalaqa ẓilālan – God has made for you, from that which He has created, shades, Q16:81

> allāhu yabda'u al-khalqa thumma yu^c^īduh – God begins creation; then He will repeat it, Q30:11

Coherence can also be attained through the pronoun-initial nominal sentence with a main verb, as in:

> innā naḥnu nuḥyi wa numīt – It is We who give life and cause death, Q50:43

where coherence is achieved through the nominal status of the sentence (ismiyyat al-jumlah). The nominal status affirms a given notion, which is God's exclusive power to give life and cause death. In order to make this notion salient, the stylistic pattern of the sentence has to be in this grammatical structure. The affirmation mechanisms involved are: the employment of auxiliary (inna), the (-nā) of the subject, the employment of the majestic plural pronoun (nahnu), and the overall nominal status of the sentence. Similarly, in:

> allāhu dhū al-faḍl al-ᶜaẓim – God is the possessor of great bounty, Q57:29

where the notion of (faḍl – bounty) is confirmed with reference to its earlier occurrence in the same āyah. Thus, on the cohesion level, lexical cohesion has been achieved and coherence has also been attained through the employment of the no-main-verb nominal sentence, which is the most relevant stylistic pattern for coherence. The lexeme (faḍl) has occurred three times. The nominal sentence affirms the notion that 'bounty' is possessed by God alone. Q57:29 is intertextually related to Q57:21 where the same no-main-verb nominal sentence occurs, which also highlights the notion of (faḍl – bounty).

6 **Coherence through the use of sentence-initial emphatic particle (inna) + a noun (rabbakum – your Lord) + a noun + a relative pronoun (alladhī – who) + subject noun (allāhu – God) + the main verb:** Thus, we get a nominal sentence with a main verb as in the following examples:

> inna rabbakumu allāhu alladhī khalaqa al-samāwāti wal-arḍa . . . – Indeed, your Lord is God who created the heavens and the earth, Q10:3

rather than a verb-initial sentence structure:

(khalaqa allāhu rabbukum al-samāwāti wal-arḍa . . .). The illocutionary force has changed dramatically. To achieve contextual coherence with the preceding text segment Q10:2 which is on prophethood, Q10:3 provides details on God's omnipotence. To substantiate Q10:3, the nominal sentence structure is chosen with emphatic (inna) followed by two nouns: (rabbakum allāhu – your Lord is God).

inna allāha maᶜa alladhīna ittaqaw walladhīna hum muḥsinūn – Indeed, God is with those who fear Him and those who are doers of good, Q16:128. This is the conclusion of Q16, and usually the conclusion bears confirmation of the text producer. To confirm God's continuous support to the (ittaqaw – the conscious of God) and the (muḥsinūn – the doers of good), the concluding statement needs to be coherent. This is achieved through the syntactic mechanism of the nominal sentence (inna allāha – Indeed, God is . . .), which provides the text producer's perlocutionary effect in terms of [+ Continuity (of God's support to the conscious of God and to the doers of good)], [+ Permanency (of God's support to the conscious of God and to the doers of good)], and [– Renewability (i.e., God's support is not renewed every now and then but rather is continuous to this category of people)]. A verb-initial sentence would have failed the text producer's intended meaning and would have undermined the illocutionary force of the message. Thus, in terms of coherence, it is inappropriate to say (yanṣuru allāhu alladhīna ittaqaw walladhīna hum muḥsinūn – God supports those who fear Him and those who are doers of good). This is due to the fact that the illocutionary force of the text's thought is [– Continuity], [– Permanency], and [+ Renewability].

Coherence can also be realized through the sentence-initial emphatic particle (inna) + a no-main-verb nominal sentence, as in:

> inna hādhā lahuwa ḥaqqu al-yaqīn – Indeed, this is the true certainty, Q56:95

where we have three affirmation tools to affirm the notion of prophethood as a rebuttal to the deniers of Muḥammad's prophethood. These tools are: the auxiliary (inna), the /lām/ of affirmation cliticized onto the detached pronoun (huwa), and the detached pronoun (ḍamir al-faṣl) (huwa – it (meaning the Qur'an)).

7 **Coherence through the use of conjunctive particles and affirmation tools:** To make the message make sense and to make the thoughts interrelated within the text, a given conjunctive particle is chosen rather than the other, as in the following examples:

> fa'idhā sawwaituhu . . . faqaᶜū lahu sājidīn. fasajada al-malā'ikatu kulluhum ajmaᶜūn – When I have proportioned him . . . fall down to him in prostration. So the angels prostrated – all of them entirely, Q15:29–30

> faja ᶜalahum kaᶜaṣfin ma'kūl – He made them like cropped stubble, Q105:5

where the conjunctive particle /f/ (al-fā') designates the illocutionary force [+ Immediately], i.e., no delay is expected. This conjunctive particle is contrasted with the conjunctive particle (thumma – then), which designates the illocutionary force [– Immediately], i.e., delay in the action taken is expected, as in:

> walaqad khalaqnā al-insāna min sulālatin min ṭin. thumma jaᶜalanāhu nuṭfatan . . . thumma khalaqnā al-nuṭfata ᶜalaqatan . . . thumma innakum baᶜda dhālika lamaiyitūn. thumma innakum yawma al-qiyāmati tubᶜathūn – Certainly did We create man from an extract of clay. Then, We placed him as a sperm-drop . . . Then We made the sperm-drop into a clinging clot . . . Then indeed, after that you are to die. Then indeed, on the day of judgement, will be resurrected, Q23:12–16

A high level of assertiveness is achieved through the employment of the affirmation tools like (inna, anna), the /l/ letter (lām al-tawkīd), the detached pronoun, and the conjunctive particle (qad):

> inna al-insāna lafī khusr – Indeed, mankind is in loss, Q103:2 (inna + the letter /l/)

> anna ᶜadhabī huwa al-ᶜadhābu al-alīm – That it is My punishment which is the painful punishment, Q15:50 (anna + the detached pronoun (huwa))

> innā lanaḥnu nuḥyī wanumītu – Indeed, it is We who give life and cause death, Q15:23 (inna + the letter /l/ + the detached pronoun (naḥnu))

where the affirmation particle ((lām al-tawkīd) la – indeed, verily) is used with the majestic plural pronoun (naḥnu – We).

> inna rabbaka huwa yaḥshuruhum – Indeed, your Lord will gather them, Q15:25 (inna + the detached pronoun (huwa))
>
> innā laṣādiqūn – Indeed, we are truthful, Q15:64 (inna + the letter /l/)
>
> laqad khalaqna al-insāna min ṣalṣālin – We did certainly create man out of clay, Q15:26 (the letter /l/ + qad)
>
> laqad kāna lakum fī rasūl allāhi uswatan ḥasanatan – There has certainly been for you in the messenger of God an excellent pattern, Q33:21 (the letter /l/ + qad)

In terms of coherence and context, it is also interesting to observe the purposeful selection of the cohesive devices (idhā – if, when), (in – if), and (law – if). The conjunctive particle (idhā) has the pragmatic functions of [+ Certainty] of something to take place and [+ Multitude] of something taking place, i.e., when we are absolutely sure that something will take place and it is not merely an assumption, the particle (idhā) occurs, as in (idhā jā'a naṣru allāhi wal-fatḥ – When the victory of God has come, Q110:1). Also, in: (idhā qumtum ilā al-ṣalāti . . . in kuntum junuban . . . in kuntum marḍā aw ᶜalā safarin . . . – when you rise to perform prayer . . ., if you are in a state of janābah . . ., if you are ill or on a journey . . ., Q5:6) where the employment of (idhā) designates something that takes place frequently, i.e., the five daily prayers. However, the conjunctive particle (in) co-occurs with something that is merely assumed to take place but it does not or something that does not exist, i.e., not true, as in (in istaṭaᶜta an tabtaghī nafaqan fī al-arḍi – if you are able to seek a tunnel into the earth . . ., Q6:35), (in kāna lil-raḥmāni walad – if the most merciful had a son, Q43:81). Thus, (in) designates something impossible to take place. Similarly, the conjunctive particle (law) has a higher level of impossibility than the particle (in), as in (law anzalnā hādhā al-qur'āna ᶜalā jabalin . . . – If We had sent down the Qur'an upon a mountain, . . ., Q59:21) where the particle (law) designates the semantic componential feature [+ Impossible], i.e., it is not possible to send down the revelation on a mountain.

Coherence is context based; thus, we have contextual coherence. Context plays a decisive role in the purposeful selection of a given affirmation particle rather than another:

> alam tara ilā alladhīna tawallaw qawman ghaḍiba allāhu ᶜalaihim . . . yaḥlifūna ᶜalā al-kadhib wahum yaᶜlamūn. aᶜadda allāhu lahum ᶜadhāban shadīdan . . . ittakhadhū aimānahum junnatan faṣaddū ᶜan sabīl allāh . . . ulā'ika aṣḥābu al-nār . . . yawma yabᶜathuhum allāhu fayaḥlifūna lahu kamā yaḥlifuna lakum wayaḥsabūna annahum calā shai'in alā innahum hum al-kādhibūn. istaḥwadha ᶜalaihim al-shaitānu fa'ansāhum dhikra allāh ulā'ika ḥizbu al-shaiṭān alā inna hizba al-shaiṭān hum al-khāsirūn – Have you not seen

> (Prophet) those who give their loyalty to people with whom God is angry? . . . They knowingly swear to lies. God has prepared a severe torment for them . . . They have used their oaths to cover up their false deeds, and barred others from the path of God . . . They will be the inhabitants of hell . . . On the day God will resurrect them all, they will swear to Him as they swear to you, thinking that it will help them. Unquestionably, it is they who are the liars. Satan has gained control over them and made them forget God. They are the party of Satan. Unquestionably, the party of Satan will be the losers, Q58:14–19

The context is about those with whom God has become angry, who knowingly swear to lies, and who have become on Satan's side, i.e., they are members of the party of Satan. To achieve contextual coherence and continuity of thought, the following coherence-based mechanisms have been employed by the text producer in order to relay God's performative intent:

i The cohesive device (fa – al-fā') is employed with (prefixed to) the verbs (ṣaddū – to bar others, to avert them), (yahlifūn – swear, take oath), and (ansāhum – make them forget), and also prefixed to the prepositional phrase (lahum – to them). The cohesive device (fa) is semantically oriented and enjoys the semantic componential features of [+ Immediate Action], i.e., [– Delay]. In other words, an immediate action will take place without any delay.

ii The employment of the purposefully selected lexeme (istaḥwadha – to gain control over someone, to overcome someone) to make salient the pivotal thought of Satan's overcoming those with whom God has become angry, who knowingly swear to lies, and who have become on Satan's side.

iii The employment of the particle (alā – unquestionably), which has a dynamic pragmatic function serving the text producer's performative intent. The particle (alā) has the illocutionary force of warning. Thus, the reader is warned of the category of people mentioned in the text.

iv The employment of the no-main-verb nominal sentence for the pragmatic function of affirmation: (innahum hum al-kādhibūn – It is they who are the liars), (ulā'ika ḥizbu al-shaiṭān – they are the party of Satan), and (inna ḥizba al-shaiṭān hum al-khāsirūn – the party of Satan will be the losers).

> innā khalaqnā al-insāna min nuṭfatin amshājin nabtalīh faja^calnāhu samī^can baṣirā – Indeed, We (God) created man from a sperm-drop mixture that We may try him; and We made him hearing and seeing, Q76:2.

However, we encounter more affirmation tools in:

> innā naḥnu nazzalnā ᶜalaika al-qur'āna tanzīlā – Indeed, it is We (God) who have sent down to you (O Muḥammad), the Qur'an progressively, Q76:23

There is one affirmation particle used in Q76:2, which is the pronoun (innā – We). The reason is that the context of this statement is about the theme of creation (khalaqnā), which is the thought of this speech act. The addressee of Q76:2 is a believer in God as the creator of mankind, i.e., the disbelievers of Quraish used to believe that God created mankind. This is backed up by Q31:25 and Q39:38 (wala'in sa'altahum man khalaqa al-samāwāti wal-arḍa layaqulunna allāhu – If you ask them (the disbelievers of Quraish): 'Who created the heaven and earth?' they would surely say: 'God'). For this reason, there is no need to overload the speech act with confirmation particles because both the believers and the disbelievers share the same common ground (belief in God as the creator of mankind). However, the gap gets wider with the addressee in Q76:23 in terms of the major thought of this speech act. The main theme (thought) of Q76:23 is the revelation (the Qur'an), which the disbelievers reject as being the Word of God. To achieve coherence and substantiation of the theme, the affirmation load is increased where there are three affirmation tools employed since the thought of revelation is more significant than the thought of creation. Q76:23 involves three elements: (i) the source of revelation, i.e., God, (ii) the revelation, i.e., the Qur'an, and (iii) the person to whom the revelation is sent down, i.e., Muḥammad. Therefore, to achieve a coherent text, Q76:23 employs six affirmation mechanisms:

1 the auxiliary verb (inna),
2 the (na) of the first person singular pronoun (anā – I),
3 the majestic pronoun (naḥnu – We),
4 the attached plural pronoun (-nā – We) of the verb (nazzala) → (nazzalnā – We revealed),
5 the absolute object (al-mafᶜūl al-muṭlaq) → (tanzīlā – progressive revelation), and
6 the nominal status of the sentence (ismiyyat al-jumlah).

It is worthwhile to note that, in Qur'anic discourse, we have two more mechanisms of affirmation:

i Affirmation that is achieved through morphology and lexis: This is sub-classified into three categories:

   1 Lexical affirmation (al-tawkīd al-lafẓi) through the absolute object: The absolute object is a recurrent affirmation mechanism that contributes to the realization of coherence and continuity of sense. The absolute object is a stylistic mechanism which is morphology based and performs the following functions:

      a a pragmatic function of assertiveness (affirmation),
      b an embellishment rhetorical function of polyptoton, and
      c a semantic function of lexical cohesion through the reiteration of the initial verb from which the absolute object is coined.

   2 Lexical affirmation through the reiteration of a lexeme or a whole sentence: This is another stylistic mechanism whose pragmatic function is affirmation, as in (al-qāriᶜatu. mā al-qāriᶜatu. wamā

adrāka mā al-qāriᶜatu – The striking calamity. What is the striking calamity. What can make you know what the striking calamity is?, Q101:1–3) where the word (al-qāriᶜatu – the striking calamity) is repeated, and (kallā sawfa taᶜlamūn. thumma kallā sawfa taᶜlamūn – No! You are going to know. Then, no! You are going to know, Q102:3–4) where the entire verbal sentence is repeated.

3 Semantic affirmation (al-tawkīd al-maᶜnawī) through a given lexeme to confirm the meaning: This type of affirmation occurs in Qur'anic discourse and contributes to the attainment of coherence and continuity of thought. However, there is a set of lexemes like (kulluhum – all of them), (ajmaᶜūn – all of them), and (kāmilatun – complete). Such affirmation lexical items that occur for the pragmatic function of affirmation, such as (jamīᶜan – all together) in (fa'aghraqnāhu wamān maᶜahu jamīᶜan – We have drowned him and those with him, Q17:103) where (jamīᶜan) is employed for affirmation to the statement (fa'aghraqnāhu wamān maᶜahu – We have drowned him and those with him) that also signifies (all of them). Thus, (jamīᶜan) has the illocutionary force of affirmation. The other word that performs the same function is (kāmilatun – complete) in (tilka ᶜasharatun kāmilatun – Those are 10 complete days, Q2:196) where the lexeme (ᶜasharatun – 10) is affirmed by the lexeme (kāmilatun). We also encounter double affirmation through the semantic affirmation mechanism, as in (fasajada al-malā'ikatu kulluhum ajmaᶜūn – So the angels prostrated – all of them entirely, Q15:30, Q38:73) where we have two semantic affirmation tools, (kulluhum – all of them) and (ajmaᶜūn – entirely).

ii Phonetics-based affirmation: This is achieved through the addition of an extra consonant nasal sound /n/ called the affirmation /n/ (nūn al-tawkīd) to enrich the verb with more semantic force, as in (layusjanann walayakūnann . . . – He will surely be imprisoned and will be . . ., Q12:32) where the affirmation /n/ is added to the main verb (yasjun – to imprison) and (yakūn – to be). The transliteration of the Arabic words does not reflect this phonetic feature.

8 **Coherence through the use of a specific word:** Let us consider the following examples of lexemes that have been employed in Qur'anic discourse for contextual coherence, i.e., the selection of a context-based word:

Example 1

(raib – doubt, Q2:2), which is a nominalized noun and is semantically contrastive with the nominalized noun (shakk – doubt). The expression (raib) semantically designates the componential features of [+ Ill Intention (think badly of someone or something (ḍann al-sū'))], [+ Psychological Confusion (a disturbed, muddled, bewildered person)], and [+ Disliked (someone or something disliked (makrūh))], [+ Arrogance], [+ Sceptical], [+ Doubt Based on Accusation (shakk ma^{c}a tuhmah)], and [+ Disbelieve (reject, deny, renounce, disavow)]. The noun (raib) is the result of the noun (shakk).

However, the lexeme (shakk) has the componential features [+ Doubt not Based on Accusation (shakk bilā tuhmah)], [+ Undecided (mutaraddid)], [+ Bewildered until Evidence is Provided (muḥtār ḥattā yatawaffar al-dalīl)]. Based on the above semantic features, the lexemes (raib) and (shakk) are not interchangeable due to contextual coherence → (in kuntum fi raib mimmā nazzalnā ^{c}alā ^{c}abdinā – If you are in doubt about what We have sent down upon Our servant, Q2:23) → (fa'in kunta fī shakk mimmā anzalnā ilaika – If you are in doubt (O Muḥammad) about that which We have revealed to you, Q10:94). When Muḥammad is addressed in Q10:94, the noun (shakk) is employed since it fits in well in the context of someone who is undecided but not accusing someone else of something evil, is not disbelieving the revelation, but he is merely confused and looking for the truth to reach certainty. However, for the polytheists, the expression (raib) is employed in Q2:23 because they are sceptical of the revelation, they accuse Muḥammad of being a magician and a mad person, and they are dubbing the Qur'an as poetry. Thus, (raib) is used in a context where there is doubt, an accusation, and disliking Muḥammad's message.

Example 2

(munqa^{c}ir – uprooted, Q54:20) where the adjective (munqa^{c}ir – uprooted) is employed but in (ka'annahum a^{c}jāzu nakhlin khāwiyah – like hollow palm-trunks, Q69:7) the adjective (khāwiyah – hollow) is chosen. The adjective (munqa^{c}ir) is conditioned by its context, which is the verb (tanzi^{c} – to sweep away). The context is about the violent wind which destroyed the people of ^{c}Ād. People were swept away like uprooted trunks of palm trees, i.e., people are swept away from their homes (uprooted) like uprooted trunks of palm trees which are swept away. There is sarcasm involved in the illocutionary force of the adjective (munqa^{c}ir): a comparison is made between the violent force of the wind and the light weight of a person: (tanzi^{c}) → (munqa^{c}ir) → (ka'annahum a^{c}jazu nakhlin munqa^{c}ir – like uprooted palm-trunks, Q54:20).

However, a different adjective is employed in Q69:7, while the reference is also to the people of ^{c}Ād. To achieve contextual coherence, the adjective (khāwiyah – hollow) is used, which denotes a fallen-out empty (lightweight) palm-trunk resting helplessly on the ground. To achieve coherence, the feebleness of people who are in a helpless state is compared to fallen out empty palm-trunks. In the earlier context, people are described as (ṣar^{c}ā – fallen, Q69:7); thus, the adjective (khāwiyah) is well suited for the description of the state of (nakhl – palm-trees): (ṣar^{c}ā) → (khāwiyah).

Example 3

(munīr – Q25:61) where the adjective is employed for contextual coherence and succinctness. It entails a reflector of light. Thus, it collocates with (qamar – moon) → (qamar munīr – luminous moon). However, the word (sirāj – a burning lamp, Q25:61) is also used to attain contextual coherence and succinctness since it entails a source of light + heat. Thus, it collocates with (shams – sun) → (jaᶜala fīha sirāj – God placed in the sky a burning lamp).

Example 4

(shaghafa – to impassion with love, Q12:30) is an allegorical imagery which depicts an emotional situation in which someone is deeply in love with someone else. Joseph has impassioned the governor's wife with love, that his love has consumed her heart, his love has penetrated the covering layer of her heart, and Joseph's love has settled in the bottom of her heart → (qad shaghafahā ḥubbā – Joseph has impassioned her with love).

Example 5

(baṭshata – a powerful strike, Q26:130, Q28:19, Q44:16, Q85:12) echoes an onomatopoeia which achieves through its phonetic features the illocutionary force of retribution. This expression portrays an action of a mighty force being used against an opponent to inflict colossal damage → (yawma nabṭishu al-baṭshata al-kubrā innā muntaqimūn – The day We (God) will strike with the greatest assault; indeed, We will take retribution).

Example 6

(iḥtanaka – to lead someone by the nose, Q17:62), which depicts an allegorical imagery of someone being led by a rope around his/her neck, i.e., it is a metaphor with the illocutionary force of misguidance and misleading. The imagery is taken from an animal being led by the rope around its neck → (la'aḥtanikanna dhurriyyatahu – I (Satan) will lead the descendants of Adam by the nose).

Example 7

(yatafajjar minhu al-anhār – from which rivers burst forth, Q2:74) (yashshaqqaq fayakhruju minhu al-mā' – split open and water comes out, Q2:74). Based on the context of the two speech acts, the verb (yatafajjar – burst forth) is employed for the illocutionary force of multitude (al-kathrah). However, an alternative verb (yashshaqqaq – split open) is used because the context has changed, i.e., the verb (yashshaqqaq) is used for the illocutionary force of paucity (al-qillah). Thus, we have (yatafajjar) → (anhār – rivers which contain massive quantities of water) but (shaqq – a split in the ground) → (mā' – water in small quantities).

Example 8

(kubkibū – to be overturned into the hellfire, Q26:94), which depicts a vivid imagery of people being hurled into hell.

Example 9

(yaqhar – to oppress, be harsh with, Q93:9), (yanhar – to rebuke, chide, repel, Q93:10) where each lexical item has a specific context and has its collocational pattern: (yaqhar) co-occurs with (yatīm – orphan): (yaqhar → yatīm). However, (yanhar) co-occurs with (sā'il – petitioner, one who asks for help): (yanhar → sā'il). Thus, (yaqhar) and (yanhar) semantically are not interchangeable. In Qur'anic Arabic, one can neither say (ammā al-yatīma falā tanhar – So as for the orphan, do not rebuke) nor (ammā al-sā'ila falā taqhar – So as for the petitioner, do not oppress).

Contextual coherence and continuity of thought can only be achieved through adherence to collocational pattern: (ammā al-yatima falā taqhar – As for the orphan, do not oppress) and (ammā al-sā'ila falā tanhar – As for the one who asks for help, do not rebuke).

Example 10

(ṣayaṣīhim – fortresses, castles, Q33:26), which depicts the image of someone being inside his/her well-fortified castle. The image brings to mind the picture of a cow defending itself with its two strong horns. Coherence is fortified by the lexemes (qadhafa – to cast, to throw violently) + (al-ruᶜba – fear, panic). The verb (qadhafa) has been used with the truth being hurled against falsehood in Q21:18. In modern standard Arabic, from the verb (qadhafa), we get the military word (qadhīfah – an artillery shell) and (qādhifah – a bomber). Thus, today, we can imagine a fortified castle being shelled and the residents being shelled by panic and fear.

Example 11

(turāb – dust): Context plays a major role in the selection of a particular lexeme to achieve contextual coherence. In terms of contextual coherence, we can make the following observations:

i The word (turāb) is employed in the context of pride and boasting with family name (al-ghurūr wal-tafākhur bil-nasab), as in Q18:37 and Q30:20,
ii Denotatively, the lexeme (turāb) designates the semantic componential feature [– Valuable], i.e., something that has no significant value. In other words, it is worthless in comparison to the lexeme (mā' – water), which is the source of life and living,
iii The lexeme (turāb) is employed to designate the underlying meaning of the thought (theme) of the creation of Jesus. Through the word (turāb), the text producer aims to relay the underlying message of God's

omnipotence, i.e., that the creation of Jesus is extremely simple. Thus, through the employment of (turāb), the thought of the creation of Jesus has been made to sound like an extremely simple task. This is a rebuttal to a denier addressee who believes that Jesus is the son of God (Q3:59),

iv The employment of the lexeme (turāb) glorifies the notion of God's omnipotence, and

v The lexeme (turāb) collocates with the lexeme (nuṭfah – sperm-drop), which pragmatically also designates something of no value and minute, i.e., its illocutionary force is belittling the effort required for the creation of Jesus.

Example 12

(ṭīn): In terms of contextual relevance, we can provide the following observations:

i The major constituents of the lexeme (ṭīn) are (turāb + mā' – water + dust, Q37:11),

ii The employment of the lexeme (ṭīn) glorifies the notion of God's omnipotence, and

iii The selection of the lexeme (ṭīn) reminds the reader/hearer of God's favours (Q5:110).

We have argued so far that coherence can be attained through the use of a specific word. In other words, the 'specific' lexeme should not be a polyseme (involving semantic/lexical ambiguity). However, in Qur'anic discourse we also encounter polysemy. We can argue that such a selection of a polysemous word is justified because there are disambiguating lexemes in the same sentence, as:

falladhīna āmanū bihi wa ᶜazzarūhu wa naṣarūhu wa ittabaᶜū al-nūra alladhī unzila maᶜahu ulā'ika hum al-mufliḥūn – So they who have believed in him, honoured him, supported him and followed the light which was sent down with him – it is those who will be successful, Q7:157

where the lexeme (ᶜazzara) is a polyseme which means:

i to punish by hitting (al-taᶜzīr), and

ii to honour, glorify, to be generous to someone.

In Q7:157, (ᶜazzara) means (yukrim, yuᶜaẓẓim – to honour and glorify someone) because of the disambiguating lexical co-text such as (āmanū bihi – believed in him), (naṣarūhu – supported him), and (ittabaᶜū al-nūra – followed the light). Thus, the lexeme (ᶜazzara) cannot be interpreted as (to hit for punishment).

Example 13

(dusur): We have a purposeful selection of (dusur) but not its alternative partial synonym (al-fulk), as in:

ḥamalnāhu ᶜalā dhāti alwāḥin wa dusur – We carried him along on a vessel of planks and nails, Q54:13

The lexical item (dusur – vessel) refers to the vessel built by Noah. The word (dusur) is favoured over its counterpart (al-fulk – the ship). Thus, we could have: (ḥamalnāhu calā al-fulk – We carried him along on a ship). The word (dusur) is selected on purpose because it designates specific meanings: (strength, precision, and meticulous constructional details of the vessel). However, the word (al-fulk) does not possess these significations.

Example 14

(al-baḥr – sea, Q20:77–78) is semantically contrastive with the noun (al-yamm – sea). Both expressions (al-baḥr) and (al-yamm) semantically designate similar componential features of [+ Wide] and [+ Deep]. The lexeme (al-baḥr) has occurred 33 times in the Qur'an in the context of God's omnipotence and God's blessings bestowed upon mankind because the 'sea' is depicted as a source of blessing in terms of fresh meat (Q5:96), jewellery (Q16:14), and transport (Q31:31). However, the word (al-yamm) has occurred eight times in the context of the parable of Moses, and all statements make reference to 'be perished by the sea'. Thus, (al-yamm) is depicted as a means of retribution and destruction (fantaqamnā minhum fa'aghraqnāhum fī al-yamm – So We took retribution from them, and We drowned them in the sea, Q7:136) and (fa'akhadhnāhu wajunūdahu fanabadhnāhum fī al-yamm – So We took him and his soldiers and threw them into the sea, Q28:40). While the lexeme (al-baḥr) refers to [+ Overpower] and [+ Rescue], the lexeme (al-yamm) refers to [+ Overpower] and [– Rescue]. Moses and his followers from the Children of Israel were not overpowered by the sea but instead were rescued by their Lord. This is to depict God's omnipotence in terms of demonstrating that although the sea usually overwhelms and drowns people, Moses and his followers were saved. However, Pharaoh and his soldiers were overpowered by the sea and were drowned by the sea. In Q20:77, the lexeme (al-baḥr) is employed since the statement talks about Moses and his followers. Semantic support to this word's meaning is provided by: (laqad awḥainā ilā mūsā an asri biᶜibādī faḍrib lahum tarīqan fī al-baḥri yabasan lā takhāfu darakan walā takhshā – We (God) have inspired to Moses to travel by night with My servants and strike for them a dry path through the sea; you will not fear being overtaken (by Pharaoh) nor be afraid of drowning, Q20:77). Intertextuality through Q2:50 also provides support to the semantic features of (al-baḥr) (wa'idh faraqnā bikum al-baḥra fa'anjainākum – Recall when We parted the sea for you and saved you). However, semantic support is given to (al-yamm) by Q20:78 (fa'atbaᶜahum firᶜawnu bijunūdihi faghashiyahum min al-yamm mā ghashiyahum – So, Pharaoh pursued them with his soldiers and was overwhelmed by the sea) where Pharaoh and his soldiers co-occur with (al-yamm), which designates 'being overwhelmed by the sea and be drowned'.

However, it is interesting to note that the lexeme (al-yamm) in Q20:39 and Q28:7 (an aqdhifīhi fī al-tābūti faqdhifīhi fī al-yamm falyulqihi al-yamm bil-sāḥil – Put your baby (baby Moses) into the chest, then place him in the river. Let the river wash him on to its bank) where the lexeme (al-yamm) occurs in the context of making reference to the parable of Moses when he was a newly born baby and his mother is instructed by God to put him into a chest, then place him in the river. One can argue that this is related to God's omnipotence in terms of saving baby Moses although he was thrown into the sea, i.e., (al-yamm). In other words, although the [– Rescue] is a semantic feature of the word (al-yamm), God's power overrides this semantic feature and baby Moses is rescued. This is supported by the occurrence of the [+ Rescue] implicit meaning of the clauses (fal-yulqihi al-yammu bil-saḥil – Let the river wash him (baby Moses) on to its bank, Q20:39) and (lā takhāfī wa lā taḥzanī – Do not fear and do not grieve, Q28:7).

9 **Coherence through the use of a sound-based word:** The selection of a context-based word can also be conditioned by its phonetic features. In other words, the phonetic characteristics of a lexeme can also contribute in the realization of coherence. Thus, phonological factors play a role in Qur'anic discourse for contextual coherence, as in the following examples:

Example 1

(al-ṭāmmah – overwhelming calamity, Q79:34) is one of the names of the day of resurrection. It enjoys a special phonetic feature through its voiceless velarised denti alveolar plosive /ṭ/ sound, which makes it compatible to portray the horror of the day of judgement. Its sounds: the voiceless velarised denti alveolar plosive /ṭ/ sound, the long vowel /ā/, and the geminated nasal sound /m/ lend it the feature of fear. Denotatively, however, (al-ṭāmmah) designates the meaning that everything will be covered (ṭamma – to cover), such as mountains, rivers, seas, high buildings, houses, and trees. Since the major illocutionary force which (al-ṭāmmah) aims to achieve is to instil fear and horror in the mind of the reader/hearer, the text producer has selected a befitting word for the continuity of the thought (theme) of eschatology. On the macro text level, Q79 is hinged upon frightening and intimidation (al-takhwīf wal-tahwīl wal-tarhīb) to attain a heightened psychological impact on the reader/hearer in terms of the horror of the day of judgement. Thus, it cannot be substituted by its alternative (al-ṣākhkhah) due to contextual relevance reasons.

Example 2

(al-ṣākhkhah – the deafening blast, Q80:33) is one of the names of the day of resurrection. It enjoys a special phonetic feature through its voiceless velarised denti alveolar plosive /ṭ/ sound, the long vowel /ā/, and the geminated semi-voiced uvular fricative /kh/ sound, which all make this lexeme compatible to portray a high-pitched piercing cry or sound. Its phonological characteristics depict:

- i a shrieking noise of a fire alarm system,
- ii the imagery of a chaotic scene of people running away from fire in a building,
- iii the imagery of people being horrified by the deafening and ear-piercing noise, and
- iv the imagery of people being preoccupied by the fear of being burned out.

On the macro text level, Q80 is hinged upon the story of the blind Muslim ᶜAbd Allāh b. Maktūm in terms of the fear from the day of judgement. Thus, the overall scenario of Q80 is less in terms of frightening and intimidation than that of Q79.

Example 3

(hawā' – literally meaning 'air', Q14:43), which collocates in the phrase (af'idatuhum hawā' – their hearts are void). This is a highly interesting example of the interrelation between phonetics, semantics, and pragmatics in Qur'anic discourse.

Example 4

(ḥasḥas – to be evident, Q12:51), which collocates with (al-ḥaqq – the truth) and designates the meaning '(the truth) has become evident and known to people after it has been suppressed'. The consonant sounds /ḥ/ and /ṣ/ are the appropriate sounds for the context. Similarly, we have:

wakhashaᶜat al-aṣwātu lil-raḥmān falā tasmaᶜu illā hamsā – All voices will be stilled before the most merciful, so you will not hear except a whisper of the footsteps, Q20:108 where the voiceless sounds /sh/, /ṣ/, /s/, and /h/ reflect the context of meeting the Lord and standing before Him on the day of judgement.

Example 5

(taj'arūn – to cry for help, Q16:53), which is to depict an image of people crying for God's help when they are touched by adversity. The sound of the word is also that of an ox.

Example 6

(kaẓīm – to suppress grief, Q16:58), which is compatible with the context of a father being informed of the birth of a female. As he is in shock at the news, he tries to suppress his grief. Other morphological forms (kāẓimīn – to restrain anger, Q3:134 and 'filled with distress' Q40:18) and (makẓūm – distressed, Q68:48) occur in the context of anger and distress. The inter-dental sound /ẓ/ depicts a vivid image of someone biting his/her tongue to suppress one's rage or grief.

Example 7

(shaṭaṭā – excessive transgression, Q18:14), whose two sounds /ṭ/ peculiar phonetic feature which have made this lexeme most appropriately suitable for coherence and compatible with the context of rejecting polytheism and never to invoke besides God any deity.

10 **Coherence through the use of metonymy**: Metonymy is employed for the illocutionary force of decadence and as a means to achieve tactful communication, as in:

> (yamsasnī – to touch me, Q3:47, lāmastum – to contact, Q4:43, tamassūhunna – to touch them, Q2:237, bāshirūhunna – to have relations with them (women), Q2:187, rafath – sexual relations, Q2:197, and yaskun – to dwell in security, Q7:189) have been employed as a metonymy whose underlying meaning is (to have sexual intercourse). Similarly, (ḥaqq – desire, Q11:79 and hamma – to determine to seduce, Q12:24) have been employed as a metonymy whose underlying meaning is (sexual desire or sex interest), the expression (al-fāḥishah – unlawful sexual intercourse, Q4:15 and Q7:80) act as a metonymy whose underlying meaning is (fornication), and (al-ghā'iṭ – the place of relieving oneself, Q5:6) is a metonymy for (toilet, the place where someone answers the call of nature).

11 **Coherence through the use of the superordinate:** This is concerned with hyponymy (hyponym) that refers to the relationship between specific and general words. When the meaning of one word is included in the meaning of another, the relationship is called hyponymy. For instance, (*horse*) is the hyponym of (*animal*). This means that the word (*horse*) is included in (part of) the word (*animal*). An example of this semantic relation is (mukallabin, Q5:4), which acts as a superordinate because it subsumes all types of hunting animals such as dogs and hunting birds such as falcons. These different types of hunting animals and hunting birds are semantically referred to as co-hyponyms of the superordinate (mukallabīn). Thus, pragmatically, it has achieved succinctness. Similarly, the superordinate phrase (kulla dhī ẓufurin) subsumes all types of birds with claws (makhlab) and all types of animals with hooves (ḥāfir). These different types of birds with claws and all animals with hooves are semantically referred to as co-hyponyms of the superordinate phrase (kulla dhī ẓufurin). A superordinate is employed for the illocutionary force of brevity.

12 **Coherence through configuration of text segments:** Qur'anic discourse is characterized by a stylistic mechanism referred to as foregrounding and backgrounding. For contextual coherence, the interlocutor provides a marked

(unusual) word order in which a specific text segment occupies an unusual place. Thus, the stylistic pattern which involves foregrounding or backgrounding is referred to as a marked word order, i.e., a grammatically unusual arrangement of sentence constituents. The configuration of text segments achieves the following text linguistic, pragmatic, and rhetorical functions:

a the text linguistic function of saliency and contextual coherence,
b the pragmatic function of specificity (al-takhṣīṣ), which fulfils the performative intent of the text producer and the illocutionary force (communicative function) of the text, and
c the phonetically based rhetorical function of assonance at the āyah-final position.

The above three major functions achieved through the arrangement of text segments are discussed in what follows:

i Coherence through backgrounding: This is a stylistic technique through which saliency is given to the backgrounded text elements to achieve the illocutionary force (communicative function) of specificity (al-takhṣīṣ), as in:

> qāla faman rabbukumā yā mūsā – (Pharaoh) said: 'So who is the Lord of you two?', Q20:49

where the lexeme (mūsā – Moses) is backgrounded for the rhetorical purpose of assonance. The backgrounding (the placement at the end) of (mūsā) achieves phonetic coherence. This is due to the macro text phonetic co-text where the āyah-final word ends with the long vowel /ā/. The phonetic macro co-text starts from Q20:33–84. A similar configuration of the same text segment (mūsā) has occurred in Q20:57, 67, 70, and 83 where the lexeme (mūsā) is placed at the end of the sentence to achieve the phonetically based rhetorical function of assonance. However, in Q28:19, we find the same lexeme (mūsā) placed in its usual position (i.e., foregrounded) in the sentence: (qāla yā mūsā aturīdu an taqtulanī – He said: 'O Moses, do you intend to kill me?'), i.e., instead of (qāla aturīdu an taqtulanī yā mūsā). This is because the macro text phonetic co-text of Q28:19 is marked by āyah-final words that end with the nasal sound /n/.

It is interesting to note that the configuration of sentence constituents (lexemes, words) can be based on intertextuality and compatibility with the macro text. For instance, in Q91:8 (fa'alhamahā fujūrahā wa taqwāha – He (God) inspired it (the human soul) with discernment of its wickedness and its righteousness), we encounter the placement of the connotatively negative lexeme (fujūrahā – discernment of its wickedness) before the connotatively positive lexeme (taqwāhā – its righteousness, piety), although both words can achieve the phonetically based rhetorical function of assonance through the word-final long vowel /ā/, which is the macro text phonetic co-text. I believe that the major reason for the configuration of (fujūrahā) first is due to the influence of the Qur'anic macro text that can be explained by the text linguistics standard of intertextuality represented by the notion that wickedness (al-fujūr) is more common than righteousness, as in (wamā aktharu al-nāsi walaw ḥaraṣta bimu'minin – Most of the people, although you strive for it, are not believers, Q12:103), (waqalīlun min ᶜibādiya al-shakūr – Few of My servants are grateful, Q34:13), and (la'aḥtanikanna dhurriyyatahu illā qalīlā –, Q17:62I will surely destroy his descendants, except for a few).

ii Coherence through assonance (assonance-based coherence): This is also represented by the couplet epithets (al-tawwāb al-raḥīm – the accepting of repentance, the merciful, Q2:37, 54, 128, and 143) and (ghafūr raḥīm – forgiving and merciful, Q2:173, 182, 192, 199, and 218). Thus, we can also claim that the configuration of āyah-final epithets like where the epithet (al-tawwāb – the accepting of repentance) is foregrounded and the epithet (al-raḥīm – the merciful) is foregrounded (placed at the end of the āyah) can be attributed to the fact that such configuration-based coherence aims to achieve the phonetically based rhetorical function of assonance through the word-final nasal sound /m/ where the nasal sounds /n/ or /m/ dominate the macro text phonetic co-text.

It is worthwhile to note that assonance-based coherence is not always related to the configuration of text segments like (mūsā) or epithets like (raḥīm) at āyah-final position. Coherence that is related to the phonetically based rhetorical function of assonance at the āyah-final position can be achieved through one of the following two mechanisms:

a the addition of a sound that is compatible with the macro text phonetic co-text: This is represented by Q33:10, 66, and 67 where we encounter (al-ẓunūnā – assumptions, ill thoughts), (al-rasūlā – the Messenger), and (al-sabīlā – the right way), respectively. In order to achieve phonetic coherence through assonance, a long vowel /ā/ is added at the end of these three words. The expected words should have no long vowel /ā/, and their orthographic form should be (al-ẓunūn), (al-rasūl), and (al-sabīl), respectively. Thus, to achieve phonetic coherence, the macro text phonetic co-text has to be taken into consideration where the macro text phonetic co-text is the long vowel /ā/.

b the use of a sound-based lexeme that is more befitting than its synonym: In order to achieve coherence through assonance, the text producer opts for a lexeme rather than its expected synonym, as in Q54:8 where, for assonance-based coherence, the lexical item (ᶜasir – difficult) is appropriately well selected instead of its synonym (ᶜasīr – difficult). This is attributed to the fact that the macro text phonetic co-text is the consonant sound /r/ that is preceded by a consonant + a short vowel /i/ (kasrah) rather than a long vowel /ī/. Thus, for phonetic (assonance) reasons, the

> synonym (ᶜasīr) cannot achieve assonance-based coherence. On the rhetorical level, the lexeme (ᶜasīr) achieves the text producer's performative intent of cognitive allegory (majāz ᶜaqlī) because (ᶜasir) depicts hard times experienced by the deniers who are awaiting their punishment.

Similarly, in Q54:13, the word (dusur – nails) is a metonym for the word (al-safinah or al-fulk – the ship). The lexeme (dusur) semantically signifies a ship that is powerful and well built because many nails have been used. The synonyms (al-safīnah or al-fulk) cannot achieve assonance-based coherence.

13 **Coherence through āyah-final couplet epithets:** Qur'anic discourse is characterized by āyah-final epithets. However, the occurrence of epithets is not haphazard. Rather, the macro lexical (semantic) context plays a pivotal role in the selection of befitting epithets which contribute to the achievement of coherence, as in (ghafūr raḥīm – forgiving and merciful, Q2:173, 182, 192, 199, 218, and 226). We can argue that the employment of such epithets serves:

i the performative intent of the text producer, and
ii the continuity of thought.

Due to the influence of the macro text semantic co-text or context, the āyah-final epithet (ghafūr raḥīm) achieves coherence since there is continuity of thought through the following:

The context of Q2:173 allows the employment of (ghafūr raḥīm) since the āyah talks about the foods that are forbidden such as dead animals, blood, the flesh of swine, and that which has been dedicated to other than God. However, the āyah refers to an exemption, and we are informed that whoever is forced by necessity, neither desiring it nor transgressing its limit, there is no sin upon such an individual. Then the āyah concludes that God is (ghafūr raḥīm – forgiving and merciful). Thus, coherence is established by the text producer through the continuity of thought and relevance of the couplet epithets.

The context of Q2:182 allows the employment of (ghafūr raḥīm) because the āyah refers to someone who fears from the bequeather some error or sin and corrects that which is between the concerned parties. In this case, we are informed that there is no sin upon such an individual. Then the āyah concludes that God is (ghafūr raḥīm – forgiving and merciful). Coherence has, thus, been achieved by the text producer through the continuity of thought and relevance of the couplet epithets.

The context of Q2:192 allows the employment of (ghafūr raḥīm) because the context of Q2:192 (Q2:190–192) refers to self-defence when the disbelievers attack the believers. However, we are informed that when the disbelievers cease their attack, then God is (ghafūr raḥīm – forgiving and merciful). Therefore, coherence has been attained by the text producer through the continuity of thought and relevance of the couplet epithets.

The context of Q2:199 allows the employment of the āyah-final epithets (ghafūr raḥīm) because the context of the āyah refers to the pilgrimage rituals and the pilgrims are urged to depart from the place from where all the people depart and ask forgiveness of God. Thus, the āyah concludes with the thought represented by the epithets which describe God as (ghafūr raḥīm – forgiving and merciful).

The context of Q2: 218 allows the employment of (ghafūr raḥīm) because the āyah refers to those who have believed and those who have emigrated and fought in the cause of God and that this category of people expect the mercy of God. The end of the āyah provides reassurance to this specific category of people through the āyah-final epithets (ghafūr raḥīm – forgiving and merciful).

Similarly, the context of Q2:226 allows the employment of the āyah-final epithets (ghafūr raḥīm) because the context of the āyah refers to those who swear not to have sexual relations with their wives. They are informed that if they do so, they should have a waiting time of four months. However, if they return to normal relations with their wives, then they are assured by the āyah-final epithets that God is (ghafūr raḥīm – forgiving and merciful). Thus, coherence and continuity of thought are achieved by the text producer.

In an interesting example of how the āyah-final couplets are conditioned by relevance and context, we refer to Q26 in which the couplets (al-ᶜazīz al-raḥīm – the exalted in might, the merciful) has occurred eight times in Q26:9, 68, 104, 122, 140, 159, 175, and 191. Context and relevance have played a pivotal role in the employment of these sentence-final expressions. For more details, see Section 5.10.1.1.3.1.

To achieve coherence through the continuity of thought, we encounter in Q73:20 the employment of (ghafūr raḥīm – forgiving and merciful) because of the preceding context in the same āyah (istaghfirū allāh – Seek forgiveness of God, Q73:20).

14 **Coherence through number (singular/dual/plural):** The occurrence of a noun in the singular, dual, or plural form is appropriately selected to achieve coherence:

i the singular noun: The employment of a noun in the singular rather than in the plural is another linguistic mechanism through which coherence is achieved. This is explicated in the following examples:

> wamā kuntu muttakhidha al-muḍillīna ᶜaḍudā – I do not take the misguiders as a supporter, Q18:51 rather than (wamā kuntu muttakhidha al-muḍillīna aᶜḍādā – I would not have taken the misguiders as

supporters), i.e., the employment of a singular noun (ᶜaḍudā – a supporter) rather than its expected plural form (aᶜḍād – supporters) → (wamā kuntu muttakhidha al-mudillīna aᶜḍādā). To achieve contextual coherence, the singular noun (ᶜaḍudā) is employed to achieve contextual coherence with what has preceded this statement. We have been informed earlier in the text about Satan (iblīs), who is described as (fasaqa ᶜan amri rabbih – He (Satan) disobeyed his Lord's command), and we are warned not to (tattakhidhūnahu wadhurriyyatahu awliyā'a min dūnī – take him (Satan) and his offspring as your masters instead of Me (God), Q18:51). We can observe the semantically oriented coherence link between the verb (fasaqa – disobey (singular, masculine)) and the masculine singular noun (ᶜaḍudā) in (wamā kuntu muttakhidha al-mudillīna ᶜaḍudā – I do not take the misguiders as a supporter). We can also claim that to intensify the illocutionary force of the message, the employment of a singular noun designates the weakness of 'one' person rather than a plural noun which has an implicit power. Thus, the singular (ᶜaḍudā) serves the text producer's perlocutionary intent in terms of sarcasm and weakness of Satan.

ayaṭma ᶜu kullu imri'in minhum an yudkhala jannata naᶜīm – Does every person among them aspire to enter a garden of pleasure?, Q70:38

To appreciate the role of the singularity of the noun in the achievement of coherence and continuity of thought and senses, we need to investigate the preceding context, which starts from Q70:36–37. In these two statements, we are informed about the disbelievers who run away (disbelieving) (muhṭiᶜīn) from Muḥammad, sitting in groups at the Kaᶜbah, peering at him and mocking him (ᶜan al-yamīni waᶜan al-shimāli cizīn) while he was praying and reading the Qur'an by the Kaᶜbah. Q70:38 introduces through the denial interrogative particle (a – hamzat al-istifhām al-inkāri) prefixed to the verb (yaṭmaᶜu – aspire, literally meaning 'is greedy to acquire something') the illocutionary force that their wish to enter paradise is impossible. Every one of them aspires to have 'a garden of pleasure' exclusively for himself. Thus, the disbeliever does not want to share his own garden of pleasure with others. The lexeme (imri'in – a person) is used in the singular. The sense of singularity continues further in the same sentence through two mechanisms:

- i through the singularity of the noun (jannata – a garden) rather than (jannāta – gardens), and
- ii through the indefiniteness of the noun (naᶜīm – pleasure, bliss).

In order to achieve specificity (al-khuṣūṣiyyah) and exclusiveness of the garden of pleasure to one person only, singularity is required, i.e., the noun (jannata – a garden) should be employed in the singular, and most importantly the noun (naᶜīm – pleasure, bliss) should be employed in the indefinite form. Thus, we have: singular noun + indefinite noun. This is the prerequisite for the continuity of thought that each person aspires to have his own garden of bliss exclusive to him. However, the continuity of thought and contextual coherence will be disturbed had we employed the noun (naᶜīm) in the definite form (al-naᶜīm – the pleasure). The definite noun (al-naᶜīm) signifies that the garden of pleasure is shared by all people. Thus, specificity (exclusiveness) has diminished, and the text producer's performative intent is hampered.

The above text linguistic analysis of Q70:38 also applies to Q56:89 (farawḥun waraiḥānun wa jannatu naᶜīm – Then, for him/her is rest and bounty and a garden of pleasure) where we have the noun (jannatu – a garden) in the singular and indefinite form, and the noun (naᶜīm – pleasure) also occurs in the singular and indefinite form to signify the text producer's performative intent that each one of those who will be brought near to God (al-muqarrabin) will have his/her own (jannatu naᶜīm – a garden of pleasure) exclusive to him/her. Thus, we can observe the following text linguistic facts:

- a singularity and indefiniteness signify specificity, speciality, and exclusiveness,
- b the thought (theme, leitmotif) of (jannah) is made salient through singularity and indefiniteness, and
- c continuity of thought is also achieved through singularity and indefiniteness.

In (rabbu al-mashriq wal-maghrib – He is the Lord of the East and the West, Q73:9), we encounter the lexeme (al-mashriq – East) and the lexeme (al-maghrib – West) in the singular. To achieve continuity of thought and relevance, the singular is more appropriate to achieve coherence since it designates the direction, i.e., it refers to the Lord of one direction at a time: the Lord of the East as well as the Lord of the West. Thus, God is the Lord of the two directions, i.e., whatever direction you turn to, He is the same and one Lord. Thus, the notion of monotheism is affirmed, and the reader is admonished to take this one Lord as the disposer of one's affairs (lā ilāha illā hū fattakhidhhu wakīla – There is no deity except Him. So take Him as disposer of your affairs). In terms of co-text and the influence of the macro text on the occurrence of lexemes, we can also argue that the lexeme (al-lail – the night, Q73:2, 6) has occurred in the singular, and the lexeme (al-nahār – the day, Q73:7) has also occurred in the singular.

Similarly, in Q56:89, we encounter the singular noun (jannatu – a garden). This is because reference has already been made to a singular noun (kāna min al-muqarrabīn – the one who is brought near God, Q56:88). Thus, stylistically, the singular is more befitting than the plural noun (jannāt – gardens). However, in Q56:12, we encounter a plural noun (jannāt). This is because reference has been made to a plural noun in Q56:11 (al-muqarrabun – the ones who are brought near God). Thus, relevance of selection of lexemes is achieved. This case is also related to context, i.e., the selection of a singular or a plural noun is context-based.

ii the dual noun: In (rabbu al-mashriqain wa rabbu al-maghribain – He is the Lord of the two sunrises and the Lord of the two sunsets, Q55:17), we encounter the lexeme (al-mashriqain – two sunrises) and (al-maghribain – two sunsets) in the dual. One sunrise is for the summer season and the other sunrise is for the winter season. Similarly, one sunset is for the summer season and the other sunset is for the winter season. In terms of co-text and the impact of Q55 macro text, we can argue that the dual noun is employed throughout the sūrah, as in (khalaqa al-insān ᶜallamahu al-bayān – (He) created man and taught him eloquence, Q55:3–4), (al-shamsu wal-qamar – the sun and the moon, Q55:5), (al-samā'a . . . al-mizān – the heaven . . . the balance, Q55:7), (al-arḍa . . . al-nakhlu . . . – the earth . . . the palm trees, Q55:11), (al-ḥabbu . . . al-raiḥānu – the grain . . . the scented plants, Q55:12), (maraja al-baḥrain yaltaqiyān – He released the two seas meeting side by side, Q55:19).

iii the plural noun: In (falā uqsimu birabbi al-mashāriq wal-maghārib – So I swear by the Lord of all risings and settings, Q70:40), we can observe the occurrence of the lexeme (al-mashāriq – risings) and the lexeme (al-maghārib – settings) in the plural form. The plural noun refers to the points at which the sun, the moon, and the stars rise and set according to season and every position of observation. In terms of continuity of thought and the macro text, we can argue that Q70:40 is an oath employed to demonstrate the Lord's ability to destroy the deniers and affirms the extent of His lordship. Q70:40 is an example of God's omnipotence. This statement is also a glorification to the Lord since the different sunrises and sunsets in different countries all over the globe mean people continue to pray to Him and glorify Him continuously throughout the day and the night, in different seasons throughout the year. Through the employment of the plural, this thought can be achieved. Thus, coherence is attained.

Similarly, in (inna fi dhālika la āyāt lil-mutawassimīn – Indeed in that are signs for those who discern, Q15:75), we observe the occurrence of the lexeme (āyāt – signs) in the plural, but in (inna fi dhālika la āyah lil-mu'minīn – Indeed in that is a sign for the believers, Q15:77), the lexeme (āyah – a sign) occurs in the singular.

15 **Coherence through the saliency of a thought in an antithesis structure:** This is a common presentation technique encountered in Qur'anic discourse used for reward and punishment as a tenet of faith where a notion is made salient (gains prominence) through antithesis (oppositeness), as in:

> al-shaiṭānu yaᶜidukum al-faqra waya'murukum bil-faḥshā'/allāhu yaᶜidukum maghfiratan wafaḍlā – Satan threatens you with poverty and orders you to immorality/God promises you forgiveness from Him and bounty, Q2:268

man ya^cmal sū'an yujza bihi/man ya^cmal min al-ṣāliḥāti min dhakarin aw unthā wahuwa mu'minun fa'ulā'ika yadkhulūna al-jannata walā yuẓlamūna naqīrā – Whoever does a wrong will be recompensed for it/ Whoever does righteous deeds, whether male or female, while being a believer – Those will enter paradise and will not be wronged, even as much as the speck on a date seed, Q4:123–124

inna rabbaka ladhū maghfiratin/wadhū ᶜiqābin alīm – Your Lord is a possessor of forgiveness/He is a possessor of a painful penalty, Q41:43

wāwuffiyat kullu nafsin mā ᶜamilat wahuwa aᶜlamu bimā yafᶜalūn. wasīqa alladhīna kafarū ilā jahannama zumarā ḥattā idhā jā'ūhā futiḥat abwābuhā waqāla lahum khazanatuhā alam ya'tikum rusulun mikum yatlūna ᶜalaikum āyāti rabbikum wayundhirūnakum liqā'i yawmikum hādhā qālū balā walākin ḥaqqat kalimatu al-cadhābi ᶜalā al-kāfirīn. qīla adkhulū abwāba jahannama khālidīna fihā fabi'sa mathwā al-mutakabbirīn. wasīqa alladhīna attaqaw rabbahum ilā al-jannati zumarā ḥattā idhā jā'ūhā wafutiḥat abwābuhā waqāla lahum khazanatuhā salāmun calaikum ṭibtum fadkhulūhā khālidīn. waqālū al-ḥamdu lillāhi alladhī ṣadaqanā waᶜdahu wa'awrathnā al-arḍa natabawwa'u min al-jannati ḥaithu nashā' faniᶜma ajru al-ᶜāmilin – Every soul will be fully compensated for what it did; and He is most knowing of what they do. Those who disbelieved will be driven to hell in groups until, when they reach it, its gates are opened and its keepers will say: 'Did there not come to you messengers from yourselves, reciting to you the āyāt of your Lord and warning you of the meeting of this day of yours?' They will say: 'Yes, but the decree of punishment has come into effect upon the disbelievers'. To them, it will be said: 'Enter the gates of Hell to abide eternally therein, and wretched is the residence of the arrogant'. But those who feared their Lord will be driven to paradise in groups until, when they reach it while its gates have been opened and its keepers say: 'Peace be upon you; you have become pure; so enter it to abide eternally therein'. And they will say: 'Praise to God, who has fulfilled for us His promise and made us inherit the earth so we may settle in paradise wherever we will. And excellent is the reward of righteous workers', Q39:70–74

We can make the following text linguistic observations:

- i We observe the continuity of thought in the text where the thought of God being the most knowing of what people do (huwa aᶜlamu bimā yafᶜalūn – He (God) is the most knowing of what people do) occurs at the beginning (Q39:70). Then the text also ends with the thought of doing (faniᶜma ajru al-ᶜāmilīn – how excellent is the reward of those who do righteous deeds, Q39:74).
- ii The text represents the Qur'anic presentation technique of reward and punishment where antithesis is employed to make salient a given thought.
- iii We also observe that the text involves the antithesis of two text segments:

a The first text segment represents those who disbelieved and who will be driven to hell, and

b The second segment represents those who believed and who will be driven to paradise.

iv We can observe that the thought (leitmotif) of reward and punishment is made salient through the oppositeness (antithesis) between disbelievers and believers and between hell and paradise.

> . . . ja^cala kalimata alladhīna kafarū al-suflā wa kalimatu allahi hiya al-^culyā – He (God) made the word of those who disbelieved the lowest, while the word of God is the highest, Q9:40

where coherence and continuity of thought are achieved through the antithesis between the two text segments: (kalimata alladhīna kafarū al-suflā – the word of those who disbelieved the lowest) and (kalimatu allāhi hiya al-^culya – the word of God is the highest). In this example, the text producer has adopted the grammatical mechanism of shift from the accusative case in (kalimata – the word (i.e., a direct object of the verb (ja^cala – to make)) to the nominative case (kalimatu – the word) i.e., (kalimatu allāhi – the word of God) is the mubtada' in the nominative case whose khabar is (al-^culyā – the highest) for a well-planned performative intent. The performative intent and continuity of thought can only be achieved through the grammatical technique of shift: to enforce the illocutionary force of [– Continuity] and [+ Certainty] through the verbal sentence (ja^cala kalimata). In other words, (the word of the disbelievers is certainly the lowest and does not remain in a fixed state) because the past tense designates an action that has certainly finished. However, to give the thought (the word of God is the highest) the illocutionary force of [+ Saliency], [+ Continuity], and [+ Permanency], it has to be employed in a no-main-verb nominal sentence stylistic pattern. Also, further grammatical support to the thought 'God's word is the highest' is given by the employment of the detached pronoun (hiya – it, i.e., the word of God). We can also claim that the expression (manṣūb – in the accusative case, i.e., figuratively means 'made low') connotatively designates something or someone 'low'. However, the expression (marfū^c – in the nominative case, i.e., figuratively means 'elevated') connotatively designates something or someone 'high'. For this reason, the alternative style: (. . . ja^cala kalimata alladhīna kafarū al-suflā wa <u>kalimata</u>hu hiya al-^culyā – He (God) made the word of those who disbelieved the lowest, while His (God's) word is the highest) is avoided because (kalimata – word, i.e., the word of God (<u>kalimata</u> + hu)) occurs in the accusative case. The art of syntax beautifies style.

5.6 Coherence and relevance

In this discussion, we are concerned with micro level coherence, which is the word level. By relevance, we mean the following:

i How far (a) a specific lexeme, (b) its position in the text, or (c) its grammatical function fits in well in the text,
ii How: (a) a specific lexeme, (b) its position in the text, or (c) its grammatical function is suitable in the circumstances, and
iii How far one of the above three mechanisms (a–c) serves coherence and the continuity of thoughts.

With regards to the relationship between the appropriate positioning of a sentence constituent and coherence, we can provide a set of reasons in support of our claim:

i Coherence plays a central role in the achievement of the text producer's communicative goals which he/she wants to deliver to the hearer/reader,
ii The relevant arrangement of *thoughts* in a given text makes it easy for the *thought* to get across to the text receiver and to be unequivocally understood,
iii Effective communication depends on the relevant organization of sentence constituents,
iv Effective communication depends on the relevant selection of a specific lexeme of a specific morphological form and/or grammatical function,
v Word order signifies *thoughts* order. In other words, the organization of lexical items in a sentence represents the organization of the text producer's *thoughts* (messages), and
vi Saliency (prominence) of a *thought* expressed via a lexical item is achieved through word order.

Based on these factors, we can provide an explicated account of the interdependence between a sentence constituent positioning, grammatical form and coherence.

According to Beaugrande and Dressler (1981:20), the relations of *thoughts* to each other affect the arrangement of words in sentences.

However, we believe that the interrelationship between the thoughts expressed by a specific text's segments influences:

i the linearization of lexemes, and
ii the selection of a specific syntactic function of the lexeme in the text.

It is worthwhile to note that our approach to coherence has not been accounted for by text linguists. It can, therefore, be claimed that our approach to coherence is Qur'an specific. However, it can be of value to other related or unrelated languages to Arabic. Let us consider the following examples to substantiate our argument in terms of coherence, continuity of senses, linearization of words, the selection of specific grammatical functions, and/or grammatical structure:

> dhālika al-kitābu lā raiba fīhi hudan lil-muttaqīn. alladhīna yu'minūna bil-ghaibi wayuqīmūna al-ṣalāta wamimmā razaqnāhum yunfiqūn – This is the

Book about which there is no doubt, a guidance for those conscious of God. Who believe in the unseen, establish prayer, and spend out of what We (God) have provided for them, Q2:2–3.
wamā hum bikhārijīn min al-nārr – They are never to emerge from the fire, Q2:167
ulā'ika alladhīna ṣadaqū wa'ulā'ika hum al-muttaqūn – Those are the ones who have been true, and it is those who are the righteous, Q2:177.
sawā'un ᶜalaikum adaᶜawtumūhum amm antum ṣāmitūn – It is all the same for you whether you invite them or you are silent, Q7:193.
wa'inna jahannama lamuḥīṭatun bil-kāfirīn – Indeed, hell will encompass the disbelievers, Q9:49.
falayaᶜlamanna allāhu alladhīna ṣadaqū walayaᶜlamanna al-kādhibīn – God will surely make evident those who are truthful, and He will surely make evident the liars, Q29:3

The above examples demonstrate the Qur'anic text linguistics fact that the text producer's perlocutionary intent is accomplished through the selection of a specific syntactic function of the lexeme in each text. The text Q2:2 represents a nominal sentence whose illocutionary force is to make salient the thought that the revelation is true and is a guidance to those who are mindful of God. The illocutionary force of the nominal construction is the substantiation to the theme (the pivotal thought) of Q2:2. Thus, this thought is fortified by the employment of the active participle (muttaqin – those conscious of God), which enjoys the pragmatic functions of [+ Permanency], [+ Continuity], and [– Renewability] through which the active participle (muttaqin) represents a category of people whose faith is firmly established. Had the text producer used a verb (yattaqūn) instead: (dhālika al-kitābu lā raiba fīhi hudan lilladhīna yattaqūn – This is the Book about which there is no doubt, a guidance for those conscious of God), the major features of this category of people would have changed to [– Permanency], [– Continuity], and [+ Renewability], which designate a category of people whose faith is shaky. The employment of a verb would have undermined the first thought (dhālika al-kitābu lā raiba fīhi – This is the Book about which there is no doubt). The same applies to Q2:177, Q7:193, and Q29:3 where the active participles (muttaqūn – righteous), (ṣāmitūn – silent), and (kādhibīn – liars) are used instead of their alternative verb forms (alladhīna yattaqūn – who are righteous), (am ṣamattum – to keep silent), and (alladhīna kadhabū – who lied). The negative impact of using the verb is demonstrated by the verb's pragmatic functions of [– Permanency], [– Continuity], and [+ Renewability]. Similarly, in Q2:167, the active participle (khārijīn) is selected instead of its alternative verb form (yakhrujūn – (they) to emerge) in order to portray the impossibility of their emergence from the punishment of the fire, i.e., the active participle designates the thought of perpetual punishment. However, the use of the verb (yakhrujūn) can lead to the thought that their punishment is not perpetual, i.e., [– Permanency], [– Continuity], and [+ Renewability], i.e., their punishment is renewed every other time but not constantly. Similarly, the selection of the active participle (muḥitatun – encompass) designates the perlocutionary intent of the text producer that the encompassing of hell to the disbelievers is perpetual, continuous, and not renewed every now and then.

Another example of how the text producer's perlocutionary intent is appropriately achieved is (mā khalqukum wamā baᶜthukum illā kanafsin wāḥidatin – Your creation and your resurrection will not be but as that of a single soul, Q31:28) where the selection of the no-main-verb nominal sentence is appropriately selected by the text producer to substantiate two communicative goals:

i God's omnipotence (mā khalqukum illā kanafsin wāḥidatin – Your creation is but as that of a single soul), and
ii the affirmation of eschatology (mā baᶜthukum illā kanafsin wāḥidatin – Your resurrection will not be but as that of a single soul).

The relationship between coherence and the appropriate selection of a grammatical structure is also manifested by the following example:

> Yā aiyuhā al-nāsu idhkurū niᶜmata allāhi ᶜalaikum hal min khāliqin ghairu allāhi yarzuqukum min al-samā'i wal-arḍi lā ilāha illā hū fa'annā tu'fakūn – O mankind, remember the favour of God upon you. Is there any creator other than God who provides for you from the heaven and earth? There is no deity except Him. So how are you deluded?, Q35:3.

where the no-main-verb nominal sentence (lā ilāha illā hū – There is no deity except Him) is employed by the text producer as rebuttal to a denier addressee and as substantiation of monotheism and God's being the only provider of provision. Thus, the continuity of senses is attained.

> awalam yaraw ilā al-ṭairi fawqahum ṣāffāt wa yaqbiḍn? – Do they not see the birds above them with wings outspread and sometimes their wings folded in?, Q67:19

where we have a shift from the noun (active participle – ism fāᶜil) → (ṣāffāt – outspread wings) to a verb → (yaqbiḍn – they (the birds) occasionally folded in wings). The verb (yaqbiḍn) is grammatically regarded a full verbal sentence: verb + subject (they). The active participle noun designates [+ Permanency] and [+ Continuity] (al-thubut), while the verb designates [+ Renewability] (al-tajaddud) and [+ Action] (al-huduth). This example illustrates the semantic and pragmatic distinction between the active participle (the noun) and the verb. The text producer of Q67:19 could have provided either:

i active participle + active participle → ṣāffāt + qābiḍāt, or
ii verb + verb → yaṣfufn + yaqbiḍn

It is worthwhile to note that during flying, the birds' permanent physical characteristic is to outspread their wings throughout their flying process but occasionally fold them in. Therefore, the verb (yaqbiḍn) is required to demonstrate that the occasional folding in of wings is renewed every now and then. However, to outspread them is a normal permanent flying procedure. Therefore, the active participle noun (ṣāffāt) is selected. We have claimed earlier that the effective communication depends on the appropriate selection of a specific lexeme of a specific morphological form and/or grammatical function. This is demonstrated by the relevant selection of the lexeme (mutahharah – purified, Q2:25) as a passive participle in order to designate [+ Continuity] and [+ Perpetual State]. We could have the same lexeme in the verb form (yataṭahharn – to purify themselves) for the same sentence, but the illocutionary force will be undermined, i.e., the text producer's perlocutionary intent is violated. However, to achieve coherence, in Q7:82 and Q27:56, the appropriate lexeme occurs in the verb form (yataṭahharūn – to keep oneself pure). This is context-specific coherence where relevance dictates the employment of the verb since it designates [– Continuity] and [– Perpetual State], i.e., one needs to renew one's purity every now and then.

The text linguistic interrelationship between coherence and relevance can also be demonstrated through the appropriate selection of a singular or plural noun. For instance, the noun (jannah – garden) is intentionally employed in both the singular, where it occurs 66 times (Q2:35, 214), and in the plural, where it occurs 69 times. Coherence here has not been affected since a singular noun is more relevant for a context than a plural noun and vice versa. The perlocutionary intent of the text producer underlying this text linguistic phenomenon is to demonstrate the thought that (jannah) as a reward has different categories depending on the achievement of the individual during his/her present life. In other words, there are different types of (jannah). The employment of the noun (jannah) in the singular or the plural is more relevant to the notion of multiple categories of (jannah). Thus, coherence is intact.

However, the intentional employment of the noun (nārr – fire) in the singular echoes the perlocutionary intent of the text producer. The text linguistic phenomenon of singularity of (nārr – fire) in Qur'anic discourse underlies the thought that the (nārr) is a place for punishment and that there is only one such place in the hereafter.

In terms of coherence and relevance, the perlocutionary intent of the text producer applies to intentional application of singularity for the noun (sabīl – way, path) whose synonym is (ṣirāṭ) rather than its plural form (subul – ways, paths), as in:

> wa'anna hādha ṣīrātī mustaqīman fattabiᶜūhu walā tattabiᶜū al-subul fatafarraqa bikum can sibīlih – This is my path which is straight; so follow it and do not follow other ways for you will be separated from His (God's) way, Q6:153).

The continuity of the text producer's thought is maintained through the intentional selection of the singular noun (sabīl – way, path), which is relevant to the intentionality (underlying meaning) of the text producer. In other words, the singular (sabīl) designates the meaning that there is only one way of God, while the plural (subul – ways, paths) designates the different ways of evil.

The example that follows makes the relationship between coherence and relevance more lucid:

> allāhu waliyyu alladhīna āmanū yukhrijuhum min al-ẓulumāt ilā al-nūr walladhīna.
>
> kafarū awliyā'uhum al-ṭāghūt yukhrijūnahum min al-nūr ilā al-ẓulumat – God is the ally of those who believe. He brings them out from depths of darkness into the light. Those who disbelieve, their allies are false gods who take them out of the light into the depths of darkness, Q2:275).

where we can observe how coherence (the continuity of the thought (theme, leitmotif) of monotheism and the continuity of the thought (theme, leitmotif) of polytheism) is maintained through relevance (the selection of the most relevant/appropriate lexeme). This is illustrated below:

> (allāh – God) → singular → (nūr – light) → singular
> (ẓulumāt – depths of darkness) → plural

In other words, (nūr) represents the light, i.e., the truth, which is one (monotheism), while (ẓulumāt) represents darkness, disbelief, doubt, and error.

For more details on coherence and number, see Section 6.4, point (13). For more details on the interrelationship between relevance, coherence, and continuity of thought, see Section 6.8.

5.6.1 Coherence, relevance, and embellishments

We have discussed the purposeful selection of a relevant word for the achievement of coherence and the text producer's performative intent. However, it is worthwhile to note that the selection of a given lexeme is conditioned by contextual coherence rather than by embellishment which is employed for the decorative rhetorical façade of the text. Qur'anic discourse, in particular, is marked by embellishments, and the most commonly occurring types are polyptoton (the different morphologically related derivations of a word) and antithesis (oppositeness in meaning between two or more text segments). Yet in Qur'anic discourse, meaning overrides embellishments (rhetorical features). The text producer's performative intent is paramount. Let us consider the following examples:

> The lexeme (kubbārā, Q71:22) is an example which illustrates why embellishments are subsidiary to coherence and relevance. This lexeme has occurred only once in the Qur'an, during Noah's parable:
>
> > makarū makran kubbārā – They conspired an immense conspiracy, Q71:22

The word (kubbārā – immense, grand) is a hyperbole adjective (ṣifah mushabbaha) purposefully selected for the illocutionary force of [+ Extreme Hyperbole] and

[+ Affirmation]. However, its counterpart lexeme (kabīrā – great, big) is unable to achieve the same illocutionary force. It is worthwhile to note that both lexemes (kubbārā) and (kabīrā) can achieve assonance. Therefore, it is not a matter of embellishment through the sentence-final assonance but a matter of coherence and relevance. In terms of coherence and relevance, the two words are not interchangeable.

For instance, Q50 starts with prophethood (Q50:1–2), followed by scepticism about eschatology (Q50:3). To rebut this scepticism, God's omnipotence is presented and made salient to the text receiver (Q50:6–11). Therefore, Q50:11 is part of the previous substantiating statement. In this statement, imagery is presented, and a mental image is put forward to the reader the tenet of faith of eschatology (kadhālika al-khurūj – thus is resurrection): Water is sent down from the sky (Q50:9–11) to generate fruits as sustenance for people and most importantly to give life to dead land (Q50:11). Then, the conclusion at the end of the statement reminds the sceptics that resurrection will take place in the same fashion, i.e., the dead bodies will be given life as well. Thus, we can claim that although Q50:11 ends with a /j/ rhyme different from the surrounding statements, the text has progressed coherently and smoothly. In other words, coherence and textual progression in Qur'anic discourse have nothing to do with assonance. Rhyme (assonance) as an embellishment can be violated in the interest of coherence.

5.6.2 Coherence and relevance of conjunctions

In this discussion, we are concerned with micro level coherence, which is the particle level. In Section 6.3, we have argued that cohesion is a prerequisite of coherence. To back up our earlier claim, we can consider the following examples, which lend support to the Qur'anic text linguistic fact that the occurrence or non-occurrence of a conjunctive particle in a text depends on its relevance to the current context of situation. In other words, the employment of a given conjunctive element (cohesive device) should be relevant to the circumstance in order to achieve coherence. A case in point is the relevant employment of the additive conjunctive element (wa – and (al-wāw)), as in the following examples:

Example 1

> sīqa alladhīna kafarū ilā jahannama zumarā ḥattā idhā jā'ūhā futiḥat abwābuha – Those who disbelieved will be driven to hell in groups until when they reach it, its gates are opened, Q39:71.

where we observe a zero-cohesion, i.e., the absence of conjunction (a conjunctive element) before the lexeme (futiḥat – are opened). However, in Q39:73, we observe the occurrence of conjunction, i.e., the employment of the additive conjunctive element (wa – and) before the same lexeme (futiḥat) → (wa futiḥat – and are opened): sīqa alladhīna ittaqaw rabbahum ilā al-jannati zumarā ḥattā idhā jā'ūhā **wa** futiḥat abwābuhā – Those who feared their Lord will be driven to paradise in groups until when they reach it, its gates open, Q39:71

One may question the relevance of the non-occurrence or occurrence of the additive conjunctive element (wa) to the current matter of disbelievers driven to hell versus believers driven to paradise. This is not a haphazard linguistic choice but rather a well-calculated Qur'an-bound stylistic mechanism adopted by the text producer. This is not merely a matter of coordination (al-ᶜaṭf), i.e., polysyndeton, or lack of coordination (asyndeton) on the grammatical level. The additive conjunctive element (wa) is referred to in Arabic syntax as (wāw al-thamāniyah – the 'and' of the eight elements, i.e., the (wāw) that occurs before the eighth element in the sentence).

Grammatically, the (wāw al-thamāniyah – the 'and' of the eight elements) is employed before the eighth element (lexeme) in a list of eight elements (lexemes). In other words, there is no conjunction between the seven lexemes. Conjunction through the additive conjunctive device (wa – and) is used only before the eighth lexeme, as in: aḥmad ᶜālim dhakī karīm basīṭ ghanī wafi naqī **wa** taqī – Ahmad is knowledgeable, clever, generous, simple, wealthy, loyal, pure, **and** pious.

Example 2

al-tā'ibūn al-ᶜābidūn al-ḥāmidūn al-ṣā'iḥūn al-rākiᶜūn al-sājidūn al-āmirūn bil-maᶜrūf **wa** al-nāhūn ᶜan al-munkar – The repentant, the worshippers, the praisers of God, the travellers for His cause, those who bow and prostrate in prayer, those who enjoin what is right **and** forbid what is wrong, Q9:112.

where we have the (wāw al-thamāniyah) employed before the eighth noun (al-nāhūn can al-munkar).

The three major Qur'anic conjunctions (adwāt al-rabṭ, literally meaning tools for binding sentence elements (constituents)) are:

- i the (wa – and), i.e., al-wāw: Its grammatical function is to coordinate (combine, bind) between two text segments like nouns, verbs, adjectives, prepositional phrases. It is used for listing items.
- ii the (fa – then), i.e., al-fā': Its grammatical function is to coordinate between two text segments and to deliver the illocutionary force of [+ Immediately], i.e., there is no lapse of time and no time gap between the two actions denoted by the coordinated verbs.
- iii the (thumma – then): Its grammatical function is to coordinate between two text segments and to deliver the illocutionary force of [– Immediately], i.e., there is a lapse of time, a certain time gap between the two actions denoted by the coordinated verbs. The above three conjunctions are:
  - a coordination particles (adwāt ᶜaṭf),
  - b context-based, and

c contribute to the continuity of sense and the coherence of a given Qur'anic text segment.

Example 3

mā tilka biyamīnika yā mūsā? qāla hiya ᶜaṣāiy: (1) atawakka'u ᶜalaihā/**wa** (2) ahushshu bihā ᶜalā ghanamī/**wa** (3) liya fīhā ma'āribu ukhrā. qāla alqihā yā mūsā. **fa** (4) alqaha/**fa** (5) idha hiya ḥaiyyatun tasᶜa – Moses, what is that in your right hand? He said: 'It is my stick: (1) I lean on it/**and** (2) restrain my sheep with it/**and** (3) I have other uses for it'. God said: 'Throw it down, Moses'. (4) **Immediately**, he throws it down/**Immediately** (5) it has become a fast-moving snake, Q20:17–20.

where we have the employment of the (wa – and) between the text segments (1–3). Moses has answered the question and listed the purposes of the stick that he is holding. This is followed by text segments that have employed the immediate action conjunctive particle (fa) in segments (4–5). God commands Moses to throw down his stick. Thus, Moses should not hesitate at all, and there should not be any waiting time between Moses' response to God's command and the moment he throws down the stick. Therefore, the (wāw) is employed for listing, while the (fa) is employed for the purpose of immediate action.

Example 4

However, when there is a time gap between two actions denoted by the verbs, the conjunctive particle (thumma) is employed, as in:

> khalaqnākum min turabin/**thumma** min nutfatin/**thumma** min ᶜalaqatin/**thumma** min muḍghatin mukhallaqatin wa ghairi mukhallaqatin . . . /**thumma** nukhrijukum ṭiflan/**thumma** litablughlū ashuddakum – We created you from dust/**then** from a sperm-drop/**then** from a clinging clot/**then** from a lump of flesh formed and unformed . . . /**then** We bring you out as a child/**then** you may reach maturity, Q22:5

This text segment deals with the different stages of the creation of the foetus in the womb followed by the birth of the child and his/her growing up as an adult. In terms of coherence and continuity of the thought of creation and other stages, the text producer has employed the conjunctive particle (thumma – then) to designate the time gap between the stages of creation, birth, and growing up. Thus, we have:

stages of creation in the womb → birth → growing up

For more details on conjunction and the different types of conjunctive element, see Chapter 6, Section 6.5.4.

5.7 Coherence and saliency

In this discussion, we are concerned with micro level coherence, which is the word level. Saliency is to make a pivotal idea (notion, theme) prominent. Saliency is achieved when the text segment that carries the pivotal idea of a statement is foregrounded (placed sentence-initially). Saliency is concerned with a prominent, most noticeable, or important text segment, i.e., a text segment that bears an information value. In terms of coherence, the salient segment:

i stands out more than others in terms of its information value,
ii contributes to the awakening of the listener's/reader's attention to an important matter,
iii contributes to the delivery of the text producer's performative intent,
iv contributes to the sequentiality (continuity) of thoughts, and
v attains a pivotal role for the text producer in persuasion and interpersonal communication.

We can, therefore, claim that the text producer achieves saliency through grammatical and semantic deviation. Syntactic and morphological deviation lead to saliency through the different forms of shift and the different forms of foregrounding.

However, semantic deviation leads to saliency through rhetorical devices such as antithesis, epizeuxis, metaphor, metonymy, polyptoton, simile, and zeugma. The illocutionary force of a salient word/phrase is to awaken the reader/hearer and draw his/her attention to it.

For Beaugrande and Dressler (1981:165), salient elements are readily assigned to the subject or direct object slots of English sentences to bring them into a prominent perspective. Saliency is the phenomenon of linguistic highlighting and is related to motivated prominence in order to make a text segment stand out in some way (Halliday 1973). For Simpson (2004), the salient element draws attention to itself.

5.7.1 Saliency mechanisms

The relations of *thoughts* to each other affect the arrangement of words in sentences (Beaugrande and Dressler 1981:20). We can claim here that saliency is related to appropriateness. In other words, the marked (unusual) word order is more appropriate than the unmarked (usual) word order in the realization of saliency and coherence.

The text receiver gives attention to the salient segment through which he/she can deliver his/her performative intent. Through saliency, the Qur'anic discourse makes the audience pay attention to a specific unit of information through the following techniques:

1 Shift: Through shift in the grammatical function of a word, the reader's/hearer's attention can be diverted towards a specific text segment which has

made shift in grammatical function. In other words, because of the value of information which a text segment bears, it is made salient through changing its original grammatical function in order to raise attention to this particular word, as in the following examples:

Example 1

qul amara rabbī bil-qisṭ wa aqīmū wujūhakum ᶜinda kulli masjid – Say: 'My Lord commands justice. Direct your worship straight to Him wherever you pray', Q7:29

where the salient text segment is (aqīmū – to direct, to maintain) whose grammatical function is a verb. However, grammatically speaking, it should have the grammatical function of a nominalized noun (maṣdar) because it is coordinated to (maᶜṭūf ᶜalā) the first nominalized noun (al-qisṭ – justice). Thus, we expect the grammatical structure of Q7:29 to be like the following:

(qul amara rabbī bil-qisṭ wa bi'iqamat wujūhakum ᶜinda kulli masjid – Say: 'My Lord commands justice and the direction of your worship straight to Him wherever you pray').

However, due to the significance of praying to God in every place of worship rather than praying to false gods, the audience needs to be made aware of this theological fact and alert them. To achieve the illocutionary force of value information, the grammatical function of the word needs to be changed to awaken the audience.

Example 2

innā sakhkharnā al-jibāla maᶜahu yusabbiḥna bil-ᶜashiyi wal-ishrāq – Indeed, We (God) subjected the mountains with him (David) which exalt God in the late afternoon and after sunrise, Q38:18

where the salient text segment is (yusabbiḥna – to exalt God), which is employed in the present tense form for the text linguistic function of saliency. However, grammatically speaking, it should have the grammatical function of an active participle (ism fāᶜil) that designates the semantic componential feature of [+ Continuity] and also because the exaltation (tasbīḥ) of the mountains took place in the past during the lifetime of Prophet David. Thus, we expect the grammatical structure of Q38:18 to involve the active participle:

(innā sakhkharnā al-jibāla maᶜahu musabbiḥātin bil-ᶜashiyi wal-ishrāq – Indeed, We (God) subjected the mountains with him (David) exalting God in the late afternoon and after sunrise).

Due to the fact that the exaltation of the mountains is considered a unique theological notion in the Qur'an, the audience's attention has to be drawn to this matter through the shift from the active participle to the present tense verb. The present tense carries the action of the mountains from the past during David's lifetime to the present time and gives it a vivid imagery, setting the scene for God's omnipotence in terms of the creation of mountains.

Example 3

The past tense is employed to achieve the illocutionary force of threat, as in:

atā amru allāhi falā tastaᶜjilūh – The command of God is coming, Q16:1

wayawma yunfakhu fī al-ṣūri fafaziᶜa man fī al-samāwāti wamān fī al-arḍi – And warn of the day the horn will be blown, and whoever is in the heavens and whoever is on the earth will be terrified, Q27:87

where the salient text segment is the verb (atā – is coming) in Q16:1 and (faziᶜa – to be terrified), which are both employed in the past tense. However, the day of judgement has not taken place, yet while the past tense designates an action that has taken place already. However, the employment of the past tense has the semantic componential feature of [+ Certainty of Something to Happen]. Thus, to make the notion of eschatology vivid in the text, tense shift is employed as a technique of saliency to draw the attention of the text receiver to this notion. When something indeed took place, it possesses the status of reality, i.e., the truth value. However, the expected tense in Q16:1 and Q27:87 is the future or present tense (saya'tī/ya'tī) and (sayafzaᶜu/ yafzaᶜu). The same applies to Q39:69–72 and Q50:19–24 where there is saliency of the text segments that have been employed in the past tense while they should have been employed in the present or future tense. This is again for the illocutionary force of threat and awakening the audience.

Example 4

To bring the importance of performing the daily prayer to the audience, and to make this notion prominent, the text producer grants it saliency through tense shift as in:

innamā tundhiru alladhīna yakhshawna rabbahum bil-ghaibi wa aqāmū al-ṣalāta – You can only warn those who fear their Lord unseen and have established prayer, Q35:18

where we have shift from the present tense (yakhshawna – to fear) to past tense (aqāmū – established, performed) in order to draw the reader's attention to the valuable information signalled by the text segment (aqāmū al-ṣalāta – established prayer). Thus, through shift, the notion of performing the prayer is made salient. It is through the stylistic mechanism of shift that the distinction between the two actions denoted by the two verbs (yakhshawna – to fear) and (aqāmū – established, performed) is highlighted to us. It is through shift that we can distinguish between two distinct situations: The first is the fear of the Lord, and the second is the establishment of prayer. Shift has made the second situation salient.

2 Word order: In Qur'anic discourse, we account for saliency in terms of word order, i.e., the word's position in the sentence, such as foregrounding. Saliency through word order (foregrounding) takes the following forms:

i Subject in sentence-initial position (foregrounded subject): The salient text segment is the subject of the sentence and occurs at sentence-initial position, as in the following examples:

Example 1

allāhu yaḥkum bainakum yawma al-qiyāmah – God will judge between you on the day of resurrection, Q22:69

where saliency by sentence-initial position aims to achieve coherence and prominence to the thought. The text segment (allāhu – God) is given saliency through initial position because it is the pivotal thought where an alternative structure with a verb at sentence-initial position is ruled out because the continuity of thought and coherence will be obstructed. The saliency of the noun at the initial position of the sentence delivers the illocutionary force of specificity, i.e., the action denoted by the verb is God specific. Thus, we cannot expect:

(yaḥkum allāhu bainakum yawma al-qiyāmah – God will judge between you on the day of resurrection).

Example 2

The same applies to numerous examples in Qur'anic discourse, as in Q2:212, 245, Q3:156, Q13:8, Q16:19, 70, 71, 78, 81, Q24:45, Q37:96, and Q76:23, 28.

allāhu lā ilāha illā hū – God! There is no god but Him, Q64:13

ii Theme (foregrounded noun): This is a Theme-Rheme sentence structure (al-muḥaddath ᶜanhu wa al-muḥaddath), which grammatically is referred to as mubtada' and khabar (subject and predicate). The Theme (al-muḥaddath ᶜanhu) is given saliency through sentence-initial position for its high information value, which distinguishes it from other text segments. Let us consider the following interesting example of a salient noun in a sentence-initial position. The following syntactic structure represents a marked (uncommon) word order, which is referred to as Theme-Rheme (al-muḥaddath ᶜanhu). Theme-Rheme sentences involve saliency to their sentence-initial words. This is a syntactic process in which the initial noun (phrase) acts as a Theme (al-muḥaddath ᶜanhu) and the rest of the sentence acts as the Rheme (al-muḥaddath). Grammatically, the Theme is a foregrounded noun (phrase), but most importantly it takes the nominative case regardless of its underlying (original) grammatical function and case ending. It is worthwhile to note that the Theme-Rheme syntactic structure is a marked (unusual) word order.

Example 3

tilka al-rusulu faḍḍalnā baᶜḍahum ᶜalā baᶜḍ – Those messengers, some of them We caused to exceed others, Q2:253

where the Theme is the noun phrase (tilka al-rusulu – those messengers), the Rheme is (faḍḍalnā baᶜḍahum ᶜalā baᶜḍ – some of them We caused to exceed others), and the coreferential pronoun is (-hum – them), referring to the foregrounded object noun phrase (tilka al-rusulu) acting as a Theme. This is a marked word order whose unmarked (usual) word order is: (faḍḍalnā baᶜḍa tilka al-rusuli ᶜala baᶜḍ) where the object noun phrase has regained its original accusative case /ā/ implicitly → (tilka al-rusula) and the coreferential pronoun (-hum) attached to the first word (baᶜḍ) is dropped. The reason why (al-rusuli) occurs in the genitive case /i/ is because of the impact of (baᶜḍa).

Example 4

al-nāru waᶜadahā allāhu alladhīna kafarū – It is the fire which God has promised those who disbelieve, Q22:72

where the Theme is the noun (al-nāru – the fire), the Rheme is (waᶜadahā allāhu alladhīna kafarū – has promised those who disbelieve), and the coreferential pronoun is (-hā – it), referring to the foregrounded object noun (al-nāru) acting as a Theme.

This is a marked word order whose unmarked word order is: (waᶜada allāhu alladhīna kafarū al-nāra) where the object noun has regained its original accusative case /ā/ → (al-nāra) and the coreferential pronoun (-hā) attached to the first word (al-nāru) is dropped.

In the above example, (al-nāru – the fire) is foregrounded for saliency and coherence. To rearrange the configuration of sentence constituents, saliency and coherence will not be achieved. Neither of the following syntactic structures can achieve saliency for the word (al-nāru) or coherence and continuity of the thought of punishment:

(allāhu waᶜada alladhīna kafarū al-nāra – God has promised those who disbelieve the fire).

(wa ᶜada allāhu al-nāra alladhīna kafarū – God has promised the fire to those who disbelieve).

Example 5

al-nāru yuᶜraḍūna ᶜalaihā – The fire, they are exposed to it, Q40:46

where the Theme is the noun (al-nāru – the fire), the Rheme is (yuᶜraḍūna ᶜalaihā – are exposed to it), and the coreferential pronoun is (-hā – it), referring to the object noun (al-nāru) acting as a Theme. This is a marked word order whose unmarked word order is: (yuᶜraḍūna ᶜalā al-nāri) where the object noun has regained its original genitive case /i/ (majrūr) → (al-nāri) and the coreferential pronoun (-hā) attached to the preposition (ᶜalā) is dropped.

Example 6

al-mawtā yabᶜathuhum allāhu – The dead, God will resurrect them, Q6:36

where the Theme is the noun (al-mawtā – the dead), the Rheme is (yabᶜathuhum allāhu – God will resurrect them), and the coreferential pronoun is (-hum – them), referring to the object noun (al-mawtā) acting as a Theme. This is a marked (unusual) word order whose unmarked (usual) word order is: (yabᶜathu allāhu al-mawtā) where the object noun has regained its original genitive case /ā/ (manṣūb) → (al-mawtā) and the coreferential pronoun (-hā) attached to the verb (yabᶜathu) is dropped. It is worthwhile to note that the Theme (al-mawtā) is a noun that ends with a vowel. Thus, neither the nominative nor the accusative case will appear at the end of the word.

iii Object noun sentence-initially (foregrounded object): Saliency can also be achieved through the foregrounding of the direct object. This is a syntactic structure through which saliency is given to the object noun through sentence-initial position due to its high information value, which distinguishes it from other text segments, as in the following examples:

jahannama yaslawnahā – Hell which they will enter to burn, Q14:29

where we have a marked (unusual) sentence structure with a foregrounded object noun (jahannama – hell) rather than the unmarked (usual, expected) verb-initial construction (yaslawna jahannama). However, through the marked Q14:29, coherence is achieved through the saliency of (jahannama), which provides continuity of senses to the preceding sentence Q14:28, whose notion is hell but is referred to through the metonymy (dār al-bawār – the home of ruin). Thus, in terms of coherence and continuity of senses, we have:

(dār al-bawār) → (jahannama).

al-arḍa madadnāhā – The earth We (God) have spread it out, Q15:19

al-jānna khalaqnāhu min qablu min nāri al-samūm – The jinn We (God) created before from the fire of scorching wind, Q15:27

iyyāka naᶜbudu – It is You we worship, Q1:5

al-anᶜāma khalaqahā – The grazing livestock He has created, Q16:5, 8

al-arḍa baᶜda dhālika daḥāhā – After that He spread the earth, Q79:30, 32

al-arḍa madadnāhā – The earth We have spread, Q15:19

iv Noun phrases and prepositional phrases within the sentence (foregrounding inside the sentence): These are also made salient inside the sentence, as in:

> alam ta^{c}lam anna allāha ^{c}alā kulli shai'in qadīr – Do you not know that God is over all things competent?, Q2:106

> alladhī aḥsana kulla shai'in khalaqahu – who perfected everything which He (God) created, Q32:7

where the salient text segments are (^{c}alā kulli shai'in/ kulla shai'in – all things). The text producer has resorted to word order change to give saliency to the segment (kulli shai'in) in Q2:106. Linguistically, Q2:106 is a marked (unusual) word order. The unmarked (usual) word order is: (inna allāha qadīr ^{c}alā kulli shai'in). To achieve coherence and continuity of thoughts, (^{c}alā kulli shai'in) is given saliency (prominence, importance) to catch the addressee's attention. Thus, in terms of coherence, the text segment (^{c}alā kulli shai'in) is more important than the notion of (qudrah – competence) represented by the segment (qadīr – competent). The foregrounding of (^{c}alā kulli shai'in) has the illocutionary force of rebuttal and has the communicative function of dispelling doubt in the mind of either a denier (munkir) or a floating (mutarddid) addressee about God's infinite abilities. The same applies to Q2:109.

In similar vein, Q32:7 is a marked word order. The unmarked order is: (allāhu alladhī aḥsana khalqa kulli shai'in). However, to give focus and importance to the segment (kulli shai'in), word order change is necessary to provide saliency to (kulli shai'in), which has attained more importance than the notion of (khalq – creation), which has been postponed and backgrounded.

Let us consider the following examples:

> fallāhu huwa al-mawlā wahuwa yuḥyī al-mawtā wahuwa ^{c}alā kulli shai'in qadīr – God, He is the protector, and He gives life to the dead, and He is over all things competent, Q42:9

In the above example, the text segment (^{c}alā kulli shai'in) is given saliency in the context of listing. To substantiate that God's omnipotence encompasses infinite abilities, i.e., God has more than just two features: (al-mawlā – the protector) and (yuḥyī al-mawtā – He gives life to the dead). Thus, (^{c}alā kulli shai'in) is brought in as a rebuttal to a denier addressee who thinks that God's power is finite. The context of listing and saliency also applies to Q57:2–3 (lahu mulku al-samāwāti wal-arḍi yuḥyī wayumītu wahuwa ^{c}alā kulli shai'in qadīr. huwa al-awwalu wal-ākhiru wal-ẓāhiru wal-bātinu wahuwa bikulli shai'in ^{c}alīm – He is the dominion of the heavens and earth. He gives life and causes death, and He is competent over all things. He is the first and the last, the ascendant and the intimate, and He is knowing of all things) where the text segments (ᶜalā kulli shai'in – over all things) and (bikulli shai'in – of all things) are made salient.

Also, in the following marked (unusual) word order:

> wamā arsalnāka illā <u>kāffatan</u> lil-nāsi bashīran wanadhīran – We (God) have sent you (Muḥammad) only to bring good news and warning to <u>all</u> people, Q34:28

where the noun (kāffatan – all) is made salient due to its position preceding the prepositional phrase (lil-nāsi – to people). Its original position in the sentence should be after the prepositional phrase: (wamā arsalnāka illā lil-nāsi {kāffatan} bashiran wanadhīran).

v Prepositional phrase in sentence-initial position (foregrounded prepositional phrase): This is concerned with foregrounding a prepositional phrase. This stylistic pattern represents a marked (unusual) word order, as in the following examples:

> <u>bil-ākhirati</u> hum yūqinūn – They have firm faith <u>in the hereafter</u>, Q2:4
>
> <u>ilā allāhi</u> marjīᶜukum jamiᶜan – You will all return <u>to God</u>, Q5:48

where the prepositional phrases (bil-ākhirati – in the hereafter) and (ilā allāhi – to God) are given saliency through sentence-initial position (foregrounding). The unmarked (usual) word orders are:

> (hum yūqinūn bil-akhirati – They have firm faith in the hereafter).
>
> (marji ᶜukum jamīᶜan ilā allāhi – You will all return to God).

where the prepositional phrases (bil-ākhirati – your return) and (ilā allāhi – to God) are not given saliency because they are not foregrounded, i.e., they are backgrounded (placed sentence-finally).

In the following example, we have two salient text segments:

> <u>ilā allāhi</u> marjiᶜukum/huwa <u>ᶜalā kulli shai'in</u> qadir – <u>To God</u> you will all return, and He has power <u>over everything</u>, Q11:4

The first salient text segment is the prepositional phrase (ilā allāhi – to God) and the second salient text segment is (ᶜalā kulli shai'in – over everything). The first case of saliency is achieved through sentence-initial position (foregrounding), while the second case of saliency is achieved through rearrangement of sentence constituents. The unmarked (usual) word order of Q11:4 is:

> (marjiᶜukum ilā allāhi wa huwa qadir ᶜalā kulli shai'in – You will all return to God, and He has over everything power).

It is worthwhile to note that the prepositional phrase is not always a salient text segment. For example, in Q6:72 (huwa alladhī <u>ilaihi</u> tuḥsharūn – It is He to whom you will be gathered), the prepositional phrase (ilaihi – to Him (whom)) is salient. The unmarked (usual, expected) word order of Q6:72 is (huwa alladhī tuḥsharūn ilaihi). However, in Q6:73 (huwa alladhī khalaqa al-samāwāti wal-arḍa bil-ḥaqqi – It is He who created the heavens and earth in truth), the prepositional phrase (bil-ḥaqqi – in truth) is not salient. Thus, Q6:73 is an unmarked word order.

> ᶜalā allāhi falyatawakkal al-mu'minūn – Upon God let the believers rely, Q64:13

where the prepositional phrase (ᶜalā allāhi – on God) is made salient by placing it sentence-initially for the illocutionary force of specificity of the action of trust should be made only to God. The unmarked word order is (falyatawakkal al-mu'minūn ᶜalā allāhi).

It is worthwhile to note that the illocutionary force of specificity of some feature that is God specific can also be encountered in the following examples:

> biyadika al-khair – In Your hand is all good, Q3:26

> ilā allāhi al-maṣīr – To God is the final destination, Q3:28

> lahu al-mulk yawma yunfakhu fi al-sur – To Him belongs sovereignty on the day the horn is blown, Q6:73

The matters that are specific to God and which are made salient include: (all that is good, control over all things, sovereignty, reliance, and the return on the day of judgement).

It is also worthwhile to note that the foregrounding for saliency can take place in the middle of the sentence, as in:

> lam yakun lahu kufuwan aḥadun – There is not any equivalent to Him, Q1124

where the prepositional phrase (lahu – to Him) is foregrounded for saliency in order to make the notion of 'nothing is equivalent to God' as a God-specific feature. The unmarked word order of Q112:4 is: (lam yakun aḥadun kufuwan lahu).

Having considered the above unmarked word order which does not involve saliency, we can observe that two foregrounding processes have taken place in the marked word order Q112:4:

i The foregrounding of (kufuwan – equivalent), which is the predicate (khabar) of the auxiliary verb (yakun – to be). The subject (ism) of (yakun) is (aḥadun – one), which is backgrounded (mu'akhkhar), i.e., placed sentence-finally.

ii The foregrounding of the prepositional phrase (lahu – to Him), which is placed before the first foregrounded word (kufuwan). Thus, the prepositional phrase (lahu) is made salient.

The illocutionary force of foregrounding (lahu) is to highlight the feature of 'nothing is equivalent to God' and make this feature God specific. Q112:4 is intertextually related to Q22:73 (inna alladhīna tadᶜūna min dūni allāhi lan yakhluqū dhubāban walaw ijtamaᶜū lahu – Indeed, those you invoke beside God will never create as much as a fly even if they gather for that purpose) and also to Q16:20 and Q25:3.

3 Relative clauses: Saliency also features in relative clauses, as in:

> yajᶜalu man yashā'u ᶜaqīmā – He (God) renders whom He wills barren, Q42:50

where the text segment (man yashā'u – whom He wills) is given saliency through foregrounding while the segment (ᶜaqīmā – barren) is backgrounded.

4 Conditional clauses: Saliency also occurs in conditional clauses, as in:

> huwa ᶜalā jamᶜihim idhā yashā'u qadīr – He (God), for gathering them, if He wills, is competent, Q42:29

where the text segment (idhā yashā'u – if He wills) is given saliency through foregrounding while the segment (qadir – competent) is backgrounded.

5 A lexical item: In terms of coherence and relevance, a word is purposefully selected through which two text linguistic objectives are achieved:

i the performative intent of the text producer, and
ii coherence and continuity of thought.

Therefore, we can claim that although the selected lexical item has either a partial synonym or has a verb form alternative, the two words are not interchangeable, as in the following examples:

i (mu'minūn – believers, Q5:88): This lexical item is employed in the active participle to deliver the illocutionary force [+ Continuity] of belief in God. It represents the text producer's performative intent, i.e., it is purposefully selected in this grammatical form to achieve the intended pragmatic function of continuity. However, had we changed it to a verb form (tu'minun – to believe), the meaning has dramatically changed. The verb designates the illocutionary force [– Continuity] of belief in God, i.e., [+ Renewability]. Therefore, we can claim that it is not a matter of assonance where both (mu'minun) and its alternative word (tu'minun) end with /-ūn/.

ii (khāliq – creator, Q6:102): This lexical item occurs in the active participle form. To investigate its relevance and contribution to the continuity of thought and coherence, we need to be aware of the following:

a The text producer's performative intent that is hinged upon (khāliq),
b The pivotal thought that has occurred in the previous statements, and
c The cognitive status of the text receiver (audience).

Based on the above, we can make the following observations:

1. Q6:100 is a counter-argument where the opponent's viewpoints (premises) are cited: (ja^c^alū lillāhi shurakā'a al-jinna – They (the polytheists) made the jinn partners with God) and (kharaqū lahu banīn wabanāt – They attributed sons and daughters to God).
2. The cognitive status of the addressee is a denier.
3. Rebuttal to the opponent's premises is cited in the following text segments:

   i In Q6:95–99 where God's omnipotence is listed in terms of God's ability in bringing out the living from the dead and the dead from the living, making the dawn break, the creation of the stars, the creation of people, and the sending down of water from the sky.

   ii Rebuttal is also cited in Q6:100 (khalaqahum – It was God who created the jinn).

   iii In Q6:100 (bighair ^c^ilm – without any true knowledge, i.e., the polytheists made the jinn partners with God without any true knowledge).

   iv In Q6:100 through the theological expression (subḥānahu – Glory be to God) that affirms the oneness of God (monotheism): (subḥānahu wata^c^ālā ^c^ammā yushrikūn – Glory be to Him! He is far higher than what they ascribe to Him).

   v Rebuttal through the no-main-verb nominal sentences (Q6:101–102), which affirms the notion of monotheism: (badī^c^u al-samāwāti wal-arḍ – The creator of the heavens and earth), (huwa bikulli shai'in ^c^alīm – He has full knowledge of all things), (dhālikum allāhu rabbukum – This is God, your Lord), (lā ilāha illā hū – There is no deity except Him), (khāliqu kulli shai'in – The creator of all things), (huwa ^c^alā kulli shai'in wakīl – He is in charge of everything).

   vi Rebuttal through the denial interrogative question: (annā yakūnu lahu waladun walam takun lahu ṣāḥibatun – How could God have children when He has no spouse, when He created all things, and He has full knowledge of all things, Q6:101). Having said the above with regards to the rebuttal of the opponent's thesis about polytheism, the lexical item (khāliq) as an active participle fits in well to deliver the illocutionary force of monotheism as a perpetual status of God [+ Continuity] and the perpetual status of being the creator of all things including the jinn. Therefore, to employ a verb form (yakhluq – to create) will fail to deliver the perpetual status of the oneness of God and His being the creator all the time of all things. In other words, the semantic features [+ Creator All the Time] and [+ Creator of All Things] are specific to the active participle (khāliq) and not the alternative verb (yakhluq). Thus, coherence and continuity of thought have been achieved through the purposeful selection of the relevant word (khāliq).

For more details on through-argumentation and counter-argumentation, see Chapter 3, Section 3.10.

iii (al-akram – the most bountiful one, Q96:3): This word has occurred once in the Qur'an as a modifier (adjective) of the noun (rabb – Lord) and so has its counterpart (karīm – generous, Q82:6).

> iqra' warabbuka al-akram – Recite, and your Lord is the most generous, Q96:3

> yā aiyuhā al-insānu mā gharraka birabbika al-karīm – O mankind, what has deceived you concerning your Lord, the generous, Q82:6

One may wonder, if the two words have the same grammatical function as modifiers of the same noun (rabb), why the lexeme (al-akram) is more relevant in terms of coherence and continuity of thought than (karīm). One may be lured by the generosity of a person. Thus, the word (yaghtarr – to be lured, tempted, attracted) collocates with (karīm). Also, the word (karīm) semantically designates [+ Wisdom]. Thus, generosity without wisdom is classified as wastefulness and squandering of wealth. Due to the Lord's wisdom-based generosity, man becomes tempted to ignore the Lord's commands, thinking that God is generous in forgiveness. The word (karīm) fits in well in the context of the creation of man, which is considered as only one blessing of the Lord (khalaqaka fasawwāka faᶜadalaka – (The Lord) has created you, proportioned you, and balanced you, Q82:7). Due to the fact that the context of Q96:3 is different, the word (al-akram) is selected, as it is relevant to achieve coherence and continuity of thought. This word fits in well in the context of more than one blessing. In Q96:1–6, we are informed of the Lord's two blessings: (i) the blessing of the creation of man and (ii) the blessing of the knowledge given to man. It is the blessing of knowledge that has made man different from animals. This knowledge is referred to as (al-ᶜaql – reason, the power to think, understand, and form judgements logically).

iv (mawᶜidatin, Q9:114): This word is contrasted with (waᶜd, Q4:122). Both (mawᶜidatin) and (waᶜd) mean (a promise). However, in Qur'anic Arabic, they are partial synonyms used in different contexts. The lexeme (mawᶜidatin) designates the following semantic characteristics:

1 It has occurred only once in the Qur'an and is rarely used,
2 It refers to a promise that does not last to the end but stops at a point of time,
3 It designates something unusual, as we are informed by Q9:114, in which Abraham requests forgiveness for his father who is a disbeliever, and most importantly,
4 The promise does not last for ever, i.e., when it became apparent to Abraham that his father was an enemy to God, Abraham dissociated himself from his father. In other words, Abraham stopped his promise he made earlier to his father.

Based on the context, the above semantic traits of (maw^{c}idatin) fits in well with the text producer's performative intent. Thus, (maw^{c}idatin) achieves coherence and continuity of thought.

The above cannot be made by the word (wa^{c}d). This word has occurred several times in the Qur'an and designates continuity and truthfulness of a promise. Thus, we encounter the collocations (ṣādiqa al-wa^{c}d – to be true to one's promise, 19:54), (kāna wa^{c}d rabbī ḥaqqā – The promise of my Lord is ever true, 18:98).

5.8 Coherence, continuity of thought, and relevance

In the present discussion, we are concerned with micro level coherence which takes place at both the word level and the sentence level. The text producer wants to achieve a communicative goal, i.e., to deliver a performative intent. This is his/her thought, which can represent a theme (notion), a point of view, or an argument. Each interlocutor (text producer) has to bear in mind his/her audience (addressee, text receiver). The text producer has to make his/her thoughts well arranged. In other words, he/she is required to meet the coherence requirement, namely, the continuity (sequentiality) and good arrangement of thoughts. He/She has to provide appropriately relevant (well-selected) lexical items, relevant grammatical structures, and stylistic patterns, which contribute to the continuity of the pivotal thought that carries his/her performative intent. To put what I have said into practice, let us consider the following example that will illuminate the above claim:

> (saqar – hell): This is one of the names of fire, which is the place of punishment. It has occurred in Q54:48 and Q74:26. This lexeme has occurred three times in Q74 (Q74:26, 27, and 42). Thus, Q74 will be taken as the contextual launching pad for this text linguistic analysis of (saqar) in terms of coherence, continuity of thought, and relevance. We can provide the following observations:

- i Based on the reasons for revelation (asbāb al-nuzūl), the statements Q74:14–25 constitute the context for Q74:26 in which (saqar) has occurred.
- ii We are informed by the reasons for revelation that Q74:14–25 refer specifically to al-Walīd b. al-Maghīrah, who used to attack the Qur'an and Muḥammad (Q74:24–25). He claimed that the Qur'an was magic imitated from others.
- iii As a consequence for the enormity of al-Walīd's allegations and scepticism, we can claim that (saqar) is the most relevant, befitting, appropriately selected, and context-based lexeme. So far, (saqar) has served well the interlocutor's performative intent (communicative goal).
- iv Denotatively, (saqar) designates the meanings:
  1. very tall flames of fire, and
  2. fire with an extreme high temperature.

- v The most salient semantic componential feature of (saqar) is [+ Extremely High Temperature].
- vi Semantically, due to the very high temperature of the fire, the complexion of the face or the body turns extremely black, as we are informed by Q74:29 (lawwāḥatan lil- bashar – Blackening the skins).
- vii In terms of the illocutionary force which (saqar) delivers, the text producer has successfully managed to employ this lexeme to make the punishment compatible with the offense committed by al-Walīd b. al-Maghīrah.
- viii In terms of continuity of thought, we need to consider Q74:22. This refers to al-Walīd, who frowned (ᶜabasa) and whose face turned black as a result of his rage (basara) when he heard the Qur'an. The expression (ᶜabasa wa basara) is an idiom that refers to extreme rage where the Arabic describes the person's face as becoming black due to his/her anger.
- ix In terms of relevance, (saqar) has achieved relevance since it means the fire that turns the person's skin black.
- x In terms of continuity of thought, Q74:22 is followed by the statement where (saqar) is employed (Q74:26).
- xi In terms of relevance, we can observe cause and effect. In other words, the punishment by (saqar) to blacken his skin is as a result of and is compatible with al-Walīd's scepticism.
- xii The lexeme (saqar) is morphologically related to (saqqār), which means (laᶜᶜān), i.e., someone who curses and accuses others for nothing, a person who blemishes people's reputation for no reason. Thus, we encounter the Islamic legal ruling of (al-liᶜān) when someone makes a false accusation against an innocent person, as in Q24. Thus, al-Walīd has accused Muḥammad of producing a fake Qur'an and of being a magician. In terms of Islamic law, al-Walīd should face the punishment of (al-liᶜān) in the hereafter. Therefore, the lexeme (saqar) is well selected for this pragmatic function. In other words, (saqar) is the fair punishment for a person who is (saqqār).
- xiii In terms of continuity of thought and relevance, the interlocutor has employed a lexeme (saqar) that is morphologically related to the punishment, the person's attitude, and the crime committed.
- xiv In terms of the macro text, the lexeme (saqar) occurs in the context where the deniers (disbelievers) reject their Prophets and argue that they (the deniers) are more appropriate for the task of prophethood than the Prophets, as we are informed by Q74:52 and Q54:24–25.
- xv On the phonetic macro text level, (saqar) is marked by the initial sibilant consonant sound /ṣ/. We can argue that the phonetic co-text has influenced the selection of the lexeme (saqar). In Q74:17, 22, 23, 24, and 26, the sibilant consonant sound /ṣ/ has occurred. This lends support to (saqar).

We move now to sentence-level coherence. An interesting example that demonstrates coherence, continuity of thought and relevance is Q2:270. Through this example, we can claim that the macro text has an impact on the configuration of text segments to achieve coherence, continuity of thought and relevance:

> mā anfaqtum min nafaqatin aw nadhartum min nadhrin fa'inna allāha yaᶜlamuh – Whatever you spend of expenditure or make of vows, indeed God knows of it, Q2:270.

In this example, we have a specific configuration of text segments:

> (mā anfaqtum min nafaqatin – whatever you spend of expenditure] + [nadhartum min nadhrin – make of vows] + [inna allaha yaᶜlamuh – indeed God knows of it).

However, we may expect the alternative configuration of the same text segments:

> [inna allāha yaᶜlamu] + [mā anfaqtum min nafaqatin] + [nadhartum min nadhrin] – Indeed God knows of whatever you spend of expenditure or make of vows.

The alternative word order of text segments is ruled out because of the impact of the macro text, which abounds with the lexeme (yunfiq – spend). Most importantly, the thought (leitmotif) of spending one's wealth in God's cause is focal and recurrently employed in the macro text Q2:261–274. Thus, the configuration of Q2:270 achieves coherence, continuity of thought, and saliency of the pivotal thought. The continuity of the focal thought of spending has resulted in placing first the text segments which include the sense of spending. Thus, saliency of thought is achieved.

Let us consider Q39:68–75 where we can observe coherence, continuity of thought and relevance:

> wanufikha fī al-ṣūri . . . wa'ashraqat al-arḍu binūri rabbihā wawuḍiᶜa al-kitābu . . . waquḍiya bainahum bil-ḥaqq . . . wawuffiyat kullu nafsin mā ᶜamilat wahuwa aᶜlamu bimā yafᶜalūn. wasīqa alladhīna kafarū ilā jahannama zumarā . . . wasīqa alladhīna attaqaw rabbahum ilā al-jannati zumarā . . . waqālū al-ḥamdu lillāhi alladhī ṣadaqanā waᶜdahu . . . faniᶜma ajru al-ᶜāmilīn . . . waquḍiya bainahum bil-ḥaqq . . . – The horn will be blown . . . The earth will shine with the light of its Lord, and the record of deeds will be placed . . . and it will be judged between them in truth . . . Every soul will be compensated for what it did, and He is most knowing of what they did. Those who disbelieved will be driven to hell in groups . . . Those who feared their Lord will be driven to paradise in groups . . . They will say: 'Praise to God who has fulfilled for us His promise . . . and excellent is the reward of righteous workers'. It will be judged between them in truth, Q39:68–75.

The above text is coherent due to the text linguistic factors of:

i the continuity of thought within the text, and
ii the relevance of a given thought in the text.

In Q39:68–75, we have the thought of resurrection (eschatology) and the thought of reward and punishment. The continuity of the thought of resurrection starts at Q39:68–69. The other thought that is made relevant is God's judgement in truth between believers and disbelievers according to their deeds. This thought is represented by the expression (waquḍiya bainahum bil-ḥaqq – it will be judged between them in truth, Q39:69), which occurs at the beginning of the text and at the end of the text in Q39:75. In the above text, the thought of reward and punishment is made salient through antithesis between the disbelievers (Q39:71–72) and the believers (Q39:73–74).

At the sentence-level coherence, Q7:26–27 represent an interesting example of the continuity (sequentiality) and good arrangement of thoughts:

> yā banī ādama qad anzalnā ᶜalikum libāsan yuwārī saw'ātikum warīshan walibāsu al-taqwā dhālika khair dhālika min āyāt allāh laᶜallāhum yadhdhakkarūn. yā banī ādama lā yaftinannakum al-shaiṭānu kamā akhraja abawaikum min al-jannati yanziᶜu ᶜanhumā libāsahumā liyuriyahumā saw'ātihimā innahu yarākum huwa waqabīluhu min ḥaithu lā tarawnahum innā jaᶜalnā al-shayāṭīna awliyā'a lilladhīna lā yu'minūn – O children of Adam, We have bestowed upon you clothing to conceal your private parts and as adornment. But the clothing of righteousness – that is best. That is from the signs of God that perhaps they will remember. O children of Adam, let not Satan tempt you as he removed your parents from paradise, stripping them of their clothing to show them their private parts. Indeed, he sees you, he and his forces, from where you do not see them. Indeed, We have made the devils allies to those who do not believe, Q7:26–27.

where the focal thought in Q7:26 is represented by 'clothing to conceal people's private parts', which is presented as one of God's favours bestowed upon mankind. However, to achieve coherence and continuity of thought with this leitmotif (thought, theme), Q7:27 makes reference to Satan, who caused Adam and Eve to slip out and managed to remove them from the state they were enjoying in paradise where they were dwelling (Q2:36, Q7:20). Satan has made Adam and Eve fall through deception (Q7:22). Satan whispered to them and made them taste the forbidden tree (Q7:20).

Having tasted the tree, their private parts became apparent to them, i.e., became naked, and began to fasten together over themselves from the leaves of paradise (Q7:22). Thus, Q7:27 provides continuity with the previous thought of 'clothing that is used to cover people's private parts'.

At the sentence-level coherence, Q3:26 provides another example of the continuity of thoughts and how the pivotal thought (leitmotif) is fortified by subsequent text segments that have opted for the configuration of specific segments to prop up the main thought:

> qul allāhumma mālika al-mulki tu'tī al-mulka man tashā'u watanziᶜu al-mulka mimman tashā'u watuᶜizzu man tashā'u watudhillu man tashā'u biyadika al-khairu innaka ᶜalā kulli shai'in qadīr – Say: 'O God, owner of sovereignty, You give sovereignty to whom You will and You take sovereignty away from whom You will. You honour whom You will and You humble whom You will. All that is good lies in Your hand. Indeed, You are over all things competent'.

In the above example, the āyah-final no-main-verb nominal sentences (biyadika al-khairu – All that is good lies in Your hand) and (innaka ᶜalā kulli shai'in qadīr – Indeed, You are over all things competent) have foregrounded expressions (biyadika – in Your hand) and (ᶜalā kulli shai'in – over all things), which have effectively contributed to the continuity of the pivotal thought at the beginning of the statement and have substantiated it, too:

> (allāhu mālika al-mulki/allāhu yu'ti al-mulka man yashā'u/allāhu yanziᶜu al-mulka mimman yashā'u/allāhu yaᶜizzu man yashā'u/allāhu yadhillu man yashā'u – God is the owner of sovereignty/God gives sovereignty to whom He wills/God takes sovereignty away from whom He wills/God honours whom He wills/God humbles whom He wills).

To achieve continuity of the above thought, the foregrounding of (biyadika) and (ᶜalā kulli shai'in) is a prerequisite. In Chapter 4, Section 4.3.2 (Qur'anic deductive argument), we have claimed that the premises are linked with the conclusion through the process of deductive reasoning. The example Q3:26 represents a deductive argument where its continuity of thought is achieved through the conclusion which includes the foregrounding of text segments to substantiate the pivotal thought at the beginning of the statement.

We have argued so far that the text producer takes into account his/her audience and rearranges his text segments to deliver his/her performative intent. Thus, the rearrangement of thoughts takes place. However, this is not a haphazard text linguistic phenomenon. The rearrangement of thoughts (represented by words) is to achieve continuity of thought and, ultimately, coherence, as in the following example:

> yā'aiyuhā alladhīna āmanū kūnū qawwāmīna bil-qisṭi shuhadā'a lillāh – O you who have believed, be persistently standing firm in justice, witnesses for God, Q4:135.

where we have two text segments: (qawwāmīna bil-qisṭi – be persistently standing firm in justice) + (shuhadā'a lillāh – witnesses for God). However, in Q5:8, we encounter a different configuration of the same text segments:

> yā'aiyuhā alladhīna āmanū kūnū qawwāmīna lillāh shuhadā'a bil-qisṭi – O you who have believed, be persistently standing firm for God, witnesses in justice, Q5:8.

where we have two text segments: (qawwāmīna lillāh – be persistently standing firm for God) + (shuhadā'a bil-qisṭi – witnesses in justice).

Having considered the co-text of each configuration of text segments, we can claim that in Q4:135, the pivotal relevant thought is 'justice', as we are admonished by (man yaᶜmal sū'an yujza bihi – whoever does a wrong will be recompensed for it, Q4:123 as well as (wa'in taqūmū lil-yatāmā bil-qisṭi – that you maintain for orphans their rights in justice, Q4:127). Thus, the configuration of text segments in Q4:135 is co-text sensitive. Therefore, the thought (bil-qisṭi – in justice) has occurred first in Q4:135.

However, the configuration of the text segments in Q5:8 is also conditioned by co-text where the pivotal relevant thought is (God and piety). Thus, we have reference to ablution for performing the prayer in Q5:6 and reference to piety in Q5:7 (wattaqū allāha – fear God, Q5:7). Therefore, the configuration of text segments in Q5:8 is co-text-sensitive. Accordingly, the thought (lillāh – for the sake of God) has occurred first in Q5:8.

An interesting example of the interrelationship between relevance, coherence, and continuity of thought is the text segment (kubbārā, Q71:22). This lexeme has occurred only once in the Qur'an during Noah's parable:

> makarū makran kubbārā – They conspired an immense conspiracy, Q71:22.

The word (kubbārā – immense, grand) is a hyperbole adjective (ṣifah mushabbaha) purposefully selected as relevant to achieve contextual coherence because it designates the text producer's performative intent through (kubbārā), whose illocutionary force is [+ Extreme Hyperbole] and [+ Affirmation]. However, its counterpart lexeme (kabīrā – great, big) is unable to achieve the same illocutionary force. It is interesting to note that both lexemes (kubbārā) and (kabīrā) can achieve assonance. Therefore, it is not a matter of sentence-final assonance but a matter of coherence. In terms of coherence and relevance, the two words are not interchangeable.

For details on macro level coherence and continuity of thought, see Section 5.10.1.2.

5.9 Context-based coherence

This is an account of the relationship between coherence and context at the micro (sentence) level. We can argue here that context influences the purposeful selection of a lexeme through which coherence is achieved. Let us consider the following examples:

> inna fī dhālika la'āyatan liqawmin yatafakkarūn – There truly are signs in this for those who use their reason, Q16:11.

In Q16:11, we have the verb (yatafakkarūn – to give thought, to reflect), which has occurred in the context of rain, which symbolizes God's favours upon people. We are informed that the rain is the source of vegetation (shajar – plants, shrubs), (sharāb – drinking water), and (tusīmūn – (water) that enables you to pasture animals, Q16:10). Thus, it is the source of the continuation of living on planet Earth since it causes the growing of crops, olives, palm trees, grapevines, and all types of fruit. Therefore, in terms of coherence, the text receiver expects the verb (yashkurūn – to be grateful (to God)). However, the employment of (yatafakkarūn) is not without a good reason. The illocutionary force of (yatafakkarūn) is to urge people to ponder and reflect upon God's omnipotence. Q16:11 does not aim to give saliency to the notion of thankfulness and gratitude to the Lord's favours. Thus, the lexical item (yatafakkarūn) is relevant and is successfully employed to attain coherence between the two sentences Q16:10 and Q16:11. Our claim is supported by Q16:12 and Q16:13 where the verbs (yaᶜqilūn – to use one's reason) and (yadhdhakkarūn – to remember), respectively, are coherently employed to provide saliency to God's omnipotence in terms of the subjugation of the night, the day, the sun, the moon, and the stars for the service and benefit of people (sakhkhara lakum) and also to give prominence to God's omnipotence with regards to the several kinds of many-coloured things such as fruits and trees. The text producer's illocutionary force is to reason and remember the power of the creator of these things. In other words, coherence is through cause and effect: to reflect on the cause (which is water) and its effects (which are too many and which lead to the continuation of life on Earth).

However, the context has changed in Q16:14 where the verb (tashkurūn – to give thanks, to be grateful to someone) occurs. This lexical item fits in well in terms of coherence since the context is about making the sea of benefit to people to get fresh fish and bring out jewellery from it and also to use the sea as a means of transport through the ships. Q16:12 is concerned with benefits to people. Thus, coherence is successfully attained by the relevant word (tashkurūn) since saliency is given to (laḥman ṭariyyan – tender meat), (ḥilyatan – jewellery), and (al-fulk – ships).

Let us consider Q6:102 which is a series of nominal sentences that echo sequentiality (continuity) of interlocutor's (text producer's) thought:

> (dhālikum allāhu rabbukum – That is God, your Lord) + (lā ilāha illā hū – There is no deity except Him) + (khāliqu kulli shai'in – The creator of all things) Q6:102.

Based on context, the above nominal sentences represent continuity of thought with the previous statements whose underlying theme (leitmotif) is polytheism:

> mā qadarū allāha ḥaqqa qadrih – They did not appraise God with true appraisal, Q6:91.
> man aẓlamu mimman iftarā ᶜalā allāhi kadhiban – Who is more unjust then one who invents a lie about God, Q6:93.

taqūlūna ᶜalā allāhi ghaira al-ḥaqq – You used to say against God other than the truth, Q6:93.
kuntum ᶜan āyātihi tastakbirūn – You have been arrogant toward His āyāt, Q6:93.
jaᶜalū lillāhi shurakā' – They have attributed to God partners, Q6:100.

Similarly, the nominal sentences of Q6:102 represent continuity of thought with the previous statements whose underlying thought is God's omnipotence:

inna allāha fāliqu al-ḥabbi wal-nawā yukhriju al-ḥaiya min al-maiyiti . . . – Indeed, God is the cleaver of grain and date seeds. He brings the living out of the dead . . ., Q6:95.

The chaining (relatedness) of thought and thematic sequentiality among the different segments of the text (Q6:91–102) have unfolded, and the continuity of senses among these segments has been established. The context of Q6:102 leads us to believe that this statement has been employed as a rebuttal to the previous thought of polytheism. Also, the last segment of 102 is an imperative segment (faᶜbuduh – So, worship Him), which adds more coherence to 102 and its previously related text segments. In Q16, we encounter three distinct sets of text:

Set one: Q16:90–97, whose thought is about good conduct: (God orders justice and good conduct and giving to relatives and forbids immorality and bad conduct . . . Fulfil the covenant of God . . . Do not break oaths . . . Do not be like she who untwisted her spin thread after it was strong . . Do not take your oaths as means of deceit between you . . . Do not exchange the covenant of God for a small price). The pivotal thought of this segment is admonition urging the reader to do justice and good conduct, to fulfil the covenant of God and not to exchange it for a small price, not to take one's oaths as means of deceit.

Set two: Q16:98–100, whose thought is about Satan and warns the reader to seek refuge in God from Satan when reciting the Qur'an.

Set three: Q16:101–105, whose thought is about the revelation, confirmation of Muḥammad's prophethood, and the disbelievers who invent falsehood about the revelation and Muḥammad.

5.10 Coherence system

Qur'anic discourse is marked by micro level and macro level coherence. Micro level coherence refers to coherence at word and sentence level, while macro level coherence is concerned with connectivity of thought between two consecutive sūrahs or within the same sūrah.

5.10.1 Types of coherence

At the textual level, we encounter two different categories of coherence:

i micro level coherence, and
ii macro level coherence.

5.10.1.1 Micro level coherence

Qur'anic statements (āyahs) interlock and get engaged with each other by overlapping themes (concepts). This is a sentence-level coherence and is concerned with the continuity (sequentiality, connectivity) of thought in the following categories:

i coherence between consecutive sentences,
ii coherence between consecutive sentences that, on the surface, are incoherent and unrelated,
iii coherence within the same sentence through a purposeful selection of a lexeme or a configuration of lexemes, and
iv coherence through sentence-final lexemes.

The above micro level coherence categories are discussed in what follows:

1 Coherence between consecutive sentences

An example of coherence and textual progression at a micro textual level is Q40:3. The prefatory statement of Q40:2 introduces the thought of prophethood (tanzīlu al-kitāb – the revelation of the Book (the Qur'an)) and ends with God's epithet couplet (al-ᶜazīz al-ᶜalīm – the exalted in might, the knowing). To achieve coherence for the sake of continuity of the introductory thought which is prophethood, substantiating statements are required for the rebuttal of sceptics of revelation and Muḥammad's prophethood. To achieve powerful substantiation and effective rebuttal, syntax-based coherence becomes a prerequisite. The most befitting mechanism for this text linguistic role is the no-main-verb nominal sentence structure. Thus, a series of six no-main-verb nominal sentences is employed to achieve continuity of thought and rebuttal to those who dispute the revelation:

> ghāfir al-dhanb + wa qābil al-tawb + shadīd al-ᶜiqāb + dhi al-ṭawl + lā ilāha illā hū + ilaihi al-maṣīr – The forgiver of sin + the acceptor of repentance + the severe in punishment + the owner of abundance + there is no deity except Him + to Him is the destination, Q40:3

In terms of continuity of senses, it is interesting to note that further rebuttal is provided in the subsequent statements Q40:4 (No one disputes concerning the signs of God except those who disbelieve, so be not deceived by their uninhibited movement throughout the land), Q40:5 (They disputed by using falsehood to attempt to invalidate thereby the truth). Finally, the use of the retribution statement Q40:6 against those who dispute the revelation (Thus has the decree of your Lord come into effect upon those who disbelieved that they are companions of the fire).

Another example of textual thematic progression and continuity of thought at a micro textual level is Q50:11. Q50 starts with prophethood (Q50:1–2), followed by scepticism about eschatology (Q50:3). To rebut this scepticism, God's omnipotence is presented and made salient to the text receiver (Q50:6–11). Therefore, Q50:11 is part of the previous substantiating statement. In this āyah, imagery is provided and a mental image is put forward to the reader to bring home the tenet of faith of eschatology (kadhālika al-khurūj – thus is resurrection): Water is sent down from the sky (Q50:9–11) to generate fruits as sustenance for people, and most importantly to give life to dead land (Q50:11). Then the conclusion at the end of the āyah reminding the sceptics that resurrection will take place in the same fashion, i.e., the dead bodies will be given life as well:

> (nazzalnā min al-samā'i mā'an mubārakan – We have sent down blessed rain from the sky) → (anbatnā bihi jannāt – We made grow thereby gardens) → (ḥabba al-ḥaṣīd – the harvest grain) → (al-nakhla bāsiqāt – lofty palm trees) → (aḥyainā bihi baldatan maitā – We have given life thereby to a dead land) → (kadhālika al-khurūj – Thus is resurrection).

We can also claim that although Q50:11 ends with a /j/ rhyme different from the surrounding āyahs, the text has progressed coherently and smoothly. In other words, textual progression in Qur'anic discourse has nothing to do with rhyme.

It is worthwhile to note that in Qur'anic discourse, presentation technique is directly related to textual progression and continuity of thought (leitmotif, theme, or notion). In other words, some tenets of faith co-occur with a given thought. The tenet of faith of monotheism, for instance, is accompanied by other leitmotifs such as God's omnipotence, as in Q10:3 where the thought of monotheism is presented and followed by God's omnipotence details (Q10:3–6) as a means of substantiation to the thought. This demonstrates textual progression and continuity of thought.

However, the tenet of faith of reward and punishment is accompanied by antithesis, as in Q18:110, which can be taken as an example of textual progression at the micro text level. The text segment that needs to be investigated for textual progression and continuity of thought starts from Q18:100 where the first unit of antithesis starts: (We will present on display hell that day to the disbelievers). This is followed by reference to the theme of polytheism: (Do those who disbelieve think that they can take My (God's) servants instead of Me (God) as allies?, Q18:102) then, reference to reward and punishment and eschatology is made: (. . . Their deeds have become worthless. We will not assign to them any weight on the day of resurrection . . . Their recompense will be hell, Q18:105–106). The second unit of antithesis starts from Q18:100–108: (hell will be presented to the disbelievers . . . paradise will be the lodging for the believers). Reference to the notion of prophethood is made: (I (Muḥammad) am only a human being, like you, Q18:110). This is culminated by reference to the notion of monotheism, which is the pivotal thought of the argument: (Your God is one, Q18:110). This illustrates how coherence and the continuity of thought are achieved through conceptual (thematic) dovetailing (chaining, sequentiality of thought).

The reader/listener may believe there is a breakdown of continuity of senses between two consecutive sentences. However, when elaboration is required on a given lexical item or notion, the sentence which includes a specific lexical item or notion occurs after the sentence that does not need elaboration. For instance, Q82:13 refers to (al-abrār – the righteous), but there is no elaboration required for this word. However, Q82:14 refers to (al-fujjār – the wicked). In terms of coherence, sentence 14 occurs after sentence 13 because of the elaboration provided on (al-fujjār) in sentences 15–19.

2 Coherence between consecutive sentences that, on the surface, are incoherent

Let us consider Q2:254:

> yā aiyuhā alladhīna āmanū anfiqū mimmā razaqnākum . . . – You who believe, give from what We (God) have provided for you, Q2:254

Whose major thought is (al-infāq mimmā razaqnākum – spending from what God has provided us).

On the surface, Q2:254 is unrelated to the previous sentence Q2:253, which makes reference to different Prophets and people who fought each other after their Prophets passed away. Similarly, on the surface, Q2:254 is unrelated to the following sentence Q2:255, whose major thought is monotheism. However, we need to investigate the surrounding context and macro text in order to establish the continuity of the thought of (al-infāq mimmā razaqnākum). Q2:245 urges the reader to spend, and God will multiply his/her charity many times over. Q2:261–281 urge the reader to be charitable, spend in the way of God, spend one's wealth by night and by day, and to avoid taking interest on a loan. Thus, Q2:243 occurs in the middle of sentences which have the same thought (theme, leitmotif, notion) of being charitable.

Within Q22:5, we encounter an example which seems to have unrelated thoughts. In other words, on the surface, there is lack of coherence between the thoughts (themes) of text's segments:

yā aiyuhā al-nāsu in kuntum fī raibin min al-baᶜthi fa'innā khalaqnākum min turābin thumma min nuṭfatin thumma min ᶜalaqatin thumma min muḍghatin mukhallaqatin waghairi mukhallaqatin linubaiyina lakum wanuqirru fī al-arḥāmi mā nashā'u ilā ajalin musammā thumma nukhrijukum ṭiflan thumma litablughū ashuddakum waminkum man yutawaffā waminkum man yuraddu ilā ardhali al-ᶜumuri likailā yaᶜlama min baᶜdi ᶜilmin shai'ā watarā al-arḍa hāmidatan fa'idhā anzalnā ᶜalaiha al-mā'a ihtazzat warabat wa'anbatat min kulli zawjin bahīj – O people, if you should be in doubt about the resurrection, then consider that indeed, We (God) created you from dust, then from a sperm-drop, then from a clinging clot, and then from a lump of flesh, formed and unformed, that We may show you. And We settle in the wombs whom We will for a specified term, then We bring you out as a child, and then We develop you that you may reach your time of maturity. And among you is he who is taken in early death, and among you is he who is returned to the most decrepit old age so that he knows, after once having knowledge, nothing. And you see the earth barren, but when We send down upon it rain, it quivers and swells and grows something of every beautiful kind, Q22:5

On the surface, there is no coherence between the two segments:

i (waminkum man yutawaffā waminkum man yuraddu ilā ardhali al-ᶜumuri likailā yaᶜlama min baᶜdi ᶜilmin shai'ā – And among you is he who is taken in early death, and among you is he who is returned to the most decrepit old age so that he knows, after once having knowledge, nothing), and

ii (watarā al-arḍa hāmidatan fa'idhā anzalnā ᶜalaihā al-mā'a ihtazzat warabat wa'anbatat min kulli zawjin bahīj – And you see the earth barren, but when We send down upon it rain, it quivers and swells and grows something of every beautiful kind).

Q22:5 involves a jigsaw of different thoughts in different segments of the text. The theme (thought) of the first segment is about some people who either die early or have a very long life span. However, the main thought of the second segment is about the barren earth which is revived by rain. However, a close-up look reveals the continuity of thoughts and senses among the text's segments. Our search for coherence and the relations between the thoughts starts from the first segment of the text whose theme is the sceptics who have doubted eschatology (raibin min al-baᶜth). As an inherent Qur'anic presentation technique, rebuttal is provided to the sceptics through the presentation of God's omnipotence represented by reference to the stages of creation in the womb. The thought of the other segment is concerned with the life span after birth. The last segment informs us about the barren earth (al-arḍa hāmidatan) whose underlying sense is 'the dead'. We are told that when the rain is sent down, the barren 'dead' earth is revived→ (ihtazzat warabat wa'anbatat – quivers and swells and grows).

By logical reasoning, the reader can conclude that, likewise, the dead can be revived. Thus, the thought of resurrection is substantiated and the sceptics are rebutted.

For more details on superficial incoherence, i.e., U-turn sentences, see Section 5.10.1.1.2.

3 Coherence within the same sentence through a purposeful selection of a lexeme or a configuration of lexemes

This category of micro level coherence involves two types:

a Sentence-level coherence through configuration of lexemes: This is concerned with the purposeful employment of a noun or a noun phrase at sentence-initial position. The occurrence of a lexeme sentence-initially contributes to the achievement of coherence in terms of saliency, relevance, and continuity of thought. For the purpose of coherence, continuity of thought, and saliency, a noun at sentence-initial position is employed. For instance, we encounter the occurrence of the noun (allāh – God) as a subject at sentence-initial position preceding the verb, as in:

> allāhu lā yuḥibu al-fasād – God does not like corruption, Q2:205

where the subject noun (allāh – God) is placed sentence-initially before the negated verb (lā yuḥibbu – does not like).

> allāhu ya^clamu mā taḥmilu kullu unthā wamā taghīḍu al-arḥāmu wamā tazdād – God knows what every female carries and what the wombs lose prematurely or exceed, Q13:8

where the sentence-initial subject noun (allāh – God) is well suited for the purpose of saliency and coherence. For this purpose, the subject noun (allāh) occurs before the verb (ya^clam – know).

> allāhu yabda'u al-khalqa thumma yu^cīduh – God begins creation, then He will repeat it, Q30:11

> allāhu yabsuṭu al-rizqa liman yashā'u wayaqdir – God extends provision for whom He wills and restricts it, Q13:26

The occurrence of (allāh) as a subject at sentence-initial position preceding the verb (yabda'u) in Q30:11 and (yabsuṭu – to extend) in Q13:26

When God's omnipotence is the major thought of the text, the noun (allāh – God) is given saliency through sentence-initial position, as in:

> allāhu akhrajakum min buṭūni ummāhatikum – God has extracted you from the wombs of your mothers, Q16:78

> allāhu ja^cala lakum min buyūtikum sakanan – God has made for you from your homes a place of rest, Q16:80

> allāhu ja^cala lakum mimmā khalaqa ẓilālan – God has made for you, from what He has created, shade, Q16:81

To understand the achievement of continuity of thoughts and thematic sequentiality, we need to go back to Q16:77 (inna allāha ᶜalā kulli shai'in qadīr – Indeed, God is over all things competent), which is the springboard for the continuity of senses with Q16:78–81.

However, when God's omnipotence is not the major thought of the message, we encounter the occurrence of the verb at sentence-initial position. Our claim is based on the fact that coherence is also concerned with the appropriateness of a given lexeme or a grammatical function. Thus, the verb is given saliency and is appropriately employed in the following contexts which do not highlight God's omnipotence:

> ḍaraba allāhu mathalan . . . – God presents an example, Q16:75

> ḍaraba allāhu mathalan . . . – God presents an example, Q16:76

These examples are also related to the semantic co-text Q16:74 (falā taḍribū lillāhi al-amthāla – Do not assert similarities to God) in which the verb (ḍaraba) occurs.

Similarly, for the purpose of coherence, continuity of thought, and saliency, a prepositional phrase is placed sentence-initially (foregrounded), as in:

> ilā allāhi turjaᶜu al-umūr – To God all matters return, Q2:210

where the sentence-initial prepositional phase (ilā allāhi – to God) carries the pivotal thought of the sentence. This prepositional phrase contributes effectively to the realization of coherence and making the prepositional phrase salient. For more details on saliency, see Sections 5.7 and 5.7.1, point 2 (v).

b Sentence-level coherence through a purposeful selection of a lexeme: Also, for the purpose of coherence, continuity of thought, and saliency, a specific lexeme is purposefully selected in a given sentence, as in:

> lā takūnū kallatī naqaḍat ghazlahā min baᶜdi quwwatin ankāthan – Do not be like she who untwisted her spun thread after it was strong, Q16:92 where the employment of the lexeme (naqaḍat – to untwist) fits in well with the semantic co-text of the lexeme (ᶜahd – covenant, pledge, Q16:90) and the collocation of (yafī bil-ᶜahd – to fulfill the covenant, Q16:90) and (yanquḍ al-aimān – to break oaths, Q16:90). Thus, we have (yanquḍ al-aimān) → (yanquḍ al-ghazl – to unravel a thread). The continuity of thoughts is achieved through the simile of the lady who has unravelled the thread she has firmly spun in order to depict a vivid imagery of the importance of not breaking oaths after we have sworn them.

Micro level coherence is also related to the purposeful selection of a lexeme rather than the other, as in:

> . . . liqawmin yasmaᶜūn – for a people who listen, Q16:65
>
> . . . liqawmin yaᶜqilūn – for a people who reason, Q16:67

The two examples above are semantically coherent. In Q16:65, the verb (yasmaᶜūn – listen) occurs to achieve continuity of thoughts with the previous statement Q16:64, whose context is the revelation which the polytheists have rejected: (We have not revealed to you (Muḥammad) the Book (the Qur'an) except for you to make clear to them (the polytheists)). Thus, Q16:65 is not incoherent where it is just because it talks about rain. One may be tempted to claim that statement 65 should use the lexeme (yubṣirūn – to see) to achieve coherence with statement 64, since 'rain' can be seen but not 'something you listen to'! In fact, coherence between statements 64 and 65 lies in the fact that the underlying thought of 65 is to present to the polytheists an example of God's omnipotence through reference to rain, and this should be sufficient for them to ponder upon the rain's effect in terms of reviving the barren earth and the growing of vegetation. By logical conclusion, the polytheists should 'listen' to Muḥammad and the revelation.

In Q16:67, the lexeme (yaᶜqilūn – to reason) is appropriately employed in a context (Q16:66–67) whose major thoughts are God's omnipotence and the benefits of the grazing livestock, their milk, the fruits of palm trees, and grapevines. These should have provided a clear lesson (ᶜibrah) to the polytheists if they use their reason (ᶜaql).

4 Coherence through sentence-final lexemes

This is concerned with sentence-level coherence through āyah-final epithets. Micro level coherence is also concerned with the sentence-final epithets that are employed to achieve thematic sequentiality and continuity of thought, as in:

> al- ᶜazīz al-ḥakīm – the exalted in might, the wise, Q16:60 where the first epithet (al-cazīz – the exalted in might) fits in well to achieve contextual coherence in terms of polytheism which has been referred to earlier in Q16:51 (lā tattakhidhū ilāhain ithnain innamā huwa ilāhun wāḥid – Do not take for yourselves two deities. He is the one God). However, (al-ḥakīm – the wise) is more related to the preceding co-text where we have (sā'a mā yaḥkumūn – How ill they judge!, Q16:59). Thus, we have (ḥakīm) → (yaḥkum).
>
> lā tudrikuhu al-abṣār wa huwa yudriku al-abṣār wa huwa al-laṭīf al-khabīr – Vision does not perceive Him (God), but He perceives all vision, and He is the subtle, the acquainted, Q6:103

In this example, we can observe that each of the sentence-final epithets is linked to an earlier thought in the same sentence and that each epithet designates specificity of a given quality of God:

(al-laṭīf – the subtle) → (lā tudrikuhu al-abṣār – vision does not perceive Him). In other words, because God is subtle, no vision can perceive Him.

(al-khabīr – the acquainted, the aware) → (huwa yudriku al-abṣār – He perceives all vision). In other words, because God is well acquainted and well aware of everything, He can perceive all vision.

ghulibat al-rūm . . . hum min ba^cdi ghalabihim sayaghlibūn . . . lillāhi al-amr . . . yawma'idhin yafraḥu al-mu'minūna binaṣri allāh yanṣuru man yashā'u wahuwa al-cazīz al-raḥīm – The Byzantines have been defeated in nearby land. They will reverse their defeat with a victory in a few years' time – God is in command, first and last. On that day, the believers will rejoice at God's help. He helps whoever He pleases: He is the mighty, the merciful, Q30:2–5

In Q30:5, the statement ends with two epithets (al-ᶜazīz al-raḥīm – the mighty, the merciful). However, we have reference to the Byzantines of the Eastern Roman Empire. The earlier statements (Q30:2–5) are historical information about the defeat of the Byzantines in Syria at the hands of the Persians (613–614 CE) and also the news that the Byzantines will achieve victory later on which, in fact, truly took place in 624 CE. One may wonder why the text producer in Q30:5 employs the words (al-cazīz al-raḥīm) and whether they have achieved coherence and continuity of thought with what has been said earlier. Semantically, the word (al-ᶜazīz – the Mighty) designates the meaning: (having might and power to overcome adversaries, be in total control, and most importantly, the possessor of granting victory and help to whoever God pleases, the subjugator over His servants (qāhir), the prevailing (qahhār), and He is over all things competent (qādir/qadīr)). Thus, the first epithet fits in well in the context of the Byzantines' defeat. The word (al-raḥīm – the merciful) semantically denotes the meaning: (mercy to all mankind especially the helpless and the unjustly treated, the defeated, i.e., the 'bullied'). Thus, the second epithet also contributes to the continuity of thought which is concerned with the defeat of the Byzantines and has, therefore, fit in well in the context of Q30:2–5.

5.10.1.1.1 SENTENCE-FINAL WORDS COHERENCE

This micro level coherence is concerned with the lexeme(s) that occurs at the end of the āyah. The lexeme is a content word (a lexical item) that can be either a noun, a phrase, or an adjective (God's epithet). Coherence with regards to the occurrence of the final word in the sentence is realized through one of the following requirements:

1 Interchangeable words: There are two words like proper nouns, and either of them can occur sentence-finally, as in (mūsā – Moses) and (hārūn –Aaron):

rabbi mūsā wa hārūn – The Lord of Moses and Aaron, Q7:122, Q26:48, Q37:114, 120 where (mūsā) occurs first. When Pharaoh's magicians were overcome by Moses' magic, they fell down in prostration to God and said: 'We have believed in the Lord of the worlds. The Lord of Moses and Aaron (Q7:122). This also applies to Q26:48. Thus, it is the direct speech of the magicians. The phonetic impact of sentence-final assonance where the nasal consonant /n/ has been employed in all the surrounding sentences of Q7:122, Q26:48, Q37:114, 120. Thus, the sentence ends with the word (hārūn), which ends with the nasal consonant /n/ and can now achieve assonance'. However, Q37:114 and 120 are the direct speech of God. The word order (mūsā) + (hārūn) seems to be the unmarked (usual) word order. However, this word order is reversed where (hārūn) occurs first, as in:

> rabbi hārūn wa mūsā – The Lord of Aaron and Moses, Q20:70

Although Q20:70 is also the direct speech of the magicians, the word order has been changed to (hārūn) + (mūsā) due to the phonetic impact of sentence-final assonance where the long vowel /ā/ has been employed in Q20. Thus, the sentence ends with the word (mūsā), which ends with the long vowel /ā/ and can now achieve assonance.

However, we can also claim that the macro context of Q20 leads us to believe that the word (hārūn) has to occur first before (mūsā) since the macro context highlights Aaron as the prominent figure of the sūrah more than Moses in terms of personal potential qualities. We can observe macro context evidence for our claim. Moses is in need of Aaron: (to appoint Aaron a minister, Q20:29–30), (Aaron will be a source of strength to Moses, Q20:31), (to let Aaron share Moses' task, Q20:32), and (Aaron will help Moses to glorify and remember God much and often, Q20:33–34). These reasons may justify the occurrence of Aaron before Moses in Q20:70.

2 Lexical co-text: The occurrence of a lexeme can influence its repetition at the end of the sentence, as in:

> fayantaqimu allāhu minhu wallāhu ᶜazīzun dhū intiqām – God will take retribution from him. God is exalted in might and owner of retribution, Q5:95

where lexical co-text is represented by the lexeme (yantaqīmū – to take retribution). This has influenced the occurrence of the sentence-final phrase (dhū intiqām – owner of retribution).

> litaᶜlamū anna allāha yaᶜlamu mā fī al-samāwāti wamā fī al-arḍi wa'anna allāha bikulli shai'in ᶜalīm – So you may know that God knows what is in the heavens and what is in the earth and that God is knowing of all things, Q5:97

Thus, through the lexical co-text of Q5:95 and 97, coherence has be attained. Similarly, through the lexical co-text of Q5:95 and 97, cohesion is achieved through reiteration.

3 Synonymy: The occurrence of synonyms leads to micro level coherence, as in:

> afalā yatūbūna ilā allāhi wa yastaghfirūnahu wallāhu ghafūrun raḥīm – So will they not repent to God and seek His forgiveness? God is forgiving and merciful, Q5:74

where the lexemes (yatūbūna – to repent) and (yastaghfir – to seek forgiveness) are synonyms of (ghafūrun raḥīm – forgiving and merciful).

> laqad ᶜafā allāhu ᶜanhum inna allāha ghafūrun ḥalīm – God has already forgiven them.

Indeed, God is forgiving and forbearing, Q3:155

where the lexeme (ᶜafā – to forgive) is a synonym of (ghafūrun ḥalīm – forgiving and forbearing). Thus, through synonymy, coherence is attained.

4 Antonymy: The employment of antonymy (oppositeness) can lead to micro level coherence at sentence-final position, as in:

> yaghfiru liman yashā' wa yuᶜadhdhibu man yashā' wallāhu ghafūrun raḥīm – God forgives whom He wills and punishes whom He wills. God is forgiving and merciful, Q3:129

where the final phrase (ghafūrun raḥīm – forgiving and merciful) is an antonym of the initial phrase (yuᶜadhdhibu man yashā' – He punishes whom He wills).

> anna allāha shadīdu al-ᶜiqābi wa anna allāha ghafūrun raḥīm – God is severe in penalty and God is forgiving and merciful, Q5:98

where the final phrase (ghafūrun raḥīm – forgiving and merciful) is an antonym of the initial phrase (shadīdu al-ᶜiqābi – severe in penalty).

> inna rabbaka sarīᶜu al-ᶜiqābi wa'innahu laghafūrun raḥīm – Indeed, your Lord is swift in penalty, but indeed, He is forgiving and merciful, Q6:165

where the final phrase (ghafūrun raḥīm – forgiving and merciful) is an antonym of the initial phrase (sarīᶜu al-ᶜiqābi – swift in penalty).

> in taᶜuddū niᶜmata allāhi lā tuḥṣūhā inna allāha laghafūrun raḥīm – If you should count the favours of God, you could not enumerate them. Indeed, God is forgiving and merciful, Q16:18

where the final phrase (ghafūrun raḥīm – forgiving and merciful) is employed in response to the context where people can never count the blessings of God (in taᶜuddū niᶜmata allāhi lā tuḥṣūhā). Yet God is 'forgiving' and 'merciful' to them. Semantically, however, (in taᶜuddū niᶜmata allāhi lā tuḥṣūhā) entails the meaning (ungrateful to God's blessings) whose antonym is (ghafūrun raḥīm). Thus, through antonymy, both lexical cohesion and coherence are achieved.

5.10.1.1.2 SUPERFICIAL INCOHERENCE BETWEEN CONSECUTIVE SENTENCES

The present analysis is concerned with the superficial incoherence between consecutive statements. The expression 'incoherence' refers to absence of coherence, lack of thematic relatedness, incongruity between two consecutive statements due to discontinuity of thought, and thematic disjointedness between two consecutive statements. The analysis of the following examples demonstrates that some text segments which are adjacent to each other lack thematic connectivity and that they, on the surface, do not provide continuity of thought. However, an in-depth examination of the two superficially incongruent text segments reveals coherence links and thematic relatedness between them.

Example 1

Q2:62 is an example of superficial incongruity between consecutive statements:

> inna alladhīna āmanu walladhīna hādū wal-naṣārā wal-ṣābi'īna man āmana billāhi wal-yawmi al-ākhiri wa^{c}amila ṣālihan falahum ajruhum ^{c}inda rabbihim walā khawfun calaihim walā hum yaḥzanūn – The Muslim believers, the Jews, the Christians, and the Sabians – all those who believe in God and the last day and do good – will have their rewards with their Lord. No fear for them, nor will they grieve, Q2:62

Thus, this sentence refers to four categories of people: the Muslims, the Jews, the Christians, and the Sabians. To understand the coherence and conceptual relatedness of Q2:63 to other text segments, we need to investigate the previous and following text segments. The statements from Q2:40–61 and from Q2:63–103 constitute one information unit, namely details about the Children of Israel. Therefore, the occurrence of Q2:62 seems inappropriate since it deals with a distinct theme and involves other categories of people. Based on continuity of thought and coherence, Q2:62 is a parenthetical statement. The pivotal thought of the first text segment Q2:40–61 focuses on how the Children of Israel were blessed by God, favoured over other people, saved from the injustice of Pharaoh's people, were reminded to honour their pledge to Him, and to fear no one except Him. The details of God's blessings to them continue until we come to a point where we are informed that they broke their pledge with God when Moses was away on Mount Sinai and did a terrible wrong through which they wronged themselves when they took to worshipping the calf instead of God. In this text segment, the Children of Israel are also urged to repent, but we are informed of how they persistently disobeyed Moses. As a result, they were struck with humiliation and wretchedness and incurred the wrath of God because they persistently rejected God's message and killed prophets. The pivotal thought of the second text segment Q2:63–103 also focuses on the same theme but with reference to different incidents such as the story of the cow.

As a Qur'anic presentation technique, reward and punishment statements are employed as a means of persuasion and encouraging the audience to repent and win the garden as a reward. That is exactly the major purpose of Q2:62, which intervenes between the two text segments Q2:40–61 and Q2:63–103. Thus, the continuity of thought has not been interrupted, and coherence has been maintained between the text segments. Having disobeyed Moses, the Children of Israel were struck with humiliation and wretchedness and incurred the wrath of God. They are urged in Q2:62 to 'believe in God and the last day and do good, and they will have their rewards with their Lord. No fear for them, nor will they grieve'. Therefore, the thought of Q2:62 is that the gate of God's mercy is always open for all categories of people who have wronged.

Example 2

> sayaqūlu al-sufahā'u min al-nāsi mā wallāhum ᶜan qiblatihim allatī kānū ᶜalaihā qul lillāhi al-mashriqi wal-maghribi yahdī man yashā'u ilā ṣirāṭin mustaqīm – The foolish among the people will say: 'What has turned them away from their qiblah which they used to face?' Say: 'To God belongs the east and the west. He guides whom He wills to a straight path', Q2:142.

The main thought of Q2:142 is the qiblah (the direction faced in prayer). After the migration from Makkah to Madinah, the Muslims used to face Jerusalem in prayer. This direction was changed to Makkah (Kaᶜbah) later on. However, on the surface, the reader/listener may believe that Q2:142 does not achieve coherence since there is no continuity of senses (thought) with the preceding text segments whose main thought is Abraham and monotheism. To determine whether Q2:142 achieves coherence with the preceding text, one needs to investigate the macro text segment beginning from Q2:124–141. In the preceding text segment, we are told about Abraham and the Kaᶜbah (al-bait – the House), which is made for Abraham and all people a place of return, security, and a place of prayer. Thus, we are informed about the Kaᶜbah as the qiblah for Abraham and his followers. in terms of the text linguistics standard of intertextuality, there is conceptual relatedness, thematic chaining, and continuity of thought between Q2:142 and the preceding text segments. In other words, Q2:142 achieves coherence with the previous text segment.

Example 3

Q4:42–43 represent an interesting example of coherence and thematic (conceptual) chaining between consecutive statements of a given sūrah:

> yawma idhin yawaddu alladhīna kafarū waᶜaṣaw al-rasūla law tusawwā bihim al-arḍu walā yaktumūna allāha ḥadīthā – That day, those who disbelieved and disobeyed the Messenger will wish they could be covered by the earth. They will not conceal from God a single statement, Q4:42

and:

> yā aiyuhā alladhīna āmanū lā taqrabū al-ṣalāta wa antum sukārā ḥattā . . . – O you who believe, do not approach prayer while you are intoxicated until . . ., Q4:43 where, on the surface level, there seems to be a U-turn in statement and lack of coherence, i.e., Q4:43 is not conceptually related to Q4:42. A deeper exegetical account of Q4:43 provides an insight into the continuity of thought, conceptual chaining, and logical thematic link between the two statements. While we are told about the agony and hopelessness of the unbelievers on the day of judgement by Q4:43, we are told about a number of Islamic legal rulings with regards to prayer and what to do in preparation for it. Thus, one may conclude that the two statements are unrelated thematically. However, considering the larger context, such as Q4:40–41, we are informed about God's justice, that our good deeds will be multiplied on the day of judgement, reference to prophethood is made, the horrors on the day of resurrection, and the despair and disappointment of the disbelievers on this day. Thus, the reader is psychologically prepared and alarmed. The second step, in terms of Qur'anic presentation technique, is to provide the admonition to the reader. Thus, Q4:43 refers to the importance of prayer and good deeds in order to be fully prepared for the day of judgement in order to avoid the fate of the unbelievers. In a similar vein, Q4:42 and Q4:43 are thematically linked through the theme of prophethood through the expressions (kafarū – disbelieved, al-rasūla – the Prophet, Q4:42) and (yā aiyuhā alladhīna āmanū – O you who have believed (in the prophethood of Muḥammad), Q4:43). At the macro textual level, coherence is established through the thematically related expressions (la yaẓlimu – (God) does not do injustice, Q4:49) and (ᶜafuwwan ghafūran – (God) is ever pardoning and forgiving, Q4:43) where the two expressions in both statements are synonymous. Thus, lexical and textual cohesion is achieved.

Example 4

yurīdūna an yakhrujū min al-nāri wamā hum bikhārijīna minhā walahum ᶜadhābun muqīm – They will wish to come out of the fire but they shall not come out of it, Q5:37.

al-sāriqu wal-sāriqatu faqṭaᶜū aidiyahumā jazā'an bimā kasabā nakālan min allāh – Now as for the man who steals and the woman who steals, cut off their hands in requital for what they have wrought, as a deterrent ordained by God, Q5:38.

In Q5:37, reference is made to the unbelievers who are trying in vain to get out of the hellfire, while in Q5:38 reference is made to the Islamic legal ruling about the punishment of whoever steals. In an earlier text segment (Q5:33), we encounter the Islamic legal ruling of those who strive to spread corruption on earth and that their hands and feet should be cut off from opposite sides. Then reference is made in Q5:37 to the unbelievers in the hellfire, followed by Q5:38, which refers to those who commit robbery. Based on Islamic law, robbery represents a hostile opposition and disregard to God's instructions and Muḥammad's tradition and is also a crime that leads to the spread of corruption on earth by robbers' ill behaviour who have not attained firm faith. Robbers, therefore, are from the category of people (who wage war against God and His messenger, Q5:33). Consequently, robbery deserves the same severe punishment of cutting off the hand. Coherence and continuity of thought can also be observed from reference to God as being forgiving and merciful in both Q5:34 and Q5:38.

Example 5

qālū lawlā nuzzila ᶜalaihi āyatun min rabbih . . . – They (unbelievers) say: 'Why has no miraculous sign been bestowed upon him from his Lord?', Q6:37.

mā min dābbatin fī al-arḍi walā ṭā'irin yaṭīru bijanaḥaihi illā umamun amthālukum . . . – There is no creature on the earth or bird that flies with its wings except that they are communities like you, Q6:38.

Q6:37 is a statement made by deniers of Muḥammad's prophethood. The unbelievers challenge Muḥammad to bring forward a miraculous sign as evidence of his prophethood. However, one can be surprised to encounter in Q6:38 reference to creatures and birds. In terms of argumentation, Q6:38 is a rebuttal to the unbelievers' claim. It tells them that nature is the best manifestation of God's omnipotence. They are instructed to ponder upon the ever-recurring miracles of God's creation such as the animals living on the earth, the different creatures living in water, as well as the birds. The existence of these creatures is similar to our existence: Everything and every creature, whether animals, birds, or humans, is subject to God's plan and will. Thus, coherence, continuity of thought, and thematic relatedness between Q6:37 and Q6:38 are established.

Example 6

On the surface discontinuity of thought is represented by Q6:94 and Q6:95. This superficial lack of coherence can be explained: In Q6:93–94, we are informed about people who invent a lie about God (man aẓlamu mimman iftarā ᶜalā allāhi kadhiban – Who is more unjust than one who invents a lie about God), who wrongly claim that a revelation has been sent down to them from God (ūḥiya ilaiya walam yūḥa ilaihi shai' – It has been inspired to me while nothing has been inspired to him), and who claim they can reveal something like what God has revealed (sa'unzilu mithlamā anzala allāhu – I will reveal something like what God revealed). There is also reference to their associates who are taken as their intercessors (shufaᶜā'akum). Q6:95 sets the scene for a rebuttal to Q6:93–94. The rebuttal text segment is from Q6:95–101, which represents God's omnipotence to demonstrate the opponent's invalid argument and that their claim does not have a truth value. Thus, one can pinpoint the continuity of thought and coherence between the text segments Q6:94 and Q6:95. These consecutive statements are logically related.

Example 7

> qad khasira alladhīna qatalū awlādahum safahan bighairi ᶜilmin waḥarramū mā razaqahum allāhu iftirā'an ᶜalā allāhi – Lost indeed are those who kill their own children out of folly, with no basis in knowledge, forbidding what God has provided for them, fabricating lies against Him, Q6:140.
>
> wahuwa alladhī ansha'a jannātin maᶜrūshātin waghaira maᶜrūshātin wal-nakhla wal-zarᶜa mukhtalifan ukuluhu wal-zaitūna wal-rummāna . . . kulū min thamarihi idhā athmara . . . – For it is He (God) who has brought into being gardens – both the cultivated ones and those growing wild – and the date-palm, and fields bearing multiform produce, and the olive tree, and the pomegranate, . . ., Q6:141.

In Q6:140, we have reference to those who kill their children for fear of poverty and invent lies against God by forbidding themselves eating foods which are not prohibited by God. However, Q6:141 makes reference to the different types of produce as a sign of God's omnipotence and mercy for people. When Q6:140 refers to people who slay their children out of ignorance, Q6:141 reminds them of God's mercy and that God is the sustainer of every creature on the earth. Q6:141 is a statement about the economic resources available, urging those who kill their children to make use of the resources but warning not to waste them. We can claim that while Q6:140 provides information about the ignorance of the unbelievers and their evil practice of murder, Q6:141 is a reminder to mankind not to fear poverty, that the provision of everyone is taken care of by God, and that the wasting of our natural resources rather than looking after our children leads to poverty. Therefore, coherence is established between Q6:140 and Q6:141.

Example 8

> falaᶜallaka bākhiᶜun nafsaka ᶜalā āthārihim in lam yu'minū bihādhā al-ḥadīthi asafā. innā jaᶜalnā mā ᶜalā al-arḍi zīnatan linabluwahum aiyuhum aḥsanu ᶜamalā. wa'innā lajāᶜilūna mā ᶜalaihā ṣaᶜīdan juruzā – Thus, perhaps you (Muḥammad) would kill yourself through grief over them if they do not believe in this message. Indeed, We have made that which is on the earth adornment for it that We may test them as to which of them is best in deed. Indeed, We will make that which is upon it into a barren ground, Q18:6–8.

On the surface, there seems to be no coherence, i.e., a breakdown of continuity of senses, between statements 6 and the subsequent statements 7 and 8. In Q18:6, we are told about Muḥammad worrying too much because people have disbelieved his message. In Q18:7, we are told about something completely different where reference is made to how the earth is adorned by God with attractive things but

God may test people when He reduces the adornment to barren dust. However, the coherence cue between Q18:7 and 8 lies in (linabluwahum – that We (God) may test them). Thus, reference is made to 'the deniers of Muḥammad's prophethood'. We are informed by Q18:7 that the unbelievers are given in the present life (zīnatan – adornment, i.e., attractive things, prosperous life) so that they may be grateful to God. However, they have become ungrateful and denied this favour. Elaboration on this is made by Q18:8, which is a warning to the unbelievers that God's wrath is imminent, i.e., the (zīnatan) they are enjoying now will be taken out of them and their land will be reduced to barren dust. This is backed up intertextually by Q18:2 (liyundhira ba'san shadīdan min ladunhu – warning of severe punishment from Him). Grammatically, the employment of the particle (inna – indeed) at the āyah-initial position is for justification (al-ta^{c}līl), whose pragmatic function is reassurance to Muḥammad and which is intertextually related to Q18:6 (fala^{c}allaka bākhi^{c}u nafsaka ^{c}alā ātharihim – O Muḥammad, are you going to worry yourself to death over the unbelievers?). Thus, the thematic meaning of Q18:7–8 is: (Although God has given a prosperous life to the unbelievers and are financially better than Muḥammad, their prosperity will come to an end. Economic prosperity does not necessarily lead to believing in Muḥammad's prophethood). Thus, we can say that (people enjoy a prosperous life but have disbelieved Muḥammad. Yet their prosperity can be ruined by God). Thus, coherence is attained as sentences 7–8 constitute reassurance to Muḥammad to persevere and not to worry too much.

Example 9

Let us consider whether there is coherence between the text segment Q25:50–52 and the preceding and following text segments:

> walaqad ṣarrafnāhu bainahum liyadhdhakkarū fa'abā aktharu al-nāsi illā kufūrā. walaw shi'nā laba^{c}thnā fī kulli qaryatin nadhīrā. falā tuṭi^{c} al-kāfirīna wajāhidhum bihi jihādan kabīrā – We have certainly distributed it among them that they might be reminded, but most of the people refuse except disbelief. If We had willed, We could have sent into every city a warner. So do not obey the disbelievers, and strive against them with it (the Qur'an) a great striving, Q25:50–52

The above text segment's thought is the rejection of the revelation (ṣarrafnāhu – distributed (the Qur'an)), i.e., the disbelief in Muḥammad's prophethood (fa'abā aktharu al-nāsi illā kufūrā – but most of the people refuse except disbelief). As a major presentation technique in Qur'anic discourse, a given tenet of faith such as prophethood is usually either preceded or followed by rebuttal details, which I refer to as God's omnipotence to substantiate the tenet of faith. Now, the text linguistics notion of coherence unfolds to us: In Q25:50–52, the tenet of faith is introduced. This, however, has not resulted in a breakdown of coherence with the preceding and the following text segments. Our claim is supported by the fact that the text segment Q25:50–52 is sandwiched between two text segments that have the illocutionary force of rebuttal to the deniers of Muḥammad's prophethood. The text segment Q25:45–49 and the text segment Q25:53–54 represent God's omnipotence with the performative intent of substantiation of Muḥammad's prophethood. Such a textual insight leads us to believe that there is continuity of senses and sequentiality of thought among the sentences:

> wahuwa alladhī arsala al-riyāḥa bushrā baina yadai raḥmatihi wa'anzalnā min al-samā'i mā'an ṭahūrā. linuḥyi bihi baldatan maitan wanusqīhi mimmā khalaqnā anᶜāman wa'anāsiyya kathīrā – It is He who sends the winds as good tidings before His mercy and We send down from the sky pure water that We may bring to life thereby a dead land and give it as drink to those We created of numerous livestock and people, Q25:48–59.

Example 10

> wamin āyātihi an yursila al-riyāḥa mubashshirātin waliyudhīqakum min raḥmatihi walitajriya al-fulku bi'amrih walitabtaghū min faḍlih walaᶜallakum tashkurūn – Another of His (God's) signs is that He sends out the winds bearing good news, giving you a taste of His grace, making the ships sail at His command, enabling you to journey in search of His bounty so that you may be grateful, Q30:46.
>
> walaqad arsalnā min qablika rusulan ilā qawmihim fajā'ūhum bil-baiyināti fantaqamnā min alladhīna ajramū . . . – Before you (Muḥammad), We sent messengers, each to their own people; they brought them clear proofs and then We punished the evildoers . . ., Q30:47.

where the theme of Q30:46 is God's omnipotence, telling us about the wind and the ships, while the theme of Q30:47 is concerned with sending Prophets to past nations. We need to expand our textual analysis in search for coherence, continuity of thought, and thematic relatedness among consecutive statements. Thus, we need to go further to Q30:48, which also provides further God's omnipotence details. Thus, the textual structure of Q30:46, 47, and 48 is like the following:

> God's omnipotence details → past unbelieving nations → God's omnipotence details.

Before we account for the superficial incongruity between the consecutive statements Q30:46 and Q30:47, it is worthwhile to note that Q30:47 refers to God's omnipotence details, which is a Qur'anic argumentation technique which delivers the following types of illocutionary force:

i signs to ponder upon,
ii example for deductive reasoning,
iii substantiation of God's might,
iv substantiation of monotheism,

v proof of divinity,

vi substantiation of God's mercy to mankind since God's omnipotence details refer to the causes of sustenance and benefits to all human and non-human creatures, and

vii rebuttal to deniers who disbelieve in the tenets of faith (monotheism, prophethood, eschatology, and reward and punishment).

For more details on the function of God's omnipotence details in argumentation, see Chapter 4.

We also need to note that Q30:47 is sandwiched between two sets of God's omnipotence details. Since the major function of the argumentation strategy of God's omnipotence is to substantiate God's might, monotheism, and His mercy to mankind, Q30:47 fits in well with Q30:46 and Q30:48 and has successfully achieved thematic connectivity and relatedness with the previous and the following statements.

Disbelieving people in Q30:47 are reminded of God's might, oneness, and bounty. People are informed that they should be grateful to God's blessings bestowed upon them through the many causes of bounty, sustenance, and welfare, such as the wind, the rain, the sea, the sun, the night, the daylight. If not, God will take retribution from those who commit crimes and incumbent upon God, as they are informed by Q30:47 (fantaqamnā min alladhīna ajramū – We punished the evildoers).

Example 11

Another example of coherence between consecutive statements is Q40:6 and Q40:7 where in Q40:6 the thought is about the punishment of those who disbelieved and who will be the companions of the fire: (Thus has the decree of your Lord come into effect upon those who disbelieved that they are companions of the fire). However, on the surface, Q40:7 seems to have done a U-turn from the thought of the fire punishment, and the reader may wonder why the thought in Q40:7 is unrelated to that of Q40:6. In Q40:7, the text producer introduces the thought of the angels who carry God's throne and exalt Him with praise. In terms of text linguistics, there seems to be no coherence because there is a breakdown of continuity of senses between Q40:6 and Q40:7. However, with a close look at Q40:7 and the presentation technique of Qur'anic discourse, we can recognize coherence and continuity of thought:

i Antithesis is a presentation technique employed to make a given thought salient. Thus, we have disbelievers sceptics of the Qur'an and Muḥammad's prophethood in Q40:6 followed by the angels as firm believers of the Lord, and

ii Q40:7 carries the text producer's performative intent with the illocutionary force of encouragement to abandon disbelief. Q40:7 includes good news for those who are willing to repent and follow God's way and that they will be rewarded by being protected from the punishment of hellfire. The continuity of thought of this reward is found in Q40:8 where we are informed that the disbelievers who repent will be admitted to the gardens of perpetual residence. Thus, in terms of coherence, there is continuity of thought and relatedness between Q40:6 and Q40:7.

Example 12

There seems to be superficial incoherence between Q13:7 and 8. In other words, there is no thematic relatedness between these two statements, and there is discontinuity of thought between them. In Q13:7, the disbelievers argue against Muḥammad's prophethood and claim that if he is truly a Prophet, he should have presented to them a sign from his Lord. However, the following statement refers to God's knowledge of what every female carries in her womb, the normal period of pregnancy, and the number of foetuses. To demonstrate the coherent relationship between statements 7 and 8 of Q13, we can make the following observations:

- i We need to refer to Qur'anic modes of persuasion and argumentation techniques. In terms of argumentation, the topos of the text segment 7 is slander. In terms of types of argumentation, the text segment represents a counter-argument where a premise (thesis) is presented by an antagonist (opponent) whose cognitive state of mind is a denier (munkir). This premise is followed by a substantiation statement, i.e., a rebuttal to refute the antagonist's argument. As a Qur'anic substantiation and presentation technique, God's omnipotence details are provided to contest the opponent's premise. Thus, statement 8 is employed.
- ii In terms of modes of persuasion, we have statement 8 used as a logos which provides supporting evidence. The impact of logos on the audience is called 'the argument's logical appeal' or 'persuading by the use of reasoning'. Logos in statement 8 appeals to the audience's reason. The antagonist needs to employ deductive reasoning (logical deduction), which is a cognitive activity through which the reader can infer the truth value of a statement. Since statement 8 is a logos, it employs deductive reasoning, signalling to the opponent that the Lord who possesses such potential qualities is surely able to send a sign to Muḥammad.
- iii The other mechanism of Qur'anic rebuttal and substantiation of statement 8 is the employment of a no-main-verb nominal sentence: (innamā anta mundhir – You are only a warner, Q13:7) and (likulli qawmin hād – You are a guide for every people, Q13:8). Having said the above, one can conclude that there is coherence between statements 7 and 8 of Q13.

Example 13

Similarly, on the surface, statement 25seems to be unrelated to statement 26 of Q13. Statement 25 talks about those who break the covenant of God after a contract, who spread corruption on earth, who are cursed, and whose home will be the fire in the hereafter. However, statement 26 deals with (i) the abundance of God's favours, (ii) God is able to either extend or restrict provision for people, and (iii) that the worldly life is no more than a fleeting comfort compared to the ever-lasting life and comfort in the hereafter. We can make the following observations:

- i As a Qur'anic argumentation technique, statement 26 represents the persuasion mode of pathos, which is a persuasion technique that focuses on the emotions of the audience in a persuasive act to sway the mind of the audience. In other words, pathos is associated with emotional appeal (vivid and emotional language and sensory details) when persuading an audience by appealing to their emotions. Thus, Q13:26 invokes sympathy from the audience to drive the message home, to influence the antagonist's belief and convince him/her to change his/her opinion and attitude.
- ii Statement 25 is a through-argumentation where the text producer (protagonist) has put forward own thesis and follows it by a substantiating statement to defend own premise.
- iii As a Qur'anic persuasion technique, Qur'anic pathos includes details to win the hearts and minds of the opponents through reference to God's ability to provide financial welfare for those who do not break the covenant of God after a contract and who do not spread corruption on earth. Qur'anic pathos also includes details to warn the opponents that God is able to withhold financial support from whoever breaks the covenant of God and from whoever spreads corruption on earth. Therefore, pathos is related to the tenet of faith of reward and punishment.

Having said the above, one can conclude that there is continuity of thought between statements 25 and 26 of Q13, that they are coherently linked and share thematic relatedness. For more details on argumentation, see Chapter 3.

5.10.1.1.3 MICRO LEVEL COHERENCE TECHNIQUES

The present discussion is concerned with the sentence-final expressions (a word or a phrase) and their contribution to the continuity of thought and the logical link either with the previous sentence or within the same sentence. Among the major micro level coherence techniques are: (1) enablement, (2) lexical cohesion, and (3) antithesis and antonymy. These are discussed in what follows:

5.10.1.1.3.1 Enablement for coherence By enablement, we mean inaugural details occur to set the scene for the sentence-final expression and enable it to the following objectives:

- a to fit in well in the sentence,
- b to achieve coherence and continuity of thought with the surrounding context, and
- c to avoid semantic incongruity within the sentence.

Let us consider the following examples of enablement:

Example 1

man kāna yurīdu al-ḥayāta al-dunyā wazīnatahā nuwaffi ilaihim aʿmālahum fīhā wahum fīhā lā yubkhasūn. ulā'ika alladhīna laisa lahum fī al-ākhirati illā al-nāru waḥabiṭa mā ṣanaʿū fīhā wabāṭilun mā kānū yaʿmalūn – Whoever desires the life of this world and its adornments – We fully repay them for their deeds therein, and they therein will not be deprived. Those are the ones for whom there is not in the hereafter but the fire. Lost is what they did therein, and worthless is what they used to do, Q11:15–16.

where details mentioned in the beginning are foundational and have set the scene for the occurrence of the sentence-final word (yaʿmalūn – to do). Thus, cohesion and continuity of thought have been achieved.

Example 2

qālū yā shuʿaibu aṣalawātuka ta'muruka an natruka mā yaʿbudu ābā'unā aw an nafʿala fī amwālinā mā nashā'u innaka la'anta al-ḥalīmu al-rashīdu – They said: 'O Shuʿaib, does your prayer (religion) command you that we should leave what our fathers worship or not do with our wealth what we please? Indeed, you are a tolerant and discerning man', Q11:87.

where details mentioned in the beginning of the sentence have set the scene for the occurrence of the sentence-final words (al-ḥalīmu al-rashīdu – tolerant and discerning). The word (ṣalawāt – prayer or religion) has set the scene for the occurrence of the word (al-rashīdu – tolerant) since prayer and religion should make the person forbearing with regards to abandoning the wrong practice of worship on the one hand and sensible with how to spend his/her money wisely on the other.

Example 3

qālū yā shuʿaibu mā nafqahu kathīran mimmā taqūlu wa'innā lanarāka fīnā ḍaʿīfan walawlā rahṭuka larajamnaka wamā anta ʿalainā biʿazīz – They said: 'O Shuʿaib, we do not understand much of what you say. Indeed, we consider you among us as weak. If not for your family, we would have stoned you to death. To us, you are not respected', Q11:91.

where the sentence-final negated word (ʿazīz – respected) has been enabled to fit in well with the surrounding context of the sentence and has successfully managed to achieve coherence through its relatedness to the previous details mentioned in the sentence such as (mā nafqahu kathīran mimmā taqūlu – we do not understand much of what you say), (innā lanarāka fīnā ḍaʿīfan – Indeed, we consider you among us as weak), and (lawlā rahṭuka larajamnāka – If not for your family, we would have stoned you to death). These details are negative feedback from the

Prophet Shu^c^aib's people, and the sentence-final word (^c^zīz) has also occurred in the negative sense because it is negated by (mā – not). Thus, (mā) + (^c^azīz) → mā anta bi^c^azīz = You are not respected.

Example 4

waradda allāhu alladhīna kafarū bighaiẓihim lam yanālū khairan wakafā allāhu al-mu'minīna al-qitāl wakāna allāhu qawiyyan ^c^azīzan – God repelled those who disbelieved, in their rage, not having obtained any good, and spared the believers from fighting. He (God) is strong and mighty, Q33:25.

The reasons for revelation are the major factor in understanding what set the scene for the occurrence of the sentence-final words (qawiyyan ^c^azīzan – strong and mighty). Q33:25 is based on the Battle of the Trench, which took place in March/April 627 (during the fifth year after migration of Muḥammad (5/626)). The disbelievers were camping outside the Madinah surrounding the Muslims. Before the Battle, a violent chilly storm blew which tore apart the tents of the disbelievers causing fear and chaos among them. As a result, their military leader, Abu Sufyān, ordered his army to withdraw and go back to Makkah. Thus, it was the wind sent by God that caused the defeat of the disbelievers. This sets the scene for the occurrence of the sentence-final words (qawiyyan ^c^azīzan – strong and mighty), which semantically signals that, thanks to God, the disbelievers were defeated.

Example 5

likai lā ta'saw ^c^alā mā fātakum walā tafraḥū bimā ātākum wallāhu lā yuḥibbu kulla mukhtālin fakhūr – In order that you not despair over what has eluded you and not exult in pride over what He has given you. God does not like everyone self-deluded and boastful, Q57:23.

Three observations can be made:

1 The continuity of thought is achieved through the antithesis between the text segments (lā ta'sū ^c^alā mā fātakum – that you not despair over what has eluded you) → (lā tafraḥū bimā ātākum – not exult in pride over what He has given you),
2 The sentence-final segment (mukhtālin fakhūr – self-deluded and boastful) has been enabled to occur in its position, i.e., the previous text segment (likai lā ta'saw calā mā fātakum wa lā tafraḥū bimā ātākum – In order that you not despair over what has eluded you and not exult in pride over what He has given you) has set the scene for the occurrence of (mukhtālin fakhūr – self-deluded and boastful), and
3 Semantic incongruity has been avoided between (allāhu lā yuḥibbu – God does not like) and (mukhtālin fakhūr – self-deluded and boastful). In other words, by deductive reasoning, the reader can understand the intended meaning of the text segment: (allāhu lā yuḥibbu kulla mukhtālin fakhūr – God

does not like everyone self-deluded and boastful), which, based on intertextuality, entails the following conclusion:

> inna allāha lā yuḥibbu man kāna mukhtālan fakhūrā – God does not like those who are self-deluded and boastful, Q4:36
>
> inna allāha lā yuḥibbu al-fariḥīn – Indeed, God does not like the exultant, Q28:76
>
> inna allāha lā yuḥibbu kulla mukhtālin fakhūr – Indeed, God does not like everyone self-deluded and boastful, Q31:18

Example 6

An interesting example of enablement occurs in Q26 where the sentence-final couplet (al-ᶜazīz al-raḥīm – the mighty, the merciful) has occurred eight times (Q26:9, 68, 104, 122, 140, 159, 175, and 191) due to the same context which has furnished the details that contributed to each occurrence. The eight contexts refer to different Prophets (Muḥammad, Moses, Abraham, Noah, Hud, Ṣāliḥ, Lot, and Shuᶜaib). We encounter in these contexts details on:

- i Disbelief in the Prophet of a given nation he is sent to,
- ii Each Prophet is ridiculed and rejected by his people,
- iii The Prophets have reminded people of the blessings of God,
- iv The Prophets were called 'mad' or 'affected by magic',
- v The disbelievers called the Prophets' followers 'the lowest class of people' – al-ardhalūn, Q26:111),
- vi News of the past nations who disbelieved and rejected their Prophets,
- vii News of how the past disbelieving nations were destroyed,
- viii The repetition of the same statement in each of the eight contexts: (inna fī dhālika la'āyatan wamā kāna aktharuhum mu'minīn – Indeed, in that is a sign, but most of them were not to be believers),
- ix Divine legislations or Scriptures were given to people by their relevant Prophets, but these were turned down, and
- x The employment of the word (rabb – Lord), which semantically entails divine care, love, compassion, and bestower of blessings.

Therefore, the most befitting sentence-final words that can achieve coherence, relevance, and continuity of thought are (al-ᶜazīz al-raḥīm – the mighty, the merciful) for the following contextual reasons:

1 The word (al-ᶜazīz – the mighty) entails the semantic componential feature [+ Able to Avenge] from the wicked (al-fujjār),
2 The word (al-ᶜazīz) semantically entails ability to deliver destruction (al-halāk),
3 The word (al-raḥīm – the merciful) entails the semantic componential features [+ Giving Respite] before vengeance is taken (mā ahlaknā min qaryatin illā

lahā mundhirūn – We did not destroy any city except that it had warners, Q26:208), [+ Mercy], and [+ Bestower of Blessings], and
4 The word (al-raḥīm) semantically entails respite (al-imhāl).

Having considered the contextual details before the couplet (al-ᶜazīz al-raḥīm), we can argue that people have been sent Prophets with instructions to follow, they have been warned of the consequences of mocking and disbelieving their relevant Prophets, they were given generous respite, and blessings were bestowed upon them regardless of their disbelief. Thus, the most relevant words for such contexts are (al-ᶜazīz al-raḥīm – the mighty, the merciful). This is intertextually linked to Q3:11 (kadhdhabu bi'ayatina fa'akhadhahum allāhu bidhunūbihim wallāhu shadīdu al-ᶜiqāb – They denied Our (God's) signs, so God punished them for their sins. God is severe in penalty) and is also related to (wamā kāna rabbuka muhlika al-qurā ḥattā yabᶜatha fī ummihā rasūlan yatlū ᶜalaihim āyātinā wamā kunnā muhlikī al-qurā illā wa'ahluhā ẓālimūn – Your Lord would never destroy towns without first raising a messenger in their midst to recite Our messages to them, nor would We destroy towns unless their inhabitants were evildoers, Q28:59).

5.10.1.1.3.2 Lexical cohesion for coherence By lexical cohesion, we mean the sentence-final lexeme is morphologically related to another lexeme within the same sentence. In addition to the achievement of lexical cohesion, the rhetorical feature of polyptoton is also realized. Let us consider the following examples of lexical cohesion and how coherence is achieved at the micro level:

Example 1

rabbanā lā tuzigh qulūbanā baᶜda idh hadaitanā wahab lanā min ladunka raḥmatan innaka anta al-wahhāb – Our Lord, let not our hearts deviate after You have guided us and grant us from Yourself mercy. Indeed, You are the bestower, Q3:8.

where continuity of thought is achieved through the lexical cohesion between the imperative verb (hab – to grant) and the sentence-final word (al-wahhāb – the bestower).

Example 2

ulā'ika alladhīna khasirū anfusahum . . . lā jarama annahum fī al-ākhirati hum al-akhsarūn – Those are the ones who will have lost themselves . . . Assuredly, it is they in the hereafter who will be the greatest losers, Q11:21–22.

where continuity of thought is achieved through the lexical cohesion between the verb (khasirū – have lost) and the sentence-final word (al-akhsarūn – the greatest losers).

Example 3

artaqibū innī ma^{c}akum raqīb – So watch. Indeed, I am with you a watcher, Q11:93.

where continuity of thought is achieved through the lexical cohesion between the imperative verb (artaqibū – to watch) and the sentence-final word (raqīb – a watcher).

Example 4

anẓur kaifa faḍḍalnā ba^{c}ḍahum ^{c}alā ba^{c}ḍin wal-ākhiratu akbaru darajātin wa'akbaru tafḍīlā – Look how We have favoured in provision some of them over others. But the hereafter is greater in degree of difference and greater in distribution, Q17:21.

where continuity of thought is achieved through the lexical cohesion between the verb (faḍḍalnā – to favour) and the sentence-final word (tafḍīlā – greater in distribution).

Example 5

qāla lahum mūsā wailakum lā taftarū ^{c}alā allāhi kadhiban fayusḥitakum bi^{c}ad-habin waqad khāba man iftarā – Moses said to the magicians: 'Woe to you! Do not invent a lie against God or He will exterminate you with a punishment, and whoever invents such falsehood will fail', Q20:61.

where continuity of thought is achieved through the lexical cohesion between the verb (taftarū – to invent) and the sentence-final verb (iftarā – to invent).

5.10.1.1.3.3 Antithesis and antonymy for coherence Through antithesis among text segments and antonymy (oppositeness) among lexemes, the continuity of thought can be achieved. In other words, the second text segment or the second antonym can be predicted, as in the following examples:

Example 1

qul allāhumma mālika al-mulki tu'tī al-mulka man tashā' wa tanzi^{c}u al-mulka mimman tasha' wa tu^{c}izzu man tashā' wa tudhillu man tashā' – Say: 'O God, owner of sovereignty, You give sovereignty to whom You will and You take sovereignty away from whom You will. You honour whom You will and You humble whom You will. In Your hand is all good. Indeed, You are competent over all things', Q3:26.

where continuity of thought is achieved through the antithesis between the text segments (tu'tī al-mulka man tashā' – You give sovereignty to whom You will) → (tanzi^{c}u al-mulka mimman tashā' – You take sovereignty away from whom

You will) and (tuᶜizzu man tashā' – You honour whom You will) → (tudhillu man tashā' – You humble whom You will).

Example 2

falyaḍḥakū qalīlan wal yabkū kathīran – Let them laugh a little and weep much, Q9:82.

where continuity of thought is achieved through the antithesis between the text segments (yaḍḥakū qalīlan – laugh a little) → (yabkū kathīran – weep much).

Example 3

likai lā ta'saw ᶜalā mā fātakum wa lā tafraḥū bimā ātākum – In order that you not despair over what has eluded you and not exult over what He has given you, Q57:23.

where continuity of thought is achieved through the antithesis between the text segments (lā ta'sū ᶜalā mā fātakum – you not despair over what has eluded you) → (lā tafraḥū bimā ātākum – not exult over what He has given you).

Example 4

fa'ammā man aᶜṭā wattaqā waṣaddaqa bil-ḥusnā fasanuyassiruhu lil-yusrā wa'ammā man bakhila wastaghnā wakadhdhaba bil-ḥusnā fasanuyassiruhu lil-ᶜusrā – As for he who gives and fears God and believes in the best reward, We will ease him toward ease. But as for he who withholds and considers himself free of need and denies the best reward, We will ease him toward difficulty, Q92:5–10.

where continuity of thought is achieved through the antithesis between the text segments (fa'ammā man aᶜṭā wattaqā waṣaddaqa bil-ḥusnā fasanuyassiruhu lil-yusrā – As for he who gives and fears God and believes in the best reward, We will ease him toward ease) → (wa'ammā man bakhila wastaghnā wakadhdhaba bil-ḥusnā fasanuyassiruhu lil-ᶜusrā – as for he who withholds and considers himself free of need and denies the best reward, We will ease him toward difficulty).

Example 5

allāhu yaqbiḍ wa yabsuṭ – God withholds and grants, Q2:245.

where we have oppositeness (antonymy) between the lexemes (yaqbiḍ – withhold) and (yabsuṭ – grant).

Example 6

mā yastawī al-aᶜmā wal-baṣīr walā al-ẓulumāt walā al-nūr walā al-ẓillu walā al-ḥarūr wamā yastawī al-aḥyā' walā al-amwāt – The blind and the seeing are not equal. The darkness and the light are not equal. The shade and the heat are not equal. The living and the dead are not equal, Q35:19–22.

where we have oppositeness (antonymy) between the lexemes (al-a[c]mā – the blind) and (al-baṣīr – the seeing), (al-ẓulumāt – darkness) and (al-nūr – light), (al-ẓillu – shade) and (al-ḥarūr – heat), and between (al-aḥyā' – the living) and (al-amwāt – the dead).

Example 7

qul hal yastawī alladhīna ya[c]lamūn walladhīna lā ya[c]lamūn – Say: 'Are those who know equal to those who do not know?', Q39:9.

where we have oppositeness between the lexemes (alladhīna ya[c]lamūn – those who know) and (alladhīna lā ya[c]lamūn – those who do not know).

5.10.1.1.3.4 Avoiding embellishment for coherence Embellishment is a decorative rhetorical technique to beautify the text stylistically. It includes, among other rhetorical features, antithesis and polyptoton. In Qur'anic discourse, antithesis, at times, is avoided for a performative intent that needs to be achieved through the use of a different word. Let us consider the following examples:

Example 1

In Q14:6, we find the word (nisā'akum – your women) occur rather than the expected word (banātakum – your daughters):

> . . . yasūmūnakum sū'a al-[c]adhābi wayudhabbiḥūna abnā'akum wayastaḥyūna nisā'akum – . . . who were inflicting terrible suffering on you, slaughtering your sons and sparing only your women, Q14:6

The two words (nisā'/banāt) have distinct componential features:

(nisā') → [+Adult] and [± Married] while (banat) → [–Adult] and [–Married].

Considering Q14:6, the lexeme (banāt) is more appropriate for the achievement of antithesis (antonymy) with the lexeme (abnā' – sons). Thus, Q14:6 could have achieved antithesis:

(. . . yasūmūnakum sū'a al-[c]adhābi wayudhabbiḥūna <u>abnā'akum</u> wayastaḥyūna <u>banātakum</u> – . . . who were inflicting terrible suffering on you, slaughtering your <u>sons</u> and sparing only your <u>daughters</u>).

Q14:6 has avoided antithesis and opted for (nisā') in order to achieve the illocutionary force of humiliation, which the alternative word (banāt) could not have done. Based on context, the women from the Children of Israel were left to grow old and be left unmarried to inflict humiliation on them. The employment of (banāt) would not have achieved the illocutionary force of humiliation.

Example 2

mathaluhum kamathali alladhī istawqada nāran falammā aḍā'at mā ḥawlahu dhahaba allāhu binūrihim watarakahum fi ẓulumātin lā yubṣirūn – Their example is that of one who kindled a fire, but when it illuminated what was around him, God took away their light and left them in darkness so they could not see, Q2:17.

where we have two partial synonyms (ḍaw' – light) and (nūr – light), which are morphologically related to (aḍā'at – to kindle) and (anāra – to lighten), respectively. The two words (ḍaw'/nūr) have distinct componential features:

(ḍaw') → [+ Excessive Light] and [+ Large Quantity] while (nur) → [+ Light] and [– Large Quantity]. Thus, we encounter this meaning in (huwa alladhī jaᶜala al-shamsa ḍiyā'an wal-qamara nūran – It is He who made the sun a shining light and the moon a derived light, Q10:5), which distinguishes between the light of the sun and the moon. In Q2:17 enablement is not achieved because we have expected the word (ḍaw'ihim – their light) and not (nūrihim – their light). The purposeful selection of (nūr) is due to the text producer's performative intent. The lexeme (nūr) negates completely the existence of any light for the hypocrites (nūr) designates: [– Large Quantity] while (ḍaw') denotes [+ Large Quantity].

Having observed enablement in Q2:17, we would have achieved polyptoton:

(mathaluhum kamathali alladhi istawqada nāran falammā aḍā'at mā ḥawlahu dhahaba allāhu biḍaw'ihim watarakahum fī ẓulumātin lā yubṣirūn – Their example is that of one who kindled a fire, but when it illuminated what was around him, God took away their light and left them in darkness so they could not see).

Polyptoton is the repetition of a word in different forms that are morphologically related to it, i.e., the repeated words are derived from the same root. Although polyptoton is a vital embellishment for rhetorical decoration of the text, it is abandoned in the interest of the illocutionary force of (nūr), which entails total darkness based on the meaning of the clause (dhahaba allāhu binūrihim – God took away their light completely), i.e., the existence of light is negated → non-existent light. Thus, affirmation is introduced by the last text segment (watarakahum fī ẓulumātin lā yubṣirūn – God left them in darkness so they could not see).

Example 3

wamā anta bimu'minin lana walaw kunnā ṣādiqīn – But you would not believe us, even if we were truthful, Q12:17.

where we have expected polyptoton, as in:

> (wamā anta bimuṣaddiqin lanā walaw kunnā ṣādiqīn – But you would not believe us, even if we were truthful).

Or:

> (wamā anta bimu'minin lanā walaw kunnā mu'minin – But you would not believe us, even if we were truthful).

In other words, the phrase (wamā anta bimu'minin) is semantically different from (wamā anta bimuṣaddiqin). There is a semantic distinction between the lexemes (muṣaddiq) and (mu'min). The word (muṣaddiq) signifies [+ Believe], i.e., that someone trusts someone else and has faith in him/her, while (mu'min) signifies [+ Believe] and [+ Grant Security]. In other words, Joseph's brothers have employed the word (mu'min) because they want their father (i) to believe their fake story and (ii) to pardon them, not to punish them but grant them security. It can be claimed, therefore, that Q12:17 has avoided polyptoton as an embellishment in the interest of the illocutionary force of belief and avoiding punishment.

> fa'adhāqahā allāhu libās al-jūᶜi wal-khawf – God made it taste the envelopment of hunger and fear for what they had been doing, Q16:112.

where we have expected semantic relatedness between (yadhūq – to taste) and (ṭaᶜm – the taste of something), as in:

> (fa'adhāqahā allāhu taᶜma al-juᶜi – God made it taste the taste of hunger and fear for what they had been doing).

The expression (libāsa al-jūᶜi wal-khawf – the envelopment of hunger and fear) represents imagery: People have become ungrateful to their Lord's blessings, and as a result, they have been clothed with hunger and fear. The word (libās – clothes) entails that the whole body is covered. Thus, the illocutionary force of (libās) is [+ Whole], i.e., totality or wholeness. In other words, the ungrateful people have experienced total hardship as a punishment. Although the alternative word (adhāqa – to taste) would have achieved the rhetorical beauty of polyptoton, it would have achieved only [– Whole], i.e., the ungrateful people have only experienced partial hardship in terms of hunger and fear. Tasting is by the tongue only → partial, while the garment (clothes) → all the body, whole.

5.10.1.2 Macro level coherence

This is a macro text level coherence that is concerned with the continuity of thought within either a whole Qur'anic chapter (sūrah) or between consecutive chapters.

The examples demonstrate that coherence holds within the same Qur'anic chapter and among Qur'anic chapters. Thus, Qur'anic chapters interlock and get engaged with each other by overlapping themes (concepts, leitmotifs, notions).

This text linguistic phenomenon has led to thematic (conceptual) connectivity (sequentiality, chaining, dovetailing) in Qur'anic discourse through the mutually related themes which designate either:

i different notions (such as God's omnipotence, righteousness, admonition), or
ii different tenets of faith (mabādi' al-īmān) such as monotheism, prophethood, reward and punishment, and eschatology (resurrection).

5.10.1.2.1 TYPES OF MACRO LEVEL COHERENCE

This is concerned with how two macro text segments interlock and get engaged with each other by overlapping themes (notions). Macro level coherence takes place within the same Qur'anic chapter, between the beginning of two consecutive Qur'anic chapters, the beginning of a Qur'anic chapter and the end of either a previous or following chapter, the beginning and the end of the same Qur'anic chapter, and the end of a chapter and the beginning of a following chapter. It is worthwhile to note that these forms of macro level coherence are Qur'an specific and a text linguistic feature of Qur'anic discourse.

1 Within the same sūrah

Thematic chaining (connectivity) takes place within the same Qur'anic chapter. For instance, in Q16, we encounter thematic connectivity and intertextuality between the major themes in this sūrah. The major themes are:

i eschatology: Q16:1, 21, 27, 38–40, 61, 77, 109, 111, 122
ii monotheism: Q16:1–2, 22, 36, 49–57, 120, 123
iii God's omnipotence: Q16:3–17, 65–72, 78–81
iv polytheism: Q16:20, 35, 62, 73
v reward and punishment: Q16:29–34, 85–88
vi prophethood: Q16:43–44, 64, 89, 98, 101–105, 123
vii admonition: 75–76, 90–99, 125–128

In Q22, the major themes through which thematic connectivity and intertextuality are established within the same sūrah include:

i eschatology: Q22:1–7, 55
ii reward and punishment: Q22:9, 14, 19–25, 50–51, 56–59, 72
iii polytheism: Q22:12, 17, 71, 73
iv prophethood: Q22:16, 42, 49, 52, 54–55, 67–69, 72
v God's omnipotence: Q22:61, 63–66
vi admonition: Q22:26–48, 60, 74–78
vii monotheism: Q22:1, 31, 34, 62, 69, 74–76, 78

In short sūrahs, however, we encounter one major theme, as in the following examples:

Q93:3–8 prophethood
Q94:1–8 prophethood
Q112:1–4 monotheism

We also encounter two major themes only:

Q99:1–6 eschatology, 7–8 reward and punishment
Q101:1–5 eschatology, 6–11 reward and punishment

Allusion, thematic connectivity, and intertextuality can be demonstrated through the text segment Q2:35–39 and the text segment Q2:40–43. In Q2:35–39, we are told about the story of Adam and Eve, how they were misled by Satan, a reference to disbelievers and a reference to reward and punishment. In Q2:40, we are informed about the Children of Israel. Q2:40 is a reminder to the Children of Israel which warns them of the danger which Adam and Eve faced when they were misguided by Satan. Therefore, Q2:40 harks back to Q2:35–39. Thus, continuity of thought, thematic relatedness, and intertextuality are established between the two text segments.

Q27 is an illustration of macro text level coherence and continuity of thought. We can observe the following:

i A series of Prophets' parables depicting disbelief in their message of monotheism (Q27:1–58),
ii Reference to polytheism (Q27:59), and
iii A series of five denial interrogatives (istifham inkari) (a'ilahun maca allah), i.e., denying (rebutting, disproving) polytheism (Q27:60–64). In brief:

Prophets' parables → polytheism → denial interrogatives

For details on micro level coherence and continuity of thought, see Section 6.8.

2 Beginning and end of same sūrah

This is a macro text account of the occurrence of a tenant of faith as a theme at the beginning of a sūrah and which interlocks with the same theme that occurs at the end of the same sūrah. This establishes thematic connectivity (textual chaining) between the beginning and end of the same sūrah, as in:

Q6

Beginning: monotheism, Q6:1–3
End: monotheism, Q6:162–165

Q22

Beginning: eschatology, Q22:1
End: monotheism + admonition, Q22:78

Q36

Beginning: prophethood, Q36:2–3
End: monotheism, Q36:83

Q64

Beginning: monotheism, Q64:1
End: monotheism, Q64:13, 18

Q69

Beginning: eschatology, 1–3
End: monotheism, Q69:52

Q101

Beginning: eschatology, Q101:1–5
End: reward and punishment, Q101:6–11

3 End and beginning of two sūrahs

This is a macro text feature of the occurrence of a tenant of faith as a theme (notion, leitmotif) that has occurred at the end of a sūrah and which interlocks with the same theme that occurs at the beginning of the same sūrah. Through this thematic engagement, textual connectivity (chaining, dovetailing) between the end and the beginning of the same sūrah is achieved, as in:

Q36 and Q37

End of Q36:83 monotheism
Beginning of Q37:4 monotheism

Q38 and Q39

End of Q38:87 prophethood
Beginning of Q39:1 prophethood

Q37 and Q38

End of Q37:180–182 monotheism
Beginning of Q38:1 prophethood

Q54 and Q55

End of Q54:55 monotheism → God's epithet (malīk muqtadir – sovereign, perfect in ability)
Beginning of Q55:1 monotheism → God's epithet (al-raḥmān – the most merciful)

Q56 and Q57

End of Q56:96 monotheism
Beginning of Q57:1 monotheism

Q75 and Q76

End of Q75:37–39 God's omnipotence → the creation of man from a drop of sperm
Beginning of Q76:2 God's omnipotence → the creation of man from a drop of sperm

5.11 Macro context and coherence

This is an account of the relationship between coherence and the macro context. For instance, macro context determines the occurrence of the final phrase in the sentence, as in the following examples:

Example 1

wa'in ta^{c}uddū ni^{c}mata allāhi lā tuḥṣūhā inna al-insāna laẓalūmun kaffār – If you should count the blessings of God, you could not enumerate them. Indeed, mankind is most unjust and ungrateful, Q14:34.

wa'in ta^{c}uddū ni^{c}mata allāhi lā tuḥṣūhā inna allāha laghafūrun raḥīm – If you should count the blessings of God, you could not enumerate them. Indeed, God is forgiving and merciful, Q16:18.

where in Q14:34, the phrase (inna al-insāna laẓalūmun kaffār – Man is truly unjust and ungrateful) occurs, while in Q16:18, the phrase (inna allāha laghafūrun raḥīm – God is truly most forgiving and most merciful) is employed. These examples illustrate the strong bond between macro context and the selection of lexical items in a given sentence. We can observe two salient elements in the two macro contexts:

i the disbelievers as in Q14:28–30 and Q16:20–29, and
ii God's favours represented by God's omnipotence as in Q14:32–33 and Q16:5–16 where the verb (sakhkhara – to subject something for the benefit of someone) is employed.

In Q14, there are two major salient elements that have preceded sentence 34:

i The first is represented by (alladhīna baddalū ni^{c}mata allāhi kufran – those who exchanged the favour of God for disbelief, Q14:28).
ii The second is represented by (ātākum min kulli mā sa'altumūh – God gave you from all you asked of Him, Q14:34).

However, the occurrence of the sentence-final phrase (inna al-insāna laẓalūmun kaffār – People are truly unjust and ungrateful, Q14:34) is more influenced by the second salient element (ātākum min kulli mā sa'altumūh – God gave people from all they asked of Him, Q14:34). This is attributed to the fact that this element is an address to all people regardless of their faith, race, or colour who appeal to their Lord for small and big favours, and their appeal is answered. However, some people have (baddalū niᶜmata allāhi kufran – have exchanged the God's favour for disbelief, Q14:28). Thus, to achieve coherence, the phrase (al-insāna laẓalūmun kaffār – People are truly unjust and ungrateful, Q14:34) is well selected. Also, in terms of coherence, we can argue that:

i the selection of the word (kaffār – ungrateful, Q14:34) is morphologically related to the verb (kafara – to disbelieve). Thus, semantically, it is coherently (morphologically) related to earlier words of the same root and meaning: (kāfirīn – disbelievers, Q14:2), (kafartum – you disbelieved, Q14:7), (kafarnā – we disbelieved, Q14:9), (kafarū – they disbelieved, Q14:13, 18), (kafartu – I disbelieved, Q14:22), and (kufran – disbelief, Q14:28), and

ii the selection of the adjective (ẓalūm – unjust, Q14:34) is morphologically related to the verb (ẓalama – to be unjust). Thus, semantically, it is coherently related to earlier words of the same root and meaning: (al-ẓālimīn – the wrongdoers, Q14:13, 22, 27).

Therefore, in terms of coherence, the sentence-final phrase (inna al-insāna laẓalūmun kaffār – Man is truly unjust and ungrateful) fits in well in the sentence and most appropriately selected for the macro context.

In Q16, there are two salient elements of the macro context that have preceded and followed sentence 18:

i The first is monotheism (lā ilāha illā anā fattaqūni – There is no deity except Me; so fear Me, Q16:2) and (ilāhukum ilāhun wāḥidun – Your god is one God, Q16:22).

ii The second is the interrogative sentence (afaman yakhluqu kaman lā yakhluq – Is God who creates like one who does not create?, Q16:17), whose pragmatic function has an illocutionary force of denial (rebuttal) of opponent's premise (thesis). In other words, the one who does not create is of limited power, i.e., Q16:17 is a denial question for the illocutionary force of rebuttal whose intended meaning is 'the opponent's premise is false'. This is also related to (alladhīna yadᶜūna min dūni allāhi lā yakhluqūna shai'an wahum yukhlaqūn – Those who invoke other than God create nothing, and they themselves are created, Q16:20). Thus, in terms of coherence, we can argue that the selection of the sentence-final phrase (inna allāha laghafūrun raḥīm – God is truly most forgiving and most merciful, Q16:18) fits in well with the macro context. This is due to the fact that God's epithets (ghafūr raḥīm – most forgiving and most merciful) usually occur in the context of monotheism for the illocutionary force of:

  i 'encouragement' to disbelievers to abandon polytheism, and
  ii 'reassurance' to disbelievers since God is (most forgiving and most merciful).

Let us consider the following interesting example:

> kallā bal tuḥibbūna al-ᶜājilah. watadharūna al-ākhirah – Truly you (people) love this fleeting world, and neglect the hereafter, Q75:20–21.

Example 2

The following observations must be taken into consideration when looking into the relationship between coherence and the macro text and why the two statements 20–21 occur in the middle of Q75:

- i Q75 is made up of 40 āyahs whose title is 'resurrection',
- ii The major theme of Q75 is resurrection,
- iii The two āyahs 20–21 fall in the middle of Q75,
- iv Q75:1–19 refer to the theme of resurrection and God's omnipotence + the two statements 20–21 + statements 22–40 refer to resurrection and God's omnipotence,
- v The two statements 20–21 represent antonymy (oppositeness) where the word (tuḥibbūna – to love) is the antonym of (tadharūna – to hate (to neglect)). Also, the word (al-ᶜājilah – the fleeting world (the present life)) is the antonym of (al-ākhirah – the hereafter),
- vi The selection of the antonym expression coherently fits in with the macro context theme of Q75.

Example 3

fa'ajā'ahā al-makhāḍu ilā jidhᶜ al-nakhlati . . . wahuzzī ilaiki bijidhᶜi al-nakhlati tusāqiṭ ᶜalaiki ruṭaban janiyyā – When the pains of childbirth drove her to cling to the trunk of a date palm . . . If you shake the trunk of the palm tree towards you, it will deliver fresh ripe dates for you, Q19:23, 25.

One may wonder whether there is any coherence or continuity of thought in the above example with regards to Mary's story of having a baby and of the date palm tree. We can make the following observations to set the scene for continuity of senses:

1. We need to consider the relevance of the word (jidhᶜ – trunk).
2. The two statements could have ignored (jidhᶜ) and employed only the word (al nakhlati – a date palm).
3. The word (jidhᶜ) semantically entails it had no leaves (saᶜfu al-nakhlati) and no head (ra'su al-nakhlati); it was just a lifeless trunk of a palm tree with no fresh dates on.
4. The place was barren, and there were no surrounding date palm trees.
5. Because there were no trees near the dead palm tree, we can conclude that there was no male date palm tree.
6. Because there was no male palm tree nearby, the trunk could not have been fertilized. Therefore, it could not have been able to produce fresh dates.

Therefore, through deductive reasoning, we can make five inferences:

i Mary had no physical contact with a male partner (a man). Yet she got pregnant and gave birth to a baby boy, Jesus.
ii The dry date palm trunk was the only tree in that place, and there was no male date palm tree nearby to get the female dead palm tree fertilized and be able to produce fresh dates.
iii The trunk's situation is identical to Mary's. Both have had no contact with a male partner but both have managed to produce.
iv It was God who caused Mary to give birth to a baby boy and it was God who caused the date palm trunk to produce fresh dates.
v The two stories entail God's omnipotence.

The continuity of this thought ends in Q19:35 (mā kāna lillāhi an yattakhidha min waladin subḥānahu idhā qaḍā amran fa'innamā yaqūlu lahu kun fayakūn – It would not befit God to have a child. He is far above that: when He decrees something, He says only: 'Be' and it is).

Example 4

lā taqtulū awlādakum min imlāqin naḥnu narzuqukum wa'iyyāhum – Do not kill your children in fear of poverty – We will provide for you and for them, Q6:151.

lā taqtulū awlādakum khashyata imlāqin nahnu narzuquhum wa'iyyākum – Do not kill your children in fear of poverty – We will provide for them and for you, Q17:31.

The problem lies in the two word orders of the two sentence units: (naḥnu narzuqukum wa'iyyāhum – We will provide for you and for them) and (naḥnu narzuquhum wa'iyyākum – We will provide for them and for you). One may wonder whether the word order in each unit has impact on the coherence and meaning of each sentence. Both sentences are instructions which prohibit the murder of own children by parents. However, each sentence has a distinct purpose of killing own children by parents.

In Q6:151, the provision is provided first to the parents (narzuqukum – We will provide for you (parents)), then reference to the provision for children comes later (wa'iyyāhum – and for them (children)). Thus, we have:

Provision → Parents → Children

However, in Q17:31, the provision is provided first to the children (narzuquhum – We will provide for them (children)), then reference to the provision for parents comes later (wa'iyyākum – and for you (parents)). Thus, we have:

Provision → Children → Parents

How can the two sentences be coherent when, on the surface, they focus on the same theme, namely the killing by parents of their own children for fear of poverty, but they have different grammatical structures?

In Q6:151, both the parents and the children are stricken by poverty. The poor parents used to kill their own children for fear of more hardship and poverty. Thus, the provision for parents comes first (narzuqukum – We will provide for you (parents)) to reassure poor parents that they will be cared for financially. Then the reference to the provision for children is made (wa'iyyāhum – and for children). Thus, the illocutionary force of this word order (Provision → Parents → Children) is reassurance to the poor parents that they will be cared for financially and they will be able to look after their children.

In Q17:31, the parents are well off and have no financial problems. The well-off parents used to feel insecure financially and have groundless fear about their children's financial future. To save their children from wrongly anticipated poverty, they used to murder them. Thus, the provision for the children (narzuquhum – We will provide for them (children)) comes first, then reference to the provision for parents is made later (wa'iyyākum – and for you (parents)). Therefore, the illocutionary force of this word order (Provision → Children → Parents) is reassurance to the wealthy parents that their children will be cared for financially in the future.

Example 5

> wahuwa alladhī arsala al-riyāḥa bushran baina yadai rahmatihi wa'anzalnā min al-samā'i mā'an ṭahūrā. linuḥyiya bihi baldatan maitan wanusqiyahu mimmā khalaqnā an^{c}āman wa'anāsiyya kathīrā – It is He (God) who sends the winds as good tidings before His mercy (i.e., rainfall), and We send down from the sky pure water. That We may bring to life thereby a dead land and give it as drink to many animals and people, Q25:48–49.

where we have Cause and Effect relationship between the above two statements:

Cause: riyāḥa – the winds
Effect: mā'an – water (i.e., rain)
Cause: mā'an – water (i.e., rain)
Effect 1: linuḥyiya bihi baldatan maitan – to revive a dead land with it (i.e., water, rain)
Effect 2: nusqiyahu mimmā khalaqnā an^{c}āman – Give it as a drink to many animals
Effect 3: nusqiyahu anāsiyya kathīrā – Give it as a drink to many people

In terms of coherence, the continuity of thought is as such: the thought is based on the rain (water) from the sky which occurs first, then the thought of the dead land being revived by the rain occurs next, then animals benefit from the water as a drink, and finally people benefit from water as a drink:

(rain) → (dead land) → (animals) → (people)

Because prosperous life of people starts from the revival of the dead land, the notion of reviving the dead land occurs as the first effect of the rain. Also, because prosperous life of people depends on having livestock to live on. Livestock need pasture (a revived land watered by the rain) and water to drink. Lastly, people can have a prosperous life when they have a revived land through water, healthy livestock, and water to drink. This is the continuity of thought and coherence in the two statements.

5.12 Summary

We have discussed micro level coherence which takes place at a word, sentence, or particle level and macro level coherence which takes place at the larger text (sūrah) level. Coherence is hinged on saliency and relevance of a given thought that is delivered through different mechanisms. We have discussed how coherence is based on grammatical, semantic, morphological, stylistic, and phonetic saliency and relevance in order to deliver the illocutionary force of the thought expressed by the text producer's (interlocutor's) message. These mechanisms are achieved either at word level or sentence level. Grammatical saliency and relevance are demonstrated by Q18:51 (Section 5.5, point (14 (i))), which is an example of syntax-based coherence. Semantic saliency and relevance is demonstrated by Q2:2 (Section 5.5, point 8) and Q5:4 (Section 5.5, point (11)), which are examples of semantics-based coherence. Morphological saliency and relevance are demonstrated by Q76:24 (Section 5.5, point (3)), which is an example of morphology-based coherence. Stylistic saliency and relevance are demonstrated by Q2:4 (Section 5.5, point (1)), Q1:2 (Section 5.5, point 5 (i)), and Q16:19 (Section 5.5, point 5 (ii)), which are examples of stylistics-based coherence. Phonetic saliency and relevance are demonstrated by Q79:34 (Section 5.5, point 9), which is an example of phonetics-based coherence. In Section 5.6, we have explained the relationship between the relevance of a particular lexeme and the position it occupies in the sentence for the purpose of coherence. In Section 5.7, we have discussed why a text producer purposefully makes a specific text segment more salient than others through word order and sentence position for the purpose of coherence. In Section 5.8, we have focused on how some text lexemes are purposefully selected for coherence, continuity of thought, and relevance. In 5.10.1.1, we have discussed micro level coherence at sentence level. Section 5.10.1.2 deals with macro level coherence which is at text level.

6 Cohesion in Qur'anic discourse

6.1 Introduction

The present chapter provides an insight into the cohesion system of Qur'anic discourse. It provides a detailed account of what Halliday and Hasan (1976:274) call the different types of grammatical cohesion such as reference, substitution, ellipsis, and conjunction. The textual analysis accounts in detail for the notion of cohesion in Qur'anic Arabic, its textual purpose, and Qur'anic cohesive devices, which include: (1) reference (endophoric and exophoric), (2) ellipsis (verbal, nominal, and clausal), (3) substitution (nominal and clausal), (4) conjunction (additive, adversative, causal, and temporal), and (5) lexical cohesion (the general noun, reiteration, synonymy, antonymy, collocation, hyponymy, and meronymy). It is worthwhile to note that the present discussion will focus only on the discourse connectives that occur in Qur'anic discourse. The present discussion is of value to translation studies, contrastive linguistics, and Qur'anic corpus linguistics. The sentences between brackets () represent statements which do not flout cohesion, i.e., the ellipted elements are brought back but are non-Qur'anic. A tree diagram of cohesive devices is at the end of this chapter (Figure 6.1).

6.2 What is cohesion?

Cohesion is a text-centred notion and is a constitutive principle of effective communication. Cohesion accounts for text connectedness through cohesion elements (lexical cohesion, ellipsis, reference, substitution, and conjunction). These cohesive mechanisms indicate how statements relate to each other. Thus, cohesion is employed as a tool to analyse the text beyond the sentence level and to characterize text structure. For Halliday and Hasan (1976:4), cohesion occurs when the interpretation of some element in the discourse is dependent on that of another.

Cohesion is the set of resources for constructing relations in discourse that transcend grammatical structure (Halliday 1994:309). For Martin (2015:61), cohesion is one part of the study of texture, which considers the interaction of cohesion with other aspects of text organization. It is the process whereby meaning is channelled into a digestible current of discourse. Thus, without cohesion, communication slows down and may break down.

6.3 The textual purpose of cohesion

Sentences represent facts and actions. However, these facts and actions need to be presented to the listener/reader in an acceptable sequence. Thus, the cohesion system of language is a regulator that organizes the facts and the sequence of actions in an orderly cohesive pattern appropriate for a cohesive text. The employment of a specific cohesive device provides a logical sense and sequence to the sentence. For instance, the use of (and) in (I am in Leeds and York at 9 a.m.) makes the speech act unacceptable and contradictory. However, we can rectify the illogical property of this sentence through the employment of (either . . . or). Thus, we can say (I am in either Leeds or York at 9 a.m.). Through cohesion, sentences of a text fit together in a sensible way and become related to each other.

Cohesion makes the text hang together. It is the potential that the speaker or writer has at his/her disposal (Halliday and Hasan 1976:18). Cohesion is a process which always involves one item pointing to another, i.e., one item provides the source for the interpretation of another (ibid:19). It is the set of meaning relations that is general to all classes of text, that distinguishes text from non-text and interrelates the substantive meanings of the text with each other. Cohesion does not concern what a text means; it concerns how the text is constructed as a semantic edifice. It is a potential for relating one element in the text to another (ibid:26–27).

Discourse connectives have two distinct functions as distinguished by Cohen (1984):

i enabling faster recognition of coherence relations by the reader (the hearer), and
ii allowing the recognition of coherence relations which could not be inferred in the absence of a connective.

Redeker (1991:1168), who worked in speech research, defined a discourse connective (discourse operator) as 'a linguistic signal of textual coherence link'. It is 'a word or phrase that is uttered with the primary function of bringing the listener's attention to a particular kind of linkage of the upcoming utterance (clausal unit) with the immediate discourse context'. For Fraser (2009:295), discourse markers (pragmatic markers) signal aspects of the message the speaker wishes to convey. In our discussion, the discourse connectives (discourse markers, pragmatic markers, discourse connectives, discourse operators) include clausal indicators of discourse structure (e.g., let me tell you a story), deictic expressions like (now, here, today), and anaphoric pronouns.

6.4 Cohesion in Qur'anic discourse

Cohesion is a prerequisite of the texture of any text. As a linguistic resource and a standard of textuality, cohesion plays a vital role in making the Qur'anic text connected together. The text becomes cohesive through the different ties within it such as reference, ellipsis, substitution, conjunction, and lexical cohesion. In other words, through cohesion, the components (words, phrases, clauses) of the

Qur'anic text become associated semantically, grammatically, or both, and the sentences are linked together.

6.4.1 Flouting cohesion in Qur'anic discourse

While cohesion is a requirement of any text type (genre), different languages employ different cohesive mechanisms to suit their linguistic and stylistic norms. In other words, some components of cohesion can be flouted. For instance, in Qur'anic discourse, reiteration is a prominent cohesive element, as in:

> inna minhum lafarīqan yalwūna alsinatahum bil-kitābi litaḥsabūhu min al-kitābi wamā huwa min al-kitābi – Indeed, there is a party who alter the Scripture with their tongues so you may think it is from the Scripture, but it is not from the Scripture, Q3:78.
>
> yaqūlūna huwa min ᶜind allāh wamā huwa min ᶜind allāh – They say, 'This is from God, but it is not from God', Q3:78.

where the noun phrase (al-kitābi – the Scripture) and the noun (allāh – God) are reiterated to achieve the illocutionary (communicative) force of affirmation. However, this does not apply to English, which would have applied the cohesive component of reference, i.e., employing a pronoun referring to the noun (phrase). In other words, in terms of reference (pronominalization or coreferentiality), Q3:78 has flouted reference and should read as:

> (inna minhum lafarīqan yalwūna alsinatahum bil-kitābi litaḥsabūhu min**hu** wamā huwa min**hu** – Indeed, there is a party who alter the Scripture with their tongues so you may think it is from **it**, but it is not from **it**).
>
> (yaqūlūna huwa min ᶜind allāh wamā huwa min ᶜindih – They say, 'This is from God, but it is not from **Him**').

Also in:

> bal kadhdhabū bil-sāᶜati wa'iᶜtadnā liman kadhdhaba bil-sāᶜati saᶜīrā – But they have denied the hour and We have prepared a blaze for those who deny the hour, Q25:11.
>
> (bal kadhdhabū bil-sāᶜati wa'iᶜtadnā **lahum** saᶜīrā – But they have denied the hour and We have prepared a blaze for them).

Similarly, in:

> wamin āyātihi al-lailu wal-nahāru wal-shamsu wal-qamaru. lā tasjudū lil-shamsi walā lil-qamari wasjudū lillāhi alladhī khalaqahunna in kuntum iyyāhu taᶜbudūn – And of His signs are the night and the day and the sun and the moon. Do not prostrate to the sun or to the moon, but prostrate to God who created them if it should be Him that you worship, Q41:37.

where reference has been flouted and we expect Q41:37 to read as:

> (wamin āyātihi al-lailu wal-nahāru wal-shamsu wal-qamaru. lā tasjudū **[lahumā]** wasjudū lillāhi alladhī khalaqahunna in kuntum iyyāhu ta[c]budūn – And of His signs are the night and the day and the sun and the moon. Do not prostrate to (**them**), but prostrate to God who created them if it should be Him that you worship, Q41:37).

where the noun phrase (al-shams wal-qamar – the sun and the moon) is reiterated for the illocutionary function of affirmation and warning. In other words, the notion of monotheism is highlighted through reiterating the noun phrase (al-shams wal-qamar) to set the scene for the notion that 'prostration should be made to God only'.

In Q29:53, we observe the flouting of reference because Qur'anic Arabic favours reiteration over reference for the illocutionary force of affirmation:

> wayasta[c]jilūnka bil-[c]adhāb walawlā ajalun musamman lajā'ahum <u>al-[c]adhāb</u> walaya'tiyannahum baghtatan wahum lā yash[c]urūn – They challenge you to hasten the punishment. If not for the decree of a specified term, punishment would have reached them. But it will surely come to them suddenly and catch them unawares, Q29:53.

where the underlined noun phrase (<u>al-[c]adhāb</u> – the punishment) is repeated, while the expected grammatical structure should be:

> (wayasta[c]jilūnka bil-[c]adhāb walawlā ajalun musamman lajā'ahum () walaya'tiyannahum baghtatan wahum lā yash[c]urūn – They challenge you to hasten the punishment. If not for the decree of a specified term, (it) would have reached them. But it will surely come to them suddenly and catch them unawares, Q29:53).

where the anaphoric reference pronoun (it) is implicit in the verb (jā'a – to come). However, in the verb (ya'tiyanna – to come), the implicit anaphoric reference pronoun (it) has been employed without the reiteration of the noun phrase (al-[c]adhāb – the punishment).

A striking feature of Qur'anic Arabic is the stylistic feature of shift. Shift in Qur'anic discourse occurs at different levels. However, in terms of cohesion, we are concerned only with coreferential pronoun shift, which is encountered frequently in the Qur'anic text. Pronoun shift, we can argue, is a representation of flouting cohesion, i.e., the breaking of the pronominalization rule, as in:

> man aslama wajhahu lillāh wa huwa muḥsiniun falahu ajruhu [c]inda rabbih walā khawfun [c]alaihim walā hum yaḥzanūn – Whoever submits himself in Islam to God while being a doer of good will have his reward with his Lord. And no fear will there be concerning them, nor will they grieve, Q2:112.

The above example flouts the textual standard of cohesion. This is because the cohesion component of reference (coreferentiality) has been defied.

In Q2:112, we have a pronoun shift from the third person masculine singular (huwa – he), which is also represented by the (-hu – he) of (falahu – he will have), the (-hu – his) of (ajrahu – his reward), and (rabbahu – his Lord) to third person masculine plural (-him – them) of (ᶜalaihim – concerning them), (hum – they), and the (-nūn – plural masculine (they)) of (yaḥzanūn – they grieve). If we want to apply the cohesion component of reference to Q2:112, we need to preserve cohesion through reference, i.e., to apply the coreferential pronoun (he) throughout the sentence. Thus, we get:

> (man aslama wajhahu lillāh wa huwa muḥsiniun falahu ajruhu ᶜinda rabbih walā khawfun ᶜalaihi walā huwa yaḥzan).

which is marked by a poor style, as opposed to the sublime style of Q2:112 due to its stylistic glitter and colourful stylistic façade, which add a psychological impact on the reader, namely to mentally alert the reader, i.e., the flouting of cohesion (reference) acts like a bell of an alarm clock.

Similarly, the shift from first person singular masculine pronoun (I) to first person plural masculine pronoun (we) in Q1:5 where the implicit subject first person pronoun flouts cohesion and reference because it occurs in the plural form (naḥnu – we) in (naᶜbud – we worship) and (nastaᶜīn – we ask for help), which are both implicit first person masculine plural pronoun rather than in the expected first person singular (aᶜbud – I worship) and (astaᶜīn – I ask for help). Thus, the number agreement is violated (singular → plural). However, this is not without a good pragmatic reason. Cohesion is flouted in Q1:5 for the pragmatic function of involving the 'plural' → 'we', i.e., more than one speaker to demonstrate the notion of collective supplication to the Lord. Another interesting example of the flouting of cohesion in terms of reference due to coreferential pronoun shift is the following:

> waᶜada allāhu alladhīna āmanū minkum waᶜamilū al-ṣāliḥāti layastakhlifannahum fī al-arḍi kamā istakhlafa alladhīna min qablihim walayumakkinanna lahum dīnahum alladhī irtaḍā lahum walayubaddilannahum min baᶜdi khawfihim amnā yaᶜbudūnanī lā yushrikūna bī shai'an – God has promised those who have believed among you and done righteous deeds that He will surely grant them succession to authority upon the earth just as He granted it to those before them and that He will surely establish for them therein their religion which He has preferred for them and that He will surely substitute for them, after their fear, security. They will worship Me (God) and do not associate anything with Me, Q24:55.

where we have the verb (waᶜada – to promise), the subject (allāhu – God), and the object (alladhīna āmanū minkum waᶜamilū al-ṣāliḥāti – those who have believed among you and done righteous deeds) where there is no pronoun shift in this part of the sentence, i.e., cohesion is observed where there is subject pronoun agreement, i.e., reference (pronominalization or coreferentiality) is achieved because the pronoun agrees with its verb in terms of number. However, cohesion is violated because a pronoun shift has occurred in the second part of the sentence:

> yaᶜbudūnanī lā yushrikūna bī shai'an – They worship Me and do not associate anything with Me, Q24:55.

where the verb (yaᶜbudūnani – to worship Me) has violated cohesion, i.e., the subject pronoun number agreement is not applied. In other words, the implicit pronoun (Me) within the verb occurs in the first person singular rather than the expected third person singular (Him). If cohesion is observed, we expect to see (yaᶜbudūnahu – to worship Him). The flouting of cohesion has produced a shift from the third person singular → the first person singular.

Similarly, while English can achieve verbal substitution through the verb (do), Arabic can't. For this reason, while English has three types of substitution (nominal, verbal, and clausal), Qur'anic Arabic has only two (nominal and clausal). The same applies to ellipsis where English has three types of ellipsis (nominal, verbal, and clausal), Qur'anic Arabic has only two (nominal and clausal).

This leads us to conclude that languages like English and Qur'anic Arabic which are linguistically and culturally incongruent employ different linguistic and stylistic mechanisms, including that of cohesion.

6.5 Cohesive devices in Qur'anic discourse

We encounter different types of cohesive devices in a macro text. These cohesive devices need to be studied in actual situations of use, i.e., in a text, rather than through invented examples. In Qur'anic discourse, we encounter five major cohesive devices:

> (i) reference, (ii) ellipsis, (iii) substitution, (iv) conjunction, and (v) lexical cohesion.

6.5.1 Reference

According to Halliday and Hasan (1976:130, 226), reference is a semantic relation. Through reference, a word is linked to its pronoun. For Salkie (1995:64), there are special words which need help from their environment to determine their full meaning. Because of this, they are important in creating cohesion in texts. Thus, reference words do not have a full meaning in their own right. To find out about the meaning of a reference word, we have to refer to something else in the same sentence or in earlier sentences. Thus, when Halliday and Hasan regard reference as a semantic relation, Salkie (ibid:65) reiterates that reference is a relation between the meaning of a word and its environment.

In Qur'anic discourse, pronouns refer to persons, things, and places. We can distinguish between two types of reference:

1 Text-bound reference: Different pronouns within different texts refer to different people, things, or places. Thus, from the text we can retrieve the information about what a specific pronoun refers to. This is text-bound reference, as in Q2:255. Endophoric reference is text bound. For more details, see Section 6.5.1.1.1.
2 Context-bound reference: From the context, we can also retrieve information about what a given pronoun refers to, i.e., there is no person/thing mentioned in the text. This is context-bound reference, as in Q18:44 and Q33:11 where the reference word (ulā'ika – there) occurs. Exophoric reference is context bound. For more details, see Section 6.5.1.1.2.

Reference is a relationship between a lexical item and its pronoun. Reference refers to nouns, determiners, personal and demonstrative pronouns, implicit pronouns within a verb, and adverbs, as in:

> allāhu lā ilāha illā huwa . . . lā ta'khudhuhu sinatun walā nawmun lahu mā fī al-samāwāti . . . man dha alladhī yashfa^c^u ^c^indahu illā bi'idhnihi ya^c^lamu mā baina aidīhim wamā khalfahum walā yuḥīṭūn bishai'in min ^c^ilmihi illā bimā shā' . . . wasi^c^a kursiyyuhu al-samāwāt wal-arḍ wa lā ya'uduhu ḥifẓihimā wa huwa al-^c^aliyyu al-^c^aẓīm – God – there is no deity except Him . . . Neither drowsiness overtakes Him nor sleep. To Him belongs whatever is in the heavens . . . Who is it that can intercede with Him except by His permission? He knows what is present before them and what will be after them, and they do not encompass a thing of His knowledge except for what He wills . . . His kursi extends over the heavens and the earth and their preservation does not tire Him, and He is the most high, the most great, Q2:255.

Form the above text, we can retrieve the information about what each pronoun refers to:

i The pronouns (huwa – He, Him), (-hu – Him) of (ta'khudhuhu – overtake Him), (-hu – Him) of (lahu – to Him), (-hu – Him) of (^c^indahu – with Him), (-hi – His) of (bi'idhnihi – by His permission), the implicit pronoun (huwa – He) in the verb (ya^c^lamu – He knows), the pronoun (-hi – His) of (^c^ilmihi – His knowledge), the implicit pronoun (huwa – He) of (shā' – He wills), the pronoun (-hu – His) of (kursiyyuhu – His kursi), and the pronoun (-hu – Him) of (ya'uduhu – tire Him) refer to (allāhu – God).
ii The pronoun (-humā – their (dual)) of (ḥifẓihimā – their preservation) refer to (al-samāwāt wal-arḍ – the heavens and the earth).
iii The pronouns (-him – them/their) of (aidīhim – (literally) their hands), (-hum – them) of (khalfahum – after them), and the implicit masculine plural pronoun (-ūn – they) of (yuḥīṭūn – they encompass) refer to the plural noun

represented by the exegetically based clause (all those who have the intellect and are living either in the heavens or on earth).

> allāhu waliyyu alladhīna āmanū yukhrijuhum min al-ẓulumāt ilā al-nūr walladhīna kafarū awliyā'uhum al-ṭāghūtu yukhrijūnahum min al-nūr ilā al-ẓulumāt ulā'ika aṣḥābu al-nār hum fihā khālidūn – God is the ally of those who believe. He brings them out from darknesses into the light. And those who disbelieve their allies are ṭāghūt. They take them out of the light into darknesses. Those are the companions of the fire; they will abide eternally therein, Q2:257

where the pronoun (-hum – them) of (yukhrijuhum – (He) brings them out) refers to (alladhīna āmanū – those who believe), and the pronoun (-hum – them) of (yukhrijūnahum – (they) bring them out) refers to (alladhīna kafarū – those who disbelieve). From the context of Q2:257, we can find out that the demonstrative pronoun (ulā'ika – those) refers to (alladhīna kafarū) because the phrase (aṣḥābu al-nār – the companions of the fire) is mentioned.

> yawma yafirru al-mar'u min akhīh wa ummih wa abīh wa ṣāḥibatih wa banīh – On the day, a man will flee from his brother and his mother and his father, Q80:34–36.

where the pronoun (-h – his) in (akhīh), (ummih), (abīh), and (ṣāḥibatih) refers to the word (al-mar'u – a man), i.e., the noun (al-mar'u) is linked to its pronoun through the reference element (-h). Thus, pronouns are used as reference items that can be used either to relate to the person or thing that has been mentioned earlier in the sentence.

> alladhīna yunfiqūn amwālahum fī sabīl allāh . . . – (those) who spend their wealth in the way of God . . ., Q2:261, 262, 265.

where the implicit plural subject pronoun (-ūn – they) of the verb (yunfiqūna – spend) and the possessive plural pronoun (-hum – their) refer to the subject plural relative pronoun (alladhīna – who)

> alladhīna yunfiqūn amwālahum fī sabīl allāh. . . . lahum ajruhum ᶜinda rabbihim walā khawfun ᶜalaihim walā hum yaḥzanūn – (those) who spend their wealth in the way of God . . . will have their reward with their Lord, and there will be no fear concerning them, nor will they grieve, Q2:262.

where the implicit plural subject pronoun (-ūn – they) of the verb (yunfiqūna – they spend), the possessive plural pronoun (-hum – their), the plural pronoun (-hum – them) of (lahum), the plural possessive pronoun (-hum – their) of (ajruhum – their reward) and (rabbihim – their Lord), the plural object pronoun (-him – them) of (ᶜalaihim – upon them), the pronoun (hum – they), and the implicit plural subject pronoun (-ūn – they) of the verb (yaḥzanūn – they grieve) refer to the same subject plural relative pronoun (alladhīna – who).

> hunālika al-walāyatu lillāhi al-ḥaqq – There the authority is completely for God, Q18:44.
>
> hunālika ibtuliya al-mu'minūna . . . – There the believers were tested, Q33:11.

In Q18:44, the reference word (hunālika – there) is an adverb of place that refers to the day of judgement. Contextually, (hunālika) means (on the day of judgement). In other words, the sentence is like: (On the day of judgement, the authority is completely for God). However, in Q33:11, the reference word (hunālika – there) is an adverb of place that refers to the Battle of the Trench (maᶜrakat al-khandaq) that took place in 5/627.

6.5.1.1 Classification of reference

Items of reference are classified into endophoric reference and exophoric reference. These two types of reference are discussed in what follows:

6.5.1.1.1 ENDOPHORIC REFERENCE

Endophoric reference is text bound. In other words, it refers to someone or something within the text where different pronouns in a text refer to different people, things, or places. Through the text, we can retrieve the information about what a specific pronoun refers to. Endophoric (text-bound) reference includes:

i personal reference,
ii general reference,
iii anaphoric reference,
iv cataphoric reference,
v demonstrative reference,
vi extended demonstrative reference, and
vii comparative reference.

These types of endophoric reference are illustrated in what follows.

6.5.1.1.1.1 Personal reference Personal reference is concerned with detached personal pronouns (ḍamīr munfaṣil), such as (innī – I), (anā – I), (huwa – he), (hiya – she), (hunna – they (feminine, plural)), (anta – you (singular, masculine)), (antum – you (masculine, plural)), and with attached pronouns (ḍamīr muttaṣil), which can be attached to either a verb, a noun, or a preposition or which can be an implicit pronoun within a verb. Possessive pronouns are also personal pronouns and are referred to as 'determiners' and represent a personal reference such as (-ī – my (kitābī – my book)), (-hu – his (kitābuhu – his book)), (-hā – her (kitabuhā – her book)). Let us consider the following examples:

innanī anā allāhu lā ilāha illā anā – Indeed, I am God. There is no deity except Me, Q20:14.
idhhab anta wa'akhūka – Go you and your brother, Q20:42.
allāhu lā ilāha illā huwa – God – there is no deity except Him, Q2:255, Q3:2.
hum lil-kufri yawma'idhin aqrabu minhum lil-īmān yaqūlūna bi'afwāhihim mā laisa fī qulūbihim – They were nearer to disbelief that day than to faith. Saying with their mouths what was not in their hearts, Q3:167.
ijnubni wabaniyya an na^c^buda al-aṣnām rabbī inna hunna aḍlalna kathīran min al-nāss – Keep me and my sons away from worshipping idols. My Lord, indeed they have led astray many among the people, Q14:35–36.
. . . ilā nisā'ikum hunna libāsun lakum wa antum libāsun la hunna – . . . to your wives. They are clothing for you and you are clothing for them, Q2:187.

The following are examples of determiners (possessive pronouns) as personal reference items:

iqra' kitābaka kafā binafsika al-yawma ^c^alaika ḥasībā – Read your record. Today your own soul is enough to calculate your account, Q17:14.
yā aiyuhā al-nabiyyu qul li'azwājika wa banātika wanisā'i al-mu'minīn yadnīna ^c^alaihinna min jalābībihinna – Prophet, tell your wives, your daughters, and women believers to make their outer garments hang low over them, Q33:59
inna allāha yudkhilu alladhīna āmanū wa^c^amilū al-ṣāliḥāt jannāt tajrī min taḥtihā al-anhār yuḥallawna fīhā min asāwira min dhahabin walu'lu'an walibāsuhum fīhā ḥarīr – Indeed, God will admit those who believe and do righteous deeds to gardens beneath which rivers flow. They will be adorned therein with bracelets of gold and pearl, and their garments therein will be silk, Q22:23

In Q17:14, the determiner (-ka – your (second person singular masculine)) of (kitābaka – your book) represents the personal reference. The determiner (possessive pronoun) personal reference in Q33:59 is (hinna – their (feminine plural)) of (jalābībihinna – their outer garments). In Q22:23, the determiner is (-hum – their (third person plural masculine)) of (libāsuhum – their garments) is the personal reference. It is also worthwhile to note that the personal reference item (-hā – them) of (taḥtihā – beneath them (gardens)) and of (fīhā – in them (gardens)) refers to the adverb noun (jannāt – gardens).

6.5.1.1.1.2 General reference The general reference items are like (aḥadu – one), (ākharu – other), (al-awwal – the first), as in:

> watlu ^{c}alaihim naba'a ibnai ādama bil-ḥaqqi idh qarrabā qurbānan fatuqubbila min aḥadihimā walam yutaqabbal min al-ākhari – Recite to them the story of Adam's sons, in truth, when they both offered a sacrifice and it was accepted from one of them but was not accepted from the other, Q5:27.
> waqāla al-ākharu innī arānī aḥmilu fawqa ra'sī khubzan – The other said: 'I dreamed that I was carrying bread on my head', Q12:36.
> yā ṣāḥibai al-sijni ammā aḥadukumā fayasqī rabbahu khamrā – Fellow prisoners, one of you will serve his master with wine, Q12:41.
> wa ākharūn i^{c}tarafū bidhunūbihim – And there are others who have acknowledged their sins, Q9:102.
> an taḍilla iḥdāhumā fatudhakkira iḥdāhumā al-ukhrā – So that if one of the two women errs, then the other can remind her, Q2:282.
> wa'idh ya^{c}idukum allāhu iḥdā al-ṭā'ifatain – When God promised you one of the two groups, Q8:7.
> qālat iḥdāhumā yā abatī . . . One of the women said: 'O my father . . . ', Q28:26.
> fi'atun tuqātilu fī sabīl allāh wa ukhrā kāfiratun – One fighting in the cause of God and another of disbelievers, Q3:13.
> waqālat ulāhum li ukhrāhum famā kāna lakum ^{c}alainā min faḍlin – The first of them will say to the last of them: 'Then you had not any favour over us', Q7:39.
> minhu āyātun muḥkamātun hunna umm al-kitābi wa ukharu mutashābihāt – In it are āyāt that are precise – they are the foundation of the Book – and others are mutashābihāt, Q3:7.
> ya'kulhunna sab^{c}un ^{c}ujāfun wasab^{c}u sunbulātin khuḍrin wa ukharu yābisāt – Eaten by seven lean, and seven green spikes of grain and others dry, Q12:43.

where the general reference words are (aḥadi/iḥdā – one of), (al-ākhari/ukharu/ukhrā/ākharūn – the other, the others).

6.5.1.1.1.3 Anaphoric reference Anaphoric reference takes place when a noun occurs first then is followed by its reference pronoun. Anaphoric reference is the unmarked word order, i.e., the expected and the normal word order in Qur'anic Arabic. Examples that represent anaphoric reference are:

> nisā'ikum hunna libāsun lakum – Your wives, they are clothing for you, Q2:187.

where the noun (nisā' – wives) is mentioned first then is followed by its anaphoric reference pronoun (hunna – they).

6.5.1.1.1.4 Cataphoric reference Cataphoric reference takes place when a reference pronoun occurs first then is followed by the noun it refers to. Cataphoric reference is the marked word order, i.e., the unexpected and the unusual word order in Qur'anic Arabic. Examples that represent cataphoric reference are:

> **huwa** allāhu alladhī lā ilāha illā huwa – **He** is God, other than whom there is no deity, Q59:22–23.
> **huwa** allāhu al-khāliqu al-bāri'u al-muṣawwiru lahu . . . – **He** is God, the creator, the inventor, the fashioner, to Him . . ., Q59:24.
> qul **huwa** allāhu aḥad – Say: '**He** is God', Q112:1.

where the pronoun (**huwa** – He) occurs first before the noun (allāhu – God) to which it refers.

6.5.1.1.1.5 Demonstrative reference Demonstrative pronouns refer to something either nearby or farther away. Demonstratives are words like (hādhā – this (masculine, singular)), (hādihi – this (feminine, singular)), (dhālika – this, that), (ulā'ika – those), and (hā'ulā' – those (masculine, plural)), as in the following examples:

> hādhā rabbī hādhā akbar – This is my lord, this is bigger, Q6:78.
> lā taqrabā hādihi al-shajarata – Do not approach this tree, Q2:35.
> dhālika al-kitābu lā raiba fīh – This is the Book about which there is no doubt, Q2:2.
> ulā'ika hum al-mufliḥun – Those who are the successful, Q2:5.
> famāli hā'ulā' al-qawmi lā yakādūna yafqahūna ḥadīthā? – What is the matter with those people that they can hardly understand any statement?, Q4:78.
> hādhihi jahannamu allatī kuntum tūᶜadūn – This is the hellfire which you were promised, Q36:63.

6.5.1.1.1.6 Extended demonstrative reference There is a semantic difference between a demonstrative reference and an extended demonstrative reference:

> mazzaqa al-muᶜallimu al-kitāba – The teacher tore the book.

(i) hādhā kitābun mufīd – This is a useful book.
(ii) hādhā ᶜamalun aḥmaq – This is foolishness.

Based on the above examples, we can distinguish between the two forms of (hādhā – this). In (i), (hādhā) is a demonstrative reference referring to (kitābun – a book), while in (ii), (hādhā) is an extended reference referring to (tamzīq al-kitāb – the action of tearing the book) rather than (al-kitāba – the book). Examples of extended demonstrative reference are:

> hādhā min ᶜamali al-shaiṭān – This is from the work of Satan, Q28:15.

where the extended demonstrative pronoun (hādhā – this) refers to the action performed by Moses (fawakazahu mūsā faqaḍā ᶜalaih – Moses struck him and killed him, Q28:15).

> hādhā mā tūᶜadūna liyawmi al-ḥisāb – This is what you are promised for the day of account, Q38:53.

where the extended demonstrative pronoun (hādhā – this) refers to (the good final return for the pious, such as paradise and chaste wives, Q38:49–52).

> hādhā mā tūᶜadūna likulli awwābin ḥafīẓ – This is what you were promised – for every returner to God and keeper of His covenant, Q50:32.

where the extended demonstrative pronoun (hādhā – this) refers to paradise which will be brought near to the pious, Q50:31.

6.5.1.1.1.7 Comparative reference Cohesion can also be achieved when two or more things are compared in a text. Comparative reference is concerned with reference words such as (akbar – bigger, greater), (kabīr – big, large), (aṣghar – smaller), (ṣaghīr – small, little), (afḍal – more/most, better), (aqall – fewer, less), (qalīl – little), (kathīr – many, much), (akthar – more, most), (aswa' – worse), (aqall – smaller, less), (kathura – become large, much), as in the following examples:

> ikhrāju ahlihi minhu akbar ᶜinda allāh . . . al-fitnatu akbar min al-qatl – The expulsion of its people therefrom is greater evil in the sight of God . . . The fitnah is greater than killing, Q2:217.
> falammā ra'ā al-shamsa bāzighatan qāla hādhā rabbī hādhā akbar – When he saw the sun rising, he said: 'This is my lord, this is bigger', Q6:78.
> wamā yaᶜzubu ᶜan rabbika min mithqāli dharratin fī al-arḍi walā fī al-samā'i walā aṣghar min dhālika walā akbar illā fī kitābin mubīn – And not absent from your Lord is any part of an atom's weight within the earth or within the heaven or anything smaller than that or bigger but that it is in a clear register, Q10:61, Q34:3.
> walā tas'amū an taktubūhu ṣaghīran aw kabīran ilā ajalih – Do not be too weary to write it, whether it is small or large, Q2:282.
> walā yunfiqūna nafaqatan ṣaghīratan walā kabīratan . . . – Nor do they spend an expenditure, small or large . . ., Q9:121.
> . . . lā yughādiru ṣaghīratan walā kabīratan illā aḥṣāhā – . . . that leaves nothing small or great, Q18:49.
> walā aṣghar min dhālika walā akbar – smaller than that or greater, Q10:61, Q34:3.
> inna kathīran min al-nāsi ᶜan āyātinā laghāfilūn – Indeed, many among the people, of Our signs, are heedless, Q10:92.
> falyaḍḥakū qalīlan walyabkū kathīran – So let them laugh a little and weep much, Q9:82.

lā yashtarūna bi'āyāti allāhi thamanan qalīlā – They do not exchange the āyāt of God for a small price, Q3:199.
anā akthar minka mālan wa a^cazzu nafarā – I am greater than you in wealth and mightier in numbers of men, Q18:34.
anā aqall minka mālan wawaladā – I am less than you in wealth and children, Q18:39.
fasaya^clamūna man aḍ^caf nāṣiran wa aqall ^cadadā – They will know who is weaker in helpers and less in number, Q72:24.
liyukaffira allāhu ^canhum aswa' alladhī ^camilū – That God may remove from them the worst of what they did, Q39:35.
walanujziyannahum aswa' alladhī kānū ya^cmalūn – We will surely recompense them for the worst of what they had been doing, Q41:27.
lil-rijāli naṣībun mimmā taraka al-wālidāni wal-aqrabūna walil-nisā'i naṣībun mimmā taraka al-wālidāni wal-aqrabūna mimmā qalla minhu aw kathura – Men shall have a share in what their parents and closest relatives leave, and women shall have a share in what their parents and closest relatives leave, whether the legacy be small or large, Q4:7.

where (akbar – bigger), (aṣghar – smaller), (ṣaghir – small), (kabīr – large), (aswa' – worst), (qalla – small, little), (qalīl – little), (aqall – less), (kathīr – many), (kathura – large, much), (akthar – greater) are comparative reference words.

Comparative reference is also concerned with comparative sentences in which two things are said to be either the same (mutashābih) or different (mukhtalif), as in:

huwa alladhī ansha'a jannātin ma^crūshātin waghaira ma^crūshātin wal-nakhla wal-zar^ca mukhtalif ukuluhu wal-zaitūna wal-rummāna mutashābih waghaira mutashābih – He it is who causes gardens to grow trellised and untrellised, and palm trees and crops of different kinds of food and olives and pomegranates, similar and different, Q6:141.

where (mukhtalif – different) and (mutashābih – the same, similar) are comparative reference words.

6.5.1.1.2 EXOPHORIC REFERENCE

This is a context-bound reference. In other words, it applies to someone or something that has not been mentioned in the text. However, through the context, we can identify the person or thing which the pronoun refers to and retrieve the information about what a given pronoun specifically refers to.

6.5.1.1.2.1 Generalized exophoric reference In Qur'anic discourse, the generalized exophoric reference is context bound and is represented by the following reference items:

i the reference items (-hi – it (singular masculine), (-hā – it (singular feminine)), and (-t – (singular feminine)), as explained in what follows:

fa'asarrahā yūsufu walam yubdihā – But Joseph kept it within himself and did not reveal it, Q12:77

where the generalized exophoric reference item (-hā) in (fa'asarrahā) and (yubdihā) can be understood through the context of situation as a reference to an underlying item (kalimah – a word), which has not been mentioned in the text.

mā taraka ᶜalaihā min dābbah – He would not have left upon it any creature, Q16:61

where the generalized exophoric reference item (-hā) in (ᶜalaihā) can be understood through the context of situation as a reference to an underlying item (al-arḍ – Earth), which has not been mentioned in the text.

walaw yu'ākhidh allāhu al-nāsa bimā kasabū mā taraka ᶜalā ẓahrihā min dābbah – If God were to impose blame on the people for what they have earned, He would not leave upon it any creature, Q35:45

where the generalized exophoric reference item (-hā) in (ẓahrihā) can be understood through the context of situation as a reference to an underlying item (al-arḍ – Earth), which has not been mentioned in the text.

fa'atharna bihi naqᶜā – Stirring up thereby dust, Q100:4

where the generalized exophoric reference item (-hi) in (bihi) is understood through the context of situation as a reference to an underlying item (al-wādī – the valley), which has not been mentioned in the text. This is because the valley is the place from which dust can be raised.

ḥattā tawārat bil-ḥijāb – until it (i.e., the sun) disappeared into the curtain of darkness, Q38:32

Through the context of situation, the reader/hearer understands that the generalized exophoric reference item (-t) in (tawārat – disappear) refers to the underlying noun (al-shams – the sun).

ii The generalized exophoric reference is also represented by the reference item (aḥad – one), which has a generalized exophoric use in which the referent is treated as being as it were immanent in all contexts of situation (Halliday and Hasan 1976:53). Thus, the generalized exophoric reference needs to be distinguished from the general reference (aḥad – one), which has been discussed in Section 6.5.1.1.2.1. This semantic distinction is due to the fact that the generalized exophoric reference means 'any human individual, i.e., unspecified person' while the general reference means 'one of the two individuals or groups of people' mentioned in the same text. Examples of generalized exophoric reference are:

ayawaddu aḥadukum an takūna lahu jannatun min . . . – Would one of you like to have a garden of . . ., Q2:266

kutiba ᶜalaikum idhā ḥaḍara aḥadukum al-mawtu . . . – Prescribed for you when death approaches any one of you . . ., Q2:180

fa'innī uᶜadhdhibuhu ᶜadhāban lā uᶜadhdhibuhu aḥad min al-ᶜālamīn – Indeed, I will punish him with a punishment by which I have not punished anyone among the worlds, Q5:115

ayuḥibbu aḥadukum an ya'kula laḥma akhīhi maitan fakarihtumūh – Would one of you like to eat the flesh of his brother when dead?, Q49:12

fayawma'idhin lā yuᶜadhdhabu ᶜadhābuhu aḥad – So on that day, none will punish as severely as His (God's) punishment, Q89:25

ᶜālimu al-ghabi falā yuẓhiru ᶜalā ghaibihi aḥad – He is knower of the unseen, and He does not disclose His knowledge of the unseen to anyone, Q72:26

6.5.2 Ellipsis

Ellipsis is a lexicogrammatical relation in which a word is specified through the use of a grammatical signal indicating that it is to be recovered from what has gone before (Halliday and Hasan 1976:308). Between substitution and ellipsis, the difference in meaning is minimal. Semantically, ellipsis and substitution are very close, i.e., ellipsis can be interpreted as a substitution without a substitute. Grammatically, however, the two are different (ibid:92). Ellipsis is the substitution by zero, and substitution is explicit ellipsis (ibid:317). The distinction between substitution and ellipsis is scarcely noticeable and can be treated for practical purposes as a matter of free variation (ibid:318). There are two categories of ellipsis: verbal and nominal. These are discussed in what follows.

6.5.2.1 Verbal ellipsis

Verbal ellipsis deals with ellipsis within the verbal group. Verbal ellipsis is characteristic of responses to yes/no questions, i.e., the verbal proposition is ellipted, as in:

> qāla awalam tu'min? qāla balā – God said: 'Have you not believed?' He (Abraham) said: 'Yes', Q2:260.

where the verbal proposition (u'min – I believe, i.e., I believe in God's ability to give life to the dead) is ellipted from the response.

Another example of verbal ellipsis is encountered in Q7:44:

> wanādā aṣḥābu al-jannati aṣḥāba al-nāri an qad wajadnā mā waᶜadanā rabbunā ḥaqqan fahal wajadtum mā waᶜada rabbukum ḥaqqan? qālū naᶜam – The companions of paradise will call out to the companions of the fire: 'We have already found what our Lord promised us to be true. Have you found what your Lord promised to be true?' They will say: 'Yes', Q7:44.

An elliptical verbal group presupposes one or more words from a previous verbal group (Halliday and Hasan 1976:167). In other words, in the verbal group, there is only the verb itself like (wajada – to find) in the embedded question (hal wajadtum mā wa^{c}ada rabbukum ḥaqqan? – Have you found what your Lord promised to be true?) of the example.

Ellipsis is also characteristic of responses to WH-questions where we have the ellipsis of all elements except the one required, as in:

> hal wajadtum mā wa^{c}ada rabbukum ḥaqqan? qālū na^{c}am – Have you found what your Lord promised to be true? They will say: 'Yes', Q7:44.

where the ellipsis-free sentence is:

> (hal wajadtum mā wa^{c}ada rabbukum ḥaqqan? qālū na^{c}am (wajadnā mā wa^{c}adanā rabbunā ḥaqqan) – Have you found what your Lord promised to be true? They will say: 'Yes, (we have found what our Lord promised us to be true')).
>
> ḥattā idhā jā'athum rusulunā yatawaffawnahum qālū aina mā kuntum tad^{c}ūna min dūn allāh? qālū ḍallū ^{c}annā – Until, when Our angels come to them to take them in death, they will say: 'Where are those you used to invoke besides God?' They will say: 'They have deserted us', Q7:37.

where the WH-question is represented by the interrogative word (aina – where). The sentence which is free from ellipsis is:

> (ḥattā idhā jā'athum rusulunā yatawaffawnahum qālū aina mā kuntum tad^{c}ūna min dūn allāh? qālū (mā kānū yad^{c}ūna min dūni allāhi) ḍallū ^{c}annā – Until, when Our angels come to them to take them in death, they will say: 'Where are those you used to invoke besides God?' They will say: 'They (who used to invoke besides God) have deserted us').
>
> a'idhā mitnā wakunnā turāban wa^{c}iẓāman a'innā lamab^{c}ūthun? awa'ābā'unā al-awwalūn? qul na^{c}am – When we have died and become dust and bones, are we indeed to be resurrected? And our forefathers as well? Say: 'Yes', Q37:16–18.

where we have two WH-questions through the interrogative particle (a), whose answer is by (na^{c}am – Yes), and the ellipted elements represent clauses (a'idhā mitnā wakunnā turāban wa^{c}iẓāman a'innā lamab^{c}ūthun – When we have died and become dust and bones, are we indeed to be resurrected) and (awa'ābā'unā al-awwalūn? – And our forefathers as well?).

To bring back the ellipted clauses, we get the following ellipsis-free statement:

> (a'idhā mitnā wakunnā turāban wa^{c}iẓāman a'innā lamab^{c}ūthun? awa'ābā'unā al-awwalūn? qul na^{c}am (satub^{c}athūn/annakum lamab^{c}ūthūn idhā mittum

wakuntum turāban wa^ciẓāman) (wasayub^cathu ābā'ukum al-awwalūn) – When we have died and become dust and bones, are we indeed to be resurrected? And our forefathers as well? Say: 'Yes, (you will be resurrected when you have died and become dust and bones) (and your forefathers will be resurrected as well')).

6.5.2.2 Nominal ellipsis

Nominal ellipsis deals with how a noun, a noun phrase, or an adjective is ellipted. Let us consider the following examples:

> tilka ᶜasharatun kāmilatun – Those are ten complete, Q2:196.

where the noun (aiyām – days) is ellipted and the expected grammatical structure is: (tilka ᶜasharatu (aiyām) kāmilatun – Those are ten complete (days)).

> qul hal unabbi'ukum basharrin min dhālika mathūbatan ᶜinda allāh? – Say: 'Shall I inform you of what is worse than that as penalty from God?', Q5:60.

where the ellipted noun phrase is (yā ahla al-kitāb – O People of the Book). Thus, the non-elliptical sentence is: (qul (yā ahla al-kitāb) hal unabbi'ukum basharrin min dhālika mathūbatan ᶜinda allāh? – Say: '(O People of the Book) Shall I inform you of what is worse than that as penalty from God?').

> kāna warā'ahum malikun ya'khudhu kulla safinatin ghaṣbā – There was after them a king who seized every ship by force, Q18:79.

where there is an ellipted adjective (ṣāliḥatin – good, i.e., in a good seaworthy condition). The non-elliptical sentence structure is: (kāna warā'ahum malikun ya'khudhu kulla safīnatin (ṣāliḥatin) ghaṣbā – There was after them a king who seized every (good) ship by force).

> yaqūlūna matā hādhā al-waᶜdu in kuntum ṣādiqīn? qul ᶜasā an yakūna radifa lakum baᶜḍa alladhī tastaᶜjilūn – They say: 'When is this promise, if you should be truthful?' Say: 'Perhaps it is close behind you – some of that for which you are impatient', Q27:71–72.

where the noun (al-ᶜadhāb – punishment) is ellipted. The non-ellipted sentence structure is: (qul ᶜasā an yakūna radifa lakum baᶜḍa (al-ᶜadhāb) alladhī tastaᶜjilūn – They say: 'When is this promise, if you should be truthful?' Say: 'Perhaps it is close behind you – some of (the punishment) for which you are impatient'). This is intertextually related to Q29:54 (yastaᶜjilūnaka bil-ᶜadhāb – They urge you to hasten the punishment).

qul man rabbu al-samāwāti wal-arḍ? qul allāh – Say: 'Who is the Lord of the heavens and earth?' Say: 'God', Q13:16.

where the noun phrase (rabbu al-samāwāti wal-arḍ – the Lord of the heavens and earth) is ellipted and the non-elliptical sentence is: (qul allāh rabbu al-samāwāti wal-arḍ – Say: 'God is (the Lord of the heavens and earth')).

yaqūlūna matā hādhā al-wa^cdu in kuntum ṣādiqīn? qul innamā al-^cilmu ^cinda allāh – They say: 'When is this promise, if you should be truthful?' Say: 'The knowledge is only with God', Q67:25–26.

where the ellipted noun phrase is: (bihādhā al-wa^cdi – this promise). Thus, the ellipsis-free sentence is: (qul innamā al-^cilmu (bihadhā al-wa^cdi) ^cinda allāh – Say: 'The knowledge of (this promise) is only with God').

6.5.2.3 Clausal ellipsis

Clausal ellipsis is concerned with how a verbal clause is ellipted. Let us consider the following examples:

yas'alūnaka mādha yunfiqūn? qul al-^cafwa – They ask you what they should spend. Say: 'The excess', Q2:219.

where the verbal clause (yunfiqūn) is ellipted. This is treated as a verbal clause because we have the verb (yunfiq – to spend) + the plural subject pronoun (-ūn – they (masculine)). Thus, the non-elliptical sentence is: (yas'alūnaka mādhā yunfiqūn? qul (yunfiqūn) al-^cafwa – They ask you what they should spend. Say: '(They spend) the excess').

qul man biyadihi malakūtu kulli shai'in wa huwa yujīru wa lā yujāru ^calaih in kuntum ṣādiqīn? sayaqūlūna lillāh – Say: 'In whose hand is the realm of all things – and He protects while none can protect against Him – if you should know?' They will say: 'To God', Q23:88–89.

where the ellipted verbal clause is (malakūtu kulli shai'in wa huwa yujīru wa lā yujāru ^calaih). Thus, the non-elliptical sentence should be: (sayaqūlūna ('biyadihi malakūtu kulli shai'in wa huwa yujīru wa lā yujāru ^calaih') lillāh – They will say: ('In His hand is the realm of all things – and He protects while none can protect against Him')).

wala'in sa'altahum man khalaqa al-samāwāti wal-arḍa layaqūlunna allāhu – If you ask them: 'Who created the heavens and earth?' They would surely say: 'God', Q31:25.

where the ellipted verbal clause is (khalaqahunna – they were created). Thus, the non-elliptical sentence structure should be: (wala'in sa'altahum man khalaqa al-samāwati wal-arḍa layaqulūnna (khalaqahunna) allāhu – If you ask them: 'Who created the heavens and earth?' They would surely say: ('They were created by) God').

> yā abatī innī qad jā'anī min al-ᶜilmi mā lam ya'tika fattabiᶜnī ahdika ṣirāṭan sawiyyā – O my father, indeed there has come to me of knowledge that which has not come to you, so follow me; I will guide you to an even path, Q19:43.

This is a conditional sentence where (in – if) is the conditional particle. The conditional sentence, i.e., the protasis (jumlat al-sharṭ), is (in tattabiᶜanī – if you follow me), but it is ellipted. It should have occurred after the imperative verb (fattabiᶜnī – Therefore, follow me). Thus, we can have a non-elliptical conditional sentence: (yā abatī innī qad jā'anī min al-ᶜilmi mā lam ya'tika fattabiᶜnī (in tattabiᶜnī) ahdika ṣirāṭan sawiyyā – O my father, indeed there has come to me of knowledge that which has not come to you, so follow me; (if you follow me), I will guide you to an even path). Thus, the apodosis (jawāb al-sharṭ) is (ahdika ṣirāṭan sawiyyā – I will guide you to an even path). For clarification, we say:

> The conditional sentence (the protasis (jumlat al-sharṭ)) is (in tattabiᶜanī – if you follow me) + the apodosis (jawāb al-sharṭ), which is (ahdika ṣirāṭan sawiyyā – I will guide you to an even path).
>
> in yukadhdhibūka faqad kudhdhibat rusulun min qablika – If they disbelieve you (O Muḥammad) – the messengers before you were already denied, Q35:4.

This is also a conditional sentence whose protasis (jumlat al-sharṭ) is (in yukadhdhibūka – if they disbelieve you). However, its apodosis (jawāb al-sharṭ) is ellipted. The ellipted apodosis is (faṣbir – be patient). Therefore, the non-elliptical conditional sentence structure is (in yukadhdhibūka (faṣbir) faqad kudhdhibat rusulun min qablika – If they disbelieve you, (be patient); the messengers before you were already denied).

> afaman sharaḥa allāhu ṣadrahu lil-islām fahuwa ᶜalā nūrin min rabbihi fawailun lil-qāsiyati qulūbuhum min dhikr allāh – So is the one whose heart God has opened and he is guided by a light from his Lord? Alas for those whose hearts are hardened against the mention of God, Q39:22.

where the ellipted verbal clause is (kaman qasā qalbuhu – like the one whose hear has hardened), which should have occurred after the noun (rabbihi – his Lord). Thus, the non-elliptical sentence structure should be: (afaman sharaḥa allāhu ṣadrahu lil-islām fahuwa ᶜalā nūrin min rabbihi (kaman qasa qalbuhu) fawailun lil-qāsiyati qulūbuhum min dhikr allāh – So is the one whose heart God has opened and he is guided by a light from his Lord (like the one whose hear has hardened)? Alas for those whose hearts are hardened against the mention of God).

6.5.3 Substitution

Substitution is a process within the text which indicates the replacement of one item by another to avoid repetition. It is the most strictly cohesive relation, a purely textual relation whose major function is to cohere one piece of text to another (Halliday and Hasan 1976:226). Substitution is a lexicogrammatical cohesive relation in which a word is specified through the use of a grammatical signal indicating that it is to be recovered from what has gone before. The lexicogrammatical level is the level of grammar and vocabulary. Thus, substitution is similar, in a way, to ellipsis because the two are the same process. Because ellipsis is a kind of substitution, it is also on the lexicogrammatical level. However, substitution is the replacement of one item by another, while ellipsis is the omission of an item, i.e., ellipsis is a form of substitution in which the item is replaced by nothing, i.e., ellipsis is substitution by zero. Although the two are the same process, substitution and ellipsis involve different mechanisms (Halliday and Hasan 1976:88–89, 308).

Substitution is a relation in the wording rather than in the meaning. It is a relation between linguistic items, such as words or phrases. However, reference is a relation between meanings where the recoverability of meaning is derived from the environment. Thus, reference is a relation on the semantic level, i.e., the cohesion lies in the semantic identity, whereas substitution is a relation on the lexicogrammatical level (of grammar and vocabulary) (ibid:88–89). For Halliday and Hasan (ibid:145), substitution is essentially a textual relation; it exists primarily as an anaphoric or cataphoric device.

6.5.3.1 Types of substitution

We have said earlier that substitution is a lexicogrammatical relation, i.e., a relation in the wording rather than in the meaning. Therefore, the different types of substitution are defined grammatically rather than semantically (Halliday and Hasan 1976:90). In Qur'anic discourse, we encounter two types of substitution. In Qur'anic discourse, the substitute may function either as a noun or as a clause. Thus, we have (i) nominal substitution and (ii) clausal substitution. A substitute has the same grammatical function as that for which it is substituting.

It is worthwhile to note that English has verbal substitution through the verbal substitutes (do, be, have). However, Arabic does not have verbal substitution. This is due to the linguistic fact that Arabic does not have verbal substitutes. Instead, Arabic favours to reiterate (repeat) the main verb, as in:

> wamā kafara sulaimānu walākinna al-shayāṭīna kafarū – It was not Solomon who disbelieved but the devils did, Q2:102.

where the verb (kafara – disbelieved) is repeated at the end of the sentence, while English employs the linguistic mechanism of verbal substitution through the verbal substitute (did). The same applies to the English verbal substitute (be (am, is, are, was, were)) and (have (has, have, had)). An alternative translation of Q2:102 is to have the verb (kafara) translated to (has disbelieved) or to a noun (disbeliever):

> wamā kafara sulaimānu walākinna al-shayāṭīna kafarū – It is not Solomon who has disbelieved but the devils have, Q2:102.
>
> wamā kafara sulaimānu walākinna al-shayāṭīna kafarū – It was not Solomon who was a disbeliever but the devils were, Q2:102.

Thus, while English has the linguistic mechanism of verbal substitution through the verbs (have) and (were) at the end of the sentence, Qur'anic Arabic reiterates the first verb (kafara). The observation that can be made here is that the linguistic verbal (kafara – disbelieved, has disbelieved) or nominal (kāfir – disbeliever) element is not repeated in English but is replaced by a substitution item (do), (has), or (be).

Also, in:

> ulā'ika yalᶜanuhum allāhu wa yalᶜanuhum al-lāᶜinūn – God rejects them, and so do others, Q2:159.

where the verb (yalᶜanu – to curse) is reiterated.

Similarly in:

> . . . fastamtaᶜū bikhalāqihim fastamtaᶜtum bikhalāqikum kamā istamtaᶜa alladhīna min qablikum bikhālaqihim wakhuḍtum kalladhī khāḍū – They have enjoyed their portion and you have enjoyed your portion as those before you enjoyed their portion, and you have engaged like that in which they engaged, Q9:69.

where Arabic repeats the verbs with their objects (fastamtaᶜū bikhalāqihim – they have enjoyed their portion) → (fastamtaᶜtum bikhalāqikum – you have enjoyed your portion) → (istamtaᶜa alladhīna min qablikum bikhālaqihim – those before you have enjoyed their portion), and (wakhuḍtum – you have engaged) → (khāḍū – they have engaged).

> wa'alqi mā fī yamīnika talqaf mā ṣanaᶜū innamā ṣanaᶜū kaidu sāḥir – Throw down what is in your right hand; it will swallow up what they have produced. They have only done the tricks of a sorcerer, Q20:69.

where the verb (ṣanaᶜū – to produce) is repeated in Q20:69 but is substituted in English by the verb (to do):

> innamā <u>ṣanaᶜū</u> kaidu sāḥir – They have only <u>done</u> the tricks of a sorcerer.
>
> faqḍi mā anta qāḍin innamā taqḍī hādhihi al-ḥayāta al-dunyā – So decide whatever you will. You can only decide matters of this present life, Q20:72.

where the verb (aqḍi – to decide) is repeated in Q20:72 but is substituted in English by the verb (to do):

> faqḍi mā anta qāḍin innamā taqḍi hādhihi al-ḥayāta al-dunyā – So decide whatever you will. You can only do so for the matters of this present life.
>
> bal kadhdhabū bil-sāᶜati wa'aᶜtadnā liman kadhdhaba bil-sāᶜati saᶜīrā – But they have denied the hour and We (God) have prepared for those who deny the hour a blaze, Q25:11.

where the verb (kadhdhaba – to deny) is repeated in Q25:11, but in English it is substituted by the verb (to do):

> . . . wa'aᶜtadnā liman kadhdhaba bil-sāᶜati saᶜīrā – . . . and We (God) have prepared for those who have done so a blaze.
>
> . . . rabbanā hā'ulā'i alladhīna aghwainā aghwaināhum kamā ghawainā – 'Our lord, these are the ones we caused to deviate. We caused them to deviate as we ourselves did', Q28:63.

where the verb (aghwā/ghawā – to deviate) is repeated in Q28:63, but in English it is substituted by the verb (to do).

> in tadᶜuhum lā yasmaᶜū duᶜā'akum walaw samiᶜū mā istajābū lakum – If you call them, they cannot hear you. If they could, they wouldn't answer you, Q35:14.

where the verb (yasmaᶜ – to hear) is reiterated, while in English it is substituted by the auxiliary verb (could).

> man tazakkā fa'innamā yatazakkā linafsih – Whoever purifies himself does so for his own benefit, Q35:18.

where the verb (yatazakkā – to purify) is reiterated, while in English it is substituted by the auxiliary verb (do).

6.5.3.1.1 NOMINAL SUBSTITUTION

The nominal substitutes are like the demonstrative pronoun (hādhā – this), the personal pronoun (huwa – he), the demonstrative pronoun (ulā'ika – those), a general word, and the pronoun (-hum – they) attached to the auxiliary verb (inna). Examples of nominal substitution are:

> jannātu ᶜadnin mufattaḥatan lahum al-abwāb . . . ᶜindahum qāṣirātu al-ṭarfi atrāb. **hādhā** mā tūᶜadūna liyawmi al-ḥisāb . . . – Gardens of perpetual residence whose doors will be opened to them. With them will be women limiting their glances and of equal age . . . **This** is what you are promised for the day of account, Q38:50–53.

where the demonstrative pronoun (hādhā – this) substitutes for the no-main-verb nominal sentences (jannātu ᶜadnin mufattaḥatan lahum al-abwāb – Gardens of perpetual residence whose doors will be opened to them) and (ᶜindahum qāṣirātu al-ṭarfi atrāb – With them will be women limiting their glances and of equal age).

> inna lil-ṭāghīna la sharra ma'āb . . . **jahannama** yaṣlawnahā – Indeed, for the transgressors is an evil place of return – **hell**, in which they will burn, Q38:55–56.

where the general word (jahannama – hell) substitutes for the noun phrase (sharra ma'āb – an evil place of return).

> wal-qur'ān dhi al-dhikr . . . **huwa** naba'un ᶜaẓīmum . . . in **huwa** illā dhikrun lil-ᶜālamīn – By the Qur'an containing reminder . . . **It** is great news . . . **It** is but a reminder to the world, Q38:1, 67 and 87.

The above text includes nominal substitution where the pronoun (huwa – it) substitutes for the noun phrase (al-qur'ān dhi al-dhikr – the Qur'an containing reminder). If we bring back what the pronoun (huwa) has substituted, the result will be the following text that lacks both cohesion and coherence:

> (al-qur'ān dhi al-dhikr . . . (**al-qur'ān dhi al-dhikr**) naba'un ᶜaẓimum . . . in (**al-qur'ān dhi al-dhikr**) illā dhikrun lil-ᶜālamin – By the Qur'an containing reminder . . .
>
> {**The Qur'an containing reminder**} is great news . . . (**The Qur'an containing reminder**) is but a reminder to the world).

al-sābiqūn al-sābiqun. **ulā'ika** al-muqarrabūn – The forerunners, the forerunners. **Those** are the ones brought near to God, Q56:10–11. This is a cohesive sentence which involves nominal substitution where the demonstrative pronoun (ulā'ika – those) substitutes for the noun phrase (al-sābiqūn al-sābiqūn – the forerunners, the forerunners). To bring back to the text what substitution has replaced will lead to lack of cohesion and coherence, as can be observed in the following text:

> (al-sābiqūn al-sābiqūn. (**al-sābiqūn al-sābiqūn**) al-muqarrabūn – The forerunners, the forerunners. (**The forerunners, the forerunners**) are the ones brought near to God).
>
> aṣḥābu al-shimāli mā aṣḥābu al-shimāl. fī samūmin waḥamīm. waẓillin min yaḥmūm. lā bāridin walā karīm. inna**hum** kānū qabla dhālika mutrafīn – The companions of the left – what are the companions of the left? They will be in scorching fire and scalding water, and a shade of black smoke, neither cool nor beneficial. Indeed, **they** were, before that, indulging in affluence, Q56:41–45.

where the masculine third person plural pronoun (-hum – they), which is attached to (inna), substitutes for the noun phrase (aṣḥābu al-shimāli – the companions of the left).

> mathalu al-jannati allatī wu^c^ida al-muttaqūn tajrī min taḥtihā al-anhāru ukuluhā dā'imun wa ẓilluhā **tilka** ^c^uqbā aladhīna ittaqaw – The example of paradise which the righteous have been promised is that beneath it rivers flow. Its fruit is lasting, and its shade. **That** is the consequence for the righteous, Q13:35.

where the demonstrative pronoun (tilka – that) substitutes for the noun (al-jannati – paradise).

6.5.3.1.2 CLAUSAL SUBSTITUTION

In clausal substitution, the presupposed is not a single word or a noun phrase but rather a whole clause with a main verb. The clausal substitutes are like the demonstrative pronoun (dhālika – that), the personal pronoun (ulā'ika –), the demonstrative pronoun (hādhā – this), the pronoun (huwa – he), and the pronoun (hā'ulā' – those). Let us consider the following examples:

> zuyyina lil-nāsi ḥubbu al-shahawāti min al-nisā'i wal-banīna wal-qanāṭīri al-muqantarati min al-dhahabi wal-fiḍḍati wal-khaili al-musawwamati wal-an^c^āmi wal-ḥarthi **dhālika** matā^c^u al-ḥayāti al-dunyā – Beautified for people is the love of that which they desire – of women and sons, heaped-up sums of gold and silver, fine branded horses, and cattle and tilled land. **That** is the enjoyment of worldly life, Q3:14.

where the demonstrative pronoun (dhālika – that) substitutes for the clause (ḥubbu al-shahawāti min al-nisā'i wal-banīna wal-qanāṭīri al-muqantarati min al-dhahabi wal-fiḍḍati wal-khaili al-musawwamati wal-an^c^āmi wal-ḥarthi – the love of that which they desire – of women and sons, heaped-up sums of gold and silver, fine branded horses, and cattle and tilled land).

> yā aiyuhā alladhīna āmanū lā tulhikum amwālukum wa lā awlādukum ^c^an dhikr allāh wa man yaf^c^al **dhālika** fa'ulā'ika hum al-khāsirūn – O you who have believed, let not your wealth and your children divert you from the remembrance of God. Whoever does **that** – then those are the losers, Q63:9).

where the demonstrative pronoun (dhālika – that) substitutes for the clause (lā tulhikum amwālukum wa lā awlādukum ^c^an dhikr allāh – let not your wealth and your children divert you from the remembrance of God).

> lā taj^c^al ma^c^a allāhi ilāhan ākhara . . . waqaḍā rabbuka allā ta^c^budū illā iyyāhu wabil-wālidaini iḥsānā . . . falā taqul lahumā uffin walā tanharhumā waqul lahumā qawlan karīmā wakhfiḍ lahumā janāḥa al-dhulli min al-raḥmati waqul rabbī irḥamhumā kamā rabbayānī ṣaghīrā . . . wa'āti dhā al-qurbā ḥaqqahu wal-miskīna . . . walā taj^c^al yadaka maghlūlatan ilā ^c^unuqika . . . walā taqtulū

awlādakum khashyata imlāqin . . . walā taqrabū al-zinā . . . lā taqtulū al-nafsa allatī ḥarrama allāhu illā bil-ḥaqq . . . lā taqrabū māla al-yatīmi illā billatī hiya aḥsan . . . ūfū bil-cahdi . . . ūfū al-kaila . . . lā taqfu mā laisa laka bihi ᶜilm . . . lā tamshī fī al-arḍi maraḥan . . . kullu **dhālika** kāna saiyi'uhu ᶜinda rabbika makrūhā. **dhālika** mimmā awḥā ilaika rabbuka min al-ḥikmati – Do not make as equal with God another deity . . . Your Lord has decreed that you not worship except Him, and to parents, good treatment . . . Do not say to them so much as 'uff' and do not repel them but speak to them a noble word. Lower to them the wing of humility out of mercy and say: 'My Lord, have mercy upon them as they brought me up when I was small' . . . Give the relative his right and the poor . . . Do not make your hand chained to your neck . . . Do not kill your children for fear of poverty . . . Do not approach unlawful sexual intercourse . . . Do not kill the soul which God has forbidden, except by right . . . Do not approach the property of an orphan, except in the way that is best . . . Fulfil commitment . . . Give full measure . . . Do not pursue that of which you have no knowledge . . . Do not walk upon the earth exultantly . . . All **that** (i.e., the aforementioned) – its evil is ever destroyed in the sight of your Lord. **That** is from what your Lord has revealed to you, (O Muḥammad), of wisdom, Q17:22–39.

where the demonstrative pronouns (dhālika – that) substitute for all the clauses that have been said before in Q17:22–37.

i'itūnī zubura al-ḥadīd ḥattā idhā sāwā baina al-ṣadafain qāla infukhū ḥattā idhā jaᶜalahu nāran qāla i'tūni ufrigh ᶜalaihi qiṭrā. famā isṭāᶜū an yaẓharūhu wamā isṭatāᶜū lahu naqbā. qāla **hādhā** raḥmatan min rabbī – 'Bring me sheets of iron' – until, when he had levelled them between the two mountain walls, he said: 'Blow with bellows' until when he had made it like fire, he said: 'Bring me, that I may pour over it molten copper'. So they (i.e., Gog and Magog) were unable to pass over it, nor were they able to effect in it any penetration. (Dhu al-Qarnain) said: '**This** is a mercy from my Lord', Q18:96–98.

where the demonstrative pronoun (hādhā – this) substitutes for the clauses (i'itūnī zubura al-ḥadīd ḥattā idhā sāwā baina al-ṣadafain qāla infukhū ḥattā idhā jaᶜalahu nāran qāla i'tūni ufrigh ᶜalaihi qiṭrā – 'Bring me sheets of iron' – until, when he had levelled them between the two mountain walls, he said: 'Blow with bellows' until when he had made it like fire, he said: 'Bring me, that I may pour over it molten copper'), (famā isṭāᶜū an yaẓharūhu – were unable to pass over it) and (wamā istaṭāᶜū lahu naqbā – nor were they able to effect in it any penetration).

hal tanqamūna minā illā an āmannā billāhi wamā unzila ilainā wamā unzila min qablu . . . qul hal unabbi'ukum bisharrin min **dhālika** mathūbatan ᶜinda allāh man laᶜanahu allāhu waghaḍiba ᶜalaihi wajaᶜala minhum al-qiradata wal-khanāzīra waᶜabada al-ṭāghūta **ulā'ika** sharrun makānan wa'aḍallu ᶜan sawā' al-sabīl – Do you resent us except for the fact that we have believed in God

> and what was revealed to us and what was revealed before . . . Say: 'Shall I inform you of what is worse than **that** as penalty from God? It is that of those whom God has cursed and with whom He became angry and made of them apes and pigs and slaves of ṭāghūt. **Those** are worse in position and further astray from the sound way', Q5:59–60.

where the demonstrative pronoun (dhālika – that) substitutes for the clause (āmannā billāhi wamā unzila ilainā wamā unzila min qablu – we have believed in God and what was revealed to us and what was revealed before). However, the pronoun (ula'ika – those) substitutes for the clauses (man laᶜanahu allāhu – those whom God has cursed) and (waghaḍiba ᶜalaihi wajaᶜala minhum al-qiradata wal-khanāzīra waᶜabada al-ṭāghūta – with whom He became angry and made of them apes and pigs and slaves of ṭāghūt).

> alladhīna āmanū waᶜamilū al-saliḥāti fī rawḍāti al-jannāti lahum mā yashā'ūna ᶜinda rabbihim **dhālika** huwa al-faḍlu al-kabīr – Those who have believed and done righteous deeds will be in lush regions of paradise having whatever they will in the presence of their Lord. **That** is what is the great bounty, Q42:22.

where (dhālika – that) substitutes for the clause (fī rawḍāti al-jannāti lahum mā yashā'ūna ᶜinda rabbihim – in lush regions of paradise having whatever they will in the presence of their Lord).

> la'ākilūna min shajarin min zaqqūm. famāli'ūna minhā al-buṭūn. fashāribūna ᶜalaihi min al-ḥamīm. fashāribūna shurba al-hīm. **hādhā** nuzuluhum yawma al-dīn – You will be eating from trees of zaqqūm, and filling with it your bellies, and drinking on top of it from scalding water, and will drink as the drinking of thirsty camels. **This** is their accommodation on the day of recompense, Q56:52–56.

where (hādhā – this) substitutes for the clauses (la'ākilūna min shajarin min zaqqūm – You will be eating from trees of zaqqūm), (famāli'ūna minhā al-buṭūn – filling with it your bellies), (fashāribūna ᶜalaihi min al-ḥamīm – drinking on top of it from scalding water), and (fashāribūna shurba al-hīm – and will drink as the drinking of thirsty camels).

> wa huwa alladhī yabda'u al-khalqa thumma yuᶜīduh wa **huwa** ahwanu ᶜalaih – It is He who begins creation; then He repeats it, and **that** is easier for Him, Q30:27.

where (huwa – this, that) substitutes for the clause (yabda'u al-khalqa thumma yuᶜīduh – He begins creation then He repeats it).

> fa'āti dhā al-qurbā ḥaqqahu wal-miskīna wa ibn al-sabīl **dhālika** khairun lilladhīna yurīdūna wajha allāh wa **ulā'ika hum** al-mufliḥūn – So, give the

relative his right, as well as the needy and the traveller. **That** is best for those who desire the countenance of God, and **it** is **they** who will be the successful, Q30:38.

where (dhālika – that) substitutes for the clause (fa'āti dhā al-qurbā ḥaqqahu wal-miskīna wa ibn al-sabīl – So, give the relative his right, as well as the needy and the traveller) and the demonstrative pronoun (ulā'ika – those) and the detached pronoun (hum – they) substitute for (alladhīna yurīdūna wajha allāh – who desire the countenance of God). The same applies to (mā ātaitum min zakātin turīdūna wajha allāh – What you give in zakāt desiring the countenance of God, Q30:39).

allāhu alladhī khalaqakum thumma razaqakum thumma yumītukum thumma yuḥyīkum hal min shurakā'ikum man yafᶜal **dhālikum** min shai' – God is the one who created you, then provided for you, then will cause you to die, and then will give you life. Are there any of your partners who does anything of **that**?, Q30:40.

where (dhālikum – that) substitutes for the clause (khalaqakum thumma razaqakum thumma yumītukum thumma yuḥyīkum – created you, then provided for you, then will cause you to die, and then will give you life).

wahal atāka naba'u al-khaṣmi idh tasawwarū al-miḥrāb idh dakhalū ᶜalā dāwūda fafaziᶜa minhum . . . inna hādhā akhī lahu tisᶜun watisᶜūna naᶜjatan waliya naᶜjatun wāḥidatun faqāla akfilnīhā waᶜazzanī fī al-khiṭāb qāla laqad ẓalamaka bisu'āli naᶜjatika ilā niᶜājih wa'inna kathīran min al-khulaṭā'i layabghī baᶜḍuhum ᶜalā baᶜḍin . . . waẓanna dāwūdu annamā fatannāhu fastaghfara rabbahu wakharra rākiᶜan wa'anāb faghafarnā lahu **dhālika** – Has there come to you the news of the adversaries when they climbed over the wall of his prayer chamber – when they entered upon David and he was alarmed by them? They said: 'Fear not. We are two adversaries, one of whom has wronged the other, so judge between us with truth and do not exceed it and guide us to the sound path. Indeed this, my brother, has ninety-nine ewes and I have one ewe; so he said: "Entrust her to me" and he overpowered me in speech'. David said: 'He has certainly wronged you in demanding your ewe in addition to his ewes. Indeed, many associates oppress one another, except for those who believe and do righteous deeds – and few are they'. David became certain that We had tried him, and he asked forgiveness of his Lord and fell down bowing in prostration and turned in repentance to God. So We forgave him **that**, Q38:21–25.

where (dhālika – that) substitutes for the clause (laqad ẓalamaka bisu'āli naᶜjatika ilā niᶜājih wa'inna kathīran min al-khulaṭā'i layabghī baᶜḍuhum ᶜalā baᶜḍin – 'He has certainly wronged you in demanding your ewe in addition to his ewes. Indeed, many associates oppress one another').

> man kāna yurīdu al-cājilata cajjalnā lahu fīhā . . . man arāda al-ākhirata wa sacā lahā sacyahā wahuwa mu'minun . . . kullan numiddu **hā'ulā'** wa **hā'ulā'** – Whoever should desire the fleeting life – We speed up whatever We will in it . . . Whoever desires the hereafter and exerts the effort due to it while he is a believer . . . To each We extend – to **those** and to **those**, Q17:18–20) where the first (hā'ulā' – those) substitutes for the clause (man kāna yurīdu al-cājilata – whoever should desire the fleeting life) but the second (hā'ulā' – those) substitutes for the clause (man arāda al-ākhirata wa sacā lahā sacyahā wahuwa mu'minun – whoever desires the hereafter and exerts the effort due to it while he is a believer).

According to Halliday and Hasan (1976:91), there is a borderline where substitution shades into lexical cohesion involving the use of general words like (dhālika – that) in a cohesive function, as in the following examples:

> wamin āyātihi an khalaqa lakum min anfusikum azwājan litaskunū ilaihā wajacal bainakum mawaddatan waraḥmatan inna fī **dhālika** la'āyāt liqawmin yatafakkarūn – Of His signs is that He created for you from yourselves mates that you may find tranquility in them; and He placed between you affection and mercy. Indeed, in **that** are signs for a people who give thought, Q30:21.
> wamin āyātihi khalqu al-samāwāti wal-arḍi wakhtilāfi alsinatikum wa'alwānikum inna fī **dhālika** la'āyāt lil-cālimīn – Of His signs is the creation of the heavens and the earth and the diversity of your languages and your colours. Indeed, in **that** are signs for those of knowledge, Q30:22.
> wamin āyātihi manāmukum bil-laili wal-nahāri wabtighā'ikum min faḍlih inna fi **dhālika** la'āyāt liqawmin yasmacūn – Of His signs is your sleep by night and day and your seeking of His bounty. Indeed, in **that** are signs for a people who listen, Q30:23.
> wamin āyātihi yurīkum al-barqa khawfan waṭamacan wayunazzilu min al-samā'i mā'an fayuḥyī bihi al-arḍa bacda mawtihā inna fī **dhālika** la'āyāt liqawmin yacqilūn – Of His signs is that He shows you the lighting causing fear and aspiration, and He sends down rain from the sky by which He brings to life the earth after its lifelessness. Indeed, in **that** are signs for a people who use reason, Q30:24.

where in sentence (21), (dhālika – that) substitutes for the clauses (khalaqa lakum min anfusikum azwājan litaskunū ilaihā – He created for you from yourselves mates that you may find tranquility in them) and (wajacal bainakum mawaddatan waraḥmatan – and He placed between you affection and mercy), in (22), (dhālika) substitutes for the clauses (khalqu al-samāwāti wal-arḍi – the creation of the heavens and the earth) and (wakhtilāfi alsinatikum wa'alwānikum – the diversity of your languages and your colours), in (23), (dhālika) substitutes for the clauses (manāmukum bil-laili wal-nahāri – your sleep by night and day) and (wabtighā'ikum min faḍlih – and your seeking of

His bounty), and in (24), (dhālika) substitutes for the clauses (yurīkum al-barqa khawfan waṭamaᶜan – He shows you the lighting causing fear and aspiration) and (wayunazzilu min al-samā'i mā'an fayuḥyī bihi al-arḍa baᶜda mawtihā – He sends down rain from the sky by which He brings to life the earth after its lifelessness).

> al-shamsu tajrī limustaqarrin lahā **dhālika** taqdīru al-ᶜazīz al-ᶜalīm – The sun runs on course toward its stopping point. **That** is the determination of the exalted in might, the knowing, Q36:38.

where (dhālika – that) substitutes the main verb nominal sentence (al-shamsu tajrī limustaqarrin lahā – the sun runs on course toward its stopping point).

> alladhīna yastaḥibbūna al-ḥayāta al-dunyā ᶜalā al-ākhirati wa yaṣuddūna ᶜan sabīl allāh wa yabghūnahā ᶜiwajan **ulā'ika** fī ḍalālin baᶜīd – The ones who prefer the worldly life over the hereafter and avert people from the way of God, trying to make it crooked. **Those** are in extreme error, Q14:3.

where the demonstrative pronoun (ulā'ika – those) substitutes the clause (alladhīna yastaḥibbūna al-ḥayāta al-dunyā ᶜalā al-ākhirati wa yaṣuddūna ᶜan sabīl allāh wa yabghūnahā ᶜiwajan – The ones who prefer the worldly life over the hereafter and avert people from the way of God, trying to make it crooked).

6.5.4 Conjunction

Conjunction is a type of cohesive semantic relation but is not an anaphoric relation. Thus, it is different from reference, substitution, and ellipsis (Halliday and Hasan 1976:226, 228). Conjunction represents forms of systematic relationships between sentences (Halliday and Hasan 1976:320). Thus, conjunction is a process that keeps words and sentences semantically connected. In other words, conjunctive relations are text-forming relations. For Salkie (1995:xi), conjunctive (cohesive) devices are one of the factors in making a text coherent and are a good place to start the study of text and discourse.

A variety of labels were used in literature to express words with a similar function to that of the discourse connectives: cue phrases (Knott and Dale 1994), discourse connectives (Blakemore 1987, 1992), discourse operators (Redeker 1991), discourse particles (Schorup 1985), discourse signalling devices (Polanyi and Scha 1983), pragmatic connectives (Stubbs 1983), pragmatic markers (Fraser 2009), semantic conjuncts (Quirk et al. 1985), and sentence connectives (Halliday and Hasan 1976).

In Qur'anic discourse, the conjunctive adjunct usually occurs sentence-initially and has as its domain the whole of the sentence; thus, its meaning extends over the entire sentence, as in:

> min ajli dhālika katabnā ᶜalā banī isrā'īla annahu man qatala nafsan bighairi nasin . . . – Because of that, We (God) decreed upon the Children of Israel that whoever kills a soul unless for a soul . . ., Q5:32.

In Qur'anic discourse, we encounter two kinds of conjunctive adjuncts (cf. Halliday and Hasan 1976:231):

i simple adverbs (coordinating conjunctions) like (walākin – but), (lihādhā – so), (thumma – then), and
ii compound adverbs (prepositional expressions) like (lihādhā/ᶜalaihi – therefore, thereupon), (min ajli dhālik/bisababi dhālik – whereat, because of that, Q5:32), (ᶜalāwatan ᶜalā dhālik – furthermore), (maᶜa dhālik – nevertheless), (ᶜalā kulli ḥāl – anyway), (ᶜalā al-raghmi min dhālik – in spite of that), (badalan min dhālik – instead of that), (iḍafatan ilā dhālik – besides), (ᶜalā al-ᶜaks min dhālik – on the contrary), (iḍāfatan ilā dhālik – in addition to that), and (bisabab – because of).

There are four major types of conjunction:

1 additive conjunction (wa – and),
2 adversative conjunction (lākin – but),
3 causal conjunction (min ajli dhālik – because of that), and
4 temporal conjunction (thumma/baᶜda idhin/baᶜda dhālik – then), (qabla/baᶜda – before/after).

For details on coherence and relevance of conjunctions, see Chapter 5, Section 5.6.2.

6.5.4.1 Additive conjunction

The most recurrent additive conjunction in Qur'anic Arabic is (wa – and), which joins between the following sentence elements:

i The additive conjunction (wa) joins between nouns, as in (al-samāwāti wa al-arḍi wa al-jibāli – the heavens and the earth and the mountains, Q33:72).
ii The additive conjunction (wa) joins between pronouns, as in (innaka maiyitun wa innahum maiyitūn – Indeed, you are to die, and indeed, they are to die, Q39:30) and (sakhkhara al-shamsa wal-qamara – He subjected the sun and the moon, Q36:78).
iii The additive conjunction (wa) joins between relative pronouns, as in (man kāna yurīdu ḥartha al-ākhirati nuzid lahu fi ḥarthih wa man kāna yurīdu ḥartha al-dunyā nu'tihi minhā – Whoever desires the reward of the hereafter – We increase for him in his reward. Whoever desires the benefits of this world – We give him thereof, Q42:20).
iv The additive conjunction (wa) joins between verbs, as in (yukawwiru al-laila ᶜalā al-nahār wa yukawwiru al-nahāra ᶜalā al-lail wa sakhkhara al-shamsa wal-qamar – He wraps the night over the day and wraps the day over the night and has subjected the sun and the moon, Q39:5; wa ḍaraba lanā mathalan wa nasiya khalqah – And he presented for Us an example and forgot his own creation, Q36:78).

v The additive conjunction (wa) joins between adjectives, as in (al-ṣābirīna wa al-ṣādiqīna wa al-qānitīna wa al-munfiqīna wa al-mustaghfirīna – The patient, the true, the obedient, those who spend in the way of God, and those who seek forgiveness, Q3:17).

vi The additive conjunction (wa) joins between prepositional phrases, as in (ᶜalaihi tawakkaltu wa ilaihi unīb – Upon Him I have relied and to Him I return), Q11:88.

vii The additive conjunction (wa) joins between nominalized nouns (maṣdar), as in (qiyāman wa quᶜūdan – standing and sitting, Q4:103).

The conjunctive elements (wa – and), (aw – or), and (fa – so) express a structural logical relation of coordination. While Qur'anic and written modern standard Arabic abound with the sentence-initial coordination conjunct (wa – and), written English employs it in the middle of the sentence. The coordination relation through the conjunctive (wa – and) appears between a pair of nouns, nominal groups, verbs, verbal groups, clauses, adverbs, adverbial groups, prepositions, or prepositional groups. As a semantic relation, the conjunctive element (wa – and) is additive and gives cohesion to the text. We also encounter the conjunctive element (wa) before other conjuncts like (wa lammā – and when, Q43:30, 57, 63) and (wa lawlā – and if, Q43:33) occurring in sentence-initial position. It is worthwhile to point out that the two together function as a single conjunctive element but take into consideration that the second element is the major one, i.e., (lammā – when) and (lawlā – if).

In Qur'anic discourse, the additive elements (wa) and (fa) occur alternatively at the micro level, as in:

> fa nabadhnāhu bil-ᶜarā'i wa huwa saqīm wa anbatnā ᶜalaihi shajaratan min yaqṭīn wa arsalnāhu ilā mi'ati alfin aw yazīdūn fa āmanū fa mattaᶜnāhum ilā ḥīn – But We threw him onto the open shore while he was ill. And We caused to grow over him a gourd vine. And We sent him to his people of a hundred thousand or more. And they believed, so We gave them enjoyment of life for a time, Q37:145–148.

Qur'anic discourse employs double additive conjunctive elements, such as (mā . . . wa – not . . . and), (lā . . . wa lā – neither . . . nor), (ammā . . . wa ammā . . . – either . . . or), (mā . . . wa mā – neither . . . nor), and (ammā . . . fa . . . – as for . . ., . . .):

> mā yastawī al-aᶜmā wa al-baṣīr – not equal are the blind and the seeing, Q35:19.
> wa lā al-ẓulumātu wa lā al-nūr wa lā al-ẓillu wa lā al-ḥarūr – Nor equal are the darkness and the light, nor are equal the shade and the heat, Q35:20–21.
> lā al-shamsu yanbaghī lahā an tudrika al-qamara wa lā al-lailu sābiqu al-nahār – It is not possible for the sun to reach the moon, nor does the night overtake the day, Q36:40.

mā anzalnā ᶜalā qawmihi min baᶜdihi min jundin min al-samā'i wa mā kunnā munzilīn – And We neither sent down upon his people after him any soldiers from the heaven, nor would We have done so, Q36:28.
mā ᶜallamnāhu al-shiᶜra wa mā yanbaghī lahu – We neither gave him (Muḥammad) knowledge of poetry, nor is it befitting for him, Q36:69.
lā yuqḍā ᶜalaihim fayamūtū walā yukhaffafu ᶜanhum min ᶜadhābihā – (Death) is neither decreed for them so they may die, nor will its fire torment be lightened, Q35:36.
fa lā yastaṭiᶜūna tawṣiyatan wa lā ilā ahlihim yarjiᶜūn – So, they will neither be able to give any instruction, nor to their people can they return, Q36:50.
fa al-yawma lā tuẓlamu nafsun shai'an wa lā tujzawna illā mā kuntum taᶜmalūn – So, today no soul will be wronged at all, and you will not be recompensed except for what you used to do, Q36:54.

The conjunctive element (aw – or) expresses the relation of alternative, as in:

qāla labithtu yawma aw baᶜḍa yawm – He (the man) said: 'I have remained a day or part of a day', Q2:259.

qālū lan nu'mina laka ḥattā tafjura lanā min al-arḍi yanbūᶜan aw takūna laka jannatun min nakhīlin . . . aw tusqiṭa al-samā'a . . . aw yakūna laka baitun . . . aw tarqā fī al-samā' – They said: 'We will not believe you until you break open for us from the ground a spring or until you have a garden of palm trees . . . or you make the heaven fall . . . or you have a house . . . or you ascend into the sky', Q17:90–93.

where the relation of alternative expressed by the cohesive device (aw – or) can be between nouns or verbal sentences.

The other additive conjunctive elements are (fa ammā . . . fa – as for . . ., . . .), as in:

fa ammā al-yatīma fa lā taqhar wa ammā al-sā'ila fa lā tanhar wa ammā biniᶜmati rabbika faḥaddith – So as for the orphan, do not oppress him, and as for the petitioner, do not repel him, but as for the favour of your Lord, report it, Q93:9–11.

The additive conjunctive elements (fa ammā . . . fa – as for . . ., . . .) are also encountered in Q2:26 (fa ammā alladhīna āmanū fayaᶜlamūna annahu al-ḥaqq – So as for those who have believed, they know that it is the truth) and Q32:19–20.

The conditional conjunctive element (in – if) expresses an additive relation, as in:

in tamsaskum ḥasanatun tasu'hum wa in tuṣibkum saiyi'atun yafraḥu bihā wa in taṣbirū wa tattaqū lā yaḍuruukum kaiduhum shai'ā – If good touches you, it distresses them, and if harm strikes you, they rejoice at it. And if you are patient and fear God, their plot will not harm you at all, Q3:120.

The conditional conjunctive elements (law . . . la – if . . ., . . .), (idhā . . . fa – if . . ., . . .), and (in . . . fa – if . . ., . . .) are also additive, as in:

> law annahum ṣabarū . . . lakāna khairan lahum – If they had been patient . . . it would have been better for them, Q49:5, Q4:46.
> fa idhā qaḍaitum al-ṣalāta fa idhkurū allāh qiyāman wa quᶜūdan – When you have completed the prayer, remember God standing and sitting, Q4:103.
> fa in lam tafᶜalū wa lan tafᶜalū fa ittaqū al-nāra . . . – But if you do not – and you will never be able to – then fear the fire, Q2:24.
> in yamsaska allāhu biḍurrin falā kāshifa lahu illā hū wa in yuridka bikhairin falā rādda lifaḍlihi – If God should touch you with adversity, there is no remover of it except Him; and if He intends for you good, then there is no repeller of His bounty, Q10:107.

The negative form of the additive relation is expressed in the Qur'an as (mā . . . walā – neither . . . nor), as in:

> mā yastawī al-aᶜmā wal-baṣīr walā al-ẓulumāt walā al-nūr – Neither the blind nor the seeing are equal, and neither the darkness nor the light are equal, Q35:19–20.
>
> mā yastawī al-aḥyā' walā al-amwāt – Neither the living nor the dead are equal, Q35:22.

(lā . . . walā – neither . . . nor), as in:

> lā yuqḍā ᶜalaihim fayamūtū walā yukhaffafu ᶜanhum min ᶜadhābihā – (Death) is neither decreed for them so they may die, nor will its (fire) torment be lightened, Q35:36.
> wa'in tubtum falakum ru'ūsu amwālikum lā taẓlimūn walā tuẓlamūn – If you repent, you may have your capital – thus, you do no wrong, nor are you wronged, Q2:279.
> fa lā yastaṭiᶜūna tawṣiyatan wa lā ilā ahlihim yarjiᶜūn – They will neither be able to give any instruction, nor to their people can they return, Q36:50.

A complex comparative additive relation is expressed through the conjunctive elements (mathal . . . kamathal – the example . . . is that of) and (mathal . . . ka . . . – the example of . . . is like), as in:

> mathaluhum kamathali alladhī istawqada nāran falammā aḍā'at mā ḥawlahu dhahaba allāhu binūrihim . . . – Their example is that of one who kindled a fire, but when it illuminated what was around him, God took away their light, Q2:17.
> inna mathala ᶜĪsā ᶜinda allāhi kamathali ādam . . . – The example of Jesus to God is like that of Adam, Q3:59.

mathaluhu kamathali al-kalbi in taḥmil ᶜalaihi yalhath aw tatrukhu yalhath – His example is like that of the dog: If you chase it, it pants, or if you leave it, it still pants, Q7:176.
mathalu al-ḥayāti al-dunyā kamā'in anzalnāhu min al-samā' – The example of this worldly life is like rain which We (God) have sent down from the sky, Q10:24.
mathalu nūrihi ka mishkātin . . . – The example of His (God's) light is like a niche . . ., Q24:35.

Other examples of the comparative additive relation are Q2:171, 261, 264, 265, Q3:117, Q11:24, Q14:18, 26, Q18:45, Q29:41, Q57:20, Q59:16, Q62:5.

6.5.4.2 Adversative conjunction

An adversative relation means contrary to expectation (Halliday and Hasan 1976:250), as in (lākin – but):

wa mā ẓalamūnā wa lākin kānū anfusahum yaẓlimūn – They did not wrong Us but they were wronging themselves, Q2:57.

wa mā kāna allāhu liyaẓlimahum wa lākin kānū anfusahum yaẓlimūn – God would not have wronged them but it was they who were wronging themselves, Q29:40, Q30:9.

Thus, the conjunctive element (lākin – but) expresses an adversative relation. Most frequently, however, (lākin) is preceded by the additive conjunctive element (wa – and), which does not affect the adversative relation.

The adversative conjunction element (lākin – but) occurs with an initial negative element (mā – no) or (lā – no); thus, we have (mā . . . wa lākin – not . . . but) or (lā . . . wa lākin – not . . . but) as in:

wa mā ẓalamūnā wa lākin kānū anfusahum yaẓlimūn – They did not wrong Us but they were wronging themselves, Q2:57, Q7:160.
wa mā ẓalamnāhum wa lākin ẓalamū anfusahum – We did not wrong them but they wronged themselves, Q11:101.
wa mā ẓalamnāhum wa lākin kānū anfusahum yaẓlimūn – We did not wrong them but they were wronging themselves, Q16:118.
wa mā ẓalamahum allāhu wa lākin anfusahum yaẓlimūn – God did not wrong them but they had wronged themselves, Q3:117, Q16:33.
fa mā kāna allāhu liyaẓlimahum wa lākin kānū anfusahum yaẓlimūn – God would never have wronged them but they were wronging themselves, Q9:70, Q29:40, Q30:9.
inna allāha lā yaẓlimu al-nāsa shai'an wa lākin al-nāsa anfusahum yaẓlimūn – God does not wrong people at all but it is people who are wronging themselves, Q10:44

6.5.4.3 *Causal conjunction*

There is a limited number of causal conjunctions in Qur'anic discourse. These include (min ajli dhālika/min ajli hādhā – because of that), (bimā – because of), (laᶜalla – so that), and the letter /f/, i.e., (fa – so, because), as in the following examples:

> min ajli dhālika katabnā ᶜalā banī isrā'īla annahu man qatala nafsan bighairi nafsin . . . – Because of that, We (God) decreed upon the Children of Israel that whoever kills a soul unless for a soul . . ., Q5:32.
> lan yatamannawhu abadan bimā qaddamat aidīhim – They will never wish for it because of what their hands have put forth, Q2:95.
> fakaifa idhā aṣābathum muṣībatun bimā qaddamat aidīhim – So how will it be when disaster strikes them because of what their hands have put forth, Q4:62.
> dhālika bimā qaddamat yadāka – That is for what your hands have put forth, Q22:10.
> in tuṣibhum saiyi'atun bimā qaddamat aidīhim idhā hum yaqnaṭūn – If evil afflicts them for what their hands have put forth, they despair immediately, Q30:36.

The letter /f/, i.e., (fa – so, because) designates a causal conjunction meaning (so, for this reason), which usually occurs sentence-initially, as in:

> faᶜaqarū al-nāqata – So, they hamstrung the she-camel . . . fa'akhadhathum al-rajfatu . . . – So the earthquake seized them . . ., Q7:77–78.
> fafarartu minkum lammā khiftukum . . . – So I fled from you when I feared you, Q26:21.

The causal conjunction (fa) can also mean (therefore), as in:

> falammā nasū mā dhukkirū bihi fataḥnā ᶜalaihim abwāba kulli shai'in . . . – Therefore, when they forgot that by which they had been reminded, We opened to them the doors of every thing . . ., Q6:44.
> faḥaqqa ᶜalainā qawlu rabbinā – Therefore, the decree of our Lord has come into effect upon us, Q37:31.
> fa'innahum yawma'idhin fī al-ᶜadhābi mushtarikūn – Therefore, on that day, they will be sharing in the punishment, Q37:33.
> . . . laᶜallakum tattaqūn – . . . so that you may fear God, Q2:21, 183, Q6:153.
> idhkurū mā fīhi laᶜallakum tattaqūn – Remember what is in it so that you may fear God, Q7:171.

6.5.4.4 *Temporal conjunction*

Qur'anic temporal conjunction is realized through the elements (thumma/baᶜda idhin / baᶜda dhālik – then), (qabla/baᶜda – before/after), (kullamā – whenever, every time), (āl'āna – now), (an – before), and (idh/idhā – when). Through temporal conjunction, two parts of a sentence or two separate sentences can be linked by the same logical relations of succession in time. The time sequence has become a cohesive agent. This semantic relation has a cohesive function (Halliday and Hasan 1976:228), as in:

> kullamā naḍajat julūduhum baddalnāhum julūdan ghairahā – Every time their skins are roasted through We will replace them with other skins, Q4:56.
> kullamā dakhala ᶜalaihā zakariyyā al-miḥrāba wajada ᶜindahā rizqā – Every time Zachariah entered upon her in the prayer chamber, he found with her provision, Q3:37
> kullamā dakhalat ummatun laᶜanat ukhtahā – Every time a crowd enters, it will curse its fellow crowd, Q7:38
> āl'āna waqad ᶜaṣaita qablu wakunta min al-mufsidīn – Now? And you had disobeyed before and were of the corrupters?, Q10:91
> min nuṭfatin khalaqahu . . . thumma al-sabīla yassarahu thumma amātahu . . . thumma idhā shā'a ansharahu – From a sperm-drop He (God) created him (man) . . . Then He eased the way for him . . . Then He causes his death . . . Then when He wills, He will resurrect him, Q80:19–22.
> For more examples on (thumma – then), see Q23:13–16, Q30:20, 25, 27, and Q40:67.
> idhā al-shamsu kuwwirat wa idhā al-nujūmu inkadarat wa idhā al-jibālu suyyirat wa idhā al-ᶜishāru ᶜuṭṭilat – When the sun is wrapped up, and when the stars fell dispersing, and when the mountains are removed, and when full-term she-camels are neglected, Q81:1–4.
> For more examples on (idhā – when), see Q81:1–8.

The other temporal conjunctive element is (an – before) meaning (qabla – before), as in:

> wa lā ta'kulūhā isrāfan wa bidāran an yakburū – and do not consume it wastefully and in haste before they grow up, Q4:6.

6.5.5 Lexical cohesion

Lexical cohesion is concerned with lexical ties, which we encounter in a macro text. Semantically related items produce a semantic chain that links the related lexemes. Thus, lexical cohesion plays a role in the semantic continuity of a text because the semantically chained lexical items refer to the same thing. For Halliday and Hasan (1976:282), lexical cohesion is the reiteration of a lexical item in a context of grammatical cohesion, the cohesion being simply a matter of reference. In other words, since lexical cohesion is lexical reiteration, we find the reference identical and usually made explicit by means of an anaphoric reference item. This means that the present sentence is related to the previous sentence because both have a reference to the same thing, notion, fact, or person: one lexical item refers to another. Thus, lexical cohesion is 'associated with grammatical reference' (Halliday and Hasan 1976:282).

Lexical cohesion in a text is achieved by the selection of vocabulary. In other words, lexical cohesion is attained by one of the following lexical mechanisms:

> (i) the general noun, (ii) reiteration, (iii) synonymy, (iv) antonymy, (v) collocation, (vi) hyponymy, and (vii) meronymy.

Lexical cohesion is the function of one of the above seven mechanisms (cf. Halliday and Hasan 1976:274). The seven forms of lexical cohesion are cohesive agents and play a major role in making the text hang together. What these seven lexical mechanisms have in common is that one lexical item refers to another. In other words, they operate anaphorically.

6.5.5.1 The general noun

In Qur'anic discourse, lexical cohesion is achieved through the repetition of the replacement general noun. By a replacement noun, we mean a substitute noun that is anaphoric to the noun, noun phrase, or a whole clause mentioned earlier. The general lexeme is a category of reiteration and is very general in meaning. Let us consider the cohesive effect that is achieved through the selection of vocabulary in the following examples:

1 ḥattā idhā jā'a aḥaduhum al-mawtu qāla rabbī arjiᶜūnī laᶜallī aᶜmal ṣāliḥan fimā taraktu kallā innahā kalimatun huwa qā'iluhā – When death comes to one of them, he cries, my Lord, let me return so as to make amends for the things I neglected. Never! This will not go beyond his words, Q23:99–100

2 wanādā nūḥun rabbahu faqāla rabbi inna ibnī min ahlī . . . qāla yā nūḥụ innahu laisa min ahlika. innahu ᶜamalun ghairu ṣāliḥ – Noah called to his Lord and said: 'My Lord, indeed my son is of my family' . . . God said: 'O Noah, indeed he (your son) is not of your family. Indeed, he is one whose work was other than righteous', Q11:41–46

3 waqālū lan yadkhula al-jannata illā man kāna hūdan aw naṣārā. tilka amāniyyuhum – They say: 'None will enter paradise except one who is a Jew or a Christian'. That is merely their wishful thinking, Q2:111

4 waqalāt al-yahūdu laisat al-naṣārā ᶜalā shai'in waqālat al-naṣāra laisat al-yahūdu calā shai'in wahum yatlūn al-kitāba. kadhālika qāla alladhīna lā yaᶜlamūna mithla qawlihim . . . – The Jews say: 'The Christians have nothing true to stand on', and the Christians say: 'The Jews have nothing to stand on', although they both recite the Scripture. Thus do those who do not know speak the same as their words', Q2:113

5 al-ṭalāqu marratān. fa'imsākun bimaᶜrūfin aw tasrīḥun bi'iḥsān. walā yaḥillu lakum an ta'khudhū mimmā ātaitumūhunna shai'an illā an yakhāfā allā yuqīmā ḥudūd allāh. fa'in khiftum allā yuqīmā ḥudūd allāh falā junāḥa ᶜalaihimā fimā iftadat bih. tilka ḥudūd allāh falā taqrabūhā. waman yataᶜadda

ḥudūd allāh fa'ulā'ika hum al-ẓālimūn – Divorce is twice. Then after that either keep her in an acceptable manner or release her with good treatment. It is not lawful for you to take anything of what you have given them unless both fear that they will not be able to keep within the limits of God. But if you fear that they will not keep within the limits of God, then there is no blame upon either of them concerning that by which she ransoms herself. These are the limits of God, so do not transgress them. Whoever transgresses the limits of God – it is those who are the unjust, Q2:229

6 wamā min dābbatin fī al-arḍi walā ṭā'irin yaṭīru bijanāḥaihi illā umamun amthālukum – There is no creature on the earth or bird that flies with its wings except that they are communities like you, Q6:38

7 min warā'ihi jahannam wayusqā min mā'in ṣadīd. yatajarra^{c}uhu walā yakādu yusīghuhu waya'tīhi al-mawtu min kulli makān – Hell is before him and he will be given a drink of purulent water. He will gulp it but will hardly be able to swallow it. Death will come to him from everywhere, Q14:16–17

8 inna fī khalqi al-samāwāti wal-arḍi wakhtilāfi al-laili wal-nahāri wal-fulki allatī tajrī fī al-baḥri bimā yanfa^{c}u al-nāsa wamā anzala allāhu min al-samā'i min mā'in fa'aḥyā al-arḍa ba^{c}da mawtihā wabaththa fīhā min kulli dābbatin wataṣrīfi al-riyāḥi wal-saḥābi al-musakhkhari baina al-samā'i wal-arḍi la'āyāt liqawmin ya^{c}qilūn – Indeed, in the creation of the heavens and the earth, and the alternation of the night and the day, and the ships which sail through the sea with that which benefits people, and what God has sent down from the heavens of rain, giving life thereby to the earth after its lifelessness and dispersing therein every kind of moving creature, and His directing of the winds and the clouds controlled between the heaven and earth are signs for a people who use reason, Q2:164

9 wamin āyātihi an khalaqa lakum min anfusikum azwājan litaskunū ilaihā waja^{c}al bainakum mawaddatan waraḥmatan inna fī dhālika la'āyāt liqawmin yatafakkarūn – And of His signs is that He created for you from yourselves mates that you may find tranquility in them; and He placed between you affection and mercy. Indeed in that are signs for a people who give thought, Q30:21

10 wamin āyātihi khalqu al-samāwāti wal-arḍi wakhtilāfi alsinatikum wa'alwānikum inna fī dhālika la'āyāt lil-^{c}ālimin – And of His signs is the creation of the heavens and the earth and the diversity of your languages and your colours. Indeed in that are signs for those of knowledge, Q30:22

11 wamin āyātihi manāmukum bil-laili wal-nahāri wabtighā'ikum min faḍlih inna fī dhālika la'āyāt liqawmin yasma^{c}ūn – And of His signs is your sleep by night and day and your seeking of His bounty. Indeed in that are signs for a people who listen, Q30:23

12 wamin āyātihi yurīkum al-barqa khawfan waṭama^{c}an wayunazzilu min al-samā'i mā'an fayuḥyi bihi al-arḍa ba^{c}da mawtihā inna fī dhālika la'āyāt liqawmin ya^{c}qilūn – And of His signs is that He shows you the lightning causing fear and aspiration, and He sends down rain from the sky by which He brings to life the earth after its lifelessness. Indeed in that are signs for a people who use reason, Q30:24

13 dhālika jazā'uhum jahannamu bimā kafarū . . . – That is their recompense – hell – for what they denied, Q18:106

In the above examples, the general nouns perform a cohesive function. The lexical cohesion is as follows:

In example (1), lexical cohesion is achieved by the general noun (kalimatun – a word, a saying), which is anaphoric, i.e., referring to (rabbī arjiᶜūnī laᶜallī aᶜmal ṣāliḥan fīmā taraktu – my Lord, let me return so as to make amends for the things I neglected).

In example (2), the lexical cohesion is achieved through the general noun (ᶜamal – work, act), which is anaphoric to (inna ibnī min ahlī – indeed my son is of my family).

In example (3), the lexical cohesion is achieved through the general noun (amāniyyuhum – their wishful thinking), which is anaphoric and harks back to (lan yadkhula al-jannata illā man kāna hūdan aw naṣārā – None will enter paradise except one who is a Jew or a Christian).

In example (4), the lexical cohesion is achieved through the general noun (qawl – words (i.e., speech)), which refers to (waqālat al-yahūdu laisat al-naṣārā ᶜalā shai'in waqālat al-naṣara laisat al-yahūdu ᶜalā shai'in wahum yatlūn al-kitāba – The Jews say: 'The Christians have nothing true to stand on', and the Christians say: 'The Jews have nothing to stand on', although they both recite the Scripture).

In example (5), the lexical cohesion is achieved through the general noun (ḥudūd allāh – the limits of God), which is anaphoric to (al-ṭalāqu marratān. fa'imsākun bimaᶜrūfin aw tasrīḥun bi'iḥsān. walā yaḥillu lakum an ta'khudhū mimmā ātaitumūhunna shai'an illā an yakhāfā allā yuqīmā ḥudūd allāh. fa'in khiftum allā yuqīmā ḥudūd allāh falā junāha ᶜalaihimā fīmā iftadat bih – Divorce is twice. Then after that either keep her in an acceptable manner or release her with good treatment. It is not lawful for you to take anything of what you have given them unless both fear that they will not be able to keep within the limits of God. But if you fear that they will not keep within the limits of God, then there is no blame upon either of them concerning that by which she ransoms herself).

In example (6), the lexical cohesion is achieved through the general noun (umamun – communities), which refers to (dābbatin fī al-arḍi walā ṭā'irin yaṭīru bijanāḥ – creature on the earth or bird that flies with its wings).

In example (7), the lexical cohesion is achieved through the general noun (makān – everywhere), which is anaphoric to the place noun (jahannam – hell).

In example (8), the lexical cohesion is achieved through the general noun (āyāt – signs), which is anaphoric and refers to (inna fī khalqi al-samāwāti wal-arḍi wakhtilāfi al-laili wal-nahāri wal-fulki allatī tajrī fī al-baḥri bimā yanfaᶜu al-nāsa wamā anzala allāhu min al-samā'i min mā'in fa'aḥya al-arḍa baᶜda mawtihā wabaththa fihā min kulli dābbatin wataṣrifi al-riyāḥi wal-saḥābi al-musakhkhari baina al-samā'i wal-arḍi – Indeed, in the creation of the heavens and the earth, and the alternation of the night and the day, and the ships which sail through the sea with that which benefits people, and what God has sent down from the heavens of rain, giving life thereby to the earth after its lifelessness and dispersing therein every kind of moving creature, and His directing of the winds and the clouds controlled between the heaven and earth).

However, in examples 9, 10, 11 and 12, the lexical cohesion is achieved through the general noun (āyāt – signs), which has occurred twice, at the beginning and at the end of the sentence, while the fact (notion) which the general noun refers to has occurred in the middle. The general noun (āyāt – signs) which occurs at the beginning of the sentences (9, 10, 11 and 12) is cataphoric to the fact clause, while the general noun (āyāt – signs) which occurs at the end of the sentences (9, 10, 11 and 12) is anaphoric to the fact clause.

The general noun (āyāt – signs) which occurs at the end of the sentence (9) is anaphoric to the fact clause (khalaqa lakum min anfusikum azwājan litaskunū ilaihā waja^c al bainakum mawaddatan waraḥmatan – He created for you from yourselves mates that you may find tranquility in them; and He placed between you affection and mercy).

In example (10), the lexical cohesion is achieved through the general noun (āyāt – signs), which refers (anaphoric) to the fact clause (khalqu al-samāwāti wal-arḍi wakhtilāfi alsinatikum wa'alwānikum – the creation of the heavens and the earth and the diversity of your languages and your colors).

In example (11), the lexical cohesion is achieved through the general noun (āyāt – signs), which refers (anaphoric) to the fact clause (manāmukum bil-laili wal-nahāri wabtighā'ikum min faḍlih – your sleep by night and day and your seeking of His bounty).

In example (12), the lexical cohesion is achieved through the general noun (aȳāt – signs), which refers (anaphoric) to the fact clause (yurīkum al-barqa khawfan waṭama^c an wayunazzilu min al-samā'i mā'an fayuḥyi bihi al-arḍa ba^c da mawtihā – He shows you the lightning causing fear and aspiration, and He sends down rain from the sky by which He brings to life the earth after its lifelessness).

In example (13), the lexical cohesion is achieved through the general noun (jahannamu – hell), which is anaphoric to the fact (notion) noun (jazā' – recompense, reward).

Having discussed the general noun (āyāt – signs) in examples 9, 10, 11, and 12 of Q30:21, 22, 23 and 24, respectively, we can also observe that the general word (āyāt – signs) has occurred cataphorically, i.e., at the beginning of the sentences (9, 10, 11 and 12), referring forward to a whole fact clause mentioned after the general noun (āyāt). The general word (āyāt – signs) refers cataphorically, i.e., referring forward to the same whole clause mentioned after it. Thus, the general noun (āyāt) cataphorically refers to (khalaqa lakum min anfusikum azwājan litaskunū ilaihā waja^c al bainakum mawaddatan waraḥmatan – He created for you from yourselves mates that you may find tranquility in them; and He placed between you affection and mercy), (khalqu al-samāwāti wal-arḍi wakhtilāfi alsinatikum wa'alwānikum – the creation of the heavens and the earth and the diversity of your languages and your colours), (manāmukum bil-laili wal-nahāri wabtighā'ikum min faḍlih – your sleep by night and day and your seeking of His bounty) and (yurīkum al-barqa khawfan waṭamaᶜan wayunazzilu min al-samā'i mā'an fayuḥyī bihi al-arḍa baᶜda mawtihā – He shows you the lightning causing fear and aspiration, and He sends down rain from the sky by which He brings to life the earth after its lifelessness) in examples 9–12 respectively.

However, in Qur'anic Arabic, the general noun which is a replacement (substitute) noun can also occur as cataphoric only to the whole clause mentioned after it, as in:

1 wamin āyātihi an khalaqakum min turāb – And of His signs is that He created you from dust, Q30:20
2 wamin āyātihi an taqūma al-samā'u wal-arḍu bi'amrih – And of His signs is that the heavens and earth remain by His command, Q30:25

In the above two examples, the general nouns (āyāt – signs) perform a cohesive function. The lexical cohesion in example (1) is achieved through the general noun (āyātihi – His signs), which is cataphoric to (khalaqakum min turāb – He created you from dust). In example (2), the lexical cohesion is achieved by the general noun (āyātihi – His signs), which is cataphoric, i.e., referring forward to (an taqūma al-samā'u wal-arḍu bi'amrih – that the heavens and earth remain by His command).

It is worthwhile to note that lexical cohesion through general nouns is related to Qur'anic exegesis and translation studies. The understanding of the semantic relationship between the general noun and its anaphoric/cataphoric reference has significant impact on the accuracy of exegesis, translation, and the preservation of the intended meaning of the text producer (the source text).

6.5.5.2 Reiteration

Reiteration (repetition) is a form of lexical cohesion which involves the repetition of the same lexeme many times in the same sentence or in consecutive sentences of a macro text. It is one of the cohesive characteristics of language and a means of linking the various parts of a text (Halliday and Hasan 1976:278, 318; Crystal 2003:394).

The repeated lexical items have the same referent. In other words, there is identity of reference between the two lexical items, i.e., between the lexeme and its repeated form. Reiteration can also be achieved through a synonym when the two occurrences have the same referent. It is worthwhile to note that repetition is not restricted to the same morphological form. Let us consider the following examples:

1 al-ṭalāqu marratān. fa'imsākun bimaᶜrūfin aw tasrīḥun bi'iḥsān. walā yaḥillu lakum an ta'khudhū mimmā ātaitumūhunna shai'an illā an yakhāfā allā yuqīmā

ḥudūd allāh. fa'in khiftum allā yuqīmā ḥudūd allāh falā junāḥa ^{c}alaihimā fīmā iftadat bih. tilka ḥudūd allāh falā taqrabūhā. waman yata^{c}adda ḥudūd allāh fa'ulā'ika hum al-ẓālimūn . . . fa'in ṭallaqahā . . . falā junāḥa ^{c}alaihimā an yatarāja^{c}ā in ẓannā an yuqīmā ḥudūd allāh. watilka ḥudūd allāh yubaiyinuhā liqawmin ya^{c}lamūn – Divorce is twice. Then after that either keep her in an acceptable manner or release her with good treatment. It is not lawful for you to take anything of what you have given them unless both fear that they will not be able to keep within the limits of God. But if you fear that they will not keep within the limits of God, then there is no blame upon either of them concerning that by which she ransoms herself. These are the limits of God, so do not transgress them. Whoever transgresses the limits of God – it is those who are the unjust. If he has divorced her . . . There is no blame upon them (i.e., the woman and her former husband) for returning to each other if they think that they can keep within the limits of God. These are the limits of God which He makes clear to a people who understand, Q2:229–230

2 waqad makarū makrahum wa^{c}inda allāhi makruhum wa'in kāna makruhum litazūla minhu al-jibāl – They had planned their plan, but with God their plan is recorded, even if their plan had been sufficient to do away with the mountains, Q14:46

3 qul hal min shurakā'ikum man yabda'u al-khalqa thumma yu^{c}īduh qul allāhu yabda'u al-khalqa thumma yu^{c}īduh – Say: 'Are there of your partners any who begins creation and then repeats it?', Q10:34

4 qul hal min shurakā'ikum man yahdī ilā al-ḥaqqi qul allāhu yahdī lil-ḥaqqi – Say: 'Are there of your partners any who guides to the truth?' say: 'God guides to the truth', Q10:35

5 yurīdu allāhu an yuḥiqq al-ḥaqq bikalimātihi wayaqṭa^{c}a dābira al-kāfirīn liyuḥiqq al-ḥaqq wayubṭil al-bāṭil walaw kariha al-mujrimūn – God intended to establish the truth by His words and to eliminate the disbelievers. That He should establish the truth and abolish falsehood, even if the criminals disliked it, Q8:7–8

6 wamā ja^{c}alahu allāh illā bushrā . . . wamā al-naṣru illā min ^{c}ind allāh inna allāh . . . cazīzun ḥakīm – God made it not but good tidings . . . Victory is not but from God . . . exalted in might, wise, Q8:10

7 wa'inna minhum lafariqan yalwūna alsinatuhum bil-kitāb litaḥsabūhu min al-kitāb wamā huwa min al-kitāb wayaqūlūna huwa min ^{c}ind allāh wamā huwa min ^{c}ind allāh wayaqūluna ^{c}alā allāh al-kadhiba wahum ya^{c}lamūn – Indeed, there is among them a party who alter the Scripture with their tongues so you may think it is from the Scripture, but it is not from the Scripture. They say: 'This is from God', but it is not from God. They speak untruth about God while they know, Q3:78

8 laisa ^{c}alā al-a^{c}mā ḥarajun walā ^{c}alā al-a^{c}raji ḥarajun walā ^{c}alā al-marīḍi ḥarajun walā ^{c}alā anfusikum an ta'kulū min buyūtikum aw buyūti ābā'ikum aw buyūti ummahātikum aw buyūti ikhwānikum aw buyūti akhawātikum aw buyūti a^{c}māmikum aw buyūti ^{c}ammātikum aw buyūti akhwālikum aw buyūti khālātikum aw mā malaktum mafātiḥahu aw ṣadiqikum laisa ^{c}alikum junāḥun an ta'kulū jamī^{c}an aw ashtātan fa'idhā dakhaltum buyūtan fasallimū ^{c}alā

anfusikum taḥiyyatan min ᶜind allāh mubārakatan ṭaiyibatan – There is not upon the blind any constraint nor upon the lame any constraint nor upon the ill any constraint nor upon yourselves if you eat from your own houses or the houses of your fathers or the houses of your mothers or the houses of your brothers or the houses of your sisters or the houses of your fathers' brothers or the houses of your fathers' sisters or the houses of your mothers' brothers or the houses of your mothers' sisters or from houses whose keys you possess or from the house of your friend. There is no blame upon you whether you eat together or separately. But when you enter houses, give greetings of peace upon each other – a greeting from God, blessed and good. Thus does God make clear to you the āyāt of ordinance that you may understand, Q24:61

9 wayastaᶜjilūnka bil-ᶜadhābi walawlā ajalun musamman lajā'ahum al-ᶜadhābu walaya'tiyannahum baghtatan wahum lā yashᶜurūn – They challenge you to hasten the punishment. If not for the decree of a specified term, punishment would have reached them. But it will surely come to them suddenly and catch them unawares, Q29:53

Lexical cohesion is achieved through the repetition of the noun phrase (ḥudūd allāh – the limits of God) in example (1); the repetition of (makrahum – their plan) in example (2); the repetition of (yabda'u al-khalqa thumma yuᶜiduh – begins creation and then repeats it) in example (3); the repetition of (yahdī ilā al-ḥaqqi – guides to the truth) in example (4); the repetition of (yuḥiqq – establish) and (yubṭil – abolish) in example (5); the repetition of (allāh – God) in example (6); the repetition of (al-kitāb – the Scripture) and (allāh – God) in example (7); the repetition of (ḥarajun – constraint), (ta'kulū – eat), (buyūt – houses) in example (8); and the repetition of (al-cadhābu – punishment) in example (9).

The noun phrases (ḥudūd allāh) and (makruhum), and the clauses (yabda'u al-khalqa thumma yuᶜīduh) and (yahdī ilā al-ḥaqqi) cohere with the earlier occurrences of their relevant noun phrases and clauses because they have the same referent, i.e., the referent is identical. Thus, there is a referential relationship between these noun phrases and clauses.

Examples of reiteration at the micro level, i.e., within the same sentence, can be demonstrated through the referential relationship between pronouns, as in:

alladhīna lā yu'tūna al-zakāta wa hum bil-ākhirati hum kāfirun – Those who do not give zakāt and in the hereafter they are disbelievers, Q41:7 where the pronoun (hum – they) is repeated.

We have claimed earlier that repetition is not restricted to the same morphological form. An example of reiteration of a lexeme at the macro Qur'anic text is (qāla – to say). For instance, the verb (qultu) has occurred 6 times in the first person masculine singular, (aqul) has occurred 6 times in the first person masculine singular, (aqūl) has occurred 9 times in the first person masculine singular, (naqūl) has occurred 11 times in the first person masculine plural, (qulnā) has occurred 27 times in the first person masculine plural, (taqūl) has occurred 12 times in the second person masculine singular, (qultum) has occurred 9 times in the second person masculine plural, (taqūlū) has occurred 16 times in the second person masculine plural, (taqūlūn) has occurred 11 times in the second person masculine plural, (qulna) has occurred twice in the imperative second person feminine plural, (qūlā) has occurred three times in the imperative second person masculine dual, (qāla) has occurred 529 times in the third person masculine singular, (yaqūl) has occurred 68 times in the third person masculine singular, (yaqūlā) has occurred once in the third person masculine dual, (qālat) has occurred 43 times in the third person feminine singular, (qālā) has occurred 3 times in the third person masculine dual, (qālatā) has occurred twice in the third person feminine dual, (qālū) has occurred 331 times in the third person masculine plural, (yaqūlū) has occurred 17 times in the third person masculine plural, (yaqūlūn) has occurred 92 times in the third person masculine plural, (qul) has occurred 332 times in the imperative masculine singular form, (qūlū) has occurred 12 times in the imperative masculine plural form, (qīla) has occurred 49 times in the passive form, (al-qawla/al-qawlu/al-qawli) has occurred 52 times as a definite nominalized noun (maṣdar), (qawlan) has occurred 19 times as an indefinite nominalized noun, and (al-aqāwīl) has occurred once as a definite plural nominalized noun.

Another example of reiteration of a lexeme at the macro Qur'anic text level is (allāh – God), which has occurred 980 times in the Qur'an, the lexeme (rabb – Lord) has occurred 84 times, the singular lexeme (ilāh – God/god) has occurred 80 times, and the plural lexeme (ālihah – gods) has occurred 18 times. The lexeme (al-arḍ – the earth) has occurred 451 times, the singular lexeme (al-samā' – heaven) has occurred 120 times, and the plural lexeme (al-samāwāt – heavens) has occurred 190 times.

A unique cohesion feature of Qur'anic discourse is represented by the different types of reiteration:

1 single-clause reiteration, as in Q55, which provides an interesting example of reiteration of a whole clause as in the interrogative question (fabi'aiyyi ālā'i rabbikumā tukadhdhibān – So, which of the favours of your Lord would you deny?), which has occurred 31 times. In Q77, we also encounter single clause reiteration through (wailun yama'idhin lil-mukadhdhibīn – Woe, that day, to the deniers), which has occurred 10 times. Similarly, we encounter the prepositional phrase (bi'idhnī – with My permission), which has occurred four times in Q5:110 for (a) the perlocutionary effect of God's omnipotence, and (b) the theological notion that Jesus is but a human and cannot perform the miracles mentioned in Q5:110 without God's leave.
2 multiple-clause reiteration, where different but complete clauses have occurred, as in Q26 where a multiple-clause has been reiterated seven times: (inna fī dhālika la'āyatan wamā kāna aktharuhum mu'minīn. wa'inna rabbaka lahuwa al-ᶜazīzu al-rahim – Indeed in that is a sign, but most of them were not to be believers. And indeed, your Lord, He is the exalted in might, the merciful) in 8–9, 67–68, 103–104, 139–140, 190–191. Multiple-clause reiteration has also occurred in Q26:123–126 (kadhdhabat ᶜādun al-mursalīn. innī lakum

rasūlun amīn. fattaqū allāha wa'aṭiᶜūn – ᶜĀd denied the messengers. Indeed, I am to you a trustworthy messenger. So fear God and obey me), 141–144 (kadhdhabat thamūdu al-mursalīn. innī lakum rasūlun amīn. fattaqū allāha wa'aṭīᶜūn – Thamūd denied the messengers. Indeed, I am to you a trustworthy messenger. So fear God and obey me), 161–163 (kadhdhabat qawmu lūṭin al-mursalīn. innī lakum rasūlun amīn. fattaqū allāha wa'aṭīᶜūn – The people of Lot denied the messengers. Indeed, I am to you a trustworthy messenger. So fear God and obey me), and Q26:109, 127, 145, 164, and 180 (wamā as'alukum ᶜalaihi min ajrin. in ajriya illā ᶜalā rabbi al-ᶜālamīn – I do not ask you for it any payment. My payment is only from the Lord of the worlds).

3 no-main-verb nominal sentence reiteration, as in (inna fī dhālika la'āyah – Indeed, in that is a sign), which is repeated eight times (Q26:8, 67, 103, 121, 139, 158, 174, and 190), the no-main-verb sentence (wamā kāna aktharuhum mu'minīn – but most of them were not to be believers), which is repeated eight times (Q26:8, 67, 103, 121, 139, 158, 174, and 190), and the no-main-verb sentence (wa'inna rabbaka lahuwa al-cazīz al-raḥīm – And indeed, your Lord, He is the exalted in might, the merciful), which is repeated eight times (Q26:9, 68, 104, 122, 140, 159, 175, and 191).

4 function word chain reiteration: This is conjunctive element reiteration, as in (idh and idhā – when, Q2:124–127), (idh – when, Q5:110–112), and (idhā – when, Q81:1–13, Q82:1–3).

6.5.5.3 Synonymy

Synonymy and near-synonymy (partial synonymy) are a category of reiteration and have the same referent. In other words, as Halliday and Hasan (1976:282) put it, 'there must be identity of reference between the two, i.e., between the lexeme and its synonym or near-synonym'. Synonym is a major type of sense relation between lexical items that can occur when these items are close enough in their meaning (Salkie 1995:9; Crystal 2003:450), as in (sanah – year) and (ᶜāmm – year), (baḥar – sea) and (yamm – sea), (yakhāf – to fear) and (yakhshā – to fear), (tafjur – to break open) and (tufajjir – to gush forth), (wāqq – protector) and (waliy – protector). We have called the semantic relationship between these pairs of words, i.e., between the synonym and its near (partial) synonym, semantic contrastiveness. For more details, see Abdul-Raof (2018:97).

Complete synonymy is very rare in language. Complete synonymy takes place when two words have exactly the same meaning and we can have the choice to use any of them without making any difference in the meaning of the sentence, as in (I sleep at 11 p.m.) or (I go to bed at 11 p.m.). However, partial (near) synonyms are not very similar in meaning. We cannot substitute one synonym for the other in different contexts. Near synonyms have different shades of meaning and different connotations. Although (brave/courageous) are synonyms, we can say: (Liz does not want to go to the dentist. She is not brave). However, we cannot say: (Liz does not want to go to the dentist. She is not courageous). Partial synonyms are like: (big → large), (almost → nearly), (brave → courageous). Therefore, formal and informal style and different contexts create partial synonyms (Abdul-Raof 2015:79).

It is worthwhile to note that although we encounter in English and modern standard Arabic register differences like formal register as in (ḥumāt al-qānūn/minions of the law) and colloquial register like (abu ismāᶜil – cops (Iraqi Arabic)), this does not apply to Qur'anic discourse, which represents the syntactic canon of Arabic.

In Q2:249, we encounter lexical cohesion through the verbs (shariba – to drink) → (ṭaᶜama – to taste) → (shariba – to drink). However, (ṭaᶜama – to taste) is classified as a contextual synonym of (shariba – to drink) since the context of the statement is that of liquid where the (nahar – river) occurs.

6.5.5.4 Antonymy

Antonymy is also a category of reiteration. It is employed as part of the study of oppositeness of meaning (Crystal 2003:27), as in (ghaib – the unseen) and (shahādah – the witnessed), (naᶜīm – pleasure) and (jaḥīm – hell), (ḥasanah – good) and (saiyi'ah – evil), (ḥaqq – truth) and (bāṭil – falsehood), (yuḍlil – misguide) and (yahdī – guide), (mu'min – believer) and (kāfir – disbeliever), (jannah – garden) and (nārr – fire), (nūr – light) and (ẓulumāt – darkness).

6.5.5.5 Collocation

Collocation is the co-occurrence of individual lexical items (Crystal 2003:82), i.e., lexical items that regularly co-occur (Halliday and Hasan 1976:284). Lexical cohesion takes place through the occurrence of a different lexical item that is systematically related to the first one, as a synonym or superordinate of it (ibid). There is always the possibility of cohesion between any pair of lexical items which are in some way associated with each other in the language. Certain words collocate with other specific words. In other words, a lexical item has its own collocational environment within the text. We can observe the following facts about the words that have collocational cohesion (ibid:286):

i Such words share the same lexical environment,
ii They occur in collocation with one another,
iii They appear in similar contexts,
iv They generate a cohesive force if they occur in adjacent sentences,
v They weave in and out of successive sentences, and
vi They occur freely both within the same sentence and across sentence boundaries.

Examples of such words in modern standard Arabic are: (jāmiᶜah – university), which collocates with (ṭālib – student), (imtiḥān – exam), which collocates with (su'āl – question), (kalb – dog), which collocates with the verb (yanbaḥ – to bark), (saḥābah – a cloud), which collocates with (maṭar – rain), (nuktah – a joke), which collocates with the verb (yaḍḥak – laugh), (marīḍ – ill), which collocates with (ṭabīb – doctor), (shaᶜar – hair), which collocates with (mishṭ – comb), and (mustashfā –

hospital), which collocates with the noun (radhah – ward). The occurrence of such pairs generates a cohesive effect in the text. In Qur'anic Arabic, however, (nadhīr – warner) collocates with (mubīn – clear), (^{c}adhāb – punishment) collocates with (alīm – painful) or (mubīn – clear), (yaghfir – forgive) collocates with (dhanb – sin), (yastaghfir – seek forgiveness) collocates with (rabb – Lord), (khalaqa – create) collocates with (allāh – God), (yu'tī – give) collocates with (zakāt), and (yuqīm – establish) collocates with (ṣalāt – prayer) or (ḥudūd allāh – the limits of God).

Thus, collocation produces cohesive chains as a result of the lexical relations between such words. In Qur'anic text linguistics, collocation is concerned with the co-occurrence of words that are associated with one another and occur in similar environments. The study of Qur'anic lexical behaviour is of value to Qur'anic textual cohesion. Examples of chains of Qur'anic collocational cohesion are:

Example 1 (Q13)

(samāwāt – heavens) . . . (^{c}arsh – throne) . . . (shams – sun) . . . (qamar – moon) . . . (yajrī – running its course); (arḍ – earth) . . . (rawāsī – set mountains) . . . (anhār – rivers) . . . (thamarāt – fruits) . . . (zawjain – two mates) . . . (al-lail – the night) . . . (al-nahār – the day) . . . (arḍ – earh) . . . (qiṭa^{c}un – plots) . . . (jannāt – gardens) . . . (a^{c}nāb – grapevines) . . . (zar^{c} – crops) . . . (nakhīl – palm trees) . . . (mā' – water) . . . (akl – quality of fruit); (kafarū – disbelieved, denied) . . . (aghlāl fī a^{c}nāqihim – shackles upon their necks) . . . (aṣḥāb al-nār – the companions of the fire) . . . (fīhā khālidūn – they will abide therein eternally); (al-lail – the night) . . . (al-anhār – the day) . . . ; (al-lail – the night) . . . (al-nahār – the day) . . . ; (saiyi'ah – evil) . . . (ḥasanah – good) . . . (rabb – Lord) . . . (maghfirah – forgiveness) . . . (nāss – people) . . . (ẓulm – wrongdoing) . . . (rabb – Lord) . . . (shadīd al-^{c}iqāb – severe in penalty); (unthā – female) . . . (arḥām – wombs); (barq – lightning) . . . (saḥāb – clouds) . . . (ra^{c}d – thunder) . . . (malā'ikah – angels) . . . (ṣawā^{c}iq – thunderbolts) . . . (mā' – water, rain) . . . (sama' – sky) . . . (mā' – water, rain) . . . (awdiyah – valleys) . . . (iḥtamala – carry) . . . (sail – torrent) . . . (zabad – foam) . . . (zabad – foam) . . . (zabad – foam); (yūqid – to heat) . . . (nār – fire); (ābā' – fathers) . . . (azwāj – spouses) . . . (dhurriyyah – descendants) . . . (jannah – paradise) . . . (muttaqūn – the righteous) . . . (anhār – rivers) . . . (ukul – fruits) . . . (ẓil – shade); (azwāj – spouses) . . . (dhurriyyah – descendants).

Example 2 (Q14)

(rīḥ – wind) . . . (yawm ^{c}āṣif – a stormy day) . . . (jahannam – hell) . . . (bi'sa al-qarār – the settlement is wretched); (dār al-bawār – the home of ruin) . . . (jahannam – hell) . . . (bi'sa al-qarār – the settlement is wretched) . . . (al-nār – the fire); (samā' – sky) . . . (mā' – rain) . . . (thamarāt – fruits) . . . (rizq – provision); (mujrimīn – criminals) . . . (muqarranīn fi al-aṣfād – bound together in shackles) . . . (sarābiluhum min qaṭirān – their garments of liquid pitch) . . . (al-nār – the fire).

Example 3 (Q24:61)

laisa ᶜalā al-aᶜmā ḥarajun walā ᶜalā al-aᶜraji ḥarajun walā ᶜalā al-marīḍi ḥarajun walā calā anfusikum an ta'kulū min buyūtikum aw buyūti ābā'ikum aw buyūti ummahātikum aw buyūti ikhwānikum aw buyūti akhawātikum aw buyūti aᶜmāmikum aw buyūti ᶜammātikum aw buyūti akhwālikum aw buyūti khālātikum aw mā malaktum mafātiḥahu aw ṣadiqikum laisa ᶜalikum junāḥun an ta'kulū jamīᶜan aw ashtātan fa'idhā dakhaltum buyūtan fasallimū ᶜalā anfusikum taḥiyyatan min ᶜind allāh mubārakatan ṭaiyibatan – There is not upon the blind any constraint nor upon the lame any constraint nor upon the ill any constraint nor upon yourselves if you eat from your own houses or the houses of your fathers or the houses of your mothers or the houses of your brothers or the houses of your sisters or the houses of your fathers' brothers or the houses of your fathers' sisters or the houses of your mothers' brothers or the houses of your mothers' sisters or from houses whose keys you possess or from the house of your friend. There is no blame upon you whether you eat together or separately. But when you enter houses, give greetings of peace upon each other – a greeting from God, blessed and good. Thus does God make clear to you the āyāt of ordinance that you may understand, Q24:61.

where the chains of Qur'anic collocational cohesion are represented by (al-aᶜmā . . . al-aᶜraji . . . al-marīḍi – the blind . . . the lame . . . the ill), (buyūt . . . ābā'ikum . . . ummahātikum . . . ikhwānikum . . . akhawātikum . . . aᶜmāmikum . . . ᶜammātikum . . . akhwālikum . . . khālātikum . . . ṣadiqikum . . . – houses . . . your fathers . . . your mothers . . . your brothers . . . your sisters . . . your fathers' brothers . . . fathers' sisters . . . mothers' brothers . . . your mothers' sisters . . . your friend), (jamīᶜan . . . ashtātan – together . . . separately), and (sallimū ᶜalā anfusikum taḥiyyatan min ᶜind allāh mubārakatan ṭaiyibatan – give greetings of peace upon each other – a greeting from God, blessed and good).

Example 4 (Q4:22–23)

An example of chains of Qur'anic collocational cohesion at the micro level is:

(abb – father), (umm – mother), (akh – brother), (ukht – sister), (bint – daughter), (ᶜammah – father's sister), (khālah – mother's sister), (bint al-akh – brother's daughter), (bint al-ukht – sister's daughter), Q4:22–23

6.5.5.6 Hyponymy

Hyponymy (hyponym) refers to the relationship between specific and general words. When the meaning of one word is included in the meaning of another, the relationship is called hyponymy. For instance, the word (horse) is a specific word, but the word (animal) is a general word because there are many other types of animals. Therefore, (horse) is the hyponym of (animal). Also, (chair) is the hyponym of (furniture), (orange) is the hyponym of (fruit), and (chicken) is the hyponym of (bird).

This means that the word (horse) is included in (part of) the word (animal), the word (chair) is included in (furniture), the word (orange) is included in (fruit), and the word (chicken) is included in (bird). However, there are other words included in (animal), (furniture), and (fruit). For instance, the other words included in (animal) are: (camel, cat, lion, tiger, cow, calf, bull, sheep, lamb, ram, ewe, stallion, mare, horse, donkey, dog, pig), which are all animals. Therefore, these words are called the co-hyponyms of the superordinate word (animal). It is worthwhile to note that the superordinate is a category of reiteration. Therefore, we can claim that hyponymy is related to entailment (Abdul-Raof 2015:85).

In Qur'anic discourse, hyponymy is also a relationship between specific and general words, i.e., when the meaning of one word is included in the meaning of another, the relationship is called hyponymy. For instance, the word (jānn – a snake) is included in (part of) the word (thuᶜbān – a serpent). Semantically, (thuᶜbān) is the superordinate (it has the generic meaning), while (jānn) is a co-hyponym (it has a specific meaning). The semantic componential features of (thuᶜbān) include: [+ Big], [+ Male], [+ Adult], [+ Long], and [– Fast]. However, the semantic componential features of (jānn) are: [– Big], [± Male], [– Adult], [– Long], and [+ Fast]. The word (thuᶜbān) is employed in Q7:107 to entail its enormous size and to depict an image of horror to the people involved in the scene, while the word (jānn) is used in Q27:10 to entail its tiny size, speed, and agility. The major semantic distinction in the lexical shift from (thuᶜbān) to (jānn) is the fear generated by the size of each reptile, i.e., the componential features of each word (Abdul-Raof 2018:106).

In Qur'anic discourse, we encounter the superordinate noun (insān – human being) and its co-hyponyms (rajul – a man, Q2:282), (mu'min – a he-believer, Q23:1), (imra'ah – a woman, Q4:128), (ṭifl – a child, Q24:31), (mu'minah – a she-believer, Q2:221), (ḥawāriyyūn – the disciples, Q3:52), (munāfiq – a hypocrite, Q9:64), (kāfir – a he-disbeliever, Q2:41), (al-kafirūn – the disbelievers, Q29:47), (nabiy – a prophet, Q33:32), (rasūl – messenger, Q5:41), (qawm – people, Q5:51), (ahl al-kitāb – the People of the Book, Q2:109), (banī isrā'īl – the Children of Israel, Q2:40), (malik – King, Q18:79).

6.5.5.7 Meronymy

Meronymy is a category of reiteration. Meronymy refers to the whole–part relationship between words, such as (hand–finger) where the (hand) is the whole and the (finger) is the part. In other words, the (hand) is bigger than the (finger). Also, the word (tree) represents the whole, but the words that are part of the whole are (trunk, branch, leaf). This applies to Qur'anic discourse where we have (shajarah – tree, Q2:35), which designates the whole, and its related parts are (jidhᶜ – trunk, Q19:23), (waraq – leaves, Q7:22). Similarly, we have the whole in (ṣadr – chest, Q16:106) whose part is (qalb – heart, Q3:159).

Therefore, we can define meronymy as something which is a part of something else, or something which has something else. Thus, a (finger) is a part of the (hand), and a (hand) has (fingers). Other examples of meronymy are: (car–engine), (house–room), (telescope–lens), (door–handle). Meronymy is also related to entailment. For instance, we have the meronymy (cockpit/airplane). Therefore, if we say (David is in the cockpit), this sentence entails (David is in the airplane).

6.6 Summary

Cohesion is concerned with how sentences are interrelated. However, it is not sentence centred but text centred. In other words, cohesion is concerned with the analysis of the text beyond the sentence level and aims to characterize text structure. Cohesion is a prerequisite of successful communication because text segments have to be tied up by cohesive devices. The inappropriate employment of a cohesive device can result in an illogical and contradictory statement. The major cohesive devices are (see Figure 6.1):

1 Reference: This is a relationship between a lexical item and its pronoun. Reference refers to nouns, determiners, personal and demonstrative pronouns, implicit pronouns within a verb, and adverbs. Reference includes:

   i endophoric reference, which is text bound. It refers to someone or something within the text where different pronouns in a text refer to different people, things, or places. With the help of the text, we can recover the information about what a specific pronoun refers to. Endophoric reference includes: personal reference, general reference, anaphoric reference, cataphoric reference, demonstrative reference, extended demonstrative reference, and comparative reference and
   ii exophoric reference, which refers to someone or something that has not been mentioned in the text. Through the context, we can identify the person or thing which the pronoun refers to.

2 Ellipsis: This has three categories:

   i verbal ellipsis, which deals with ellipsis within the verbal group as in responses to yes/no questions, i.e., the verbal segment is ellipted, i.e., it has been taken out. An elliptical verbal group, i.e., a verbal group which involves ellipsis, presupposes one or more words from a previous verbal group,
   ii nominal ellipsis, which deals with how a noun, a noun phrase, or an adjective is ellipted, and
   iii clausal ellipsis, which is concerned with how a verbal clause is ellipted,

3 Substitution: This indicates the replacement of one item by another to avoid repetition. Substitution is either:

   i nominal substitution, which involves nominal substitutes like the demonstrative pronoun (hādhā – this), personal pronoun (huwa – he), the demonstrative pronoun (ulā'ika – those), a general word, and the pronoun (-hum – they) attached to the auxiliary verb (inna), or

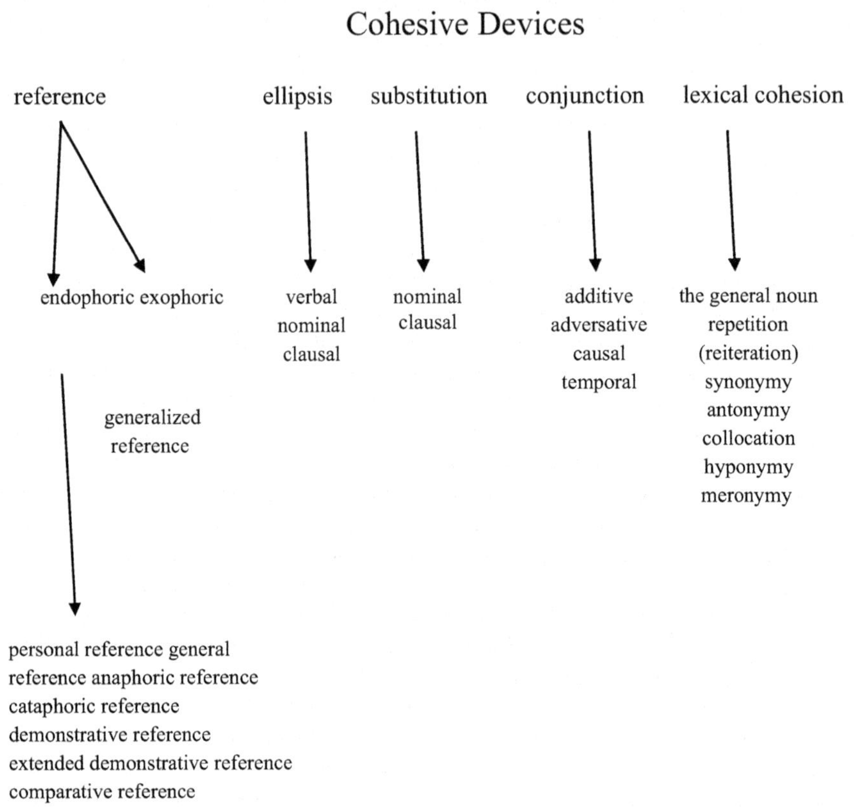

Figure 6.1 Cohesion network in Qur'anic discourse

ii clausal substitution, which is concerned with a whole clause with a main verb. In Qur'anic discourse, the clausal substitutes are like the demonstrative pronoun (dhālika – that), the personal pronoun (ulā'ika – those), the demonstrative pronoun (hādha – this), the pronoun (huwa – he), and the pronoun (hā'ulā' – those).

4 Conjunction: This involves additive conjunction (such as (wa – and)), adversative conjunction (such as (lākin – but)), causal conjunction (such as (laᶜalla – so that)), and temporal conjunction (such as (qabla – before)).
5 Lexical cohesion: This can be achieved through one of the linguistic mechanisms, such as the general noun, reiteration, synonymy, antonymy, collocation, hyponymy, and meronymy.

7 Linguistic inimitability of Qur'anic discourse

7.1 Introduction

This is an investigation of the notion of Qur'anic discourse inimitability with regards to the linguistic and stylistic aspects only. The present chapter argues that the notion of inimitability is concerned with the naturalness and eloquence of Qur'anic discourse and that grammatical, morphological, semantic, and phonetic congruity are the major constituents of inimitability. The notion of inimitability is defined in detail and its major criteria are discussed. The discussion makes reference to the views of Muslim theologians, and a historical account is also provided of how this notion has evolved since the third/ninth century. Reference is also made to the major scholars who have dealt with the notion of inimitability and to the relationship between the notion of piecemeal revelation and inimitability.

7.2 What is inimitability?

The expression 'inimitability' is referred to in Arabic as (i^{c}jāz). Linguistically, the expression i^{c}jāz is a nominalized noun derived from the transitive verb (a^{c}jaza – to make someone unable to do something) and is also morphologically related to the expression mu^{c}jizah (a miracle). For Muslim linguists, Qur'anic genre is free from any form of stylistic, linguistic, or phonetic incongruities which are commonly found in non-Qur'anic discourses. Theologically, however, inimitability denotes the miraculous nature of the Qur'an and its divine source. Thus, the translation of i^{c}jāz is given as 'inimitability' since it is related to the notion that no one can imitate what God makes.

During the very early years of the revelation of the Qur'an, ^{c}Utbah b. Rabī^{c}ah (died 2/624), a disbeliever from Quraish, a dignitary and businessman, was an expert and well-known authority in Arabic rhetoric and especially in the figures of speech and eloquence of Arabic. He admitted that Qur'anic discourse was unique and was not poetry. The same applies to al-Walīd b. al-Maghīrah (died 1/622).

The Qur'an refers to the notion of inimitability in the following statements:

> am yaqūlūna taqawwalahu bal lā ya'uminūn. falya'tū biḥadīthin mithlihi in kānū ṣādiqīn – Do they say: 'He (Muḥammad) made it (the Qur'an) up

himself'. Rather, they do not believe. Let them produce one like it, if what they say is true, Q52:33–34.

am yaqūlūna iftarāhu qul fa'tū bi^{c}ashri siwarin mithlihi muftarayātin wad^{c}ū man istaṭa^{c}tum min dūni allāhi in kuntum ṣādiqīn – If they say: 'He (Muḥammad) has invented it (the Qur'an) himself', say: 'Then produce ten invented sūrahs like it, and call in whoever you can beside God, if you are truthful', Q11:13.

am yaqūlūna iftarāhu qul fa'tū bisūratin mithlihi wad^{c}ū man istaṭa^{c}tum min dūni allāhi in kuntum ṣādiqīn – Do they say: 'He (Muḥammad) has devised it (the Qur'an)?' Say: 'Then produce a sūrah like it, and call on anyone you can beside God if you are telling the truth', Q10:38.

in kuntum fī raibin mimmā nazzalnā ^{c}alā ^{c}abdinā fa'tū bisūratin min mithlihi wad^{c}ū shuhadā'akum min dūni allāhi in kuntum ṣādiqīn. fa'in lam taf^{c}alū walan taf^{c}alū fattaqū al-nāra allatī waqūduhā al-nāsu wal-ḥijāratu u^{c}iddat lil-kāfirīn – If you have doubts about the revelation We have sent down to Our servant, then produce a single sūrah like it – enlist whatever supporters you have other than God – if you truly think you can, Q2:23–24.

In the above statements, the Qur'an challenges the deniers to produce something like the Qur'anic discourse. In other words, the Qur'an makes an implicit reference to its inimitability. However, in terms of inimitability, it is worthwhile to note that the text produced by a denier of the divine source of the Qur'an should not only be based on assonance (al-saj^{c}). To take the challenge, the text produced should emulate the inimitability criteria discussed in what follows.

The Qur'an also defends its genre as unique, as we are informed by:

walaw kāna min ^{c}indi ghair allāhi lawajadū fīhi ikhtilāfan kathīran – If the Qur'an had been from any other than God, they would have found within it much contradiction, Q4:82.

The notion of inimitability of Qur'anic discourse has been a controversial issue among Muslim and non-Muslim scholastics since the ninth/ninth century. Occasional debates took place between the Syriacs, Buddhists, and Magians with the Muslim scholastic theologians and linguists. The notion of inimitability was also controversial among Muslim scholastics and non-scholastics. Inimitability is correlated to the linguistic (grammatical and semantic), phonetic, and rhetorical architecture of Qur'anic genre. In other words, what makes Qur'anic discourse unique and of divine origin rather than man-made (walaw kāna min ^{c}indi ghair allāhi lawajadū fīhi ikhtilāfan kathīran – If the Qur'an had been from any other than God, they would have found within it much contradiction, Q4:82). Since the early decades of the third/ninth century, linguists and rhetoricians expressed particular interest in the notion of stylistic inimitability of Qur'anic genre.

In terms of translation studies, Muslim theologians do not accept the expression 'Qur'an translation'. For them, Qur'anic language is divine, while the translation, no matter how accurate, remains a human language and vulnerable to error.

Secondly, for Muslim theologians, the Qur'anic Arabic is the only 'container' that has room, i.e., linguistic mechanisms, large enough to accommodate the divine message of the Qur'an. By comparison, other languages are smaller-size containers, i.e., they do not possess similar linguistic mechanisms that can accommodate the linguistically and stylistically oriented meanings of Qur'anic Arabic. The difference in the size of the two containers will ultimately lead to an overflow in the small-size container. In translation studies, this is referred to as under-translation. Therefore, theologically, inimitability denotes the miraculous nature of the Qur'an and its divine source. Thus, the translation of i^{c}jāz is given as 'inimitability' since it is related to the notion that no human can imitate what God makes. For Muslim theologians, the Qur'an is the word of God, translation is the word of man. However, they suggest to use the expression 'The Translation of the Meanings of the Qur'an' but not 'The Translation of the Qur'an'.

7.3 Criteria of inimitability

To provide a definition of the notion of inimitability, we need to know what this notion is concerned with, and we also need to diagnose its major criteria. These two points are discussed in what follows:

1. Inimitability is concerned with naturalness and eloquence of discourse (purity of language). An eloquent discourse should possess grammatical, morphological, semantic, and phonetic congruity. An eloquent discourse should be grammatically and lexically well formed.
2. Inimitability is measured by the linguistic, phonetic, stylistic, and rhetorical criteria of congruity, succinctness, eloquence, coherence, cohesion, and elegance in terms of initiation of locution and word order. In other words, inimitability deals with discourse that is free from sluggish sentences (syntactically incongruent) and sluggish style. An inimitable style should be sublime (solid) (raṣīn) and free from stylistic complexity and stylistic impurity and oddity (ibtidhāl, gharābah).
3. Inimitability is also concerned with rhetorical elegance in terms of the word order (al-naẓm) of Qur'anic discourse, the figures of speech (^{c}ilm al-bayan, such as simile, allegory (metaphor), and metonymy), and embellishments (^{c}ilm al-badī^{c}, such as alliteration, antithesis, assonance, chiasmus, epizeuxis, euphemism, hyperbole, polyptoton, pun, rhetorical question, sarcasm, and shift). Both figures of speech and embellishments are considered beautifying mechanisms of discourse. This is referred to as rhetorical inimitability.
4. An inimitable discourse is marked by textual weaving (sibākat, ḥabk al-nass), i.e., the cohesiveness of the overall text is maintained. A text which does not apply the cohesion mechanisms is not a text and lacks textuality. Thus, inimitability is concerned with cohesion at the micro (sentence) level. Qur'anic discourse is marked by both cohesiveness and textuality, as in the following example.

> qālat rabbi annā yakūnu lī waladun walam yamsasnī basharun qāla **kadhālik** allāhu yakhluqu mā yashā' – She (Mary) said: 'My Lord, how will I have a child when no man has touched me?' The angel said: '**Such** is God. He creates what He wills. When He decrees a matter, He only says to it: "Be", and it is', Q3:47

In this text, the word (kadhālik – such) is the cohesive tie that has made the text cohesive and substituted for a whole clause. To remove (kadhālik), the text will not hang together, i.e., it will have neither cohesion nor coherence:

> (qālat rabbi annā yakūnu lī waladun walam yamsasnī basharun qāla (**yakūnu laki waladun walam yamsaski basharun**) allāhu yakhluqu mā yashā' – She (Mary) said: 'My Lord, how will I have a child when no man has touched me?' The angel said: (You will have a child when no man has touched you). 'God creates what He wills. When He decrees a matter, He only says to it: "Be", and it is'). For more details on cohesion, see Chapter 7.

5 Inimitability is also concerned with the configuration of sentence constituents, i.e., the order of words in a sentence. This accounts for many things such as the noun-initial nominal sentence with a main verb. This is where the subject (al-fā^{c}il) of a given sentence is placed sentence-initially (foregrounded) before its verb in order to achieve the illocutionary force of affirmation, as in:

> allāhu yabda'u al-khalqa thumma yu^{c}īduh – God begins creation; then He will repeat it, Q30:11

where the subject noun (allāhu – God) is placed sentence-initially to deliver the text producer's performative intent that it is God only who can begin the creation and who can repeat the creation.

6 Shift is a major feature of inimitability. It refers to stylistic and grammatical change at different levels of language and occurs at different places of the Qur'anic text for different purposes, such as:

i grammatical, morphological, and semantic harmony,
ii collocation and semantic componential features inherent to a given word,
iii stylistic symmetry,
iv phonetic harmony (for cadence and assonance), and most importantly
v perlocutionary effect, i.e., an illocutionary (communicative) force.

Shift in Qur'anic discourse occurs (i) at the micro level within the sentence boundary and (ii) at the macro level beyond the sentence boundary.

Shift in Qur'anic discourse occurs at two levels of Qur'anic Arabic (Abdul-Raof 2018:142):

i at the micro level within the sentence boundary, and
ii at the macro level beyond the sentence boundary.

Qur'anic genre provides intriguing manifestation of the impact of context and co-text on the variation in style in Qur'anic Arabic. Qur'anic discourse is rich with shift which occurs due to one of the following eight factors (ibid):

a Syntactic factors which generate 10 types of stylistic shift: word order, grammatical case endings, person, tense, number (singular/plural form), definiteness (definite/indefinite form), gender (feminine/masculine form), morphological form, substitution, and ellipsis (stylistic ellipsis and grammatical ellipsis).
b Semantic factors which generate five types of stylistic shift: componential features, collocation, surface structure semantic incongruity, semantic redundancy, and violation of selection restriction rule.
c Phonetic factors which generate two types of stylistic shift: assimilation and onomatopoeia.
d Co-textual factors which generate three types of stylistic shift: grammatical co-text which involves five sub-types of stylistic shift (grammatical category, morphological form, number, tense, and word order), lexical co-text, and phonetic co-text.
e Contextual factors which generate three types of stylistic shift: lexical, grammatical, and word order.
f Pragmatic factors which mark the departure from the unmarked (usual) verb-initial word order to the marked (unusual) subject noun-initial word order for three pragmatic reasons: rebuttal/substantiation, affirmation, and specification.
g Repetition which generates four types of stylistic shift: lexical items, formulas, leitmotifs, and parables.
h Surface structure ungrammaticality which generates five types of stylistic shift: number (singular/plural form), morphological form, gender (masculine/feminine form), grammatical case, and anaphoric reference.

Let us consider the following example of shift:

i fayaghfiru liman yashā'u wa yu^{c}adhdhibu man yashā'u – He will forgive whom He wills and punish whom He wills, Q2:284
ii yu^{c}adhdhibu man yashā'u wa yaghfiru liman yashā'u – He will punish whom He wills and forgive whom He wills, Q5:40

Sentence (i) has also occurred in Q3:129, Q5:18, and Q48:14. Structurally, both sentences (i) and (ii) are made of two units:

Unit one: (fayaghfiru liman yashā'u – He will forgive whom He wills), and
Unit two: (yu^{c}adhdhibu man yashā'u – He will punish whom He wills).

The stylistic variation between sentence (i) and sentence (ii) lies in the order of these constituent units. This stylistic shift is not without a good reason. The unmarked (usual) order in Qur'anic genre is the occurrence of the verb (yaghfiru – to forgive) before its antonym counterpart (yu^{c}adhdhibu – to punish) as we have seen in sentence (i) (Q2:284). The pragmatic function of the unmarked word order is to highlight the leitmotif of God's forgiveness that always precedes His wrath. Due to the change in the context of situation surrounding sentence (ii), i.e., Q5:40, a stylistic variation takes place. This is represented by sentence Q5:38, which deals with the male and female thieves and refers to the Islamic legal ruling pertinent to their crime. In order to establish intertextuality between sentences Q5:38 and Q5:40, the verb (yuᶜadhdhibu – to punish) is right-dislocated (placed sentence-initially). Thus, stylistic variation occurs (Abdul-Raof 2018:155).

7 Inimitability is also concerned with phonetic congruity, i.e., the discourse should be free from repugnant sounds and tongue-twisting words. Phonetic congruity is concerned with phonetically close words where their place of articulation is taken into consideration so that phonetic and pronunciation smoothness is achieved in particular and assonance is not hampered in general. Let us consider the phonetic features of the word (al-ṭāmmah – overwhelming calamity, Q79:34) and how it is most relevant to the context in which it has occurred. This word is one of the names of the day of resurrection. It enjoys a special phonetic feature through its voiceless velarised denti alveolar plosive /ṭ/ sound, which makes it compatible to portray the horror of the day of judgement. Its sounds: the velarised denti alveolar plosive /ṭ/, the long vowel /ā/, and the geminated nasal sound /m/ lend it the feature of fear. Denotatively, however, (al-ṭāmmah) designates the meaning that everything will be covered (ṭamma – to cover) such as mountains, rivers, seas, high buildings, houses, and trees. Since the major illocutionary force which (al-ṭāmmah) aims to achieve is to instil fear and horror in the mind of the reader/hearer, the text producer has selected a befitting word for the continuity of the thought (theme) of eschatology. On the macro text level, Q79 is hinged upon frightening and intimidation (al-takhwīf wal-tahwīl wal-tarhīb) to attain perlocutionary effect and heightened psychological impact on the attitude and opinion of the reader/hearer in terms of the horror of the day of judgement. Thus, it cannot be substituted by its alternative (al-ṣākhkhah) due to contextual relevance reasons. Qur'anic assonance achieves both phonetic beauty and coherence. In other words, the āyah-final couplet epithets are neither haphazardly employed nor are they used for the mere purpose of sound (assonance). Rather, the assonance-oriented ayah-final couplets have a text linguistic function, namely coherence. Let us consider the couplet epithets (al-tawwāb al-raḥīm – the accepting of repentance, the merciful, Q2:37, 54, 128, and143) and (ghafūr raḥīm – forgiving and merciful, Q2:173, 182, 192, 199, and 218). The configuration of āyah-final epithets like where the epithet (al-tawwāb – the accepting of repentance) is foregrounded and the epithet (al-raḥīm – the merciful) is foregrounded (placed at the end of the āyah) can be attributed to the fact that such coherence-based configuration aims to achieve the phonetically based rhetorical function of assonance through the word-final nasal sound /m/ where the nasal sounds /n/ or /m/ dominate the macro text phonetic co-text.

8 Eloquence as a major criterion of inimitability is concerned with the purposeful selection (most relevant) of a lexical item in order to achieve the performative intent of the interlocutor (text producer) and to achieve textual coherence. For instance, in (waqadimnā ilā mā ᶜamilū min ᶜamalin fajaᶜalnāhu habā'an manthūrā – We will approach what they have done of deeds and make them as dispersed dust, Q25:23), the lexical item (qadimnā – to approach, i.e., to regard) is selected as a relevant word which depicts an imagery of someone who has come from a long journey (qadima – to arrive from a journey). Thus, the speaker, who is likened to a traveller, has arrived and has given the audience some time to think. However, when he comes to meet them, he has found them in a state completely different from what he has commanded them to do. This was a surprise for him, and he makes their wrong deeds like dispersed dust. Similarly in (muñir – luminous, Q25:61) where the adjective is employed for contextual coherence and succinctness. It entails a reflector of light. Thus, it collocates with (qamar – moon) → (qamar munīr – luminous moon). However, the word (sirāj – burning lamp, Q25:61) is also used to attain contextual coherence and succinctness since it entails a source of light + heat. Thus, it collocates with (shams – sun) → (jaᶜala fīhā sirāj – God placed in the sky a burning lamp).

9 One of the major criteria of inimitability is the well-formedness of the sentence. Eloquence as a major criterion of inimitability is also concerned with the well-formedness of the sentence (sabk al-jumlah). For instance, in (yaḥsabūna kulla ṣaiḥatin ᶜalaihim hum al-ᶜaduwu faḥdharhum – They think that every shout is against them. They are the enemy, so beware of them, Q63:4), if we make changes in terms of words and word order, the eloquence of the sentence would have disappeared and we get a stylistically ill-formed sentence: (yaḥsabūna kulla ṣaiḥatin (wāqiᶜah) ᶜalaihim (wahum ᶜaduwu faḥdharhum)).

10 Succinctness as a major criterion of inimitability is concerned with brevity of the information provided. In other words, it is related to Paul Grice's maxim of quantity: to make your contribution as informative as is required, i.e., do not make your contribution more informative than is required (Grice 1975). Examples of succinct statements are: (fanbidh ilaihim ᶜalā sawā' – Throw their treaty back to them, putting you on equal terms, Q8:58), which means you can go to war against them, but you should never be treacherous to them and inform your enemy that their time is over; (latajidannahum aḥraṣa al-nāsi ᶜalā ḥayāt – You will surely find them the most greedy of people for life, Q2:96), which means they are more greedy for more years to live, i.e., the expression (mazīdin min – for more) is deleted for brevity. Thus, we have (latajidannahum aḥraṣa al-nāsi ᶜalā (mazīdin min) al-ḥayāt).

Inimitability is also related to succinct sayings of wisdom, such as: (walā yaḥīqu al-makru al-saiyi'u illā bi'ahlih – The evil plot does not encompass except its own people, Q35:43). The evil plot does not encompass except its own people, (innamā baghyukum ᶜalā anfusikum – Your injustice is only against yourselves, Q10:23), (kullu nafsin dhā'iqatu al-mawt – Every soul will taste death, Q21:35), (kullu nafsin bimā kasabat rahīnah – Every soul will be retained for what it has earned, Q74:38), (qul kullun yaᶜmalu ᶜalā shākilatihi – Say: 'Each works according to his manner', Q17:84), (walā tansa naṣībaka min al-dunyā – Do not forget your share of the world, Q28:77), (taḥsabuhum jamīᶜan waqulūbuhum shattā – You think they are together, but their hearts are diverse, Q59:14), (walā taziru wāziratun wizra ukhrā – No bearer of burdens will bear the burden of others, Q6:164), and (kullu ḥizbin bimā ladaihim fariḥūn – Each faction is rejoicing in what it has, Q23:53).

11 Inimitability is also concerned with coherence at the micro level (word, phrase, and sentence) and at the macro level, which is the larger text. A major text linguistic criterion of inimitability is relational coherence, i.e., the interrelatedness between different text segments to achieve sequentiality (continuity, chaining) of the thought's illocutionary force, as in the following example whose text segment is taken from Q28:88:

> 1 (walā tadᶜu maᶜa allāhi ilāhan ākhar – Do not invoke with God another deity) → 2. (lā ilāha illā hū – There is no deity except Him) → 3. (kullu shai'in hālikun illā wajhahu – Everything will be destroyed except His face) → 4. (lahu al-ḥukmu – He is the judgement) → 5. (ilaihi turjaᶜūn – To Him you shall all be brought back) where we have a series of different messages (text segments) but all have the same thought and intended meaning and, most importantly, all point to one illocutionary force intended by the text producer, namely 'monotheism'. Thus, there is a relationship between the appropriate positioning of a sentence constituent and coherence.

Coherence between consecutive sentences is a criterion of inimitability. Let us consider Q40:3 as an example of coherence and textual progression at a micro textual level. The prefatory statement of Q40:2 introduces the thought of prophethood (tanzīlu al-kitāb – the revelation of the Book (the Qur'an)) and ends with God's epithet couplet (al-ᶜaziz al-ᶜalīm – the exalted in might, the knowing). To achieve coherence for the sake of continuity of the introductory thought which is prophethood, substantiating statements are required for the rebuttal of sceptics of the revelation and Muḥammad's prophethood. To achieve powerful substantiation and effective rebuttal, syntax-based coherence becomes a prerequisite. The most befitting mechanism for this text linguistic role is the no-main-verb nominal sentence structure. Thus, a series of six no-main-verb nominal sentences is employed to achieve continuity of thought and rebuttal to those who dispute the revelation:

> ghāfir al-dhanb + wa qābil al-tawb + shadīd al-ᶜiqāb + dhi al-ṭawl + lā ilāha illā hū + ilaihi al-maṣīr – The forgiver of sin + the acceptor of repentance + the severe in punishment + the owner of abundance + there is no deity except Him + to Him is the destination, Q40:3

In terms of continuity of senses, it is interesting to note that further rebuttal is provided in the subsequent statements Q40:4 (No one disputes concerning the signs of God except those who disbelieve, so be not deceived by their uninhibited movement throughout the land), Q40:5 (They disputed by using falsehood to attempt to invalidate thereby the truth). Finally, the use of the retribution statement Q40:6 against those who dispute the revelation (Thus has the decree of your Lord come into effect upon those who disbelieved that they are companions of the fire). For more details on coherence, see Chapter 5.

12 A major feature of inimitability of Qur'anic discourse is thematic chaining between consecutive chapters. This is to do with the sequentiality of thought among running chapters. Qur'anic chapters are chained (dovetailed) to each other where the beginning of a chapter harks back to either the beginning or end of the previous chapter, the end of a chapter harks back at the beginning of the same chapter or at the end of the previous chapter, and so on. Thus, chaining is achieved. Let us consider the end of Q54:1, which harks back at the end of Q53:57 where both text segments have the thought (theme, leitmotif) of eschatology (resurrection) and reference is made to the hour. Similarly, the beginning of Q55:1 harks back at Q54:55 where both have made reference to the same thought which is God: the Lord of mercy (al-raḥmān) → the all-powerful sovereign (malīk muqtadir). Then the end of Q55:78 harks back at the beginning of Q55:1 where both refer to God. For more details on Qur'anic coherence, see Abdul-Raof (2003, 2005a).

13 Inimitability is concerned with foregrounding (al-taqdīm) for the purpose of saliency. Foregrounding is the accurate configuration of sentence constituents and is a major grammatical feature of Qur'anic discourse, as in:

> bil-ākhirati hum yūqinūn – In the hereafter they firmly believe, Q2:4

where we have a sentence-initial prepositional phrase (bil-ākhirati – in the hereafter) rather than a verb-initial sentence (yūqinūn bil-ākhirati – They firmly believe in the hereafter). The context is about 'those conscious of God, who believe in the unseen', Q2:2–3. Thus, to achieve coherence, saliency is given to eschatology as a tenet of faith 'in the hereafter' since it is the focus of the text producer's message rather than the verb (yūqin – believe firmly).

14 A requirement of inimitability is the purposeful selection of a specific grammatical form through which the text producer's performative intent is achieved and the illocutionary force is delivered to the audience, as in:

> dhālika al-kitābu lā raiba fīhi hudan lil-muttaqīn – This is the Book about which there is no doubt, a guidance for those conscious of God, Q2:1

where the active participle (muttaqūn – the conscious of God) is purposefully selected rather than the alternative verb form (yattaqūn) or the alternative grammatical pattern (alladhīna yattaqūn – who are conscious of God)

→ (dhālika al-kitābu lā raiba fīhi hudan lilladhīna yattaqūn – This is the Book about which there is no doubt, a guidance for those {who are} conscious of God).

15 A requirement of inimitability is the purposeful selection of a specific grammatical structure through which the text producer's performative intent is achieved and the illocutionary force is delivered to the audience. In other words, the no-main-verb nominal sentence is purposefully employed as a stylistic technique for the achievement of coherence and the illocutionary force of affirmation, as in:

> al-ḥamdu lillāh rabb al-ᶜālamīn – All praise is due to God, Lord of the worlds, Q1:2

where this nominal sentence initiates the message through the nominalized noun (masdar) → (al-ḥamdu) to achieve the illocutionary force of [+ Continuity] and [+ Permanency] of our praise to God. Through the nominalized grammatical structure, the praise becomes continuous, and there is no interruption whatsoever to our praise to the Lord. However, this illocutionary force ceases through the alternative verbal form:

> (naḥmid allāh rabb al-ᶜālamīn – We give all due praise to God, Lord of the worlds). This verbal syntactic form designates the illocutionary force of [+ Renewability] and [– Continuity], which do not befit God. In other words, the verb-initial text means our praise to the Lord is interrupted and not continuous.

16 A major feature of inimitability is semantic contrastiveness, which is concerned with partially synonymous words, but each has distinct semantic componential features, entailment, collocation, and most importantly, different illocutionary force, as in (thuᶜbān) and (jānn). The noun (thuᶜbān – snake, Q7:107) and the noun (jānn – small snake, serpent, Q27:10) occur in the context of the story of Moses and Pharaoh. The denotative meaning of both nouns represents a reptile. However, the difference between the two nouns stems from their innate semantic componential features. This subtle semantic difference can also be captured through the semantic relationship of hyponymy, which is a relationship between specific and general words, i.e., when the meaning of one word is included in the meaning of another, the relationship is called hyponymy. Thus, the word (jānn) is included in (is part of) the word (thuᶜbān). In semantics, (thuᶜbān) is the superordinate (it has a generic meaning), while (jānn) is a co-hyponym (it has a specific meaning). For instance, (furniture) has a generic meaning, but (chair) has a specific meaning. Thus, (furniture) is the superordinate, while (chair) is a co-hyponym.

The semantic componential features of (thuᶜbān) include: [+ Big], [+ Male], [+ Adult], [+ Long], and [– Fast]. However, the semantic componential features of (jānn) are: [– Big], [± Male], [– Adult], [– Long], and [+ Fast]. The word (thu^{c}bān) is employed in Q7:107 to entail its enormous size and to depict an image of horror to the people involved in the scene, while the word (jānn) is used in Q27:10 to entail its tiny size, speed, and agility. The major semantic distinction in the lexical shift from (thu^{c}bān) to (jānn) is the fear generated by the size of each reptile, i.e., the componential features of each word.

For more details on semantic contrastiveness, see Abdul-Raof (2018:97).

Similarly, a semantic distinction is made between the partial synonyms (sanah – year) and (^{c}amm – year) where each has a different contextual meaning. The word (sanah) occurs in the context of hard times, financial hardship, and adverse economic situations, as in Q12:47. However, the word (^{c}amm) occurs in the context of affluence and economic prosperity, as in Q12:49.

17 Antithesis and antonymy are major criteria of inimitability. These are one of the major linguistic characteristics of Qur'anic discourse, as in:

> qul allāhumma mālika al-mulki tu'tī al-mulka man tashā' wa tanzi^{c}u al-mulka mimman tashā' wa tu^{c}izzu man tashā' wa tudhillu man tashā' – Say: 'O God, owner of sovereignty, You give sovereignty to whom You will and You take sovereignty away from whom You will. You honour whom You will and You humble whom You will', Q3:26

where antithesis is between the text segments (tu'tī al-mulka man tashā' – You give sovereignty to whom You will) → (tanzi^{c}u al-mulka mimman tashā' – You take sovereignty away from whom You will) and (tu^{c}izzu man tashā' – You honour whom You will) → (tudhillu man tashā' – You humble whom You will).

> falyaḍḥahū qalīlan wal yabkū kathīran – So, let them laugh a little and then weep much, Q9:82

where antithesis is between the text segments (yaḍḥahū qalīlan – laugh a little) → (yabkū kathīran – weep much).

> fa'ammā man a^{c}ṭā wattaqā waṣaddaqa bil-ḥusnā fasanuyassiruhu lil-yusrā wa'ammā man bakhila wastaghnā wakadhdhaba bil-ḥusnā fasanuyassiruhu lil-^{c}usrā – As for he who gives and fears God and believes in the best reward, We will ease him toward ease. But as for he who withholds and considers himself free of need and denies the best reward, We will ease him toward difficulty, Q92:5–10

where antithesis is between the text segments (fa'ammā man a^{c}ṭā wattaqā waṣaddaqa bil-ḥusnā fasanuyassiruhu lil-yusrā – as for he who gives and fears God and believes in the best reward, We will ease him toward ease) → (wa'ammā man bakhila wastaghnā wakadhdhaba bil-ḥusnā fasanuyassiruhu lil-^{c}usrā – as for he who withholds and considers himself free of need and denies the best reward, We will ease him toward difficulty).

> mā yastawī al-aᶜmā wal-baṣīr walā al-ẓulumāt walā al-nūr walā al-ẓillu walā al-ḥarūr wamā yastawī al-aḥyā' walā al-amwāt – The blind and the seeing are not equal, nor are the darknesses and the light, nor are the shade and the heat, and nor are the living and the dead, Q35:19–22

where we have antonymy (oppositeness) between the lexemes (al-aᶜmā – the blind) and (al-baṣīr – the seeing), (al-ẓulumāt – the darknesses) and (al-nūr – the light), (al-ẓillu – the shade) and (al-ḥarūr – the heat), and between (al-aḥyā' – the living) and (al-amwāt – the dead).

18 Repetition is another feature of inimitability. Recurrence (repetition), according to Beaugrande and Dressler (1981:55), is prominently employed to assert and affirm.

This is represented by the repetition of single words, formulas, sentences, and Prophets' parables:

i repetition of single words, as in (al-qāriᶜah. mā al-qāriᶜah. wamā adrāka mā al-qāriᶜah – The striking calamity. What is the striking calamity? And what can make you know what the striking calamity is?, Q101:1–3) and (al-ḥāqqah. mā al-ḥāqqah. wamā adrāka mā al-ḥāqqah – The inevitable reality. What is the inevitable reality? And what can make you know what the inevitable reality is?, Q69:1–3) for the illocutionary force of glorification and arousing fear.

ii repetition of formulas, as in (fabi'aiyī ālā'i rabbikumā tukadhdhibān – So which of the favours of your Lord would you deny?, Q55), which has been repeated 31 times. Also (a'ilāhun maᶜa allāh – Is there a deity with God?, Q27:60–64), which is repeated five times.

iii repetition of sentences, as in (kallā sawfa taᶜlamūn. thumma kallā sawfa taᶜlamūn – No! You are going to know. Then, no! You are going to know, Q102:3–4) and (mā adrāka mā yawm al-dīn. thumma mā adrāka mā yawm al-din – What can make you know what the day of recompense is? Then, what can make you know what the day of recompense is?, Q82:17–18) for the illocutionary force of threat. However, the repetition of sentences like (afara'aitum mā tumnūn . . . afara'aitum mā taḥruthūn . . . afara'aitum al-mā'a alladhī tashrabūn . . . afara'aitum al-nāra allatī tūrūn – Consider the semen which you eject? . . . Consider the seeds you sow in the ground . . . Consider the water you drink . . . Consider the fire you kindle, Q56:58, 63, 68, 71) has the illocutionary force of highlighting God's blessings upon mankind and God's omnipotence. The repetition of sentences like (inna fī dhālika la'āyatan wamā kāna aktharuhum mu'minīn – Indeed in that is a sign, but most of them were not to be believers, Q26:8, 67, 103, 121, 139, 174, 190) has the illocutionary force of reminding, i.e., learning a lesson from the fate of past unbelieving nations. The repetition of (laqad yassarnā al-qur'āna lil-dhikri fahal min muddakir – We have made it easy to learn lessons from the Qur'an, Q54:17, 22, 32, 40) for the illocutionary force of glorification of the Qur'an. The repetition of (fakaifa kāna ᶜadhābī wanudhur – How terrible was My punishment and My warnings!, Q54:16, 21, 30) is for the illocutionary force of threat.

iv repetition of Prophets' parables, such as the parable of Noah, which has occurred in the Qur'an 23 times: Q4:163, Q6:84, Q7:59–64, Q9:70, Q10:71–73, Q11:25–49, Q14:9, Q17:17, Q21:76–77, Q23:23–30, Q26:105–122, Q29:14–15, Q33:7, Q37:75–82, Q40:5, Q42:13, Q50:12–14, Q51:46, Q53:52, Q54:9–16, Q57:26, Q66:10, and Q71:1–28. Although the parable of Noah has occurred 23 times at different places and in varying lengths, in all these 23 instances, different stylistic patterns and linguistic structures have been employed. The parable of Moses has occurred 10 times in the Qur'an: Q7:103–157, Q10:75–93, Q11:96–101, Q20:9–99, Q23:45–68, Q27:7–14, Q3–44, Q40:23–56.

It is worthwhile to note that repetition is not periphrasis (al-ishāb, al-ḥashu), i.e., Qur'anic discourse is free from irrelevant details.

19 Mutashābihāt (linguistically similar but stylistically dissimilar sentences) is one of the most intriguing features of inimitability. The occurrence of mutashābihāt sentences is a major textual feature of Qur'anic discourse. For instance, the linguistic structure of (wamā uhillā bihi lighair allāh – That which has been dedicated to other than God, Q2:173) is similar to (wamā uhillā lighair allāh bihi – That which has been dedicated to other than God, Q5:3, Q6:145, and Q16:115). Also in: (waqālū lan tamassanā al-nāru illā aiyāman ma^{c}dūdah – And they said: 'Never will the fire touch us except for a few numbered days', Q2:80) and (waqālū lan tamassanā al-nāru illā aiyāman ma^{c}dūdat – And they said: 'Never will the fire touch us except for a few numbered days', Q3:24). Although they are structurally similar, the stylistic differences between any two mutashābihāt sentences are not merely cosmetic. There is a significant semantic difference between any pair of mutashābihāt sentences. To unearth the semantic distinction between two mutashābihāt sentences, we need to take into consideration three major factors:

i the context in which a pair of mutashābihāt sentences occur,
ii the need to achieve grammatical or stylistic symmetry, and
iii the grammatical, lexical, and stylistic co-text.

Co-text is defined as the linguistic context and the relevant textual environment in which a word or a sentence occurs. The surrounding co-text can influence the meaning of a word (Abdul-Raof 2018:63).

An interesting example of mutashābihāt is:

> lā taqtulū awlādakum min imlāqin naḥnu narzuqukum wa'iyyāhum – Do not kill your children in fear of poverty. We will provide for you and for them, Q6:151

> lā taqtulū awlādakum khashyata imlāqin naḥnu narzuhum wa'iyyākum – Do not kill your children for fear of poverty. We will provide for them and for you, Q17:31

where in Q6:151, the notion of provision to parents (naḥnu narzuqukum – We will provide for you (parents)) precedes the notion of provision to their children (wa'iyyāhum – and will provide for them). However, in Q17:31, the notion of provision to children (naḥnu narzuhum – We will provide for them) precedes the notion of provision to their parents (wa'iyyākum – and will provide for you (parents)). The reason for the shift in word order is attributed to the fact that in Q6:151, the whole family were suffering from poverty, i.e., both the parents and their children were poor. In order to avoid further financial hardship (poverty), the poor parents resorted to killing their own children as a precautionary measure. Thus, it is the parents who are primarily concerned in Q6:151, and the text segment that refers to the parents' provision is placed before (i.e., foregrounded, given focus and saliency) the other text segment that refers to the children. This is a stylistic measure to reassure the poor parents that they should not worry about their provision, i.e., to send a message to the parents that their provision is guaranteed by God.

However, the word order in Q17:31 is attributed to the fact that the parents were financially well off, i.e., the parents were not poor. The well-off parents are worried that, in the future, their children may be poor, i.e., their children will suffer from wrongly anticipated financial hardship. Due to the parents' groundless apprehension about their children's poverty, the text segment that refers to the children's poverty is placed first (i.e., foregrounded, given saliency) before the text segment that refers to the parents. This is a stylistic measure to reassure the rich parents that they should not worry about their children's provision. In other words, to send a message to the well-off parents that their children's provision in the future is guaranteed by God.

20 The argumentation technique of God's omnipotence as a means of persuading the deniers of eschatology (resurrection) and a rebuttal to their argument, as in:

> wanazzalnā min al-samā'i mā'an mubārakan fa'anbatnā bihi jannātin waḥabba al-ḥaṣīd. wal-nakhla bāsiqātin lahā ṭalᶜum naḍīd. rizqan lil-ᶜibād wa'aḥyainā bihi baldatan maitan kadhālika al-khurūj – We (God) have sent down blessed rain from the sky and made grow thereby gardens and grain from the harvest. And lofty palm trees having fruit arranged in layers – as provision for the servants, and We have given life thereby to a dead land. Thus, is the resurrection, Q50:9–11

> alam yaku nuṭfatan min maniyyin yumnā. thumma kāna ᶜalaqatan fakhalaqa fasawwā. fajaᶜala al-zawjaini al-dhakara wal-unthā. alaisa dhālika biqādirin ᶜalā an yuḥyiya al-mawtā? – Had he (man) not been a sperm from emitted semen? Then, he was a clinging clot, and God created his form and proportioned him and made of him two mates, the male and the female. Is not that creator able to give life to the dead, Q75:37–40

Through deductive reasoning, the deniers of eschatology will reach a sound conclusion that God who has given life to a dead land by the rain (Q50:11) and who is the creator of man (Q75:40) is equally able to resurrect the dead.

For more details on deductive reasoning, see Chapter 4, Section 4.3.2.

21 Intertextuality is a major feature of inimitability in Qur'anic discourse. Intertextuality is one of the seven standards of textuality which refers to the dependence of one text on another. For Beaugrande and Dressler (1981:10), a text is dependent upon the knowledge of one or more previously encountered texts. It subsumes the ways in which the production and reception of a given text depend upon the participant's knowledge of other texts (ibid:182). Examples of Qur'anic intertextuality are:

> waqālū hādhihi an^{c}āmun waḥarthun ḥijrun lā yaṭ^{c}amuhā illā man nashā'u biza^{c}mihim wa'an^{c}āmun ḥurrimat ẓuhūruhā wa'an^{c}āmun lā yadhkurūna ismā allāhi ^{c}alaihā iftirā'an calaihi sayajzīhim bimā kānū yaftarūn – They say: 'These animals and crops are forbidden. No one may eat from them except when we will', according to their claim. There are those camels whose backs are forbidden by them and those upon which the name of God is not mentioned – all of this is an invention of untruth about Him. He will punish them for what they were inventing, Q6:138

which is intertextually related to (explained by) Q10:59:

> qul ara'aitum mā anzala allāhu lakum min rizqin faja^{c}altum minhu ḥarāman waḥalālan qul a'allāhu adhina lakum am ^{c}alā allāhi taftarūn – Say: 'Have you seen what God has sent down to you of provision of which you have made some lawful and some unlawful?' say: 'Has God permitted you to do so, or do you invent something about God?', Q10:59

The text segment that follows involves a semantically ambiguous object noun phrase (nāqata allāhi wasuqyāhā – the she-camel of God or her drink):

> faqāla lahum rasūlū allāhi nāqata allāhi wasuqyāhā – The messenger of God (Prophet Ṣālih) said to them: 'The she-camel of God or her drink', Q91:13

The above sentence is intertextually related, disambiguated, and explained by the following sentences:

> qāla hādhihi nāqatun lahā shirbun walakum shirbu yawmin ma^{c}lūm. walā tamassūhā bisū'in faya'khudhakum ^{c}adhābu yawmin ^{c}aẓīm – He ((Prophet Ṣāliḥ) said: 'This is a she-camel. For it is a specified time of drink and for you is a specified time of drink. Each is on a known day. Do not touch her with harm, lest you be seized by the punishment of a terrible day'), Q26:155–156

22 Inimitability is also concerned with imagery which provides vivid depiction of different situations. An instance of imagery is like an attractive painting by a skilful portraitist, as in the following examples:

- i imagery of a false charitable person who shows off his charitable deeds, i.e., he spends his wealth for fame only. We have the image of a large smooth stone upon which is dust. This person wrongly thinks this is a fertile piece of land. However, heavy rain falls and leaves the large, smooth stone completely bare. The truth has unfolded. It is not a fertile land but merely a useless stone. Thus, his effort went to waste and he earns no reward for his deeds: (O you who have believed, do not invalidate your charities with reminders of it or injury as does one who spends his wealth only to be seen by the people and does not believe in God and the last day. Such a person is like a large smooth stone upon which is dust and is hit by a downpour that leaves it bare. Such people are unable to keep anything of what they have earned. God does not guide the disbelievers, Q2:264).
- ii imagery of a true charitable person who spends his wealth to gain God's approval. Such a genuine charitable person is like a garden on a hill which produces double its normal yield when heavy rain falls. No matter how little effort he makes, he will still be rewarded. The garden produces fruits regardless of the quantity of rain: (The example of those who spend their wealth seeking means to the approval of God and assuring reward for themselves is like a garden on a high ground which is hit by a downpour – so it yields its fruits in double. Even if it is not hit by a downpour, then a drizzle is sufficient. God is seeing of what you do, Q2:265).
- iii imagery of a camel trying to enter into the eye of a needle: (Indeed, those who deny Our (God's) statements and are arrogant toward them – the gates of heaven will not be opened for them, nor will they enter paradise until a camel enters into the eye of a needle, Q7:40).
- iv imagery of a person who has been endowed with knowledge but he leaves it aside and becomes busy with worldly affairs: (Tell them the story of the man to whom We (God) gave knowledge of Our messages but he detached himself from them; so Satan pursued him, and he went astray. If We had willed, We could have elevated him thereby, but he adhered instead to the earth and followed his own desires – he was like a dog that pants with a lolling tongue whether you drive it away or leave it alone. Such is the image of those who reject Our signs. Tell them the story so that they may reflect, Q7:175–176).
- v imagery of people who are trying on the day of judgement to put together their deeds. Their work now is like a person who is trying to collect flying ashes on a stormy day: (The deeds of those who reject their Lord are like ashes that the wind blows furiously on a stormy day: they have no power over anything they have gained. That is extreme error, Q14:18).

vi imagery of a person who assigns partners to God: (Devote yourselves to God and do not associate anything with Him. The person who does so is like someone who has been hurled down from the skies and snatched up by the birds or flung to a remote place by the wind, Q22:31).

vii imagery of billions of people like swarming locusts are summoned on the day of judgement to a horrific event rushing towards God. People are leaving their graves, their eyes downcast, and are crying: (Their eyes are humbled; they will emerge from their graves as if they were spreading locusts, Q54:9).

7.4 Differences among theologians

This is a discussion of the theological differences between Muslim theologians who represent the scholastics and the non-scholastics, i.e., the differences between Mu^ctazilites and non-Mu^ctazilites in terms of inimitability. Scholastic (al-mutakallimūn), i.e., Mu^ctazili, theologians view the notion of inimitability differently. From a stylistic perspective, the major differences between Mu^ctazili and non-Mu^ctazili linguists with regards to inimitability of Qur'anic discourse are:

i whether the inimitability of Qur'anic style is attributed to its eloquence (al-faṣāḥah) or to its order system (al-naẓm), and

ii whether the Arabs are able to imitate the style of the Qur'an but God has discouraged them to do so or the Arabs are unable to imitate the style of the Qur'an.

However, it is important to note that in terms of i^cjāz and rhetorical studies, the two jargons 'eloquence' (al-faṣāḥah) and 'order system' (al-naẓm) have been employed by Mu^ctazilites, i.e., scholastics, and non-Mu^ctazilites interchangeably, i.e., they are synonymous expressions.

7.5 Historical overview of inimitability

The notion of inimitability of Qur'anic discourse has been a controversial issue among Muslim and non-Muslim scholastics since the third/ninth century. Occasional debates took place between the Syriacs, Buddhists, and Magians with the Muslim scholastic theologians and linguists. The notion of inimitability was also controversial among Muslim scholastics and non-scholastics. Since the early decades of the third/ninth century, linguists, and rhetoricians expressed particular interest in the notion of stylistic inimitability of Qur'anic genre.

The early years of the Abbasid era (132–655/749–1257) was characterized by the emergence of the notion of inimitability around which there was debate between linguists and the scholastics. As a result, we witness the evolution of al-ṣarfah (dissuasion, discouraging), a notion which was introduced by Ibrāhīm b. Saiyār al-Naẓẓām (d. 231/845), a Mu^ctazili linguist. The notion of al-ṣarfah was first coined by the Mu^ctizili theologian Wāṣil b. ^cAṭā' (d. 131/748) and then adopted by Ibrāhīm al-Naẓẓām. Later on, the notion of al-ṣarfah was challenged by linguists like Abu ᶜUthmān ᶜAmru b. Baḥr b. Maḥbūb al-Jāḥiẓ (d. 255/868), who was a Muᶜazili linguist, the founder of Arabic rhetoric, and a student of al-Naẓẓām.

Other linguists who opposed the al-ṣarfah notion were Abu Bakr Muḥammad b. al-Ṭaiyib al-Bāqillānī (d. 403/1012), ᶜAbd al-Qāhir b. ᶜAbd al-Raḥmān al-Jurjānī (d. 471/1078 or 474/1081), and Fakhr al-Dīn al-Rāzī (d. 606/1209). The inimitability-oriented linguistic approach was led by the iconic rhetorician al-Jurjānī, who wrote *Dalā'il al-Iᶜjāz*, in which he introduced his theory of word order (al-naẓm) in Qur'anic discourse, and al-Zamakhsharī (d. 538/1143), who put al-Jurjānī's theory into practice in his exegesis book *al-Kshshāf.*

The tip of the iceberg began during the third/ninth century when Muslim scholastics (al-mutakallimūn) and linguists responded to the claims by Qur'an critics that the language of the Qur'an was imitable. In response to the sceptics of the inimitability of the Qur'an, al-Jurjānī wrote *Dalā'il al-Iᶜjāz*, which was about the innate linguistic and rhetorical characteristics of Qur'anic discourse.

During the modern phase of Qur'anic exegesis, scholarship on the notion of Qur'anic inimitability continued. However, the approach to the notion of inimitability has taken two different forms of scholarship:

- i The first form is an extension of the linguistic scholarship that evolved during the recording phase (third/ninth century onwards) of Qur'anic exegesis.
- ii The second form of research has been developed during the 20th century and is scientifically based. This falls outside the scope of the present chapter.

Thus, we have two approaches to Qur'anic inimitability: (i) linguistically oriented and (ii) scientifically oriented.

Modern scholars like ᶜOdat Allāh al-Qaisī (1996) have mentioned two major features of linguistic inimitability:

- i semantic inimitability (al-iᶜjāz bil-maᶜānī), and
- ii word order inimitability (al-iᶜjāz bil-naẓm).

However, al-Qaisī (ibid) mentions a third feature (al-iᶜjaz bil-ghaib – inimitability through the unseen), which falls outside the scope of our interest in the present chapter.

7.5.1 Dissuasion versus inability to emulate

During the third/ninth century, linguists expressed particular interest in the notion of stylistic inimitability of Qur'anic discourse. As a result, this notion took centre stage in linguistic scholarship and became controversial. This linguistic controversy led to the birth of the theological notion of the al-ṣarfah (dissuasion, aversion) notion, which was adopted by Ibrāhīm b. Saiyār al-Naẓẓām (d. 231/845), who claimed that Qur'anic discourse was inimitable but the Arabs could not challenge its genre and match its style because God dissuaded them to challenge Qur'anic style. In other words, the Arabs could have produced a discourse similar in style to that of the Qur'an, but God discouraged them to do so. al-Naẓẓām's proposition is intertextually related to the following statements:

> sa'aṣrifu ᶜan āyātī alladhīna yatakbbaruna fī al-arḍi bighairi al-ḥaqqi – I will keep distracted from my signs those who behave arrogantly on Earth, Q7:146.
>
> ṣarafa allāhu qulūbahum – God has turned away their hearts, Q9:127.

This claim is echoed in Qur'anic exegesis as: (ṭabaᶜa allāhu ᶜala qulūbihim – God has sealed the Arabs' hearts from imitating the Qur'an) with reference to statements like Q4:155, Q7:101, Q9:87 and 93, Q16:108, Q47:16, and Q63:3.

The inimitability-oriented linguistic approach is hinged on the premise that although the contemporary Arabs at the time of the revelation of the Qur'an reached the peak of their linguistic proficiency and competence, they found it impossible to compose sentences that could match Qur'anic genre. Classical and modern inimitability-oriented linguists hold the view that the Qur'an has come up with unparalleled discourse features such as stylistic patterns, linguistic structures, and textual chaining of coherence which the Arabs were unaware of and, thus, were unable to emulate. The inimitability-oriented premise is referred to by Q10:38 (Do they say about Muḥammad: 'He invented the Qur'an'? Say: 'Then, bring forth a sūrah like it and call upon for assistance whomever you can besides God, if you should be truthful') and Q11:13 (Do they say about Muḥammad: 'He invented the Qur'an'? Say: 'Then, bring ten sūrahs like it that have been invented and call upon for assistance whomever you can besides God, if you should be truthful). Most importantly, the major argument of the notion of inimitability is hinged upon: (walaw kāna min ᶜindi ghair allāhi lawajadū fīhi ikhtilāfan kathīran – If the Qur'an had been from anyone other than God, they would have found much inconsistency in it', Q4:82).

Muᶜtazili linguists like al-Rummāni and Ibn Sinān believed in the theological notion of al-ṣārfah and that āyah-final expressions (fawāṣil al-āyāt), assonance (al-sajᶜ), and eloquence (al-faṣāḥah) represented features of Qur'anic inimitability. However, non-Muᶜtazili linguists like al-Bāqillānī, al-Jurjānī, and al-Rāzī and some Muᶜtazili linguists like al-Jāḥiẓ and al-Zamakhsharī disagreed and argued that Qur'anic inimitability was attributed to the order system (al-naẓm) of Qur'anic discourse.

There are different views held by different rhetoricians with regards to the notion of inimitability. For al-Rummānī (d. 386/996), for instance, āyah-final expressions and assonance are prototypical features of the inimitability of Qur'anic genre. This is counter to the view held by other rhetoricians like al-Jāḥiẓ, who has attributed the notion of inimitability to the order system (al-naẓm) of Qur'anic Arabic. For other rhetoricians such as ᶜAbd al-Jabbār, Ibn Qutaibah, and al-Khaṭṭābī, the notion of inimitability is also attributed to the order system of Qur'anic genre. For al-Jurjānī, inimitability is attributed to both Qur'an-bound stylistic features and its order system but not to Qur'an's individual lexical items or their significations. In other words, the notion of inimitability for al-Jurjānī is not attributed to the lexical items' linguistic, semantic, or phonetic features but rather to the Qur'an's ad hoc order system. Thus, inimitability, for al-Jurjānī, is attributed to both the order system and eloquence since the notion of eloquence is not attributed to individual lexical items. This illustrates that interest in the linguistic feature of word order and its correlation with the notion of inimitability has attracted both Muᶜtazilite and Ashᶜari rhetoricians.

Some Muᶜtazili linguists like al-Jāḥiẓ and al-Zamakhsharī and non-Muᶜtazili linguists rejected the notion of al-ṣarfah. This is because to believe in the theological notion of al-ṣarfah is to dismiss the linguistic notion of inimitability. The well-known exegete al-Ṭabari (d. 310/922) was also against the al-ṣarfah notion and was an advocate of inimitability that is based on the order system (al-naẓm) of Qur'anic sublime style.

For modern linguists and exegetes like Muṣṭafā Ṣādiq al-Rāfiᶜī (1880–1937), the notion of inimitability is attributed to euphony represented by cadence and the phonetic order system. For Saiyid Quṭb (1906–1966), inimitability is based on artistic imagery (al-taṣwīr al-fannī) that abounds in Qur'anic discourse and argues that if the imagery changes, meaning will change, too.

7.5.2 Scholarship on inimitability

This is concerned with the scholarship that has focused on the inimitability-oriented stylistic analysis of Qur'anic genre. Research on the inimitability of Qur'anic discourse has dealt with the archetypal Qur'anic features that are analysed, such as grammatical, rhetorical, and phonetic features. This approach evolved during the third/ninth century and has been also adopted by modern linguists. Scholars of this linguistic approach include Ibn Qutaibah (d. 276/889) (*Ta'wīl Mushkīl al-Qur'ān*), ᶜAlī b. cĪsā al-Rummāni (d. 386/996) (*al-Nukāt fī Iᶜjāz al-Qur'ān*), Aḥmed b. Muḥammad al-Khaṭṭābī (d. 388/998) (*al-Bayān fī Iᶜjāz al-Qur'ān*), Abu Bakr Muḥammad b. al-Ṭaiyib al-Bāqillānī (d. 403/1012) (*Iᶜjāz al-Qur'ān*), Abu Muḥammad ᶜAbd Allāh Ibn Sinān al-Khafājī (d. 466/1073) (*Sirr al-Faṣāḥah*), ᶜAbd al-Qāhir b. ᶜAbd al-Raḥmān al-Jurjānī (d. 471/1078 or 474/1081), who wrote two books (*Dalā'il al-Iᶜjāz*) in which he introduced his theory of word order (al-naẓm) in Qur'anic discourse and (*Asrār al-Balāghah*), al-Zamakhsharī (d. 538/1143), who put al-Jurjānī's theory into practice in his exegesis book *al-Kshshāf*, Fakhr al-Dīn al-Rāzī (d. 606/1209) (*Nihāyat al-Ijāz fī Dirāyat al-Iᶜjāz*), Sirāj al-Dīn Yusuf al-Sakkākī (d. 626/) (*Muftāḥ al-ᶜUlūm*), and Ibn Qayyim al-Jawziyyah (d. 751/1350) (*al-Fawā'id al-Mushawwiq ilā ᶜUlūm al-Qur'ān waᶜUlūm al-Bayān*). Among linguists of the modern phase who have adopted this linguistic approach are al-Rāfiᶜī (*Iᶜjāz al-Qur'ān*), ᶜĀ'isha ᶜAbd al-Raḥmān Bint al-Shāṭi' (*al-Iᶜjāz al-Bayānī lil-Qur'ān*), whose approach is similar to that of al-Zamakhsharī, Muḥammad ᶜAbd al-Khāliq ᶜIḍīmah (*Dirāsāt li-Islūb al-Qur'ān al-Karīm*), Muḥammad Muḥammad Abu Mūsā (*al-Balāghah al-Qur'āniyyah fī Tafsīr al-Zamakhsharī wa Atharuhā fī al-Dirāsāt al-Balāghiyyah*), and Tammām Ḥassān (*al-Bayān fī Rawā'iᶜ al-Qur'ān*).

7.6 Inimitability, revelation, and compilation of the Qur'an

The notion of inimitability of Qur'anic Arabic is also correlated to the notion of piecemeal revelation (al-tanjīm). The argument that Qur'anic discourse is unparalleled and matchless can also be attributed to the different stages and amount of revelation through which the Qur'an as a text has taken shape. Piecemeal revelation provides further support to the argument that Qur'anic Arabic is distinctive and incomparable to the Arabic language used during the revelation of the Qur'an. This premise is hinged upon the following two factors:

1 Although it took 23 years to complete the Qur'an, its transcendent style remained unique. In the view of the inimitability-oriented premise, this long period of time is impractical for any human faculty. The human mind, practically speaking and under the circumstances, cannot produce statements with accurate and sophisticated linguistic and stylistic consistency. It is impractical to deliver a large text that enjoys textual and stylistic precision over a period of 23 years, especially under extremely difficult circumstances, harsh environment, and hostile opposition. Such circumstances exert psychological pressure on the author and, thus, can derail one's focus and cognitive skills. However, the aesthetic effects remained unchanged, the stylistic splendour was maintained, and the sublime word order (al-naẓm) was preserved throughout. Similarly, it is impractical for a human to produce a large text with logical cohesion and stylistic precision while relying mainly on his memory rather than writing down what was said 3 or 16 months ago.
2 Although Qur'anic statements (āyahs) and chapters evolved (i) in a piecemeal form and (ii) in two different phases, i.e., the Makkan and Madīnan phases, and that (iii) there were long, medium, and short time intervals, sometimes 3–16 months, among some statements or chapters, Qur'anic discourse maintained its logical coherence and cohesion.

7.7 Summary

Muslim theologians have referred to the Qur'an as muᶜjizah (a miracle) and have considered Qur'anic genre as free from stylistic, linguistic, or phonetic inconsistencies which are frequently encountered in non-Qur'anic discourses. Theologically, inimitability refers to the miraculous nature of the Qur'an and its divine source. Discussion of the notion of inimitability has begun since the third/ninth century. The major criteria of linguistic inimitability are naturalness and eloquence of discourse (purity of language). An eloquent discourse enjoys grammatical, morphological, semantic, and phonetic congruity, i.e., Qur'anic genre statements are both grammatically and lexically well formed. In other words, inimitability is concerned with discourse which is free from sluggish sentences (syntactically incongruent) and sluggish style. Muslim linguists have measured inimitability by the linguistic, phonetic, stylistic, and rhetorical criteria of congruity, succinctness, eloquence, coherence, cohesion, and elegance in terms of initiation of locution and word order. A major feature of inimitability for them is shift, which refers to stylistic and grammatical change at different levels of language and which occurs at different places of the Qur'anic text for different purposes. For Muslim linguists, the mutashābihāt (linguistically similar but stylistically dissimilar sentences) is one of the most intriguing features of inimitability.

The early years of the Abbasid era (132–655/749–1257) were characterized by the emergence of the notion of inimitability, around which there was debate between linguists and scholastics. In other words, there has been a difference of opinion about the notion of inimitability among Muslim linguists (al-mutakallimūn) represented by the Muᶜtazili scholars and the non-Muᶜtazili linguists with regards to inimitability of Qur'anic discourse. This is with regards to whether the inimitability of Qur'anic style is attributed to its eloquence (al-faṣāḥah) or to its order system (al-naẓm), whether the Arabs are able to imitate the style of the Qur'an but God has discouraged them from doingso, and whether the Arabs are unable to imitate the style of the Qur'an.

Muslim theologians have also argued that although it took 23 years to complete the Qur'an, its transcendent style remained unique. In other words, the piecemeal revelation over the two different phases (Makkan and Madīnan), which involves a long period of time, has not disturbed the stylistic elegance, precision, textuality, and coherent textual structure. For them, this is impractical for any human faculty.

8 General observations on Qur'anic text linguistics

This is a bird's-eye view of the text linguistic approach to Qur'anic discourse which highlights the major thoughts derived from the previous discussion in the chapters of this book. The present points of view can be of value to the notion of linguistic universality that binds languages from different language families. The discussion is also useful for contrastive text linguistics and translation studies.

1 Neither word- nor sentence-level analysis, on their own, are appropriate approaches to the study of language. Neither of them can provide an insight into many linguistic features that are beyond the sentence level, such as the argumentation structure of language, the coherence network of language, the 'textness' of a text, and the interpersonal relationship between the text producer and the text receiver.
2 The text carries the performative intent of its producer and a perlocutionary force that influences its receivers.
3 In terms of contrastive linguistics, we can claim that in English, the grammatical/stylistic patterns of declarative, interrogative, and conditional sentences remain the same regardless of the text producer's performative intent. In other words, the illocutionary force of the English speech act can be relayed through the same syntactic structures. However, Qur'anic speech acts are regulated by grammatical mechanisms and have pragmatic functions. We encounter in Qur'anic Arabic grammatical/stylistic variations depending on the text producer's performative intent and the illocutionary force relayed by the speech act. This leads us to safely conclude that, in Qur'anic discourse, grammatical mechanisms play a pivotal role in inter-personal communication and have communicative functions. This applies to all marked (unusual) word order such as the noun-initial (nominal) sentences with a main verb, no-main-verb nominal sentences, and sentence-initial (foregrounded) prepositional phrases (ᶜalā allāhi falyatawakkal al-mu'minūn – Upon God, let the believers rely, Q5:11) and (ᶜalā allāhi fatawakkalū in kuntum mu'minūn – Upon God rely, if you should be believers, Q5:23). Each of these grammatical/stylistic constructions signifies a specific illocutionary force and contextual relevance. However, in no-main-verb nominal sentences, the prepositional phrase occurs in the middle position of the sentence but not

sentence-finally. Thus, it remains a foregrounded text segment, as in (allāhu ᶜalā kulli shai'in qadīr – God is over all things competent, Q5:17, 19). The no-main-verb nominal sentence remains pivotal in Qur'anic genre due to its powerful perlocutionary effect upon the text receiver, as in (inna kathīran min al-nāsi lafāsiqūn – Indeed, many among the people are defiantly disobedient, Q5:49), which involves two affirmation particles (inna + the /l/ letter) and is preferred over the alternative main verb nominal sentence (kathīrun min al-nāsi yafsiqūn – Many among the people disobey) or the verbal sentence (yafsiqu kathīrun min al-nāss – Many among the people disobey).

4 Coherence and cohesion are the major components of a communicative text. A text should be cohesive in terms of grammatical structures and should also be coherent in terms of the logical presentation of its constituent sentences. In other words, the text segments should be cohesively and coherently linked.

5 A text (spoken or written) needs cohesion. However, cohesion is not merely a glue to stick sentence constituents (nouns, verbs, adjectives, prepositional phrases) together haphazardly. The cohesive devices are rule governed, regulated by context, conditioned by the text producer's performative intent (communicative goal). Thus, cohesive devices are pragmatically and semantically oriented. The reason why a text needs cohesion is due to the fact that without cohesion, interpersonal communication slows down and may break down.

6 A text is not merely a piece of language made up of jumbled-up text segments. These text segments can be words of different grammatical functions and of different morphological forms. They can be sentences in a running text, or they can be sentences in different parts of the macro text. On the contrary, the text segments hark back to each other. The text segments are tied up to different social circumstances: Who am I talking to? What am I talking about?

7 A coherent text has conceptual (thematic) unity which is based on the major text's ideas (notions, leitmotifs), the logical organization of these ideas, and the development of the text's conceptual (thematic) content.

8 Cohesion and coherence give the text texture. Thus, a text that lacks texture is not a text because its sentences have no relationship to each other. Texture is the semantic interdependence within the text. Each sentence in any text should be linked coherently to the previous sentence. The texture of the text is also concerned with the internal ties within the text. In other words, the sentences, clauses, and words are structured because they are internally cohesive.

9 Qur'anic genre flouts cohesion at times for the perlocutionary effect of either affirmation or glorification, as in (lā uqsimu bihādhā al-balad. wa'anta ḥillun bihādhā al-balad – I swear by this city (Makkah) and you (Muḥammad) are free of restriction in this city, Q90:1–2) where the noun (al-balad – the city) is repeated in the second text segment, which should be replaced by the an anaphoric reference pronoun (-hi – it), which refers to the same noun

(al-balad) in the first text segment. The flouting of cohesion here is to achieve the illocutionary force of glorification of Makkah. Similarly, Q3:78 flouts reference:

> yaqūlūna huwa min ᶜind allāh wamā huwa min ᶜind allāh – They say, 'This is from God, but it is not from God', Q3:78

where the expected sentence should have pronominalization (coreferential pronoun):

> (yaqūlūna huwa min ᶜind allāh wamā huwa min ᶜind**ih** – They say, 'This is from God, but it is not from **Him**') where the coreferential pronoun (-ih – Him) (God) refers to the noun (allāh – God).

10 Pronoun shift represents a violation of pronominalization, i.e., pronoun shift flouts reference in terms of cohesion:

> man aslama wajhahu lillāh wa huwa muḥsiniun falahu ajruhu ᶜinda rabbih walā khawfun ᶜalai**him** walā hum yaḥzanū**n** – Whoever submits himself in Islam to God while being a doer of good will have his reward with his Lord. And no fear will there be concerning them, nor will they grieve, Q2:112

The above sentence flouts cohesion because reference (coreferentiality) has been defied because of pronoun shift from third person singular (huwa – he) to third person plural (-him – them) and (-ūn – they). To include reference back, we get:

> (man aslama wajhahu lillāh wa huwa muhsiniun falahu ajruhu ᶜinda rabbih walā khawfun **ᶜalaihi** walā yaḥzan – Whoever submits himself in Islam to God while being a doer of good will have his reward with his Lord. And no fear will there be concerning **him**, nor will **he** grieve).

11 In terms of cohesion, Qur'anic Arabic does not have verbal substitution, i.e., Arabic does not have verbal substitutes and favours to reiterate the main verb. However, English has verbal substitution through the verbal substitutes (do, be, have). Let us consider the following examples:

> sawā'un ᶜalaihim astaghfarta lahum am lam tastaghfir lahum lan yaghfira allāhu lahum – It makes no difference whether you ask forgiveness for them or you do not. God will not forgive them, Q63:6

where the verb (istaghfara – to ask for forgiveness) is repeated, but in English it can be substituted by the verbal substitute (do).

> wamā kafara sulaimānu walākinna al-shayāṭīna kafarū – It was not Solomon who disbelieved but the devils did, Q2:102

where the verb (kafara – disbelieved) is repeated at the end of the sentence, while English employs the linguistic mechanism of verbal substitution through the verbal substitute (did).

12 The absence of the cohesion process of reiteration and lexical cohesion does not affect the coherence of the text, as in the following example:

> bal kadhdhabū bil-sāᶜati wa'aᶜtadnā liman kadhdhaba bil-**sāᶜati** saᶜīrā – But they have denied the hour, and We have prepared for those who deny the **hour** a blaze, Q25:11

where the noun (sāᶜati – hour) is repeated for lexical cohesion. Thus, it flouts the cohesion process of reference. In other words, the co-referential pronoun (-hā – it (the hour)). Thus, we should have:

> (bal kadhdhabū bil-sāᶜati wa'aᶜtadnā liman kadhdhaba bi(**hā**) saᶜīrā – But they have denied the hour, and We have prepared for those who deny (**it**) a blaze).

However, both types of the above text are coherent. For more details, see Chapter 5, Section 5.3.

13 The absence of the cohesion process of ellipsis does not affect the coherence of the text, as in the following example:

> laisa ᶜalā al-aᶜmā ḥarajun wa **lā ᶜalā** al-aᶜraji **ḥarajun** wa **lā ᶜalā** al-marīḍi **ḥarajun** wa **lā ᶜalā** anfusikum an ta'kulū min buyūtikum aw . . . – There is not upon the blind any constraint **nor upon** the lame **constraint, nor upon** the ill **constraint, nor upon** yourselves when you eat from own homes or . . ., Q24:61

where the negative particle (lā – not) + the preposition (ᶜalā – upon) and the noun (ḥarajun – constraint) are repeated, but their repetition can be avoided, i.e., they can be ellipted. Thus, we have:
(laisa ᶜalā al-aᶜmā wal-aᶜraji wal-marīḍi wa'anfusikum ḥarajun an ta'kulū min buyūtikum aw . . . – There is not upon the blind, the lame, the ill, and yourselves any constraint when you eat from own homes or . . .).

However, ellipsis is avoided to achieve reiteration. For more details, see Chapter 5, Section 5.3.

14 In terms of cohesion, the demonstrative pronoun (dhālika – that) is the most recurrent means of clausal substitution where the presupposed is a whole clause with a main verb, as in:

> zaᶜamā alladhīna kafarū an lan yubᶜathū qul balā warabbī latubᶜathunna thumma latunabba'unna bimā ᶜamiltum wa **dhālika** ᶜalā allāhi yasīr – Those who disbelieved have claimed that they will never be resurrected. Say: 'Yes, by my Lord, you will surely be resurrected; then you will surely be informed of what you did. **That**, for God, is easy', Q64:7

where the demonstrative pronoun (dhālika – that) substitutes for the clause (latubᶜathunna thumma latunabba'unna bimā ᶜamiltum – you will surely be resurrected; then you will surely be informed of what you did).

15 As two standards of textuality, cohesion and coherence complement each other. A cohesive text is not necessarily coherent, but a coherent text is necessarily cohesive. This leads us to conclude that cohesion is a prerequisite of coherence.

16 In the interest of the illocutionary force of affirmation, Qur'anic discourse flouts anaphoric reference, i.e., the noun (phrase) is reiterated rather than using its pronoun, as in:

> wayasta^{c}jilūnka bil-^{c}adhāb walawlā ajalun musamman lajā'ahum al-^{c}adhāb walaya'tiyannahum baghtatan wahum lā yash^{c}urūn – They challenge you to hasten the punishment. If not for the decree of a specified term, punishment would have reached them. But it will surely come to them suddenly and catch them unawares, Q29:53

where the underlined noun phrase (al-^{c}adhāb – the punishment) is repeated while the expected grammatical structure should be:

> (wayasta^{c}jilūnka bil-^{c}adhāb walawlā ajalun musamman lajā'ahum (al-^{c}adhāb) walaya'tiyannahum baghtatan wahum lā yash^{c}urūn – They challenge you to hasten the punishment. If not for the decree of a specified term, (it) would have reached them. But it will surely come to them suddenly and catch them unawares, Q29:53).

where the anaphoric reference pronoun (it) is implicit in the verb (jā'a – to come). However, in the verb (ya'tiyanna – to come), the implicit anaphoric reference pronoun (it) has been employed without the reiteration of the noun phrase (al-^{c}adhāb – the punishment).

For more details on flouting cohesion, see Chapter 6, Section 6.4.1.

17 There is a communicative purpose for each text segment, regardless of its length. The communicative purpose of the text is the performative intent of the text producer. The text producer, to be successful in the delivery of his/her intended meaning, needs to take into consideration the cognitive status of his/her text receiver (the audience, i.e., listeners/readers).

18 Language is not a random use of words or sentences. There is a purposeful manipulation of language. The text producer provides a text through which he/she can capture the hearts and minds of the audience. This cannot take place without resort to the different mechanisms of language on the grammatical, lexical, morphological, phonetic, rhetorical, and stylistic levels.

19 To capture the hearts and minds of the listeners/readers (audience), the text producer is required to be aware of the cognitive status of the text receiver (audience). The text producer is required to take into consideration the cognitive status of his/her audience before the employment of the different mechanisms of language. Awareness of the cognitive status of who we are addressing influences the way we manipulate language. Having diagnosed whether the addressee is open-minded (a likely supporter), a sceptic (a floater, one who has not made up his/her mind), or a denier (an antagonist, an

opponent who rejects), we can select the most appropriate word that can best serve our communicative purpose, and we can select the most effective configuration of words, i.e., whether we employ a marked (unusual) word order with foregrounding or an unmarked (usual) word order.

20 Having known the cognitive status of the addressee, the text producer can select the topos of his/her statement.

21 Having known the cognitive status of the addressee, the text producer can employ specific means of rebuttal to the opponent's premise.

22 Having known the cognitive status of the addressee, the text producer can employ specific means of substantiation to validate own premise.

23 Having known the cognitive status of the addressee, the text producer can employ specific statements which include either deductive reasoning or admonition such as reward and punishment. For instance, in Q62:10, the audience are open-minded who are believers: (idhā ra'aw tijāratan aw lahwan infaḍḍū ilaihā watarakūka qā'iman – On the occasion when they saw a transaction or a diversion, they rushed to it and left you standing). Because the addressees are open-minded, the text producer employs a low level of assertiveness (no affirmation tools) in the subsequent admonition statement to be used by the audience for deductive reasoning: (mā ᶜinda allāhi khairun min allahwi wamin al-tijārati wa allāhu khairu al-rāziqīn – What is with God is better than diversion and a transaction, and God is the best of providers, Q62:11). Furthermore, the two text segments (mā ᶜinda allāhi khairun min allahwi wamin al-tijārati) and (allāhu khairu al-rāziqīn) are no-main-verb nominal sentences whose illocutionary force is affirmation of their moral instructions.

24 Having known the cognitive status of the addressee, the text producer can employ effectively the three major rhetorical and stylistic strategies of persuasion. A successfully persuasive text is hinged upon logical reasoning (logos), character (ethos), and emotions (pathos).

25 The level of assertiveness (affirmation) depends primarily upon the cognitive status of the audience. In other words, we have observed that statements addressing an open-minded addressee have a low level of assertiveness, i.e., they include no affirmation tools. The statements addressing a sceptic addressee have a mid level of assertiveness, i.e., they include one affirmation tool. However, the statements addressing a denier (an antagonist, opponent) include a high level of assertiveness, i.e., they include two or more affirmation tools. For more details on the cognitive status of the addressee and the number of affirmation tools, see Chapter 3, Sections 3.9.1 and 3.9.2.

26 The rebuttal to an opponent's premise can be grammatically based, i.e., the text producer resorts to the employment of specific syntactic structures such as no-main-verb nominal sentence and the employment of a marked word order, such as foregrounding.

27 In both through-argumentation and counter-argumentation, God's omnipotence details and reward and punishment are employed recurrently in Qur'anic discourse.

28 In both through-argumentation and counter-argumentation, God's omnipotence details are employed recurrently in Qur'anic discourse as either rebuttal to or substantiation of monotheism. For instance, through deductive reasoning, Abraham reaches the conclusion: (innī wajjahtu wajhiya lilladhī faṭara al-samāwāti wal-arḍa ḥanīfan wamā anā min al-mushrikīn – Indeed, I have turned myself toward He who created the heavens and the earth, inclining towards truth, and I am not of those who associate others with God, Q6:75–79).

Similarly, in Q7:54, the premises are: (inna rabbakumu allāhu alladhī khalaqa al-samāwāti wal-arḍa fī sittati aiyāmin – Indeed, your Lord is God who created the heavens and earth in six days), (istawā ᶜalā al-ᶜarshi – He established Himself upon the throne), (yughshī al-laila al-nahāra yaṭlubuhu ḥathīthā – He covers the night with the day, another night chasing it rapidly), (wal-shamsa wal-qamara wal-nujūma musakhkharātin bi'amrihi – The sun, the moon, and stars are subjected by His command), and (alā lahu al-khalqu wal-amru – Unquestionably, His is the creation and the command). Thus, the conclusion is monotheism: (tabāraka allāhu rabbu al-ᶜālamīn – Blessed is God, Lord of the worlds).

Also, in Q2:164, parallel examples are cited to enable the reader/listener reach a sound conclusion on monotheism based on deductive reasoning: (inna fī khalqi al-samāwāti wal-arḍi wakhtilāfi al-laili wal-nahāri wal-fulki allatī tajrī fī al-baḥri bimā yanfaᶜu al-nāsa wamā anzala allāhu min al-samā'i min mā'in fa'aḥyā bihi al-arḍa baᶜda mawtihā wabaththa fīhā min kulli dābbatin wataṣrīf al-riyāḥi wal-saḥābi al-musakhkhari baina al-samā'i wal-arḍi la'āyātin liqawmin yaᶜqilūn – Indeed, in the creation of the heavens and the earth, and the alternation of the night and the day, and the ships which sail through the sea with that which benefits people, and what God has sent down from the heavens of rain, giving life thereby to the earth after its lifelessness and dispersing therein every kind of moving creature, and His directing of the winds and the clouds controlled between the heaven and earth are signs for a people who use reason, Q2:164). In these text segments, God's omnipotence examples are listed to substantiate the previous statements: (ilāhukum ilāhun wāḥidun lā ilāha illā huwa al-raḥmānu al-raḥīmu – Your god is one God. There is no deity worthy of worship except Him, the entirely merciful, the especially merciful, Q2:163). These examples are: (khalqi al-samāwāti wal-arḍi – the creation of the heavens and the earth), (wakhtilāfi al-laili wal-nahāri – the alternation of the night and the day), (wal-fulki allatī tajrī fī al-baḥri bimā yanfaᶜu al-nāsa – the ships which sail through the sea with that which benefits people), (wamā anzala allāhu min al-samā'i min mā'in fa'aḥya bihi al-arḍa baᶜda mawtihā wabaththa fīhā min kulli dābbatin – what God has sent down from the heavens of rain, giving life thereby to the earth after its lifelessness and dispersing therein every kind of moving creature,), (wataṣrīf al-riyāḥi – His directing of the winds), and (wal-saḥābi al-musakhkhari baina al-samā'i wal-arḍi – the clouds controlled between the heaven and earth).

29 In both through-argumentation and counter-argumentation, God's omnipotence details are employed recurrently in Qur'anic discourse as either rebuttal to or substantiation of eschatology (resurrection), as in: (allāhu alladhī arsala al-riyāḥa fatuthīru saḥāban fasuqnāhu ilā baladin maiyitin fa'aḥyainā bihi al-arḍa ba^cda mawtihā kadhālika al-nushūr – It is God who sends the winds, and they stir the clouds, and We drive them to a dead land and give life thereby to the earth after its lifelessness. Thus is the resurrection, Q35:9) and (wamin āyātihi annaka tarā al-arḍa khāshi^catan fa'idhā anzalnā ^calaihā al-mā'a ihtazzat warabat. inna alladhī aḥyāhā lamuḥyi al-mawtā innahu ^calā kulli shai'in qadīr – Of His signs is that you see the earth stilled, but when We send down upon it rain, it quivers and grows. Indeed, he who has given it life is the giver of life to the dead. Indeed, he is competent over all things, Q41:39). Thus, eschatology is substantiated through citing the above parallel examples to enable the reader/listener to reach a sound conclusion on eschatology based on deductive reasoning, i.e., that eschatology is certain to take place based on the example of the dead land that is revived by the rain.

30 In both through-argumentation and counter-argumentation, admonition details that refer to past unbelieving nations as well as reward and punishment details are employed recurrently in Qur'anic discourse as either rebuttal to or substantiation of eschatology (resurrection). For instance, the polytheists' deny resurrection and put forward their premises: (in hiya illā mawtatunā al-ūlā / mā naḥnu bimunsharīn – There is nothing beyond our one death. We will not be resurrected, Q44:35). Their conclusion is based on deductive reasoning: (Because you cannot bring back our forefathers, therefore, there is no resurrection, i.e., what you say about resurrection is not true) → (fa'ātū bi'ābā'inā in kuntum ṣādiqīn – If what you say is true, bring back our forefathers, Q44:36). Rebuttal to the deniers' thesis is put forward through reference to the unbelieving nation of Tubba^c (Q44:37), reference to God's omnipotence with regards to the creation of heavens, and reference to reward and punishment in Q44:40–57.

31 God's omnipotence details are based on deductive reasoning and primarily deal with God's signs as tools of persuasion and the verification (substantiation) of the text producer's thesis (argument, premise). These include: the creation of the heavens and earth, the creation of mankind, the creation of livestock, the creation of horses, mules, and donkeys, the sending down of water for drink and for growing trees, making the night, the day, the sun, the moon and the stars of benefit to mankind, making the many coloured things on earth of benefit to mankind, making the sea of benefit to mankind, making the mountains stand firm on the earth, making rivers on the earth, making paths on the earth for people to find their way, and the creation of stars to guide people through the desert or the sea at night.

32 The antagonist's premise is concerned with one of the following notions:

i Monotheism: This refers to the oneness of God, i.e., the theological notion of divinity, the unity of God, whether God has partners, and the worship of idols in the form of different deities.

ii Prophethood: This refers to whether someone is entrusted with a divine message, whether the teachings he is advocating are instructed by God, and whether the scripture he has is the word of God,
iii Eschatology: This refers to the disbelief in resurrection, i.e., there is no life after death, and
iv Reward and punishment: This refers to whether the antagonist (opponent) will be rewarded with paradise or punished with fire.

33 The no-main-verb nominal sentence is the major substantiation and rebuttal linguistic technique which is employed by the text producer to describe the notion of reward and punishment, as in: (inna jahannama kānat mirṣādā. lilṭāghīna ma'ābā. lābithīna fīhā aḥqābā . . . inna lil-muttaqīna mafāzā. ḥadā'iqa wa'aᶜnābā. wakawāᶜiba atrābā. waka'san dihāqā – Indeed, hell has been lying in wait for the transgressors, a place of return, in which they will remain for ages unending . . . Indeed, for the righteous is attainment – gardens and grapevines and full-breasted companions of equal age and a full cup, Q78:21–23, 31–34).

The argumentative nominal sentence is usually decorated by active participle words as extra linguistic tools to consolidate the premise and to make the audience accept the conclusion without qualms. The active participle is the centrepiece which occurs recurrently in the no-main-verb nominal sentences. One may wonder why the verb-initial sentence structure is avoided. This is due to the pragmatic fact that the nominal sentence has a powerful illocutionary force which the verb-initial sentence lacks.

Thus, the latter sentence structure is avoided, as in the following examples: (allāhu laṭīfun biᶜibādih – God is gentle with His servants, Q42:19). To change this nominal sentence to a main verb sentence (allāhu yalṭufu biᶜibādih), the illocutionary force will disappear and the text producer's performative intent will not be achieved.

In (allāhu ᶜalā kulli shai'in qadīr – God is competent over all things, Q3:29), the illocutionary force is focused on God's power. A main verb alternative stylistic pattern will fail to deliver the text producer's performative intent: (allāh yaqdiru ᶜalā kulli shai'in) or (yaqdiru allāh ᶜalā kulli shai'in).

Similarly, in (ilāhukum ilāhun wāḥid lā ilāha illā huwa al-raḥmān al-raḥīm – Your god is one God. There is no deity except Him, the entirely merciful, the especially merciful, Q2:163), we have two no-main-verb nominal sentences: (ilāhukum ilāhun wāḥid – Your god is one God) and (lā ilāha illā huwa al-raḥmān al-raḥīm – There is no deity except Him, the entirely merciful, the especially merciful), with the second having two active participles. The two no-main-verb nominal sentences reflect the text producer's performative intent of monotheism. These nominal sentences are employed as substantiation linguistic techniques to validate monotheism and rebut polytheism.

34 In any textual communication, coherence plays a vital role in the success of the text producer's performative intent at the interpersonal communication level and as a persuasion process.

35 On the macro level of Qur'anic discourse, there is interrelationship between coherence and the skill of initiating a text. The beginning of a text segment such as the beginning of a sūrah is a well-calculated initiative. In other words, the beginning of a sūrah relies on the end of the previous sūrah, the beginning of the previous sūrah, the end of the same sūrah, the beginning of the subsequent sūrah, or the end of the subsequent sūrah. By doing so, the text producer has achieved two major text linguistic objectives:

   i intertextuality between the initiating text segment and the relevant previous or subsequent text segment, and
   ii coherence between the initiating text segment and the relevant previous or subsequent text segment. Thus, the text producer has successfully achieved continuity of thought and thematic chaining (dovetailing, sequentiality, connectivity).

36 The mutashābihāt (the stylistically different but thematically or grammatically similar structures) are an intriguing macro text feature of Qur'anic discourse. In Qur'anic discourse, we encounter two syntactic structures which occur at different places but are intertextually related through the common leitmotif (theme) shared by the two sentences.

37 Linguistic mechanisms are employed to relay the text producer's performative intent. Such mechanisms perform different types of illocutionary force such as substantiation, rebuttal, and affirmation. The no-main-verb nominal sentence, the active participle, and the passive participle are examples of this form of locution, as in (in anā illā nadhīrun wa bashīr – I am not except a warner and a bringer of good tidings, Q7:188) → no-main-verb nominal sentence; (anna ṣāliḥan mursalun min rabbih – Ṣāliḥ is sent from His Lord, Q7:75) → no-main-verb nominal sentence = passive participle (mursal – is sent) to affirm prophethood; and (ilāhukum ilāhun wāḥidun/lā ilāha illā huwa/al-raḥmānu/al-raḥīmu – Your god is one God/There is no deity worthy of worship except Him/the entirely merciful/the exceptionally merciful, Q2:163) → no-main-verb nominal sentences + active participles (epithets) to affirm monotheism.

38 Based on text linguistics, we can safely conclude that the marked (unusual) word order dominates Qur'anic genre. This is not without a good reason. The marked word order, with or without embellishments, is pragmatically more powerful than the unmarked (usual) word order in the delivery of the text producer's performative intent. It is the marked word order of Qur'anic discourse that has motivated ᶜAbd al-Qāhir al-Jurjānī (d. 471/1078 or 474/1081) to write his *Dalā'il al-Iᶜjāz*.

39 Based on text linguistics, we can also conclude that the pivotal sentence structure in Qur'anic argumentative genre is the nominal sentence, which carries a heavy weight perlocutionary effect on the audience, as in (lā tadᶜu

ma^c^a allāhi ilāhan ākhar – Do not invoke with God another deity, Q28:88), which is a an imperative informing sentence (jumlah inshā'iyyah) indirectly imposing persuasion upon the antagonist audience. This carries the notion of monotheism, which is backed up stylistically by a series of nominal informing sentences: (lā ilāha illā hū/kulla shai'in hālikun illā wajhah/lahu al-ḥukm/ilaihi turja^c^ụn – There is no deity except Him/Everything will be destroyed except Himself/His is the judgement/To Him you will be returned, Q28:88). Similarly, the opponent's premise (ittakhadha allāhu waladā – God has taken a son, Q10:68) is rebutted by a series of nominal sentences: (subḥānahu/huwa al-ghaniy/lahu mā fī al-samāwāti wamā fī al-arḍ/in ^c^indakum min sulṭānin bihādhā? – He is exalted/He is the one free of need/To Him belongs whatever is in the heavens and whatever is in the earth/You have no authority for this claim, Q10:68). The nominal sentence is the grammatical/stylistic tool that is manipulated by the text producer to win the argument and persuade the antagonist.

Bibliography

Abdul-Raof, Hussein (2003). 'Conceptual and textual chaining in Qur'anic discourse'. In *Journal of Qur'anic Studies*, vol. 5, issue 2, (Edinburgh University Press); pp. 72–94.

——— (2005a). *Consonance in the Qur'an: A Conceptual, Intertextual and Linguistic Analysis*. Muenchen: Lincom Europa Academic Publications.

——— (2005b). 'Textual progression and presentation technique in Qur'anic discourse: An investigation of Richard Bell's claim of "disjointedness" with especial reference to Q17–20'. In *Journal of Qur'anic Studies*, vol. 7, issue 2; pp. 36–60.

——— (2006). *Arabic Rhetoric: A Pragmatic Analysis*. London and New York: Routledge.

——— (2015). *Semantics: A Coursebook for Students of English as a Foreign Language*. Muenchen: Lincom Europa Academic Publications.

——— (2018). *New Horizons in Qur'anic Linguistics: A Syntactic, Semantic and Stylistic Analysis*. London and New York: Routledge.

Abū Ḥaiyān, Muḥammad b. Yūsuf al-Andalusī (2001). *al-Baḥr al-Muḥīṭ*. 8 vols. Beirut: Dār al-Kutub al-cIlmiyyah.

Adams, Charles J. (1978). 'Qur'an'. In *The Encyclopedia of Religion*. Vol. 12. Edited by Mircea Eliade. New York: Macmillan Publishing Company; pp. 156–176.

al-Baiḍāwī, Abu Sacīd cAbd Allāh b. cUmar (1999). *Anwār al-Tanzīl wa Asrār al-Ta'wīl*. 2 vols. Beirut: Dār al-Kutub al-cIlmiyyah.

al-Bāqillānī, Abu Bakr Muḥammad b. al-Ṭaiyib (1994). *Icjāz al-Qur'ān*. Beirut: Dār Iḥyā' al-cUlūm.

al-Baqrī, Aḥmad Māhir (1986). *Dirāsāt Naḥwiyyah fī al-Qur'ān*. Alexandria: Mu'assasat Shabāb al-Jāmicah.

al-Biqācī, Burhān al-Dīn Abū al-Ḥasan Ibrāhīm b. cUmar (1995). *Naẓm al-Durar*. 8 vols. Beirut: Dār al-Kutub al-cIlmiyyah.

al-Darwīsh, Muḥyi al-Dīn (1992). *Icrāb al-Qur'ān wabayānuh*. Beirut: Dār Ibn Kathīr.

——— (1979). *The Structures and Functions of Discourse*. Lectures at the University of Puerto Rico, Rio Piedras.

——— (1980). *Macrostructures*. NJ: Erlbaum.

al-Farrā', Abū Zakariyya Yaḥyā (2002). *Macānī al-Qur'ān*. 3 vols. Beirut: Dār al-Kutub al-cIlmiyyah.

al-Jurjānī, cAbd al-Qāhir (1984). *Dalā'il al-Icjāz*. Cairo: Maktabat al-Khānachi.

al-Khāzin, cAlī b. Muḥammad al-Baghdādī (1995). *Lubāb al-Ta'wīl fī Macānī al-Tanzīl*. 4 vols. Beirut: Dār al-Kutub al-cIlmiyyah.

al-Naḥḥās, Abū Jacfar Aḥmad b. Muḥammad b. Ismācīl (2001). *Icrāb al-Qur'ān*. 5 vols. Beirut: Dār al-Kutub al-cIlmiyyah.

al-Nasafī, ᶜAbd Allāh b. Aḥmad (1996). *Madārik al-Tanzīl waḥaqā'iq al-Ta'wīl*. 4 vols. Beirut: Dār al-Nafā'is.

al-Qurṭubī, Abu ᶜAbd Allāh Muḥammad b. Aḥmad (1997). *al-Jāmiᶜ li-Aḥkām al-Qur'ān*. 20 vols. Beirut: Dār al-Kitāb al-ᶜArabī.

al-Rāfiᶜī, Muṣṭafā Ṣādiq (1990). *Iᶜjāz al-Qur'ān*. Beirut: Dār al-Kitāb al-ᶜArabī.

al-Rāzī, Fakhr al-Dīn Muḥammad b. ᶜUmar b. al-Ḥusain (1990). *Mafātīḥ al-Ghaib*. 32 vols. Beirut: Dār al-Kutub al-ᶜIlmiyyah.

al-Suyūṭī, Jalāl al-Dīn (1976). *Asrār Tartīb al-Qur'ān*. Cairo: Dār al-Iᶜtiṣām.

al-Ṭabarī, Abu Jaᶜfar b. Jarīr (2005). *Jāmiᶜ al-Baiyān fi Ta'wīl al-Qur'ān*. 12 vols. Beirut: Dār al-Kutub al-ᶜIlmiyyah.

al-Zarkashī, Badr al-Dīn (1988). *al-Burhān fī ᶜUlūm al-Qur'ān*. 4 vols. Beirut: Dār al-Kutub al-ᶜIlmiyyah.

Allen, James (2007). 'Aristotle on the disciplines of argument: Rhetoric, dialectic, analytic'. In *Rhetorica*, vol. 25; pp. 87–108.

Aristotle (1924). *Rhetoric*. Translated by W. Rhys Roberts. Mineola, NY: Dover.

——— (2007). *On Rhetoric*. 2nd edition. Translated by George A. Kennedy. Oxford, UK: Oxford University Press.

b. cĀshūr, Muḥammad al-Ṭāhir (n.d.). *al-Taḥrīr wal-Tanwīr*. 30 vols. Tunis: al-Dār al-Tunisiyyah lil-Nashr.

b. cAṭiyyah, Abu Muḥammad ᶜAbd al-Ḥaqq (1991). *al-Muḥarrir al-Wajīz*. 15 vols. Doha: Wizārat al-Awqāf.

Bakhtin, Mikhail Mikhailovich (1981). *The Dialogic Imagination: Four Essays*. University of Texas Press Slavic Series. Vol. 1. Translated by Caryl Emerson and Michael Holoquist. Austin: University of Texas Press.

Barth, Jacob (1916). 'Studien zur kritik und exegese des Qorans'. In *Der Islam*, vol. 6; pp. 113–148.

Barthes, Roland (1973). *The Pleasure of the Text*. Paris: Editions du Seuil. Translated by Richard Miller (1975). New York: Hill and Wang.

Beard, Adrian (ed.) (2008). *Working with Texts*. London and New York: Routledge.

Beaugrande, Robert (1980). *Text, Discourse, and Process*. Norwood, NJ: Albex. London: Longman.

Beaugrande, Robert and Dressler, Wolfgang (1981). *Introduction to Text Linguistics*. London: Longman.

Bell, Richard (1932). 'The men on the Aᶜraf (Sūrah vii:44)'. In *The Muslim World*, vol. 22; pp. 43–48.

——— (1937). 'Muḥammad's pilgrimage proclamation'. In *The Journal of the Royal Asiatic Society*; pp. 233–244.

——— (1945). 'Muḥammad's knowledge of the old testament'. In *Studia Semitica et Orientalia*, vol. 2; pp. 1–20.

——— (1953). *Introduction to the Qur'an*. Edinburgh: The Edinburgh University Press.

——— (1991). *A Commentary on the Qur'an*. 2 vols. Edited by C. Edmund Bosworth and M. E. J. Richardson. Manchester: University of Manchester.

Besnard, Philippe and Hunter, Antony (2008). *Elements of Argumentation*. Cambridge, MA: The MIT Press.

Blakemore, Diane (1987). *Semantic Constraints on Relevance*. Oxford: Blackwell.

_______ (1992). *Understanding Utterances*. Oxford: Blackwell.

Bosworth, C. Edmund and Richardson, M. E. J. (1991). 'Editors' introduction'. In *A Commentary on the Qur'an*. 2 vols. Edited by C. Edmund Bosworth and M. E. J. Richardson. Manchester: University of Manchester; pp. xiii–xviii.

Braet, Antoine C. (1996). 'On the origin of normative argumentation theory: The paradoxical case of the *Rhetoric to Alexander*'. In *Argumentation*, vol. 10; pp. 347–359.

Brook, G. L. (1979). *Varieties of English*. London: Palgrave Macmillan.

Brown, Gillian and Yule, George (1996). *Discourse Analysis*. Cambridge: Cambridge University Press.

Burton, Gideon O. 'Invention'. Brigham Young University. Retrieved 13th October 2013. www5.csudh.edu/ccauthen/350S11/ethosdef.htm

Carnap, Rudolf (1956). *Meaning and Necessity*. Chicago: Chicago University Press.

Carter, Ronald A. and Malmkjær, Kirsten (2002). 'Text linguistics'. In *The Linguistics Encyclopedia*. 2nd edition. Edited by Kirsten Malmkjær. London and New York: Routledge; pp. 540–552.

Childs, Peter and Fowler, Roger (2006). *The Routledge Dictionary of Literary Terms*. London and New York: Routledge.

Clark, Billy (2013). *Relevance Theory*. Cambridge, USA: Cambridge University Press.

Cockcroft, Robert and Cockcroft, Susan (2005). *Persuading People: An Introduction to Rhetoric*. 2nd edition. New York: Palgrave Macmillan.

Cohen, Robin (1984). *A Computational Theory of the Function of Clue Words in Argument Understanding*. In Proceedings of the 10th international conference on computational linguistics. Stanford, California: Coling; pp. 251–258.

Corbett, Edward P. J. (1990). *Classical Rhetoric for the Modern Student*. Oxford, UK: Oxford University Press.

Crane, Paul (n.d.). 'Texture in text: A discourse analysis of a news article using Halliday and Hasan's model of cohesion'; pp. 131–156. Retrieved 23rd July 2014. www.scribd.com/doc/36550727/Discourse-Analysis

Crowley, Sharon and Hawhee, Debra. (2008). *Ancient Rhetorics for Contemporary Students*. New York: Longman.

Crystal, David (2003). *A Dictionary of Linguistics and Phonetics*. Oxford: Blackwell Publishing.

Crystal, David and Davy, Derek (1969). *Investigating English Style*. London: Longman.

Cutting, Joan (2002). *Pragmatics and Discourse: A Resource Book for Students*. London and New York: Routledge.

Dirven, René and Vespoor, Marjolijn (eds.) (2004). *Cognitive Exploration of Language and Linguistics*. Philadelphia: John Benjamins Publishing Co.

Dressler, Wolfgang U. (ed.) (1978). *Current Trends in Text Linguistics*. Vol. 2. Berlin: Walter de Gruyter.

Eemeren, F. H. van and Grootendorst, R. (2004). *A Systematic Theory of Argumentation: The Pragma-Dialectical Approach*. Cambridge, USA: Cambridge University Press.

Egg, Markus and Redeker, Gisela (2012). *Modelling Textual Organisation: Coherence and Cohesion*. Netherlands: Centre for Language and Cognition Groningen, University of Groningen.

Enkvist, Nils Erik (1984). 'Contrastive linguistics and text linguistics'. In *Contrastive Linguistics: Prospects and Problems*. Edited by Jacek Fisiak. Berlin: Walter de Gruyter; pp. 45–67.

Fahnestock, Jeanne and Secor, Marie (1983). 'Grounds for argument: Stasis theory and the topoi'. In *Argument in Transition*. Edited by D. Zarefsky, M. O. Sillars, and J. Rhodes. Annandale, VA: Speech Communication Association; pp. 135–146.

Fraser, Bruce (2009). 'An account of discourse markers'. In *International Review of Pragmatics*, vol. 1; pp. 293–320.

Freeborn, Dennis (1996). *Style: Text Analysis and Linguistic Criticism*. London: Palgrave Macmillan.

Grice, Paul (1975). 'Logic and conversation'. In *Syntax and Semantics: Speech Acts*. Vol. 3. Edited by P. Cole and J. Morgan. New York: Academic Press; pp. 41–58.

Halliday, Michael Alexander K. (1973). *Explorations in the Functions of Language*. London: Edward Arnold.

——— (1994). *An Introduction to Functional Grammar*. London: Edward Arnold.

Halliday, Michael Alexander K. and Hasan, Ruqaiya (1976). *Cohesion in English*. London: Longman.

——— (1985). *Language, Context, and Text: Aspects of Language in a Social-Semiotic Perspective*. Australia: Deakin University Press.

Hasan, Ruqaiya (1979). 'On the notion of text'. In *Text vs. Sentence: Basic Questions of Text Linguistics*. Edited by J. S. Petofi. Hamburg: Helmet Buske.

——— (1984). 'Coherence and cohesive harmony'. In *Understanding Reading Comprehension*. Edited by J. Flood. Newark: IRA.

Hatim, Basil (1997). *Communication across Cultures: Translation Theory and Contrastive Text Linguistics*. Exeter: Exeter University Press.

Hatim, Basil and Mason, Ian (1990). *Discourse and the Translator*. London: Longman.

Hatim, Basil and Munday, Jeremy (2004). *Translation: An Advanced Resource Book*. London and New York: Routledge.

Ḥawwah, Saᶜīd (2003). *al-Asās fī al-Tafsīr*. 11 vols. Cairo: Dār al-Salām.

Hirschfeld, Hartwig (1902). *New Researches into the Composition and Exegesis of the Qur'an*. London: Royal Asiatic Society.

Ibn Ḥajar, Aḥmad b. ᶜAlī al-ᶜAsqalānī (1997). *Fatḥ al-Bārī*. 13 vols. Damascus: Dār al-Faiḥā'.

Ibn Kathīr, Abū al-Fidā' Ismāᶜil (1993). *Tafsīr al-Qur'ān al-ᶜAẓīm*. 4 vols. Beirut: Mu'assasat al-Kutub al-Thaqāfiyyah.

Ice, Richard (2012). *Rhetoric in Civic Life*. State College, PA: Strata Publishing Inc.

Irving, Washington (1850). *The Life of Mahomet*. London: George Routledge & Co.

Johnstone, Barbara (2002). *Discourse Analysis*. Oxford, UK: Blackwell Publishers.

Katz, Jerrold J. and Fodor, Jerry A. (1963). 'The structure of a semantic theory'. In *Language*, vol. 39; pp. 170–210.

Knott, A. and Dale, R. (1994). 'Using linguistic phenomena to motivate a set of coherence relations'. In *Discourse Processes*, vol. 18; pp. 35–62.

Leighton, Stephen (1982). 'Aristotle and the emotions'. In *Phronesis*, vol. 27; pp. 144–174.

——— (2009). 'Passions and persuasion'. In *A Companion to Aristotle*. Edited by G. Anagnostopoulos. Oxford, UK: Blackwell Publishers; pp. 597–611.

Lichtenstadter, Ilse (1974). 'Qur'an and Qur'an exegesis'. In *Humaniora Islamica*, vol. 2; pp. 3–28.

Lyons, John (1977). *Semantics*. 2 vols. Cambridge, USA: Cambridge University Press.

Margoliouth, David S. (1914). *The Early Development of Mohammedanism*. London: Williams and Norgate.

Manser, Martin H. (2006). *The Facts on File Guide to Style*. New York: Facts On File, Inc.

Martin, J. R. (2015). 'Cohesion and texture'. In *The Handbook of Discourse Analysis*. Vol. 1. 2nd edition. Edited by D. Tannen, H. E. Hamilton, and D. Schiffrin. West Sussex: Wiley Blackwell; pp. 61–81.

McCabe, Anne (2011). *An Introduction to Linguistics and Language Studies*. London: Equinox.

McGregor, William B. (2009). *Linguistics: An Introduction*. London and New York: Continuum International Publishing Group.

Muir, Sir William (1923). *The Life of Mohammad*. Edinburgh: John Grant.

ᶜOdat Allāh Manīᶜ al-Qaisi (1996). *Sirru al-Iᶜjāz fī al-Qur'ān*. ᶜAmman: Dār al-Bashīr.

Ogiermann, Eva (2009). *On Apologising in Negative and Positive Politeness Cultures*. Amsterdam: John Benjamins Publishing Co.

Ohlander, Erik S. (2005). 'Fear of God (taqwa) in the Qur'an: Some notes on semantic shift and thematic context'. In *Journal of Semitic Studies*, vol. 50, issue 1; pp. 137–152.

Paltridge, Brian (2012). *Discourse Analysis: An Introduction*. London and New York: Bloomsbury Academic.

Paret, I. R. (1983). 'The Qur'an'. In *Arabic Literature to the End of the Umayyad Period*. Edited by A. F. L. Beeston, T. M. Johnstone, R. B. Serjeant, and G. R. Smith. Cambridge, USA: Cambridge University Press; pp. 186–227.

Polanyi, Livia and Scha, Remko (1983). 'The syntax of discourse'. In *Text*, vol. 3; pp. 261–270.

Quirk, Randolph, Greenbaum, Sidney, Leech, Geoffrey, and Svartvik, Jan (1985). *A Comprehensive Grammar of the English Language*. London: Longman.

Ramage, John D. and Bean, John C. (1998). *Writing Arguments*. 4th edition. Needham Heights, MA: Allyn & Bacon.

Redeker, Gisela (1991). 'Linguistic markers of discourse structure'. In *Studies in International Linguistics*. Vol. 5. Cambridge, USA: Cambridge University Press; pp. 1139–1172.

Rippin, Andrew (2001). *The Qur'an and Its Interpretive Tradition*. Aldershot: Ashgate; pp. 639–647.

Robinson, Neal (1996). *Discovering the Qur'an: A Contemporary Approach to a Veiled Text*. London: SCM Press.

Robzin, Hartmut (1996). '"A treasury of heresies": Christian polemics against the Koran'. In *The Qur'an as Text*. Edited by Stefan Wild. Leiden: E. J. Brill; pp. 157–175.

Salkie, Raphael (1995). *Text and Discourse Analysis*. London: Routledge.

——— (2005). *Text and Discourse Analysis*. London: Routledge.

Schorup, Lawrence (1985). *Common Discourse Particles in English Conversation: 'Like', 'Well', 'Y'know'*. New York: Garland.

Searle, John R. and Vanderveken, Daniel (1985). *Foundations of Illocutionary Logic*. Cambridge, USA: Cambridge University Press.

Simons, Herbert W., Morreale, Joanne, and Gronbeck, Bruce (2001). *Persuasion in Society*. London: Greater Kailash.

Simpson, Paul (2004). *Stylistics: A Resource Book*. London and New York: Routledge.

Sperber, Dan and Wislon, Deirdre (1986). *Relevance: Communication and Cognition*. Oxford, UK: Blackwell Publishers.

Sternberg, Robert (2009). *Cognitive Psychology*. Belmont, CA: Wadsworth.

Stubbs, Michael (1983). *Discourse Analysis*. Chicago, IL: The University of Chicago Press.

Tannen, Deborah, Hamilton, Heidi, and Schiffrin, Deborah (2015). *The Handbook of Discourse Analysis*. Vol. 1. 2nd edition. West Sussex: Wiley Blackwell.

Tanskanen, Sanna-Kaisa (2006). *Collaborating Towards Coherence: Lexical Cohesion in English Discourse*. Amsterdam, Philadelphia: John Benjamins.

Torrey, Charles Cutler (1933). *The Jewish Foundation of Islam*. New York: Jewish Institute of Religion Press.

Trappes-Lomax, Hugh (2004). 'Discourse analysis'. In *The Handbook of Applied Linguistics*. Edited by A. Davies and C. Elder. Oxford, UK: Blackwell Publishers; pp. 133–164.

Trask, Larry (1997). *A Student's Dictionary of Language and Linguistics*. London: Edward Arnold.

Trosborg, Anna (ed.) (1997). *Text Typology and Translation*. Amsterdam: John Benjamins Publishing Co.

van Dijk, Teu A. (1977). *Text and Context: Explorations in the Semantics and Pragmatics of Discourse*. London and New York: Longman.

Walton, Douglas (1989). *Informal Logic*. New York: Cambridge University Press.

——— (2006). *Fundamentals of Critical Argumentation*. Cambridge, USA: Cambridge University Press.

——— (2007). *Media Argumentation*. New York: Cambridge University Press.

Walton, Douglas, Reed, Christopher, and Macagno, Fabrizo (2008). *Argumentation Schemes*. Cambridge, USA: Cambridge University Press.

Wansbrough, John (1977). *Qur'anic Studies: Sources and Methods of Scriptural Interpretation*. Oxford, UK: Oxford University Press.

Wardhaugh, Ronald (1993). *Investigating Language: Central Problems in Linguistics*. Oxford, UK and Cambridge, USA: Blackwell.

Weil, Henri (1844). *De l'ordre des mots dans les langues anciennes comparées aux langues modernes*. Paris: Joubert.

______ (1887). *The Order of Words in the Ancient Languages Compared with that of the Modern Languages*. Boston: Ginn.

Widdowson, Henry G. (2007). *Discourse Analysis*. Oxford, UK: Oxford University Press.

Woods, Nicola (2006). *Describing Discourse*. London: Hodder Arnold.

Yule, George (1985). *The Study of Language*. Cambridge, USA: Cambridge University Press.

Websites

www.scribd.com/doc/36550727/Discourse-Analysis

www.u.arizona.edu/ic/polis/courses021/ENGL_102-78/EthosPathosLogos

Index